Rehound 1980

STUDIES

IN THE ITALIAN RENAISSANCE

STORIA E LETTERATURA

RACCOLTA DI STUDI E TESTI

—— 51 ——

B. L. ULLMAN

STUDIES
IN THE ITALIAN RENAISSANCE

SECOND EDITION
WITH ADDITIONS AND CORRECTIONS

ROMA 1973
EDIZIONI DI STORIA E LETTERATURA
VIA LANCELLOTTI, 18

EDIZIONI DI STORIA E LETTERATURA
Roma - Via Lancellotti, 18

Illi
quae quadraginta quinque annos
multis modis me adiuvit
hoc qualecumque dedico.

PREFACE

This book consists in part of old material, in part of new, and some of the old articles have been considerably enlarged. One reason for republishing the older articles is to make them more generally available. It is not surprising that the older articles on the Renaissance published in American periodicals, especially classical periodicals, have not been widely known to European scholars. One example is an article on Petrarch's books, first published in 1923 (now reprinted in chapter VI). A knowledge of some of the facts (not opinions) in it would have prevented the repetition of incorrect views about Petrarch's library.

A few of the chapters attempt a broad survey of the Italian Renaissance with the aim of putting it in proper perspective. It is hoped that they may contribute to some degree, however slight, to refurbishing the reputation of the Renaissance as one of the great epochs in the world's history. Most of the chapters, however, deal with details, insignificant in themselves perhaps, but necessary to a restoration of the great mosaic which the Renaissance was. The chief figures in this book are Petrarch, whose great merits as a humanist have been widely recognized, and Coluccio Salutati, whose achievements are insufficiently known. If it should be suggested that I have attempted to follow in the footsteps of that illustrious master, Remigio Sabbadini, I shall be more than content.

To the learned and enthusiastic Maecenas who has made possible this and the other volumes of that splendid series Storia e Letteratura, *don Giuseppe De Luca, I offer my most grateful thanks.*

B. L. U.

In this second edition I must mention with deep sorrow the passing of don Giuseppe, a warm friend and a great humanist. At the same time I record my appreciation to his sister Maddalena De Luca and to Romana Guarnieri for bravely carrying on his work.

I have made a number of changes and have added six new chapters. I have had the benefit of corrections and suggestions by Dr. R. W. Hunt and by reviewers of the first edition.

B. L. U.

La presente seconda edizione era molto avanzata quando l'Autore morì improvvisamente a Roma il 21 giugno 1965. La tipografia aveva approntato pochi giorni prima le terze bozze. Rimaneva da rifare l'« Index of names » per adeguarlo alla nuova numerazione, ai numerosi mutamenti e al più ricco contenuto del volume. In realtà si presentarono subito alcuni problemi editoriali e il compito di quanto restava da fare, assunto principalmente dal più vecchio e dal più giovane degli amici italiani di B. L. Ullman, risultò più lento e complesso del previsto. Dirò ciò che la casa editrice ha fatto per curare e migliorare la presentazione e il contenuto stesso del volume in modo degno della sua importanza e del suo Autore.

La nuova revisione delle bozze fece affiorare parecchie difficoltà e indicò la necessità di ulteriori controlli e interventi, resi più delicati, per la responsabilità di chi doveva operarli, dalla scomparsa dell'Autore. Fu subito deciso di aggiungere l'« Index of manuscripts », che mancava nella prima edizione: un sussidio che sempre più si è venuto generalizzando per libri di ricerca quale il presente, e che è nella pratica delle Edizioni di Storia e Letteratura. Infine si presentò l'opportunità di una integrazione del contenuto. Vivo e attivo l'Autore, questa raccolta dei suoi saggi di argomento umanistico poteva considerarsi, per così dire, aperta: altri scritti della stessa natura, troppo recenti per esservi compresi, e altri futuri che la sua sempre fresca attività poteva far prevedere nonostante l'età avanzata, avrebbero potuto essere raccolti in una terza edizione o in un separato volume; ma la sua scomparsa creava una prospettiva nuova. Decisi così, confortato anche dall'opinione autorevole di comuni amici, G. Billanovich e P. O. Kristeller, di aggiungere ai sei capitoli nuovi (XXI-XXVI) altri due scritti recentissimi. L'integrazione mi sembrava tanto più opportuna in quanto l'uno e l'altro erano strettamente legati a due dei più importanti capitoli del volume: la discussione sui manoscritti liviani di Poggio (XXVII) è un necessario complemento del cap. XV, e l'esame dei marginalia del Pontano in un antico codice di Ovidio (XXVIII) riprende e allarga la materia del cap. XXII.

Nel solo lavoro scritto in italiano (XXVI) avremmo potuto introdurre alcuni ritocchi stilistici, quali ogni redazione dovrebbe eseguire o suggerire a un autore straniero. Non avendo potuto farlo quando Egli era in vita, abbiamo preferito non mutare niente dell'edizione originale: quelle piccole imperfezioni sono la prova che la stesura è opera sua, e dunque della sicurezza con cui Egli maneggiava la nostra lingua, e lo scritto ci è caro anche per questo.

Gli studiosi che già conoscono e usano la prima edizione avranno il piacere di scoprire in questa, oltre i capitoli nuovi, molti miglioramenti e anche importanti aggiunte, ai quali l'Autore ha accennato con eccessiva semplicità e modestia nelle righe che precedono questa nota. Nello stesso modo aveva preparato la prima edizione, per i capitoli che non erano nuovi: I-VII, XII, XV-XVIII (gli altri erano allora inediti: VIII-XI, XIII, XIV, XIX, XX). Lo stesso ha fatto per quasi tutti gli scritti vecchi e nuovi della nuova edizione. Appunti dei suoi ultimi giorni, che ho potuto vedere tra le sue carte (relativi per es. al cap. IX, sul suo Salutati), mostrano che la stessa vigile attenzione si sarebbe esercitata ancora sulle bozze di questo volume se avesse potuto seguirne la stampa fino alla fine. Servirsi di quegli appunti per qualche nota aggiunta, a cui Egli solo avrebbe potuto dare forma, sarebbe stato indiscreto da parte nostra; e ancora più introdurre altri aggiornamenti bibliografici. Ma Ullman ha avuto come pochi fede nel progresso continuo degli studi e senso della collaborazione tra studiosi; proseguire la sua ricerca, anche discutendo con Lui, dovrà essere sentito come un dovere dai lettori di questo volume: quelli che hanno avuto la fortuna di essere suoi amici e discepoli, e quelli che li seguiranno.

Hanno collaborato alla revisione delle bozze (come già nella fase precedente il compianto Alfredo Rizzo) in primo luogo Berthe M. Marti, poi Rino Avesani e chi scrive. L'Indice dei nomi è stato integrato e rielaborato da Rino Avesani, che ha anche compilato ex novo, con grande competenza e diligenza, l'Indice dei manoscritti, in molti casi identificando manoscritti citati solo indirettamente o senza segnatura, in altri scoprendo errori nelle segnature, che solo per questa via hanno potuto essere corretti anche nel testo.

Pochi anni dopo la prima edizione di questo libro (1955), la collezione aveva ospitato The Origin and Development of Humanistic Script (1960, n. 79). Solo tre anni dopo, Ullman ci aveva dato The Humanism of Coluccio Salutati (Padova 1963). Il lavoro qui annunziato a p. 173 sulla biblioteca fiorentina di S. Marco, a cui Egli lavorò fino all'ultimo senza poterlo finire, è poi divenuto un grosso volume per l'opera devota ed esperta di un più giovane collega (B. L. Ullman and Ph. S. Stadter, The Public Library of Renaissance Florence, Padova 1972). Con questi libri e con le esemplari edizioni di Sicco Polenton e di due opere del Salutati, Ullman ha dato agli studi sull'Umanesimo italiano, nella linea di Sabbadini a cui amava ricollegarsi, un contributo tra i più alti del nostro secolo e un esempio, ancora più prezioso, di coerente e sostanzioso lavoro. Ma non è ancora tutto. Come Sabbadini, Egli era professionalmente filologo classico, ma non aveva mai sentito come distinti o separati gli altri suoi interessi nel campo medioevale o umanistico. Infaticabile come sempre, in quello stesso anno 1965 aveva preparato il materiale di un volume di saggi parallelo al presente, di Classical and Mediaeval Studies. La raccolta, ampliata fino a formare due volumi di « Storia e Letteratura », sarà curata dal suo allievo Francis Newton. Parecchi di questi saggi interessano non meno i classicisti e i medievisti che i lettori del presente volume. Anche con la nuova raccolta di studi che le Edizioni di Storia e Letteratura hanno il piacere di annunziare il caro vecchio amico che ci ha lasciato continuerà a essere per tutti un maestro.

A. C.

CHAPTER I

RENAISSANCE

THE WORD AND THE UNDERLYING CONCEPT [1]

The extraordinary confusion which reigns today about the Italian Renaissance impels me to write this introductory chapter for a book whose title contains the word Renaissance. Strange as it may seem, there are those who deny the existence of any such movement as the Renaissance, others label it « so-called », thereby warning the public against it as if it were a spurious commodity, or insist that it was no different from similar movements in the Middle Ages, or maintain that it produced only evil. Inconsistently, some assert several of these views at the same time. It has become a favorite sport (to which I raise no objection) to criticize Burckhardt, but the trouble is that these critics generally read only one another's discussions instead of the documents of the period. On the other hand, it must be admitted that the term Renaissance has been given ever widening meanings by Burckhardt and others to cover many phases of human existence and thought where it is not appropriate. Hence those who noticed this inappropriateness were led to challenge the whole idea [2].

---

[1] Originally published in *Studies in Philology*, XLIX (1952) p. 105.

[2] I shall not discuss or list the great number of books that have dealt with the question. Suffice it to mention the following: Franco Simone, « La coscienza della rinascita negli umanisti », *La rinascita*, 2 (1939), p. 838; 3 (1940), p. 163 (reprinted in part in *La coscienza della rinascita negli umanisti francesi* [Rome, 1949], p. 27); Wallace K. Ferguson, *The Renaissance in Historical Thought* (Boston, 1948); E. H. Wilkins, « On the Nature and Extent of the Italian Renaissance », *Italica*, XXVII (1950), p. 67. Ferguson's excellent and thorough survey has a good bibliography. His title is ambiguous; it might better have been *The « Renaissance » in Historical Thought*.

It does not seem to me correct to consider the Renaissance, even in its narrowest sense, equivalent to humanism, much less to the Revival of Learning, which was but one outgrowth of the Renaissance, to judge from the attitude of contemporaries. That attitude is the prime concern of this chapter. It is my thought merely to call attention to documents which, for the most part, are thoroughly familiar. The word Renaissance is French and relatively late in origin, the phenomenon is Italian and early. The metaphor involved in it is only one of several that were current. Too much concern with the word that came into use several centuries after the concept was born has been partly to blame for misapprehensions about the movement itself.

One of Petrarch's *Epistulae metricae* suggests some interesting speculations. In III, 3 Petrarch wrote (at Vaucluse):

> Hic longo exsilio sparsas revocare Camenas,
> Hic Graios Latiosque simul conferre poetas
> Dulce fuit.

« Longo exsilio » recalls Campesani's « longis a finibus exul ». Had Petrarch seen this poem? Elsewhere I have suggested that Petrarch obtained a copy of Catullus when he was in Verona in 1345, and that in obtaining it he was aided by his good friend Guglielmo da Pastrengo of Verona [3]. Petrarch's poem is addressed to this same Guglielmo; the date assigned to it is one year later, 1346 [4]. This seems too striking to be mere coincidence.

The point I wish to emphasize is that the founders of the Renaissance were creative artists, poets chiefly, and that it was their poetic achievements that indicated to their contemporaries that something new was stirring, that a thousand years of creative torpor had ended. Even in the early dawn of the Renaissance some of the leading figures, such as Mussato at Padua, were

---

[3] *Studi in onore di Luigi Castiglioni* (Florence, 1960), p. 1043. I made this suggestion before seeing Petrarch's poem.

[4] Diana Magrini, *Le epistole metriche di Francesco Petrarca* (Rocca S. Casciano, 1907), p. 130; E. H. R. Tatham, *Francesco Petrarca* (London, 1926), II, p. 377, n. 1. E. Bianchi, in Francesco Petrarca, *Rime, Trionfi e poesie latine* (*La letteratura italiana, storia e testi*, VI, Milan, 1951), p. 785, reverts to Fracassetti's date, 1338 or 1339, which Magrini rightly decided was incorrect. For a possible reminiscence of Catullus in this poem see Chapter VIII.

poets [5]. It is unnecessary to remark that Petrarch achieved fame through his Italian poems, written in his youth, but hoped that his glory would rest on the product of his mature manhood, the Latin epic *Africa*. Boccaccio too was a poet in both Latin and the vernacular. Indeed we are told by Petrarch that Boccaccio destroyed some of his Italian poems because he did not wish to be third to Dante and Petrarch [6]. Even Coluccio Salutati, the founder of the Florentine circle, wrote verse, both Italian and Latin, though his fame rests on other accomplishments.

The extreme importance which the early humanists attributed to poetry must not be overlooked. Petrarch, Boccaccio, Salutati defend it. The last of this triad asserts that poetry presupposes « totum trivium, quadrivium, philosophiam omnem, humana divinaque et omnes prorsus scientias » [7]. All the arts are, in his opinion, mere handmaids to poetry.

The idea of awakening from slumber implies a return to an earlier state of wakefulness. This and other figures used by the humanists all suggest a return to the old life of ancient Rome, not the hewing out of new paths in new and strange lands. The reading of classical Latin literature was associated with literary creation from the very beginning of the Renaissance, though I shall not attempt to say which came first. We need only recall the preoccupation of the early Paduan school of « prehumanists » with the *Tragedies* of Seneca and the surreptitious reading of Virgil, Cicero, and other classics by the schoolboy Petrarch. Though most of the early examples of metaphors associated with the concept of Renaissance are concerned with the writing of literature, the earliest I have been able to find deals with the discovery of a classical poet, and such discovery is, of course, a phase of humanism. This fact perhaps indicates that the fortunes of humanism and creative literature, reading and writing, were inextricably associated, and therefore they cannot be separated, at least for the early Renais-

---

[5] For a survey of the earliest period see R. Weiss, *The Dawn of Humanism in Italy* (London, 1947).

[6] Petrarch, *Sen.* V, 3 (1365).

[7] *Epistolario di Coluccio Salutati,* ed. F. Novati, IV (Rome, 1905), p. 230.

sance. At any rate, the example I have in mind has not, I believe, been cited for our present purpose.

Early in the fourteenth century Benvenuto Campesani of Vicenza, who died in 1323, wrote a short poem about the discovery of a manuscript of Catullus. The title reads: « Versus domini Benvenuti de Campexanis de Vicencia de resurectione Catulli poete Veronensis ». The poem begins with this line: « Ad patriam venio longis a finibus exul » [8]. The word « resurrection » attracts notice; even more, the word « exile ». Plattard has shown that in sixteenth-century France one of the metaphors in use was that of literature returning from exile by the legal principle of *postliminium* (« return to one's home ») [9]. One example he cites is from Tiraqueau (1524): « Litterae illae quae ... humanae vocantur ... veluti postliminio revertantur ». His other instances are from Rabelais and Budé. Earlier Poliziano speaks of the ancient authors who « suam hanc in patriam reverterunt » [10].

Yet the return of one Roman poet did not mean that they would all come trooping back, and that the people of the fourteenth century could become true Romans in the sense that they could have access to all Roman literature as the ancients presumably had. When Petrarch laments the loss of many of the books of the ancients, he realizes that most of them will never be found in spite of all his efforts and those of his contemporaries and his successors. At best he and his fellows have prevented posterity from being completely ignorant of antiquity. He blames the « soporem ac torporem » of an age that was too much concerned with things it should not have cared about and too little with matters of real significance [11]. There is no suggestion here of an awakening.

---

[8] Quoted in editions of Catullus, e.g., that of E. Cazzaniga (Turin, 1945), p. 127; M. Schuster (Leipzig, 1949), p. 100. In a review of the first edition of the present book R. Weiss suggested that Campesani's poem was written between 1303 and 1307 (*Classical Review*, LXX, 1956, p. 310).

[9] J. Plattard, « 'Restitution des bonnes lettres' et 'Renaissance' », *Mélanges offerts par ses amis et ses élèves à M. Gustave Lanson* (Paris, 1922), p. 128.

[10] *Opera* III (Lyon, 1537), p. 107, quoted by Simone, *op. cit.*, p. 851 (*Coscienza... francesi*, p. 38).

[11] *Rerum memorandarum libri*, I, 19, ed. G. Billanovich (Florence, 1943).

When it comes to the writing rather than the reading of poetry, the contemporary commentators are fully agreed that an awakening has come, that once more there are poets of commanding stature. In one of his earliest extant letters, written before 1360, Coluccio Salutati told Nelli that the latter and his friend Petrarch had revived poetry [12]: « Meonidas longo situ etatis nostre vitio et vetustate obductas iuvenescere ad cantus amenitatem et melos: et iandiu desiccatum Pegasicum hippofontem scaturire novas undas Cyrreosque lacus abundare liquoribus letasque sorores hedera redimitas et olea ad vestrum concentum ducere choream ». The long neglected and aging Muses are growing young again, and the springs of inspiration once more are flowing full. (Coluccio does not say how long the Muses had been neglected, but from his remarks elsewhere he clearly means that no worthwhile poetry had been produced from antiquity until his own times.) Indeed, in Coluccio's eyes, the Muses are more vigorous than they ever were, for he seems at one time to be sincere in his belief that Petrarch was a greater poet than Virgil and as great a prose writer as Cicero [13].

In his *Vita di Dante* (1357-59) Boccaccio states that Dante was the first to open the way for the return of the Muses who had been banished from Italy, and by whom poetry, which had been dead, was brought back to life [14]: « Questi fu quel Dante, il quale primo doveva al ritorno delle Muse, sbandite d'Italia, aprir la via... per costui la morta poesi meritamente si può dire suscitata ». Petrarch received a copy of this *trattatello*, but he himself apparently made no similar statement anywhere, partly, no doubt, because his opinion of Dante was not so high as that held by others. When Petrarch discusses his own time, he continually criticizes its low cultural level [15]. At best he can merely hope for better times ahead, for the return of a Golden Age [16].

[12] *Epist.*, IV, p. 244.
[13] *Epist.*, I, pp. 338 ff. (1379). He changed his mind later.
[14] A. Solerti, *Le vite di Dante, Petrarca e Boccaccio* (Milan, 1904), p. 13. The shorter form of the *Vita* (which most scholars consider a revised form) omits the entire passage.
[15] See V. Rossi's edition of the *Familiari*, IV (Florence, 1942), Index, p. 405 *s. v. Moderni*.
[16] Even so he inserts a « perhaps » in the lines that best express his hopes (*Epist. Met.*, III, 33, 4): « Nam fuit et fortassis erit felicius evum ». He should

In 1372 Boccaccio wrote to Iacopo Pizzinga that individuals not unlike those of antiquity were seeking immortality under the guidance of poetry, and the tiny spark of their efforts raised hope that the lost light of antiquity would be restored [17]: « A quibus etsi non integrum deperditi luminis ytalici restituatur columen, saltem a quantumcunque parva scintillula optantium spes erigitur in fulgidam posteritatem... Verum evo nostro ampliores a celo venere viri, si satis adverto, quibus cum sint ingentes animi, totis viribus pressam [sc. poesim] relevare et ab exilio in pristinas revocare sedes mens est ». Here again is the theme of return from exile; great writers are coming to the rescue of poetry, crushed to earth, and are inviting her to return from exile to her former home. Boccaccio continues, naming Dante and Petrarch and Zanobi: « Vidimus ... Dantem Alegherii nostrum omissum a multis retroactis seculis fontem laticesque mellifluos cupientem ... et semisopitas excivisse sorores et in cytharam traxisse Phebum ». Dante goes to the Pyerian spring, neglected for many centuries, and awakens the Muses. And Petrarch clears the road to the spring for his successors, restores the Muses: « Pyeridisque iam rusticitate sordentibus in antiquum redactis decus », and climbs to the very top of Parnassus, receiving the laurel crown for the first time in a thousand years or more.

In 1381-82 Filippo Villani wrote his book on the history of Florence and its citizens [18]. Book II, dealing with the famous citizens, was an outgrowth, he tells us, of a plan to write merely on Dante. The book begins with the statement that poets were held in the highest honor by the ancients, ranking next to the

---

have been born earlier or much later, he says (note « multo post tempore »). The same « perhaps » appears in the same context in the Africa (IX, 456-457): « Poterunt discussis forte tenebris Ad purum priscumque iubar remeare nepotes ». Petrarch is thoroughly pessimistic about the dark ages in which he lives. I find a similar interpretation in U. Bosco, Petrarca (Turin, 1946), pp. 136-138; second edition (1961), pp. 119-120; Simone, op. cit. (Coscienza... francesi), p. 32, n. 19.

[17] Giovanni Boccaccio, Opere latine minori, ed. A. F. Massèra (Bari, 1928), pp. 194-195.

[18] Philippi Villani Liber de civitatis Florentiae famosis civibus, ed. G. C. Galletti (Florence, 1847).

emperors. Poets, he believes, have to know everything, which explains their rarity. Yet Florence has produced five who have passed away and is nursing others of great promise. The first poet he mentions is Claudian, who at that time was generally considered a Florentine. Next comes Dante, who died more than nine hundred years after Claudian. After Dante, Villani takes up Petrarch, Zanobi da Strada, Boccaccio, Coluccio Salutati, and Domenico Silvestri, all of whom had been alive in the sixty years since Dante's death. Making due allowance for favoritism towards contemporaries, we can understand his being struck by the fact that Dante, Petrarch, and Boccaccio are all clustered together after a long interval. At the beginning of his life of Dante he blames the withering of poetry on the weakness and avarice of the emperors and the opposition of the Church: « Post Claudianum ... Caesarum pusillanimitate et avaritia omnis pene consenuit poesis, eo etiam fortasse quod ars non esset in pretio, cum fides Catholica coepisset figmenta poetarum ut rem perniciosissimam et vanissimam abhorrere. Ea igitur iacente sine cultu, sine decore, vir maximus Dantes Allagherii, quasi ex abysso tenebrarum eruptam revocavit in lucem, dataque manu, iacentem erexit in pedes ». Villani refers only to poetry, saying that Dante brought her into the light after long neglect, raised her to her feet after a long period of prostration. Though he himself wrote in Latin, he showed more esteem for Dante than for the others and did not hold it against him that he wrote in the vernacular. He probably is echoing Florentine feeling, and we must not forget that under the leadership of Coluccio Salutati Florence was becoming the center of the new movement. Villani himself looked up to Coluccio and asked him to read and correct his history.

In 1395 Coluccio deprecates comparison between himself and Cassiodorus as an epistolographer [19]. Generalizing somewhat, he observes that excellent writers existed even in late antiquity, but a great decline set in thereafter. Then: « Emerserunt parumper nostro seculo studia litterarum; et primus eloquentie cultor fuit ... Musattus Patavinus... Emerserunt et ista lumina Florentina

---

[19] *Epist.*, III, p. 76.

(ut summum vulgaris eloquentie decus et nulli scientia vel ingenio comparandum qui nostris temporibus floruit, aut etiam cui-
piam antiquorum, Dantem Alligherium, pretermittam), Petrarca
scilicet et Bocaccius ». Here it is said that « luminaries emerged »
and that Dante ranks with the ancients.

Let us add one set of examples from the fifteenth century.
Between 1433 and 1437 Sicco Polenton finished his history of
Latin literature [20]. He says that poetical ability and eloquence
went to sleep after Juvenal: « Age, post eum [*i.e.,* Iuvenalem]
illa omnis quae suum in diem aut magna aut saltem aliqua fuerat veterum more poetandi cura, delectatio, diligentia adeo intermissa atque sopita est ut deinde multos ac multos ad annos quasi
longo et magno labore fatigatis ac fessis ingeniis dormisse omnis
poetandi facultas ac fere omnis eloquentia videatur ». Then in
discussing Dante he carries out the figure (too far, be is said!) in
remarking that the Muses were slowly waking up from a long
sleep of a thousand years, that they were moving their limbs,
were rubbing their eyes and stretching: « Iam quidem iam paulatim quasi longissimo e somno excitabantur Musae. Annos quippe
post quem nominavi Iuvenalem mortuum ad mille dormierant.
Hoc vero tempore, ut somnulenti solent, membra movere, oculos
tergere, brachia extendere coeperant ». Of Petrarch Sicco states
that in literature he surpassed all writers of the past thousand
years and that he was the leader in stirring up interest in poetry
and eloquence, which had lain dormant: « In studiis ea gravitate,
copia, gratia versatus est ut qui etiam severissime iudicant fatean-
tur ipsum excelluisse cunctos qui aut memoria sua viverent aut
superiori aetate mille prope ad annos istis in litteris claruissent.
Neque vero id negant,... ipsum esse illum qui et princeps et
auctor fuit excitandi studii et poetici et omnis eloquentiae, ut
quae perdiu neglecta fuerant et quasi sopita dormierant, ea tandem mortalium ad cognitionem usumque redirent ».

In the unpublished first edition of Sicco's history of litera-

---

[20] *Sicconis Polentoni Scriptorum illustrium Latinae linguae libri XVIII,* ed
B. L. Ullman (Rome, 1928). The three passages quoted are from pp. 125, 17;
128, 31; 139, 6.

ture, written ten or fifteen years earlier, we find some interesting differences. In the first passage he merely says that after Juvenal's death « diutissime cura poetandi missa ». In the second, he uses the figure of the awakening of the Muses in connection with his fellow Paduan Mussato instead of Dante, but without mention of the thousand years' intermission. Nor is there any in the passage about Petrarch. It may be that in the meantime he got the idea from the Florentines [21].

It would be useful, I think, to bring to light other fourteenth-century statements of the same purport. To be sure, there are those who hold that the very fact that the humanists started the idea of a rebirth or awakening is a reason for rejecting it, that the notion was artificially fostered by the drum beating of the humanists. We can ignore this view, a natural outgrowth of the cynicism aroused by modern advertising, as its proponents would,

[21] I find no merit whatever in Baron's attempt to see a difference of attitude in Sicco's two editions; he thinks that in the first Sicco has only poetry in mind, but in the second includes eloquence and other studies (H. Baron, *The Crisis of the Early Renaissance*, Princeton, 1955, II, pp. 541-542). But in the first edition Sicco discusses not merely poetry but has much to say about Petrarch's prose works: « in omni genere dicendi, Latine, patrie, metrice, solute ». Similarly about Dante. He actually uses the same words about poetry in both editions: « cura poetandi missa » (first edition), « poetandi cura... intermissa » (second edition). The difference merely is that in the second edition Sicco elaborates, as he does throughout his book. Baron had before him only the brief quotation which I gave, since (alas!) the first edition has not been published, though it has been prepared. There is now a prospect that it will soon be published. Buck in his review of my book in *Gnomon*, 28 (1956), p. 236, reproached me for overlooking Baron's point. Our books appeared in the same year, and neither of us was in a position to see the other's book. I could not be expected to see a point which I do not believe exists.

As for *studia humanitatis,* the hallmark of the fifteenth century, according to Baron, the phrase is used by Coluccio Salutati a number of times. *In Epist.,* III, p. 536, his definition of *humanitas* is very broad: « Nam non solum illa virtus que etiam benignitas dici solet hoc nomine significatur, sed etiam peritia et doctrina », for which he refers to Cicero. In his long reply to Giovanni Dominici (*Epist.*, IV, p. 205) he discusses all the liberal arts as basic for poetry, which, he says, presupposes trivium, quadrivium, philosophy, and everything else. In a letter of 1404-1405 Coluccio mentions a translation of a homily of Basil made by Leonardo Bruni in 1400-1401 at Coluccio's suggestion. In a letter to Coluccio written soon after, Bruni describes this translation as a defense against those who attack *studia humanitatis* (*Epist.,* IV, p. 185, note). In a letter of 1406 Poggio speaks of *studia haec humanitatis* in reference to Coluccio (Tonelli's edition of Poggio's letters, I, 1832, p. XIV) and frequently thereafter.

in the absence of any such statements as we have just set forth, surely be the very ones to assert that such absence was suspicious.

Boccaccio, Salutati, Villani, Polenton, all mention Dante as the first to wake the Muses from their thousand-year slumber. If the word Renaissance referred only to the revival of poetry, we should have to date its inception with Dante, whom most of us would assign to the Middle Ages. The fact that the men of the Renaissance, at least of the early Renaissance, with which I am here primarily concerned, considered that the new movement began with Dante shows the folly of the modern notion (fostered, it must be admitted, by later humanists) of setting up the Middle Ages and the Renaissance as opponents. Students are almost being forced to take sides, to applaud the one and jeer at the other. Those who are interested in both periods, or rather in the continuous flow of culture, are placed in a difficult position but can take refuge in the thought that Dante ends the Middle Ages and begins the Renaissance.

From poetry and other forms of literature, Italian and Latin, the concept of an awakening spread naturally to the other creative arts. As early as 1348-53 Boccaccio, commenting on the naturalness of the figures in Giotto's paintings, so lifelike that people mistook them for living beings, adds [22]: « E per ciò, avendo egli quella arte ritornata in luce, che molti secoli sotto gli error d'alcuni che più a dilettar gli occhi degl'ignoranti che a compiacere allo 'ntelletto de' savi dipignendo intendevano, era stata sepulta, meritamente una delle luci della fiorentina gloria dirsi puote ». Boccaccio does not indicate how many centuries the art of painting had been buried before Giotto brought her back to the light of day, but we may be sure that he means the ten centuries, more or less, since antiquity.

Similarly in 1381 Villani said that Cimabue, Giotto, and other Florentines revived the art of painting, which was almost dead: « qui artem exanguem et pene extinctam suscitaverunt ». The pictures in the churches reveal, he continues, how low Greek and Roman painting had sunk before Cimabue returned to nature: « Picturam ... coepit ad Naturae similitudinem ... revocare.

[22] *Decameron* VI, 5.

Constat siquidem ante hunc Graecam Latinamque picturam per
multa saecula subcrassae peritiae in ministerio iacuisse, ut plane
ostendunt figurae et imagines quae in tabulis atque parietibus
cernuntur sanctorum ecclesias adornare ». The phrase « per multa
saecula » is elucidated by his mention of ancient artists, as Zeuxis,
Polyclitus, Phidias, etc. [23].

Villani commented on Florentine musicians also but he made
no such claim for them as he did for the poets and painters.
He knew next to nothing about ancient music; hence he could
not say anything about a return to the ancient standards of
achievement. As a matter of fact, no comparable advance had
taken place in music, though there had been new developments
around 1300, and Florence itself saw some in the fourteenth century, as we know from Boccaccio and Salutati. But the great
changes were to come later [24]. Yet it is interesting to note that
Dante and Giotto flourished just about the time when there
were new developments in music.

Humanism, the new humanism, had its origins in the time
of Dante. To compare great with small, Dante the poet died
in 1321, Benvenuto Campesani, who because of his little poem
on the discovery of Catullus may be taken to symbolize the new
humanistic movement, died in 1323. But since humanism had
no outstanding representative before Petrarch, the impression is
given that humanism was born much later than the creative arts.

Reading of the classics concerned itself with both form and
content. To speak of the Renaissance as a mere return to the
writing of Ciceronian Latin is one of the shocking misstatements
that one encounters. The ideas expressed by the ancient authors
led readers in many directions and influenced them in many of
their thoughts and actions. Their reactions were often different
from those of their predecessors because they were different
readers: they were laymen — jurists and notaries, most of them.
The role of notaries and jurists in the movement has not been
sufficiently stressed. Indeed I can recall but one mention of it

[23] *Op. cit.,* p. 35.
[24] E. J. Dent, « Music of the Renaissance in Italy », *Proceedings of the
British Academy,* 19 (1933), p. 293.

in print, and that is quite recent [25]. The secularization of learn
ing is an important phenomenon of the time.

Worth quoting is an admirable sentence of Simone's [26]. « In-
fatti letterato quale era, il Petrarca non poteva che amare una
cultura classica a base essenzialmente letteraria e disprezzare
quella a base filosofica che aveva dominato nei grandi secoli medievali ». Classical Aristotelianism had become a theological tool
of no interest to a poet. The more professional or esoteric aspects
of philosophy held no appeal for laymen. The phase of philosophy which may be called the least professional, ethics, attracted
men like Petrarch (as it had the ancient Romans). In the early
Renaissance there was little formal philosophy, aside from Tho-
mism, beyond the watered down Platonism derived from Cicero
and Augustine, and the Stoicism of Seneca. Yet Petrarch and
Salutati were regarded as great philosophers in their day! The
chief contribution of the Italian Renaissance to philosophy would
seem to be in the understanding of Platonism as a result of the
study and translation of the Greek text of Plato. Study and
translation of other Greek texts, Aristotle, Plutarch, etc., also
contributed to this field.

Petrarch and Salutati may have absorbed their political ideas
from their environment, from the independent commune into
which Florence, like other Italian towns, had grown, but these
ideas were nourished on the reading of Cicero and Livy and Valerius Maximus. Perhaps the seed might not have grown without this nourishment. Petrarch's enthusiasm for the ill-starred
adventure of Cola di Rienzo was, of course, the direct outgrowth
of his classical reading. And Cola owed much to the same source.
Burdach made a neat point when he remarked that Cola, during
his imprisonment at Avignon, read Livy, while the cardinals read
mediaeval French love romances [27]. It is to the ancient authors

[25] Weiss, *op. cit.*, pp. 5-6. The notaries in particular, with their training
in law, literature, and *ars dictaminis,* became even more prominent later: Salutati, Bruni, Poggio, and scores of lesser lights scattered through all the communes
of Italy. A special study should be devoted to them. See *Il Notariato nella
civiltà italiana*, a cura del Consiglio Nazionale del Notariato (Milan, 1961).

[26] *Op. cit.*, p. 846.

[27] K. Burdach, *Aus Petrarcas ältestem deutschen Schülerkreise (Vom Mit
telalter zur Reformation,* IV [Berlin, 1929]), p. 134.

that Petrarch went for examples of liberty in his famous horta-
tory epistle to Cola (*Var.* 48) — his pounding insistence on the
theme is indicated by no less than thirty-three occurrences of *libertas, liberator, liber* in this single letter. It is from the same
source that Coluccio Salutati obtained fuel to keep the sacred
flame of liberty burning in the hundreds of letters he wrote
during the war between Florence and Gregory XI. It is to this
source that Leonardo Bruni went for inspiration for his central
theme of democratic liberty in his *History of Florence.*

The greater the number of ancient books the humanists read
the more they wanted. Their craving led to the famous manuscript hunts, whose dramatic qualities have tended to produce
overemphasis and misconceptions. From the search for lost Latin
authors they turned to the Greeks whom they found mentioned
and praised in Cicero and the other ancients, and thus a new
phase of the everchanging Renaissance was started. It must not
be forgotten that the Renaissance was a living, changing, growing being, not a lump of inert matter. The incredible enthusiasm with which the study of the ancient classics was pursued
by the humanists is in itself a fascinating subject of investigation,
being one of the distinguishing marks of the Renaissance. That
study had various aspects. Criticism in all its forms was developed. The genuineness of texts, the correctness of the manuscripts, the literary qualities of the works were topics for investigation and discussion. Grammar and spelling came in for attention. All that, and only that, is properly called the Revival of
Learning.

I have probed very superficially, of course, into a few fields,
such as politics, to indicate to what extent the new movement
affected those fields. Perhaps we should start anew to test, cautiously and scientifically, the impact of the Renaissance on the
various aspects of civilization. To what extent, if any, was the
demand for books created by the Renaissance responsible for the
invention of printing? Did the enormous influence of the translation of Ptolemy's *Geography* finished in 1406 [28] by Iacopo Angeli

---

[28] The usual date is 1409 or 1410, but in the *Prodromus* to the facsimile
of Ptolemy's *Codex Urbinas Graecus 82* (Leiden, 1932), p. 185, J. Fischer cites
testimony that it was finished in 1406.

da Scarperia, disciple of Salutati, have any bearing on the voyages of discovery? [29]   Perhaps these questions have been satisfactorily answered and these are unfortunate examples, but they may serve to indicate lines that might be followed.

It is a rather curious situation that, with all the awareness of the humanists of what was going on, no single word found general acceptance among them to describe the phenomenon. If any particular designation had become current in the early period it might have been « Awakening ». The idea of rebirth came into use very slowly. It is found early, in a letter of one of those first French humanists who were in touch with the Italian movement, Nicolas de Clamanges: « His ingeniosis studiis ... operam aliquantam impendi atque ipsam eloquentiam diu sepultam in Galliis quodammodo renasci novisque iterum floribus, licet priscis longe imparibus, repullulare laboravi » [30].   Machiavelli used the phrase *Roma rinata* in speaking of Cola di Rienzo [31], but Rome was not actually reborn as a result of Cola's efforts. Beginning in 1518, Melanchthon frequently spoke of *renascentes Musae* and *litterae renascentes* [32]. And others were writing of *litterae renatae*. The metaphor gained wide acceptance with Vasari's use of *rinascita* of the fine arts (1550).

Plattard has listed the many terms used of the French movement in the sixteenth century [33]: « restitution des bonnes lettres », « restauration », « postliminio reverti », especially « renaistre et florir en ce noble royaume les bonnes lettres » (Amyot in the dedication of his translation of Plutarch, 1559). Plattard repeats the familiar remark that the word *renaissance* was not used in the sixteenth century. One example has, however, turned up. In the dedicatory letter of a book describing his travels the naturalist

---

[29] On Angeli's translation cf. Dana B. Durand in *Journal of the History of Ideas,* IV (1943), p. 4: « The fact that this capital text had been overlooked by the medieval translators may be regarded as one of the momentous accidents of history; its recovery as one of the most notable successes of early scientific humanism ».   General statements about the influence of Ptolemy's *Geography* are not rare, but I have in mind the accumulation of specific details.

[30] Nicolaus de Clemengiis, *Opera omnia,* ed. I. M. Lydius (Lugduni Batavorum, 1613), No. XLVI, p. 141.

[31] Quoted by Simone, *op. cit.,* p. 842 (*Coscienza... francesi,* p. 29).

[32] *Ibid.,* p. 857 (*Coscienza... francesi,* p. 43).

[33] *Loc. cit.*

Pierre Belon has some interesting remarks of which I quote only part [34]. He pays tribute to Cardinal de Tournon by saying that « les esprits des hommes qui au paravant estoyent comme endormiz et detenuz assopiz en un profond sommeil d'ancienne ignorance, ont commencé à s'esveiller, et sortir des tenebres, ... et en sortant, ont iecté hors et tiré en evidence toutes especes de bonnes disciplines: lesquelles à leur tant heureuse et desirable renaissance, tout ainsi que les nouvelles plantes apres l'aspre saison de l'hyver reprennent leur vigueur à la chaleur du Soleil, et sont consolées de la doulceur du printemps: semblablement ayants trouvé un incomparable Mecenas, et favorable restaurateur si propice n'arresterent gueres à pulluler et à produire leurs bourgeons ». Belon seems to have most of the phrases that had been used of the Renaissance in Italy and France: the awakening from sleep (not of the Muses, however, but of men), the coming out of darkness, a renaissance — a rebirth like that of plants in the spring — a restorer, a pullulation.

Belon's book evidently enjoyed a fairly large circulation, as it passed through several editions and was even translated into Latin. Yet his word *renaissance* seems not to have caught the popular fancy, for no other example, in this use, is reported until 1675 [35]. Its wide diffusion is due, however, to Bayle [36]. The term finally received its accolade when it was permitted to enter the dictionary of the French Academy in 1718, over four hundred years after the beginning of the movement in Italy. It might be expected that after such a long period of gestation the word would enjoy a greater esteem than it does today. Certainly a part of the growing literature of criticism, even denial, of the Renaissance has been engendered by dissatisfaction with the term. The name is not the best that could have been chosen. Words have a habit of changing meanings and acquiring new ones. « Renaissance » is no more objectionable, however, than « science »,

---

[34] Pierre Belon, *Les observations de plusieurs singularitez et choses memorables trouvées en Grece, Asie, Iudée, Egypte, Arabie et autres pays estranges* (Paris, 1953). L. Thorndike first called attention to this passage in *Journal of the History of Ideas*, IV (1943), p. 68.

[35] D. Bonhours, *Remarques nouvelles sur la langue françoise* (Paris, 1675), who cites the phrase « la renaissance des lettres humaines ».

[36] Pierre Bayle, *Dictionaire historique et critique* (Rotterdam, 1697).

for example, which by etymology arrogates to itself the whole field of knowledge. In any event, the phenomenon which people have chosen to call the Renaissance, whether they include much or little under the term, « by any other name would smell as sweet » to those who love it.

It will not have escaped the reader that, in my opinion, a host of problems connected with the Renaissance remain to be investigated, not only the larger problems of reinterpretation and synthesis of known data, but also those that are more minute, involving a search for unknown details tucked away in unpublished manuscripts. And when the constantly shifting phases of the later manifestations in Italy, France, Spain, England, and Germany are taken into account, it will be seen that scholars may remain happily busy for a long, long time.

CHAPTER II

SOME ASPECTS OF THE ORIGIN
OF ITALIAN HUMANISM [1]

Improved techniques of lighting have affected not only our homes and offices, but the Middle Ages as well. The darkness of the mediaeval blackout has all but disappeared. Certain mediaeval centuries indeed are said by some to be nearly as bright as day, for we now speak of a renaissance in the ninth century and another in the twelfth. Consequently the dazzling brightness of what used to be *the* Renaissance to those who came to it from the mediaeval blackout now seems to have less candle power. Then too we have discovered mediaeval shadows lurking in the Renaissance. As a result of both of these developments some persons even maintain that they can see little or no difference in the brightness of the two periods. Furthermore the importance of the revival of letters and learning which used to bulk large in the minds of many has been diminished by the historians and other social scientists who have asserted that this movement was subsequent and subsidiary to the real Renaissance — to the development of trade, of a bourgeois society, of cities, and so on. Then too we have discovered a spiritual kinship with the Middle Ages, a discovery which has led to some rather remarkable results in the last thirty years. Among them is a depreciation of the Renaissance.

This chapter will be regarded as reactionary by some because it assumes the fundamental importance of the revival of literature and the classics in the formation of the Renaissance [2]. It is not

[1] Originally published in the *Philological Quarterly*, XX (1941), p. 20.
[2] Protests against some of the current views are rare. A welcome emphasis on the classical revival is to be found in Douglas Bush, *The Renaissance and English Humanism* (Toronto, 1939).

my ambition to present a new unified interpretation of the origin of the Renaissance, a movement so complex that no single interpretation or even many interpretations can suffice to explain it. Scholars often tend to oversimplify the phenomena they study. I must confess to a distrust of any single, simple explanation, the kind that is easily conveyed to a notebook, for so many-sided a movement. It is my intention merely to trace out a few threads of the complicated pattern. I shall confine myself almost entirely to the beginnings of the movement in Italy in the fourteenth century.

But before considering Italy let us turn to neighboring France. As a result of the ninth-century awakening many manuscripts of classical Latin authors had been copied and were lying about in the libraries of France. In the twelfth century came another renaissance. Continuing into the thirteenth century, it brought with it or was accompanied by the founding of the universities and of the Dominican and Franciscan orders. The interest turned to philosophy. The translation of works of Aristotle previously unknown was in keeping with the current interest, and all these factors led to scholasticism. It is clear that scholasticism had its roots in a revival of the classics, but it petrified into a form which was eventually regarded as the very antithesis of classical study. The scholastic movement spread everywhere, to England and to Italy. It is against this movement, in its later more quibbling form, that the early Italian humanists reacted most strongly: one classical revival against the ossified remains of another. This is not so strange as it seems, for some recent scholars have criticized the Italian Renaissance as well as certain tendencies of present-day classical study in much the same manner.

It is not without interest to note that the particular phase of scholasticism that the Italians attacked most fiercely was that of the British, whose leader was Ockham. In one of his letters, Petrarch belabors a Sicilian dialectician, i.e., a devotee of scholasticism. Scylla and Charybdis were bad enough without this new pestilence invading Sicily, says Petrarch; the pest seems to be one peculiar to islands, for in addition to the legions of British dialecticians we now have this new horde of Sicilians. Sicily first had Cyclopes, he continues, then tyrants, now it has a third pack of monsters, armed with syllogisms, and so on at some length[3]. Benvenuto da Imola, the commentator of Dante, calls « those modern English logicians » « spiders »[4]. Coluccio Salutati bewails the fact that philosophy, so-called, has fled to Britain and urges his correspondent to rid the world of sophistry and equivocation[5]. Again in a defense of poetry against certain contemporary philosophers who are always ready to talk at length on any subject, he charges that they do not understand Aristotle but instead quote certain English treatises[6]. Though the early humanists were not particularly fond of Aristotle, their attitude was one rather of indifference than of hostility.

But to return to France with its many manuscripts of classical authors which had been copied from the ninth century to the fourteenth. Here then there was a continued interest in the classics, one that waned from time to time to be sure, but the like of which did not exist in Italy before the fourteenth century. Cross-fertilization between Italy and France, it seems to me, played an important part in the revival of the classics in Italy. What was it that brought Italians, especially north Italians, into contact with French classical culture? For one thing it was the establishment of the papal court at Avignon in 1309. Hundreds of Italians came to Avignon and France during the succeeding seventy years. The papal court played somewhat the same role in spreading classical culture to Italy that the church council of Constance played a century later (1415) in spreading the new Italian humanism to other parts of Europe[7]. Even if we take the unlikely view that in France humanistic interest was at a

---

[3] *Fam.* I, 7, 5 ff. These letters are cited from the edition of V. Rossi, *Francesco Petrarca, Le Familiari*, 4 vols. (Florence, 1933-1942).

[4] F. Novati, *Epistolario di Coluccio Salutati*, III (Rome, 1896), p. 320 n.

[5] *Ibid.*, pp. 319-320.

[6] *De laboribus Herculis,* ed. B. L. Ullman (Zurich, 1951), I, 1, 2 (p. 3, 16).

[7] P. Sambin, « Ildebrandino Conti e l'introduzione dei monaci olivetani a Padova », *Benedictina*, III (1949), p. 263, accepts my view (first published in 1941) or arrived at the same conclusion independently: « Ci spostiamo ad Avignone, punto d'incontro di tante correnti e tanti uomini dell'Europa del Trecento ». See also Robert Weiss in *La parola del passato*, Fasc. XXXII (1953), p. 321, and especially Franco Simone, *Il Rinascimento francese* (Turin, 1961), pp. 3-44.

very low ebb in the early part of the fourteenth century, and that classical culture was neglected or passed on in mechanical fashion, it is still true that the manuscript treasures were there for the Italian visitors to gloat over, as today collectors of antique furniture do who find themselves in virgin territory where the houses are filled with precious pieces whose value the owners do not realize and to whose beauty they are indifferent.

Among those who came to Avignon and spent many years there or near by was Petrarch, the most remarkable figure among the early humanists, a man far ahead of his time and one who, in spite of all reservations, may still fittingly be called the first modern man. In France he found many of the manuscripts which gave him such an enthusiasm for the classics. It is this enthusiasm that is one of the most striking and significant characteristics of Petrarchan and Italian humanism. The world has seen nothing like it since.

Petrarch was in Paris (which he calls the foster-mother of learning) in 1333 and might, as Nolhac suggests[8], have been in the Sorbonne library. A catalogue of this library made in 1338 survives; in it are several of the classical treasures listed by the thirteenth-century humanist Richard de Fournival. Of at least two of these Petrarch obtained copies[9]. We thus have a direct connection between Petrarch and the French humanism of the thirteenth century. From a Greek whom he met at Avignon in 1353, Petrarch obtained the copy of Homer in the original Greek which he treasured but never learned to read. The ferment caused by this manuscript may have been partly responsible for the rise of interest in Greek among the humanists. It seems to me then that Petrarch's stay in Avignon and his travels through France were highly significant for the development of his interests and therefore for the humanistic movement in general, in which he was the dominant figure.

[8] P. de Nolhac, *Pétrarque et l'humanisme,* ed. 2, I (Paris 1907), p. 39.
[9] See below, chapter VIII. The fathers of both Petrarch and Boccaccio had been in Paris (Nolhac, *op. cit.,* p. 35). Petrarch's father bought a manuscript of Isidore there which passed to his son. He was an admirer of Cicero and his son no doubt acquired some of his own love of Cicero from his father. The father's copy of Cicero's rhetorical works (where he obtained it is unknown) was cherished by the son.

There are other indications that point the same way, that show that the curious, but intellectually somewhat narrow Italians of the fourteenth century, found in France just the right milieu for their development. Here is just one detail, dealing with a single Latin author, Seneca. In the Middle Ages Seneca's philosophical works were well known everywhere, but the plays first attracted attention in Italy in the early fourteenth century [10]. A Dominican cardinal from Prato, near Florence, became interested in the tragedies, how or why we do not know, and about 1314 wrote from Valence, not far from Avignon, to an English Dominican, Nicholas Trevet, or Trivet, to prepare a commentary on Seneca's plays, which the cardinal, with his scholastic background, found obscure [11]. He turned to Trevet, not because the latter was a humanist in any sense or had a special competence in Seneca, but because the cardinal had read and liked Trevet's commentary on Boethius and because he knew that Trevet had written a commentary on the *Declamations* of the Elder Seneca. Trevet produced the desired commentary, which is of no great consequence. The really significant point for us is that an interest in the tragedies should be awakened in the very Dominican circles which were the heart of scholasticism and that the clearing-house, so to speak, of this activity should be at Avignon. The significance of the cardinal's action is heightened when we consider, as we shall in a moment, the part that Seneca's tragedies played in the Renaissance. Incidentally the papal library at Avignon had a copy of them, with Trevet's commentary, as early as 1317 [12].

Another example of Avignon's strategic position. This time the example is Greek and of a somewhat later period. A Florentine cardinal, Pietro de' Corsini, had been imbued with the

[10] Mediaeval manuscripts of the tragedies are scarce, but some three hundred dating from the fourteenth and fifteenth centuries, written for the most part in Italy, are in existence. I have not time to go into details or to substantiate my belief that their archetype came from France.

[11] E. Franceschini, *Studi e note di filologia latina medievale* (Milan, 1938), p. 29.

[12] We know, to be sure, only that the library had a manuscript of the tragedies with a commentary, but I agree with Franceschini (*loc. cit.*) that Trevet's commentary must be the one.

humanistc spirit, probably catching it from Petrarch. In Aulus Gellius, that gossipy ancient who gives us all sorts of curious lore, the cardinal found a quotation from Plutarch's essay on anger. This impressed him so much (again we do not know why) that he seems to have kept it in mind for years and to have looked for a chance to get the entire essay. We can imagine the good cardinal asking every new acquaintance if he had seen a copy of the essay. In 1372 at the papal court of Avignon he met a Greek archbishop named Simon and asked him the usual question. The quest was ended, for Simon had a copy and translated it for his new acquaintance [13].

Avignon played a part in establishing contacts between French and Italian scholars [14]. It may be significant that the first phases of humanism in France, represented by Jean de Montreuil, Nicolas de Clémanges, the Col brothers, Gontier and Pierre, and others, died out at just about the time that Avignon abandoned its papal claims entirely and the schism came to an end. To be sure, political conditions in France, as well as the departure of the papacy, played their part too in bringing this period to a close.

Though Coluccio himself never went to Avignon he was in touch with many Italians who did, and through them he became acquainted with Frenchmen and other foreigners. So he writes to the Aragonese Juan Fernandez de Heredia, who spent much

---

[13] Dean P. Lockwood in an unpublished paper (cf. *Proceedings of the American Philological Association*, LXIV, 1933, p. lxvi). Coluccio (*Epist.*, II, p. 480) criticizes the style of this translation.

[14] A. Coville, *Gontier et Pierre Col et l'humanisme en France au temps de Charles VI* (Paris, 1934), has a chapter entitled *Les relations avec l'Italie et l'intermédiaire d'Avignon* (p. 140). R. Sabbadini, *Le scoperte dei codici latini e greci ne' secoli XIV e XV*, II (Florence, 1914), has a few hints of the same sort in his second chapter. P. Simone, stressing the importance of Avignon as an international center, is primarily concerned with Italian influence on French humanism, which he covers in a masterly survey, but also touches on our problem (« Le origini del rinascimento in Francia e la funzione storica della cultura avignonese », *Convivium, raccolta nuova*, 1951, p. 161); see too his *Il Rinascimento francese*, pp. 3-44. See also Ruth J. Dean in *Studies in Philology*, XLV (1948), p. 541. The hint that I have given of the role of Avignon should be thoroughly investigated

time in Avignon, and asks for copies of the less well-known Roman historians [15].

In spite of all the indebtedness to France which is merely hinted at in my few examples, early Italian humanism retained its independence. Otherwise it would not have developed. The mysterious urge was already there; Avignon and France furnished the opportunity. Notwithstanding his love for Vaucluse, Petrarch has some sharp things to say about French barbarism. He admits that the French are the most civilized of the barbarians, but insists that after all only Italians are real Latins. It has already been pointed out that humanism reacted strongly against scholasticism, nurtured in France. Humanism did more than that, it cancelled all mediaeval literature and started where the ancients left off. The French saw their mediaeval literature as part of their continuous tradition. The earlier French revivals could not be lightly cast aside by Frenchmen but the Italians travelled without such useless baggage.

I do not want to give the impression that Italy had no classical treasures and that the humanists found the classics only in France. Such an impression would be far from the truth. Nor do I mean to imply that the Italians found all their inspiration in France. The ghost of Dante rises to challenge any such implication. Scholars have placed him now at the end of the Middle Ages, now at the beginning of the Renaissance. The dispute is a good proof that the Renaissance did not come into being full-grown, like Minerva from the head of Jove. Dante has some humanistic qualities, though if I am forced to classify him I should prefer to put him in the Middle Ages. Except for Petrarch, the early humanists were enthusiastic admirers of Dante. Boccaccio lectured on *The Divine Comedy* in the University of Florence. Benvenuto da Imola, Dante's commentator (in Latin at that) was a friend of Petrarch and Coluccio. Dante's patriotic utterances, the prominence he gives to Virgil, and other aspects of his work had their influence in shaping humanism.

---

[15] Novati, *Epist.*, II, p. 289 and note 1. Benedict XIII may have been the intermediary (cf. Novati, *Epist.*, p. 264).

I am ready then to take into account the twelfth (and thirteenth) century French renaissance. At the same time I vehemently reject the view that the Italian Renaissance is a mere continuation of the French. To my mind it is still to be regarded as something quite new, quite as dazzling as it appeared to those who years ago saw no glimmer of light in the mediaeval darkness.

In the thirteenth century much of the classical material was taken by speakers and writers at second and third hand from handbooks and anthologies, such as the enormously popular *specula,* or encyclopaedias, of Vincent of Beauvais [16]. One striking result of the new humanistic curiosity which led to the acquisition of better libraries was that the originals were now read and quoted. Petrarch acutely characterizes the French renaissance of the thirteenth century when he accuses a certain Frenchman of having only a handful of extracts, a truly French work, and of regarding them, in accordance with Gallic lack of seriousness, as substitutes for a complete library [17]. An unusually interesting example of the difference between the two attitudes may be seen in the defense of literature by Coluccio Salutati and the attack on it by Giovanni Dominici in the early 1400's [18]. Dominici gets a large part of his material from secondary sources such as Vincent. Much of it he quotes from a faulty memory. Coluccio, on the other hand, regularly quotes scrupulously at first hand from the classical books in his library. In this way he is able to clear up many an obscurity and many a misunderstanding and to refute his opponent. « Quote correctly », he says on one occasion, « as the best manuscripts have it and as other evidence shows. If you cannot do

[16] B. L. Ullman, « Classical Authors in Certain Mediaeval Florilegia », *Classical Philology,* XXVII (1932), p. 40; « A Project for a New Edition of Vincent of Beauvais », *Speculum,* VIII (1933), p. 312.

[17] « Unum *Manipulum florum,* opus vere Gallicum, et quod Gallica levitas pro omnibus libris habet » (*Contra Galli calumnias,* in *Opera,* Basel, 1554, p. 1178; Petrarca, *Prose,* Milano, 1955, p. 770). This is an allusion to the *Manipulus florum* of Thomas Hibernicus, written or finished in Paris in 1306; see Chapter XXI. The work was very popular. Cf. *Rer. mem.* II, 91.

[18] See the edition of Edmund Hunt, *Iohannis Dominici Lucula Noctis* (Publications in Mediaeval Studies, The University of Notre Dame, IV, 1940), and below, chapter XII.

that, do not quote at all rather than offer the reader something that is open to criticism » [19].

The work which Coluccio considered his most important, as it was his longest, the *De laboribus Herculis,* was an allegorical treatment after the manner of the « moralized Ovids » and similar works which gave the Middle Ages one of its chief characteristics. But Coluccio's work reveals a broad and first-hand knowledge of the Latin classics and an interest in neglected authors which no mediaeval writer can match.

Great weight must be attached to the influence of particular Latin authors in determining the direction that the Renaissance took. Though all authors were eagerly sought, the various humanists had their favorites. For Petrarch, who did more than any one else to chart the course of humanism, it was Cicero. As a child Petrarch was fascinated by the musical sound of Cicero's words even before he could understand them [20]. When the other boys were reading Prosper and Aesop, the regular pabulum of the mediaeval school, he was racing through Cicero. He attributes such ability as he has in writing Latin to « the father of eloquence », as he calls Cicero. But he was absorbed in Cicero's *Weltanschauung* as well as his style. Through Petrarch Cicero had far-reaching effects on the development of prose style in Latin and in the vernaculars and on the tendencies of political theory. If Petrarch was the father of humanism, Cicero was its grandfather.

We are extremely fortunate in having a short list of favorite books which Petrarch put together before 1333, when he was still in his twenties. The exact nature and therefore the importance of this list has not always been realized on account of the difficulty of deciphering its faded heading. It can now be stated positively that it reads: *Libri mei peculiares. Ad reliquos non transfuga sed explorator transire soleo,* « My specially prized books. To the others I usually resort not as a deserter but as a

---

[19] *Epist.,* IV, pp. 83-84.
[20] The appreciation of the artistry of Latin literature was a fundamental characteristic of the early humanists. The Paduan group, to be mentioned below, interested themselves in the meters of Seneca.

scout » [21]. The last part of the sentence is a quotation from one of Seneca's letters. The difference between humanism and mediaevalism is well illustrated by this quotation. Petrarch employs it to head a list of favorite books in which Cicero has first place. The same sentence is quoted by a twelfth-century prior in answer to a request by an abbot of Corvey for a manuscript of Cicero. The prior writes: « Although you want to have the books of Cicero, I know that you are a Christian, not a Ciceronian. For you go into the enemy's camp not as a deserter but as a scout ». To the prior, Cicero is in the enemy's camp; the Christian writers are in his own. To Petrarch, Cicero is a most precious friend, while the Christian writers, with the one exception of Augustine, are in the enemy's camp.

But to return to Petrarch's list. Cicero's philosophical, or moral works, as Petrarch calls them, come first, headed by the sixth book of the *Republic* and the *Tusculan Disputations*. Then follow the rhetorical essays and the orations. After Cicero comes Seneca, leading off with the letters to Lucilius, the essay *De clementia*, and the *De remediis fortuitorum*, followed by the tragedies. The titles of three other essays were added later. Petrarch's enthusiasm for Seneca's philosophical works was more of an inheritance from the Middle Ages than a humanistic innovation. Aristotle's *Ethics* is squeezed in among the moral works and is the only Aristotelian work included. This too is a medieval inheritance; but of all the works of Aristotle the *Ethics* would naturally be among the few of greatest interest to the early humanists. Boethius' *Consolation of Philosophy* is also listed. After moralists come the historians: Valerius Maximus, Livy, Justinus, Florus, Sallust, Suetonius, Rufus Festus, Eutropius. History was a favorite subject with Petrarch, and Livy his favorite historian. From Cicero and Livy in particular he got his ideas about the growth of Rome, ideas which he applied to the Italy of his day. Next to appear in the list are Macrobius and Aulus Gellius. The poets listed are Virgil, Lucan, Statius, Horace, « especially in the *Odes* », Ovid, « especially in the *Metamorphoses* », and Juvenal. Virgil always had been a favorite of

---

[21] See below, chapter VI.

Petrarch's and along with Cicero's rhetorical works had been rescued from the fire into which Petrarch's father had thrown the
son's books because he spent too much time in dalliance with
them when he was supposed to be studying the practical subject
of law at Montpellier. We really owe a great debt to the law for
the many eminent persons who turned from it in distaste to pur-
sue humanistic studies. Virgil of course was no discovery of the
humanists but was now being read with greater insight and appreciation. The entry « Horace, especially in the *Odes* », attracts
our attention. The personal, lyric character of the *Odes* would
naturally appeal to the author of the *Canzoniere*. The Middle
Ages were fonder of the *Satires* and *Epistles*.

The only Christian writer in the list is Augustine, of whom
the *City of God* and the *Confessions* head the list of four works
given. Petrarch and Augustine had some qualities of tempera-
ment in common, and it is not surprising that Petrarch should
be drawn to these two books.

A slightly later list on the same page is somewhat briefer.
The poets are the same; Cicero and Seneca are still favorites but
the tragedies are expressly excepted. Aristotle and dialectic are
omitted. Livy too is absent but this must be due to accident or
to a temporary estrangement. Cicero and Livy, Virgil and Horace
were Petrarchan favorites who continued to mold the thought of
the Renaissance.

Petrarch's coolness toward Seneca's tragedies, a coolness that
is only relative, however, by contrast with his other enthusiasms,
and in another person and in a different age might be called
warmth, is for once out of line with the Renaissance movement.
About the same time that Trevet wrote his commentary for the
Italian cardinal, several persons in Padua became deeply interested in Seneca's plays—just why is one of the many unanswered
questions about the origin of the Renaissance. Franceschini has
pointed out that, although Trevet really understood Seneca scarcely more than the cardinal for whom he wrote, the Paduans
certainly did [22]. Marsilius, the famous author of the *Defensor*

----

[22] *Op. cit.*, p. 12.

pacis [23], precursor of Machiavelli, was one of the Paduans who took an interest in Seneca. But most noteworthy among the Paduan contributions was the play called the *Ecerinis*, by Mussato. This was the first and best play to imitate Seneca; it was so successful that Mussato has been called the father of Renaissance tragedy. It is perhaps true that he was chiefly responsible for making Seneca the tragic poet of the Italian and European Renaissance down to the time of Shakespeare. Perhaps we should rather say, in the absence of other Roman tragedies than Seneca's, that Mussato raised Senecan tragedy to a high place among Renaissance literary genres.

The continued influence of Seneca's tragedies is worth tracing a bit farther. Dionigi da Borgo San Sepolcro, a friend of Petrarch, who had studied and taught in Paris, wrote a commentary on the tragedies before 1342 (the date of his death) [24]. Coluccio Salutati, who with Petrarch and Boccaccio formed a triumvirate of Florentine humanism in the fourteenth century and who was largely responsible for making Florence the center of the movement in the next century, had a large library. I have located over one hundred manuscripts of this library, and of all these only one was transcribed by Coluccio himself. It is a beautiful copy, carefully made, of Seneca's tragedies, followed by Mussato's *Ecerinis*, at the end of which Coluccio proudly wrote: « I Coluccio copied this book myself ». Coluccio's chief book, on the labors of Hercules, was inspired by Seneca's play on the mad Hercules.

While we are on the subject of Seneca's plays let us skip a bit in time and out of our particular field to get a glimpse of how the Italian Renaissance spread. In the British Museum there is a manuscript of Seneca's tragedies copied by an Englishman, John Gunthorpe, in 1460 while he was studying the art of poetry in Ferrara under the famous humanist Guarino of Verona. The margins are filled with notes, presumably reproducing in part at

---

[23] My theory that Franco-Italian relations contributed to the Renaissance gets some support from the fact that this budding humanist spent a number of years in France (C. W. Previté-Orton, *The Defensor Pacis of Marsilius of Padua*, Cambridge, 1928, p. x).

[24] R. Sabbadini, *op. cit.*, II, p. 38.

least the observations of Professor Guarino [25]. Once again an Englishman writes a commentary on the tragedies, but how different a commentary and how different an Englishman from the commentary of Nicholas Trevet, written less than 150 years before! A new world had come into being. John Gunthorpe is one of the figures in that early fifteenth-century Renaissance in England which prepared for but was so completely overshadowed by the great sixteenth century that it has received less attention than it deserves.

Let us turn to another Roman poet, Ovid. Coluccio Salutati says of him: « I owe him much, for I had him as a sort of door and teacher (*ianuam et doctorem*) when my passion for this sort of study first flared up as if by divine inspiration at the end of my adolescence. Although I had no one to advise me and heard no one discuss the matter, after Ovid came into my hands, I of my own accord read all the poets and by divine gift, as it were, understood them » [26]. Ovid a door! A door to the great treasures of Roman poetry, a door into the future through the past, a door opening vistas of the coming Renaissance. By contrast, Rabanus Maurus, a product of the ninth-century renaissance, addresses God as *ianua vitae* and *doctor* [27]. Elsewhere Coluccio calls Ovid a key to poetry and its illuminator [28]. To Dante Virgil had been a guide: « Tu duca, tu signore, e tu maestro » [29], a guide into the Inferno of the life after death. To Coluccio Ovid is a door into a paradise on this earth.

Coluccio himself could not understand how he took to Ovid so easily and so violently; to him it seemed a miracle. Of unusual importance is his statement that he started his own renaissance, so to speak, without outside suggestion. Was humanism a seed

---

[25] The manuscript is Harl. 2485. R. Weiss independently noted the nature of this manuscript (*Humanism in England During the Fifteenth Century*, Oxford, 1941; second edition, 1957, p. 123). Much remains to be done with Gunthorpe's manuscripts. For Gunthorpe see C. Woodforde, *Stained Glass in Somerset, 1250-1830* (London, 1946), pp. 132-148.

[26] *De laboribus Herculis* III, 11, 25 (p. 215, 21).

[27] *Carm.* 12, 3 in E. Duemmler, *Poetae Latini Aevi Carolini,* II (Berlin, 1884), p. 175.

[28] *Op. cit.,* III, 39, 27 (p. 396, 8).

[29] *Inf.* 2, 140.

spread by the winds? Or had he at least heard or read some chance remark that germinated in his soul? Here at the beginning of the Renaissance we are confronted by the usual mystery. Significant too is the inspiration which Ovid gave him to read more widely. He was by no means the first to read Ovid; in fact Ovid was very popular in the Middle Ages, and the twelfth century has been called the *aetas Ovidiana,* the age of Ovid. But the Italian of the fourteenth century had a mysterious something, a germ or an excess of some secretion or an imbalance of salts that caused him to behave in a different way from his predecessors. Others would call it economic independence or something similar. Be that as it may, Ovid remained a favorite of the humanists, again down to the time of Shakespeare.

In this chapter I have merely hinted at the possible role of France in feeding the culture-hungry Italians of the fourteenth century and thus contributing to the origin of humanism. The sketch should be filled in with scores of minutiae. In the same way the influence of certain classical authors which I have outlined should be traced in detail. By following the procedure of Voigt, Sabbadini, and others like them we may achieve a point of view and a method which will help to correct some current views about the Renaissance.

Chapter III

THE SORBONNE LIBRARY
AND THE ITALIAN RENAISSANCE [1]

Chapter I mentioned the controversy between mediaevalists and Renaissance scholars. The former belittle the Renaissance as a mere outgrowth of the Middle Ages, the latter perhaps still think of the mediaeval period as one of darkness. Neither view is entirely true, neither is without truth. To one interested in the continuity of Latin culture through the ages both periods are important. Paradoxically, they are at the same time a continuum, yet strikingly different. The Renaissance, especially in its early Italian form, fascinates one by its enthusiasm and its freshness of outlook. A the same time, it is true that it did not spring full-grown from the head of Jove—or even of Petrarch. It grew out of the Middle Ages and preserved, at least at the start, many mediaeval aspects. Whatever inconsistency there may be is involved in the nature of human cultural tradition. The Renaissance, like a bride, wears something old and something new. In this chapter we shall concern ourselves with the old, with that part of Latin culture which the Renaissance received from the Middle Ages and, we might add, transmuted to its own uses.

The importance of the mediaeval universities in transmitting our cultural heritage is, of course, well-known. Among them Paris was one of the most influential, and in it the College of the Sorbonne stood in the front rank; indeed today the name Sorbonne is often used as a synonym for the University of Paris.

---

[1] Originally published under the title « The Library of the Sorbonne in the Fourteenth Century » in *The Septicentennial Celebration of the Founding of the Sorbonne College in the University of Paris* (Chapel Hill, 1953), pp. 33-47

Founded in the thirteenth century, the Sorbonne almost at once acquired a fine library which had much to do with spreading the University's influence.

Fortunately, we know quite a bit about the history and background of the Sorbonne Library. Thanks to that great scholar and librarian, Leopold Delisle, the material is readily available in that invaluable compilation of his, *Le Cabinet des Manuscrits de la Bibliothèque Nationale* [2]. Delisle states that the first benefactors of the college founded by Robert of Sorbon showed as much zeal in obtaining books for the faculty and students as in providing housing and income—and that too in a college founded for penniless students. A library was formed as if by magic in the first fifty years of the institution's life. Many of the early teachers left their books to the Library. Robert of Sorbon himself gave at least sixty-seven volumes to the Library, thirty-nine of which are today in the Bibliothèque Nationale, to which the Sorbonne collection of manuscripts, or what was left of it, was moved in 1796. His gifts consisted mostly of Bibles, complete or partial, Church Fathers, theological works, sermons, and a few legal books. Delisle lists the names of 168 early donors, most of whom are represented by at least one book in the Bibliothèque Nationale. Included are some men well-known to students of the Middle Ages: Godfrey of Fontaines, William Fichet, Peter of Limoges, Raymond Lull, and Thomas of Ireland (de Hibernia).

Our chief source of information about the Sorbonne Library is a catalogue prepared in 1338, which incorporated one made in 1290, less than forty years after the foundation of Robert's college. At that time the Library already had 1017 books; by 1338 it had reached the remarkable total of 1722 volumes. I say remarkable, for such it was for its time, though in comparison with the millions of books in some libraries today the total is of course remarkably low.

In 1338 the Library consisted of two parts, one of which was a small reference library of some 330 volumes which did not circulate and, to prevent unauthorized circulation, were chained to their places. This was called the *communis* or *magna libraria*.

---

[2] Paris, 1868-1881: II, p. 142; III, p. 8.

The rest of the collection, some 1090 volumes, was in the so-called small library, that is, the stacks. About 300 volumes, relist-ed from the first catalogue, are marked as missing or in circula-tion, a chronic condition of some libraries today.

The cataloguer followed a practice by no means new but one for which he is to be blessed, in that he furnished a large amount of information about each volume. He gives not only the contents, but also the name of the donor, the estimated value, and the first words on the second leaf and on the next to the last leaf. This device, intended to help identification of books belonging to the Library and to prevent mutilation, is invaluable to us in trying to identify surviving volumes of the collection. Some professors kept out books on indefinite loan, like their descendants today. Such books were appropriately called *libri vagantes,* « strays » from the sacred precincts of the Library. It should be said that usually a money deposit was required of borrowers. We even have loan records of the Library during the fourteenth century. The appraisal of each book given in the catalogue was intended to facilitate payment for books lost by borrowers. Chained books were occasionally loaned but only after a faculty vote. There was even a rudimentary inter-library loan system. And that is not all: a union list of books in the monasteries of Paris was made as early as the thirteenth century for the use of the *Sorbonnistes.* The catalogue of the reference library is in two parts, a shelf-list and a classified catalogue.

Since the Sorbonne was founded as a theological school it is only natural that theological books should be in the great majority. But even the reference library contained many others. The first classification is that of grammars, including Priscian, Huguccio, Isidore, and others. Then comes a group under the title « grammatical books in verse ». Included are not only such common school texts as Cato, Theodolus, Avianus, Pamphilus, etc., but also Ovid's *Metamorphoses* and *Fasti,* Persius, and others. The Latin Aristotle and his commentators of course play a large part, but there is also Plato in Latin dress with his *Timaeus* and *Phaedo,* Cicero's rhetorical and philosophical works, Seneca's let-ters, essays, and tragedies, Solinus, Valerius Maximus, Pliny. The Church Fathers are well represented, as are such mediaeval writers

as Hugo of St. Victor. Sermons are numerous. Even a few
French books were in the reference room, including the *Roman
de la Rose,* which, unfortunately, is marked « perditus est », in
spite of the chains.

So far I have largely summarized what anyone can glean
from the catalogues and other data published by Delisle. I now
come to two original and, I trust, not unimportant contributions
of my own to this survey of the early Sorbonne Library. One
of these contributions attempts to work back and tie the cultural
life of the Sorbonne to earlier periods, the other to work forward
and indicate an unsuspected influence of the Library on an important development in the history of Western culture, the Italian
Renaissance. First I wish to call attention to two early donors
to the Library collections. One is Gerard of Abbeville, who in
1271 willed nearly three hundred volumes to the Library, of which
118 are still preserved in the Bibliothèque Nationale. Some
indeed had been loaned to the Sorbonne before his death. Gerard
was a famous Parisian master and a neighbor of Robert of
Sorbon—they both lived in the Montagne Sainte-Geneviève. This
fact may account for his legacy. In the same year (1271) he
founded a college in his home town of Abbeville. In his will
leaving his books to Robert's new college, he mentions his theological books, his copies of the Church Fathers, his theological
notes, his collection of sermons and « questions », his books on
canon law and philosophy. His medical books and some others
were to be sold to pay his debts. It is interesting to note that,
though he left his books to the Sorbonne, he wanted them to
be accessible to all students in Paris. He particularly requested
that the books of the Church Fathers and some others be made
available to the secular masters of theology, as the religious were
already well supplied. This recalls his attacks on the Franciscans
and Dominicans, arising out of the rivalry between the secular
clergy and the newly founded and vigorous monastic orders. In
his will Gerard fails to mention poetry and other pagan works,
but among the books he left to the Sorbonne were Horace, Juvenal,
Statius, Virgil, Lucan, Priscian, Donatus, Aristotle, the Arabic
writers Avicenna, Alpharabius, and others, Seneca, Cicero's letters
and orations, philosophical and rhetorical works. His collection

was in all likelihood the first large nucleus of the Sorbonne library. He died about three years before Robert, and his gift was much larger than that of the founder of the college.

Now Gerard had lived in Amiens for some time—he was archdeacon there in 1262. Another resident of Amiens at this time was Richard of Fournival, who, among other works, has left us one called *Biblionomia,* a classification system of his library [3]. This library he made available to the people of Amiens. Now some of the unusual books and rare titles mentioned in his book are identical with those which Gerard presented to the Sorbonne. Sabbadini noted that Gerard, and hence the Sorbonne Library, had three items that were great rarities at that period [4]: Cicero's letters to his friends, the work of the Roman surveyor Junius Nipsus, and the elegies of Tibullus [5]. All three of these are in Richard's list too, and the comparison of the titles of the last two is interesting: Richard says that he found in one volume Boethius on surveying, Junius on the same, and a treatise on geometry. The Sorbonne catalogue reads: « In one volume the geometry of Boethius, the book on surveying of Junius ». Richard and the Sorbonne catalogue both mention the *epigrams* of « Albius Tybullius », though in no other catalogues and in no existing manuscripts are the elegies of Tibullus called epigrams. This title was probably suggested by a little biography of Tibullus which occurs in some manuscripts, for in it the word epigram is used. The term *elegiographus,* « writer of elegies », in the Sorbonne catalogue attracts attention. It is used nowhere else of Tibullus except in the little biography. Richard applies it to Ovid. Nor are these the only similarities. Richard describes a volume of Cicero containing *De officiis, De senectute, De amicitia,* and *Paradoxa* (79), and Gerard owned just such a volume (LI, 3). Richard mentions a manuscript containing Ptolemy's *Planisperium,* John, Herman, and Gilbert on the astrolabe, a work on a timepiece for travellers, Ralph on the astrolabe (59). The same

---

[3] *Ibid.,* II, p. 518.
[4] R. Sabbadini, *Le scoperte dei codici latini e greci ne' secoli XIV e XV,* II (Florence, 1914), p. 33.
[5] Cicero is No. 29 of Richard as given by Delisle, identical with LI, 28 of the Sorbonne catalogue; Junius is No. 44=LVI, 49; Tibullus is No. 115=LVI, 35.

miscellaneous contents occur in a Sorbonne manuscript (LVI, 19). Another manuscript described by Richard contained the *De disciplina scholarium* attributed to Boethius, his work on the trinity, Hildebert's book on the soul and the body, Bede on the nature of things (101). The same assortment of materials is found in a manuscript Gerard left to the Sorbonne (XXXVIII, 9). Others too have seen the parallelism between Gerard and Richard. Many years ago the Polish scholar Birkenmajer, noting the remarkable agreement of some of the mathematical manuscripts in Richard's catalogue and in Gerard's legacy to the Sorbonne, wrote a monograph in which he very completely and in the main convincingly demonstrated the identity of many of Richard's and Gerard's books [6]. Delisle himself had noted the striking similarity of the contents of one of Richard's books and an existing Sorbonne manuscript but had not gone beyond that point. I might add that independently of Birkenmajer I made most of the identifications he made [7].

Not to belabor the point further, let me sum up by saying that about half of the 162 books listed by Richard can be identified more or less certainly with books that Gerard gave to the Sorbonne. Unfortunately Richard did not work out his scheme in detail for legal and theological works, so that we cannot equate his books in these fields with those given by Gerard to the Sorbonne. Nearly all of Gerard's books outside of these fields can be identified in Richard's list. The statement in Gerard's will that medical and other books were to be sold seems to be confirmed by the fact that none of the twenty-eight medical books in the Sorbonne catalogue is credited to Gerard or, to be sure, to any other donor. It should also be said that some of Gerard's books may be listed in the reference library catalogue, in which donors' names are not given. Birkenmajer finds some of Richard's manuscripts in this reference library. He insists that all of Fournival's library passed into the hands of Gerard. That may be, but some of them,

---

[6] Aleksander Birkenmajer, *Bibljoteka Ryszarda de Fournival* (Polska Akademja Umiejętności, Wydzial Filologiczny, Rozprawy LV, 4; Krakow, 1922).

[7] I may perhaps publish a detailed study with some corrections of Birkenmajer.

I believe, found their way into the possession of others, including some that eventually came to the Sorbonne, as we shall now see.

A second donor to the Sorbonne to whom I wish to call attention was another native of Abbeville, a certain Stephen, who like Gerard, at one time lived at Amiens, in fact was canon there at the time of his death in 1287. Some forty books of his came to the Sorbonne as a legacy. Possibly Stephen was influenced by Gerard's example. Perhaps he even obtained some of Fournival's manuscripts from Gerard, if not from Fournival himself. The small number of the books he left makes identification with Richard's listings difficult. Ovid's *Fasti* may be one (R 118 = S XLV, 32); Aristotle's *Ethics* may be another (R 77 = XLIX, 9). This is not much to go on, but it is important for a point to be made later.

Where did these three inhabitants of the little city of Amiens—Richard, Gerard, Stephen—obtain so many books? One can only guess. I should like to point out that the famous Benedictine monastery of Corbie was only some fifteen kilometers distant. Corbie was founded in the seventh century by monks from Luxeuil, itself founded in the year 590 by the Irishman St. Columban. Corbie soon became an outstanding cultural center. Its famous scriptorium not only turned out many important manuscripts but played a large but not yet fully described part in developing the new Carolingian script, which later became a model for fifteenth-century Italian copyists and printers and hence is the ancestor of our current type fonts. Corbie had a large library for many centuries, which did not begin to disintegrate until the sixteenth century. About 400 of the most important of the remaining manuscripts were moved in 1638 to Saint-Germain-des-Prés, and later to the Bibliothèque Nationale. Another 400 are now in Amiens. Some twenty of the most precious volumes were stolen from Saint-Germain in 1791 and found their way to what is now called Leningrad.

Besides the 800 or 900 existing Corbie manuscripts we have three mediaeval catalogues of the library. Neither the books nor the catalogues have been fully exploited, although Corbie may be called one of the great centers of Western culture from the eighth to the fourteenth century. But it is more to the point to say that it has so far not been possible to establish any sure connection between the three scholars of Amiens and the great library of Corbie. Yet it seems to be an attractive hypothesis and there is some evidence to support it [8]. It is even conceivable that Gerard obtained copies of some of the oldest Corbie manuscripts of the sixth century. In that event the Sorbonne would by inheritance have a direct connection with late antiquity.

But if we must leave this alluring thought in the realm of unproved conjecture, perhaps even, some may say, of wild fancy, we can be much more positive about the link of the early Sorbonne library with the future.

A few years ago a manuscript in the Bibliothèque Nationale containing the mediaeval Latin translation of Plato's *Phaedo* was discovered to have belonged to and to have been annotated by Petrarch, the founder, if any one man can be said to be the founder, of the Italian Renaissance. It was also proved that this manuscript was copied from another existing Paris manuscript that had once been in the Sorbonne and that is listed in the 1338 catalogue of that institution [9]. The *Phaedo* is one of three Platonic works known in Latin form during the late Middle Ages. Together with the *Meno* it was translated by a certain Aristippus in the twelfth century, but the *Meno* seems to have been read very little. The third Platonic work, the *Timaeeus,* was available in an ancient translation by Chalcidius, but the obscurity of its mathematical discussion of the universe was heightened rather than reduced by the translator. Obviously Petrarch could be expected to take more interest in the immortality of the soul discussed in the *Phaedo.* Another transcript of the same Sorbonne manuscript was copied into a manuscript now in the Vatican which once belonged to the Florentine humanist, Coluccio Salutati, founder of the famous circle which made Florence the head

---

[8] This is presented in an article published in *Scriptorium* VIII (1954), p. 24. I shall discuss elsewhere Bischoff's comments on this article.

[9] L. Minio-Paluello, « Il Fedone latino con note autografe del Petrarca », *Accademia Naz. dei Lincei, Rendiconti, Sc. morali,* Serie VIII, vol. IV (1949), p. 107; Plato Latinus, II: *Phaedo,* ed. L. Minio-Paluello (London, 1950), p. xi ff. The Sorbonne manuscript is now 16581 of the Bibliothèque Nationale; Petrarch's is 6567A.

of humanistic studies in the fifteenth century [10]. Petrarch and Salutati were both Platonists, of a sort, opposed to the narrow Aristotelianism of their time and might be supposed to have welcomed the *Phaedo*. Yet they seem not to have made much use of it, perhaps repelled by its crabbed Latinity. But we know that their books were avidly sought by their humanist successors and we must grant that their two copies of the Sorbonne *Phaedo* had some influence in preparing the way for the study of Plato in the original by such scholars as Marsilio Ficino and for the new translations that they produced. Soon Italy, and later other countries, became one vast Platonic Academy.

The *Phaedo* is not, I believe, an isolated example of the influence of the Sorbonne on the Italian Renaissance. Another missionary can, I am confident, be identified. Our friend Richard of Fournival had access to a manuscript of the Roman poet Propertius, an author of exceeding rarity from antiquity down to the fifteenth century. For years I felt that Richard's copy must have gone to the Sorbonne, but I looked in vain through the catalogue of 1338. Recently, however, I found it there, hiding under the misspelling « Propicius ». That story is told below, in chapter VIII. Suffice it to say at this point that I am convinced that Richard's copy of Propertius, identical with the Sorbonne's « Propicius », is a fragmentary manuscript now in Leiden (Voss. lat. in Oct. 38). From this manuscript, at that time still complete, Petrarch's lost Propertius was transcribed, perhaps in 1333, and from Petrarch's manuscript, Coluccio Salutati's copy, which still survives (Laur. 36, 49), was made. The origin then of Petrarch's Propertius would be the same as that of his *Phaedo*.

Though Petrarch and Salutati took no great interest in Propertius, the fifteenth-century humanists did, and they first made his acquaintance in the copies that had belonged to Petrarch and Salutati. Once more the Sorbonne furnished a book which went into the humanistic hopper of the Italian Renaissance.

I believe too that Salutati's Tibullus, the only existing manuscript of that author antedating the fifteenth century (Milan, Ambr. R. 26 sup.), was copied from the Sorbonne volume bequeathed by

[10] *Ibid.*, p. xiii. The manuscript is Vat. lat. 2063. See B. L. Ullman, *The Humanism of Coluccio Salutati* (Padua, 1963), p. 186.

Gerard of Abbeville and described by Richard of Fournival. There is no question that Salutati's manuscript of Tibullus was the source for the many copies of that author which circulated in the fifteenth century and furnish evidence for the great vogue of Tibullus during the Renaissance. What is true of the ancient authors mentioned, that is, Plato, Propertius, Tibullus, may well be true of others, namely that the Sorbonne copies were transcribed for Petrarch and other Italian humanists and played a signifi- cant part in developing the humanistic interests of the book-hungry scholars of Italy. We may well say that the Sorbonne about the year 1300 played no small part in maintaining the link between ancient and modern times. Its books reached back via Amiens and perhaps Corbie to late antiquity; these same books reached forward to the eager arms of the humanists. I believe, as I have pointed out in chapter II, that Avignon as the center of the Papacy and the crossroads of the world in the fourteenth century had a huge role in developing the movement we call the Renais- sance, but we must not forget the part played by Paris and the Sorbonne. With Avignon as a focal point Petrarch travelled from one to another of the rich monastic and cathedral libraries of France and Belgium and eagerly copied many ancient treasures not available to him in Italy. We must remember that France, not Italy, was the great storehouse of classical Latin literature throughout the Middle Ages. The story that Petrarch himself tells of his finding of Cicero's speech for Archias at Liège is well-known. A recent study of great importance by Giuseppe Billanovich has shown that Petrarch's copy of all the books of Livy known in his day was based on one at Chartres—and Livy had a profound influence on the leaders of the Renaissance from Petrarch to Machiavelli [11]. One could almost write a history of Italian humanism around Livy. As Billanovich remarks, from the old masters of Chartres, such as Fulbert and John of Salisbury, to Petrarch and Lorenzo Valla, the later owner of Petrarch's Livy, « è un bel ponte, lungo e lucido ».

Petrarch was by no means the only Italian to use the treasures of the Sorbonne Library. The Florentine Roberto de' Bardi was

[11] G. Billanovich, « Petrarch and the Textual Tradition of Livy », *Journal of the Warburg and Courtauld Institutes*, XIV (1951), p. 137.

a professor at the University of Paris from 1333 to 1335 and then its chancellor from 1336 to his death in 1349. It was he who in 1340 invited Petrarch to receive the laurel wreath at Paris, an honor which Petrarch declined in favor of the crowning in Rome. Bardi's invitation seems to indicate an interest in the new learning and the new poetry of Petrarch [12]. Sabbadini's suggestion that the two may have met in Paris in 1333 [13] is an attractive one, and we may speculate that Bardi facilitated Petrarch's investigation of the treasures of the Sorbonne. Petrarch later says that Bardi was « michi et rebus meis amicissimo » (*Fam.* IV, 4). Bardi himself made a collection of the sermons of Augustine, but whether it had any wide influence in Italy remains to be investigated [14].

Another Italian, Dionigi da S. Sepolcro, studied and taught in Paris from 1317 to 1329. A close friend and correspondent of Petrarch's, he was a book collector, and it may be presumed that on his return to Italy in 1329 he took with him copies of many manuscripts he found in the Sorbonne and other French libraries. When and where did Petrarch and Dionigi become acquainted? We do not know, but the best suggestion I have seen is that they met in Avignon in 1333 and that in that year Dionigi presented to his new friend the precious pocket edition of Augustine's *Confessions* which Petrarch says he took with him when he made his celebrated ascent of Mont Ventoux and « got religion » [15]. Whether Petrarch actually climbed the mountain and had his conversion there, has recently been questioned [16]. In any case, Petrarch's copy of the *Confessions* not only made a deep impression upon him but caused him to spread its influence, for he sent copies to his brother and to his young friend Donato degli Albanzani. Near the end of his life he presented the highly prized book itself to the Florentine monk Luigi Marsigli [17]. Its further history and influence is something that needs investigation.

---

[12] It may be that Petrarch solicited the invitation; cf. Ernest H. Wilkins, *The Making of the « Canzoniere » and Other Petrarchan Studies* (Rome, 1951), p. 28.

[13] *Op. cit.*, p. 35, n. 13.

[14] This has now been done by G. Pozzi in *Miscellanea del Centro di studi medievali*, S. II (1958), p. 125; *Italia medioevale e umanistica*, I (1958), p. 139.

[15] Ugo Mariani, *Il Petrarca e gli Agostiniani* (Rome, 1946), pp. 35-36.

[16] G. Billanovich, *Petrarca Letterato* (Rome, 1947), pp. 193 ff.

[17] Petrarch, *Sen.* XV, 7.

But where did Dionigi get it in the first place? The Sorbonne Library had three copies of the *Confessions*, one of them presented by Godfrey of Fontaines early in the fourteenth century. This and one of the others still exist in the Bibliothèque Nationale (15650, 15656). Obviously copies of this work were not scarce; hence we cannot be positive that Dionigi had his copy made from one of these manuscripts, though is seems not unlikely. Nor is it unreasonable to suppose that Dionigi's large library was in part made up of copies of books discovered by him in the Sorbonne.

It may be that we shall find more manuscripts that belonged to Petrarch and other early humanists and shall be able to trace some of them back to the Sorbonne and other French centers. Some years ago Mlle. Pellegrin published an amazing paper in which she added ten manuscripts to the forty odd previously known to have belonged to Petrarch [18]. She found them in that little known library, the Bibliothèque Nationale of Paris! One or two of these came from Tournai, perhaps obtained by Petrarch in the same year (1333) that he had copies made of several Sorbonne manuscripts. So as we come to know more about the beginnings of the Italian Renaissance in the fourteenth century we may be able to see a closer connection between it and the institution founded seven hundred years ago for poor students of theology by the Robert who came from the insignificant village of Sorbon. I imagine that if Robert had lived 150 or 200 years longer he would have been shocked to see that some of the books presented to his Library would help form the Renaissance, a development he would surely not have viewed without alarm and dismay.

[18] *Scriptorium*, V (1951), p. 265. For still others see G. Billanovich in *Scriptorium*, VIII (1954), p. 115; *Journal of the Warburg and Courtauld Institutes*, XIV (1951), p. 137; *Rendiconti dell'Accademia di Archeologia, Lettere e Belle Arti di Napoli*, XXVI (1951), p. 253; *Miscellanea in memoria di Luigi Ferrari* (1952), p. 99; *Studi petrarcheschi*, VI (1954), p. 1; *Italia medioevale e umanistica*, V (1962), p. 103; L. Minio-Paluello in *Accademia Nazionale dei Lincei*, ser. VIII, IV (1949), p. 107.

CHAPTER IV

THE POST-MORTEM ADVENTURES OF LIVY [1]

To most persons who as college freshmen « took » Livy, the well-authenticated story of the Spanish admirer of this ancient Roman historian is entirely incomprehensible. Yet it is at least eighteen and a half centuries old, for it is told by the younger Pliny. A man living in Gades, the modern Cadiz, on the south coast of Spain, went all the way to Rome just to have a glimpse of the author of the much admired history. This done, he went straight back home entirely satisfied, not stopping to see any of the wonderful sights of the city that the Emperor Augustus was transforming from brick to marble. The overland journey would have taken forty days or more and the discomforts must have been great. I well remember the train trip which I made from Rome to Madrid many years ago and the wooden third class seats on which I slept for three successive nights. Italian, French, and Spanish seats were of equal hardness. And yet, that was as nothing compared with the feat of the old Gaditan. Petrarch's comment is that it would have been worth a trip from Spain to India to see Livy in the flesh.

Something of the reverential attitude of the man of Gades towards the historian who spent over forty years in setting forth the deeds of his country from its beginning to his own day revealed itself again in fourteenth-century Italy and became one of the distinguishing characteristics of the Renaissance, for the Middle Ages took relatively little interest in Livy. Between 1318 and 1324, there was discovered in Padua, the city of Livy's birth, a sepulchral

---

[1] Originally given as a lecture and published in *University of North Carolina Extension Bulletin*, XXXIV, 4 (1944; published 1945), pp. 39-53.

inscription which was thought to refer to Livy himself[2]. The error was caused by a misinterpretation. The inscription gave the name T. Livius, to be sure, but the discoverers failed to note that this Livius was called a freedman and had the cognomen Halys. This, of course, made it impossible for him to have been the famous Livy. The epitaph was accepted, however, as Livy's by fourteenth-century writers and scholars, including Boccaccio and Petrarch; in fact the error persisted even until the end of the seventeenth century. It should be said, however, that Boccaccio implies some reservations[3]. The inscription was placed in the wall of the church of Santa Giustina, part of which according to tradition was built over a pagan temple of Concord. The belief naturally arose that Livy was buried in that temple.

The next chapter in our strange tale brings us to the year 1413. This year was one of tremendous excitement in the sturdy little city of Padua. The glories of the Renaissance, with its revival of the classics of Greece and Rome, had reached this ancient town as they had the rest of Italy, and Padua's admiration for Livy, its most famous citizen, had been greatly intensified. The addition of this new interest to that aroused by the daily sight of the supposed epitaph of Livy on the walls of one of Padua's most important churches had brought about a state of receptivity and susceptibility that is psychologically very significant.

It was under such conditions that in the course of some improvements to the monastery adjoining the church of Santa Giustina a tomb was discovered in which there was a lead coffin six feet long, over a foot high and of the same width. Is it any wonder that the monk in charge of the work at once exclaimed, « It's Livy! »? He immediately sent a note to one of the town's leading scholars, the notary Sicco Polenton, to whom we owe our information about what happened. Sicco at once rushed to the church, abandoning everything in his haste, and with loving and reverent hands helped raise the casket from its resting place. He then hurried back to the city hall, now full of litigants leaving the court rooms, to acquaint the city fathers with this wonderful

---

[2] C. I. L., V, 2865. Another inscription (C. I. L., V, 2975) is today considered by many to come from the tombstone of the historian.

[3] A. Hortis, *Studi sulle opere latine del Boccaccio* (Trieste, 1879), p. 323.

discovery. Everybody agreed that a suitable mausoleum should be built and promised to contribute toward the expense. Soon the whole town was on its way to Santa Giustina, including even the butchers and cobblers. But in the meantime, before Sicco's return, a most unfortunate thing had happened through the carelessness of the guards. Certain out-of-town students who attended the University of Padua, in their desire for souvenirs, removed all the teeth from the skull. This childish behavior we may attribute in part to the youthfulness of the University, then less than two hundred years old, as well as to the fact that, as Sicco so carefully explains, these students were not natives of Padua, and were presumably not imbued with proper respect and awe for the city's most famous son. Then, when the horse (or should we say the horse's teeth?) had been stolen, what was left of the skeleton was put under lock and key.

As it happened, the abbot of the monastery was out of town. His substitute was much disturbed by the great crowds of sight-seers and apparently thought that the finding of the ancient bones might cause the excited people to return to paganism; for their attitude toward the discovery seemed to him to be that of worshipers toward God. So he decided to destroy the bones. He began by crushing the skull, which, as Sicco pathetically puts it, had remained unharmed in the bowels of the earth all these centuries. The monk who was Sicco's friend got word to him of the dastardly deed. Sicco at once gathered about him the mayor and other leading citizens with the idea of removing the bones, even, if necessary, by force. The remains of St. Livy, as we may well call him, were now placed in a wooden coffin and carried through the streets and squares of the town in a procession of Padua's most illustrious citizens. The common people and the small boys fell in behind, while crowds of spectators lined the streets. It was a great day in the history of the ancient and glorious city of Padua, this thirty-first day of August, in the year of our Lord, one thousand four hundred and thirteen. It is refreshing to us with our general attitude of indifference and sophistication to see such wild enthusiasm over the finding of the supposed bones— not of a motion picture star, or a notorious criminal, but of a mere historian who had been dead for fourteen centuries.

Of course the excitement died down as the days passed. People began to ask for proof of the identification of these bones as Livy's. Even in Padua profane scoffers were not unknown. Some went so far as to say that the skeleton was that of a woman, but physicians quickly proved that this was a gross and malicious libel. As to the rest, Sicco merely waxes ironic: there were of course no survivors to identify the body, none to testify that they had seen Livy die and that they had been present at his funeral, no document in his handwriting. Sicco's chief argument is that the tomb was found near the inscription, and he has not the slightest doubt that the inscription refers to the historian.

In the enthusiasm of the first discovery the leading citizens, as already said, decided to build a sumptuous mausoleum. The details were left to a representative committee of six, consisting of a military man, a lawyer, an « honorable », and three crafts-men: Frank the butcher, Frank the perfume maker, and Godfrey the goldsmith. Several citizens promptly agreed to meet the expense on certain conditions, but all agreed that it must be a work of the people, by the people, and for the people (« quod publici ornamenti esset de publico et in publicum fieri »). For some reason, however, the plans were never carried out. Not until 1426 was a resting place prepared in the wall of the court-house with an inscription and bust. In 1457 the bones were removed to the interior of the building, together with the inscription of Livius Halys, the freedman, and another bust was installed [4].

But to return to 1413. The news of the find quickly spread to the rest of Italy, and everywhere scholars were eager to learn the details. That indefatigable investigator, the Florentine Niccolò Niccoli, asked for information, and it is Sicco's letter to him, written in 1414, that gives the details which I have quoted [5]. Scholars quickly became familiar with this letter, and Sicco's reputation was assured. No less a man than the illustrious Leonardo Bruni himself read the letter to Pope Martin V. In the

[4] Pictures and interesting information about Livy are to be found in Luigi Ferretto, *Livius noster* (Padua, 1903).

[5] A. Segarizzi, *La Catinia, le orazioni e le epistole di Sicco Polenton* (Bergamo, 1899), letters 1, 7, 8. A briefer account is given by Sicco in his *Scriptorum illustrium Latinae linguae libri XVIII*, ed. B. L. Ullman (Rome, 1928), p. 183.

ensuing discussion someone pointed out that, according to Apollonius (by which name the poet Sidonius Apollinaris seems to be
meant) [6], Livy was a small man, whereas the newly-found bones
were those of a large corpse. Bruni wrote to Polenton for the
exact length of the tibia, so that the height of the man could be
estimated. This stirred up the indignation of the pious Sicco
and he exclaimed: « Deus bone! Of slanderers there is no end ».
He pointed out that undue scepticism led some people to say
that Livy was not born in Padua and did not die there. Others
even said that his history was not his own but was merely a
word-for-word copy of the early annals. Sicco then explains that
he had seen the skeleton when it was intact, that in the six-foot
coffin there was quite a bit of space at either end. He declares
also that only he observed the details, as the workmen were
ignorant rustics and the monk was busy bossing them. They then
moved the coffin, and this movement caused the skeleton to fall
apart and the bones to be jumbled together. Sicco vigorously
maintains that it is impossible to determine the height of a man
from the length of his tibia, but that, if one *could* tell from the
length of his tibia how tall the man was, this particular tibia
must have been that of a person of moderate height! This reminds one of the man charged with murder who said that he
was in another city at the time of the murder, and anyway, the
other man struck him first.

But that does not finish the story. In 1451 Beccadelli, better
known as Panormita, the famous Sicilian humanist and poet, was
ambassador of King Alfonso of Naples to the Venetian government. This was the Alfonso who ended a war with Cosimo de'
Medici of Florence when the latter sent him a copy of Livy as

[6] In his letter to Sicco, Bruni used the form Appollinus, if we can believe
the manuscripts examined by L. Bertalot, *Archivum romanicum*, XV (1931),
p. 323: « ut viris illustribus scribit Appollinus ». In his reply Sicco quotes the
name as Apollonius, according to Segarizzi, *op. cit.*, pp. 92 ff. In *Carm.* II,
188-190 Sidonius says: « Quicquid in aevum mittunt Euganeis Patavina volumina chartis; qua Crispus brevitate placet ». If the semicolon is ignored and
crispus is taken as an adjective (one manuscript has the meaningless *cripus*),
brevitate might be regarded as an allusion to Livy's stature. As for the *viris
illustribus* of Bruni, Sidonius addresses the senators as *egregii proceres* in vs. 129.
This solution is admittedly highly conjectural.

a peace offering.   Alfonso's physicians advised him against opening the package for fear that it might contain—not a bomb according to modern practice—but poison.   But Alfonso refused
their advice, saying that kings were under the special protection
of God.   Such is Panormita's report of the facts, but who can
say that it was not Alfonso's love of Livy that led him to throw
caution to the winds? Panormita was himself an admirer of
Livy. At one time he sold a farm in order to raise enough money
to buy a manuscript of Livy's history.   Panormita, then, having
finished the special business on which he had been sent to Venice,
wrote to the king for permission to return home. A widower of
fifty, he had recently married a young wife, and the separation
was proving irksome. It was at this time that Panormita asked
the Venetian government that the coffin containing the bones of
the newly, though unofficially, canonized saint be opened and that
one of the bones be presented to his king. The Republic of
Venice, to which Padua belonged, granted the request and sent
one of the bones of the forearm to the king. It now rests under
a large altar in the Cappella del Pontano in the Via dei Tribunali
in Naples[7]. The suggestion has been made that Beccadelli's hope
was that the gift would fill Alfonso's heart with so much joy
that he would consent to his ambassador's return. Whether the
bone of the supposititious Livy fulfilled its mission as a sort of
love charm we do not know.

Not even then did the bones rest in peace. To judge from
all that happened to them it seems that their original owner was
not duly covered over with the three handfuls of earth which
sent the spirit happily on its way across the Styx. For the
Paduans, taking advantage of the opening of the coffin for Panormita, removed the jawbone. This was enclosed in a specially
prepared gilded ball and was hung in one of the rooms of the
chancellery. It is referred to by various writers up to the year
1835. Then for some years it dropped from sight.

---

[7] R. Sabbadini, *Ottanta lettere inedite del Panormita* (Catania, 1910), p.157;
E. Cocchia in *Nuova Antologia*, CCXXXVIII (November, 1924), p. 81. A notarial
document describing the formal presentation of the bone has been published by
P. Sambin in *Italia medioevale e umanistica*, I (1958), p. 276. Sambin notes
the similarity between this ceremony and that of 1413.

In the year 1908, Oliviero Ronchi, the scholarly librarian of the Biblioteca Civica of Padua, came across a gilded ball in the museum of which the library is part [8]. At first he took it to be one of the balls which used to be attached as counter-weights to hanging lamps. On opening it he found four fragments of a jawbone, a metal plaque with Livy's name on it, and a piece of paper dated 1812, on which reference was made to the town archives for a description of the formal opening of the metal ball in the presence of various notables and of several physicians. Ronchi found no teeth in any of the fragments; the report of 1812 also comments on their absence. Another record indicates that the ball was opened in 1730. At that time it was regilded, the bones being kept in a box under lock and key, duly sealed in the presence of witnesses, until the gilding was finished. The last previous examination on record was in 1668.

In May, 1926, while I was working in the library of Padua, Sig. Ronchi once more opened the gilded ball and showed me the fragments of the jawbone that for so many centuries was thought to be that of the famous historian. It was truly a relic worth seeing. What mattered it that it was not genuine? It had filled the hearts of countless numbers of Paduan citizens with the noblest sentiments of patriotic pride and had been a real inspiration in their lives. It had made Livy's name better known to many persons throughout Italy, and it had contributed a bit to the influence of the ancients on modern life. It was not out of malice, surely, but in a spirit of wholesome good-natured fun that the shade of the great Paduan played his little trick on his descendants.

But while the adventures of the supposed corporeal remains of Livy have been strange enough, his spiritual self, the part of him that was not to die, as Horace would have said, has had an even more weird experience. At first, like his bones, his histories were allowed to rest in peace. In fact, for a long time, the very bulk of his work, with its one hundred and forty-two books, seems to have caused it to repose on dusty shelves while

[8] Oliviero Ronchi, « Titi Livi maxilla », *Atti e Memorie della R. Accademia di Scienze, Lettere ed Arti in Padova*, XXXVI (1920).

abridgments and abridgments of abridgments took its place. Livy's « Shorter Short History of the Roman People » might well be the title of the epitome called *Periochae* which has come down to us. It is evidently an abridgment that the Roman poet Martial has in mind when he speaks of the huge Livy in a vest pocket edition and says that his library is too small for the original work. Most of the writers of the Empire seem to have used only an epitome of Livy's « *maximum* » *opus*.

The mad emperor Caligula threatened to remove from the libraries all copies of the works of Homer, Virgil, and Livy; Homer because Plato had excluded him from his ideal state, Virgil for his lack of genius and learning, Livy for his verbosity and carelessness. In the Middle Ages the story was circulated that Caligula actually burned all the books except the first forty, and that these escaped because they had already been circulated far and wide outside of Italy [9]. Another mediaeval story was that the missing books of Livy had been destroyed by Pope Gregory the Great. The motive attributed to him was that Livy's style was so alluring that it kept the reader from becoming acquainted with the severer charms of sacred literature. Sicco Polenton acutely disposes of this canard by asking why Gregory should have destroyed books which contained no attack on the Christian religion and not the entire work while he was at it [10].

At any rate not all of the original 142 books seem to have survived antiquity. Of these only twenty-nine were known to the early humanists of the fourteenth and fifteenth centuries. That is the number contained in Petrarch's manuscript of Livy, which is in the Bibliothèque Nationale of Paris, and in the first printed edition of 1469. Today we have thirty-five books: I-X, XXI-XLV, and a tiny fragment of XCI.

The finding of the epitaph of Livius Halys in the fourteenth century and of the spurious bones of Livy in the fifteenth gave the impressionable scholars of these centuries a romantic thrill and made them especially keen to find the missing books and sometimes caused them to delude themselves into the belief that

---

[9] This story is told by Giovanni Colonna in the fourteenth century (R. Sabbadini in *Atti della R. Accademia delle Scienze di Torino*, XLVI, 1910-1911, p. 23).

[10] In his *Scriptorum illustrium Latinae linguae libri*, p. 182.

they had been found. Sicco Polenton, the man on whom rests
the chief responsibility for stirring up excitement about Livy, is
one of the first to voice the hope of recovering the lost books.
This hope and the attendant credulity we have inherited from
earlier centuries. The Livy ghost goes back to the time when
his epitaph and bones were thought to have been found. « The
Lost Books of Livy » will ever be a phrase to conjure with, or
in more modern parlance, they will always make the front page.
Some years ago a newspaper correspondent in telling of the results hoped for from the excavations of Herculaneum begun in
1927 mentioned « manuscripts of classics perhaps including such
longed-for treasures as the lost books of Livy and the lost plays
of Sophocles ». James Hilton was obsessed by the lost Livy; in
Good-bye, Mr. Chips (p. 47) he speaks of an irretrievable loss as
« lost like the lost books of Livy », and in Lost Horizon he writes
(p. 190): « He foresaw a time when... every treasure garnered
through two millenniums, ... all would be lost like the lost books
of Livy ». As was to be expected, the hopes of finding the lost
books were again expressed at the time of the bimillennium of
Livy in 1941 [11].

Salomon Reinach, the distinguished French archaelogist,
said [12]:

I am struck by the fact that rumours relating to the discovery
of a great Latin author have always concerned Livy; and am inclined
to think that all the rumours collected by Morhof (and a few others
since) were not all hoaxes.

The true explanation of the fact by which the credulous
Reinach was struck is, I think, the one that I have suggested,
that the discovery of the supposed epitaph and bones of Livy
attracted attention of a romantic sort to Livy that no other author
received. The « Lost Books of Livy » symbolize that continued
hope of uncovering more and more of ancient literature which
has been one of the characteristics of our culture for six centuries.

[11] Vincenzo Dattilo, Tito Livio (Naples, 1942), p. 76.
[12] In a letter to Professor Conway, quoted by the latter in the London
Times tor Sept. 18, 1924. The reference to Morhof is to his De Patavinitate
Liviana (Kiel, 1685) — which I have used in what follows — reprinted in

With the fourteenth century we begin to come upon hopes
of finding the lost books of Livy. The hopes are soon followed
by rumors. One of the first is related in a letter written by the
Florentine scholar, Coluccio Salutati, in 1397 [13]. The letter is
addressed to the Margrave of Moravia, who had told Coluccio
that he had seen a complete Livy, and had, in fact, promised him
a copy; but Coluccio had scarcely been convinced. But now the
story was repeated to him by one of the Margrave's subordinates
with such convincing detail that Coluccio was aroused. The
manuscript was said to be in a monastery near Lübeck and so
old that no one could read it. As late as 1850 the well-known
scholar, Moritz Haupt, thought that the story of the Margrave
of Moravia was worth investigating [14].

During the fifteenth century there were further rumors of
the existence of a complete Livy in Germany and Scandinavia.
In 1424 a Danish monk named Nicholas [15] swore in the presence
of a distinguished company at the court of Pope Martin V that
he had seen in the Cistercian monastery of Sorö (near Roeskilde)
two large volumes containing ten decades, i. e., one hundred
books, of Livy, and that he had, in fact, read a number of the
chapter headings. Poggio, the great humanist, who was present
on that occasion, writes: « If this is true, we shall have to cele-
brate a triumph over the Danes » [16]. By the time the story got
to Niccolò Niccoli the two volumes had become five [17]. But
investigation failed to substantiate the monk's assertion. Later
someone else appeared, this time at Mantua, to claim the existence of all the decades of Livy in still another Danish monastery.
But now Poggio was less enthusiastic, and consequently less disap-
pointed when a special investigator could find nothing. When
a third story of the same sort came to him, Poggio, to whom

Drakenborch's Livy, VII (1746), pp. 27 ff. For Reinach's remarks see also
Revue archéologique, Ser. V, XX (1924), p. 353.
    [13] P. Novati, Epistolario di Coluccio Salutati, III (Rome, 1905), p. 218.
    [14] Opuscula, I (Leipzig, 1875), p. 303.
    [15] For the identification of this monk see P. Lehmann in Zentralblatt für
Bibliothekswesen, LIV (1937), p. 261.
    [16] Epist. II, 9; cf. III, 12; V, 18; VIII, 24; XI, 12 (Poggii Epistolae, ed.
Thomas de Tonellis, 3 vols., Florence, 1832-62).
    [17] Rodney P. Robinson, « The Inventory of Niccolò Niccoli », Classical
Philology, XVI (1921), p. 251.

the cry « Livy » was now like that of « wolf », declared the witness an imposter. But hope springs eternal, and when another report of a complete Livy came down from the North in 1457 Poggio once more was afire with anthusiasm.

In 1451, the very year in which Panormita picked a bone for King Alfonso from the coffin of the putative Livy, Pope Nicholas V sent Enoch of Ascoli to the northern countries to look for classical manuscripts and especially for the complete Livy. He was gone four years. When he finally returned, he brought no Livy, though he did rescue some other important writings from oblivion.

In the same century a Venetian nobleman and humanist named Andrea Giuliano thought of going to Germany to look for Trogus Pompeius and one decade of Livy, which he had heard were there. This is reported by one Pietro Delfino on the authority of Giuliano's son Francesco [18].

With all its enthusiasm, then, the fifteenth century had no success in adding to the previously known books of Livy. In the sixteenth, new Argonauts, as one writer calls them [19], set forth in search of this Golden Fleece.

[18] In a manuscript of Justinus (Bodl., Canon. lat. 281) which Delfino bought in 1465 (H. O. Coxe, *Catalogus codicum manuscriptorum bibliothecae Bodleianae*, III, Oxford, 1854, p. 231). Giuliano (ca. 1382-1455) was a pupil of Barzizza and Guarino and at the latter's request wrote a funeral oration on Chrysoloras' death in 1415 (R. Sabbadini, *Storia e critica di testi latini*, Catania, 1914, pp. 172-173, etc). On Giuliano see also S. Troilo, *Andrea Giuliano*, in *Biblioteca dell'Archivum romanicum*, 18 (Florence, 1932).

Sabbadini's statement (*Le scoperte dei codici latini e greci ne' secoli XIV e XV*, II, Florence, 1914, p. 232) that Giuliano *intraprese* the journey to Germany is misleading; the Latin says *voluit se transferre*. The intention was obviously not carried out. Sabbadini also erred in thinking the *second* decade was the object of Giuliano's search; Delfino says merely *unam decadum Livii*. Evidently elaborating on Sabbadini, Vincenzo Dattilo (*op. cit.*, p. 43) arrives at this statement: « Un faticoso viaggio in Germania fu intrapreso da Andrea Giuliano per rintracciare la seconda Deca che si diceva colà conservata in un monastero ». No doubt the journey would have been *faticoso* if made, and probably the manuscript would have been in a monastery if it existed. Dattilo continues that it was not found because it had been destroyed in the sack of Magdeburg. The journey that Giuliano did not make would have taken place during his lifetime, before 1455, but the fire at Magdeburg occurred in 1631!

[19] Carlo Landi, « Il fantasma Liviano », *Annuario del R. Ginnasio-Liceo Tito Livio*, 1924-25 (Padua, 1926). An earlier monograph of his is *Tito Livio* (Padua, 1903).

In the preface to his edition of the letters of Pliny which he published in 1508, the famous publisher Aldus states that he had been in the habit of saying that the tales of the finding of the complete histories of Livy, Sallust, and Trogus were stuff and nonsense. But his discovery of an old manuscript including the previously unknown correspondence of Pliny and Trajan, led him to believe that the works of Livy and other authors were merely hidden somewhere and would eventually turn up, perhaps during his own lifetime. Sure enough, nine years later parts of Books XXXIII and XL of Livy were found at Mainz in a manuscript which has since disappeared. As this find inevitably led to the rumor that all of Livy had been discovered, in 1532 Pope Clement VII asked the Archbishop of Mainz to lend him the manuscript for publication [20]. Shortly before this there had been another false report. Martin Grönning of Bremen wrote to the librarian of the Vatican that he had a complete Livy which had been found at Drontheim, Norway. The librarian urged him to bring it to Rome and promised a large sum for it. But Grönning died before he could accept the invitation. This was in 1521. It is said that after Grönning's death the manuscript was torn to pieces by children and others who were ignorant of its value. One is led to think that Grönning was honest but probably mistaken.

Another report credited a complete Livy to the island of Iona in the Hebrides, said to have been brought there by Fregusius, prince of Scotland, to save it from the Danes [21]. He was supposed to have obtained it when he took part in the sack of Rome by Alaric, king of the Goths, in 410 A. D. This seems to be a later version of the tale reported as early as 1497 that ten decades had been found in an unknown place in England [22].

Finally, in 1527 Books XLI to XLV were found in Lorsch, near Worms, in Germany, the only considerable portion to be turned up in the last six centuries. Thus the stories of the exist-

---

[20] L. von Pastor, *Geschichte der Päpste* (Freiburg i. B., 1932), IV, 2, p. 764.

[21] The story is reported by Paolo Giovio in his *Descriptio Britanniae, Scotiae, Hyberniae, et Orchadum* (Venice, 1548), fol. 39v.

[22] *La bibliofilia*, XXVI (1924), p. 160. See also *I Diarii di Marino Sanuto*, ed. F. Stefani, I (Venice, 1879), col. 806, where a letter of the Venetian envoy to London, Andrea Trivixam (Trevisan) reports his finding the books on an island near Cornwall.

ence of new parts of Livy in northern Europe at last received partial though noteworthy confirmation. The building of a more pretentious monument to Livy in Padua twenty years later may perhaps be attributed in part to the interest created by this find. Erasmus was led to hope for the discovery of still more books and to suggest that rewards be offered to scholars to get them to investigate. He thought it absurd that people should dig in the ground for gold and silver while so much greater treasure was being neglected. The report got about that Erasmus himself had discovered five books [23].

In 1615, the rest of Book XXXIII was brought to light, again in Germany, at Bamberg, in a manuscript of the eleventh century which, except for some fragments in Rome and in Bamberg, is the oldest and best for the whole decade. So sceptical had people become about Livy finds that one well-known scholar, Vossius, refused to accept the book as genuine [24].

These finds, however, brought new hopes—and new disappointments. The specter of the lost books of Livy appeared now at one place, now at another. After the discoveries in Germany, at Mainz and Lorsch and Bamberg, it is not surprising that the great fire in the German city of Magdeburg, in 1631, should have given rise to the story that Livy perished in it. So big a fire demanded a big book to feed it. Perhaps the explanation of the Magdeburg story is that the Mainz manuscript was discovered in the library of Albert of Brandenburg who at the time (1517) was Archbishop of Magdeburg as well as of Mainz.

At any rate, after the Magdeburg conflagration the hopes of obtaining a complete Livy from the northern countries—hopes which had some basis of fact and which had fired the imagination of the world for a century and a half—came to a smoldering end. In the meantime, these hopes had turned from the north to the south and east. It is not surprising that the new crop

---

[23] *Scaligerana, Thuana, Perroniana, Pithoeana, et Colomesiana* (Amsterdam, 1740), II (Scaliger), p. 432.

[24] The editions of Vossius' *De historicis Latinis* (1627, 1651) speak of book « XLIII », but Drakenborch is no doubt right in changing this to « XXXIII » in his reprint of Vossius' life of Livy, as Books XLI-XLV were known long before.

5

of stories, fed purely on hope, should be even more fantastic
than the old. Near the end of the sixteenth century, an Arabic
version of the complete Livy was reported to be at La Goulette,
near Tunis. That seems to have been the first of many tales
localizing an Arabic version in various parts of the Mediterranean
world. For example, an Arabic, and even a Punic version were
said to exist in the Desert of Saint Macaire. As the name « Macaire » has more recently been used in the sense of « swindler »,
the desert would seem to have been well named [25].

How proverbial the « lost books » had become is shown by a
poem written in 1639 by Thomas Bancroft, called « Of the *Ae-
thiopian* Mountaine, *Amara* » [26]:

> On this faire Mountaine, sphericall and high,
> Stands (as fame goes) a precious Library,
> Where *Livies* whole works, *Enochs* Oracles,
> *Salomons* Physicke, and some mysteries else
> That did survive the Flood, entreasur'd lye,
> Insulting o're *Times* wastefull tyranny.
> O could I thither reach! then should I stand
> High in the *Muses* grace, and all command.

The allusion to Amara seems to have been taken from
Richard Montagu, who in turn refers to a lying Spaniard [27]. Later
in the century the hopes were centered at Fez, in Morocco.

In the very year in which the rest of Book XXXIII came to
light (1615) an Italian reported that there was a complete Livy
in the library of the Seraglio in Constantinople, and that he and
the French ambassador had tried to buy it, but the librarian could
not find it. Fifty years later, in 1665, the library burned down
and the supposed manuscript was presumably lost—if one can
speak of a supposed manuscript as lost. Not long after, however,
a Greek from the island of Chios seems to have heard of this
story, for in 1682 he came to King Louis XIV of France with
the tale that during the fire in the library of Constantinople a

---

[25] *Scaligerana*, etc., I (Pithou), p. 518.

[26] Thomas Bancroft, *Two Bookes of Epigrammes, and Epitaphs* (London,
1639), N. 200.

[27] Richard Montagu, *Apparatus ad origines ecclesiasticas* (Oxford, 1635), *Praef.*

complete Livy had been thrown out of the window and picked up by a passing Turk, from whom he (the Greek) had bought it. The Greek offered to sell the work in installments at a fabulous price, but the deal was not consummated, as delivery was not made. Presumably he expected to forge bits from time to time and from the proceeds to keep the forge in his forgery factory going.

The story about Constantinople would not down, in spite of all disappointments, and has flared up every once in a while since. In 1905 a new investigation was made at Constantinople but of course it was futile [28]. The hopes that have constantly been expressed that important Greek and Latin manuscripts would sometime be found in Constantinople are based in part on this story. On the other hand, the story itself was an outgrowth of these hopes. Thus one hope feeds another.

In 1668 it was reported in France that fragments of manuscripts of the lost books were found on battledores, similar to tennis rackets. The man who vouched for the story, a M. Chapelain, said that he had heard it forty years before from the mouth of a person of « unquestionable veracity » [29]. The manuscripts were supposed to have been given by the abbess of Fontévrault to an apothecary, who sold them to a manufacturer of battledores.

Another rumor had it that there was a complete Livy on Mt. Athos and that Colbert, minister of Louis XIV, was to send two frigates for it. Presumably it was thought that one frigate could not hold the entire one hundred and forty-two books. The story was toned down a bit by the time it reached the celebrated English librarian Humphrey Wanley. He drew up a project for collecting and studying rare manuscripts, such as the ancient manuscript of the known books of Livy that King Louis XIV had obtained from Mt. Athos. Apparently he confused the alleged Mt. Athos manuscript with the celebrated uncial manuscript which Dupuy left to King Louis and which is now in the Biblio-

---

[28] A. Muñoz in *Bollettino della Associazione archeologica romana*, XIV (1924), p. 4. E. Miller (*Académie des inscriptions et belles-lettres, Comptes Rendus*, 1865, I, p. 26) casually mentions a Livy in the Seraglio, but this obviously contained the known books.

[29] *Gentleman's Magazine*, XXXIX (1769), p. 131; *Scaligerana*, etc., I (Colomiés), p. 537.

thèque Nationale of Paris. The project was approved by a number of illustrious men, including Samuel Pepys, the diarist who seems to have spent so much of his time in going to bed [30]. At any rate, we know that Colbert instructed his diplomats to be on the lookout for Livy and other manuscripts in their trips to the Near East [31].

In 1737, Richard West wrote a letter to Walpole describing a pretended dream in which he visited the moon. There, he says, « his Lunatic Majesty shew'd me his Cabinet of *Lost Things upon Earth* », and the first thing that he saw was « Livy's Decads, complete, best Edition ». In 1771 a false report located the lost books in the Escorial Library in Spain. Finally a small palimpsest fragment of Book XCI was found in 1772, not in some remote corner of the world, but in the Vatican Library, to which it had come in 1623 from Germany. Livy's ghost seems to have played a part in this discovery, for how else can we explain the fact that the finder, a man named Bruns, was born near and educated in Lübeck, the very town in which a fourteenth-century report located the lost books? The fragment was just enough to tantalize scholars and to bring forth a new crop of rumors. By the end of the century there was again talk of the existence of an Arabic translation of the complete Livy somewhere in Morocco. One scholar even tried to get the Austrian government to send for it. Apparently it was a variant of this same story which Niebuhr told his classes in 1828-29 when he referred to the alleged discovery of an Arabic version in Saragossa, Spain [32].

With all this background, it is easy to understand the interesting happenings at Palermo in 1782 [33]. In that year a certain

---

[30] John Nichols, *Literary Anecdotes of the Eighteenth Century,* I (London, 1812), p. 101. The *Rivista Indo-Greco-Italica*, VIII (1924), fasc. 3-4 (cover), tells of an uncial Livy bought by Anthony Askew in Sicily in 1749 and lost in England among the books of one Taylor (presumably Dr. John Taylor, a correspondent of Askew). In the sales catalogue of Askew's library (*Bibliotheca Askeviana manu scripta,* London, 1785, p. 29), three copies of Livy are listed, two of the fourteenth century, the third dated 1464.

[31] L. Delisle, *Le cabinet des manuscrits de la Bibliothèque Impériale,* I (Paris, 1868), pp. 276, 296.

[32] B. G. Niebuhr, *Lectures on the History of Rome,* edited by L. Schmitz, 4th ed. (London, 1873), p. 41.

[33] I take these facts from the *Gentleman's Magazine,* LXX (1800), p. 220.

Joseph Vella, an Italian born in Malta, acted as interpreter for a distinguished Arab from Morocco who was forced by bad weather to put in at Palermo. There, among other things, the visitor was shown a number of Arabic manuscripts. The interpreter became interested in them and took it upon himself to read and explain them and thus to parade his erudition. But his inventiveness far exceeded his knowledge, and to save his face and to maintain the interest which he had aroused he came to depend entirely on his imagination. Soon he announced that he possessed an Arabic translation of Books LX-LXXXVIII of Livy's history, which had been given to him by the Grand Master of Malta. The latter, he said, had received it from a Frenchman who took it away from a thief in the church of St. Sophia in Constantinople. International intrigue and crime such as are found in the pages of a mystery thriller. Vella did not publish the new Livy, though an English lady offered to defray the expense. In 1790 it was reported that the lost books had arrived in Dublin from Palermo. This was in a letter appropriately sent to Bishop Percy [34], who in his famous *Reliques* published a collection of ancient English poems, the manuscript of which he saved from the fire to which a housemaid was about to consign them. Finally Vella issued an Italian translation of the supposed Book LX. But the entire publication consisted of a single page, for he had simply translated the well-known Epitome. After this apprenticeship he went into the forgery business on a grand scale, specializing in mediaeval letters and documents. He achieved considerable fame and wealth thereby, was made abbot and professor of Arabic. He published numerous expensive volumes out of funds which were provided by others, and some of these were translated into Latin, English, French, and German. Finally in 1794 he pretended that he had been robbed of his precious manuscripts. Testimony showed that he had shipped a large box the day before the supposed robbery. From a study of the published works, a German scholar, Hager, denounced him as a fraud and then proceeded to Palermo for further investigation. After two

---

[34] John Nichols, *Illustrations of the Literary History of the Eighteenth Century*, VII (London, 1848), pp. 509-513.

years of study, Hager set forth such a convincing array of evidence against Vella that the latter confessed and was sentenced to fifteen years' imprisonment. And this ended the Arabic period, so to speak, of Livian hopes, which like its predecessor, the Germanic, lasted a century and a half or more.

In 1783 a gentleman living in Bergamo came upon a history of the First Punic War in a Latin manuscript. Immediately leaping to the conclusion (who wouldn't after the sensational reports of preceding centuries?) that here were some of the lost books of Livy, he at once began to transcribe them with the utmost enthusiasm. Imagine his disappointment when a scholarly friend informed him that the fine Latin which he was copying was nothing but the version of Polybius made by Leonardo Bruni in the fifteenth century! [35].

We have already seen that in 1850 the Leipzig professor Moritz Haupt thought that there might be something in the early tales about the existence of the missing books. About the same time he told his friend, the novelist Gustav Freytag, in strictest confidence that under a house in a small town in Westphalia there lay the ruins of an old monastery library which quite possibly contained the lost Livian decades [36]. Freytag suggested that they visit the old curmudgeon who owned the house, drink him under the table, and make off with the manuscript. Their plan, presumably concocted over a glass of wine or two or six, came to nought, but Freytag introduced the theme into his successful novel « Die verlorene Handschrift », in wich, however, he substituted Tacitus for Livy.

In 1861 the German press falsely reported that fifty books had been discovered in Padua. What could have been more dramatic than to find them there, in Livy's home town? This seems to have been the only false alarm during the century. In 1904 a number of small fragments of a manuscript of the fourth decade written in the ancient script called uncial were found in the covers of two manuscripts in Bamberg. They were important because of their age and turned out to belong to the manuscript

[35] G. Gervasoni in *Rivista di Bergamo*, IV (1925), pp. 1953-1958.
[36] Gustav Freytag, *Erinnerungen aus meinem Leben* (Leipzig, 1899), p. 293.

from which the eleventh-century Bamberg manuscript was copied. But the importance of the find was exaggerated, and some American newspapers reported the discovery of the lost books of Livy.

Germany has bulked large both in the rumors and the finds. Not only new books but valuable manuscripts of those already known were found there. It certainly was a center of interest in Livy during the Middle Ages. For the first decade, there once was an important manuscript at Worms; another still exists at Bamberg. Another Bamberg manuscript contains the third and fourth decades, including some chapters unknown before it came to light. Part of the third and fourth decades were in a manuscript of some importance which has disappeared from Speyer. The uncial fragments at Bamberg belong to this decade, as did the lost Mainz manuscript, which contributed some new material. The fifth-century manuscript from Lorsch, our only source for the text of Books XLI-XLV, once contained the entire fifth decade. The fourth-century fragments of Book XCI probably came from Lorsch. Worms, Lorsch, Speyer, and Mainz are near one another on or near the Rhine. It is quite possible that other books of Livy once existed in this region and it is not inconceivable that fragments may still be found there or in places to which they have been removed.

Last of all, in our pursuit of the elusive Livy, after more than a century of comparative peace, comes the great hoax of 1924, or as an Italian scholar euphemistically called it, the « late Livian polemics ». On August 5 of that year there appeared a number of the *Rivista Indo-Greco-Italica,* a reputable classical periodical published in Naples, on the cover of which there was a short notice printed at the last moment. It began with the words « sensational discovery », followed by « Titi Livii ab urbe condita libri CXLII » in large letters, and went on to report that Dr. Mario Di Martino Fusco, editor of the classical periodical *Mouseion,* had found the complete works of Livy in a series of uncial manuscripts. In the next issue of the *Rivista,* which appeared several months later, the editor defends himself for publishing the original notice, in a manner so vehement that it strikes the reader as rather amusing. He states that he did so only after 1) the sending of telegrams on July 27 by Dr. Di Martino asking for subscriptions to the photographs of the Livy manuscripts; 2) repeated confirmation of the find by Dr. Di Martino to scholars and newspaper correspondents; 3) trustworthy assurances of first-class authorities in philology and palaeography. A brief letter in the London *Times* of August 21 called the attention of the world to the first notice in the *Rivista*. It created a stir at once. Newspaper correspondents besieged Di Martino. He confirmed the reports but refused to go into details or to show the books. Government officials interviewed him. Precautions were taken to prevent the manuscripts from being taken out of Italy. Di Martino was defended by some well-known scholars and attacked by others. In the London *Times* of September 12 no less a scholar than the late R. S. Conway, wrote:

Accounts which have now reached me from different sources in Italy place Dr. Di Martino's character as a man of the highest integrity and his competence as a student of palaeography beyond all doubt in my mind. I am quite convinced that he has secured large portions of Livy hitherto unknown, whether in their original form or, conceivably, in long series of extracts. . . . The suggestions of fraud and forgery which continue to be made in many newspapers are really a disgrace to our national intelligence. How can any one who has so much as looked into a Book of Livy, even in translation, conceive of a person sitting down to compose in Latin, at this date, 107 Books of the same bulk? Certainly no one who ever set eyes on an Uncial codex could dream—except in a bad nightmare— of attempting to forge 15 such bulky volumes, on vellum, and in ink of the sixth century. It would need an army of superlunatics to begin such a task. Some of them, however, do seem to find it easy to get their fancies printed in reputable newspapers. For the same reasons the hypothesis of any complete mistake on the part of a high-minded, eager, and conscientious young scholar—and such is the picture of Di Martino which I construct from the sources before me—is only a little less insane.

It seems not to have occurred to Professor Conway to question the existence of the codices. But the reactions were not all on a lofty and serious level. In *Punch* for September 10, 1924, A. P. Herbert, well-known author, humorist, and member of Parliament, protested, in the name of the « Amalgamated Society of Schoolboys, Past, Present and Future », against the finding or at least the publication of any more of Livy. He objected to having the fiery labors of Pope Gregory I nullified by an Italian whose name sounded like a cocktail. There was too much Livy as it was. And besides he did not like the idea of having a new generation know more Livy than he did. He ended his letter with the solemn adjuration: « Sir, this scandal must not be ».

To return to Di Martino. The most that he himself would say was that he was copying the second decade and that, when this was finished, he would call in other scholars to assist in transcribing the rest. The papers were full of speculation but little news. American and English newspapers vied with one another for the publication rights of the new find. Think of reading the serialized Livy in your local newspaper every morning as you gulp your breakfast! Naples was reported to be more stirred by the discovery than by almost any event of the last century. One is reminded of Padua in 1413.

The sensation took a new turn when a German, Dr. Max Funke, stated in the *Leipziger Tageblatt* of September 12 that he had had an interview with Di Martino Fusco, who was an old friend, had seen the manuscript, and had been permitted to make a facsimile copy of several lines. This facsimile was reproduced in the newspaper. Funke also revealed that the manuscript, or rather, manuscripts, had been found in the famous Castel dell'Ovo, in a niche in the wall of the old monastery. He stated that Di Martino wanted a million gold marks for the right of publication in Germany and similar sums for these rights in other countries, and that he expected to sell the manuscripts themselves for a million pounds sterling in England or America.

Such was the story which the London *Times* carried on September 13 (as hundreds of other papers did on that and following days). It included the first words of the facsimile: « Ubi multitudo hominum insperata occurrit ». Conway, who was a well-known authority on Livy, said that the style of these five words was unmistakably Livian, partly because of the use of *insperatus* instead of the Caesarian *inopinatus,* but especially because of the way in which the word was used. On September 20 the *Illustrated London News* reproduced the facsimile given by the Leipzig paper. At once Professor Hall of Oxford and Professor Housman of Cambridge, the well-known poet and classical scholar, wrote to the *Times* to point out that the fac-simile was taken from a published photograph of a manuscript of Sulpicius Severus' Life of St. Martin of Tours and thus had nothing to do with Livy. It later turned out that Funke had taken it from a Naples newspaper of September 2, in which it had been printed for what it was: merely as a specimen of uncial writing. It remains uncertain whether Funke was looking for notoriety or for newspaper employment, or whether, as seems more likely, he merely wanted to help a good joke along. Con-way's anger, it is amusing to note, was then turned against the rascally Funke, whereas Di Martino was still an innocent man deserving of sympathy.

We may even surmise with some plausibility where Funke got the inspiration for his story. As I have said, the popular German novelist, Gustav Freytag, wrote a story called « Die ver-lorene Handschrift ». In this a German *professor* finds in an *old book a reference* to a *complete manuscript* of *Tacitus* which had once existed in a German *monastery* but had been carried to a nearby *castle* by a *monk* at the time of the *Swedish invasion*. The professor concludes that the manuscript may have been writ-ten in the *sixth* century and may still be in the castle, walled up in its *thick foundations*. In his story Funke makes Di Martino Fusco find a *reference* to a *complete Livy* in an *old book* and then discover the *sixth-century manuscript* of that author in the *thick walls* of the *monastery* beneath the *Castel* dell'Ovo, where the *monks* had concealed it at the time of the *French invasion*. In his periodical *Mouseion,* Di Martino had published a short article in 1923 on a sixth-century library and scriptorium at Naples in or near the Castello, and this Funke probably had read. At any rate, Funke, perhaps under the influence of Livy's ghost, righted the wrong committed by Freytag in substituting Tacitus for Livy. Curiously enough, not a word about the supposed Livy find was ever published in Di Martino's own periodical. In 1925 Di Martino discussed the history of the Castello and its importance as a center of book production in the sixth century and in the next year he wrote in defense of some of his earlier criticism of Nardi's translation of Livy, but nothing was said about the lost books in either article.

Whatever Funke's motives, he brought the matter to a head by his obvious lies. For they seem to have acted like a pail of cold water on the befuddled Di Martino and a few days later he retracted. We can reconstruct what happened to him somewhat as follows: Four years previously, at the age of twenty-eight, he had taken his degree at the University of Naples with a thesis on Livy. He continued his studies in that author, working especially on the text tradition. He presumably learned what all students of Livy know, that a fifth-century manuscript of Livy now in Paris had been revised in the sixth century at Avellino, near Naples. In the archives of Naples he found an entry under the date 1322 which told of the payment of wages to a scribe « pro scriptura decem librorum Titi Livii de Bello Macedonico ». The ten books on the Macedonian War which the scribe copied were among those already known, but this bookkeeping entry led Di Martino to think that he was on the track of all of the books of Livy. He told his friends about it and they jumped to the conclusion that he had already found the books which he was hoping to find. Once the story got into the press he could not bring himself to deny it: the more lies he told, the more he had to tell. Finally, however, the situation became so intolerable that he went into seclusion, leaving a note for his mother to hand to the reporters; in this he said that the whole thing was a mistake. But the public appetite had been so whetted that his denial was at first received with incredulity as a mere effort to be left in peace.

At the suggestion of Benedetto Croce, Fausto Nicolini, inspector of government archives, had been put in charge of the government's investigation of Di Martino's story [37]. From the first Nicolini had been sceptical of Di Martino's claims. Rivalry between two Neapolitan newspapers had helped keep the affair alive. It had been rumored that Nicolini received a « flood of dollars » to permit the Livy manuscripts to be sold in America.

---

[37] Giovanni Artieri, « Don Fausto Nicolini e la beffa liviana », *Nuova Antologia,* 96 (1961), p. 17. In this paragraph I report Artieri's account, incredible though it may seem.

Then Nicolini did something that to me seems in rather bad taste, to put it mildly, great though the provocation was. He invented a collaborator of Di Martino and in the name of this fictitious character he wrote to the newspaper « Il Mattino » to complain of Di Martino's failure to give him credit. At the same time, to make the story more plausible, he asserted that Di Martino had found only the second decade. My objection to Nicolini's tricks is based on the fact that he was a government official in charge of the investigation. If anyone else had thought up the clever joke it would have been a delightful farce *alla napolitana*. Perhaps, however, one had to be in Naples at the time fully to appreciate Nicolini's difficult position.

There is much similarity between the stories of Funke and Nicolini. One wonders whether the two bits of fiction are related to each other.

One of the lawyers who represented Di Martino and who urged him to admit that he had not actually found the complete Livy was Vincenzo Dattilo. Presumably this is the same Vincenzo Dattilo who years later voiced the hope that the complete Livy would be found (see above, note 11). Apparently it will be a long time before Naples abandons all hope of discovering *Livius ingens*.

Strangely enough, Di Martino's scholarly career seems not to have been affected, for some years at least. Perhaps the world has formed the habit of considering a Livian lie a white lie. Di Martino continued to edit *Mouseion,* though after 1924 (is the date significant?) his name did not appear on the title page [38]. The periodical was discontinued in 1928. That year is also the last in which Di Martino's name appears as archivist in the R. *Archivio di Stato* at Naples [39].

---

[38] In one of his later articles, he claimed the discovery of the tomb of Archytas at Tarentum. One whole number he devoted to the initiation of the new excavations at Herculaneum in 1927. Copies of this number brought him letters of acknowledgment from the offices of the Pope, the King of Italy, the King of Belgium, Mussolini, and others; all the letters were published in the next number.

[39] *Minerva* for 1928. The above account about Di Martino is based chiefly on newspaper accounts, American, English, Italian, especially *The Times* (of London), *Il Mattino* (of Naples), the New York *Times*. See also the article by Cocchia (a former teacher of Di Martino) mentioned above. Other references are E. Chatelain in *Revue des études anciennes*, XXVI (1924), pp. 314-316, and

If my interpretation is correct, the hopes of Di Martino's friends and later of the public, hopes which in the course of six centuries have become part of the blood stream of all western peoples, literally forced the poor man to say things which he had no intention of saying. He was the latest victim of Livy's ghost. It has driven us from the Bosphorus to the Pillars of Hercules, from the sands of Africa to the frozen fjords of Norway, from the island of Iona to the island of Chios. It has involved Italians and Ethiopians, Arabs and Turks, English and Scotch, Frenchmen and Germans, Norwegians and Danes, Greeks and Spaniards. Its victims include kings and popes, prime ministers and apothecaries, scholars and rascals. Where it will appear next, in Siberia or South Africa, in Alpha, Oregon, or Omega, New York, we do not know, but that it will walk again is one of the few certainties of this uncertain life. Only after that reawakening of ancient spirits which we call the Renaissance loses its vigor and the classical humanities nod off into sleep will Livy's ghost be laid, and by the same token, when the Lost Books of Livy disappear into Lethe, the River of Oblivion, we shall know that the Renaissance has come to an end and another tombstone may be erected, inscribed on which will be the words: « Hic iacent studia humanitatis et spes librorum Livianorum reperiundorum; requiescant Livi manes in pace ». « Here lie humanistic studies and the hopes of finding the books of Livy; may the shade of Livy rest in peace ».

E. K. Rand in *The Classical Weekly,* XVIII (1924), p. 25. Other discussions dealing with the subject of this chapter are A. Baroni, *Tito Livio nel Rinascimento* (Pavia, 1889); Carlo Pascal, *L'opera di Livio, Codici, scoperte, incunaboli* (*Pubblicazioni dell'Atene e Roma, Sezione di Milano,* Milan, 1925); R. Sabbadini, *Le scoperte dei codici latini e greci ne' secoli XIV e XV* (Florence, 1905, 1914), especially II, pp. 231-233; G. Voigt, *Die Wiederbelebung des classischen Alterthums,* ed. 3, I (Berlin, 1893), pp. 206-207, 247-249; II, pp 200, 271.

CHAPTER V

HIEREMIAS DE MONTAGNONE
AND HIS CITATIONS FROM CATULLUS [1]

Hieremias (Jeremy) de Montagnone, a Paduan judge who was born between 1250 and 1260 and died in 1320 or 1321, put together a book of quotations from ancient and mediaeval writers which he called *Compendium moralium notabilium*. This was the most successful of his books, as indicated by the number of extant manuscripts (at least fifty-two, not to mention several we know existed at one time). It even achieved the distinction of being printed (1505). By contrast one of his other works (a medical dictionary) has been lost and a third (a collection of legal maxims) is preserved in but a single manuscript. The collection of moral quotations follows the typical pattern of the mediaeval florilegia, both those which were anonymous and those attributed to various authors [2]. Yet the work presents several unusual features which justify discussion in a book on the Italian Renaissance.

Weiss has given Hieremias first place in his valuable book on the first century of humanism [3]. He makes the interesting point that Hieremias applies the term *poeta* only to classical writers, while later versifiers have to be content with the inferior designation *versilogus*. The first to receive this appellation is

---

[1] Revised and enlarged form of an article published in *Classical Philology*, V (1910), pp. 66-82. I am indebted to Dr. Paul Pascal and Dr. Marvin Colker for checking some of the manuscripts of Jeremy.

[2] B. L. Ullman, « Tibullus in the Mediaeval Florilegia », *Classical Philology*, XXIII (1928), p. 128, and succeeding articles (XXIV, p. 109; XXV, p. 11; XXVI, p. 155; XXVII, p. 1, and especially p. 37).

[3] Roberto Weiss, *Il primo secolo dell'umanesimo* (Rome, 1949).

Avianus, who, however, is placed after Isidore in Hieremias' chronological table. Weiss draws the conclusion that Hieremias rigorously set off the classical period from the mediaeval, implying that there was a decline in the later period. This would mark the beginning of the humanistic attitude towards the two periods. But we can perhaps go farther than this: the only *philosophi* mentioned are ancient, i. e., Plato, Isocrates, Aristotle [4], Theophrastus, Seneca, Macrobius, Proclus, and Boethius. The last named is also called *religiologus,* the regular appellation for the authors of the Old and New Testaments, for the Church Fathers, and for mediaeval writers on religion. The only ones to receive the title of *historiologus* are Sallust, Valerius Maximus, Pliny, Frontinus. It is true, however, that no mediaeval historians are listed. The only *oratores* are Cicero and Quintilian; the only *rethoricus* is Cassiodorus, also called a *religiologus.* Ptolemy alone is an *astrologus*; Priscian, a *grammaticus.* By contrast the designation *doctor grammaticus* is applied to three mediaeval writers. Other mediaeval authors are left without title.

The most quoted author is Aristotle, cited 733 times in 22 works, genuine and spurious. In this respect Hieremias is still mediaeval. But Seneca the Younger is a close second, with 681 citations, including the *Tragedies.* These plays were a major concern of the early Paduan pre-Renaissance headed by Albertino Mussato [5]. Then follow Cicero and Ovid.

The most remarkable novelty in the *Compendium* is the appearance of citations from Catullus, few though they are. This author, almost more than any other, is to be identified with the Renaissance. Sabbadini began his great book on the discovery of Latin and Greek manuscripts with the story of the reappearance of Catullus in Verona [6], who was practically unknown in the Middle Ages. The oldest manuscripts were not written until after the middle of the fourteenth century. One poem alone (62) is found in a mediaeval manuscript (ninth century). Only one

---

[4] Actually no designation is given Aristotle in the Venice edition, but *philosophus* occurs regularly in the manuscripts.

[5] See above, chapter II.

[6] R. Sabbadini, *Le scoperte dei codici latini e greci ne' secoli XIV e XV,* I (Florence, 1905), p. 1.

mediaeval writer can be shown to quote him directly, Ratherius of Verona, in the tenth century [7]. No existing mediaeval catalogue of manuscripts contains a Catullus [8]. Then suddenly Catullus comes to life. Early in the fourteenth century Benvenuto de Campesanis of Vicenza writes a poem about Catullus' return home to Verona after a long exile. Hieremias quotes him, as does Benzo of Alessandria. Citations are included in a florilegium put together at Verona in 1329. Copies are made of the « lost Verona » manuscript, and Catullus is on the way to becoming one of the authors popular with the humanists. It all started in Verona and Padua in the early fourteenth century. Jeremy's quotations from Catullus, which are of great significance both for Catullus and for the humanistic movement, are the particular concern of the present discussion.

But first let us see when the *Compendium* was written, for it is important for our purpose to date it as closely as possible. The authority of Scardeone [9], who says that Hieremias died about 1300, was followed by Ellis in his large edition of Catullus [10] and by Wheeler [11]. It was, however, definitely settled by Rajna [12], by means of official documents of the city of Padua, that Hieremias became judge in 1280 and died in 1320-21. Between these two dates the *Compendium* must have been produced, for Hieremias was already judge when he published the work, as we know from the title itself. Rajna adopts 1290-1300 as a safe compromise between the two extremes, though admitting that he has no real argument for his choice. But it has been shown that the *terminus post quem* is 1295, for Jeremy cites a Latin translation of Aristotle's *Economics* which was not made until that year [13]. Weiss tentatively suggests a date between 1300

---

[7] B. L. Ullman « The Transmission of the Text of Catullus », *Studi in onore di Luigi Castiglioni* (Florence, 1960), p. 1027.

[8] Max Manitius, *Handschriften antiker Autoren in mittelalterlichen Bibliothekskatalogen* (Leipzig, 1935), p. 61

[9] B. Scardeonius, *De antiquitate urbis Patavii et claris Patavinis* (Basel, 1560), p. 235.

[10] Ed. 2 (Oxford, 1878), Prolegomena, p. ix.

[11] A. L. Wheeler, « Hieremias de Montagnone and Catullus », *American Journal of Philology*, XXIX (1908), p. 186.

[12] P. Rajna in *Studi di filologia romanza*, V (1891), pp. 193 ff.

[13] V. Rose in *Hermes*, I (1866), pp. 372-373; Weiss, *op. cit.*, p. 26.

and 1310. Even this date is so early that it is clear that Hieremias' quotation of seven passages from Catullus furnishes one of
the first *testimonia* to that author after the resurrection of his
work early in the fourteenth century.

But granting that this date is approximately correct, must we
therefore assume that Hieremias read Catullus as early as 1300?
By no means. There is evidence that the Catullus citations and
perhaps others were added later. One of the manuscripts of the
Compendium, Bodleian Canon. Lat. 212, of the fifteenth century,
omits every one of the seven Catullus passages [14]. Citations from
some other authors also are lacking in this manuscript [15]. That
these omissions were accidental is out of the question. That they
were intentional on the part of the copyist is unlikely. It would
seem, then, that this manuscript is descended from an early edition of the *Compendium,* made before the discovery of Catullus,
or at least before Hieremias had read that author. How many
editions in various states of completion there may have been it
is not possible for me to say. There is, however, some slight
evidence of one intermediate edition. Casanatensis 312 (C. iv. 11),
a manuscript dated 1398, omits the two Catullus passages that
Hieremias cites last. It is probable, of course, that these omissions are accidental, but it is not impossible that this manuscript
is descended from one which was copied from the original before
Hieremias had inserted all the quotations in his work [16]. At least
one manuscript, that in Chicago, though containing Catullus,
omits a great many passages, especially toward the end of the
volume, but generally not those omitted in the Bodleian manuscript. Ovid, Martial, Cato, the *proverbia vulgaria,* are among

---

[14] This manuscript was evidently known to R. Ellis, for in his book,
Catullus in the XIVth Century (London, 1905), he speaks of two Bodleian manu-
scripts, the other being Canon. Lat. Misc. 186, used for his large edition of
Catullus. He, however, says nothing about the omission of the Catullus passages.

[15] For example, it omits part of the Sallust quotations and the one from
Virgil's *Georgics* in III, 4, 8, of those from Ovid's *De rem. am.* and Paul,
Ad Eph., in IV, 4, 8, and of the one from *Ecclesiastes* in IV, 6, 3. This
manuscript, as well as the Chicago manuscript and others, lacks the chronological
table of authors.

[16] The omission of one passage (51, 15-16) in Paris, N. a. l. 1779 (dated
1475), and of another (39, 16) in Paris, lat. 6469 (of about the same date), I
consider accidental.

the worst sufferers. These omissions do not point to an earlier edition but to deletion after Hieremias' time. This is proved by such examples as the following. On p. 263 the scribe started to copy out a Valerius Maximus citation (V, 1, 10; fol. 127r of the Venice edition) but stopped and deleted after writing « Val li 7 ». The same thing occurred on p. 264 after he wrote the first two letters of « Augustinus » (V. 3, 1; fol. 137r of the Venice edition). The scribe himself may have decided on the omission or he may have failed at first to see deletion marks in his exemplar. As Weiss pointed out [17], there are signs of additions after Jeremy's time. He noted the presence of a Petrarch passage in an Oxford manuscript (Canon. Lat. Misc. 186, fol. 163r). This is presumably the same passage as one found in the Chicago manuscript. The latter has a number of other quotations not occurring in the Venice edition. Further light on all these matters should come from a thorough investigation of the manuscripts of the *Compendium*. If there was a second edition to which the Catullus passages were added, its date was perhaps as late as 1310-15. The Verona manuscript of Catullus does not seem to have been discovered before that time; at least, the earliest datable reference to it is by Bencius Alexandrinus, who examined it shortly before 1310 [18].

The definite contributions which I have to make in this discussion are, first, the report of an examination for the Catullus citations of a number of hitherto unused manuscripts of Hieremias' work; second, a solution, which I believe to be both simple and conclusive, of the problem which these citations present, a problem with which all students of the manuscript tradition of Catullus are familiar and for which some fantastic solutions have been proposed; and third, some interesting sidelights on the « lost Verona » manuscript of Catullus. The net result of this investigation will in my opinion be of great importance to Catullus students, for it will end in the exaltation of O to a point higher than any reached by it heretofore as a witness to the text of the Veronensis, and thus of Catullus himself.

[17] *Op. cit.*, p. 27.
[18] Sabbadini, *op. cit.*, II (1914), p. 146.

The puzzle about the Catullus passages in the *Compendium* has been the manner of citing, not according to poems as we cite from Catullus at present, but according to chapters, *capitula,* which do not correspond to our division of the poems. There cannot be the least doubt that Hieremias used the term *capitulum,* not *liber,* which is found only sporadically in the manuscripts, as may be seen from the reports given below. That the abbreviations *c.* and *ca.* are to be taken as *capitulo* and not *capite,* is perhaps not entirely proved by the abbreviations *ca°* and *c°* which are found in some manuscripts, nor by the occurrence of the full word in one passage in the Venice edition. These facts may merely show that the original abbreviation (probably *c.*) was taken as *capitulo* by the scribes. Hieremias' use of the same form in quoting from other works, prose and verse, and the interpretation of it as *capitulo* by the scribes and the Venetian printer in these passages also, serve, however, to confirm this interpretation. Moreover, a common use of *capitulum* as applied to poetry not only suggests that this is the word that Hieremias meant, but also shows how it is to be understood. The use referred to is in designation of one of a number of poems. For example, in codex R of Catullus, R[2] (fourteenth century) has written *cap^m* in the margin of poem 67 to indicate that a new poem begins there. Codex F of Propertius (fourteenth century) uses *capitulum* as a term for a new poem[19]. The word is regularly used in this sense in a manuscript of Petrarch's *Trionfi* (Bodl. Canon. Ital. 70)[20]. The forms *carmen* and *charta (carta),* which may be thought of as possible expansions of the abbreviation *c.,* may be summarily dismissed. The latter will not solve the riddle of the Catullus citations. The former seems not to have been used by Hieremias at all, even in quoting from Horace's *Odes,* if the Venice edition is to be trusted, for in this we find such forms as *Od. li. 2. c. 10* followed by *Od. li. 2. cap. 16*—the passages being from odes 10 and 16 respectively of the second book.

---

[19] III, 4. So also Baehrens' critical apparatus in his edition of Propertius (Leipzig, 1880).

[20] The term, found also in other manuscripts of the *Trionfi,* was no doubt used by Petrarch himself. See C. Appel, *Die Triumphe Francesco Petrarcas* (Halle, 1901), p. 2, note.

We see, then, that the natural way to take the word *capitulum* is as a synonym for *carmen,* poem. Since, however, this explanation does not correspond with the poem division of Catullus as shown by the manuscripts, various other interpretations have been suggested. Bywater [21] and Baehrens [22] thought that the quotations were taken from a florilegium divided into chapters, but Ellis [23] rightly objected to this explanation on the grounds that we have no evidence of the existence of such a florilegium, and especially that the *capitula* are numerically arranged to agree with the order of the poems in our Catullus manuscripts, i. e., the farther on in the Catullus collection a given poem occurs, the larger is the number of Jeremy's *capitulum* quoting from that poem. Ellis himself thought that the citations were taken from a complete manuscript of Catullus, though he did not explain the numbering of the *capitula*. In his later work he suggested that the « lost Verona » manuscript, from which he believed Hieremias drew his citations, « was divided into short books or sections, which fell out from the later transcripts, giving way to the division into separate poems, with their titles, which also formed part of the same codex » [24]. He also suggested that these sections were the original *libelli* of which the collection was formed. Wheeler put forth the theory that Hieremias' manuscript was entirely different from the manuscripts we possess, that it was, in fact, divided into ten sections on the basis of the meter employed, and that these were the *capitula* of Hieremias [25]. This theory is based on the false premise that Hieremias speaks of ten *capitula,* whereas he speaks of twelve [26]. A great deal of twisting and squeezing is also necessary to make the scheme fit the facts. Besides, it is inherently improbable that Jeremy's manuscript was not a descendant of the Veronensis. Peiper expressed the opinion that Hieremias himself divided the work into convenient sections, though making use of divisions already existing in his manuscript,

---

[21] Ellis' edition (1878), Prolegomena, p. xi.
[22] *Catulli Veronensis liber* (Leipzig, 1876), p. lviii.
[23] *Loc. cit.*
[24] *Catullus in the XVIth Century,* pp. 7, 8.
[25] *Loc. cit.*
[26] See the reports from the manuscripts at the end of this chapter.

and perhaps merely numbering sections marked off by titles [27]. It was only inherent probability that led Peiper to this conclusion, for he found no support for it in the manuscripts of Catullus, as he himself confesses: « Sein codex müsste dann allerdings sehr stark in dieser beziehung von den uns bekannten abgewichen sein ». He goes on to say that the Veronensis probably had fewer titles than the existing manuscripts.

While we are dealing with false theorizing we may have a little amusement by quoting an article by E. Wölfflin, entitled « Paläographisches und unpaläographisches » [28]. After chiding, quite appropriately, several scholars for their mistakes in reading manuscripts, he comments, briefly and categorically, on Peiper's and Baehrens' quotation from Jeremy: « cap. 12 *et pultb* ist auf-zulösen: *et proverbialiter* ». As a matter of fact, Peiper indicated that one of his manuscripts had *et plt'*, the other two *et pult'*. Baehrens, correctly understanding this but wishing to make it clearer, wrote *et pult'*. The abbreviation, of course, stands for *et penultimo*. This, then, is the « unpaläographisches » in Wölfflin's note, though not in the application he intended: it is *unpaläo-graphisch* in that he read Peiper incorrectly by dreaming up a *b* and then expanded the abbreviation wrongly.

If Peiper had examined Jeremy's usage for other authors more thoroughly at the time when he wrote his book, he would have found strong support for his suggestion. He did, it is true, note that the *Tobias* of Matthew of Vendôme had been divided by Hieremias into chapters for the purpose of quotation, but he did not work out the details of this division. It seems strange that no student of Catullus, and especially Peiper, has called atten-tion to the fact that Seneca's *Tragedies* and Terence are quoted by *capitula* exactly as Catullus is. The Seneca citations were later published by Peiper himself, who noted that Hieremias numbered the separate scenes and *cantica* in his manuscript as « chap-

---

[27] R. Peiper, *Q. Valerius Catullus, Beiträge zur Kritik seiner Gedichte* (Breslau, 1875), p. 22.
[28] *Philologus*, XXXVI (1877), p. 182.

ters » [29]. Coluccio Salutati also cites the *Tragedies* by chapters [30].

It is not difficult to harmonize Jeremy's chapters with the scene divisions of Seneca [31]. I have used the 1902 edition of R. Peiper and G. Richter and controlled it with a Harvard manuscript (MS. Lat. 47, dated 1432) and four incunabula of 1491, 1492, 1493, and 1498 (Hain 14665, 14666, 14668, 14670). I do not report their variations where Jeremy agrees with Peiper and Richter. In *Hercules furens* Jeremy quotes eleven chapters—he twice mentions « 11 fi(nali) ». These check with the scene divisions in Peiper and Richter except that the report of chapter 5 for vss. 735-736 in the Venice edition of Jeremy is an error for 6, the reading which Peiper reports for his best Breslau manuscript and which I find in two Vatican manuscripts. In *Troades* the chapters agree with the scene divisions of the Harvard manuscript (including those not indicated in Peiper and Richter at vs. 705, where all four incunabula have a scene heading, and vs. 736, where three of the incunabula have one). The last quoted is « 12 pe(nultimo) ». In the Venice edition one of four references to this chapter wrongly gives 11 for 12, and even there Peiper's report of the Breslau manuscript indicates the latter, as do two Vatican manuscripts. There is agreement in the five chapters of *Phoenissae* (the last is numbered « 5 et fi ») and in the first seven (all that are cited) of *Medea*. So too the ten chapters cited from the *Phaedra* check with the first ten scene divisions. In *Oedipus* there is agreement to the last of the fourteen chapters. *Agamemnon* can be made to harmonize by assuming scene divisions at vss. 695 and 867, as in the Harvard manuscript and the four incunabula. Jeremy's quotations indicate that there were fourteen chapters. In *Thyestes* there is agreement throughout the twelve chapters. In *Hercules Oetaeus* several adjustments must be made. A scene division at vs. 225, as in the Harvard manuscript and the four incunabula, must be assumed. With this adjustment quotations through chapter 8 check. Beyond that point there is only

---

[29] R. Peiper, *De Senecae tragoediarum uulgari lectione* (A) *constituenda* (Breslau, 1893) p. 21 (*Festschrift zur 250jährigen Jubelfeier des Gymnasiums zu St. Maria Magdalena zu Breslau*, p. 146).

[30] *Colucii Salutati De laboribus Herculis,* ed. B. L. Ullman (Zurich, 1951), IV 2, 1, 6 (p. 527, 3).

[31] There are some errors in Peiper's reports in the *Festschrift*.

one quotation, in « 26 fi », which must be an error by Jeremy,
perhaps, for 16. By assuming no scene division at vs. 1290 (as in
some manuscripts) we arrive at sixteen scene divisions in the
play. There is some difficulty in *Octavia*. Jeremy cites from
nineteen chapters, and only fourteen are marked in Peiper and
Richter. By assuming a scene division at vs. 100, as in some
manuscripts and in the four incunabula, at vss. 201, 222, and
possibly at 174, where some manuscripts indicate a lacuna, we
can place vs. 323 in chapter 8, as Jeremy does. We must also
postulate another scene division not indicated in the editions
somewhere between vss. 593 and 845, perhaps at vs. 669 or
vs. 806, at both of which the Harvard manuscript has headings.

The chapters in Terence agree with the scene divisions in the
Oxford text of Kauer and Lindsay except as noted below. The
periocha is always treated as chapter 1 and the prologue as chapter 2. Thus in the *Andria* vss. 60-61, 67-68, 77-78, 142-143 are
in chapter 3; vs. 191 in 4 [32]. In agreement with one group of
manuscripts Jeremy's manuscript apparently had no division at I,
3 (vs. 206). Then vs. 266 appears in chapter 6; vss. 305-308 in 7.
In agreement with all the manuscripts Jeremy's manuscript
evidently had no scene heading at II, 3 (vs. 375), for vss. 426-427
are in chapter 10; vs. 555 in 14. In the *Heauton timorumenos*
vss. 202, 208-209, 210 are in 4 [33]; vss. 221-222 in 5; vs. 314 in 7;
vss. 421-422, 483-485, 503-506 in 9; vss. 521-522 in 10; vs. 573
in 11; vs. 666 in 12; vs. 675 in 13; vs. 796 in 16; vss. 805-806
in 17; vss. 887, 922-923 in 20; vss. 991-993 in 21. The scene
heading was omitted, in agreement with some manuscripts, at
vs. 954. In the *Eunuchus* the *periocha* is lacking in most manuscripts. Thus the prologue becomes chapter 1 and vss. 42-43
are quoted from it; vss. 56, 59-63 are in 2; vs. 732 in 16; vss. 761-
762 in 17; vss. 789, 812-813 in 18; vs. 832 in 19; vss. 874-875 in
20; vss. 931-933 in 22. Assuming a new scene at vs. 943, as in
one class of manuscripts, we find vss. 960-961 in 23; vs. 994
in 24. In the *Phormio* vss. 41-42 are in 3; vss. 77-78 in 4; vs. 203
in 6; vss. 241-246 in 7; vs. 454 in 10; vs. 562 in 13; vss. 696-697

---

[32] The Venice edition puts vss. 60-61 in 2, but two Vatican manuscripts
which I have checked put them in 3.

[33] The Venice edition wrongly has 8; the Vatican manuscripts have 4.

in 17. In the *Hecyra* both prologues seem to have been included in one chapter, as in manuscripts Eb, according to Prete's apparatus; vss. 201-203 are in 5; vs. 310 in 8; vss. 343-344 in 9; vs. 380 in 10; vs. 608 in 15. In the *Adelphi* vss. 55-58, 65-67, 69-75 are in chapter 3; vss. 98-99 in 4. The « librorum consensus » shows no scene heading at vss. 141 and 196, where they are introduced by Kauer-Lindsay. In addition, however, we must assume either that Jeremy made a mistake or that his manuscript had no division at II, 2 (vs. 209), for vss. 216, 240-241 are in 5; vss. 254, 256-257 in 6; vss. 269-270 in 7. Kauer-Lindsay has no break at vs. 364 but indicates that all the manuscripts except the Bembine and one other indicate a new scene. Taking this into account, we find vss. 386-388, 415-416, 431 in 11. Kauer-Lindsay's heading at vs. 435 is supported by no manuscripts and is to be ignored for our purpose. So too at vs. 511, where one class of manuscripts has no new scene. We find that vss. 605-607 are included in 15 [34]. At IV, 7 (vs. 719), some manuscripts omit a scene heading but they do not belong to the group with which Jeremy regularly agrees. Including this heading we find that vss. 803-804, 833-834 are correctly in 22; vss. 855-858, 860-861 in 23. Passing over V, 5 (vs. 882), at which point only one manuscript of the class to which Jeremy's belongs begins a new scene, we find that vss. 953-954 correctly fall in 26.

The presence or absence of certain scene headings in Jeremy's manuscript, as noted above, indicates that it belonged to the gamma class. This is confirmed by the order in which he quotes the plays. In three passages he gives three quotations in a row, in eleven passages he gives two, always in the same order. This order agrees with the gamma class in every instance. For example, the order *Hecyra, Phormio* occurs three times, and this order occurs in the gamma, not the delta class.

That a title (in red ink) was a common criterion for determining the beginning of a chapter is shown by Jeremy's quotations from Valerius Maximus. These are cited by book and chapter, but usually *titulus* is substituted for *capitulum*, and the actual title used by Valerius is given: « titulo de felicitate » (Val. VII,

---

[34] The Venice edition has 14, but two Vatican manuscripts have 15.

1) and « titulo sapienter dicta aut facta » (Val. VII, 2) in Jeremy I, 2, 4. Sometimes both are given: « titulo de amore et dilectione capitulo 7 et penultimo » (Val. IV, 7) in II, 3, 4. Less common are merely *titulo* or *capitulo* with the numeral. Similarly the *Digest* and the *Codex* are always quoted by the title.

The *Disticha Catonis* are cited according to chapters, five in number (the last is called « finale »). These correspond to the *Sententiae* and the four books of the printed editions. In some early printed texts, and presumably also in many manuscripts, the terms *Sententiae* and *Libri* are not used, the five parts being distinguished merely by large initials [35].

The twelfth-century *Tobias* of Matthew of Vendôme is quoted by Jeremy in 68 chapters. In the fifteenth-century edition of this work printed in the *Auctores octo morales* (Harvard Inc. 8572. 1 = Hain 1913?) the text is divided into sections by titles. Some have large woodcut initials, others indentions of 2 or 3 lines with catch letters, still others indentions of one line without catch letters. The sections produced by the large initials total 66, very close to the Jeremy figure.

The *Poetria*, or *Ars versificatoria*, of Matthew of Vendôme is also cited by Jeremy, who divides the work into two books, each with a number of chapters. Faral divides into four books and very many short chapters, evidently his own [36]. But he mentions one manuscript that divides the work into two parts [37], and his apparatus shows that the manuscript on which he based his text has the rubric « Explicit liber primus, incipit secundus »

[35] This may be seen in the facsimiles of two incunabula given in Joseph Nève, *Catonis Disticha* (Liège, 1926), pp. 47 ff. E. Baehrens in his edition of Cato in *Poetae latini minores*, III (Leipzig, 1881), p. 214, reports that the Zurich manuscript omits all book titles. See also the edition by M. Boas (Amsterdam, 1952). There are some errors in the Venice edition. It twice quotes III, 4 as being in chapter 8 instead of chapter 4 (at II, 2, 4 and II, 2, 8); some manuscripts of Jeremy have it correct. I, 36 is put in chapter 3 by the edition and one Vatican manuscript, in 4 by another manuscript; it should be 2 (at II, 4, 9). II, 14 is assigned to chapter 2 instead of 3 in the edition and the manuscripts (at II, 6, 8). II, 28 is credited to chapter 2 in the edition and one manuscript, while the other correctly has 3 (at IV, 4, 12). II, 3 is combined with I, 22 under chapter 2 in the edition, but one manuscript correctly assigns it to 3 (at V, 4, 7).

[36] E. Faral, *Les arts poétiques du XIIe et XIIIe siècle* (Paris, 1923), p. 109.
[37] *Ibid.*, p. 13.

at the end of the first book, none at all at the end of the second, and merely a chapter heading at the end of the third. The titles in Faral's manuscript, if they are all reported by him, are capricious in that few occur at the beginning, but later they are found at almost every one of Faral's chapters. Hieremias cites up to chapter 22 or 23 in the first book, which Faral divides into 118 chapters. There were fourteen chapters in Jeremy's manuscript of the second book (he cites « c. 13 et penultimum »), whereas Faral has 149 chapters in his books II-IV. It seems likely that Jeremy's manuscript had titles only at the points where he indicates new chapters. A study of the existing manuscripts might settle the matter. Bourgain, using a manuscript that differed greatly from Faral's in text and length, divides into three parts, the first of which has 21 divisions, as compared with Jeremy's 22 or 23, the second and third have 17 and 10 respectively, for both of which Jeremy has only 14 [38].

Geoffrey of Vinsauf's *Poetria nova*, of somewhat later date, is cited by Jeremy in 110 chapters, if we assume that 101 is a misprint for 110 in the Venice edition. A division into that number of chapters can be made to accommodate Jeremy's references and to fit more or less Faral's paragraphing [39]. A Harvard manuscript (Lat. 154) divides into 98 sections by means of interlinear titles in red ink. In addition it has a number of marginal titles in red. In most cases it has a new division where I have assumed one, even where Faral has no paragraph indention.

The elegiac poem *Pamphilus* of the end of the twelfth century is also cited by Hieremias according to chapters. This poem is largely in dialogue form but is not a true drama. According to Cohen's edition only the more recent manuscripts give the names of the characters before each speech [40]. Be that as it may, Jeremy's manuscript of this work must have had such names or at least left a space between dialogues. For convenience, Cohen divided into 61 sections but he was inconsistent in his method. My own division, based on Jeremy, creates 64 sections, one more

---

[38] *Matthaei Vindocinensis Ars versificatoria,* ed. L. Bourgain (Paris, 1879).
[39] *Op. cit.,* p. 197. Some chapters have to be begun at points where Faral has no paragraph indentions and some of his paragraphs have to be ignored.
[40] Gustave Cohen, *La « Comédie » latine en France,* II (Paris, 1931), p. 191.

than the number which Goldast, dividing into separate elegies, is reported to have suggested, presumably on the basis of manuscripts or earlier editions [41].

Jeremy quotes the Pamphilus as follows [42]:

Verse	Chapter
12, 16	1
37, 53-54, 57-58	2
71, 83-88, 93-94, 101-102, 104, 105, 107, 109-114, 117, 123-124, 125-139, 141-142	3
207-208	9
259-260, 267-270, 271-272, 279	13
293-294, 295-296 [43]	14
305-306	15
335-338	18
350, 352	19
370-372	20
385-386	22
413-415, 418	25
430	27
450	28
463-466 [44], 467-468, 469	30
479 [45], 481-482 [46]	32
491-492	34
497-498	35
501, 502, 503-504 [47]	36
506	37

[41] *Ibid.*, p. 181. I agree with Cohen up to section 19 but I begin section 20 at vs. 355, where the old woman stops talking to Pamphilus and turns to Galatea. Similarly I begin new sections (52 and 53) at vss. 651 and 657. In the former the old woman stops talking to Galatea to see who is at the door; in the latter, she starts speaking to Pamphilus. Cohen himself follows this principle at vs. 549, where there is no change of speaker. In quoting chapter 64 Jeremy adds « et fi(nale) ».

[42] Based on the printed edition. Unless otherwise noted its chapter number agrees with mine. When the same verse is quoted more than once and the correct chapter is given in one case the incorrect number is ignored.

[43] Both these passages are credited to chapter 18 in the edition, but the manuscripts have 14 (in one case 13).

[44] The edition reads 20, the manuscripts have 30.

[45] Quoted twice with the number 30, apparently an error of Jeremy's, as two manuscripts also give that number.

[46] The edition has 31, the manuscripts have 32.

[47] The edition and a manuscript have 37.

Verse	Chapter
519-520	39
525-526	40
549-550, 561-562 [48], 569	43
597-598	47
619-620	50
731	60
769-771, 773-774	64

The extreme variation in the length of the chapters (2-72 verses) is a guarantee of the correctness of the foregoing explanation.

I have also examined the edition of 1499 (Cop. 4588). This divides the text into 75 sections, each section preceded by a *sententia* (summary) and followed by a *constructio* (grammatical explanation). Some of these sections give the act and scene division of the manuscripts. The relation of these to my chapter division may be seen in the following table:

Verse	Chapter	Act or Scene	
1	1	Act 1	Sc. 1
25	2		Sc. 2
143	4		Sc. 3
163	5	Act 2	
245	13		Sc. 2
285	14	Act 3	
339	19		Sc. 2 [49]
441	28		Sc. 3
549	43	Act 4	
661	54	Act 5	

Other sections of the text correspond to divisions based on change of speakers. Still others are sense divisions, evidently due to the author of the *sententiae*. These account for the greater total of divisions. All of them occur near the beginning. Only chapters 6, 7, 52, 53 of my division (based on Jeremy) are not represented in the 1499 edition. Baudouin's edition (Paris, 1874), based largely on that of 1499, divides into 59 scenes.

A Berlin manuscript which contains the *Pamphilus* in the original Latin together with a Venetian version has been published

---

[48] The edition has 83, but a Vatican manuscript has 43.

[49] By an obvious misprint called Scene 3.

by Tobler[50]. Marginal titles, or rather scene-headings, divide the poem into 57 sections. There may have been another division at vs. 723, which has been torn away.

The Berlin manuscript's 57 or 58 sections, the 1499 edition's 75, Goldast's 63, Baudouin's 59, and Cohen's 61 are close enough to Jeremy's 64 to confirm that change of speaker, indicated by a heading, was the basis of the chapter division.

Another poem Jeremy quotes by chapters is the *Facetus*, the less well-known of the two which survive under that title. It is the one beginning « Moribus et vita quisquis vult esse facetus », published by A. Morel-Fatio[51]. This edition indicates breaks at vss. 385, 439, 455, 467, 489. The poem contains 509 lines. Morawski observes that each chapter (that is the term he uses) begins with an invocation to the Muse (*Musa, Camena, Calliope*)[52]. That is not quite true; rather, the mention of the Muse is one way of marking some of the chapters. Such mention is found in vss. 61, 132, 385, 439, 455, 467. Jeremy divides the work into ten chapters, quoting within these ranges:

Chapter	2: 9-30		Chapter	6: 365-374[53]
Chapter	3: 85-90		Chapter	7: 421-438
Chapter	4: 101-130		Chapter	8: 453-454
Chapter	5: 137-316		Chapter	10: 479-504

My division is as follows, with indication of content:

Chapter	1: 1-4	Introduction
Chapter	2: 5-60	Character and behavior
Chapter	3: 61-96	Training
Chapter	4: 97-130	Recreation
Chapter	5: 131-320	*Ars amandi*
Chapter	6: 321-384	*Remedium amoris*
Chapter	7: 385-438	Friendship
Chapter	8: 439-454	Advice to judges

---

[50] A. Tobler in *Archivio glottologico italiano*, X (1886-88), p. 177.

[51] *Romania*, XV (1886), p. 224.

[52] J. Morawski, *Le Facet en Françoys* (Poznańskie Towarsystwo, II, 1, Poznań, 1923), p. xxvi.

[53] Vss. 387-390, 393-395, 399, 433-436 are attributed to chapter 6 in the Venice edition, though the last passage is quoted again under chapter 7. The error was either in Jeremy's notes or in the edition.

Chapter 9: 455-466   Advice to physicians
Chapter 10: 467-488   Advice to soldiers
Chapter 11: 489-509   Advice to the aged

Jeremy combined the last two chapters.

The poems of Godfrey of Winchester are cited by Hieremias under the name of Martial, but he distinguishes the two writers by citing the genuine Martial by book under the title *Epigrammaton*, while Godfrey is quoted by chapter under the title *Libro undique suscepto*. By assuming a few errors in the Venice edition, which together with the Chicago manuscript, is all that I have consulted for this purpose, we can, I think, discover the explanation of the chapter division [54]. Wright, presumably following the manuscripts, gives first the two-line poems (numbered 1-101), then those of four lines (102-198), then the six-line epigrams (199-218), those with eight lines (219-231), finally those with ten or more lines (232-237) [55].

Hieremias cites various epigrams as follows, according to the Venice edition, within these ranges:

Chapter 1: *Praef.*, 83
Chapter 2: 2-104
Chapter 3: 104-190
Chapter 4: 91-218
Chapter 5: 220-237
Chapter 6: 207-237
Chapter 8: 207

This does not look very hopeful, but a few simple corrections make clear that Hieremias cited as follows:

Chapter 1: *Praef.*
Chapter 2: 2-99 (2-line poems)
Chapter 3: 102-190 (4-line poems)
Chapter 4: 202-218 (6-line poems)
Chapter 5: 220-229 (8-line poems)
Chapter 6: 232-237 (poems of 10 or more lines)

[54] I cite from the edition of Godfrey in Thomas Wright, *The Anglo-Latin Satirical Poets and Epigrammatists of the Twelfth Century*, II (London, 1872), pp. 103 ff.

[55] For some reason the last poem (238) has only eight lines.

The corrections to be made in the Venice edition are these:
83 should be given as in chapter 2, not 1. The first three lines
of 104 are quoted twice, first as being in chapter 2, then in 3.
Obviously the former is a misprint or an error in the tradition.
Similarly 91, 1 is quoted twice, once in chapter 2, which is correct, again in chapter 4, which is wrong. Again, 237, 3 is quoted
as being in chapter 5, but 237, 5-6, 8 in chapter 6; the former
is wrong (the Chicago manuscript agrees with the edition in the
wrong number 5; for 6 it has ii). The attribution of 207 to
chapter 8 must be an error for 4, which is what the Chicago
manuscript has. This is the only attribution to chapter 8; there
is none to chapter 7 [56].

We may accordingly state Hieremias' principle of numbering in the case of those poetical works in which no scheme of
numbering existed, as follows: he gave a consecutive numbering
to the sections formed by the interposition of red-letter titles or
headings or by spaces.

This pedestrian solution of the Catullus problem, which will
be proved in the following, may seem to some rather disappointing by comparison with the ingenious, even sensational, theories
of Ellis and Wheeler [57]. It was, however, arrived at by marshal-
ing facts, for which no subtle reasoning nor wide knowledge
can be a substitute. One wonders to what extent philological
scholarship is built on frail foundations of unsupported theory.

For the sake of convenience I group here the passages which
Hieremias quotes from Catullus and the « chapters » to which he
assigns them. The text is given farther on.

22, 18-20	= *cap.* v
39, 16	= *cap.* v
51, 15-16	= *cap.* v
64, 143-148	= *cap.* viii
66, 15-16	= *cap.* ix
68, 137	= *cap.* ix
76, 13	= *cap.* xi, *et penult.*

---

[56] The Chicago manuscript omits the passage or the chapter number for the
passages on which it is not quoted.

[57] It should be said, however, that Wheeler withdrew his theory when
confronted by the evidence I presented in the first publication of this essay

Jeremy's manuscript, therefore, was divided, presumably by red titles, into twelve sections. Did the « lost Verona » manuscript present any such appearance? We know from the agreement of manuscripts O and G [58] that many, though by no means all, of the poems were separated from each other by a blank space of one verse. This divided the manuscript into at least 27 sections— obviously not the ones Hieremias numbers. Other poems were distinguished merely by some mark, as in O. In these places neither O nor G left a space. The omission by O of all titles, even at the beginning, makes it more difficult to say what titles the Verona manuscript had. Nearly all the titles in G and all those in R are by second hands. Before inserting these red-ink titles, R^2 (in a few cases R^1) put catch titles of black ink in the margins as a guide. R^1 supplied the catch titles for 4, 5, and 6 [59]. R^2 altered the form of these somewhat in copying them. In G at these points it was G^1, not G^2, who wrote the titles, and what is more, in the form in which R^1 gives the catch titles. The book heading at the beginning (*Catulli Veronensis liber Incipit*) was also written by G^1, but no other titles were made by him. Evidently these titles were found by GR in their exemplar, and probably they were also in the Veronensis. Probability becomes certainty when we examine O. This manuscript leaves room for a colored initial by putting the first letter in the margin as a catch letter and by indenting the first two lines in poems 1, 2, 4, 5, 8 (three lines are indented in the first poem). In poems 7

(A. L. Wheeler, *Catullus and the Tradition of Ancient Poetry*, Berkeley, 1934, p. 250, n. 11).

[58] It is universally conceded that O (Oxford, Bodl. Canon. Lat. 30) and G (Paris lat. 14137) are very close to the « lost Verona » manuscript. That R (Vat. Ottob. lat. 1829) is the ancestor of most of the other manuscripts, including M and D, and is on a par with G, is a conclusion which is bound to be accepted sooner or later by all scholars. Hale believed that O was a direct copy of the Veronensis, and that G and R were copies of a lost copy of the Veronensis (*Classical Philology*, III, 1908, pp. 233 ff.). His position is adopted in this chapter. See too my article cited in note 7. I regret to note that Weiss (*op. cit.*, p. 36) considers probable the unhappy suggestion of M. Lenchantin de Gubernatis (*Il libro di Catullo Veronese*, Torino, 1927, p. xlv) that there were two « lost Verona » manuscripts. One might quote the comment that Sabbadini made on the suggestion that there were two manuscripts of Cicero's letters to Atticus in Verona: « ci vuole un certo coraggio » (*Storia e critica di testi latini*, Catania, 1914, p. 71).

[59] Hale, *op. cit.*, pp. 246 f.

and 9-60 there is no space left for an initial, and there is no
catch letter, the first letter being part of the line [60]. The only
thing that distinguishes the poems is the blank space of one line
preceding them and the use of very slight catch paragraph
marks (//), which, however, are missing in 7. The colored initials
were supplied for 1 and 2 (at a later time?) but not for the
others. In as faithful a copy as O certainly is, as we shall see,
we have a right to believe that the difference in treatment of
poems 1, 2, 4, 5, 8 is based on a difference in the Veronensis.
We see from GR that the Verona manuscript probably had titles
for 1 [61], 4, 5, and 6. Thus OGR point to an unusual appearance
in the Veronensis for 1, 4, and 5. This unusual appearance, to
my mind, was the presence of colored titles and initials. According
to O, the same was true for 8, to judge from its indention
there, but according to GR, it was true, not of 8, but of 6, to
judge from their first-hand titles to 6. O does not even leave a
space before 6, but merely has the catch paragraph marks. In
other places where this occurs in O, G^1 has left no indication
of a separation, G^2 putting in a marginal title and a paragraph
mark. In this case, however, G^1 left a space, inserted a title,
and indented for the initial. The title which R^1G^1 have is *ad se
ipsum*, changed by R^2G^2 to *ad flauium*. The *ad se ipsum* title
obviously does not belong to 6, but to 8, which is *just a page*
farther on, and there is where it was placed by R^2G^2. O is therefore right: the Verona manuscript had no break at 6, but did
have a break with title *ad se ipsum* and initial at 8. The exemplar of GR wrongly placed this title one page farther back,
before 6. Again the faithful O points to title and initial in the
Verona manuscript for poem 2, though no title is given by R^1G^1.
No doubt the Veronensis had one, and the exemplar of GR failed
to copy it. These titles and initials thus divided the first 60 poems
of the Veronensis into five section, as follows:

Poem 1   = Section 1
Poems 2-3 = Section 2

---

[60] Except that in 13, 14, and 15 there is a catch letter, but without indention.
[61] Rather a book heading, not title, above 1. That the Veronensis had a
book heading from the beginning is not certain, but the argument here made is
not affected.

$$\text{Poem} \quad 4 \quad = \text{Section } 3$$
$$\text{Poems } 5\text{-}7 \quad = \text{Section } 4$$
$$\text{Poems } 8\text{-}60 = \text{Section } 5$$

It will be seen that Hieremias cites 22, 18-20; 39, 16; 51, 15-16 from *capitulum* 5, and that all three fall into our fifth section. Thus the greatest difficulty about the citations has been explained, the fact that four *capitula* preceded poem 22, while one *capitulum* included at least 22 to 51.

Let us now see how the rest of the Veronensis must have appeared. In O poem 60 ends on fol. 14v, the rest of the page (five lines) is left blank, and 61 is started on the next page after another space of one line Nowhere else does O leave a space at the bottom of a page merely in order to begin a new poem at the top of the next page. For example, poem 50 begins two lines from the bottom of fol. 12v after a space of one line. It seems to me that we are justified in assuming that there was more than a mere space of one line in the Veronensis before 61, that very probably there was a title. This would be the beginning of section 6. It may well be that the Veronensis also began 61 on a new folio, after leaving several lines blank on the previous page, as in O. In this state of affairs we may perhaps see a trace of the putting together of the Catullian *liber*. Perhaps one of the ancestors of the Veronensis, or even the Veronensis itself, was put together from two (or more) manuscripts, the first one (or ones) containing poems 1 to 60, the second one (or group of ones) containing poems 61 to 116. Possible confirmation of this suggestion is found in the *Explicit epithalamium* which follows 61 in O. This gives a distinctive air to the poem, as if it had once stood alone, for nothing like it is found with any other poem [62]. At any rate, the phrase (perhaps in red ink in the Veronensis) emphasizes the division between poems 61 and 62. Thus our section 7 begins with 62. G begins 63 as a new poem, with space and initial, but O merely has the catch paragraph marks without break. We may follow the more trustworthy O and consider 63 as part of section 7. In the case of 64, O simply leaves a space

---

[62] Another hint of the same sort is found below.

of one line. This would not be sufficient to permit us to assume a new section beginning with 64. But at the beginning of this poem there are glosses and variants in O by the same hand that wrote glosses and variants at the beginning of the book [63]. These notes at the beginning are surely derived from the Veronensis. Compare in 3, 14 the superscribed *i. pulcra* in both O and G (by G[1]) and the striking agreement of the marginal notes to 2 with the remarks of Guilelmus de Pastrengo, who therefore must have used the Veronensis or O itself [64]. It is thus extremely likely that the glosses in 64 too were to be found in the Verona manuscript. These alone would attract attention to the poem and would serve to distinguish it from the preceding poem, even if there was no title. The marginal note to the first line, especially (*narrat hic ystoriam aurei velleris*), attracts attention to the break. Thus the eighth section of the Veronensis began with 64. Hieremias quotes 64, 143-148, assigning the passage to *capitulum* 8.

Beginning with 65 a different method of indicating new poems is adopted in O. In addition to the one-line space, there is an illuminated initial (different in style from those in poems 1 and 2) in the margin; the second letter is a capital in line with the first letters of the other lines; then the rest of the word is written close to it without the usual space between. I give an illustration from 72:

$$\mathbf{D} \begin{array}{l} \text{Icebas} \\ \text{L \quad esbia} \\ \text{D \quad ilexi} \end{array}$$

Other poems are distinguished in the same way, with two exceptions: there is no one-line space preceding them (nor is there any in G) and instead of an illuminated initial there is only a catch letter. It is possible that the striking difference between the treatment of new poems in the earlier and later parts of the book is due merely to the caprice of the scribe of O. Two reasons lead me to believe that this is not true; first because

---

[63] See facsimile of the page in E. Chatelain, *Paléographie des classiques latins* (Paris, 1884), Pl. XV, A, or Merrill's *Catullus* (Boston, 1893).

[64] See K. P. Schulze in *Hermes,* XIII (1878), p. 57.

O in other respects is so faithful in reproducing just what he found; and second, because the reading *Vltas* instead of *Multas* in 101, 1, which both G and R (and therefore their exemplar) originally had, makes it certain that the Veronensis had the word in a form very similar to that of O: *m Vltas* (catch letter *m*). A second possibility is that the scribe of the Veronensis introduced the new system into the later poems, or that these were written by another scribe. Lastly, it may be that the Veronensis or one of its ancestors was put together from separate *libelli*, as has been suggested above, and that a new *libellus* began with poem 65. However this may be, O gives us little help from 65 on for determining the sections of Hieremias. We may assume that 65 with its new system began a new section—section 9. Hieremias quotes 66, 15, 16 from *capitulum* 9 (there is no break at 66). 68, 137, also, is quoted from the ninth chapter. There is no break at 67 in OG, but there is one at 68 which we must ignore. There are breaks in OG at 69 and 72, which began sections 10 and 11 of Hieremias' division, for 76, 13 is quoted from chapter 11, which at the same time is called the penultimate chapter. After 76 there are breaks at 77, 80, and 89 in OG. The twelfth and last chapter must begin with one of these. Our choice is not difficult: in R there is found in the margin of 77 a catch title *ad ruffum* by the first hand [65]. As this title no doubt comes from the Veronensis, we are safe in letting section 12 begin with this poem. G's failure to preserve the title suggests that he failed to preserve other titles. If the exemplar of GR was equally negligent occasionally, we can see why no titles have come down to us for some of the other sections.

The scheme of division, then, that Hieremias, following the indications of his manuscript, used was as follows:

Poem 1	= *Capitulum* i
Poems 2-3	= *Capitulum* ii
Poem 4	= *Capitulum* iii
Poems 5-7	= *Capitulum* iv
Poems 8-60	= *Capitulum* v
Poem 61	= *Capitulum* vi

---

[65] Hale, *op. cit.*, p. 247.

Poems 62-63 = *Capitulum* vii
Poem 64 = *Capitulum* viii
Poems 65-68 = *Capitulum* ix
Poems 69-71 = *Capitulum* x
Poems 72-76 = *Capitulum* xi
Poems 77-116 = *Capitulum* xii

Whether Hieremias imposed this numbering on the Veronensis itself or on a copy it is impossible to determine.

Let us stop to summarize briefly. O, by its indentions, shows us that the first sixty poems of the Veronensis were divided into five sections. In four cases out of the five, confirmation is added by three first-hand titles in G and R which must go back to the Verona manuscript. After poem 60 there are the following indications of new sections: the unusual space of five verses in O after poem 60, with the consequent beginning of 61 on a new folio; the « Explicit epithalamium » at the end of 61 in O; the glosses in the margin of O in 64; the new method of beginning poems in O from 65 on; the first-hand catch title in R at 77. Thus we have indications of various kinds for the beginnings of ten of the twelve sections. We have had no serious conflicting evidence to be explained away, nor do we have any for the remaining two sections. We are confronted here merely by a lack of evidence. We know from the manuscripts that there *may* have been new sections at 68, 69, 72, 80, and 89, and that there could have been no others. Now that we have established the agreement of Hieremias' sections with those indicated by OGR for the Veronensis, we may be allowed, on Hieremias' authority, to select 69 and 72 as the beginnings of sections, and to reject 68, 80, and 89. It is to be noted that the argument is based on the numbers which Hieremias indubitably assigned to the *capitula*, according to the evidence of the manuscripts, and that in no case has emendation been resorted to.

Two possible objections to the explanation given must be anticipated. In a Verona florilegium of 1329 we find the phrase *Catullus ad Varum* followed by a quotation of 22, 19-21. This quotation was no doubt taken from the « lost Verona » manuscript. Since in G also we find the title *Ad Varum* (in the margin by G[2]) it has been generally assumed that this title existed in the Veronensis. But in R the second hand first wrote *Ad suf-fenum* in the margin; later he deleted the second word and replaced it by *Varum*. This is the form which he used for his colored title. Hale showed that G^2 corrected G on M, while the latter is a copy of R as corrected by R^2. Therefore if the Veronensis had any title here, it must have been that which R^2 originally wrote, *Ad suffenum*, not *Ad Varum*. I have no hesitation in saying that it had neither. The author of the *Flores* had no difficulty in making up his title from the first line, possibly following the analogy of the title which he found for 8, *ad se ipsum*. In the same way R^2 arrived at his title—after being misled into making it *Ad suffenum*, by the first word of the poem, which is *Suffenus*. The other possible objection is similar. Bencius Alexandrinus introduces a quotation of 35, 1-4 with the words « Catullus poeta Veronensis ad amicum Aurelium scribens » [66]. As poem 35 is not addressed to Aurelius, Sabbadini was at a loss to explain the words. But if we look at O, we see that there is no break at 35 and that the first preceding break is at 21, which is addressed to Aurelius, as can readily be seen from the first word, the vocative *Aureli*. R^2 and G^2 give titles *Ad Aurelium*, but I do not believe that these go back to the Veronensis. Bencius, like the author of the *Flores*, invented the title [67].

We may make here another comment on Bencius' quotation. In quoting 35, 2 he gives the reading *occilio*. This is the reading of O alone. Bencius could not have used O, which was written at least a generation after his time. The other manuscripts give *cecilio*, which is the right reading. O's reading, then, is not an error on his part but is derived from the Veronensis. The reading *cecilio* must be an emendation, perhaps from vs. 18, where the name occurs again, though corrupted in the manuscripts to *cecilia* [68]. I mention this here to illustrate O's striking trustwor-

---

[66] R. Sabbadini in *Rheinisches Museum,* LXIII (1908), p. 225. Bencius certainly used the Veronensis.

[67] See Also Hale's fuller discussion of Bencius' citation, in « Benzo of Alexandria and Catullus », *Classical Philology,* V (1910), p. 56. This is based upon an argument of the same nature.

[68] I do not believe that the Veronensis had a double reading.

thiness, thus supporting my case as just presented. If we had not the evidence of Bencius, no one would hesitate to say that the Veronensis had *cecilio*, non *occilio*.

Further evidence of O's being in many ways the most faithful descendant of the Veronensis that we have is presented by an examination of the Hieremias quotations as I restore them from the manuscripts. In 22, 18, the form *nec* which Hieremias surely wrote, is the reading of O as against the *neque* of GR and the editors. I believe that O has the reading of the Veronensis. In 64, 145 Hieremias seems to have had *p'gestit*, as in O. The abbreviation probably was meant for *pregestit*, but in O should be taken as *postgestit*, which GR originally had. In the same line O has *adipisci*, with *pro adipisci* added above and to the right, which the Veronensis probably had in the same form, since G originally had *adipisci*, while R has *apisci*. Hieremias seems to have had *apisci*, with *al' adipisci* written above. Only a reading very similar to O's will account for the readings of GR and Hieremias. In the same way, in 60, 5 the *conteptam* of R and the *contentam* of G (corrected by G² to *conteptam*) are best explained by assuming a reading like O's (*conteptam* with *n* inserted above) for the Veronensis and the exemplar of GR (the caret perhaps being omitted in the latter).

The form *Catulus* which Hieremias used is probably not a slip on his part. Perhaps the Veronensis did not have a book heading at the time when Hieremias examined it or got his copy from it. O has none by the first hand. It is to be noticed that Hieremias is the only one of his period, except the compiler of the Verona *Flores*, to mention Catullus without adding *Veronensis* or *poeta Veronensis* [69]. This designation seems to have come into the Verona manuscript as a book heading with the epigram of Benvenuto de Campesanis (cf. the title of this poem in G:

---

[69] So Benzo, Petrarch, Pastrengo. This, of course, applies only to those who speak of Catullus in such a way that it is evident that they read some of his poems. It is significant that in the two places in which Pastrengo's mention of Catullus is certainly the result of an examination of a manuscript of that poet he uses the expression *Veronensis poeta*, while in the two quotations of Catullus which are drawn from Pliny and Isidore simply the name of the author is given.

Catulli poete Veronensis). If Jeremy examined the Verona manuscript before it had a heading he would have had to look into
the poems themselves for the name of the author. O in the
majority of cases where the name occurs in the poems has the
form *Catullus*, but in the first three cases (6, 1; 7, 10; 8, 1) has
the single l. The last example is particularly striking. It is in
the first line of the poem which, as has been shown above, was
introduced by the title *ad se ipsum* in the Veronensis. If in our
faith in O we can trust it to have reproduced here the spelling
of the Veronensis, we can easily understand how Hieremias came
to use the form *Catulus*. In turning over the first few pages of
the manuscript his attention would immediately be attracted to
the title *ad se ipsum* and the vocative *Catule* in the first line of 8.

The surprising faithfulness of O as shown in one case by the
evidence of Benzo and in a number of cases by that of Jeremy
is of considerable importance for any attempt to reconstruct the
« lost Verona » manuscript of Catullus. This task is made much
more difficult in that we can not be sure that an apparently correct
reading of GR (such as *cecilio*), differing from O, existed in the
Veronensis. In other words, the value of O is not equivalent to
the combined value of G and R but is greater than it. There may
be dozens of cases like *occilio* and *nec*.

I add a list of manuscripts of the *Compendium* known to
me, beginning with those I have examined. I indicate the *siglum*
for those which I used in the collation of the Catullus quotations.

A = Milan, Ambros. P. 117 sup., dated 1419.

Ag = Milan, Ambros. P. 29 sup., dated 1468 (the work
is attributed to Giovanni de Grapanis but is taken bodily from
Hieremias). Some of the Catullus passages seem to be lacking, but
since the arrangement is different, one cannot be certain.

B = Oxford, Bodleian Canon. Lat. Misc. 186, *s.* XV.

Bol = Bologna, Univ. 2600, *s.* XIV.

Br = London, British Museum Add. 22801, *s.* XV.

C = Rome, Casanatense 312 (C. IV. 11), dated 1398
(omits the last two citations).

Ch = Chicago, Univ. Library Ms. 482 (Pa V289 P), *s.* XV.

Cm = Cambridge, Univ. Library E e II. 29, *s.* XV.

E = Escorial II h 11, dated 1402.

F = Florence, Laur. Acq. e Doni 393, s. XIV.

K = H. P. Kraus, New York, s. XIV.

M = Madrid H. h. 21, s. XIV-XV [70].

Mn = Munich 14317, s. XV.

N = Naples, Naz. VII E 2, s. XV.

New = Oxford, New College (Bodleian) 100, s. XV [71].

P$_1$ = Paris, Bibl. Nat. lat. 6469, ca. 1475 (omits 39, 16).

P$_2$ = Paris, Bibl. Nat. N. a. l. 1779, dated 1475 (omits 51, 15-16).

P$_3$ = Paris, Bibl. Nat. N. a. l. 2469, copied 1404 by Henricus Rintfleis for Ludovicus de Malliciis, at the University of Padua. Possibly this is the manuscript mentioned in the inventory dated 1428 of a Lodovicus in Padua [72].

Pal = Rome, Vatican Pal. lat. 402, s. XV-XVI.

Pe = Perugia, Com. E. 34, s. XIV.

Pie = Rome, Vatican Bas. S. Pietro H. 48, s. XIV.

R = Rome, Vatican Reg. lat. 1526, s. XIV (?).

V$_1$ = Rome, Vatican lat. 4278, s. XIV (?).

---

[70] My notes on this manuscript are incomplete; they fail to report on the second and seventh passages.

[71] Ellis (Catullus in the XIVth Century, p. 9) says that this manuscript is dated 1400. That date is found at the end but seems rather to refer to the composition of the sermon to which it is appended.

[72] G. Valentinelli, Bibliotheca manuscripta ad S. Marci Venetiarum, VI (1873), p. 254. My conjecture has been confirmed by the kindness of Professor Paolo Sambin of the University of Padua. He calls my attention to I. P. Tomasini, Gymnasium Patavinum (Utini, 1654), p. 236: « Iisdem temporibus [ca. 1440] Dominicus de Ponte Venetus, et Thadaeus Vicomercatus Mediolanensis Decretalia sunt interpretati, et post eos Ludovicus de Malitia Patavinus Abbas Prataleae, et Prosdocimus à Limena Sacerdos ». Prof. Sambin supplied me with the following extract from MS. B. P. 804 of the Biblioteca Civica of Padua, containing material from the Archivio Pratalense on the monastery of Praglia (Caps: A. N. 23, fol. 44): « 1419. Lodovico I: de Militiis governò dalli 23: Giugno 1419: fino al 1° 7bre 1424: in cui morì ». Prof. Sambin calls attention to the character of Lodovico's library, as listed in the inventory, consisting largely of juristic works and Paduan chronicles and statutes, as befitted a professor of law, such as Ludovicus de Malliciis was. He received the doctorate in canon law on September 1, 1410, when he was prior of the monastery of St. Benedict in Padua (Archivio Curia Vescovile, Diversorum, vol. 13, fol. 59); he is mentioned as a « decretorum doctor » and vicar of the bishop in documents of 1414 (Archivio di Stato di Padova: Archivio notarile, 40, fols. 325, 326v).

V_2 = Rome, Vatican lat. 1168, s. XIV *ex.* (fragmentary; ends IV, 2, 3, omitting the last four Catullus quotations).

Ve = Venice, Marc. Lat. Cl. VI, 100, s. XIV [73].

Ven = Venice edition, 1505.

The following do not contain the Catullus passages:

Bologna, Univ. 2614, s. XIV-XV (extends only to I, 1, 32, before the Catullus citations begin; rest lost).

Oxford, Bodleian Canon. Lat. 212, s. XV.

From Peiper [74] I take readings from:

Vra = Breslau I F 129, s. XV.

Vrb = Breslau I F 246, s. XV.

Vrc = Breslau IV F 50, s. XV.

Others known to me are: :

Viterbo, Cap. 35 (Weiss gives the number as II. d. 15), s. XV (end missing).

Bruges, Bibl. Publique 494, s. XV (A. de Poorter, *Catalogue des manuscrits de la bibliothèque publique de la ville de Bruges,* Gembloux, 1934, p. 572).

Darmstadt, dated 1410 (F. Osann, *Vitalis Blesensis Amphytryon et Aulularia,* Darmstadt, 1836, p. vii).

Leipzig, Karl W. Hiersemann (*Manuskripte des Mittelalters und späterer Zeit,* Leipzig, 1906, No. 61), dated 1376 (?).

Zeitz, Stiftsbibliothek, philos. 8, dated 1422, Padua (Peiper, *De Senecae,* etc., p. 145).

Florence, Laur. Gadd. Rel. 46 (Rajna, *loc. cit.*).

Florence, Riccard. 250 (Rajna, *loc. cit.*).

Florence, Riccard. 816 (Rajna, *loc. cit.*).

Florence, Naz. Magliab. Palch. IV, cod. 128, fol. 121 (contains only the Italian proverbs; Rajna, *loc. cit.*).

---

[73] Valentinelli, *op. cit.,* IV (1871), p. 188, says that this manuscript was written by Hieremias himself, but I agree with Rajna (*op. cit.,* p. 198, n. 3), who emphatically denies this. Actually it was not Valentinelli who made this claim but an early owner, the well-known humanist Ioannes Marchanova: « 1437. Ioannes Marchanova artium et medicinae doctor pecunia sua empsit Patavii. Propria compositoris manu ».

[74] *Loc. cit.* Neither Ellis nor Peiper is absolutely trustworthy. Their silence, especially, cannot be trusted. Ignorance of this fact led Wheeler astray.

Modena, Est. XII, K, 12, *s.* XV (Rajna, *loc. cit.*).

Valladolid (I. Carini, *Gli archivi e le biblioteche di Spagna,* I, Palermo, 1884, p. 269).

Berlin, Lat. fol. 489 (now in Tübingen).

Berlin, Theol. lat. fol. 696 (now in Tübingen).

Munich, Univ. Fol. 98.

Salzburg, Studienbibl. M II 191, *s.* XV.

Salzburg, Studienbibl. M II 324, 1449.

Salzburg, Studienbibl. M II 346, *s.* XV.

Vienna, Dominikaner, ms. 194/159 a.

Krakow, Jaguellonska, ms. 700 (CC VIII 25).

Poznań, Raczynski, ms. II H d 4 [75].

Trotti Collection (now dispersed; F. Novati in *Giornale storico della letteratura italiana,* IX, 1887, p. 147) [76].

Padua, Bibl. Antoniana (I. F. Tomasini, *Bibliothecae patavinae manuscriptae,* Utini, 1639, p. 56); the manuscript has disappeared or is unidentified.

Krakow, Univ. CC. VI. 39 (1596), dated 1415 (Weiss, *op. cit.,* p. 29).

Seville, Colombina 5. 6. 16 (*ibid.,* p. 30).

Belluno, Lolliniana 34 (*ibid.*).

Udine, Com. 21 (*ibid.*).

Aldenburg (now lost; *ibid.*).

Collection of Palla Strozzi, 1431 (now lost; *ibid.*).

Collection of Francesco Gonzaga, 1407 (now lost; *ibid.,* p. 50) [77].

---

[75] The preceding nine I learned of through the kindness of Prof. P. O. Kristeller.

[76] Novati says that the Trivulzio-Trotti collection was sold as a whole to an American dealer. The Hieremias is the one described in *Incunabula Treasures and Medieval Nuggets from the Trivulzio Library of Milan,* New York. George A. Leavitt and Co., 1888, p. 50, No. 148, 189 fols., illuminated initials and coat of arms, dated 1453. Very few manuscripts of Trivulzio origin, and no Hieremias, are listed in S. de Ricci, *Census of Medieval and Renaissance Manuscripts in the United States and Canada,* III, Indices (New York, 1940) or in the *Supplement* by C. U. Faye and W. H. Bond (New York, 1962).

[77] Weiss' statement (p. 30) that there is a manuscript in the Biblioteca Angelica, Rome (a. 6. 7), rests on a misinterpretation of Sabbadini, *Le scoperte,*

Munich 3941, *s.* XV (tables only) [78].

Munich 18394, dated 1481 (*ibid.*).

Peniscola, Library of Benedict XIII (now lost; *ibid.*).

Escorial. From P. B. Fernandez, *Antigua lista de manuscritos latinos y griegos inéditos del Escorial* (Madrid, 1902), pp. 13, 21, it appears that in the year 1600 or thereabouts there were two manuscripts in this library, one of which was the one mentioned above.

St. Eustorgio, Milan, end fifteenth century, now lost (Thomas Kaeppeli, in *Archivum Fratrum Praedicatorum*, XXV, 1955, No. 673).

The text of the quotations from Catullus is now given. No attempt at a complete critical apparatus is made, since no critical examination and comparison of the manuscripts was undertaken. Perhaps there are better manuscripts extant than any of those used, perhaps even Hieremias' own copy still exists. It seems, however, that the text of the Catullus quotations can safely be restored from the manuscripts listed. The oldest of my manuscripts seem to be the best: the Casanatensis, the two Vaticani latini, the Matritensis, the Escorialensis. I report only such readings as are of interest for my purpose. It is to be remembered that the text has strong manuscript support where no readings are given. Several facts can conveniently be grouped together at the outset.

Catulus is found in 137 cases (122 in my manuscripts; 15 in Peiper's) [79].

Catullus is found in 24 cases (5 in Pie, 4 in P_1, 2 in E, A, and Ch, 1 in Bol, Ag, and P_5; 6 in Ven).

c. is found in 134 cases (111 in my manuscripts; 5 in Ven; 18 in Peiper's manuscripts).

c^0. is found in 8 cases (5 in C, 3 in V_2).

ca. is found in 16 cases (7 in Pal, 5 in Ch, 2 in B_1 and Pe).

I, p. 219, n. 1. Sabbadini used the Angelica copy (a. 6. 7) of the printed edition of 1505. Weiss also mentions Paris. lat. 2846, but this is an error of some sort.

[78] R. Weiss in *Italian Studies*, VI (1951), p. 24, n. 188.

[79] I did not regularly note the usage in the chronological table, but A, V_1, V_2 have *Catulus*, Ag has *Cattulus*, Ven has *Catullus*.

ca⁰. is found in 13 cases (7 in V_1, 6 in Mn).

capitilo is found in 1 case (Bol.).

capitulo is found in 1 case (Ven.).

l. or li. is found in 8 cases (1 in New, Cm, Br, Mn, P_3, M, 2 in R; 5 of these are in the third quotation and probably point to a common archetype for some of the manuscripts in which they occur).

l' is found in 1 case in Ven (first quotation).

I, 3, 8
(Cat. 22, 18-20)

Catulus c. V. Omnes fallimur nec est quisquam quem non in aliqua re videre suffenum possis suus cuique attributus est error.

V $C V_1 V_2 E N$ New Cm B P_2 Mn Pal Pie Pe.

5 $K M R P_1 P_3$ Bol Br Ve Ven.

5 alias 2 F.

7 Vra Vrb Vrc [80].

4 A.

nec $C V_1 V_2 M E N$ New Cm B P_1 Mn Pal.
Pie Ve Vra Vrb Vrc Pe A.

neque $K R P_2 P_3$ Bol Br F Ven.

II, 1, 5
(Cat. 68, 137)

Catulus c. IX. Ne nimium simus stultorum more molesti.

IX $C V_2 E$ New Cm P_2 Pie Pe.

VIIII $V_1 N B$ Mn Pal.

9 $K R P_1 P_3$ Bol Br Ve F Ven Vra A.

nono Vrb Vrc.

III, 4, 8
(Cat. 51, 15-16)

Catulus c. V. Ocium et reges prius et beatas perdidit urbes.

V $C V_1 V_2 E N$ New Cm B Mn Pal Pie.

5 $K M R P_1 P_3$ Br Ve F Ven A Ag.

quinto Bol.

IV. 4, 8
(Cat. 39, 16)

Catulus c. V. Risu inepto res ineptior nulla est.

V $C E N$ New Cm B P_2 Mn Pal Pie Pe.

5 $K V_1 M R P_3$ Bol Br Ve F Ven A Ag.

7 Vra Vrb Vrc [80].

---

[80] Peiper evidently mistook the early form of arabic 5 for 7.

IV, 5, 11 Catulus c. VIII. Nulla viro iuranti femina credat
(Cat. 64, 143- Nulla viri speret sermones esse fideles
148)   Quid dum aliquid cupiens animus p'gestit
      al' adipisci
      apisci
      Nil metuunt iurare nil promittere parcunt
      Set simul ac cupide mentis saciata libido est
      Dicta nichil metuere nichil periuria curant.
      VIII *C E N New Cm B P₂ Mn Pal Pie.*
       8 *K V₁ M R P₁ P₃ Bol Br Ve Ven Vra Vrb*
       Vrc A.
      9 *F.*
      p(re)gescit *E.*
      pregestit *Bol.*
      p(re)gessit *New B Mn Pal Pie Ven.*
      pregessit *Br Vra Vrb.*
      p(re)gesit *Ve.*
      p(re)grescit *R.*
      p(re)gressit *M N A.*
      p(re)grossit *Vrc.*
      pregressit *K P₂ P₃.*
      pigrescit *C V₁ Cm.*
      pigresscit *F.*
      p(er)egre scit *P₁.*
      aspici. al' adipisti (*in text*) *M.*
      apisci *K V₁ P₁ P₂ Bol Br F.*
      apisti *N.*
      aspici *R P₃ Vra Vrb Vrc.*
      aspici *Ve.*
      adipisci *C Ven A.*
      ipsi *E New Cm Mn Pie* [81].
      et ipsi *B Pal.*
(Cat. 76, 13) Idem c. XI et pe. Difficile est longum subito
      deponere amorem.
      XI *E New Cm B P₂ Mn Pal Pie Pe.*

---

[81] In these five manuscripts, and in these only, *animus* (abbreviated) follows the reading for *pregestit* instead of preceding it.

11 *K* V_1 *M R* P_1 P_3 *Bol Ve F Ven* (*Ven has arabic* 11, *not roman* II, *as Ellis reports*) *Vrc A Ag*.

.. (*sic*) *N*.

12 *Br Vra Vrb*.

et pe. *N New Cm B* P_1 *Mn Pal Bol Ve F Ven*.

et plt' *K M* P_2 *Vrc A*.

et ple' *R*.

et pult' *Vra Vrb*.

et penl't V_1.

et pe(n)ult' *E*.

et pel't P_3.

om. Pie Br Pe Ag.

IV, 6, 3   Catulus poeta c. IX. Est ne novis nuptis odio
(Cat. 66, 15, 16)   venus atque parentum frustrantur falsis gaudia
          lacrimulis

IX *E B* P_2 *Mn*.

VIIII *N Pal Pie*.

9 *K* V_1 *R* P_1 P_3 *Bol Br Ve F Ven Vra Vrb Vrc A*.

4 *New Cm*.

Chapter VI

PETRARCH'S FAVORITE BOOKS [1]

One of the most notable contributions to the history of the Renaissance is Pierre de Nolhac's *Pétrarque et l'humanisme* [2]. Its peculiar importance is due to the fact that it gives in minute detail the literary influences that affected the « first modern man ». As Nolhac says (I, p. 33), antiquity was revealed to Petrarch by its writers, and the history of his library, if one could have it in complete form, would be the history of his soul. The present contribution to the history of his library may therefore not be without interest to all humanists, whether they be specialists in ancient or in modern literature and history. As Petrarch's modernness consisted in his enthusiasm for antiquity, he serves well as a tie that binds together all humanists.

In 1896 Leopold Delisle, the famous palaeographer, published an article on a manuscript once owned by Petrarch [3]. It contains Cassiodorus' *De anima* and Augustine's *De vera religione*. On the flyleaf at the end there appears a list of books in Petrarch's handwriting. Besides printing it, Delisle gave an excellent reproduction. The list has a heading which can now be read only with difficulty. Delisle read it *libri mei. Peculiares ad religionem, non transfuga, sed exul* (?)... F. Novati improved this by reading *non transfuga, sed explorator* [4]. He pointed out that this was an

---

[1] Originally published in *Transactions of the American Philological Association*, LIV (1923), pp. 21-38.

[2] Second edition (Paris, 1907).

[3] *Notice sur un livre annoté par Pétrarque (Ms. latin 2201 de la Bibliothèque Nationale) tiré des Notices et extraits des Manuscrits*, XXXV, p. 2.

[4] In a review of Delisle's article in *Giornale storico della letteratura italiana*, XXIX (1897), pp. 524-525.

allusion to Seneca, *Ep.* I, 2, 5: « Soleo enim et in aliena castra transire, non tamquam transfuga, sed tamquam explorator ». He interpreted the heading as follows: the books in the list are pagan works; books peculiar to religion are mentioned in another list. Sabbadini went still farther in deciphering and interpreting the heading [5]. He saw that the last two words (after *explorator*) are *transire soleo,* found in the Senecan passage. He connected *peculiares* with the preceding words *libri mei* and interpreted them to refer to the books which belonged to Petrarch personally. The rest of the heading was taken to mean that the field of Petrarch's researches is the pagan, whereas in the Christian field he makes his bow only occasionally. He pointed out the familiar fact that Petrarch did not begin to take a great interest in the Christian writers until he reached middle age. Nolhac (II, p. 293 ff.) [6] takes much the same view.

After four such eminent scholars as Delisle, Novati, Sabbadini, and Nolhac had dealt with this point there would seem to be nothing left that could be added. But I have one small contribution to make which entirely changes the interpretation of a document which Nolhac (II, p. 296) calls extremely precious for the intellectual biography of Petrarch and the history of humanism itself.

Apparently all the scholars who have examined the manuscript in Delisle's facsimile have been handicapped by too great a knowledge of Petrarch's life: knowing of Petrarch's early indifference to Christian literature, they thought they saw the word *religionem,* when as a matter of fact Petrarch clearly wrote *reliquos,* as several persons, including those skilled and those unskilled in palaeography, said of their own accord when I showed them the facsimile [7]. The meaning then is: « My specially prized books. To the others I usually resort not as a deserter but as

---

[5] « Il primo nucleo della biblioteca del Petrarca », *Rendiconti del R. Istituto Lombardo di Scienze e Lettere,* Ser. II, XXXIX (1906), pp. 369-388.

[6] References in parenthesis are to the book of Nolhac's previously mentioned. Vol. II, pp. 293-296 (Excursus VII) are reprinted with unimportant changes from the *Revue des bibliothèques,* XVI (1906), pp. 341-344.

[7] The excellent heliogravure is quite as clear as the original manuscript, which I examined.

a scout ». For the meaning of *peculiares* we may compare, if necessary, the use in the Vulgate, *Deut.* 14, 2, *in populum peculiarem*, and 26, 18, *populus peculiaris.*

There seems to be a dot after *peculiares,* and so Sabbadini prints it. In any case, Petrarch must first have written the general title *Libri mei* and then decided to add *peculiares,* which he put in a separate line for emphasis and because he wanted to explain it with the quotation from Seneca. By this he means that the books listed are his intimate friends, whereas others he merely glances at occasionally as a scout in the enemy's camp, not as a deserter who goes over to the enemy for good and all. This interpretation is amply confirmed by a similar comparison in one of the letters: « Legi semel apud Ennium, apud Plautum, apud Felicem Capellam, apud Apuleium, et legi raptim, propere, nullam nisi ut alienis in finibus moram trahens. Sic pretereunti multa contigit ut viderem, pauca decerperem, pauciora reponerem eaque ut comunia in aperto et in ipso, ut ita dixerim, memorie uestibulo » (*Fam.* XXII, 2, 11; *anno* 1359). The thought (and in part the language) of this sentence is similar to that of the same letter of Seneca. Compare the latter's « certis ingeniis inmorari ... oportet, si velis aliquid trahere... omnia cursim et properantes transmittunt... cum multa percurreris, unum excerpe ». The point of Seneca's letter is to stress the importance of having a few favorite books to which one should come back again and again—exactly the thought of Petrarch's *libri mei peculiares.* If one has this habit, says Seneca, then one may take an occasional dip elsewhere: « non tamquam transfuga », etc.

The Senecan passage is quoted also in a well-known letter sent to Wibald, Abbot of Corvey, by a prior of Hildesheim about 1150 [8]: « Quamvis Tullii libros habere desideres, scio tamen te Christianum esse non Ciceronianum. Transis enim et in aliena castra », etc. Nothing brings out in more striking fashion an

---

[8] Quoted in F. W. Hall, *Companion to Classical Texts* (Oxford, 1913), p. 70, and translated in J. E. Sandys, *A History of Classical Scholarship,* I, ed. 3 (Cambridge, 1921), p. 619. That outstanding humanist, Ben Jonson, used « tanquam explorator » as a motto which he inscribed in the books of his library (cf. e.g,. the edition of Ben Jonson by C. H. Herford and P. Simpson, Oxford, 1925, pp. 250-271).

essential difference between the Middle Ages and the Renaissance than the different way in which the mediaeval prior and the first modern man adapt the quotation from Seneca.

It may be noted here that Seneca himself had in mind the following passages: Horace, *Carm.* III, 16, 22-24, « Nil cupientium nudus castra peto et transfuga divitum partis linquere gestio »; *Epist.* I, 1, 15, « quo me cumque rapit tempestas, deferor hospes »; Cicero, *Fam.* IX, 20, 1, « in Epicuri nos, adversari nostri, castra coniecimus ».

Sabbadini and Nolhac, as a result of their false reading of the heading, have drawn from the list a number of inferences about Petrarch's library which would be extremely important if true. Sabbadini calls the list the first nucleus of Petrarch's library, Nolhac makes it the first library of Vaucluse. Delisle, with instinctive caution, saw in it a catalogue « of a+ least a part » of Petrarch's books. It should be said that there appear to be three lists, but the first and third were written at the same time and should be considered one. The second list was written later, as shown by its contents[9]. The handwriting of the first is cursive and is similar to that used by Petrarch in his earlier years. It reappears in a note in another manuscript dated March 21, 1337, and Sabbadini thinks that our list must date from about that time. But the cursive style is also found much later in Petrarch autographs, as may be seen from Monaci's facsimiles[10]. Two other entries of Petrarch's in our manuscript are dated 1335 and 1338, showing that it was in Petrarch's hands at least as early as 1335.

But Sabbadini and Nolhac, taking the list as a complete catalogue of Petrarch's books (his pagan books at least) at the time it was made, date it from the absence of certain volumes. So Nolhac assigns it to the year 1337 because it does not mention two manuscripts bought by Petrarch in Rome in that year

[9] Nolhac (I, p. 222; II, p. 294, n. 6) goes so far as to suppose that the two lists with identical titles indicate that Petrarch owned two copies of the books mentioned! Sabbadini thinks that the secund list consists of books intended for a journey.

[10] E. Monaci and C. Paoli, *Archivio paleografico italiano* (Rome, 1882-1897).

(I, p. 42, n. 2; p. 295). Sabbadini argues that the date must be later than April 17, 1338, because Virgil figures in the list, and Petrarch's Virgil, now in the Ambrosian Library at Milan, was stolen in 1326 and not recovered until April 17, 1338, as attested by a manuscript note of Petrarch's. But it is impossible to believe that Petrarch was without a copy of his favorite poet's works for twelve years. It is to be remembered that he had another copy before he obtained the Ambrosian manuscript, for he tells us that his Virgil was rescued from the flames to which his father had consigned his classical books. This cannot be identified with the Ambrosian Virgil, which shows no trace of contact with fire, as Sabbadini himself notes. Nolhac is probably wrong in his distinction between the earlier and later styles of Petrarch's handwriting; otherwise his statement that there is no trace of the earlier style (so-called) in the marginal notes of the Ambrosian Virgil (I, p. 144) would show that Petrarch did not make much use of this manuscript until his later years. At any rate, the death notices of friends and relatives which the manuscript contains date from 1348 to 1372 (II, p. 283). All this shows that before 1338 Petrarch must have made much use of another copy.

But before going into the question of the date of the list, let us consider its arrangement and interpretation. In the following I shall show how well this list agrees with Petrarch's express statements about the books he read, with his quotations, and with his annotations. First of all, I shall reproduce the list, as nearly as possible as it is presented in the manuscript. Letters in square brackets are no longer visible. Parentheses are used to indicate that the letters included are in abbreviation. The expansions are not always certain. Thus *ex* with a superscript cursive *a,* prefixed to Macrobius and Gellius, was interpreted as *excerpta* by Delisle and others, though Nolhac seemed a bit dubious. It is more likely to stand for *exempla.* Petrarch's *Rerum memorandarum libri* is a collection of *exempla,* imitative of that of Valerius Maximus, and in it he used Macrobius and Gellius a great deal, especially Macrobius' quotations from Tiro's collection of Cicero jokes, another *exempla* book. Petrarch uses the word *exempla* a number of times in alluding to the stories he quotes (e.g., II, 14, 5; 15, 8; 81, 2).

List I

Libri mei

Peculiares. ad reliquos n(on) tra(n)sfu-
ga sed explorator tra(n)sire soleo.

M. tullii

Moral(ia)
  Eth(ica) { Ar(istotelis)
  Sen(e)ca

Recth(orica) {
  VI(us) Rei pu(bli)ce
  Tusculan(um)
  Offitia
  Lelius
  Catho maior
  divinat(i)o
  Hortensi(us)
  Na(tura) deor(um)
  Paradox(orum)
  Inve(n)tion(is)
  Ad h(er)ennium
  de orato(r)e
  Invect(ive)
  or(ati)o(n)es co(mun)es

Ad Lucillu(m)
Ad nerone(m)
Remedia fort(uitorum)
Traged(ie)
D(e) tranq(ui)llitate a(nim)i. d(e) (con)sol(atione). d(e) bre(vitate) vite

ystor(ica) {
  Valeri(us)
  Livius
  Iustin(us)
  Flor(us)
  Salust(ius)
  Sueton(ius)
  Festus
  Eutropi(us)
  Saturnalia
  Agelli(us)

Bo(ethius) i(n) (con)solat(ione)

Poet(ica) {
  Virg(ilius)
  Lucan(us)
  Stati(us)
  Hor(atius) p(re)s(er)ti(m) in od(is)
  Iuvenal(is)
  Ovid(us)[sic] p(re)s(er)ti(m) i(n) maio(r)i

Gram(matica) {
  Priscian(us)
  Papias. Donat(us)
  Catholic(on)

Dyal(ectica)   Tractat(us) (et) n(ichi)l ult(ra)

Astrol(ogia)   Spera

Macrobi(us) s(ed)
iste intelligit(ur)
accessori(us) trac[ta]-
tui suo. fi(r)m[icus]
(et) reliq(ui) com(m)e(n)tatores.

List II

Iste
Tusculan(um)
VI. rei pu(blice)
Leli(us)
offitior(um)
Catho maior
paradox(orum)

bo(ethius) d(e) (con)sol(atione)
Ad Lucillu(m) (et) c(etera) p(re)t(er) trag(edias)
Valeri(us). Iustin(us). Flor(us). Sal(ustius)
Priscian(us). d(e) poetis d(i)c(itur) ut s(upra)

List III

de civitate dei ⎫
Confessionu(m) ⎬
de orando deo ⎫
Soliloquior(um) ⎬

In listing his favorite books it is clear that Cicero's works came to Petrarch's mind first and foremost, and among these the « moral » works held first place. Apparently he first put down the titles of Cicero's philosophical books under the heading *Moralia*. Petrarch's interest in the moral side of the books he read can easily be shown[11]. It is clear that the rhetorical works were added to the list and not jotted down at once from the fact that the name *M. Tullii* is written opposite the center (fifth) line of the philosophical titles.

That Cicero should be given the place of honor in the list of Petrarch's books will surprise no one. His influence on Petrarch was as great as it is well-known (I, pp. 11, 59, 123, 213, 217, 220, 221, 22; II, p. 90). If Petrarch was the father of humanism, Cicero was its grandfather.

It is not certain when Petrarch came into possession of the Cicero manuscript now at Troyes (Bibl. Mun. 552). From the handwriting of the notes, Nolhac judges that it must have been in Petrarch's hands not much later than 1344. But he may have owned it earlier, though probably not as early as the time he made up his list of favorite books. It may be that the

---

[11] Nolhac, I, p. 19: « il travaille plutôt en moraliste qu'en historien » (in his historical composition); II, p. 32: « moraliste du XIVe siècle, disciple attardé de Cicéron et de Sénèque ».

manuscript was made expressly for Petrarch (I, p. 227), which would explain why it contains all the works mentioned in the list but one, the sixth book of the *Republic.* As in the list, so in the Troyes manuscript the *Moralia* precede the rhetorical works.

The *Tusculans,* which is second in the list, is one of Petrarch's favorites. He cites it more often than any other philosophical work (I, p. 247). The essays on friendship and old age, which hold fourth and fifth places in the list, were also special favorites of Petrarch's (I, p. 237). According to Sabbadini, the *invective* of the list refer to the Catilinarian orations, which in the Troyes manuscript have this title. But this seems unlikely, as these orations ought to be included among the *orationes comunes* of the list. Rather, the *invective* are the pseudo-Sallustian invective against Cicero and the reply. It is true that in the Troyes manuscript they are called *controversiae,* but Petrarch himself calls them invectives [12].

Next to Cicero, Seneca holds the most important place. The works of these two authors alone are enumerated in detail in the list. Petrarch has been called the modern Seneca. His writings are filled with allusions to that author [13]. Both as moralist and as stylist he is indebted to Seneca no less than to Cicero, though he holds Cicero in higher esteem (II, p. 124). The letters to Lucilius head the list, coming just below the quotation from them. These letters played a most important part in Petrarch's philosophical development (II, p. 116). Next comes the *De clementia (Ad Neronem)*, followed by the *De remediis fortuitorum,* which was the inspiration of Petrarch's *De remediis utriusque fortunae.* Then come the *Tragedies,* about which Petrarch is not so enthusiastic, though he praises them highly (II, p. 118). The next three titles (*De tranquillitate, De consolatione, De brevitate vitae*) were added at a later time, in the second style of handwriting, as Delisle saw. Furthermore, Seneca's name is centered for

---

[12] *Contra med.* I; see Nolhac, I, p. 229, n. 4. They are apparently called *Invectiva* in British Museum, Harl. 4927, newly discovered to have belonged to Petrarch: E. Pellegrin and G. Billanovich, *Scriptorium,* VIII (1954), p. 115.

[13] Nolhac, II, p. 116, says there are sixty direct quotations in the *Familiares* alone besides innumerable reminiscences. I count 117 passages in Rossi's index to the letters of Petrarch

the first four entries, not including these last titles. The three works are found together in manuscripts of the *Dialogi*.

Aristotle's *Ethics* was then entered in a crowded space between Cicero and Seneca. It is not really a later addition, as Delisle thought, for the handwriting is the same, nor is it the first in the list, as Nolhac has it (I, p. 42). Petrarch is not so fond of Aristotle as of other writers (II, p. 148). His manuscript of the *Ethics* and *Politics* (in the Latin translation of course) contains few of his notes, and all of these are on the *Ethics* (II, p. 151).

Boethius is next among the *Moralia*. His name does not seem to have been a later insertion, as Delisle thought. Petrarch was very fond of the *De consolatione* (II, pp. 106-107).

The historians come next, with Valerius Maximus heading the list. History was one of Petrarch's favorite studies (II, p. 1). Valerius served as his model in the *Liber rerum memorandarum* and is cited by him frequently elsewhere[14].

But it is Livy who was Petrarch's favorite historian (II, pp. 9, 11, 12; 1, p. 11), and Livy comes second in our list. Petrarch's two manuscripts of Livy are still extant[15]. One of them was among his handsomest books and both were profusely annotated by him.

Justinus, third in the list, is made use of by Petrarch and receives an appreciative notice from him (II, p. 35). Florus was used by Petrarch as his chief model in historical style (II, pp. 34-35). Two of Petrarch's manuscripts which are extant contain Florus (Paris, B. N. 5690, 5802), and he probably had a third. Sallust is frequently cited by Petrarch and is praised for his style (II, p. 37; cf. p. 205). Suetonius and Eutropius are found in one of Petrarch's manuscripts together with Florus (Paris, B. N. 5802), but Nolhac thinks that he must have had other manuscripts of these authors, for the one we have shows few traces

---

[14] Nolhac, II, p. 45: « Son exemplaire de Valère-Maxime devait porter beaucoup de notes de sa main ».

[15] Paris, B. N. Lat. 5690 and London, B. M. Harl. 2493. For the latter see the outstanding monograph by G. Billanovich in *Journal of the Warburg and Courtauld Institutes*, XIV (1951), pp. 137-208.

of the study which Petrarch gave them (II, p. 34). Suetonius in particular was praised by Petrarch. The Festus in the list is not Paulus Diaconus' abridgment of Festus, as Nolhac thought (II, p. 295), but Rufus Festus' *Breviarium,* similar to that of Eutropius [16].

The compilers of *Exempla* are appended directly to the historians without intervening space because it is their excerpts from history in which Petrarch was chiefly interested. Yet they are thought of as separate from the historians, as the word *ystor(ia)* is centered for the eight historians previously mentioned. Macrobius and Gellius, especially the former, held an important place in Petrarch's reading (II, p. 103). Since he often refers to Gellius' work by title only, Nolhac suggests that the author's name was unknown to him in his earlier years. But the presence of the name Agellius, the mediaeval form, in our list, which must be fairly early, as we shall see, makes this suggestion unlikely, as well as the one that the occurrence of the name in some of Petrarch's letters is due to later insertion. It should be noted further that the letter *l* in *Saturnalia* and *Agellius* has not the cursive form which it has in the words which precede. This, however, is scarcely an indication of later addition, as it occurs in other words, e.g., *Iuuenal(is)*, which cannot be a later addition because the word *poet(ica)* is centered for all the poets in the list, including Juvenal [17].

The poets come next, headed, of course, by Virgil, Petrarch's favorite poet, who was a rival with Cicero himself for the affections of our humanist (I, pp. 11, 59, 123, 180). His manuscript of Virgil, now in the Ambrosian Library at Milan (A 79 inf.), contains more of Petrarch's notations than any other of his books (I, p. 160). The epic poets Lucan and Statius follow Virgil in our list. Lucan is quoted frequently in Petrarch's writings (I, p. 194), Statius less frequently (I, p. 198). The phrase which follows, *Horatius presertim in odis,* is now quite comprehensible,

---

[16] So too Sabbadini in his review of Nolhac's book in *La Cultura,* XXVI (1907), p. 349.

[17] The use of cursive and formal elements together is found also in Petrarch's notes in the Palatine manuscript of the *Historia Augusta* (Susan H. Ballou, *The Manuscript Tradition of the Historia Augusta,* Leipzig, 1914, p. 20).

with our new light on the significance of the list. Petrarch merely means that his greatest enthusiasm is for the *Odes.* His
fondness for Horace is clear enough (I, p. 11). His letters to
classical authors include only two to Roman poets, Virgil and
Horace. It is precisely the *Odes* which he favors in his letter
to Horace, as elsewhere, in striking contrast to the attitude of
earlier centuries (I, p. 151). Horace is cited oftener than any
other poet except Virgil. *Ovidius presertim in maiori* refers to
the *Metamorphoses,* as we know from Boccaccio's similar use [18], as
well as that of others. Ovid's elegiac poems are in a class with
those of Propertius, who is not mentioned. Yet Petrarch quotes
and imitates the elegiac poems more frequently than the *Metamorphoses* (I, p. 177). They were known to him from his earliest
youth. Juvenal, last in the list, is cited frequently by Petrarch
(I, p. 186).

Then come the grammarians, with Priscian at the head.
Petrarch read Priscian in his youth and thought of him as occupy-
ing the same position in grammar that Cicero held in oratory
and Virgil in poetry (II, p. 104, n. 4). Next come Papias and
Donatus, the latter added as an afterthought in the same line in
the earlier cursive style of writing. The *Catholicon,* which comes
last, is no doubt that of Iohannes de Ianua (Balbi), as Nolhac
suggests (II, p. 295), though Petrarch does not quote him (II,
p. 213, n. 2).

Under *Dyalectica,* there is mentioned *Tractatus et nil ultra.*
No suggestion has been made as to the identity of this work.
Possibly it is the third and most considerable chapter of Cassiodorus' *Liber saecularium litterarum,* of which Petrarch's manuscript copy is extant (I, p. 205: Paris, B. N. 8500). In a note
in the Troyes Cicero, Petrarch quotes *Cassiodorus in libro secula-
rium litterarum c. de dialetica* (I, p. 243). On the other hand,
there is in the inventory made in 1426 of the library of Pavia,
into which many of Petrarch's books passed, an item which exactly
fits the entry in Petrarch's list and which may have belonged to

---

[18] I am indebted to Miss Cornelia C. Coulter for this information. She
reports that in the *Genealogia deorum* Boccaccio uses the phrase *in maiori* or
in maiori volumine six times in quoting the *Metamorphoses* (I, 10; II, 1; IV, 3;
IV, 54; IV, 68; VI, 53), but not at all in quoting other works.

him [19]: *Tractatus logice dialetice* [20] ... *Incipit « Dialetica est ars artium » et finitur « dicta sufficiant »*. This is the *ars dialectica* of Petrus Hispanus, who studied under Albertus Magnus at Paris and later became Pope John XXI. There is a manuscript of this work in the Ambrosian Library (Montfaucon, *Bibl. bibl.*, I, p. 503 c), two in the Laurentian Library (34, 1; Faes. 145). Among other manuscripts are three in Munich (8401, 12304, 18941), as Professor Lehmann informed me. I also find two mentioned in the catalogue of the Prague manuscripts (2567, 2605), and one in Paris (6657). And there are others.

In astrology, the first entry in the list is *Spera,* which stands for *Sphaera* and may be any one of several mediaeval treatises, such as that of Iohannes de Sacrobosco. An older contemporary of Petrarch, Cecco d'Ascoli, wrote a *Sphaera mundi*. It may be a mere coincidence that he taught at Bologna while Petrarch was a student there [21]. The next phrase, *Macrobius, sed iste intelligitur accessorius tractatui suo, sicut et reliqui commentatores,* must mean that Macrobius' commentary on the sixth book of Cicero's *Republic* incidentally contains astrological lore and that other commentators on ancient writers also give occasional information. But I am not entirely satisfied with the reading *sicut*. Only the first two letters are clear, and they look more like *fi*. There is room for Fi(r)mic(us). The *Mathesis* of this author is quoted by Petrarch several times and is mildly praised. He calls Firmicus an *astrologus* (II, p. 106).

Below this list there is written upside down in the cursive style *nobili viro d(omi)no hosti (ensi)* [22]. This was evidently writ-

---

[19] G. D'Adda, *Indagini storiche, artistiche e bibliografiche sulla libreria visconteo-sforzesca del Castello di Pavia,* I (Milan, 1875), No. 13; Elisabeth Pellegrin, *La bibliothèque des Visconti et des Sforza ducs de Milan, au XV⁰ siècle* (Paris, 1955), p. 77, No. 13. Another copy of Petrus Hispanus is No. 861 (p. 265) in Pellegrin's list.

[20] This word was later crossed out.

[21] G. Boffito, « Il *De principiis astrologiae* di Cecco D'Ascoli », *Giornale storico della letteratura italiana,* Suppl. VI (1903).

[22] This is a reference to the Cardinal of Ostia, Bertrando del Poggetto (1327-1352). I owe this obviously correct expansion of *hosti* to Prof. G. Billanovich in his review of the first edition of this book (*Bibliothèque d'Humanisme et Renaissance,* XVIII, 1956, p. 144).

ten first on the page. It separates the first list from the so-called third list, which, as I have said, is really part of the first list. The third list contains works of Augustine alone without the author's name and without a subject heading. The absence of the latter may suggest uncertainty as to the place of Christian writings. At any rate these came to his mind last. Augustine was his favorite among them, being cited some 600 times in the letters alone (II, p. 192). Among the bright stars of the Church he is the sun (*Fam.* IV, 15, 4). The *De civitate Dei* is mentioned first. We still have Petrarch's copy of it (Padua, Bibl. Univ. 1490). A note indicating that the book was bought in 1325 is the earliest of Petrarch's dated autographs (II, pp. 196, 197). The *Confessions,* mentioned next, was one of Petrarch's favorites (II, p. 192). He carried a copy about with him in his travels, even to the top of Mt. Ventoux (II, pp. 193, 194). It served as a model for his *Secretum.*

The second list was clearly written later, as shown by its content if not its script. It is obviously a more select list than the other. Included is one addition: the book in which the list is written, containing Cassiodorus' *De anima* and Augustine's *De vera religione.* This book naturally is put first under the designation *Iste.* Then come Cicero's philosophical works, this time with the *Tusculans* ahead of the *Republic.* As we saw, the *Tusculans* is cited by Petrarch more often than any other philosophical work. There are other changes in order. The *Divinatio, Academica, De natura deorum* are omitted, as are all the rhetorical works. Aristotle is omitted, as we might have surmised. Boethius is ahead of Seneca this time. The letters to Lucilius are expressly mentioned, since Petrarch esteemed them the most highly of Seneca's writings, whereas the *Tragedies* are expressly excepted, which is not surprising, as Petrarch had some doubts about their genuineness. We wonder why he omitted the name of his favorite historian, Livy. Was it due to accident or to a temporary estrangement or had he not possessed the copies of Livy long enough to become thoroughly enamoured of his flowing narrative? It is to be remembered that in the first list Livy takes second place after Valerius Maximus. The other historians whose names are omitted came at the end of the first list: Suetonius, Festus, Eutropius. The compilers of *Exempla* are omitted entirely. About the poets he has not changed his mind. Priscian is the only grammarian, as we might expect. The dialecticians, astrologers, and Augustine are omitted.

It is interesting to compare the names in the two lists with the authors most frequently cited by Petrarch in his writings. Augustine is cited almost 1200 times (II, p. 192, n. 3)—and Augustine is the only Christian writer in the first list. Cicero's *Tusculans* is cited more frequently than any other Ciceronian work—and it comes second among the works of Cicero in the first list, first in the second list. The *De finibus* is perhaps next in the number of quotations; it is not in the lists because Petrarch did not have a copy at the time. On the other hand, Isidore, of whose work he had a copy long before, is cited only three times and does not appear in the lists. Among the poets, Virgil takes first place in the number of citations and in the lists. In number of citations, Horace is next with 150. Then comes Ovid. Lucan is cited 40 times, Terence 30, Juvenal more than 20, Plautus 20, Statius 15, Persius more than 8, Claudian 8, Ausonius 3, Propertius 0. In the lists Lucan and Statius are placed after Virgil, ahead of Horace and Ovid, because they are epic poets. Terence, Plautus, Persius, Claudian, Ausonius, Propertius are not in the lists, the second writer because Petrarch obtained his copy later. He had a manuscript of Propertius, perhaps at the time of the lists.

Nolhac's figures may be checked by an examination of the index of Rossi's edition of the *Familiares*. Cicero takes more space than any other author (over six columns), and the *Tusculans* is well in the lead over the other works. Seneca, second among the prose writers, has two columns, with more than half devoted to the *Epistulae ad Lucilium*. Augustine is third, with most of the citations belonging to *Confessiones* and *De civitate Dei*. Virgil is well ahead of the other poets, being second only to Cicero among all the authors. Horace is next among the poets, then Ovid.

The quotations in the margins of some of Petrarch's books also confirm the inferences drawn from the two lists as to his favorite authors, though of course one must take into account the difference of content of the various books. His Virgil is particularly rich in quotations (I, pp. 156 ff.). Virgil, Macrobius, and Priscian are cited *passim*, according to Nolhac. Cicero is quoted much less frequently, 25 times in all, the *De natura deorum, Tusculanae*, and *De divinatione* being well in the lead. The other leaders are Seneca 49 (44 of these in the *Epistulae ad Lucilium*, none in the *Tragedies*), Horace 38 (22 in the *Odes*), Lactantius 33, Ovid 32 (28 in the *Metamorphoses*), Lucan 23, Isidore 18, Apuleius 17, Livy 15, Juvenal 10, Pliny 9, Statius, Pomponius Mela, and Augustine 7 each (5 in the *De civitate Dei*). Of the above, Lactantius, Isidore, Apuleius, Pliny, and Mela are not in the lists. In the notes on Petrarch's Pliny, Valerius Maximus comes next to Cicero with 10 quotations, then come Suetonius with 7, Virgil, Macrobius, and Livy with 5 each. In the manuscript of Cassiodorus and Augustine which contains our lists, Cicero is cited 19 times (*Tusculans* 9), Augustine 12, Virgil 9, Macrobius 7, Sallust 3, Boethius, Lucan, Ovid twice each, Cassiodorus (*De anima*), Cyprian, Horace (*Odes*), Juvenal, Plato, Pliny, Terence once each.

Finally, attention may be called to Petrarch's letters to the dead authors whose works he had. They include Virgil, Horace, Homer, Cicero, Seneca, Livy, Quintilian. Homer and Quintilian are not in our lists because Petrarch had not yet procured their works, as we happen to know.

Now that we have seen that the lists are not a complete catalogue, but merely a 'five-foot shelf' of favorites, we cannot use Nolhac's method of dating them by the absence of certain books the date of whose acquisition by Petrarch is known. As a matter of fact, Nolhac's interpretation was open to suspicion because Petrarch owned at least one book not in the lists long before the lists could have been made, for we still have his copy of Isidore, with the note that it was bought for him when a boy by his father. The fact that in the second list there is one addition, that of the book in which the list appears, may suggest that the first list was written soon after the acquisition of the book, before Petrarch had become thoroughly fond of it. This would be at least as early as 1335, when Petrarch copied a prayer into the manuscript. But this is a mere possibility.

While it is not safe to argue in general from the absence of titles in the lists, we may be fairly certain that Petrarch would have entered other works of Cicero in the lists if he had had them. There can be no doubt, for example, that he would have included the *Letters to Atticus*, which he acquired in 1345. This then must be a *terminus ante quem*. Another earlier *terminus* is furnished by the use of the title *Hortensius* for the *Academica*. Petrarch discovered the correct title in 1343 (I, p. 245)[23]. In fact he knew that the title *Hortensius* was incorrect before this, but we cannot say just when. It may be that the omission of the title *Hortensius* in the second list shows that it dates from the time when Petrarch was undeceived about the work, but this line of reasoning is scarcely safe. It would seem that in 1333 Petrarch got a copy of Augustine's *Confessions* (I, p. 39; Sabbadini, *Rendiconti,* p. 378; above chapter III). This date may be a *terminus post quem* for our lists, although he may have had another copy earlier. In this book he read about Cicero's *Hortensius,* and soon after (*statim*) he received a book with this title[24]. Possibly he refers to the Troyes manuscript, as Sabbadini assumes. In that case this manuscript was in Petrarch's hands in 1333 or 1334. We have seen that he may have had it when he made his lists, but it seems more likely that he did not get it till somewhat later. The lists do not include the *De fato,* or the *Partitiones,* or the *De legibus,* which are in the Troyes manuscript. This fact would seem to invalidate either the assumption that he had the Troyes manuscript when he made his lists or the suggestion that he would naturally include all the works of Cicero which he possessed. To be sure, he *may* have overlooked these works. Nolhac states (I, pp. 237-238) that with the second copy of the *De fato* (there are two in the manuscript), which is followed by the *De Legibus,* there begins a new series of quaternions. This may indicate that these works were added later and would explain the omission of the *De legibus* from the lists. On the other hand, he seems to have had a copy of the *De legibus* be-

---

[23] Bosco thinks that Petrarch did not actually make his correction in the manuscript until after 1345 (U. Bosco in *Giornale storico della letteratura italiana,* CXX, 1942, p. 82).

[24] *Sen.* XV, 1; Nolhac, I, p. 244.

fore this [25]. As to the *Partitiones*, the title in the Troyes manuscript is so vague (*liber Rhetorice sub compendio*) that the general subject heading *Rhetorica* covers it sufficiently.   In any case the works mentioned do not play the part in Petrarch's life that the *Letters to Atticus* did [26].   It would be unthinkable for him to omit these from his lists, if he had them at the time.

This is almost as true of the *De finibus*, which is neither in the lists nor in the Troyes manuscript.   Its omission in both is striking.   It was one of Petrarch's favorites and accompanied him on his journeys.   On one of them he became ill and searched in his bag for his copy, as he tells us in one of his epistles in verse [27]. The date of the epistle is 1344.   An earlier reference to the *De finibus* is in the *Secretum*, written in 1342, but revised later. There are also references in his letters *Familiarium rerum*, but it is well known that in editing them Petrarch made additions.

Another *terminus* is suggested by the phrase *orationes comunes*. *Sen.* XV, 1 (Nolhac, I, p. 260) makes clear that by *comunes* he means those to be found in many libraries.   Now in 1333 he discovered two new orations at Liège, one of which was the *Pro Archia*.   As late as 1351 his Italian friends had failed to obtain this rare work, and he supplied them with copies (I, pp. 221-222).   It does not seem likely that he would merely group this speech with the *orationes comunes*, no matter how late the list is.   It would seem then that the list must antedate the discovery of this speech in 1333.   The low place in the list occupied by Augustine favors this early date.   The ascent of Mt. Ventoux, with which is associated Petrarch's esteem of the *Confessions*, as stated above, did not take place until 1336.   There is no reason to suppose that the works listed by Petrarch were not in his hands by 1333.   He had several works of Cicero, including the *Tusculans* and one or more rhetorical works, saved from the flames, as was his Virgil.   He had another copy of Virgil by 1326 (the Ambrosian manuscript).   This also contained Statius' *Achilleid* and four odes of Horace, though the book was not

---

[25] *Sen.* XV, 1; Nolhac, I, p. 260.

[26] *De legibus* occurs but a few times in the index of Rossi's edition of the *Familiari; Partitiones* and *De fato* are not cited at all.

[27] *Epist.* II, 10; Nolhac, I, pp. 45, 223.

actually in his hands in 1333 and was not recovered until 1338. He probably had a complete manuscript of Horace, for he read the *Epistles* as a boy. He also had Priscian at the same age. He purchased the *De civitate Dei* in 1325. In one of his copies of Livy he wrote: *emptus Auinione, 1351, diu tamen ante possessus.* Billanovich has shown that this book (Paris 5690) formerly belonged to Landolfo Colonna, with whom Petrarch became acquainted in 1328 or 1329. His other Livy (British Museum Harl. 2493), discovered to be his by Billanovich, was in part written for and by him between 1325 and 1329 [28]. The Paris manuscript contains also Dictys and Florus. But Petrarch read Florus before Livy (II, p. 35), probably in another manuscript, as the two we have show too few traces of Petrarch's reading. At least part of Ovid's work was known to Petrarch in boyhood. He appears to have obtained a copy of Augustine's *Confessions* in 1333 (I, p. 39; above, chapter III). There is no reason to think that the other works in the first list were not in Petrarch's hands in 1333. The date 1333 is then the most likely for our list, though we must recognize the possibility of a date as late as 1343.

The omissions from the list are due in part to lack of interest in the books, in part to lack of possession at the time. In the former class is Isidore, which he owned in his youth. The book, still extant, has few annotations (Paris, B. N. 7595). Petrarch rarely cites Isidore in his own writings (II, p. 209) and has little use for him. Dictys may also be in this class, as this work is found in the Paris Livy manuscript. If Sabbadini (*op. cit.*, p. 376) is right in thinking that before Petrarch obtained the Troyes manuscript he owned Vat. 2193, this manuscript may have been in Petrarch's hands when the list was made. Besides Cicero, it contains Apuleius, Palladius, Frontinus, and Vegetius, none of whom is mentioned in the list. Of these only Apuleius receives more than passing notice in Petrarch's books and notes. Even Apuleius is mentioned in *Fam.* XXII, 2, 11, as we saw above, as one of the writers at whom he merely glances: he is therefore

---

[28] G. Billanovich, « Petrarch and the Textual Tradition of Livy », *Journal of the Warburg and Courtauld Institutes,* XIV (1951), p. 137.

one of the *reliquos* of our list. Possibly Propertius too is in this class: we know that Petrarch owned a manuscript but he rarely quotes from it. His manuscript was a copy of the one now in Leiden, then in France, as I have shown [29]. It is most probable that he obtained this copy in 1333, during his travels through France. Sabbadini (*op. cit.*, p. 380) has pointed out that Petrarch did a great deal of notable collecting on French soil. The Propertius should be added to the list. During the Middle Ages France was perhaps a greater storehouse of classical treasures than Italy itself. It would be idle to speculate what Petrarch would have been if his father had not taken him to France. At any rate it seems certain that the advantage of long periods of residence and travel in both France and Italy had much to do with giving him the commanding place which he held in the humanistic movement.

Among the writers whose works Petrarch obtained later are Pliny (1350), Quintilian (1350), Plautus (about 1343), Catullus (1345 or later), Nonius Marcellus (after 1350). There is uncertainty about the time when he obtained Terence [30], Persius, Caesar, Curtius Rufus, all of which he had. We can no longer argue from the absence of certain authors from the list that Petrarch did not have their works until after 1337 or 1338. Sabbadini (*op. cit.*, p. 371) thinks that Claudian and Terence came into Petrarch's hands after 1338, the date he assigns to the list, in which these authors do not appear. We cannot now accept this argument—as to the fact, we simply must say « non liquet ».

Foresti, in a paper published shortly before the original form of this chapter was written and unknown to me at the time, saw some of the difficulties in Sabbadini's conclusions and, without making the key correction of *religionem* to *reliquos*, almost reached the correct interpretation of the purpose of the lists [31].

[29] *Classical Philology*, VI (1911), pp. 282 ff.; accepted by Hosius in the second and third editions of the Teubner Propertius (Leipzig, 1922, 1932) and by others. See too chapter VIII.

[30] Bosco (*op. cit.*) plausibly argues that Petrarch must have had a copy of Terence at an early date. He believes that *Fam.* III, 4, written in 1333, contains an original, not an added, citation of Terence.

[31] A. Foresti, « Le letture del Petrarca prima del 1337 », *Rendiconti del R. Istituto Lombardo di Scienze e Lettere*, LV (1922), pp. 431. This was reprinted

His dating, however, is far from convincing. Because the writing resembles that of an autograph dated March 21, 1337, he believes the first list was written shortly before Petrarch went to Rome in 1337. But no palaeographer would consent to such precise dating on the basis of handwriting. Besides Foresti is inconsistent in trying to date by the absence of two manuscripts acquired in March, 1337, falling into the very type of error with which he reproaches Sabbadini. As the first list has the date May 12, he concludes it was made in 1336, not 1337. His statement that a prayer copied by Petrarch on the first page and dated June 1, 1335, was written before the list may well be true, but it is not supported by evidence, for it is not enough to say that it « ha tutta l'aria di essere anche stata la prima scrittura che il poeta vi inserí ». As the second list has the date February 18, Foresti puts it in the year 1338. Worst of all, he forgets his own footnote on page 46, in which he states that Petrarch obtained Augustine's *De vera religione* in the winter of 1342-43. He forgets that this work is included in the manuscript containing our lists. Petrarch could not very well have obtained the manuscript in 1342-43 and entered the lists in it in 1336 and 1338!

Since, then, our lists are select and not complete lists of the young Petrarch's books, we cannot draw the important inference that those books which are not mentioned did not come into his hands until a later period and hence did not have any influence on the development of the first humanist. To be sure, absence from the lists would indicate relatively slight influence in any case. Nor can we say that Petrarch's first library was a small one, not larger than that of some of his contemporaries, such as Jeremy of Montagnone[32]. He must have possessed scores of other books, which he read as we read most books, rapidly and once only. But the books in the select lists are those which

without change and therefore without taking into account my paper in his *Aneddoti della vita di Francesco Petrarca* (Brescia, 1928), p. 45. Bosco (*op. cit.*), perhaps influenced by Foresti, but unfortunately unacquainted with my paper, took a cautious attitude towards the interpretation of the lists, which he called mysterious. I trust that this chapter has solved the mystery to the satisfaction of everyone.

[32] Sabbadini, *op. cit.*, p. 380.

Petrarch read again and again and which remained his favorites throughout his life. He was no mere book collector, nor was he an ordinary reader of the books he so eagerly gathered about him. Perhaps the secret of his humanism may be found in the fact that he read over and over again with intense zest these few favorite books.

CHAPTER VII

THE COMPOSITION OF PETRARCH'S
« DE VITA SOLITARIA »
AND THE HISTORY OF THE VATICAN MANUSCRIPT [1]

Two manuscripts of Petrarch's works are famous because they used to be considered autographs of the great humanist. Although this view is now universally discarded, they are still considered of high importance for the texts they contain and have received much attention. The current opinion is that the two manuscripts were once bound together and were owned and in part copied by Coluccio Salutati, the too little known founder of the Florentine circle of humanists. It is my purpose to show that Coluccio neither owned nor copied any part of these manuscripts, and then to proceed to the consideration of problems concerning the composition of Petrarch's *De vita solitaria* that are suggested by one of the manuscripts. It was with regret that I came to the decision that Salutati had nothing to do with these manuscripts, for I have been engaged in a study of his humanistic activities and should have been glad to claim these two codices for his remarkable library [2].

The Florence manuscript Naz. Conv. Soppr. I. 1. 28, formerly in the monastery of St. Mark's, Florence, consists of three parts: 1) fols. 1r-8v, an early collection of Petrarch's letters; 2) fols. 17r-45v, some later letters among which is included the same author's *Itinerarium Syriacum*; 3) fols. 49r-64v three brief anony-

---

[1] Reprinted, with changes, from *Miscellanea Giovanni Mercati,* IV (Città del Vaticano, 1946), p. 107 (*Studi e testi* 124).

[2] B. L. Ullman, *The Humanism of Coluccio Salutati* (Padua, 1963).

mous works: a *Genealogia deorum*[3], an allegorical explanation of some myths, and a commentary on Martianus Capella. The Vatican manuscript lat. 3357 contains: 1) *De vita solitaria* of Petrarch; 2) his *Itinerarium*.

Francesco Novati, in his truly great edition of Salutati's letters, first stated briefly that the first part of the Florence manuscript was copied by Salutati[4]. Later he asserted that as a young man Salutati had copied these letters from the originals lent him by the recipients, Nelli, Bruni, and Lapo da Castiglionchio[5]. Still later he seemed to become more cautious, merely saying that the manuscript was *owned* in whole or part by Salutati[6]. But several years afterwards, in personal communication with Pio Rajna, he sounded a more daring note. He maintained that Salutati had copied the first two sections of the Florence manuscript and fol. 22v of the Vatican codex, tentatively identified the marginalia of the third section of the Florence manuscript as Salutati's, and, on the basis of a dovetailing foliation, held that the two manuscripts were once bound together.

Novati had apparently intended to write something about Salutati's library and during his investigations had come upon various criteria for locating and identifying books from that library. I have been doing the same sort of thing for the study I have mentioned, though apparently more intensively and extensively than Novati, for to him it was, I judge, a mere parergon. I can therefore, I believe, see how Novati's mind worked. He had discovered in various manuscripts owned by Salutati a kind of pressmark peculiar to that humanist. It consists of a library number in arabic figures followed by *Carte* (for *Chartae*, 'leaves') and a Roman numeral indicating the number of leaves in the book. In the two manuscripts under discussion Novati found *Car̄* (for *Carte*) at several points and concluded that the

[3] Not that of Paolo da Perugia nor that of Franceschino degli Albizzi and Forese Donati, published by A. Hortis, *Studi sulle opere latine di Boccaccio* (Trieste, 1879), pp. 525, 537.

[4] F. Novati, *Epistolario di Coluccio Salutati*, I (Rome, 1891), p. 331.

[5] *Giornale storico della letteratura italiana*, XXI (1893), p. 404. Novati says « Bruni », which would mean Francesco Bruni, but the one letter included is to Bruno Casini.

[6] *Epist.*, IV (1905), p. 98.

manuscripts must have belonged to Salutati. Then he turned his attention to the writing. His mind already made up about the ownership of the manuscripts, he found little difficulty in identifying the handwriting as Salutati's. Perhaps this reconstruction of Novati's procedure is incorrect but it would explain how he came to make what I consider a mistaken identification [7].

In a detailed article containing many valuable suggestions, Rajna acceptd Novati's general point of view with enthusiasm [8]. Rajna's conclusions were adopted for the most part by Piur and Rossi and no doubt also by the few scholars who concern themselves with the question but have not expressed themselves in print [9]. There are differences in detail among the four scholars mentioned and these differences furnish one of the means for their undoing, as we shall see.

At first I accepted the three main contentions, that Salutati owned both manuscripts, that he copied parts of them, and that both were at one time bound together. As I became more and more familiar with Salutati's pressmark (I have identified over one hundred books as belonging to his library) I began to have misgivings about our two manuscripts. In the first place, Coluccio invariably writes out the word *Carte,* not abbreviating it by *Car* with a line above it, as in these two manuscripts. In the second place, he usually, though not always, has his library number before *Carte.* In the third place, the letter forms of this word in our two manuscripts are not in the easily identified Salutati style. Finally, Salutati uses the *Carte* inscription only once in a single manuscript [10], whereas it occurs twice in each of our manuscripts, i.e., four times in the combined manuscript if we accept

---

[7] Although I have profound admiration for Novati's work, I have noted that he has several times been wrong in the identification of handwriting.

[8] P. Rajna, « Il codice Vaticano 3357 del Trattato *De vita solitaria* di Francesco Petrarca », *Miscellanea Ceriani* (Milan, 1910), p. 643.

[9] Piur, *Petrarca's 'Buch ohne Namen' und die päpstliche Kurie* (Halle, 1925), p. 244; V. Rossi, *Francesco Petrarca, Le Familiari* (Florence, 1933), I, p. lxi. A. Altamura, « Il 'De vita solitaria' del Petrarca », *La bibliofilia,* 45 (1943), p. 61, and in his edition of *De vita solitaria* (Naples, 1943), follows Rajna without a critical examination of the matter.

[10] There are some manuscripts in which *Carte* with a library number occurs twice, but that is due to the chance that they were bound together after Salutati's time.

the view that they were once bound together [11]. Novati apparently was led to think that *Carte* in any form was a Coluccian characteristic. I have seen a number of variations of the practice in manuscripts that certainly did not belong to him [12]. He did not invent the practice but developed an individual form of it. The upshot of all this is that what Novati thought was an argument favoring Salutati's ownership of the two manuscripts turns out to be an argument against it.

The handwriting of the text of both manuscripts is cursive or semicursive [13]. The three sections of the Florence manuscript are in three different hands of the fourteenth century [14], not just one or two hands working at different times. Three different hands produced the Vatican copy (Rajna thinks that there were at least six), none of them identical with any of those found in the Florence manuscript.

At first I accepted Novati's view that the handwriting of part of the text and marginalia was that of Salutati. But I was compelled to abandon that notion first of all with regard to the text. The handwriting of the first section of the Florence manuscript (about which Novati was most positive) resembles Petrarch's quite as much as it does Salutati's—which means that it does not closely resemble either. Novati thought that Salutati copied the Petrarch letters in his youth, presumably in or soon after 1352, the date of the most recent of these letters. A good sample of Salutati's cursive style in the year 1353 is given by Novati [15]. In an Ovid manuscript in the British Museum (Harl. 2655), Salutati's ownership claim, dated 1357, is strikingly similar. Both are entirely different from all parts of the Florence and Vatican manuscripts. Next I was forced, with Rajna, to retire from the position that the marginalia in the Rome manuscript were in Salutati's hand, on account of both their handwriting and their

---

[11] It is lacking in the second section of the Florence manuscript but may have been trimmed off in binding.

[12] I discuss these in my book (see note 2), p. 130.

[13] In the second section of the Florence manuscript almost all cursive elements have disappeared. See Pl. 1-5.

[14] I am not including the material on fol. 45, which was added in the fifteenth century.

[15] *Epist.*, IV, p. 241.

character, which will be indicated below. My last stronghold was
in the marginal notes to the third section (fol. 49r) of the Florence manuscript. In type they were like Coluccio's, consisting
of a « marginal index », i.e., the names which occur in the text.
This, of course, was not positive evidence, for such marginalia
are exceedingly common. The handwriting bore a certain resemblance to Salutati's formal hand, but careful consideration and
comparison led me to change my mind.

The disagreements among Novati, Rajna, Piur, and Rossi
weaken their arguments in favor of Salutati as copyist and owner.
It should be remembered, however, that the last three were primarily Petrarch scholars, interested in the Petrarchan problems
raised by our manuscripts and using the Coluccian evidence, such
as it was, merely to support their views on the problems with
which they were concerned. Novati held that the first two sections of the Florence manuscript and fol. 22v of the Vatican
codex were copied by Salutati. Rajna rejected (and rightly so)
that attribution for the leaf of the Vatican manuscript because
it was contrary to his explanation of the origin of that leaf. It is
not unfair to say that otherwise he would have accepted Novati's
view, and, *per contra*, that he followed Novati in attributing the
copying of two parts of the Florence manuscript to Salutati because, in dealing with *De vita solitaria,* that attribution did not
interfere with his solutions. Piur and Rossi accepted the suggestion
that the first part of the Florence manuscript was an autograph
of Salutati's but rejected that identification for the second section [16]. Rossi's chief reason is that it does not have the *Carte*
mark. This is a truly absurd reason, though I agree with his
conclusion that Salutati did not do the copying. Rossi did not
know that the presence of *Carte* elsewhere than on the first page
is an argument against Salutati ownership. He did not realize
that by eliminating this section from the combined volume of
Salutati's time he caused the whole structure to come tumbling
down. For if fols. 238-269 (this particular section) do not belong
to Salutati's joint volume, then fols. 175-190 or any other section

---

[16] Rossi wrongly states that Piur accepts the view that the second part was
copied by Salutati; see Piur, p. 246.

may be eliminated and the cogent argument based on the continuous foliation of the two manuscripts collapses. Other differences among these scholars will appear in our discussion and will still further weaken their case for Salutati's connection with the two manuscripts.

As to *De vita solitaria*, Novati thought that Salutati wrote one page of the Vatican copy and thus implied that the whole was copied in Florence or wherever Salutati was at the time. But Rajna showed the impossibility of this. From the marginalia he judged that the owner was some one in close touch with Petrarch but not living in the same place. Several of the notes are introduced by *pete* or *scito* (the imperative of *scisco*). To one of the queries the annotator later added: « dixit esse versus Iuvenalis », etc. As Rajna correctly observes, these queries must have been referred to and answered by Petrarch himself. Such notes are quite atypical as far as Salutati is concerned. Rajna held that the manuscript was copied from Petrarch's original, probably for Donato degli Albanzani at Venice in 1366, and that Donato was the annotator.

Though any thought of connecting the two volumes with Salutati must be rejected, the Novati-Rajna argument that they were once bound together in a volume which contained still more material is convincing, being based on the old dovetailing foliation in the two manuscripts. It is no serious objection that each contains the *Itinerarium*, that it would be strange to have two copies of the same work in one manuscript. Such a situation is surprisingly common.

Since there are some errors in Rajna's account of the combined manuscript, I give the contents as follows, together with the number of leaves in each of the gatherings of the extant portions:

fols. 1-107: missing
fols. 108-123 [17]: Florence; Petrarch, *Epist.*; 16
fols. 124-146: Vatican; *Vita sol.*; 10, 10+1, 2

---

[17] Rajna gives 122, which is the numbering on fol. 15 of the Florence manuscript, but fol. 16 must have been numbered 123; the figure was trimmed off in binding, as happened on other leaves

fols. 147-152: Vatican; *Itin.*; 6
fols. 153-174: missing [18]
fols. 175-190: Florence; Anon., *Geneal.*, etc.; 10, 6
fols. 191-237: missing
fols. 238-269: Florence; Petrarch, *Epist., Itin.*; 16, 16.

What did the missing portions contain? Rajna quite reason-ably suggested other works of Petrarch but could find none in the St. Mark's collection. But the reasonable is not always the right. We can tell what the contents of the missing sections were—and Petrarch's works were not among them. The answer is somewhat of a surprise which I leave to the end of this chapter. Those who cannot wait to reach the solution of the mystery may look ahead.

Some further details are of interest. In the two extant manu-scripts there are five independent sections, written in different script. *Carte,* with the number of leaves, appears at the begin-ning of each of these except one (fol. 238); as already suggested, this may have been trimmed off, or it may have been omitted. The independence of the five sections is indicated also by the gatherings and the watermarks. Fols. 108-123 constitute a single gathering of sixteen, all with the same watermark, which occurs in none of the other sections. Only the first eight leaves have writing on them. It was evidently intended that the letter to Luca Cristiani, of which only the address is found on fol. 8v, be completed and that other letters be added. Why this was not done we cannot tell; perhaps the scribe had to stop temporarily after finishing fol. 8v and thereafter the Cristiani and other let-ters were no longer available. Because a Vatican manuscript (Ottob. lat. 1554) contains thirteen of the sixteen letters that ap-pear in the part of the Florence manuscript which we are now discussing, and in the same order, but with four additional let-ters preceding and two following them [19], Piur thinks that the last two have been lost from the Florence manuscript. He says that the complete text of the Luca letter is « no longer present »,

---

[18] Through a mental slip Rajna says that 153-189 are missing. Piur follows him blindly in this error.

[19] Rossi believes that the seven (not two) which follow belong to this group; he is probably right.

that the leaves which follow « today » are blank. He thus implies that these blank leaves were added after the extant letters were copied, which is impossible as they belong to the same gathering. So the Cristiani letter cannot be said to be no longer present since it was never there! That the intention was to add this and other letters is seen from the fact that the blank sheets were included in the *Carte* number on fol. 1. This number is XV, but as it is at the extreme outside edge of the page we have a right to assume that it once was XVI, covering the eight written and eight blank leaves of the gathering [20]. On the other hand, at the beginning of the gathering of six leaves containing the Vatican *Itinerarium*, the *Carte* number is V, and the space after it shows that nothing has been trimmed off. The explanation seems to be that the text covers only five leaves and there was no intention of writing on the sixth.

The second section of the combined manuscript is *De vita solitaria* on fols. 124-146 [21]. This consists of two gatherings of ten leaves each and one of two leaves. All three have the water-mark that is perhaps the most common of all in old paper, a bow and arrow. But in the first gathering the size and shape are different from those in the second and third. The noteworthy fact—and this is true of the other sections as well—is that the amount of paper was carefully regulated so that each section became an independent unit. The only explanation is that the sections were copied at different times, and that when each section was written no further material was at hand. This is confirmed by the discovery of the contents of the missing sections, as we shall see. But it should be said that Rajna thinks that the last two leaves were pasted together, not made up of a single folded sheet, and that the rest of the gathering (again presumably a quinternion) was removed for other purposes, including the use of one large sheet (two leaves) for part of the Florence manu-

[20] Just what other letters were to be added we cannot tell, but *Var.* 53 and *Fam.* X, 1, which follow in the Ottoboni manuscript, would just about fill the space.

[21] Besides this numbering two other systems are used in the Vatican manuscript, one beginning with the parchment flyleaf, the other with the first page of the text. I follow the latter.

script. Unfortunately, not being concerned at the time with this problem, I did not check the condition of the Vatican leaves; my notes simply refer to the last two leaves of the *De vita solitaria* as a gathering of two. But Vattasso calls it a « double folio » and Mgr. E. Carusi kindly confirmed this, explaining Rajna's error as due to the reinforcements glued to these leaves to make rebinding possible [22]. In any case Rajna's conclusion seems to me impossible. All five sections were rather carefully tailored so that there would be little or no waste, i.e., the length of the gatherings was estimated beforehand so that no large amount of space would be left. The eight blank leaves in the Florence manuscript (fols. 116-123 of the combined manuscript) are no exception, for, as already explained, additional material was planned for those leaves. It will be noticed that the second gathering of this section has an added leaf. This is pasted in and serves as fol. 13 of the Vatican manuscript (fol. 136 of the combined volume). This is intended as an insertion on fol. 14. The explanation of Rajna that this addition emanated ultimately from Petrarch is unquestionably correct. The handwriting is not the same as that of the rest. Rajna thinks that apart from this hand, four others were responsible for the text of *De vita solitaria*. It seems to me that at most there are two. Fol. 22, which begins a new gathering, is in a different ink and perhaps in a different hand, though I am inclined to think not. Rajna holds that this hand wrote fol. 23r but that a different scribe was responsible for fol. 22v. The differences on fols. 16-21 seem too slight to indicate that two scribes were at work in a complicated alternation, as Rajna thinks. He would have it that a new scribe began on fol. 16r, was succeeded by the first scribe, who returned to finish the page, to be relieved again near the end of 16v, etc. It is, of course, not impossible that scribe B relieved scribe A on numerous occasions. But Rajna himself admits that the first seven and a half lines of fol. 13 are by the same scribe as the rest of the page though they are larger than the rest and not cursive [23].

[22] M. Vattasso, *I codici petrarcheschi della Biblioteca Vaticana* (Rome, 1908), p. 29.

[23] Rajna infers support in Vattasso's statement that at least two hands (one being that of fol. 13) copied the work. Vattasso's words are: « Il primo fascicolo

I explain the apparent changes of hand as follows. Throughout the book the handwriting is small and cramped, and abbreviations are numerous and drastic. Obviously the scribe was attempting to get the text into a small compass. At times, especially towards the end, he forgot himself and wrote in a larger script, only to go back to an even more crowded style. Thus he began fol. 14r in larger script but reverted to his previous style after seven and a half lines. The analogy of fol. 13, containing the Romualdus supplement added later by another scribe, is instructive. To get this on a single page a much longer line was adopted. After writing a little over seven lines in a formal hand the scribe changed to a more compact cursive, obviously to keep his material within the space determined. So the original scribe, after copying most of fol. 16r, changed to a smaller script. On fol. 17r he relapsed into larger letters but reverted to the smaller after ten and a half lines. On fol. 18r, after twenty-four lines, the writing becomes smaller. The same thing happens on fol. 19r after thirty-five lines. Somes pages are in a uniformly small script and thus have more lines. The number of lines per page varies from 46 to 68. The page that has only 46 lines is fol. 22v, the next to the last page. The scribe, realizing that he could not get the rest of the book on fol. 22v, indulged in an orgy of large characters. He returned to a smaller script on fol. 23r, taking the entire page to finish the work.

The desire to save space also led to the crowding of lines. Thus on fol. 15r the last five lines take up 15 mm. in my photographs, the preceding five lines occupy 19 mm.; even Rajna considers them the work of the same scribe. The last twenty-one lines of fol. 19r cover 71 mm., the preceding twenty-one require 79 mm.

The third extant section, covering fols. 147-152, is the Vatican *Itinerarium*. It is an entirely separate section from the preceding *De vita solitaria*, in a different script, adorned with red and blue initials, which do not occur in the preceding part. Another inno-

[he means the whole of *De vita solitaria*] sembra scritto da almeno due mani diverse; alla prima delle quali appartiene quasi tutto il fascicolo, alla seconda soltanto l'aggiunta a c. 14 » (i.e., fol. 13). This is more against than for Rajna's opinion.

vation is that the capital letters are made prominent by red lines. The writing space, too, is different. The single gathering consists of six leaves, the last of which is blank. Two different watermarks, both unlike those in fols. 124-146, are found.

The fourth of the extant sections covers fols. 175-190 and includes three anonymous items on two gatherings, the first of ten leaves, the second of six [24]. The first gathering has a stag for a watermark; the second is a mixture of sheets, some with this mark, others with a bow and arrow. Evidently the size of the second gathering was determined only after a careful estimate of the amount of paper needed to complete the text, and it was made up of whatever paper was available. The three items of text were intended to be together, for the second begins on the page on which the first ends, and similarly the third follows on the heels of the second.

The last extant section covers fols. 238-269, in two gatherings of sixteen, each having the same watermark, which differs from that of the other sections. The text consists of seven letters of Petrarch, between the second and third of which the *Itinerarium* appears, treated as if it too were a letter [25]. The text ends on fol. 266r; fols. 267-269 are blank. In the late fifteenth century other Petrarch material (the Laura note, Petrarch's epitaph) was added on fol. 266. In rebinding the Florence manuscript the second and third sections of that manuscript (the last two of the extant sections of the combined manuscript) were reversed in order, presumably to bring together the two sections containing Petrarch letters.

As the story of the composition, correction, transcription, and publication of *De vita solitaria,* which furnishes the background for the Vatican manuscript, is a complicated one, it seems desirable to present the essential portions of some of Petrarch's letters which bear on the matter [26]. In tracing that story I shall call

---

[24] Piur, *op. cit.*, pp. 246, 252, is wrong in assigning the script of this section to the fifteenth century instead of the fourteenth.

[25] Piur, *op. cit.*, p. 246, wrongly says eight letters and the *Itinerarium,* though his own listing shows seven.

[26] In what follows I shall refer to the quotations by the numbers I give them.

attention to some facts that have been overlooked and shall arrive at conclusions that differ somewhat from those which are prevalent today.

1. *Fam.* XIX, 5.   To Moggio, Milan, May 1, 1355 [27]: Non ego te ad servitium, sed ad amicitiam voco... Hunc ipsum adolescentem... meliorem et doctiorem facies... Ad hec et nugarum aliquid mearum, non nisi quantum libuerit et si libuerit, scribes; tuum erit iudicium an digne sint que tuum, rebus propriis non otiosum, calamum fatigent. In studii mei partem veni: mea michi magis probabuntur si tuo scripta sint digito. Sperabo, si quid michi vel oblivione vel incuria sit elapsum, subterfugere manus tuas ingeniumque non posse.

2. *Var.* 14.   To Socrates, Milan or Padua, 1360-61 [28]: Duos *Solitarie vite* libros scripsi olim ad Philippum Cavallicensem... Hos cupienti et oranti mittere diu distuli, et iam iam causam dilationis intelliges. Ego enim et illos sibi non negare nec subtrahere amplius institui... et te similiter horum participem facere in animo est, sed ea lege, ut vivo me nemo alius particeps per vos fiat. Ut enim quadam in parte operis advertere erit, summos hic hominum stilo attigi.

3. *Var.* 12 [29].   To Moggio, Padua [30], June 10, 1362: Recommendo vobis reculas illas meas quas dimisi vobis, nominatim *Solitariam vitam.* Libro II, ubi agitur de Paula, ad finem capituli illius, posueram signum additurus aliquid. Mutavi consilium; amoveatis signum illud. Post illud libro eodem est capitulum magnum valde de Petro heremita, quod non memini quotum sit. Ibi non nimis a principio procul est ita: « tam nichil est animi nervorum ». Nolo usque adeo famam Cesaris urgere, et ideo in utroque [31] libro mutetis et ponatis

---

[27] In deciding on dates for Petrarch's letters I gained much help from E. H. Wilkins' very useful *Modern Discussions of the Dates of Petrarch's Prose Letters* (Chicago, 1929), which has been supplanted by his even more useful and valuable *Petrarch's Correspondence* (Padua, 1960).

[28] A. Foresti, *Aneddoti della vita di Francesco Petrarca* (Brescia, 1928), pp. 402-403. For my reconstruction 1361 is preferable, as will be shown.

[29] Based on Rajna's quotation (p. 669), taken directly from the holograph letter.

[30] Foresti, *op. cit.*, p. 384.

[31] This can hardly be correct. It has been suggested that *libro* here means « copy » or « manuscript ». But there is no indication that Moggio was making two copies (he did not make even one!); but see below, n. 68. Nor does it seem likely that Petrarch would have employed *liber* in this sense just after twice using it in reference to the second book of *De vita sol.*, and just before using it once more in the same application. Therefore Petrarch perhaps intended to write *eodem* or *hoc altero* or something similar. The letter is in Petrarch's own hand.

sic: « quasi sub celo aliquid sit pulchrius ». ... Item eodem libro post tractatum de Benedicto est de quodam heremita « Marsici montis accola », etc., et ibi debet esse « Massici ».

4. *Var.* 4 [32]. To Moggio, Venice, December 9, 1362: Reliquum est ut rogem reculas illas meas vobis, frater carissime, cure esse, si vacat, saltem *Vitam solitariam*; que si transcursa erit, ut spero, minietur ligeturque solemniter per Magistrum Benedictum, et mittantur ad me exemplum et exemplar, diligenter panno cereo obvoluta inter ballas Iobannoli de Cumis.

5. *Var.* 37. To Moggio, Venice, December 20, 1362 [33]: Reculas illas habetote memorie.

6. *Sen.* V, 1. To Boccaccio, Pavia, December 22, 1365: Gaudeo hercle quod... videris... meum Philippum... Hic, ut scribis,... oravit ut librum *Vite solitarie,* olim dum Cavallicensis ecclesie presul esset, in rure suo scriptum et ei inscriptum, aliquando sibi mitterem. Iusta quidem petitio sua est, iniusta dilatio mea. Decimus enim annus est [34] ex quo opusculum illud absolvi, sed... decies vel eo amplius retentavi ita scriptum mittere ut, etsi stilus neque aures neque animum, littera saltem oculos oblectaret. Verum studio meo votoque obstitit illa de qua totiens queror nota tibi scriptorum fides, industria, nobilibus non ultima pestis ingeniis. Vix credibilia loqui dicar paucissimis mensibus scriptum opus tam multis annis non potuisse rescribi... Nunc tandem, post tot cassa primordia, scribendum illud domo abiens dimisi inter cuiusdam sacerdotis manus, que an ad scribendum sacre fuerint, ut sacerdotis, an ad fallendum faciles, ut scriptoris, nescio. Nuntiatum tamen est michi amicorum litteris iam factum esse quod iusseram; de qualitate, donec videam, mos horum certissimus me dubium facit. Solent enim (auditu mirum) non quod

---

[32] Based on Rajna's quotation (p. 673), taken directly from the holograph letter.

[33] Fracassetti gives the date as December 30, but from the holograph letter Piur corrects this in K. Burdach, *Vom Mittelalter zur Reformation*, II, 2 (Berlin, 1928), p. 335, and I have confirmed it from the facsimile in G. Vitelli and C. Paoli, *Collezione fiorentina di facsimili* (Florence, 1884), Pl. 12.

[34] This is the reading of the Venice edition of 1501. « Iniusta . . . est » is omitted by the Venice edition of 1503, the Basel editions of 1554 and 1581, and Fracassetti in his translation. In the 1503 edition *sua est* comes at the end of a line. It looks, therefore, as if the error started here, through jumping from one *est* to the next, and that the two Basel editions were based on this Venice edition. V. Develay's translation, *Lettres de François Pétrarque à Jean Boccace* (Paris, 1891), p. 166, based on a Latin text established from a Paris and a Toulouse manuscript, includes the sentence.

scribendum acceperint sed nescio quid aliud scriptitare; tantum vel ignorantie est vel inertie vel contemptus.

7. *Sen.* VI, 5.　To Philippe de Cabassoles, Venice, June 6, 1366: Olim... contigit ut duo michi libelli totidem continuos per annos in diebus quadrigesime... occurrerent, de solitaria alter vita, alter de otio religioso... Cur igitur ante non miserim quod et tuum erat... dicam. Non una quidem differendi sed plures fuerunt cause, occupatio mea ingens ac perpetua, item tarditas quedam expediendarum rerum animo insita, utraque tibi causa notissima... Accessit ad causas mora scriptorum, perfida semper inertia inersque perfidia... Hoc ipsum decies vel eo amplius ceptum opus, breve licet, fidus tandem vix explicuit sacerdos quidam, littera non tam anxie exculta quam nostre atque omni etati, nisi fallor, idonea. Adolescentia enim cunctis suis in actibus improvida et insulsa miratrix inanium, contemptrix utilium, perexiguis atque compressis visumque frustrantibus litterulis gloriari solita est, acervans omnia et coartans atque hinc spatio, hinc litterarum super litteras velut equitantium aggestione confundens, que scriptor ipse brevi post tempore rediens vix legat, emptor vero non tam librum quam libro cecitatem emat... Dilationem ipsam iam decennem... Et si enim hac [dignitate] illustrior atque altior sis, illa tamen rebus accommodatior atque aptior visa est quarum libro illo memoriam feci, quem in rure tunc tuo me dictasse prima eius in parte prefatus sum, in parte ultima, ut vicini ruris ad solitudinem ac silentium te invitans, ubi multa sunt propria illius tantum status ac temporis.

8. *Sen.* V, 4.　To Donato degli Albanzani, Pavia, September 1, 1366: Ceterum *Solitarie vite* librum, quem pene iratus iure tuo postulas, sacerdoti meo Paduano scripsi iam ut tibi transmitteret. Quem ut arbitrio tuo legas permitto, ne transcribas veto usque dum venero. Adhuc enim verbum ibi addidi. Nosti morem: alter Protogenes, nescio e tabella manum tollere.

9. *Sen.* X, 1.　To Sacramor de Pommiers, Venice, March 18, 1367[35]: Feci ego quod minimum, *Psalmos septem* misi... Librum *Vite solitarie* quem... requiris in presens mittere nequeo; duos namque necdum plures habui. Alterum tu portasti tuo ultimo digressu ad illum cui inscriptus est... Alter penes me substitit... Caruisse tamen eo nolim. At si scriptor forte (quod perrarum fateor) fidus affuerit, credo te sperare quod et hoc... faciam.

---

[35] Rossi's arguments for this date, *Scritti di critica letteraria,* II (Florence, 1930), p. 61, seem to me stronger than Foresti's for 1368, *op. cit.,* p. 106.

10. *Sen.* XVI, 3. To Francesco da Siena, Arquà, May 1, 1372:
Siquidem quod meus ille liber tuas venerit ad manus gratum habeo,...
at quod librum scripseris, non placet, et cur, dicam. Venit Venetias
nuper prior magnus Camaldulensis... Is penes amicum quendam meum
fidelissimum librum illum repperit; et erat forte quem primum scribi
feceram; atque ideo, ut fit, omnes undique margines additionibus pleni
erant. Quas cum senex legeret, et nunc hos, nunc illos prime scripture
additos videret... Romualdi vitam... ad me misit, ex qua ego... capitu-
lumque unum libro addidi... Amicus alter queri cepit quid Ioannem
quendam... relinquerem... Et nunc maxime vitam eius expecto, in qua
si quid erit ad solitudinem spectans, et hunc inseram... Quia igitur et
Romualdus hic et ille forsitan Ioannes, de quo adhuc dubius sum,
addendi erant, si videbitur, mallem scribere distulisses.

It is now generally agreed that the first draft of *De vita solitaria* was written at Vaucluse in 1346. Petrarch says that it was
written during the forty days of Lent (7). Elsewhere he says
« paucissimis mensibus » (6). The slight inconsistency could be
explained, if need be, by assuming that in the second passage
Petrarch is including the time spent in additions to the original
draft. The book was intended from the first for Philippe de
Cabassoles, but this friend, after reading the first draft, had to
wait exactly twenty years for his copy.

Petrarch gives various reasons for delay: the difficulty of
securing a satisfactory scribe (6, 7, 9), the desire to add and correct (7, 8), the fear of unpleasant reactions from persons mentioned
in the book (2). The last is referred to but once and seems
to be a temporary attitude [36]. The first receives the most emphasis and has, therefore, impressed modern scholars most. But it
really is incredible, as Petrarch himself says (6), that it took
twenty years to find an even moderately adequate scribe. During that period he had copies made of numerous books, both
his own and others, not to mention the handsome copies he made

---

[36] Avena in *Rassegna critica della letteratura italiana*, XII (1907), p. 200,
cites II, 4, 2 ff. (Francesco Petrarca, *Prose*, a cura di G. Martellotti, etc., Milan,
1955, p. 484), where kings and princes are chided for their vices and quarrels,
Charles IV for staying away from Italy, etc. That Petrarch had Charles IV
specifically in mind is proved by his request to Moggio to modify a sentence
about him (3; *Prose*, p. 488); this was overlooked by Avena. Yet Petrarch does
not hesitate to say the same things directly to Charles (*Fam.* XIX, 12).

with his own hand. The second reason is the chief one, that he was always tinkering not only with this book but with others—so much so that some were entirely suppressed. His reluctance to let his books fly away from the home nest is well-known.

In 1352 Petrarch writes to a friend that the book is not yet published but puts it at his disposal together with the rest of his library [37]. This can only mean that his friend may read it but not secure it or make a copy for himself. In 1354 the book was still unpublished, for Charles IV jokingly told its author that if he ever got hold of it he would throw it into the fire, to which Petrarch replied that he would take good care to see that Charles did not secure a copy [38].

The general view today is that the book was actually completed in 1356 and that the further delay of ten years before publication was almost wholly caused by the unavailing search for a copyist. Publication consisted in sending the dedication copy to Philippe and in allowing others to have transcripts, for it is certain that Philippe's copy was the first to be released. That this was sent in 1366 is established beyond doubt, but the other date, 1356, is not so certain. To be sure, Petrarch says (6) in 1365 that it is the tenth year since he finished the book and in 1366, in writing to Philippe, alludes to a delay of ten years. At the very least the round number indicates that we need not take these statements too literally. But possibly we should go farther. In his letter to Philippe Petrarch does not stop, so to speak, at an intermediate point such as 1356 but harks back to 1346—to the days when Philippe was at Vaucluse. Could Petrarch have made a mistake in saying ten years instead of twenty? Could he have made such a mistake twice? That does not seem reasonable, but the second letter (7) echoes much of the language of the first [39]. Avena argues for 1356 as the date of completion by

---

[37] *Fam.* IX, 14; cf. *Fam.* XVII, 5 (1353).

[38] *Fam.* XIX, 3.

[39] Foresti, *op. cit.*, p. 57, notes Petrarch's error on another occasion in using the very specific *toto decennio* for a period of nine years. In *Fam.* VIII, 3 (1349) Petrarch speaks of his twelve-year stay at Vaucluse as *decennis mora*. In *Sen.* I, 3 *prope decennium* refers to an eight-year period. In spite of Foresti's

an interpretation of a sentence in this letter about which he himself, with good reason, is dubious (« if I have not misunderstood
the passage », he says). He suggests that Petrarch wrote only
the first book in Vaucluse in 1346 and the second in Milan in
1353-56. But Petrarch is explaining why in the book he still calls
Philippe a bishop instead of giving him his later title of patriarch
of Jerusalem. He merely notes (and this is the sentence under
question) that in the first part of the book he says by way of
preface that he wrote the work in Philippe's country retreat and
that in the last part he refers to many things appropriate to 1346
and to Philippe's then status and not to his present position (7) [40].
The whole work would have to be rewritten if he were to take
cognizance of Philippe's position in 1366. In alluding to the
preface in the first part and in using the phrase « in rure tunc
tuo » he has in mind the prefatory letter of 1346, where he says
« nunc in rure tuo positus ». The allusion to the last part, « ut
(as if) vicini ruris ad solitudinem ac silentium te invitans »,
obviously refers to the tenth and last tractate of the second book,
the first chapter of which, in the printed editions, bears the title
« Tam ob virtutes ... quam ob comites ... ad solitudinem sua-
dens » [41]. So this argument of Avena's certainly misses fire.

Furthermore, there is Petrarch's own testimony to the fact
that both books had been written before 1353. In Book IV of
Invective contra medicum he mentions the fact that « duo mei
libri extant » on the life of solitude. Umberto Bosco has definitely
shown that the last three books of the Invective were finished in
the early months of 1353—before Petrarch left Vaucluse in May
of that year [42]. The preface of the Invective, written in 1355, is
really a letter to a friend who wants a copy; it was sent after the

---

explanations (p. 20), supplemented by those of C. Calcaterra (Studi Petrarcheschi,
II, 1949, p. 7), Petrarch's assertion that he spent seven years studying law
cannot be squared with the period 1316-26, the end date of which is arrived
at by another decimus annus. See too below.

[40] Fracassetti's translation is substantially correct.

[41] Though this title did not originate with Petrarch it accurately describes
the contents.

[42] Studi Petrarcheschi, I (1948), p. 97.

book had been published for at least a short time [43].   In the first
edition of *De otio* (1347) Petrarch mentions the second book of
De vita solitaria as already published [44].   Even more cogent is

[43] It occurred to me that the recipient of the prefatory letter might have
been Boccaccio, first, because we know that he requested a copy and the letter
says that the work is being sent on request; second, because the derogatory tone
of the reference to the coronation of Zanobi da Strada, which took place on
May 15, 1355, harmonizes with Boccaccio's strong feelings on the subject.   Later
I discovered that Foresti, in *Giornale storico della letteratura italiana*, LXXVIII
(1921), p. 330, had made the same suggestion, in part for the second reason.
Still later I noticed that Vat. lat. 4518, owned and annotated by Lapo da
Castiglionchio, contains the letter *after* the *Invective* and names Boccaccio as
the recipient.   G. Billanovich confirmed the attribution from other manuscripts
(*Giornale storico della letteratura italiana*, CXXV, 1948, p. 60).   He showed
that the use of the letter as a preface began with Tedaldo della Casa, whom
Vespasiano da Bisticci followed; the early printed editions are based on the
text of Vespasiano.   The date given is July 12, not June 10, as in the printed
editions (Vattasso, *op. cit.*, p. 34 f.).   Boccaccio says that he received the
manuscript while at Ravenna, and this leads Foresti to suggest the year 1357,
for Boccaccio was elsewhere in the two preceding summers.   So too Billanovich,
Petrarca letterato, I. Lo scrittoio del Petrarca (Rome, 1947), pp. 208, 210, and
E. H. Wilkins, *Petrarch's Eight Years in Milan* (Cambridge, 1958), pp. 144-146.
But the reference to Zanobi would have lost its fragrance by 1357.   The letter
was, I think, written in July, 1355, and the manuscript received in Ravenna
in September of that year after Boccaccio left Florence.   Bosco inclines to my
date of 1355, but some objection has been raised to it (e. g., Billanovich,
Petrarca letterato, I, p. 209, note 4) because Boccaccio was in Florence until the
end of August in 1355 and went to Naples in September.   But Boccaccio would
have had good reason to go to Ravenna frequently even for a short stay if his
daughter Violante and her mother lived there (Billanovich, p. 201, note 1).
Violante died at the age of seven in September of 1355 or 1362 while Boccaccio
was on his way to Naples.   He had not seen her in a year and a half.   If she
died in 1362 Boccaccio would have gone to Ravenna at the time of or just
after her birth in 1355—a very good reason for a short visit.   If Violante died
in 1355 my suggestion that Boccaccio visited Ravenna is wrong.   Another argument for the date 1355 for our letter is that in it Petrarch says that he is
sending « librum . . . et vetustissimam quam postulas cartam ».   In *Fam.* XVIII,
15, written December 20, 1355, Petrarch says that he has received the books
presented by Boccaccio and those which he returned (*remisisti*), evidently borrowed from Petrarch.   An earlier letter of thanks was lost.   If Boccaccio received
these books with the *Invective* at Ravenna in September, he could have returned
them in a month or two, in time to be acknowledged for the second time—on
December 20.

[44] G. Rotondi, « Le due redazioni del *De otio* del Petrarca », *Aevum*, IX
(1935), p. 40, note 1.   To be sure, Rotondi does not make clear when the first
edition was released by Petrarch but he gives no indication that it contains
allusions to events after 1347.   Rotondi's article is of interest for our problem.
The second edition of *De otio* (previously unknown) has about one hundred addi-

Petrarch's specific statement that both books were composed at Vaucluse at one time [45].

Avena also points out that there are indications of additions during the Milan period, before 1356. True, but there is indisputable evidence of additions and corrections between 1356 and 1366. And this is as good a time as any to discuss all the changes that were made after the original composition. Avena thinks that Petrarch's remark, « putabam enim epistolam scribere, librum scripsi » [46], shows that he intended to write only one book [47]. As a matter of fact, Petrarch goes on to say that such a letter would have been a single book. It is possible, of course, that when Petrarch stopped writing in 1346 he had put all into one book (including parts that are now in Book II) and divided the material later, though the statements referred to in the preceding paragraph seem to confute this view. The last one especially makes it clear that the natural interpretation of his remark about his original intention is that it refers to the time when he began writing the book, or even earlier. At any rate, although the evidence for the writing of a particular sentence or paragraph before a certain date is bound to be much scarcer than for composition after it since allusions to events preceding that date usually furnish no clue as to composition whereas references to later events are always significant, there are at least two sentences in Book II that betray an early origin: in II, 10, 9 (*Prose*, p. 590), the very last sentence of the book, Petrarch states that the preceding words were composed amid the rustling of the leaves in the breeze and the babbing of the nearby spring. The other sentence is in II, 10, 5 (*Prose*, p. 576), where he says that he not only can live the solitary life but has already begun to do so and

tions. The first edition is that of the printed texts. On the other hand, the first edition of *De vita solitaria* has apparently disappeared. It is to be understood, of course, that strictly speaking, we should not talk about first and second editions; rather, the first draft underwent changes from time to time.

[45] *Sen.* XIII, 11 (cf. *Sen.* XV, 15). Rosa di Sabatino shows that parts of both books were written in 1346: « Dai Dettatori al Novecento », *Studi in ricordo di C. Calcaterra* (Turin, 1953), p. 99.

[46] II, 10, 9 (*Prose,* p. 588). Avena wrongly attributes it to *Sen.* VI, 5.

[47] We are reminded of a remark in the *Invective contra medicum,* which has four books: « libellum pro epistola remisi » (end of Book I), though here, of course, *epistola* refers to the physician's letter.

wants his friend to join him. This does not sound like a later simulation of the status of 1346.

We come now to the additions. As Petrarch did not know Quintilian until a friend gave him a copy in 1350, the four quotations from that author must be later insertions. Three of the four are in Book I. The first, with the comment, takes up a large part of I, 4, 3 (*Prose*, p. 366). Petrarch says that Quintilian confirmed his own experience and states that he « inserted » (*inserui*) the quotation because it is not well-known. In I, 5, 1 (*Prose*, p. 362) quotation and comment take up the entire chapter. In I, 6, 2 (*Prose*, p. 386) the last part is devoted to Quintilian. In II, 8, 3 (*Prose*, p. 540) only a short passage deals with him.

Avena has pointed out, quite correctly, that the descriptions of Milan (II, 3, 2, 4; *Prose*, pp. 430-436) were added while Petrarch lived in that city (1353-61). The same is true of II, 6, 1 (*Prose*, p. 512). Most of this chapter is based on a manuscript which he read in the archives of the church of St. Ambrose at Milan. Nothing justifies the assumption that these additions were made in 1356 rather than at any other time earlier or later in the eight-year residence of Petrarch in the city of the Visconti. They could, of course, have been added even later.

In II, 4, 2 (*Prose*, p. 486) Petrarch says that the French and English have been fighting for five *lustra* (twenty-five years). As the Hundred Years' War began in 1337, the date would be 1362, if the round number is taken literally. In any case we have a right to assume that he is writing in a year not earlier than 1360 nor later than 1364. He goes on to mention the capture of the French king (at Poitiers in September, 1356) and his removal in chains. But the end is not yet (he continues), for the king's oldest son (Charles) is resorting to arms and the war is again raging, as the armies of the French king gather anew. This would best fit the years 1359-60, before the peace of Brétigny (May, 1360) [48]. In the same chapter Petrarch mentions the alliance of the Spanish

---

[48] I later discovered that H. Cochin, in *Société de l'histoire de France, Annuaire-Bulletin*, LIV (1917), p. 139, believed that the passage was written in 1359.

king (Peter of Aragon) with Venice against Genoa, which resulted
in the shedding of Genoese blood. The alliance was made in July,
1351, and the great disaster of the Genoese occurred in 1353 [49].
The paragraph could have been written in 1352 or 1353, but the
summer or autumn of 1353 (about the time that Petrarch went
to Venice on a mission to urge peace) is the likeliest time. An
allusion in the same chapter to the greater Spanish king, who
allows heresy and blasphemy to flourish unchecked on a narrow
rock, must refer to Pedro I of Castile (1350), who did not continue
his father's war against the Moors on Gibraltar [50]. The theme
and tone of the entire chapter are similar to those of *Fam.* XV,
7, which Cochin dates 1360 [51].

In II, 4, 3 (*Prose,* p. 488) Petrarch reproaches Charles IV
for running away from Italy after receiving the imperial crown
in April, 1355. The chapter must have been added after that
time. The language used resembles that in letters of that year
(*Fam.* XIX, 12; XX, 2) but even more that which appears in a
letter of 1361 (*Fam.* XXIII, 2). The addition, therefore, probably
falls between 1355 and 1361.

In a letter to Petrarch, Boccaccio writes from Ravenna that
Donato degli Albanzani passed on to him Petrarch's request for
the books of Pietro Damiani and for information about him.
Earlier scholars variously dated Boccaccio's letter from 1353 to
1357, but Foresti has made a plausible but not invincible case for

---

[49] The alliance is mentioned in a plea to the doge of Venice to end the
war (*Fam.* XI, 8; March 18, 1351). As the alliance was not formally concluded
until July, the letter may have to be dated 1352; but negotiations were in
progress for some time. There are other similarities between the letter and
our chapter.

[50] Vat. lat. 3357 and 4518, and the Milan edition of 1498 read: « Hispanus
ille maior *heret et* per ignaviam sinit intra *suos fines* (proh pudor!) angusto in
scopulo maiestatem Christi nefarie blasfemari ». The Wellesley College manuscript and the Strasbourg edition of 1473 agree on the italicized words. The
editions of 1496, 1501, 1503 have *h(a)eres et,* those of 1554, 1581, 1605 have
haereticus for *heret et,* and all six wrongly insert *fratres* after *fines.* I am
indebted for this and other information on the Strasbourg edition to Professor
Harry Caplan, who examined the Cornell copy for me, and to Professor Dorothy
M. Robathan for reports on the Wellesley manuscript.

[51] *Loc. cit.*

1362 [52]. Obviously the information was sought for the improve-ment of II, 3, 17 (*Prose,* p. 472) of *De vita solitaria*. I think that there are in this short chapter some traces, though slight, of Boccaccio's letter and an accompanying biography of Pietro Damiani. Petrarch refers to Damiani's writings; these Boccaccio may have sent him along with the biography. Petrarch says that he sent persons to Damiani's monastery to get information about him; Boccaccio tells us that he went there in his quest on behalf of Petrarch.

In II, 9, 2 (*Prose,* p. 546) Petrarch quotes Julius Capitolinus. As his manuscript of the *Historia Augusta,* which is still extant, was copied for him in February, 1356 [53], the quotation must have been added after that date, perhaps even several years later [54].

---

[52] F. Torraca, *Per la biografia di Gio. Boccaccio* (Rome, 1912), p. 190, placed it in 1354. Massèra suggested 1357 (Boccaccio, *Opere latine minori,* ed. A. F. Massèra, Bari, 1928, p. 331). In the early form of this essay I suggested between 1353 (when Petrarch went to Milan, where he asked Boccaccio to send the material) and 1356 (when Donato left Ravenna to live in Venice). In *Giornale storico della letteratura italiana,* XCVIII (1931), p. 73, Foresti rules out the period before 1358 because Petrarch's request to have the Damiani material sent to Milan shows that he no longer had a fixed address at Milan, as he had up to 1358. This argument, the foundation stone of Foresti's case, is not too strong. Foresti also maintains, without proof, that Petrarch's acquaintance with Donato did not begin until 1359. After that the only possible year from the standpoint of Petrarch's activities is 1362, Foresti argues, and this year best explains Boccaccio's mention of his *infortunium*. This date is accepted by Wilkins, *op. cit.,* p. 145. In any further study of this question one thing should be kept in mind. It must have taken Boccaccio some time to make the researches indicated by his letter, to read the badly worn paper copy of *Vita Damiani* (« et vetustate et incuria fere corrosum et mille seu aque seu spurcissimi liquoris alterius notis aspersum »), and then to rewrite it in a style that would appeal to Petrarch. His letter was written on January 2 of some year. Therefore Petrarch's request must have been made, not in December, as seems to be generally assumed, but between September and November of the preceding year. He seems to have remained in Milan in the summer of 1355 (Wilkins, *op. cit.,* pp. 103-107). In 1357 he left Garegnano for Milan after September 8 (Foresti, *Aneddoti,* p. 358).

[53] Pierre de Nolhac, *Pétrarque et l'humanisme,* ed. 2, II (Paris, 1907), p. 48. Apart from this one, the earliest quotation dates from 1360.

[54] Avena's assertion that the syntax at the beginning of II, 6 (*Prose,* p. 510) shows that there was an interval of time between its composition and that of the preceding chapter rests on an inadequate knowledge of Latin syntax. « Tempus erat ut finem facerem » has no reference to past time and simply means « it would be high time to end ».

A study of the Vatican manuscript reveals further secrets about the various additions antedating 1366. The margins of that manuscript disclose a series of numbers running from 1 to 63. The plausible explanation of Vattasso and Rajna is that these represent the numbering of the leaves in the original. The practice reminds one of the numbering of the *pecia,* the passage of text copied from the eight-page rented gathering used by university scribes. At some centers the *pecia* was numbered at the beginning, but at Bologna, the numbering came at the end[55]. But the numbers in our manuscript come too close together to mark the end of the *pecia*; perhaps, however, the custom of *pecia* numbering suggested the plan used in this manuscript. The *pecia* numbering was adopted primarily to make sure that no section had been omitted in copying. This may have been the reason for the numbering of the sections of the Petrarch manuscript but a possibly more likely explanation is that it facilitated reference to the original, which, as we shall see, had numerous marginal additions. This explanation implies that the owner of our manuscript had access to the original, and that is in accordance with facts that we shall now discuss. Rajna gives the number of lines in the Vatican manuscript between each of the consecutive figures. They run from about 22 lines[56] to 53 lines[57]. Rajna thinks that the original had about 30 of the Vatican lines per leaf, that the smaller numbers are to be explained by deletions and the larger ones by additions. As only ten sections run from 23 to 30 lines and twenty-four run from 31 to 38 lines, it looks as if Rajna's estimate of 30 lines for the original is a little too low even after a generous allowance for additions. Rajna also

---

[55] Jean Destrez, *La Pecia dans les manuscrits universitaires du XIIIe et du XIVe siècle* (Paris, 1935), p. 13.

[56] There is no trace of number 6 and it may, as Rajna supposes, have been trimmed off. There are only 45 lines between number 5 and 7, and that necessitates the supposition that the one section (by which I mean the group of lines between marginal numbers) consisted of only 22 lines, the other of 23. Only one other section has as few as 23 lines.

[57] In summarizing, Rajna says 49, but his table gives one instance of 53 and two of 50 lines. The number of lines in the manuscript is not an entirely reliable guide because the writing is at times smaller and more cramped and because there is variation in the amount of abbreviation. I have used the number of lines in the printed edition as a control.

notes that in the first book the average per section is 33.4 lines; in the second, 39.7 (this last figure should be 40.7). He plausibly explains this discrepancy as due to the greater number of additions in the second book (caused by the nature of the subject matter rather than by lack of time to finish it when first composed), but, to our regret, he neither employs his material to help determine what portions were added nor presents it in such fashion that we can use it for that purpose. If we accept Rajna's estimate of 30 Vatican lines per leaf in the original without marginal additions, then 63 numbered sections would have totaled 1890 lines, as against 2357 in the Vatican manuscript for those sections [58]. This last figure would represent an increase of 25 per cent due to insertions. In the first book the increase would be about 12 per cent; in the second, 36 per cent. But, as I have said, an estimate of 30 lines seems rather low. If we take 34 lines, the increase for the whole work is only 10 per cent; for the first book, none at all; for the second book, nearly 20 per cent. This estimate is probably nearer the truth.

Let us see whether the additions that we have discussed come in the longer numbered sections. The quotations from Quintilian in I, 4, 3 (*Prose*, p. 336) and I, 5, 1 (*Prose*, p. 362) are in relatively short sections, that in I, 6, 2 (*Prose*, p. 386) in a somewhat longer one. On the other hand, in the four longest sections of Book I no passages can be identified as additions. The net result is that Book I offers no confirmation of Rajna's theory. In Book II the situation is not much different. II, 3, 2; 4; 17; II, 6, 1; II, 9, 2 (*Prose*, pp. 430, 436, 472, 512, 546), which contain additions, are in sections that are of only average length. II, 4, 2 and 4 (*Prose*, pp. 486-490) are in longer sections. But the longest sections contain no easily identifiable additions: II, 3, 5-7; 13-15; 18; 4, 8—5, 2; 6, 1-3; 9,6 —10, 1 (*Prose*, pp. 438-444, 458-464, 476-482, 500-506, 518-522, 556-562). II, 3, 5 deals with Augustine but as he is tied in with Ambrose and Milan this chapter may have been added during Petrarch's Milanese period. II, 3, 18 contains an allusion to Ambrose and this may be in part a later supplement. II, 6, 1-2 deals with the Brahmans, about

[58] Rajna's figures (p. 664, note 1) are not correct.

whom Petrarch may not have had information before his Milan period. On the whole, then, the result of this part of our investigation is disappointing. Further comparison of material in the long sections with Petrarch's other works, notably the letters, may indicate the relative lateness of part of it.

The division into chapters and their length also throw some light on the additions. The chapter division went through several stages after Petrarch's time. First, smaller portions of the chapters were marked off into paragraphs or represented additions. This is the system which exists in the Vatican manuscript. Later these paragraphs became independent chapters. Later still this division formed the basis for the section and chapter division of some manuscripts and most of the printed editions. The Milan edition of 1498 has traces of the first two stages. In it the first part of Book I reveals a division into small chapters, usually though not always, identical with those in the later editions. The first 26 chapters (which are numbered) agree exactly with the chapter and paragraph divisions of the Vatican manuscript, except that two paragraph divisions of that manuscript are passed over [59]. Then, after an unnumbered chapter in the Milan edition, a dif-

---

[59] The same system is carried out to the end in the fifteenth-century Italian translation of *De vita solitaria* by Tito Vespasiano Strozzi, published in *Scelta di curiosità letterarie inedite o rare*, 170-171 (1879). There are 31 numbered chapters in the first book, 53 in the second (really 52, as there is no 48). Rotondi (see below) reports a manuscript with 33 chapters in Book I, 50 in Book II. Manuscripts in the Newberry Library, Chicago, and in the Wellesley College Library have the same plan, except that the chapters (or paragraphs) are not numbered. The Strasbourg edition of 1473 has 34 chapters (with two numbers skipped) in the first book and a sporadic numbering that is left incomplete in the second. In addition, it has an entirely independent but incomplete system of tractates, sometimes beginning at points where there are no new chapters. The Wellesley manuscript has a similar system of tractates in Book II. Most of the twenty-three manuscripts examined by Rotondi substantially agree with the Vatican manuscript, though the numbering is sometimes omitted. Two have the division into tractates or sections found in most of the printed editions. Rotondi is mistaken in saying that Vat. lat. 6394 divides the entire work into ten books. The first eight « books » agree with the corresponding chapters of other manuscripts, the ninth is the tenth chapter, the tenth is the eleventh chapter of Book II. Besides having numbered tractates and chapters, the 1501 and 1503 editions subdivide the chapters into numbered paragraphs at exactly the points where there are new paragraphs in the Vatican manuscript, but this system extends only from I, 1, 1, to I, 2, 8, inclusive.

ferent numbering sets in, beginning with 6 and running through 10. In Book II there are fifteen numbered chapters [60]. In addition, there are many paragraphs. In this edition, then, all the stages (except the last, of sections and chapters) are represented. The original chapter numbering occurs at the end of Book I and in Book II, the subdivision into paragraphs in Book II, and the consecutive numbering of the short paragraphs as chapters in Book I. Evidently the owner of a manuscript from which the edition is descended started to renumber but failed to finish the task.

The chapter and paragraph division of the Vatican manuscript is indicated by Rotondi [61]. The manuscript fails to number some of the chapters and one cannot be sure at what paragraphs they were intended to begin. This failure is reflected in other manuscripts and probably goes back to Petrarch's own copy. Rotondi's conclusions about the doubtful cases are not always correct. He would have chapter 1 begin in the middle of the Preface (p. 257 Basel). Certainly Petrarch did not intend to have it begin there but at the beginning of the treatise. Chapter 9 is skipped in the numbering. Rotondi suggests that it began at I, 6, 1, which is surely wrong, for it would make chapter 8 much too short, only half a page in the Basel edition. Perhaps there was no new chapter at all, in which case 10 should be numbered 9, as is done in some manuscripts [62].

Petrarch's division into chapters may have been something like this (I give section and page of the Basel edition of 1554, dividing the page into four parts, A, B, C, D, to give an idea of the length of each chapter; when the chapter does not coincide with the beginning of a chapter in the edition I give the first word):

---

[60] The ninth of the first book and the sixth and eleventh of the second book are skipped in the numbering.

[61] *R. Istituto Lombardo di Scienze e Lettere, Rendiconti*, Ser. II, LXIX (1936), p. 845.

[62] The manuscript fails to indicate chapters 1, 3, and 5 of Book II but does number chapters 7 and 15, though this fact escaped Rotondi's notice. There are errors in Rajna's occasional attributions of passages to chapters (pp. 650 669).

Book I			Book II		
Chap.	Sect.	Page	Chap.	Sect.	Page
1	1,1	258 C	1	1,1	285 D
2	2,1 (*Surgit*)	259 D	2	2,1	288 C
3	3,1	264 B	3	2,5	289 D
4	4,2	267 D	4	3,1	291 C
5	4,6	270 C	5	3,6	294 B
6	4,8 (*Sed quid*)	273 B	6	3,8	295 D
7	5,1	275 B	7	3,12 (*Inter nos*)	298 B
8	5,5	279 B	8	3,15	299 B
10 (9?)	6,6	284 B	9	4,1	304 A
			10	5,1	309 D
			11	6,1	311 D
			12	7,1	315 A
			13	9,1	319 C
			14	9,6	322 C
			15	10,7	328 C

Presumably the chapters were originally fairly equal in length. Yet the above table reveals wide variation. One and a half to two and a half pages of the 1554 edition seem to constitute the normal chapter. Longer ones probably contain additions. I, 5, 1, an addition suggested by the reading of Quintilian in or after 1350, is in one of the longest chapters in Book I, and I, 4, 3, also based on Quintilian, is in another fairly long chapter. II, 4, 2-3, which, as has been shown, were, at least in part, added later, fall into one of the longer chapters. Perhaps much of the rest of the section (II, 4, 4-8) was a later addition. At the end of this section Petrarch recognizes these chapters as a digression from the story of Peter the Hermit (II, 4, 1). Their common theme, as Petrarch remarks, is the criticism of the kings and nations of the West for their failure to recover Jerusalem. Another long chapter is the fourteenth, running from II, 9, 6 through 10, 6 in the edition of 1554. In 10, 1, after observing that Cabassoles perhaps has many friends, Petrarch says that the name of one, Pontius Samson, should be inserted at this point. Perhaps the word « inserendum » should not be considered particularly significant, but in any case this passage may be a later insertion. It may be just coincidence but the only two letters addressed to Samson seem to date from 1352 (*Fam.* XIV, 8; XV, 10). Perhaps the rest of the chapter is an addition, for it is a digression, from which he returns in II, 10, 2 by saying « Sed redeo ad ordinem »,. though, of course, not every digression marks an addition. II, 10, 4 deals largely with a story about Alcibiades; this is alluded to briefly in a letter of 1351 [63]. The supplements concerning Milan in II, 3, 2, 4 make the original fourth chapter a fairly long one. Perhaps the digression about women in II, 3, 3 is also supplementary. It ends with the words « Haec interfatus ad Ambrosium revertor ». II, 6, 1, which, as we have seen, contains an addition, is in a long chapter. On the whole, the chapter length seems to be more revelatory in respect to additions than the section length.

Apart from these additions which are discoverable through internal evidence, there are the changes mentioned in Petrarch's letters of 1362 (3), 1366 (8), and 1372 (10). One can, according to the point of view, say that the book was never finished, or that it was completed in 1346, or that it took final form in 1366, or even in 1361, but for 1356 there is slight evidence except Petrarch's questionable statement. It would seem that either he was in error in mentioning ten instead of twenty years or he was palliating his dilatoriness by stretching five years into ten.

In a letter to his friend Socrates (2) Petrarch writes that he has decided not to withhold the book from Philippe any longer. This clearly implies that the failure to send it previously was due to circumstances within his control and not to the lack of competent copyists. Foresti dates the letter 1360-61 and suggests that the decision took place in the latter half of 1360 on the return of Philippe from Germany and that the motive was the hope of obtaining favors for himself and Socrates [64]. This is quite possible. Could it be, however, that the reason for the decision was Philippe's prospective promotion to the patriarchate of Jerusalem, which occurred on August 18, 1361? [65]. Petrarch perhaps

---

[63] *Fam.* XI, 8. Someone (perhaps Foresti) has noted Petrarch's fondness for repeating an idea or quotation shortly after its first employment.

[64] *Op. cit.*, pp. 402-403.

[65] C. Eubel, *Hierarchia Catholica Medii Aevi* (Münster, 1898). Philippe was still acting as bishop on August 7 (U. Berlière, *Suppliques d'Innocent VI*, Rome, 1911, p. 707). The news of Socrates' death reached Petrarch August 8, as he says in a note in his Virgil quoted by Nolhac, *op. cit.*, II, p. 284. Thus Petrarch's letter to him (2) must have been written before the advancement of

felt that he had better publish the work before Philippe advanced too far and his connection with Vaucluse, the scene of the treatise, became too tenuous. In his letter to Philippe in 1366, when he finally sent the book, he goes to considerable trouble to explain why he did not take cognizance of Philippe's changed status and how unsuitable a work written about Vaucluse was to the patriarch of Jerusalem. Furthermore, 1361 is closer to 1362, when, as we shall now see, he made a serious attempt to have the treatise copied, presumably for Philippe.

Petrarch twice says, with obvious exaggeration, that he tried ten or more times to get the book copied (6, 7)[66], but the first attempt of which we know was in 1362. That attempt was due, I think, to the decision he had made the year before. In 1355 Petrarch had invited Moggio of Parma to live with him as tutor for his son and as a corrector and copyist of his works (1). In a postscript he added that he had written the letter before learning that Moggio was in the employ of Azzo da Correggio and that Moggio should do only as Azzo wished about Petrarch's offer. Moggio remained with Azzo, but it is easy to infer from later events that Moggio, in expressing his regrets, assured Petrarch that he would be glad to make transcripts of his friend's works in his spare time. So Moggio, if this interpretation is correct, was available for some six years before Petrarch decided to make use of him, at least for the copying of De vita solitaria. It was precisely in 1361 or early in 1362 that he sent the book to Moggio for transcription, for in a letter of June 10, 1362, he mentions the fact that it had been previously sent[67] and submits some correc-

---

Philippe was announced. Petrarch was in France from December, 1360, until the following March. There he might have learned about his friend's coming promotion. On his return to Milan he asked Philippe to obtain aid for him from the Pope (Var. 55; March 15, 1361). He would perhaps be more likely to make this appeal if he already knew that Philippe was to be advanced.

[66] In the letter to Boccaccio (6) this remark follows directly after the one about decimus annus and both may be far from the truth.

[67] The language used (dimisi) shows that Rajna (p. 669) is wrong in his assertion that before leaving Milan in 1361 Petrarch had entrusted (aveva commesso) the manuscript to Moggio. He sent it to Moggio at Parma before June 10, 1361, when he departed from Milan bag and baggage, or from Padua before January 10, 1362, when he left there with the intention of going to France, or soon after from Milan.

tions (3) [68]. Petrarch did not have a copy of the treatise with him when he sent these corrections and had to trust to his memory, as we can tell from his statement that he does not know the number of the chapter in which he wants a correction made [69]. Another letter of 1362 (4) contains a postscript dated December 9 in which Petrarch asks that, if the copying is finished, the manuscript be illuminated and bound, and that the copy and the original be sent him at Venice. On December 20, 1362, he reminds Moggio about his « affairs » (5) [70].

The copy that Moggio was supposed to be making was presumably intended for Philippe de Cabassoles but it was not sent to him, for we know that in December, 1365, a priest was making the copy for Philippe (6). It has, therefore, been inferred that Moggio did not make his copy at all [71]. This view I accept, though I came around to it with much reluctance. My original objections to it were: 1) the fact that Moggio *seemed* to be so near the end of his task that Petrarch gave him instructions about binding and delivery (4)—but, of course, Petrarch may merely have assumed that Moggio had nearly completed it because he had been at it so long, or may have meant his remarks as a hint; 2) the fact that Petrarch betrays no irritation toward Moggio in two later letters (*Var.* 46, 60), as might have been expected if he was left in the lurch; 3) the fact that Petrarch's own copy was not an autograph but one that was made for him (10)—and this *might* be the Moggio transcript. The compelling argument against this view is the fact that all the margins of Petrarch's copy were full of additions in 1372 (10), and most of them antedated 1366,

---

[68] Avena says that Petrarch entrusted *two* copies to Moggio. Apparently he misinterpreted Petrarch's « in utroque libro » (3). Petrarch, of course, meant the original and the copy that Moggio was supposed to be making (so too Rajna, p. 669). But see above, n. 31.

[69] As the chapters are numbered in the Vatican and other manuscripts, it is altogether likely that, in accordance with prevalent custom, they were numbered in Petrarch's copy. Another correction requested by Petrarch consisted merely of deleting a mark where he had intended to add something. This would seem to indicate that finally—but momentarily—he had decided to stop tinkering in order to get the manuscript off his hands and his mind.

[70] Petrarch does not mention *De vita solitaria* specifically, but uses *reculas*, which he had applied to this work in two preceding letters.

[71] Foresti, *op. cit.*, p. 404.

as shown in our discussion of the folio numbers of the original given in the margins of the Vatican manuscript. In fact, most of them must have antedated 1362, when Moggio was supposed to be hard at work on the new fair copy.

Another argument that has not been advanced is that Moggio did not, apparently, even act on Petrarch's request to make the corrections in the original manuscript (3), to judge from the texts of many manuscripts and the printed editions. In II, 3, 10 (*Prose*, p. 452) all the manuscripts examined and the editions (except that of 1498) have *Marsici* (or something similar) instead of the correction *Massici* [72]. Apparently Petrarch forgot about this when he got his copy back. An interesting situation confronts us in II, 4, 3 (*Prose*, p. 488). The editions have neither the original « tam nichil est animi nervorum » nor exactly the correction that Petrarch requested Moggio to make, « quasi sub celo aliquid sit pulchrius ». Instead they (and the manuscripts known to me) have « tamquam sub celo aliquid sit pulchrius » [73]. My explanation is that Petrarch, recalling his desire for a change here and the reason for it, made the alteration on the return of the copy. The slight difference in wording probably shows that he was relying on his memory and did not have before him a copy of the letter to Moggio.

[72] My reports cover the editions of 1473, 1496, 1498, 1501, 1503, 1554, 1581, 1605. This is not as formidable as it seems, for the 1501 edition appears to have been copied from that of 1496 and each of the later editions from its immediate predecessor. Altamura, on the other hand, believes that the editions of 1473, 1496, 1498, 1501, were based independently on a lost archetype, and the later editions more or less on Vat. lat. 3357. The manuscripts on which I have reports read as follows: *Marsici* Vat. lat. 3357, 4518, 4528, 6394, Pal. lat. 1730, Urb. lat. 1171, Ottob. lat. 1908, Barb. lat. 2110, Newberry; *Marsciei* Vat. lat. 4529, Pal. lat. 1596 (corrected from *Marsciei*), Urb. lat. 333; *Martinus* i. m. Vat. lat. 6394, Barb. lat. 2110; *Marcici* Wellesley. It seems rather clear that Petrarch did not discover that Moggio had failed to correct to *Massici* and that this reading in the edition of 1498 is an independent emendation. For the readings of the Vatican manuscripts on this and the following point I am indebted to my good friend, the late Mgr. E. Carusi.

[73] So Vat. lat. 3357, 4518, 4528, 4529, Pal. lat. 1596, 1730, Urb. lat. 333, Ottob. lat. 1908, Barb. lat. 2110, and most of the editions. « Tamquam sub celo sit aliquid pulcrius » is found in Vat. lat. 6394, « tamquam aliquid sub celo sit pulchrius » in Urb. lat. 1171. The editions of 1554, 1581, and 1605 omit *sit*, that of 1473 has « tanqnam (*sic*) sub celo non aliquid pulcrius ».

When Petrarch's official copy was transcribed we cannot tell, though presumably this was done early, perhaps immediately after he wrote his first draft. Nor can we tell why it was made, why he did not keep his first draft. Perhaps the transcribed copy was originally intended for Philippe and then Petrarch decided to revise the work. Some two and a half years after the unfortunate experience with Moggio Petrarch turned his official copy over to a Paduan priest to make the dedication copy. Before he found the priest he may have searched in vain for a suitable scribe, but I am inclined to believe that much of the delay is to be explained by his customary « tarditas », to use his own word (7), and by his desire for further revision. At any rate, the dedication copy was finished before December 22, 1365 (6) but was not sent until the following June. A month or more of the delay is explained by Petrarch's absence from home (he was living in Venice at the time) until January 24, 1366. When his friend Donato, who also lived in Venice, discovered that the treatise had been published, he complained that he had not received a copy[74]. But Petrarch was again away from home and so instructed his Paduan priest to send the official copy to Donato (8). Probably he had left it at Padua on his way to Pavia after sending off Philippe's copy, with the idea that the priest would make other copies if Petrarch wished him to do so. Petrarch did not need to go to the expense or the priest to the trouble of making one for Donato, who could make his own or have it made. Even so, he was not, the author warned, to make a transcript until Petrarch returned—with another addition! As Petrarch had no copy with him he must, as once before, have trusted to his memory in making the supplement, whatever it was.

In 1367 Petrarch wrote that he had once had two copies, one of which he had sent to Philippe while retaining the other (9). The retained copy was, of course, the official one which he lent to Donato. In 1372 he wrote that the head of the Camaldolensian order saw what was obviously the official copy in the house of a good friend of Petrarch's in Venice (10). Rajna's identification of this friend as the same Donato is certainly correct. Whether

---

[74] Philippe's copy had been sent off by that time (Foresti, *op. cit.*, p. 459).

Donato kept the book for five or six years [75], or borrowed it again, we cannot tell. The chances are that it stayed in Donato's hands during those years because he had facilities for getting copies made for Petrarch's friends.

Rajna showed that the Vatican manuscript was written by or for someone who was in close contact with Petrarch, preferably one who saw him frequently. He believed that this person was Donato and that the Vatican manuscript became the official copy from which others were made. There are objections to these theories, especially to the second. As to the first, Rajna was forced to admit that he was unable to see any resemblances between Donato's known handwriting and the text or the marginal notes in our manuscript. As to the second, Rajna assumed that the Vatican manuscript was not really Donato's copy but Petrarch's, and became part of his library, from which Salutati got it as he obtained others after Petrarch's death [76]. Aside from the fact that, as I think I have proved, the manuscript did not belong to Salutati, as Rajna believed, Rajna confused the copy that Donato wanted for himself and that Petrarch told him he could eventually make from the official copy being sent him (8) with an assumed new official copy which Donato was to make or have made and which would belong to Petrarch. If Donato had his own copy he probably carried it away with him to Ravenna and Ferrara, where he lived for many years after Petrarch's death [77]. As for its being a new official copy (for which there is no evidence whatever), that certainly is out of the question, for Donato showed the old official copy, with its margins full of additions, to the Camaldolite in 1371 (10). If Donato had available another copy in which the marginal supplements of the original had been incorporated into the text, he would have shown this, as being easier

[75] Foresti, *ibid.*, has established that the letter to Francesco (10) was written in 1372. In it Petrarch uses the word *nuper* of the Camaldolite's visit. Foresti refers the visit to 1371, but, of course, *nuper* is an elastic term. The fact that in 1367 Petrarch says that he has the manuscript in his possession (9) does not disprove that it was actually in Donato's hands at the moment.

[76] Rather he received copies, made at the time, but we may let that pass.

[77] He may have left Venice as early as 1372 (R. Sabbadini, *Giovanni da Ravenna*, Como, 1924, p. 47), shortly after showing Petrarch's manuscript to the Camaldolite.

to read, to the Camaldolite. Of course, a study of existing manuscripts, such as Rajna was to have made, and their relation to the Vatican manuscript may clear up the matter [78]. At the moment, the simplest solution seems to be that the Vatican copy was sent by Petrarch to one of his Florentine friends, though not Salutati, and that Donato had nothing to do with it, unless he merely supervised its transcription. To call it something rarer and more precious than an autograph seems to me sheer nonsense. It certainly would be a *rara avis* if at one and the same time it could be Donato's private copy and Petrarch's master copy, discovered in his library after his death [79].

Rajna makes much of some directions to the scribe in the Vatican manuscript. In part he misreads, in part he misinterprets them. They have nothing in common with the directions for the insertion of the Romualdus chapter. On fol. 14r we should expand the abbreviations as « R(ubrica) c(apitulum) VIII » (not « capituli »). *Rubrica* is the imperative of the verb. What we have here is a direction by the scribe to the rubricator to erase the catch words «capitulum VIII» and to write them in red letters. In other words, this direction is similar to the catch letters for initials. On fol. 1 we find « R(ubri)ca », followed by the catch title written by the scribe: « Francisci p. poete laureati vite solitarie liber primus incipit ad Philippum Cavallicensem episcopum» [80].

---

[78] Especially interesting should be a study of Laur. 26 sin. 8, copied in 1379 by Tedaldo della Casa, possibly in Padua from Petrarch's copy, as he transcribed Petrarch manuscripts there.

[79] Rotondi accepts Rajna without questioning and calls the manuscript the « codice originale », and the « ultima volontà » of the author, with all the importance of an autograph. This extravagance is scarcely justified.

[80] I have not bothered to indicate all the abbreviations. I am inclined to see significance in the abbreviation *p* for Petrarch's name. I think that it was Petrarch's custom to use this abbreviation, and that the Vatican manuscript faithfully reproduces the original, though I can quote only the following bit of evidence. In Vat. lat. 3216, at the beginning of *Psalmi poenitentiales,* there is the following heading: « Psalmi mei septem quos super miseriis propriis ipse dictavi, utinam tam efficaciter quam inculte; utrumque enim prestare studui. Franciscus P. laureatus » (Vattasso, *op. cit.,* p. 25). This heading too, obviously copied from the autograph, abbreviates the name. The language bears some similarity to that found at the end of *Bucolicum carmen* in the autograph manuscript Vat. lat. 3358 (Vattasso, p. 30). To be sure, Petrarch sometimes writes out his name in making a fair copy, as in Vat. lat. 3195 and 3359. In

As in the case of hundreds of other manuscripts, no rubricator appeared and the catch title remained, just as the catch letter *p* of the first word of text remained because nobody took the trouble to illuminate it. It was expected that the rubricator would expand the abbreviation of the poet's name, but as there was no rubricator, it was the owner presumably who deleted « p. poete » and wrote « Petrarce » above. Rajna reports that elsewhere on fol. 1 (in the middle of the Preface) occur the words « R(ubrica) capituli ». Actually it is « R(ubrica) capit(ulum) ». This may be merely a direction to the rubricator to insert a colored initial for the catch letter *q* of *Quid,* and would be a general direction to cover all following cases of the same sort, as the direction is not repeated. But it may be that the figure 1 was trimmed off and that the scribe intended the first chapter to begin here, which would, of course, be an error on his part.

As Rajna remarks, Francesco da Siena probably obtained his copy (directly or indirectly) from Cabassoles (10). No doubt others got copies from that source. The chances are that a number of copies were made from that manuscript as well as from the official copy before Petrarch added the chapter on Romualdus. It is not surprising, therefore, that it is lacking in nine out of nineteen manuscripts examined by Rotondi, in six more added by Altamura, in the Wellesley and Newberry manuscripts, in the 1498 edition, and originally in Vat. 3357, Pal. 1596, and Seville Z. 137. 20, to mention only those on which I have any information [81].

a letter written by Anastasio di Ubaldo Ghezi to Salutati in 1376 he uses the phrase « F. P. laureato poeta » of Petrarch. The letter was the copy actually sent by Anastasio, as Novati (*Epist.*, IV, p. 278) shows. Anastasio, living in Venice, was closely associated with the Paduan « school » of Petrarchists.

[81] The presence or absence of this chapter in a manuscript may be misleading. Thus at II, 1, 1 (*Prose,* p. 412) Rajna reports that the Vatican manuscript originally had *magnifice* with a marginal correction (by the author's direction, he thinks) to *premordaciter atque acriter.* The Strasbourg and Milan editions both have *magnifice,* though the former has the Romualdus chapter while the latter omits it. The Wellesley manuscript agrees with the Milan edition in both. Rajna would seem to be right in thinking that this correction, and some others that he mentions, emanated from Petrarch. There are others that probably have the same origin, e. g., *signum* substituted for *proprium* (fol. 7v; middle of I, 6, 2; *Prose,* p. 384); *celos* for *celum* (fol. 9v, end of II, 1, 10; *Prose,* p. 418). Besides the Romualdus supplement, there are only three additions that are longer

I began this paper by mentioning the esteem in which the combined manuscript was held, an esteem which at the outset I accepted without question. Let me end by noting several facts which lessen its importance. My disillusionment about it has been gradual, continuing, as new facts developed, even after I began to write this essay. The best part seems to be *De vita solitaria,* though that statement cannot be tested until and unless the critical edition projected by Rajna and left unfinished by Carrara becomes available [82]. The Vatican *Itinerarium* is full of errors, according to Lumbroso [83]. He considers it no better than either of the other two Vatican manuscripts he chose (out of pure convenience, not because of their excellence) as the basis for an interim edition. It would seem that our manuscript is several removes from the original and is just *unus multorum.* Professor Billanovich, who is preparing the *edizione nazionale* of this work, confirms this opinion. As for the first collection of letters, Rossi shows that at least two manuscripts intervened between it and Petrarch's original letters. The most that can be said about this collection of letters is that it is descended from one that was perhaps put together by one of the persons addressed [84]. Novati suggested Salutati as the collector, but there is no evidence whatever to indicate that. Piur cautiously brought out

---

than a word or two: « et sanguine rutilum ... vereque » (1, 2, 4; *Prose,* p. 310); « nec Leonardus ... solitarii » (II, 3, 12; *Prose,* p. 456); « cui appropinquare clarescere est » (II, 3, 18; *Prose,* p. 476). It is impossible to tell whether these are simply corrections of scribal omissions or later supplements suggested by Petrarch.

[82] Altamura's edition is in no sense a critical one. It is based on Vat. lat. 3357; his brief apparatus gives readings from that manuscript and the printed editions. No other manuscript is cited, though an incomplete list of manuscripts is given in the Preface, as also in his article in *La Bibliofilia,* 45 (1943), p. 61. Many readings of the Vatican manuscript are passed over, as, for example, the original reading *magnifice* mentioned in the preceding note.

[83] G. Lumbroso, *Memorie italiane del buon tempo antico* (Turin, 1889), p. 18.

[84] The most important surviving collection is one consisting of original letters by Petrarch and others to Moggio in Laur. 53, 35. Another collection is a copy of one made by Barbato da Sulmona, containing Petrarch's and Boccaccio's letters to him and his replies (Vat. Borg. 329). The presence in the manuscript of a letter of Giosia Acquaviva to the city of Sulmona shows that the manuscript was copied there, not at Naples, as Piur incorrectly states, *op. cit.,* p. 227. Piur even makes the obviously wrong suggestion that Boccaccio, not Barbato, was the collector.

Lapo da Castiglionchio as his candidate because the first letters are addressed to him. Rossi could not decide. Billanovich inclines towards Boccaccio [85]. If one must make a decision the chances favor one of the four Florentines who are the addressees of most of the letters: Lapo (three letters), Boccaccio (four), Zanobi (two), Nelli (three); these are the four who from 1348 to 1352 (when Zanobi left Florence) formed the Petrarchan «school» at Florence. One of the two non-Florentines among the recipients was Barbato da Sulmona, an old friend of Boccaccio's [86]. The original collection was made in or after 1352.

When I still had a rather high opinion of the manuscript I thought that it might have been put together over the years by some friend or admirer of Petrarch. But an examination shows that, while the early collection of letters (ending 1352) comes first, the De vita solitaria of 1366 precedes the Itinerarium of 1358. Further irreparable damage to the theory just suggested is caused by the evidence of the missing portions, as we shall soon see.

That the combined manuscript was in Florence in the four-teenth century is indicated by the following facts: 1) that part of it is there now in a collection (St. Mark's) that goes back to the fifteenth century; 2) that all but two of the letters in the first part were addressed to Florentines; 3) that, as we shall see, the entire manuscript was there at the beginning of the sixteenth century.

The Florentine and Vatican portions were still bound together in 1423 and well beyond. This may be inferred from facts supplied by a Seville manuscript (Biblioteca Colombina 84-1-5, formerly Z. 137. 20). The first part contains a fourteenth-century De vita solitaria. Then a fifteenth-century hand added the first fourteen of the letters which occur on fols. 1-8 of the Florence manuscript. As the scribe was cramped for space, he put four of the letters

<hr />

[85] G. Billanovich, Petrarca letterato, I, p. 192, n. 1.

[86] This is shown by a letter of Barbato to Petrarch published by M. Vattasso, Del Petrarca e di alcuni suoi amici (Rome, 1904), p. 14, in which he says that they were joined in a long friendship. This remark (of 1362-63) confirms Faraglia's view (Archivio storico per le provincie napoletane, IX, 1884, p. 43; Archivio storico italiano, Ser. V, III, 1889, p. 326) that Boccaccio and Bar-bato were friends from 1344 on.

on flyleaves [87]. Rossi has shown that the Seville letters were
copied from those in the Florence manuscript. The same fifteenth-
century hand added the Romualdus supplement at the end of
the text of *De vita solitaria*. Rossi did not note that this must
have been copied from the Vatican portion of our joint volume.
For at the point where the Romualdus supplement was to be
inserted the Vatican manuscript has this entry: « Hic debet scribi
pars illa: 'Sequitur hunc alius', cuius finis est: 'abiit ad eternam
vitam'. De sancto Romualdo est. Post sequitur de Petro Damiani », and at the end of the insertion: « Post [88] scribatis illud
capitulum: 'Petrus nunc occurrit', etc. ». The Seville manuscript
has this note: « Hic debet scribi et continuari id quod habes in
fine istius operis, quod incipit: 'Sequitur hunc alius', etc., cuius
finis est: 'abiit ad eternam vitam'. Postea sequitur istud capitulum: 'Petrus nunc occurrit', etc. ». The striking similarity in the
wording of the notes in the two manuscripts, coupled with the
fact that the same scribe wrote the note in the Seville manuscript
and copied the letters from the Florence manuscript, is convincing
proof that the Romualdus supplement was copied from the Vatican manuscript when it and its Florentine associate were still
bound together. The differences in the notes in the Vatican and
the Seville manuscripts are in part due to the fact that in the
Seville manuscript the supplement was written, not on an inserted leaf, but twenty-seven leaves later. As the Seville codex
contains a document of 1423 by the same hand, this date furnishes
a *terminus post quem* for the separation of our combined volume.
As a matter of fact, Rossi says the hand is of the latter part
(*inoltrato*) of the century. A *terminus ante quem* is furnished
by the presence in the Vatican manuscript of notes by Bernardo
Bembo, who died in 1519.

The Seville manuscript once belonged to a cardinal bishop
of Porto. Rossi cannot decide between Gui de Montfort and his
successor (in 1374) Pietro Corsini. The former was at one time
a friend of Petrarch, but a bitter enmity developed (*Sen.* XIII,

---

[87] I take all these statements from Rossi's edition (pp. lxii, cxxxviii),
as I have not seen the manuscript. The inferences that follow are my own.

[88] Corrected from *poste* by faint and easily overlooked deleting strokes;
this accounts for the reading *postea* of the Seville manuscript.

12), so that Petrarch's last letter to him was written in 1353, long before the publication of *De vita solitaria*. It is true, however, that as late as 1366 Petrarch states (in amazement: « illud miraculo additum ») that the pope and the bishop of Porto wanted copies of *De vita solitaria* (*Sen*. VI, 9). It is hardly likely that Montfort owned the Seville manuscript, especially since there is no reason why it should turn up in Florence after his death in 1373. On the other hand, Pietro Corsini was a famous Florentine bishop and had a fine library. By the terms of his will this was divided between his brother Filippo, who lived in Florence, and a convent near the city [89]. Additional information about the Seville manuscript kindly supplied me by Professor Billanovich confirms its ownership by Corsini. In an inventory of the cardinal's books made in 1405 there appears the following item: « Item liber Francisci Petrarche in pergameno de vita solitaria cum postibus de coreo rubeo incipit in secundo folio *gum* et finit in eodem *juda* » [90]. In the Seville manuscript fol. 2r, col. 1 begins with *gum* and col. 2 ends with *indu*. The reading *juda* in the inventory must be due to an error in copying.

Corsini died in 1405. Two or more generations later, the Florentine owner of his manuscript, as I reconstruct its history, came upon our joint manuscript and copied from it one of its collections of Petrarch letters and the Romualdus supplement. We can even tell where he saw the Florence-Rome manuscript.

As already noted, the Florence portion of our manuscript is from the library of St. Mark's, opened as a public library by Cosimo de' Medici in 1441. Rajna, looking for other Petrarch material for the missing portions, found nothing in the S. Marco inventory, presumably in the one of 1768 now in the Laurentian library. But the oldest catalogue of St. Mark's, dating from the early sixteenth century, is in Modena, though apparently it has been examined by few [91]. Now this catalogue, under the clas-

---

[89] A. Ciaconius, *Vitae et res gestae pontificum Romanorum*, I (Rome, 1630), p. 934.

[90] L. C. Barré, « Bibliothèques médiévales inédites d'après les archives du Vatican », *Mélanges d'archéologie et d'histoire*, 53 (1936), p. 364, No. 184.

[91] Mentioned in T. Gottlieb, *Ueber mittelalterliche Bibliotheken* (Leipzig, 1890), p. 199, who assigns it to the fifteenth century. I am about to publish this catalogue, at the same time identifying the existing manuscripts.

sification « In Bancho XXV ex parte occidentis 4 », has the following entry, which I have saved up as a surprise:

M. T. Ciceronis De finibus bonorum et malorum, Achademicorum, Partitiones, De caelo et mundo, De fato. Item Francisci Petrarcae Florentini De vita solitaria, Leonardi Aretini tralatio Hyconomicorum cum commento, et multae epistolae Francisci Petrarcae et Leonardi Aretini. Item Expositio super librum Martiani Capellae. Item Invectiva sive potius responsio in Leonardum Aretinum pro translatione libri Ethicorum in qua falso et ridicule carpit quendam fratrem ordinis praedicatorum. Et multa alia pulchra opuscula. In volumine satis magno rubro in papiro.

This is certainly our manuscript in its original state before the loss of the missing portions. Some items are left unmentioned, as the *Itinerarium,* presumably hiding behind the « multa alia pulchra opuscula ». But *De vita solitaria* is there, and the letters of Petrarch, though grouped together, and above all the « Expositio super librum Martiani Capellae », which is identical with the title in the Florence manuscript of today. The Cicero material must have covered the first 107 missing leaves; the translation of the *Economics* and presumably Bruni's letters were on fols. 153-174; the invective against Bruni took its place with « alia pulchra opuscula » on fols. 191-237.

The most recent work mentioned is the invective directed against Leonardo Bruni for his attack on the mediaeval version of Aristotle's *Ethics.* This must be, to judge from the description (« sive potius responsio »), the earlier and milder of two such invectives, that by Alphonso Garcia de Cartagena, written about 1430 but not available to Bruni and other Italians until 1436 [92].

The presence of this late material is disillusioning but should not cause us to lose all faith in our manuscript. It still remains true that *De vita solitaria* was transcribed in the fourteenth century and, to all appearances, directly from Petrarch's own copy.

The Modena catalogue seems to have been compiled about 1500. It contains some printed books as well as manuscripts. Unfortunately, their descriptions are too brief to identify the

---

[92] A. Birkenmajer, « Der Streit des Alonso von Cartagena mit Leonardo Bruni Aretino », *Beiträge zur Geschichte der Philosophie des Mittelalters,* XX, 5 (1922), p. 129.

editions and, to be safe, we have to assume that a particular copy belongs to the earliest edition. Three books seem not to have been published before 1496: Hugo on the *Psalms* (Hain 8972); Pico, *Heptaplus*, etc. (Hain 12992); *Cornu Copiae* (*Gesamt-katalog* 7571). One was apparently printed first in 1497, a Greek book called Urbanus, listed among grammars and dictionaries. This I take to be Hain 16098, the author of which is Urbano Bolzanio, according to the British Museum catalogue. One book may actually be as late as 1499, if the *Vocabularium* in the same list is Musurus' *Etymologicum magnum*, first printed in that year. The latest manuscript items seem to be works of Savonarola, and of these the most recent was written in 1496. One Greek manuscript in the list (VII, Occid. 6) can be identified as a Laurentian manuscript, Marc. 314, which was received by the monastery library in 1497 [93].

In later catalogues of S. Marco the complete manuscript no longer appears. It must have been taken apart shortly after the catalogue in which it is described was compiled, i.e., about 1500. Bernardo Bembo could have obtained his portion of it, not, as Rajna thought, around 1475-80, when we know that he was in Florence, but in the last twenty years of his life, which ended in 1519. It was he who « discovered » that his manuscript was copied by Petrarch, and this misinformation was gladly passed on to posterity by Fulvio Orsini, whose claims about some of the manuscripts he owned still confound scholars. Sixty years ago the claim of Bembo and Orsini was partly deflated, in that only the corrections were thenceforth called Petrarchan. Rajna let out a little more air by rejecting even this claim but at the same time puffed up the manuscript by calling it a master copy made for Petrarch and by installing it in the noble library of Coluccio Salutati. Finally, I have tried to show the unlikelihood of these theories. It remains for the future editor of *De vita solitaria* to determine, by a study of all the existing manuscripts, just what consideration this, the most valuable part of the combined manuscript, deserves.

---

[93] E. Rostagno and N. Festa in *Studi italiani di filologia classica*, I (1893), p. 182.

CHAPTER VIII

PETRARCH'S ACQUAINTANCE WITH CATULLUS, TIBULLUS, PROPERTIUS

In a valuable article Bosco reveals a wholesome scepticism towards the view of Nolhac and others that every reference to an ancient author by Petrarch indicates that the great humanist owned a manuscript of that author [1]. That his scepticism goes too far in the case of at least two authors I shall try to show in this chapter. Let us begin with the clearest case, that of Propertius. If Bosco had been familiar with a paper of mine published over fifty years ago he could not have maintained his attitude about Propertius [2]. One cannot hold that Petrarch did not have a complete Propertius just because he cites him so rarely. Petrarch possessed manuscripts of many authors that he cites rarely or not at all, as for example, Josephus and some of the works in the Troyes manuscript of Cicero and in Vat. lat. 2193, both of which he owned [3]. Bosco's principle that one cannot draw final conclusions, positive or negative, from Petrarch's citations or lack of them is admirable, but his application of that principle is in some cases open to question. That Petrarch was not a great admirer of Propertius we can admit. That he read through the poems hastily, perhaps only once, we can also admit. Propertius did not belong to the small group of Petrarchan favorites, which we discussed in chapter VI.

Let us see what the facts about Petrarch and Propertius are. On November 16, 1375, Coluccio Salutati wrote to Gaspare Broaspini of Verona: « Si prece vel precio Propertium de biblio-

[1] U. Bosco in *Giornale storico della letteratura italiana*, CXX (1942), p. 65.
[2] « The Manuscripts of Propertius », *Classical Philology*, VI (1911), p. 282.
[3] See also chapter VI.

theca illius celeberrimi viri, Petrarce inquam,... haberi posse con-
fidis, vel ut meus sit vel ut exemplari queat, deprecor ut pro-
cures » [4]. He evidently did not get his copy at once, for on July
13, 1379, he wrote to Lombardo della Seta, who had charge of
Petrarch's library after the poet's death: « De Propertio autem
nichil aliud nisi quod scribis expecto, ut videlicet exemplatum
habeam » [5]. From this letter we see that Lombardo was intending
to send a copy of Petrarch's Propertius to Coluccio. We may
assume that the intention was soon carried out, as Coluccio
begins quoting Propertius in 1381. The manuscript that Coluccio
owned is still in existence and, known as F, is one of the important manuscripts of that author (Laur. 36, 49). There is no question about its ownership, for Coluccio wrote his name in it.
But is this the manuscript that Lombardo sent and was it copied
from Petrarch's? The answer is a decided affirmative. In the
letter to Lombardo just mentioned, Coluccio speaks of a manuscript of Petrarch's *De viris illustribus* which Lombardo is having
copied for him. This manuscript is now in the Vatican (Ottob.
lat. 1883). Lombardo himself copied into it his own supplement
to Petrarch's unfinished composition and also served as technical corrector throughout. At the end is the date: « transcrip-
tus MCCCLXXX die XV novembris », followed by Coluccio's
inscription of ownership. The Laurentian Propertius was copied
by the same hand that copied the Vatican *De viris illustribus*.
Furthermore, Lombardo served as technical corrector for this
manuscript too. The third hand in both codices is that of Coluccio. There can be no possible doubt that Petrarch had a manuscript of Propertius and that F was copied from it.

There is still more evidence, unnecessary though it is, to
show that Petrarch owned a Propertius. As is well known, most
of his books passed into the Visconti library at Pavia. Many of
them have been identified in an inventory of the Pavia library
made in 1426; in it we find this notice [6]: « Monobiblos Propersii

---

[4] *Epistolario di Coluccio Salutati*, ed. F. Novati, I (Rome, 1891), p. 221.
[5] *Ibid.*, p. 331.
[6] G. d'Adda, *Indagini storiche, artistiche e bibliografiche sulla libreria vi-
scontea-sforzesca del Castello di Pavia*, I (Milan, 1875), No. 48. I examined
the original manuscript catalogue at the Brera in Milan and found d'Adda's

Aureli Naute volumen parvum in assidibus et fundo corii albi in carminibus. Incipit Cinthia prima suis, et finitur ossa vehuntur aquis ». If this were a Virgil or a Cicero, we could not be so sure that this was Petrarch's manuscript, but when we consider the scarcity of Propertius manuscripts at that time we can confidently assume that it was his. The title agrees with that in F, except for the misspelling *Propersii*. The reading *vehuntur aquis* is found only in F of the major manuscripts. The book is mentioned again in a 1459 inventory of the Pavia library, but disappeared thereafter. In 1518 an inventory of the library at Blois, to which the Pavia collection had been transferred, was finished, but the Propertius does not appear in it [7].

In my paper on the manuscripts of Propertius I proved that Coluccio's manuscript (F) was the granddaughter of A, an incomplete manuscript now in Leiden (Voss. lat. in Oct. 38). This manuscript was written in France in the thirteenth century. I suggested that A might have been the copy which Richard de Fournival of Amiens mentioned about 1250. The title he gives is « Propertii Aurelii Naute liber monobiblos ». A has « Incipit monobiblos propercii aurelii naute ad tullum ». This striking similarity, especially in the use of the certainly authentic *monobiblos*, which is not found in the oldest manuscript (N), compels a belief that A is either the manuscript which Richard had or consulted or else a close copy.

Some of the books that Richard describes in his *Biblionomia*, an ideal classification system for libraries, can be identified in the catalogue of the Sorbonne made in 1338, to which they were presented by Gérard d'Abbeville, who was archdeacon in Amiens (where Richard lived) in 1262 and who died in Paris in 1271 or soon after. Sabbadini notes that Gérard had three great rarities: Cicero's *Epist. fam.*, Iunius Nipsus, and « cimelio assai più prezioso », the elegies of Tibullus [8]. All three of these are in Rich-

report correct. See too Elisabeth Pellegrin, *La bibliothèque des Visconti et des Sforza ducs de Milan, au XVe siècle* (Paris, 1955), p. 83, A. 48.

[7] G. Mazzatinti in *Giornale storico della letteratura italiana*, I (1883), p. 53; H. Omont, *Anciens inventaires et catalogues de la Bibliothèque Nationale* (Paris, 1921). I consulted the original manuscript in Vienna.

[8] R. Sabbadini, *Le scoperte dei codici latini e greci ne' secoli XIV e XV*, II (Florence, 1914), p. 33.

ard's list. Let us compare the descriptions of the last two. Richard has: « Anitii Manlii Severini Boetii liber de agrimensura. Item Iunii Moderati liber de eadem. Item practica geometrie et stereometrie sub demonstratione. In uno volumine » [9]. The Sorbonne catalogue reads: « In uno volumine geometria Boecii, agrimensura Iunii » [10]. Richard: « Albii Tybullii liber epigrammaton »; the Sorbonne catalogue: « Epymabaton Albii Tybullii elegoagraphi » [11]. The word *epigrammata* (misspelled in the Sorbonne catalogue) is found only in these two places as applied to the elegies of Tibullus. It may have been suggested by the word *epigramma* in the *Vita* of Tibullus and by the title of Martial's epigrams, which Richard also had and for which he used the title *liber epygrammaton*. The term *elogiographus* in the Sorbonne catalogue attracts attention. Richard did not use it of Tibullus but of the *Tristia* of Ovid, which he called *libri elegyographi*. This word clearly is borrowed from the *Vita* of Tibullus. There are other authors whose titles in the two lists are much alike [12].

But what has Propertius to do with all this? His name does not appear in the Sorbonne catalogue—or does it? It is true that no one has found it heretofore. But what of this: « Propicius de virtutibus, ex legato eiusdem. Incipit in 2⁰ fol. *surgat,* in pen. *nec maii* »? [13]. Propicius is no ancient or mediaeval author that I can recall. Remember that A has the spelling Propercius. But « de virtutibus » gives us pause, as it is inexplicable. In the margin of A opposite the first line are the words « heroys prima » in a fourteenth-century hand. This is in an erasure of something which might conceivably have been the inspiration for « de virtutibus ». Or is it a corruption of A's « ad

---

[9] L. Delisle, *Le cabinet des manuscrits de la Bibliothèque Nationale,* II (Paris, 1874), p. 526, No. 44.

[10] *Ibid.,* III (1881), p. 68, No. 49.

[11] *Ibid.,* II, p. 531, No. 115; III, p. 68, No. 35.

[12] On Richard de Fournival see A. Birkenmajer, *Bibljoteka Ryszarda de Fournival* (Krakow, 1922). He thinks that Richard based his list on Gérard's library.

[13] Delisle, III, p. 62. Dr. Lester K. Born kindly checked the reading in the original manuscript catalogue (now in the Bibliothèque Nationale, N. a. l. 99) and found Delisle's report correct in every detail.

tullum »? But sceptical as this phrase may have left the reader as to the identification, his scepticism should vanish when it is pointed out to him that « Propicius » began with *surgat* on the second folio and that the second folio of A begins with this identical word! That is too much for coincidence. The first words on the penultimate folio of the Sorbonne manuscript were *nec maii*. The end of A is lost, but these words do not occur in Propertius. The penultimate folio must have been in the last elegy, which is 102 lines long. The words *nec maii* may be an error for the following words in the last poem: *nec mea* in vss. 45 and 62 or *nec matrem* in vs. 89. The last seems to be out of the question as it is too near the end of the poem and one would have to assume that the last leaf contained something other than Propertius. The same is true of vs. 62. The existing part of A generally has 24 lines to the page (25 twice, 23 once), and so the penultimate folio would begin over 48 lines before the end, i.e., before vs. 54. This leaves vs. 45 as a possible first line of the next to the last leaf. The word after *nec mea* is *mutatum*; its first two strokes might explain *ii* of *maii*. Vs. 93 would begin the last leaf, which would therefore contain the last ten lines of the book.

We can attempt to restore the rest of A from the sixteen leaves we have, though the variation in number of lines per page creates a difficulty. There is also the possibility of a few omitted lines, to judge from F, which omits lines at II, 14, 2; III, 17, 41; IV, 11, 30. But the first of these, being supplied in the margin by the technical corrector, must have been in the exemplar and therefore in A. A blank space for the third was left in F, which might indicate either a similar situation in his exemplar or a note by a reader that a line was missing. Taking 24 lines to the page and assuming that the two lines were omitted in A, we reach IV, 11, 29 as the first line of the penultimate folio. This is 16 lines before IV, 11, 45, at which we arrived by a different method. The difference can be made up by assuming sixteen pages of 25 lines each, not an unreasonable assumption when we note that there are two such pages in the first gathering, and that the missing portion covered nine gatherings.

The « Propicius » was not given by Gérard d'Abbeville but by Etienne d'Abbeville. This causes no difficulty because Etienne was canon at Amiens. His books came to the Sorbonne in 1288 [14]. If the Leiden Propertius was at the Sorbonne between 1288 and 1338, Petrarch could easily have obtained a copy when he was in Paris in 1333 [15]. One further bit of history about A. In the sixteenth century it belonged to Paul Petau, who obtained many manuscripts from French libraries, especially Fleury. One of the other libraries was the Sorbonne, for at least four of his manuscripts are definitely known to have come from that source [16].

I have said that F was the granddaughter of A. Without repeating in detail the evidence for the relation of A and F that I submitted in my earlier article, I shall give two examples out of eleven. At I, 3, 33 A has the right reading *ocellos*, but written in such a way that it can easily be taken for *ocellis* (as Baehrens did); this is the reading of F. In I, 14, 19 A has the correct *arabium*, but so written that it can easily be taken for *arabtum* (as Baehrens did); F has *arabtum*. There are other passages where a correction in A is so badly made that it is easily overlooked. In fact, Baehrens did overlook three instances. Here is one example: in I, 6, 19 AF have *securas*, which A corrected to *secures*; Baehrens, not noting the correction, reports A's reading as *securas*.

In some instances F has a better reading than A, a situation which at first thought seems to invalidate my contention that F is the granddaughter of A. I would explain some of these superior readings as emendations by Petrarch. When A and N (Wolfenbüttel, Gud. 224, the oldest and best manuscript of Pro-

---

[14] Delisle, *op. cit.*, II, p. 174.

[15] P. de Nolhac, *Pétrarque et l'humanisme*, ed. 2 (Paris, 1907) I, p. 39, makes the suggestion that Petrarch visited the library of the Sorbonne in that year. Petrarch's copy of Plato's *Phaedo* (Paris, Bibl. Nat. lat. 6567 A) is a direct copy of a manuscript still in existence which was given by Gérard to the Sorbonne (Paris, Bibl. Nat. lat. 16581), as neatly shown by L. Minio-Paluello in *Rendiconti dell'Accademia Nazionale dei Lincei*, Ser. VIII, Vol. IV (1949), p. 107. As Minio dates the writing of Petrarch's copy between 1300 and 1350, it too may have been transcribed at the time of Petrarch's visit in 1333.

[16] K. A. de Meyier, *Paul en Alexandre Petau en de geschiedenis van hun handschriften* (Leiden, 1947), pp. 118 ff.

pertius) agree in a wrong reading it is obvious that a right reading in F was due, not to transmission, but to emendation, e.g., I, 8, 17 *quodcumque* AN *quocumque* F. Such emendations I attribute to Petrarch. Other possible emendations of his may perhaps be discerned in the following readings in F: I, 2, 15 *leucupis* A *leucippis* FN; 8, 2 *sim* A *sum* FN; 12, 4 *venero* A *veneto* FN; 8 *amore* A *amare* FN; 15, 6 *quere* A *querere* FN; 42 *blandicus* A *blanditiis* FN; 16, 2 *vota* A *nota* FN; 18, 15 *fluor* A *furor* FN; 20, 17 *pegase* AN *p(er)agasse* F (I suggest that Petrarch wrote *p(ro)* *a* above, which F misread; the correct reading is *Pagase*, which Petrarch could have known from Ovid, Pliny, or Mela); II, 1, 62 *patruis* A *patriis* FN. It seems quite likely that Petrarch corrected the spelling *Propercius* in the title (so A) to *Propertius* (so F) and also indicated that a verse was missing at IV, 11, 30, where F left a line blank.

I have said that Lombardo was the technical corrector in F. There is good reason to believe that nearly everything he wrote in F was copied from Petrarch's manuscript. Thus many of the variants which he added were, I believe, the suggested emendations of Petrarch. Here are some of them [17]: I, 3, 8 *incubus* F *al' manibus* F²; 20 *innachidos* A *umachidos* F *al' inachidos* F²; 9, 19 *tigies* F *al' tigres* F² (A's *tigres* could be taken for *tigies*); 10, 2 *conctius* F *al' conscius* F²; *12, 19 *Minimeque* F *al' me neque* F² (probably Petrarch's manuscript had *Mi neque*, as in AN, above which Petrarch wrote *me* as a substitute for *Mi*, thus leading to F's error); 13, 15 *vintum* F *al' vinctum* F²; 17, 20 *Ultius* F *al' ultimus* F²; *21, 6 *ruis* AF *al' tuis* F²; 7 *perces(er)is* F *al' per cesaris* F²; *22, 10 *ferulis* AF *al' fertilis* F²N; II, 1, 38 *meneaciden* F *al' meneciaden* F²; 4, 13 *dentebus* F *al' dentibus* F²; *23 *mirantur* N *murantur* F *al' monstratur* F²; *8, 23 *cum* NF *al' cura* F²; 15, 5 *viclatis* F *al' nudatis* F²; 31 *amantes* F

---

[17] Alice Catherine Ferguson, *The Manuscripts of Propertius* (Chicago dissertation, 1934), pp. 40 ff. I have marked with an asterisk those passages where the emendation is not successful (thereby betraying that it is an emendation) in the sense that it does not agree either with NA or with modern editions. Of course emendation is not ruled out where there is such agreement. Even the worst emenders may occasionally be right! I have also quoted L, a manuscript which seems to be independently derived from Petrarch's.

al' arantes F^2; 16, 23 *semucta* F *al'* seiuncta F^2; 17, 9 *viat* F *al'* vivat F^2; 18, 9 *budis* F *al'* undis F^2; 19, 28 *Vehuntur* F *al'* venturum F^2; 22, 42 *gemos* F *al'* geminos F^2; *24, 36 *eheu* NLF *al'* heu F^2; *25, 16 *licore* LF *vel* liquore F^2; 26, 25 *audisse* F *al'* odisse F^2; *26, 39 *ratis argo* N *ratis ergo* LF *rudis argo* i. m. F^2; *43 *isdem* N *his'am* F *hys'am* L *hisdem* i. m. F^2; *27, 7 *caput* NF *vel capiti* F^2L; 29, 7 *lacivior* F *al'* lascivior F^2; 25 *Ostipui* F *al'* obstupui F^2; 32, 3 *qui* F *al'* quid F^2; III, 1, 27 *simoenta* F *vel simeunta* F^2 (according to the available indexes, Petrarch does not quote the word, but the text of his Virgil and of the accompanying Servius always has *simoenta* or *symoenta*: Aen. I, 618; III, 302; V, 261, 634, 803; X, 60); 3, 22 *cumba* F *cimba* written above F^2 (in III, 18, 24 the text has *cimba*); *8, 27 *Odi ego que* NL *Audi ego que* F *al'* odi ego quos F^2; *9, 57 *factor* N *faustor* FL *al'* fautor F^2; *11, 11 feros NL *fexos* F *al'* fessos F^2; *61 *Curius* N *Durius* LF *al'* Curcius F^2; 61 *lacivus* F *al'* lacunis F^2; *63 *Colclitis* N *Colitis* L *Collitis* F *vel coclitis* F^2; 68 *hospore* F *vel bosphore* F^2; 13, 11 *Motrana* F *matrona* i. m. F^2; 51 *lumina* LF *limina* F^2N; *58 *numquam* LF *al'nusquam* F^2N; 14, 5 *velodis* F *vel cis* F^2; 16, 29 *Hanc* F *al'* aut F^2; *18, 24 *troci* N *torci* F *vel torvi* F^2; 20, 17 *pignita* F *vel pignera* F^2; *21, 22 *Istmos* N *Ismos* L *Iomos* F *al'* ionios F^2; *24, 6 *esses* NL *essem* F *vel esset* F^2; *25, 5 *ista* NF *vel ita* F^2; *IV, 1, 16 *sollempnis* NL *solemus* F *vel solemnius* F^2; 37 *verum* F *vel nomen* F^2; 3, 4 *lictera* F *litura* i. m. F^2; *61 *agnis* NF *al'* anguis F^2; 4, 34 *tati* N *taci* L *rati* F *al'* tatii F^2; 48 *terra* F *vel terga* F^2; 69 *famille* F *al'* faville F^2; 5, 38 *panes* F *al'* pavet F^2; 39 *retentes* F *al'* recentes F^2; 40 *alterius* LF *vel alternis* F^2N; *50 *acra* NLF *al'* era F^2; *6, 50 *pictos* NL *pintos* F *pervictos al'* F^2; *50 *experiere* N *expirare* F *experiare* i. m. F^2; 86 *Iniat* F *al'* iniciat F^2; 7, 36 *infidus* F *al'* insidiis F^2; 8, 51 *resumpniat* F *al'* resupinat F^2; *9, 5 *stagnabant* NL *stanuabant* F *stagnabat* i. m. F^2; 5 *fulmine* LF *flumine* i. m. F^2; 11 *certa* F *serta* i. m. F^2; *10, 21 *inducto* NL *inducio* F *al'* induto F^2; *23 *tolumni* N *columni* L *columpni* F *al'* colo(n)ni F^2; *27 *E veii* N *E neii* F *Et neii* F^2 *Et veii* i. m. F^2L; 37 *tolinum* F *al'* tolumni F^2; *43 *virgatis* NL *nigratis* F *al'* Iurgatis F^2; 11, 23 *Sinciphe* F *al'* Sisiphe F^2. In one case Lombardo seems to have been so sure that Petrarch's marginal suggestion was right

that he made the change in the text instead of giving the reading as a marginal variant: III, 15, 22 *Invocet* N *Innocet* LF
Imictet F².

Even the scribe of F entered an occasional variant that may
be attributed to Petrarch, thus anticipating Lombardo: I, 15, 35
virabas A *vitabas* F *al' iurubas* F¹N; II, 29, 36 *voluntan* corrected
at once to *voluntatis*, then *vel tan* written above the *ta* F¹ (*voluntatis* N *volutantis* L; it looks as if Petrarch meant to emend *voluntatis* to *volutantis*); III, 9, 8 *iugo* NLF *vel rogo* F¹; IV, 6, 65
quantus NL *cantus* F *vel tantus* F¹; 10, 30 *metunt* N *metum* L
met ū F *vel metit* F¹.

Lombardo wrote several comments in the margin; some of
these will instantly be recognized as in the style of Petrarch, who
was probably originally responsible for all of them: II, 19, 9-10
« Illic te nulli poterunt corrumpere ludi Fanaque, peccatis plurima
causa tuis ». On the first line Lombardo added « quasi non », obviously intended for *nulli* [18]. On the next he wrote (but Petrarch
surely composed) « sub religionis obtentu per sepe vanitant mulieres ». On III, 1, 22, where the poet expresses his belief that
after death his fame will be doubled, Lombardo's terse comment is
« proprie ». At III, 13, 59-60 « Proloquar (atque utinam patriae
sim verus aruspex): Frangitur ipsa suis Roma superba bonis »,
Lombardo's comment on *verus* is « imo falsus ». On vs. 63 he
identifies the speaker as « divinatrix cassandra ». At III, 25, 11
Lombardo writes « imprecatio », which describes the content of
the verse. At IV, 1, 54, in comment on the prophecy that Rome
will spring from the ashes of Troy, Lombardo writes « vere ais
poeta ». A few lines later (58), where Propertius says he is inadequate to the task, the comment is «modeste». Two lines below,
when the poet proclaims that the little talent he has will be at the
service of his country, Petrarch's comment (via Lombardo) reads
«Romanum se ostendit propertius». At IV, 3, 37 « E tabula pictos
ediscere mundos », the comment reads « mappa mundi ». On IV,
4, 53 *te* is explained by a superscript « tatium » and *quem* by

---

[18] F has *nudi,* with *nulli* written above by a late hand. Evidently we can
infer that F wrote *nudi* through error, that his exemplar had *nulli.* Similarly
in the next line F had *Favaque,* corrected by Coluccio; the exemplar must have
had the right reading.

« romulum scilicet ». Similarly the note is merely « Iulius cesar » on IV, 6, 59, where Caesar is mentioned in the text, « pasiphe » at IV, 7, 58 to explain « lignea monstra bovis », « hercules » at I, 13, 23, I, 20, 16, IV, 9, 1, « forum bovarium » at IV, 9, 20 incorrectly explaining « pascua vestra forum », and « marcellus » to explain « Claudius » in IV, 10, 39. At IV, 5, 31, where the *lena* is giving advice: « Si tibi forte comas vexaverit, utilis ira », the comment reads « monitus versutissime lene ». Some lines later (53-57), in the same context, the *lena* advises the girl to consider the gold, not the hand it comes from, and to disregard the verses of poets who come with empty hands. Here the comment reads « proprie ais; in exitium propera, callida lena ». Petrarch was not one to have poetry suffer by comparison with wealth. At IV, 7, 1-2, where Propertius says that death does not end all, that the shades escape from the funeral pyre, the comment is « nota post mortem non interire animam, vel aliquid superesse ». At I, 1, 9 the note is merely « adverte ». At IV, 8, 3, where F omitted two words but left a space, we cannot be sure whether Lombardo's comment « non potuit legi in exeplari (*sic*) hoc quod deficit » is his own or Petrarch's.

How Petrarchan some of these comments are may be seen by glancing at the few examples quoted by Nolhac of notes of Petrarch's found in his manuscripts [19]. For *proprie* and *vere* cf. I, p. 238; II, pp. 73 (*quam proprie et quam vere*), 90, 98, etc.; for *modeste*, II, p. 90; for *ais*, II, p. 222. On the immortality of the soul, there is a note in his Cassiodorus (II, p. 200).

Petrarch's quotations of Propertius are extremely few. The only one that seems to occur in the published works—in the letter to Virgil (*Fam.* XXIV,4,9-10)—was probably taken indirectly from Donatus. Yet even here his manuscript of Propertius may have had a share. N and L wrongly have *Nescio quod* (II, 34, 66), and therefore presumably Petrarch's manuscript had the same. F has *Nescio quid*, with Donatus. Did Petrarch use the latter to correct his manuscript of the elegiac poet?

---

[19] It would be well worth while to publish all of the notes that Petrarch entered in his manuscripts.

Nolhac also found references to Propertius in Petrarch's notes to his Virgil [20]. At *Aen*. IV, 409 Servius comments on the short vowel in *fervere* and gives examples from Horace, including *cave*. Petrarch adds: « Sic utitur Propertius l. 2° epᵃ 11 et sepe alibi » [21]. He has in mind II, 13, 41 *cave*. This is the eleventh poem in F (the copy of Petrarch's manuscript, it should be remembered), but the tenth in N. Furthermore the poems may actually have been numbered in Petrarch's manuscript, at least in part. They are numbered in A, and F has some indications that the numbers were in its exemplar. The title of III, 2 is *Ad librum secundum* (sc. *capitulum*); of III, 3, *Tertium* (sc. *capitulum*) *somnium propertii*; of III, 4, *De triumpho quartum capitulum*; of III, 11, *De imperiis feminarum contra*, in which the meaningless *contra* is a corruption of *9ᵃ*, exactly the form regularly found in A. *Contra*, of course, can be abbreviated by a reversed *c* (similar to *9*), with a superscript *a*. In fact, Petrarch's own *9ᵃ* looks like *contra* (fol. 2v of his Virgil). But Bosco thinks that Petrarch's reference may have come from a lost commentator of Priscian whom Petrarch mentions elsewhere. The facts I have presented make this suggestion unnecessary.

Petrarch also quotes a line about Maecenas (III, 9, 1) which Bosco suggests he got from a lexicon or a gloss [22]. Again this is made unnecessary by the overwhelming evidence already presented. And the argument from supposedly lost works is always weak in the case of writers of the late Middle Ages and the Renaissance. Furthermore, if Petrarch had a Propertius—and we have proved that he did—he would have used it instead of a secondary source. That is one of the notable characteristics of the humanists. Yet though we are certain that Petrarch had a manuscript of the elegiac poet, we cannot accept Nolhac's sug-

---

[20] *Op. cit.*, I, p. 171.

[21] *Epᵃ* stands for *epistola* (so of Seneca on fol. 66v of the Virgil), for which Petrarch also uses *epl'a* or *epl'*. Nolhac, not knowing how to expand the abbreviation, avoids the issue by abbreviating still more, to *e.*, presumably for *elegia*!

[22] Actually Petrarch does not quote this line for information about Maecenas, as Bosco supposed, but to add *eques, equitis* to the similar nouns listed by Servius.

gestion that but for Petrarch Propertius might have been lost to the modern world [23].

Phillimore has listed a dozen or more possible imitations of Propertius in the *Africa* and other Latin poems of Petrarch [24]. At least a few of these seem significant, especially now that we know that Petrarch owned and read Propertius [25].

On the question of Petrarch's acquaintance with Tibullus there is far less evidence. There are no direct quotations at all. Nolhac rejects various vague reminiscences that have been pointed out and almost concludes that Petrarch knew Tibullus only by name [26]. He finds, however, one reminiscence in particular which he cannot explain away. In the tenth eclogue Petrarch alludes to Tibullus in a phrase borrowed from the first poem of the ancient poet. As this phrase occurs in florilegia containing Tibullus, Nolhac decides that Petrarch had such a florilegium. Sabbadini, however, insisted that he must have used a complete Tibullus because the florilegia do not mention the name of Delia, to whom Petrarch alludes in his verses [27]:

> Longa brevi stringens aderat suspiria cantu,
> Paupertas quem tuta iuvet, quem Delius ardor.

But Petrarch probably got Delia's name from Ovid, *Am.* II, 9, just as he got the tone of the first line from Horace, *Carm.* I, 33. The phrase *brevi cantu* may have been suggested by the poems of Propertius, with whom Tibullus is constantly associated, or from the brevity of the selections in the florilegium. As a matter

---

[23] *Op. cit.*, I, p. 172. He makes the impossible suggestion that Petrarch owned N.

[24] In Robinson Ellis, *Catullus in the XIVth Century* (London, 1905), p. 29.

[25] Of no significance is the similarity between *Epist. met.* III, 32, 40, « fortune scandere culmen », and Propertius II, 10, 23, « laudis conscendere culmen », for N and F read *carmen,* and that is what Petrarch's manuscript must have had. Wilkins believes that *Rime* I, 35 (*Son.* 28) is derived from Propertius I, 18 (E. H. Wilkins, *The Making of the « Canzoniere » and Other Petrarchan Studies,* Rome, 1951, p. 295). There is much similarity of feeling and situation but less of language. The closest parallels are Petrarch's *deserti campi* for *deserta loca* and *aspre vie* for *inculto tramite.*

[26] *Op. cit.*, I, pp. 173 ff.

[27] In a review of Smith's *Tibullus,* in *Rivista di filologia classica.* XLII (1914), p. 351.

of fact, Nolhac's guess (that is all that it was) was a good one
for it can be shown beyond doubt that Petrarch had a florilegium [28]. In the *Epistolae metricae* (I, 7, 3 ff.) he writes:

Nec tibi ficta loquar, mihi nam loquor: Absit inanis
Gloria, nil cupio, contenta est vita paratis.
Hoc primum placitis mecum concordat egestas
Aurea federibus, non sordida nec gravis hospes.
Si libet, exigui fines michi servet agelli
Angustamque domum et dulces fortuna libellos.
Cetera secum habeat vel, si libet, omnia nullo
Auferat hinc strepitu; sua sunt. Non rura requiro
Divitiasque patris, pondus grave celsa petenti
Vinclaque dura animi et cunctorum alimenta malorum.

The first lines repeat the familiar thought of Tibullus I, 1, but
the striking parallelism is in the words « requiro Divitiasque patris,
pondus grave ». With this compare the florilegia of Tibullus
(I, 1, 41; III, 3, 11):

Non ego divitias patrum fructusve requiro.
Quid prodesse potest pondus grave divitis auri?

Every word of Petrarch's is a metrical tag taken from a florilegium. I say florilegium, for the complete manuscripts of Tibullus
do not have the phrase *pondus grave* in this order and position:

Nam grave quid prodest pondus mihi divitis auri.

The seventh epistle was apparently written in 1338 [29]. Petrarch is
likely to have come upon his florilegium in France (where, as
I demonstrated in my article on Tibullus in the florilegia, the original was put together and most of the copies were made) between 1333 and 1338.

Bosco makes a good point when he asks what reason is there
to believe that Petrarch got a copy of the complete Catullus
known to have been in Verona when he did not obtain a copy
of the complete Tibullus from that city. But there is a false

[28] The following discussion is repeated from my article « Tibullus in the
Mediaeval Florilegia », *Classical Philology*, XXIII (1928), pp. 172-173.

[29] Diana Magrini, *Le epistole metriche di Francesco Petrarca* (Rocca S. Casciano, 1907), p. 84.

premise in assuming that there was a Tibullus manuscript in Verona. That assumption is based on the presence of quotations in Guglielmo da Pastrengo, Petrarch's Veronese friend, and in a florilegium made at Verona in 1329 (CLXVIII [155]). The Verona anthology, however, belongs to the tradition of the other florilegia. It has the title found only in them: « Tibulus in libro de felicitate pauperis vite ». It exhibits the arbitrary changes which characterize this whole group of florilegia, changes made to allow the excerpts to stand by themselves: *Ne* for *Nec* in I, 9, 23, *Cogit* for *Iussit* in I, 9, 28. It is true that it has two lines (I, 4, 21-22) not found in the other florilegia, but several of the others too have lines not appearing in their brother anthologies. In those two lines there is the characteristic change of text: *freta summa* becomes *longa freta*. The two quotations from Petronius in the Verona compilation were taken from the same florilegium as Tibullus, as shown by the reading *facit* for *fecit*.

As to Guglielmo da Pastrengo, he paraphrases a passage (I, 7, 29-36) not found in the known florilegia. Nevertheless it is possible that he quoted from a florilegium. He changes word order and phraseology in the same fashion as the florilegia. He quotes the *Laus Pisonis* (known to us only from the florilegia, except for one complete manuscript now lost) and in fact calls it the « Cathalectoim » of Lucan. As the florilegia alone have the running head « Lucanus in catalecton », it is obvious that Pastrengo must have used a florilegium. Furthermore Pastrengo uses the form Calphurius for Calpurnius [30]. The florilegia have Calpurius. Sabbadini suggests that Pastrengo's silence about Nemesianus indicates that he had Calpurnius only (the two are usually associated in manuscripts) and that his manuscript was the ancestor of the fifteenth-century codices that contain Calpurnius without Nemesianus. But the florilegia attribute the selections from Nemesianus to Calpurnius, and Pastrengo's silence about the former is probably due to that fact. In conclusion, then, it seems certain that both Pastrengo and the producer of the Verona *Flores* drew on one of the well-known florilegia not only for

---

[30] Sabbadini, *op. cit.,* I, p. 16, n. 82.

Tibullus but for other authors as well [31], and that no complete Tibullus existed in Verona (or for that matter, elsewhere in Italy) at that time.

That Petrarch actually owned a complete manuscript of Catullus cannot be proved, but that he had access to one and read it is beyond doubt. Nolhac was by no means the first to show this but he added substantially to the evidence. That there was a manuscript at Verona is well authenticated, but of course it does not follow that Petrarch obtained a copy of it just because he secured in that same city a copy of Cicero's letters to Atticus. It might be argued that because Coluccio asked only for Propertius and not Catullus from Petrarch's library in his letter to Gaspare de' Broaspini of Verona in 1375 he knew that Petrarch did not have a copy [32]. But he goes on to make clear that the Catullus had already been arranged for.

The evidence for Petrarch's acquaintance with Catullus depends on his quotations. These are numerous, though some were taken at second hand [33]. 1, 4, quoted in *Sen.* XI, 3 (1368) could not, apparently, have been taken from Pliny, *N. h., Praef.*, because the word order is different. Petrarch has that of the Catullus manuscripts, « meas esse aliquid putare nugas » (if we can trust the editions of the *Seniles*), whereas Pliny has « putare esse aliquid meas nugas » [34].

35, 4 is quoted by Petrarch in the margin of his Virgil (on « Lari maxime », *Georg.* II, 159). In comment on a note of Servius he cites Pliny (he acquired a copy in 1350 but had consulted

---

[31] I have treated the florilegia in a series of articles in *Classical Philology* (XXIII, 1928, p. 128; XXIV, 1929, p. 109; XXV, 1930, pp. 11, 128; XXVI, 1931, p. 21; XXVII, 1932, p. 1).

[32] Novati, *op. cit.,* I, pp. 221-222.

[33] They are conveniently listed in L. Schwabe's second edition of Catullus (Berlin, 1886), p. xv. For additions see Nolhac, *op. cit.,* I, pp. 165 ff., and Bosco, *op. cit.,* p. 108. See too B. L. Ullman, *The Transmission of the Text of Catullus,* in « Studi in onore di Luigi Castiglioni » (Florence, 1960), p. 1043.

[34] Sillig in his edition of Pliny (Hamburg, 1851) lists Petrarch's Pliny (Paris lat. 6802) but does not specifically give its reading at this point, though his silence favors the assumption that it has the vulgate reading. Mlle. Pellegrin kindly confirmed this assumption. As Petrarch's quotation involves vs. 3 of Catullus (*solet* is based on Catullus' so*lebat*), he could not have used one of the grammarians who quote vs. 4 (Marius Victorinus, Terentianus Maurus, Caesius Bassus). Petrarch is not likely to have seen the *Scholia Veronensia* on Virgil.

one before 1343-45) [35]. At a later time he added: « De hoc Catullus 'Comi menia lariumque litus' ». As this line is not quoted by any ancient or mediaeval writer except Benzo of Alessandria, whose work Petrarch surely did not know [36], we must assume that Petrarch took it from a manuscript of Catullus. This is not the place to discuss the relations of the Catullian manuscripts. Suffice it to say that to one studying closely the three earliest manuscripts it becomes obvious that G (Paris, lat. 14137) and R (Vat. Ottob. lat. 1829) are sister manuscripts whose parent may have been copied directly from the lost Verona manuscript (V). This exemplar of G and R was emended by someone. The third manuscript O (Oxford, Bodl. Canon. lat. 30) is descended directly from the Verona manuscript (though not necessarily a direct copy) and is superior, as far as the preservation of the readings of V is concerned, to the exemplar of G and R (see chapter V) [37]. Now we have an unusual situation in 35, 4. O has *veniam*, G *meniam* (corrected to *menia*), R *menia*. It would seem that V had *meniam*. If so, Petrarch may have corrected his copy to *menia*.

39, 11 is also quoted in the Virgil (on « pinguis Tyrrhenus », *Georg.* II, 193): « Catullus 'Aut parcus umber aut obesus etruscus' ». The line is quoted elsewhere only in a glossary, but with the reading *pinguis* for *parcus*, which latter is the reading of OGR and hence was that of V. Many emendations for *parcus* have been suggested, most of them with the meaning « fat ». Lindsay accepts *pinguis* and compares Persius 3, 74 *pinguibus Umbris* [38]. The less likely the reading *parcus* is thought to be, the more likely it is that Petrarch used a manuscript of the V tradition. There is one other point. OGR all have *et truscus* (the *et* represented by the usual symbol) for *Etruscus*. This has been corrected in G, but in R the variant *al' etruscus* was written above

---

[35] G. Billanovich in his edition of Petrarch's *Rerum memorandarum libri* (Florence, 1943), pp. lxii ff., xcviii ff.

[36] On Benzo's quotation see above, chapter V, and W. G. Hale, « Benzo of Alexandria and Catullus », *Classical Philology*, V (1910), p. 56.

[37] In the *Classical Review*, XX (1906), p. 160, W. G. Hale expressed the belief that O was owned by Petrarch, but he withdrew this suggestion in *Classical Philology*, III (1908), p. 233.

[38] W. M Lindsay, *Glossaria Latina*, I (Paris, 1926), p. 443.

— which probably means that it was copied from the exemplar. This example and the preceding make one wonder whether the exemplar of R and G may not have been Petrarch's copy. But that problem must be left to another occasion[39].

49, 1-3 are quoted twice by Petrarch, once in the Virgil (on Servius' note to *Aen.* I, 110 that Sallust was « Romani generis disertissimus »). Petrarch thinks this would fit Cicero better, and quotes « Catullus Veronensis poeta » as being « secretior » than the other numerous witnesses; by this he means « less well-known », thus indicating the scarcity of Catullus manuscripts in his time[40]. This quotation is followed by two from Jerome, to which Petrarch at a later time added a reference to the *Scriptores historiae Augustae.* Since his manuscript of this work was written for him in 1356, the Catullus quotation is presumably earlier than 1356. The other citation of 49, 1-3 is in *Var.* 38, 6 (1347). Petrarch ends the note in the Virgil with the words « et rel(i-qua) », thus indicating that he had the whole poem before him. It is quoted by no one else.

Poem 64 of Catullus, it will be recalled, contains a poem within a poem—the story of Ariadne embroidered on a couch cover. Petrarch twice refers to this part of the poem as the *Peplon* of Catullus, a term for it found nowhere else. It is, I believe, Petrarch's own invention. Its best source would be *Ciris* 21: « magno intexens ... peplo, Qualis Erectheis olim portatur Athenis ... Magna Giganteis ornantur pepla tropaeis ». To be sure, we are not certain that Petrarch knew the *Ciris.* He seems to refer to it in *Fam.* XXIV, 12, 25 (addressed to Homer): « Nam si ad eos quos *Iuveniles ludos* vocant, primos scilicet adolescentie sue libellos, oculum deflectis, scriptum ibi tuum nomen invenies ». The name of Homer occurs in *Ciris* 65, and an adjectival form in *Cat.* 15, 2. Today the complete *Ciris* is known only from fifteenth-century manuscripts. Petrarch's phrase

---

[39] See now my article mentioned in note 33.

[40] The nonsense that has been written about the interpretation of *secretior* is corrected by Nolhac, *op. cit.*, I, p. 270. Another example is in Petrarch's reference to his precious volume of Cicero's letters to Atticus as « locis secretioribus » (quoted by Nolhac, I, p. 257, n. 1, for another purpose). For Petrarch's calling the poem an « epistola » cf. his reference to Propertius given above The address to Cicero gives the poem the effect of a letter.

Iuveniles ludos is a puzzler. It ought to refer to the collection called « P. Virgilii Maronis iuvenalis ludi libellus », but this did not contain the *Ciris*[41]. Or did it at one time contain all the minor poems, like the lost Murbach manuscript?

If the *Ciris* gives more trouble than help we can refer to Servius (*Aen.* I, 480), who defines *peplum* as *palla picta feminea,* or better to Pilatus' translation of Homer, e.g., at *Od.* VII, 96: « Ibi pepli subtiles », which were thrown over chairs[42].

At any rate, Petrarch's reference to the *Peplon* shows that he was familiar with the whole poem, not an excerpt: « quem morem omnes in poetando sequimur, artificiali quem dicunt ordine gaudentes; naturalis enim est ystoricorum proprius. Hoc signanter servat Catullus in peplon ». Another quotation from the same poem (vs. 141) is in a comment on *Aen.* IV, 316: « sed conubia leta, sed optatos himeneos. Catullus in peplon ». The line is quoted by no one else. There is not the slightest evidence that the Ariadne episode was preserved in a separate tradition, and the chances that it was so preserved are exceedingly slight.

The six allusions or quotations just discussed cannot be explained away. They could not have come from some lost florilegium. One more quotation is probably to be added. We noted one direct quotation from poem 39. Petrarch also cites 39, 16 (*De rem.*, II, *Praef.*; 1354-66). It is true that this line is quoted by Jeremy of Montagnone (see chapter V), but there is no indication that Petrarch was familiar with Jeremy's book.

Three other quotations are clearly taken from other sources. There is nothing inconsistent in quoting Catullus both directly and indirectly. Apart from the fact that some of the indirect citations may have been made before the manuscript of Catullus was obtained, Petrarch may not have remembered passages in a poet whose work he did not constantly reread. Furthermore, the errors in V and the failure to divide poems made Catullus anything but easy reading. Bosco is quite right in his claim that Petrarch took his allusion to 3, 18 from Juvenal 6, 8 and the

---

[41] F. Vollmer in *Sitzungsberichte der Königlich Bayerischen Akademie der Wissenschaften,* 1908, No. 11.

[42] Perhaps Pilatus may explain the wrong form *Peplon.* It may be that he preserves the Greek form *peplon* for *peplum* somewhere in his translation.

scholia thereon, as Petrarch's words reveal a complete misunderstanding of the poem. He may even have failed to realize that Catulus (that is the spelling in his letter) was to be identified as Catullus. In any case, Petrarch's misunderstanding cannot shake the solid fact that six or seven quotations prove that he saw a complete Catullus.

Two quotations from poem 64 (vss. 171-172 and 327) are clearly taken from Macrobius. Here too the spelling Catulus is found, as in one of the two manuscripts of Macrobius used by Eyssenhardt in his edition (Leipzig, 1893). This is in contrast to the correct spelling in the two passages taken directly from this poem. Furthermore, the readings in the quotations agree with Macrobius rather than with the Catullus manuscripts. In vs. 171 Macrobius and Petrarch have *non*, V has *ne*. In the refrain first used in vs. 327 and frequently repeated, Macrobius has *ducenti*, Petrarch *dicenti*, V always has *ducentes*. The reading *dicenti* may be due to the text on which Petrarch was commenting (*Buc.* 4, 46): « 'Talia saecla' suis dixerunt 'currite fusis' ». Petrarch also has *sub tegmine* with Macrobius, where V has *sub tegmina* in vs. 327 but with variation thereafter.

In *De Rem.* I, 59, Petrarch writes: « Si per te ipsum illos paveris, quid nisi occupatissimus pastor eris? Officium vile, laudatum licet a multis, ante alios a Catullo Veronensi ». This is usually thought to be an error for Tibullus (I, 1; 5; II, 3). But Tibullus, though mentioning the shepherd's life, does not specifically praise it. Rather, I think that Petrarch is alluding to the *Culex*. In his Virgil (on *Georg.* II, 458; fol. 33r), where Virgil writes: « O fortunatos nimium, sua si bona norint, Agricolas », Petrarch comments: « Bona agricole. Adde bona pastoris, de quibus idem in Culice ». *Culex* 58 opens a long passage on the blessings of the shepherd's life with the words « O bona pastoris ». This, I think, is what Petrarch had in mind, but for once he made a mistake, for he, like other humans, could occasionally err.

We can agree with Bosco in rejecting most of the reminiscences of Catullus as being vague. One in particular, suggested by Nolhac, must be forcibly ejected: 64, 55 « Necdum etiam sese quae visit visere credit » is suggested as the origin for a line in one of the sonnets. But the Catullian line as printed represents the emendation of I. Vossius, whose edition appeared 310 years after Petrarch's death! The reading of V is completely unintelligible and bears no resemblance to Petrarch's line: « Necdum etiam seseque sui tui se credit ». Strange how often scholars fail to avoid such pitfalls.

There is a bare possibility that in *Epist. met.* III, 3, in which Petrarch seems to be alluding to Campesani's poem about the discovery of Catullus (see Chapter I), Petrarch may be imitating Catullus: 14 *ramis viridantibus alte*; 40 *silvestria tempe.* Compare this with Catullus 64, 229 *silvestria dona;* 285 *viridantia Tempe.* This is not too convincing. Catullus is referring to the real Tempe, Petrarch employs the word as a common noun, probably imitating Virgil's *Georgics* (II, 469). But the use of *silvestria* (in the same metrical position) and *viridantia* (not a very common word) near each other and associated with *tempe* in both poems, suggests a possible source for Petrarch.

For some reason that seems to elude us Catullus did not turn out to be one of Petrarch's favorites, in spite of what we might have expected. Perhaps he became acquainted with him too late in life, after the period of his Italian love poems [43]. We cannot set with any assurance the exact date when he became familiar with a complete Catullus. It must have been before July or August of 1347, when *Var.* 38, containing one of the direct quotations, was written [44].

[43] Perhaps James A. S. McPeek implies the right answer in his *Catullus in Strange and Distant Britain* (Cambridge, 1939), p. 42 (he is speaking of the English Petrarchists): « At first the poets responded to Catullus slowly. The formal beauty and large sufficiency of Petrarchism united with the equivocal attitude of the critics to delay the recognition of his charm ».

[44] In my article, *The Transmission of the Text of Catullus* (see note 33), I suggest 1345. It might be argued that Petrarch saw a Catullus in Avignon since a catalogue of the library of Clement VII in 1379-80 is supposed to list a copy. But this is a mistake. M. Faucon, *La librairie des Papes d'Avignon* (*Bibliothèque des Ecoles françaises d'Athènes et de Rome,* Fasc. 50), II (Paris, 1887), p. 34, has the item: « Item parvus liber multorum poetarum, primus Cat[ullus] ..., etc. ». I examined the manuscript of this catalogue in the Vatican Archives (Arch. Avign. 469). The page is mutilated at this point, but it is quite clear that the letter after *Cat* is *o*, not *u*. It must have been *Cato* or *Catonis,* i.e., the *Disticha Catonis.*

CHAPTER IX

OBSERVATIONS ON NOVATI'S EDITION
OF SALUTATI'S LETTERS

Novati's edition of Salutati's letters is an unusually fine piece of work and is not likely to be supplanted. Unfortunately Novati did not live to finish his task. Particularly to be regretted is the absence of an Appendix in which he planned to incorporate biographical data on a number of Salutati's correspondents. Nor is there any discussion of the manuscripts he used in his edition. For the interpretation of his symbols we are forced to consult a brief and incomplete table in a periodical article [1].

Novati's G^1 and G^2, in the Modena library, are copies made in the eighteenth century of two « lost » Guadagni manuscripts. Novati did not in the *Bullettino* mention two Venice manuscripts but he quotes them in his edition as M^1 and M^2. He does not realize that these are the « lost » Guadagni manuscripts, though this is quite obvious from the full description given by Mehus [2].

---

[1] *Bullettino dell'Istituto Storico Italiano,* IV (1888), p. 64 .

[2] L. Mehus, *Ambrosii Traversari ... Epistolae,* I (Florence, 1759), pp. 130, 136, 138, 253, 272, 282, 301, 304, 324, 331, 336, 353-654, 368. Guadagni 33=M^2, Marc. lat. 13. 68 (3995; Morelli 45), copied in G^1, Modena, H. 2. 26 (Campori 1017). Guadagni 34 = M^1, Marc. lat. 13. 69 (3996; Morelli 46), copied in G^2, Modena H. 2. 27 (Campori 1018). Nowhere in his edition does Novati indicate what he means by M^1 and M^2. After identifying them by their contents and readings I found a copy of the *Bullettino* article among Novati's papers in which the identification was added by hand. To make room for them M was changed to Mgl. Other additions are N^2 (but the manuscript was not named) and P^2, identified as N. a. l. 11 (evidently not completed, for it should be 1152). N was changed to N^1, P^2 to P^3. In the list as printed, N (N^1) is said to be in the « fondo Gaddiano » at Naples; this is an error, caused by confusion with one of the Laurentian manuscripts. Novati's papers and notes are in the Società Storica Lombarda at Milan. Sabbadini first called

In the *Bullettino* article Novati bewails the disappearance of the two manuscripts in « quel tristissimo traffico delle nostre ricchezze letterarie ». I suppose that there are still some Florentines who would feel that way about the transfer of their manuscripts to Venice, but Novati was not thinking of the isles of Venice but of a large island to the west.

Novati says that the Modena manuscripts are autographs of Mehus; a note on the cover of G^1 and in the Campori catalogue [3] says that the copying was done by Francesco Mouke. The catalogue also states that the two manuscripts are equipped with notes and readings based on paper and parchment manuscripts in the Riccardiana and Gaddiana (now Laurenziana) libraries. L^1 (Gadd. XC sup. 41, 3, paper) and R^1 (Ricc. 845, parchment) between them contain most of the letters in G^1 and G^2 and, to judge from Novati's apparatus, are the ones that account for many of the deviations of the Modena manuscripts. Others seem to be due to emendation. The Modena manuscripts should therefore be ignored in determining the text, except insofar as they offer attractive emendations.

The letters in M^1 and M^2 were copied continuously by the same scribe, as follows: M^1 (five gatherings of ten, numbered a-e); M^2, fols. 27-76 (five gatherings of ten numbered f-k). In binding, the first edition of *De laboribus Herculis,* copied by the same scribe but with a thicker pen, was placed at the beginning of M^2 as fols. 1-23 (fols. 24-26 are blank) [4].

As to some of the other manuscripts used by Novati, Florence, Ricc. 845 (R^1) may have been copied before Salutati's death. Presumably through inadvertence Novati fails to cite it on five

---

my attention to them many years ago, and I have had the privilege of examining them briefly on several occasions, most recently in 1950 through the kindness of Professors Besta and Secchi of the Società and especially of Professor Ghisalberti of the Centro Manzoniano.

[3] L. Lodi and R. Vandini, *Catalogo dei codici ... Campori* (Modena, 1875), p. 388.

[4] The text of the first edition is printed in my edition of *Colucii Salutati De laboribus Herculis* (Zurich, 1951); a reproduction of a page in the Venice manuscript may be found there. See too B. L. Ullman, *The Humanism of Coluccio Salutati* (Padua, 1963), pp. 271-272, where other Coluccio works copied by the same scribe are listed.

letters: II, pp. 343, 445, 470; III, pp. 135, 276. He also fails to cite L¹ (Florence, Laur. Gadd. 90 sup. 41, 3) for II, p. 302. Lucca, Archivio di Stato, Governo di Paolo Guinigi 29, contains seven letters, all original, some autograph, according to Novati. My comment is that they are all autograph. Specifically, Novati calls only four of the letters autographs, obviously because only they contain the phrase *manu propria* (III, pp. 621, 667, 669, 672). But the other three are just as certainly autographs (III, pp. 615, 668, 670).

P² is Paris N. a. l. 1152 for four letters (I, pp. 50, 72, 78, 80) and Paris 8573 for one (IV, p. 170), but in the *Bullettino* article only the latter manuscript is mentioned. Paris 8573 is quoted for III, p. 239, but not by the symbol P². In other respects the use of symbols is rather capricious. In general, they are used for manuscripts containing four or more letters, but M (Mgl), R⁴, and S have only two each. R⁴ (Florence, Ricc. 1222 C) was corrected by Coluccio himself (cf. III, p. 198, n., and IV, p. 157, n. 3, and my comment on the latter). The *Bullettino* article uses the symbol N for Naples, Naz. V. F. 13; this symbol is identical with N¹ of the edition, in which the symbol N does not appear. N² is used for a number of letters but is not identified in the *Bullettino*. Presumably it is a second Naples manuscript, but I was unable to find it in the National Library there [5].

One letter (IV, p. 106), Novati tells us, is found in about sixty manuscripts, about half of which are collections of letters of Leonardo Bruni. Apart from these, Novati uses or at least mentions about ninety manuscripts that contain one or more letters. To his list I can add about fifteen. These figures give some idea of the popularity of Salutati's letters.

How many private letters of Salutati remain unpublished it is impossible to say. Nine letters are in a Madrid manuscript

---

[5] Obviously L. Frati too was unable to determine what N² stood for, since in his *Epistolario di Pellegrino Zambeccari* (Rome, 1929), p. 31, he follows Novati in using the symbol N² without explanation. A handwritten list in the Novati collection explains « N¹ e N² » merely as *Napoletano*. N² is presumably in another Naples library.

(17652), of which seven are unpublished[6]. Professor Billanovich kindly informs me that the two published ones are II, pp. 168, 180. The others are addressed to Jean de Montreuil, Moggio, Giberto da Correggio, Donato Albanzani, Francesco Zabarella, Lombardo della Seta, and an unnamed correspondent[7].

Of the manuscripts which were not used by Novati, those containing several letters will be mentioned now, others in connection with the individual letters. British Museum, Cotton, Caligula A. 16, of the beginning of the fifteenth century, is closely related to Venice, Marc. lat. 13. 68 and 13. 69, as the letters included are identical. Another Cotton manuscript (Cleopatra C. 5) contains III, pp. 308, 310, 653. It also contains works and translations by Lapo da Castiglionchio, Leonardo Bruni, and Antonio Pasini of Todi. It therefore apparently has some relation to manuscripts in the library of Duke Humphrey of Gloucester. For Leonardo Bruni dedicated a translation to him, Lapo da Castiglionchio sent his books to him, and Antonio Pasini of Todi worked for him in Italy[8]. The spelling Collusius, found in this manuscript, was that of Humphrey's copy[9]. Manuscripts containing translations by Bruni were among the books presented to Oxford by Humphrey[10].

Prague, Univ. III. G. 18 (Truhlár 543) contains IV, p. 106; II, pp. 394, 400; III, p. 58. Prague, Chapter library 1309 (L. LXIV) appears to contain some letters; 1232 (K. XXXVII) perhaps has only official letters. Others about which I have insufficient information are Modena, Q. 7. 3; Florence, Naz. Magl. 39, 86; Munich 5350. For the Turin manuscript see chapter XIV.

---

[6] Reported briefly by N. Festa in his edition of the *Africa* of Petrarch (Florence, 1926), p. xxv. V. Rossi used the manuscript for a letter of Petrarch's (*Fam.* X, 3) in Vol. II of his edition (Florence, 1934).

[7] Billanovich plans to publish the new letters in a book called *Scuola del Petrarca* (see G. Billanovich, *Petrarca letterato*, I. *Lo scrittoio del Petrarca*, Rome, 1947, p. 293, n. 1). He and G. Ouy will publish new letters exchanged between Salutati and Jean de Montreuil.

[8] K. H. Vickers, *Humphrey Duke of Gloucester* (London, 1907), pp. 373-374.

[9] See below, chapter XVII.

[10] Henry Anstey, *Munimenta Academica* (London, 1868), Part II, p. 764; H. H. E. Craster in *Bodleian Quarterly Record*, I (1914-16), p. 131.

In the seven letters addressed to the chancellor of Lucca, Ser Guido da Pietrasanta, which are now in the Archivio di Stato of Lucca, we have, as stated above, the autograph originals sent by Salutati. In Vat. Cappon. 147 we have first drafts in Salutati's writing. Several of the existing collections of the letters belong to the official set of his works made soon after his death, which I have discussed elsewhere [11]. Another seems to have been put together by a correspondent (see chapter XIV). One collection can be identified as sent by Salutati to a friend—R[4] (Ricc. 1222 C) on which see below on IV, p. 157. There is here a good bit of parallelism to the situation in regard to Petrarch's letters, except for the important difference that Coluccio did not rework his letters as Petrarch did, at least not to the same extent.

I shall now comment on individual letters, dealing with manuscripts, chronology, and other matters.

I, p. 3. For a collation of the Turin manuscript see chapter XIV.

I, p. 9. Novati's statement that Luigi de' Gianfigliazzi died without issue contradicts Vat. Chigi G. VII. 191, which credits him with a son, Messer Giacomo, whose sons were called Lorenzo and Adoardo. On p. 10, line 1, the word *gurgustiolo* is probably taken from Apuleius, *Met.* I, 23 or IV, 10.

I, p. 17. The phrase *falcati senis* (line 10) is perhaps based on the *falcifer senex* of Ovid, *Ib.* 216, *Fast.* V, 627, or Martial, XI, 6, 1. *Salutaris fulgor ... rutilo* (lines 11-12) is from Cicero, *R. P.* VI, 17.

I, p. 21, lines 5 f. Cf. Cicero, *Off.* I, 57.

I, p. 57, line 19. The name *Gnato* for a flatterer, which Salutati uses frequently, is taken from Terence, *Eun.*

I, p. 63. Found also in Cambridge, Trinity College R. I. 35, where it occurs twice, once on the flyleaf and again on fol. 91v [12].

---

[11] See note 4.
[12] M. R. James, *The Western Manuscripts in the Library of Trinity College, Cambridge,* II (Cambridge, 1901), No. 452.

I, p. 88, n. 1. Foresti denies that there is any evidence in Petrarch that Niccolosio was an intimate friend of Boccaccio [13].

I, p. 96, line 4. For *theonino dente* and *lycambeo* cf. Horace, *Epist.* I, 18, 82 and I, 19, 25 respectively.

I, p. 119. The date 1369 is an obvious slip for 1370, as the order of letters indicates.

I, p. 130. Also in Hague, X. 131, fols. 158-160, according to Frati [14].

I, p. 149. Coluccio was chancellor at Lucca from August of 1370 to July of 1371. Political changes in the city prevented his reappointment, but he stayed on in Lucca, perhaps hoping that he might be reappointed after all. In October of 1371 he wrote to a friend in Arezzo (p. 149, line 9), stating that Santi da Valiano, a Florentine notary in Arezzo, had written a poem attacking the city of Lucca, and that he, Coluccio, had written some verses in reply, which he wanted his correspondent to hand to Santi, since he had not himself heard from the notary. It may be that Coluccio thought he might ingratiate himself with the powers at Lucca by rising to the defense of their city. At any rate, perhaps Coluccio and Santi became friends as a result of the incident. In 1387 Santi was at Poppi. In a Dante which he copied (Laur., Ashb. 834) he entered this subscription: « Anno Domini MCCCLXXXVII die X Martii expletus fuit iste liber per me Sancti olim Blasii de Valiana in castro Puppii sub illustris et magnifici viri domini comitis Karoli de Battifolle bono pacifico et tranquillo dominio tempore pontificatus domini Urbani VI ». Obviously he was employed by Carlo, probably as a notary. This Carlo di Battifolle was the brother and successor of the Roberto who was a humanist and an admirer of Petrarch, to whom Coluccio addressed a long letter about Petrarch (I, p. 176). Could it be that Coluccio obtained a position as notary for Santi with the ruler of Poppi? Coluccio kept up his friendship with this family, as we can see from his letters to Carlo's son, Roberto Novello, written about 1396 (III, pp. 150, 153). In that year

---

[13] A. Foresti, *Aneddoti della vita di Francesco Petrarca* (Brescia, 1928), p. 241.

[14] L. Frati, *Epistolario di Pellegrino Zambeccari* (Rome, 1929), p. xx.

Simone Serdini, whom Coluccio calls « frater meus dilectus », and whom he recommends warmly to Lodovico Alidosi, was in the employ of this same Roberto Novello (II, p. 383 and n. 5). Perhaps Salutati had a hand in getting Serdini this position. G. Volpi suggests that Serdini was in Roberto's employ as chancellor from 1389 [15].

Professor Billanovich tells me he has discovered a letter of Santi to Coluccio asking for information about poets laureate. Santi describes himself as chancellor of Roberto at Poppi. In view of Santi's presence in Poppi in 1387, this Roberto seems more likely to be the younger Novello rather than his uncle. The existence of this letter adds confirmation to my guess that Coluccio and Santi became friends, and that Coluccio may have been responsible for Santi's obtaining a position at Poppi. Coluccio placed an impressive number of humanists in important positions.

I, p. 150. Also in British Museum, Burney 250, following Seneca's *Tragedies*, which were copied in 1387 at San Gimignano by a certain Bartholomeus. The letter is in a different but contemporary hand.

Coluccio's scornful rejection of the popular mediaeval tale about Virgil suspended in the basket is a significant touch of the new humanism. For the story cf. J. W. Spargo, *Virgil the Necromancer* (Cambridge, Mass., 1934), pp. 62 ff., 137 ff., 383 (where this passage is mentioned).

I, p. 152, n. 1. Salutati had not forgotten what Petrarch said in *Fam.* XXIV, 5, as Novati infers, but knew only the original form of this letter, which omitted reference to the doubts about the Senecan authorship of the *Octavia* [16].

I, p. 153, line 8. In the quotation from Seneca, Novati prints *destructus*, the vulgate reading in Seneca. But two of the manuscripts of Coluccio's letters (P¹V) have *destitutus*. The reading of the Seneca manuscript which Coluccio himself copied (British Museum 11987) is *destitutus*. It seems clear that Coluccio wrote *destitutus* and that the text of the letters has in some manuscripts been corrected to that of the Senecan vulgate.

[15] *Giornale storico della letteratura italiana*, XV (1890), p. 1.
[16] Cf. V. Rossi in *Memorie dell'Accademia dei Lincei*, Ser. V, 16 (1920), p. 204, n. 1, and the critical apparatus on *Fam.* XXIV, 5, 16-17 of his edition.

I, p. 161. Barb. XI 96 (now Vat., Barb. lat. 453) was not written in the fourteenth century, as Novati states, but in 1418 or later. It is in the same hand as Barb. lat. 32 (on which see below on III, p. 65), and the two were once bound together [17]. On fol. 12v of the latter the following statement occurs in the hand of the text: « Senis in palatio potestatis tempore regiminis preclari militis atque perspicui legum doctoris domini Ugolini de farneto perusini per me Mactheum de Bondionibus de Spoleto Collateralem tunc in officio antedicto. MCCCCXVIII indictione duodecima die XIII Januarii ».

The date of this letter is troublesome. Because of its being written at Stignano, Novati is inclined to date it 1373. Actually, however, no letter in Novati's collection was sent from Stignano after 1370 and therefore the place of writing really offers no clue. In the Barberini manuscript the letter ends on fol. 107v with these words: « Colutius Pierii de Salutatis cancellarius immeritus [18] Florentinus ». This would, of course, put the letter in 1375 or later. But as Novati observes, this signature was added by another hand and may therefore be ignored in dating. Yet the form is genuine, as Coluccio elsewhere uses the phrase *cancellarius immeritus Florentinus* or something similar. One of the letters to which it is attached is III, p. 65 (see p. 70), but only in Barb. lat. 32, which, as stated above, is in the same hand as 453 and once was part of the same book. A second hand may therefore have copied it into the latter from the former.

One other trifling point is this. Coluccio's correspondent, Ser Filippo di ser Landino, was alive in 1427 and possibly long after that date. Let us assume that he was 20 when his son was born at the time of Coluccio's letter. If the date of this was 1373, then Ser Filippo was 74 in 1427; if the letter was written, let us say, in 1393, he was only 54 in 1427. The former is, of course, quite possible but a later date for the letter gives one more leeway. Our conclusion must be that no real basis for dating the letter exists.

---

[17] Before 1831 under the single number 2589. Barb. lat. 48 and 451 also formed part of this volume.

[18] Novati wrongly read *immerito*.

I, p. 164. This letter deals with the death of Giovanni da Siena, who died of the plague at Bologna. Novati assumes that the reference is to the epidemic of 1373-74 and accordingly dates the letter in one of those years. But a document has been discovered which shows that Giovanni was still alive in 1382 [19]. Therefore the plague year was that of 1383 [20], and that is the year to which Giovanni's death and Coluccio's letter must be assigned. For a collation of the Turin manuscript see chapter XIV.

I, p. 167. Foresti argues that this letter and I, p. 198, were written to Giovanni Malpaghini, not to Benvenuto da Imola, as the one manuscript containing the former and the three containing the latter indicate [21]. To deviate from this ascription requires stronger evidence than Foresti presents. Coluccio's letter was written July 25, 1374. A short postscript, written after this date, mentions the news that Petrarch had died: « ad sua sidera demigrasse ». Foresti thinks that an extant letter of Malpaghini's on the death of Petrarch was an answer to this postscript, although the manuscript does not give the correspondent's name. In it Giovanni says: « Episcole tue pars extrema ubi Petrarcham... ad astra volasse subscripseras ». The similarity of language between Malpaghini and Coluccio led Foresti to his suggestion. But this similarity is not particularly significant. In the second letter to Benvenuto (p. 198) Coluccio says: « Epistola tua, que a fine litterule quam tibi iandiu destinavi sumens auspicium, migrationem illius luminosi sideris... deplorabat ». It will be seen that *migrationem* corresponds to *demigrasse* of the first letter, and, in a way, *sideris* to *sidera*. Either his correspondent (Benvenuto) avoided the figurative language or used the same words as Coluccio. For if the correspondent is Malpaghini, and his answer to the first letter is the one that contained the words *ad astra volasse,* would not Coluccio have used these words instead of going back to his original expressions? Incidentally, Giovanni Conversino in a

---

[19] L. Frati in *Biblioteca de « l'Archiginnasio »*, V (1920), p. 239.

[20] Griffoni in L. A. Muratori, *Rerum Italicarum Scriptores,* ed. II, XVIII, 2 (Città di Castello, 1902), p. 78.

[21] *Op. cit.*, p. 449.

letter on the same theme uses language similar to Coluccio's: « Petrarce nostri migracionem »[22]. Should we, imitating Foresti, maintain that this letter was addressed to Salutati and not to Donato degli Albanzani?

In the first letter it is indicated that the correspondent had invited Coluccio to avoid the plague at Florence by coming to him. Coluccio says that on account of the influx of refugees, the plague is raging there too. This exactly fits Bologna, where Benvenuto was living. Novati quotes a contemporary document to show that Florentines were fleeing to Bologna in great numbers.

In the same letter Coluccio says that he is sending a copy of his letter about Seneca, the author of the *Tragedies*, at his correspondent's request. This letter (I, p. 150) was in demand among Salutati's contemporaries. Benvenuto used it in his commentary on Dante, as Novati points out, though Benvenuto does not mention his source. This rather conclusive evidence is ignored by Foresti. It may be worth while to compare Coluccio's and Benvenuto's statements about Seneca in order to show the latter's dependence on the former.

Coluccio (I, pp. 152 ff.):

Nonne Neronis exitus in Octavia, ubi Agrippina ab inferis accersitur, plane, prout accidit, recitatur? Que premoriens Seneca nec vidit nec, si humanam prudentiam contemplemur, potuit divinare... (Nero) ad mortem damnatus est, ut... de saxo palatii precipitaretur; que fere omnia in Octavia sunt descripta et tamen ea nemo negat post Senece obitum accidisse. Que ipsum tamen expresse prececinisse, saltem « verbera et turpem fugam », monstrum est et veri non simile, ut iam eum non moralem, non poetam, sed divinum prophetamque appellare possimus... Habeo testem assiduum atque opulentum, Sidonium scilicet; ...manifeste testatur alium fuisse Tragediarum scriptorem quam monitorem Neronis.

Benvenuto de Rambaldis (*Comentum super Dantis Aldigherii comoediam*, ed J. P. Lacaita, Florence, 1887, I, p. 180):

Seneca autem tragediarum autor, fuit alius de stirpe eius, sicut potest probari ratione et autoritate. Ratione, quia Seneca in ea tra-

[22] R. Sabbadini, *Giovanni da Ravenna* (Como, 1924), p. 221.

gedia quae intitulatur Octavia praedicit mortem Neronis, quod facere non potuit nisi fuisset propheta. Autoritate, quia Sidonius in quodam suo libro metrico dicit expresse quod duo fuerunt Senecae, quorum alter morum censor, alter tragediarum autor.

One question arises in connection with the present problem. Where was Giovanni Malpaghini at the time of Petrarch's death? Sabbadini thought that he may have been in Padua. Giovanni entered Petrarch's employ as scribe in 1364 and left him after three or more years. Sabbadini quotes a document indicating that a Giovanni of Ravenna was in Padua in 1371. He supposes that Giovanni stayed on till Petrarch's death and that in this way Coluccio's statement that Giovanni was with Petrarch *ferme trilustri tempore* (III, p. 537) is more or less correct. Even so it would be a considerable exaggeration, since from 1364 to Petrarch's death would be only ten years. Foresti rightly rejects this interpretation, argues that the Giovanni da Ravenna of the 1371 document is a different person, and emends Coluccio's phrase to *ferme lustri tempore* in order to come closer to Petrarch's *triennio et amplius*. Perhaps rather, Coluccio trusted to a faulty memory of Petrarch's phrase. In any case, Sabbadini abandoned his argument in his article in the *Enciclopedia italiana* (1933), *s. v.* « Giovanni da Ravenna ». There he corrects the chronology by having Malpaghini go to Rome in 1368 and to Avignon in 1370, where he still was in 1375. There is no indication that he went to Padua in 1374.

In the first letter Coluccio expresses his appreciation because Benvenuto is obtaining copies of Propertius and Catullus for him. Probably Benvenuto expected to get them from Petrarch's heirs, from whom the Propertius was ultimately obtained through different channels. Malpaghini would seem to have been in a less advantageous position to secure these. Nothing is said about these authors in the second letter to Benvenuto or in a third (p. 201), one which is indubitably addressed to Benvenuto. Finally in a letter to Gaspare de' Broaspini (p. 207), written a year after the first letter to Benvenuto, Coluccio states that Benvenuto had promised that Gaspare would provide the manuscripts. This seems to me to show conclusively that the first letter was written

to Benvenuto, not Malpaghini. Foresti's attempt to explain this
away is weak indeed. He cannot believe that Benvenuto waited
a year before doing anything. But if the correspondent was
Malpaghini it appears that he did not do anything at all. As I
reconstruct the circumstances, Benvenuto tried various avenues
without success, first of all approaching the circle of Petrarch in
Padua. Finally he turned to Gaspare, who was a close friend
of Lombardo della Seta, one of the Padua group, from whom
the Propertius was ultimately obtained. The friendship of Gaspare and Lombardo is attested by the letter Coluccio wrote Lombardo on Gaspare's death (II, p. 53). The date in manuscript
G of Catullus (Verona, October 19, 1375) certainly has some connection with Coluccio's quest, though I am not ready to say
with Novati (p. 222, n. 2) that some of the marginal notes in G
are in the hand of Coluccio. Most scholars agree that the date
in G is not that of the transcription of that codex but, in view
of the use of « etc. » in the subscription, of the manuscript from
which G was copied [23]. On November 16, twenty-eight days after
the date in G, Salutati writes to Gaspare (p. 222): « Catullum,
quem credo parvum libellum, aut exemplatum aut exemplandum,
rogo, transmitte. Tenent ibi Florentini ... apothecas; in ballis
quas faciunt illum iubere poteris alligari ». Obviously it was
settled that he would get his Catullus but he did not yet know
in just what form.

Foresti seizes on Novati's observation that the third letter to
Benvenuto (p. 201) is much like the second (p. 198) and is only
two months later in spite of the fact that Coluccio apologizes
for his long silence. Novati offers three possible explanations
but Foresti sees only the possibility that the second of the letters
was not addressed to Benvenuto. As a matter of fact there is a
simple explanation of such similarity as there is between these
two letters, as we shall now see. In his second letter to Benvenuto (p. 199) Coluccio writes: « De hoc tecum anxius sum: video
enim rerum suarum ministros ... pluribus libellis, quos ille forsan
incompletos reliquerat, incendium minitari ». From the word

---

[23] Against this view see B. L. Ullman, *The Transmission of the Text of
Catullus*, in « Studi in onore di Luigi Castiglioni » (Florence, 1960), p. 1047.

tecum I infer that his correspondent had expressed anxiety about the fate of Petrarch's books. No such anxiety is expressed in the letter of Giovanni Malpaghini to which the present one, according to Foresti, is the answer. We could infer further that Benvenuto returned to the theme in answering the present letter, and that this explains why Coluccio again took it up in the next letter to Benvenuto (p. 201). As a matter of fact, Coluccio says explicitly that Benvenuto began his second letter with that theme (p. 202). It may be added that there is little similarity in detail between Coluccio's treatment of the subject in the two letters.

It may be wondered why I have given so much space to demolishing so weak a case as Foresti's. The answer is that Foresti's book is rightly held in high esteem by Petrarchists and that even his impossible theory about Malpaghini might therefore be accepted without question.

I, p. 170, line 9. « In primis quidem votorum meorum diligentissimus executor dyomicenes Propertium Catullumque procuras ». The corruption *dyomicenes* has troubled me for many years. Could it be for *tu, o Mecenas?* To be sure, Maecenas is not, apparently, referred to elsewhere in the letters. Palaeographically, *tu o* could be read as *dio*; the change of *i* to *y* would be almost inevitable in a strange (presumably Greek) word. But the suggested emendation is purely tentative for want of a better. My hope is that it will stimulate others to offer one that is more convincing.

I, p. 177. The letter is dated July 25; following the date is a short postscript about Petrarch's death, written, of course, not earlier than July 25, but possibly a day or two later. Novati (p. 172, n. 1) comments on the extraordinary rapidity with which the news reached Florence, saying it took only four days. Since Petrarch died the night of July 18-19, the news took at least six, and possibly as many as nine, days to become known to Coluccio.

I, p. 180. In listing Petrarch's works Coluccio mentions *Libellus fragmentorum*, by which title, as Novati observes, Petrarch was in the habit of referring to his *Canzoniere*[24]. But

---

[24] *Rerum vulgarium fragmenta* is the title in the autograph manuscript of the *Canzoniere* (Vat. 3195).

14

Novati says that these Italian poems surely were not in Coluccio's mind (since he is talking about Petrarch's Latin works) and suggests without conviction that Coluccio may have been thinking of the letters *Sine titulo* or the *Rerum memorandarum libri*. But in III, p. 18 Coluccio clearly alludes to the *Canzoniere* by the title *Fragmentorum*. The probable explanation is this: In his list of Petrarch's works Coluccio includes some that he had not seen. Thus he follows the *Libellus fragmentorum* with the *De viris illustribus,* of which he says he is uncertain whether Petrarch published it or not. As a matter of fact, we do know that Coluccio did not obtain a copy of this work until 1380 [25]. Coluccio saw a reference to Petrarch's *Libellus fragmentorum* and assumed that it was a Latin work. Later he came upon a copy of the *Canzoniere* with this title.

I, p. 197, line 6. Cf. Cicero, *Off.* I, 85.

I, p. 198. See on I, p. 167.

I, p. 201. It seemed strange to Novati that Coluccio, writing to Benvenuto da Imola May 22, 1375, should apologize for a silence of less than two months. He even suggested that Coluccio forgot he had written the earlier letter and so wrote two answers to Benvenuto's! The explanation is rather that Benvenuto's letter included a request, as is clear from Coluccio's words: « Petita de Agellio cum presentibus accipe ». Probably the request was urgent. Benvenuto wanted a copy of a passage from Gellius for his commentary on Dante (see below on II, p. 76). He quotes Gellius several times but not before the *Purgatorio*. As we shall see (on II, p. 76), Benvenuto was working on the *Inferno* in June and July of 1374. His commentary on this is much longer than those on the other two parts. By May of 1375 he was probably writing on the *Purgatorio* or *Paradiso*. He quotes Gellius on *Purg*. I, 34 (Lacaita, III, p. 20), XII, 37 (Lacaita, III, p. 330), *Purg.* XXII, 98 (Lacaita, IV, p. 35), *Purg.* XXXII, 131 (Lacaita, IV, p. 261), *Par.* XXVI, 137-138 (Lacaita, V, p. 385). Coluccio quotes from the same passage as the third of these, though not the same words, in *Epist.*, III, p. 229 (dated 1389 or earlier; see

---

[25] *Epist.,* I, p. 331 and note.

below on III, p. 221). He quotes exactly the same words as in the last of Benvenuto's in *Epist.*, IV, p. 234 (dated 1406).

I, p. 206, line 2. Cf. Cicero, *Tusc.* I, 34.

I, p. 213, dated November, 1375, by Novati against Rigacci's 1376. The chief argument centers about a reference to a grain shortage in Florence: « Anno preterito in summa annone caritudine » (p. 216, line 20). The best argument for the date 1375 was overlooked by Novati. In a public letter written by Salutati in September, 1375, almost the same language is used: « in anno preterito, dum urbs ... annone summa caritudine laboraret » [26]. There are other similarities between the two letters.

I, p. 214, line 2. Cf. Cicero, *R. P.* III, 35, quoted by Isidore, XVIII, 1, 3.

I, p. 243. Possibly also in Wolfenbüttel 3006, fol. 217v: « Eiusdem littera ad magistrum Ludowicum heremitarum ».

I, p. 262, n. 1. Novati's inference from this letter that Coluccio did not yet have a Quintilian is unsafe and incorrect. What Coluccio wanted was a complete copy instead of the mutilated ones that were in circulation until Poggio found an *integer* at St. Gall in 1416. As a matter of fact, Coluccio quoted Quintilian as early as 1371, six years before this letter (I, p. 151), and in 1374 (I, p. 182). In 1396 Coluccio wrote: « Audio ... quod Andrevolus de Arisiis, ... repperit totum Quintilianum *De institutione oratoria*, quem habemus admodum diminutum » (III, p. 146).

I, p. 287, n. 1. The reference should be to Gregory's *Homel. in Evang.*

I, p. 304, line 12. Coluccio confused Virgil and Ovid. The reference is to Ovid, *Met.* IV, 428.

I, p. 320, n. 2. Novati quotes a document of 1398 mentioning a son of Benvenuto Rambaldi da Imola by the name of Campaldino. This is now confirmed by the Turin manuscript of Salutati's letters containing II, p. 192, for which see chapter XIV. Novati thought that the strange name Campaldino might be an

---

[26] A. Gherardi, « La guerra dei Fiorentini con Papa Gregorio XI », Appendice, in *Archivio storico italiano*, Ser. III, Tome VI, Part II (1867), p. 234.

error for Rambaldino. Quite independently I had the same idea when I first came upon the name in the Turin manuscript. We are both proved wrong. Incidentally, Benvenuto's wife was named Isabetta; she was the daughter of Iacopo di Vanondo de' Juanelli [27].

I, p. 321, n. 2, For new data on Silvestri see Pier Giorgio Ricci, « Per una monografia su Domenico Silvestri », *Annali della Scuola Normale Superiore di Pisa,* Ser. 2, XIX (1950), Fasc. I-II, pp. 13-24; cf. Roberto Weiss, *ibid.,* Fasc. III-IV; and the edition of his work, *De insulis et earum proprietatibus,* by C. Pecoraro, in *Atti d. Acc. di sc., lett. ed arti di Palermo,* S. IV, XIV, Fasc. II (1953-54), P. II.

I, p. 323, line 1. Read *Papinio* for *Papirio.* The following verses are not Coluccio's own (as Novati suggests) but are from Statius, *Theb.* I, 471-472.

I, p. 331, n. 3. Florence, Naz. I. 1, 28 did not belong to Salutati; see chapter VII.

I, p. 333, n. 1. Coluccio says that his copy of Cicero's *Post red. ad Quir.* is incomplete, concluding, as we see from the last words that he quotes, near the end of chapter 9. The complete oration contains another chapter and Novati is therefore wrong in denying Coluccio's statement that it is incomplete.

II, p. 9, n. 1. Coluccio received Gaspare de' Broaspini's manuscript containing sixty of Cicero's letters in 1377, not 1375; cf. I, p. 278.

II, p. 11. Novati used a fifteenth and an eighteenth-century manuscript for this important letter; in Vol. IV he adds the collation of the autograph first draft, Vat. Cappon. 147. Other manuscripts containing it are Vat. 8279, Corsini 33. E. 21 (già Rossi 170), fols. 83-89 [28], Vienna 3420, fol. 112r-112v (p. 28, line 10 « Erexit » to p. 31, line 21 « adimpleri »), and Bologna, Univ. 987 (1910) (p. 30, line 16 « Nec » to p. 31, line 21 « adimpleri »).

---

[27] L. Frati in *Giornale storico della letteratura italiana,* LXXII (1918), p. 90.
[28] P. Piur, *Briefwechsel des Cola di Rienzo,* in K. Burdach, *Vom Mittelalter zur Reformation,* II, 2 (Berlin, 1928), p. 223; V. Rossi in his edition of Petrarch's *Familiares,* I (Florence, 1933), p. LXV.

II, p. 47. Novati correctly identified this letter, which does not bear Coluccio's name, as emanating from him. It is an answer to Filippo Villani's request to criticize his *Liber de origine civitatis Florentie et eiusdem famosis civibus*. See below, chapter X.

II, p. 53, line 5. Cf. Terence, *Phormio* 454.

II, p. 68. See on the following letter.

II, p. 76. Novati accepts the date June 28, 1383, found in the Cambrai manuscript. But this same manuscript has indiction XII, which Novati emends to VI to fit the year 1383. Palaeographically it would be far simpler to correct the year date MCCCLXXXIII to MCCCLXXIIII, which is in the twelfth indiction. The scribe, after writing XX, made the following I an X. The new date fits the letter much better, I think, and causes some notable changes in the chronology of the commentary on Dante written by Benvenuto da Imola. The letter is addressed to Benvenuto, whom Coluccio thanks for sending him the beginning of his commentary on the *Inferno*, which he urges him to publish. He discusses various points down to *Inf.* I, 70 (Lacaita, I, p. 45). The fragment which Benvenuto sent him perhaps extended not much farther than this verse; at most, it could scarcely have gone beyond the first canto, otherwise Coluccio would have had more comments. We know that in 1373 Benvenuto heard Boccaccio read Dante in Florence and that in 1375 he himself lectured on Dante at Bologna. What more natural than that he should begin the writing of his lecture notes in the intervening year and ask his friend Coluccio to criticize a sample of them? Though Coluccio did not take up permanent residence in Florence until 1374 it is quite reasonable to suppose that he attended some of Boccaccio's Dante lectures and in that way met Benvenuto.

Nearly a month later (July 25, 1374) Coluccio wrote Benvenuto again (I, p. 167). He says that Benvenuto's letter had made him happy. The joy was presumably caused by Benvenuto's thanks for Coluccio's previous letter with its complimentary remarks on the commentary. Benvenuto also asked Coluccio for a copy of his letter about the two Senecas, which, as Novati observes, Benvenuto used in his commentary (see above on I, p. 167). He incorporates Coluccio's views in his note on *Inf.* IV, 141 (Lacaita I, p. 179). Evidently he was working on that canto at the time of the letter of July 25 but had not yet reached it when he sent the sample of his commentary to Coluccio a month earlier. If in July of 1374 he was working on the fourth canto why did he send notes on the first canto alone, nine years later, in 1383, the date Novati assigns to the June letter? If, however, we adopt the other chronology, what is more natural than that Benvenuto should have finished his notes on the first canto in June of 1374 and should be working on the fourth canto a month later? [29]

Novati associates the letter which precedes, addressed to Donato degli Albanzani (II, p. 68), with this one because, though the year of that letter is unknown, the day is the same: June 28. The evidence is against their having been written on the same date. In the letter to Donato, Marco da Castiglione, « qui nunc domesticus et commensalis meus est », i.e., had become as assistant to Coluccio, is represented as bringing a report of Donato's activities. In the letter to Benvenuto the same Marco is leaving Coluccio for bigger things. He would hardly speak on the same day of Marco's just becoming (*nunc*) an employee and of his leaving to take another position. Even if we accept Novati's reconciliation of the date of the Donato letter given in one manuscript (May 10 as against the June 28 of four others) by supposing that the letter was written May 10 but not sent until June 28, the contradictory references to Marco are not satisfactorily explained. Rather we must suppose that Marco left Florence in 1374 but returned in 1383—or whatever the date of the letter to Donato is. It must have been written in 1378 or later because it has a quotation from a letter of Cicero to Brutus, which, at the earliest, Coluccio could have obtained in the sixty-letter collection he received at the end of 1377 (I, p. 278). Actually this particular quotation becomes a favorite with him in 1383—April 26 of that year showing the first of half a dozen quotations of that passage (II, p. 67). So we might as well retain 1383 as the date for the letter to Donato. Possibly confirmation of the above

[29] Hans Baron, *The Crisis of the Early Renaissance* (Princeton, 1955), I, p. 51; II, p. 463, note 34, maintains the old date, 1383; my discussion appeared too late to be considered by him. It is a matter of some importance, since my date introduces Renaissance scepticism several years earlier than Baron thinks

view is provided by an unpublished letter of 1386 to a certain Donato, whom Billanovich identifies as Donato degli Albanzani [30]. In this letter Coluccio says that Donato intimated certain things to « ser Marcum nostrum ». If this is the same Marco as the Marco da Castiglione just mentioned then it would appear that he was still in Coluccio's employ.

One other point with reference to the date of the letter to Benvenuto: Coluccio writes that the commentary had been brought him by a « lepidus iuvenis », Antonio da Cortona. Apparently the implication is that he was rather young. It may be that he had recently finished his studies at Bologna and was on his way home or to some position. In 1385 he was named chancellor of the *anziani* at Lucca (II, p. 245). Would a person who was a « lepidus iuvenis » in 1383 be mature enough for the chancellorship two years later? Coluccio obtained a similar (but not identical) position at Lucca at the age of 38. If the letter in which Antonio is called a « lepidus iuvenis » was written in 1374, as is my view, he would be ready for the Lucca position eleven years later.

If I am right in the chronology I have indicated the only information we can glean from Coluccio is that Benvenuto's commentary on the early cantos of the *Inferno* was taking form in 1374 and 1375. When it was finally ready is another matter. See also above on I, p. 201.

I might add here an extraneous point about the commentary. Benvenuto quotes Cicero's lost *De consiliis* (Lacaita, III, p. 76). P. Toynbee comments: « Which, if his quotation be actually made at first hand, must have been extant, in part at least, in the second half of the fourteenth century » (« Index of Authors Quoted by Benvenuto da Imola », in *Eighteenth and Nineteenth Annual Reports of the Dante Society*, 1899-1900). Benvenuto found the quotation in Boethius, *Mus.* I, 1.

II, p. 77, line 25. From Cicero, *Tusc.* I, 6.

II, p. 127, n. 1. Novati's reference is wrong; it should be Livy, V, 51-54. Likewise the reference in note 2 is wrong; it should be Livy, XXII, 53.

---

[30] *Op. cit.*, p. 293. I owe my further knowledge of the letter to the kindness of Professor Billanovich.

II, p. 130. In answer to Bernardo da Moglio's request Coluccio sends a two-line epitaph to be engraved on the tomb of Bernardo's father Pietro and indicates that it may be added to the verses which Bernardo already had. These are presumably ones which Coluccio had previously sent (for Coluccio says he is sending verses for the third time) but may include the epitaph which Pietro wrote for himself, if we may trust a manuscript of Valerius Maximus in the British Museum (Ar. 7, fol. 78r), apparently copied some twenty years after Pietro's death:

> Da vocem, lector, tecum vox picta loquetur,
> Tuque loquens auditor eris dum talia promet.
> Rhetoris hoc Petri considunt membra sepulcro,
> Quo iussit Dominus migravit spiritus illo.
>
> M. P. de Mulio

Coluccio's epitaph is intended to follow something of this sort, for it does not include the name of the deceased. It starts with *Hunc* and gives only the date of death. See also chapter XIV.

II, p. 131, 141. See chapter XIV.

II, p. 159. See chapter XIV.

II, p. 162. See chapter XIV.

II, p. 168. line 5. The reference is to Cicero, *Off*. III, 77.

II, p. 168, line 15. See chapter XIV.

II, p. 170, n. 1. See comment on II, p. 194.

II, p. 173. See chapter XIV.

II, p. 180. Novati's date of February 6, 1387 (?) is based on the phrase *presentis frigoris intemperiem*; he quotes testimony to the effect that January of 1387 was very cold in Florence. The whole sentence reads: « Desine conqueri pestes et presentis frigoris intemperiem lamentari ». The plague of 1383 would be a recent memory in 1384 but not in 1387. Furthermore, Coluccio alludes to the death of Bernardo's father Pietro, who died of the plague on October 13, 1383. There would be a point to alluding to it in February, 1384, less than four months later, but much less point in 1387. It is clear that Bernardo had mentioned the death of his father in the letter to which Coluccio's is a reply, for Coluccio continues: « Quid autem de ceteris dicam, quos tanta cum affectione conquereris patrie fuisse subtractos? ». Evidently the pestilence, which caused the death of Bernardo's father and of many other prominent men, was the initial cause of Bernardo's despondency; the current cold weather was just an aggravation of the difficulties. The letter should, therefore, be dated 1384. See chapter XIV.

II, p. 192. Novati, acknowledging difficulty in dating this letter, settled on 1387-88. He was certain that it must be earlier than 1390 because of his argument for the dating of II, p. 265 as December 7, 1390. The new information furnished by the Turin manuscript shows that Benvenuto da Imola was dead when II, p. 192 was written (see chapter XIV) and, since Benvenuto died at Ferrara just before June 16, 1390, as we know from a dated epistle of Vergerio, the letter must have been written after that date. Novati's argument that it was written before 1390 rests on the following facts. In II, p. 265, dated December 7, Salutati says that he will enter his sixtieth year the following February. Thus this letter must have been written in 1390. In it he admits that he has not kept his promise of writing at least once a year. That promise was made in II, p. 192 (p. 193, line 12). The interval between the two letters, however, would be less than six months by my dating (about June 16, date of Benvenuto's death, to December 7). All we can say is that Coluccio had forgotten on December 7 just when he had written last to Bernardo. Actually Coluccio wrote him another letter (a long one too) only eight days after that of December 7 (II, p. 273) and again on the following June 7 (II, p. 279). Another point that is now established is that Benvenuto's son Campaldino was in Bologna, possibly studying there. This letter may even have been written after 1392 (see chapter XIV).

II, p. 194, n. 2. In this letter Coluccio is talking about a commentary on Martianus Capella (« quoddam scriptum super Martiano Capella »); on p. 169 he is talking about « Rethoricam Martiani » (but see chapter XIV)—an entirely different thing. The copy of the latter is in existence, as I have shown in my book on *The Humanism of Coluccio Salutati*, p. 189 (Laur. Marc. 264). The former, it can be said with some assurance, is the commentary of Rémi of Auxerre, for it is Benvenuto's son who is reported to be asking the return of the manuscript (see below, pp. 291-292), and Benvenuto cites « Remigius super Martianum » (Lacaita, *op. cit.*, III, p. 6). This perhaps was the manuscript belonging to Coluccio which once was in the Chapter Library of Genoa (see *Humanism*, p. 204): « Liber expositionis super Martinianam ». Novati's mistake in identifying the two works led him to date I, p. 192 later than I, p. 168. There is therefore no evidence to establish their relative dates.

II, p. 238. Also in Savignano, Biblioteca Comunale 75. See below on III, p. 76.

II, p. 277, n. 1. Smith differs in some details about Vergerio's life [31].

II, p. 279, n. 2. The letter is dated 1391 by Novati. In it Coluccio states that he has been interested in orthography for thirty-five years, which takes us back to 1356. Novati observes that this date must have had some particular significance for Coluccio that is unknown to us. Coluccio certainly had in mind the acquisition of his copy of Priscian in October, 1355. Either the letter should be dated 1390 or, more probably, Coluccio is using a round number [32].

II, pp. 297-298, n. 3. Coluccio mentions the names of the six authors of the *Historia Augusta* in a list of authors whose works are lost. A few lines later he lists them among the authors whose works he has. This naturally puzzled Novati. But there is an explanation. Coluccio begins the passage with a series of questions: Where are the annals of Ennius, Quadrigarius, etc.? Where are Cornelius Nepos, Tacitus, Tranquillus? Novati rightly explains that the allusions to Nepos and Suetonius are to such lost works as the *Chronica* of the former and the *De viris illustribus* of the latter. He is surprised about Tacitus, but as Coluccio does not quote Tacitus at any time it is likely that he had no manuscript, in spite of the fact that Tacitus was known to Boccaccio and other contemporaries.

But to return to the *Historia Augusta*. In the passage that immediately follows (pp. 298-299) Coluccio says that he is not looking for the common authors (whose works he has): « Non

[31] L. Smith, *Epistolario di Pier Paolo Vergerio* (Rome, 1934), pp. xiv, 53.
[32] For further details see B. L. Ullman, *The Humanism of Coluccio Salutati*, pp. 44, 109, 167.

etiam Suetonium De duodecim Cesaribus; non hystoricos illos qui incipientes ab Adriano usque in Numerianum omnes Cesares Augustos atque tyrannos stilo non incongruo descripserunt: Spar tianus, Capitolinus, Gallicanus, Lampridius, Trebellius, et Vopis cus ». It will be noted that this time he specifically mentions Suetonius' lives of the Caesars, which he has, not Suetonius in general as he did before in reference to lost works. In the same way he specifically says here that he is not looking for the lives of the Caesars from Hadrian to Numerianus, written by the six authors of the *Historia Augusta.* Earlier he mentioned these six in general. Evidently he thought that they had written other histories, or, possibly, he supposed that each had written more lives than are now extant, that the existing collection contains one life of each emperor, chosen from as many as six.

II, p. 298, n. 2. The *Historia scholastica* of Petrus Comestor is meant by Coluccio, not the *Historia tripartita* of Cassiodorus

II, pp. 340, 354. Kirner stated that these letters were written in 1393, not 1392, but he postponed discussion to a forthcoming article [33]. In IV, p. 616 Novati noted that in an unpublished paper Kirner discussed the date of these letters but gave no details. Novati later received a copy, for in his collection I found a manuscript copy of Kirner's article (93 in box 7). Kirner argued convincingly that these letters were written in 1393, not 1392. He agreed with Novati that II, p. 335 was the first letter written to Pasquino after the war between Florence and Milan and therefore is to be dated July 4, 1392. But since Coluccio in the letter on p. 340 starts by saying that this was the sixth letter or more he had written Pasquino since the establishment of peace, it is obvious that it must be dated July 16, 1393, not 1392. The allusion in the July 4 letter to Pasquino's promise to obtain Cicero's epistles for Salutati must refer to the prewar period. Of the various letters that Salutati wrote Pasquino between July 4, 1392, and July 16, 1393, only two have survived (II, pp. 375, 386). II, p. 354, to Loschi, goes with II, p. 340 and was written five days later, on July 21, 1393. Both letters refer to Florentine ambassadors at Milan, but there is no trace of such in July of

---

[33] G. Kirner in *Studi italiani di filologia classica,* IX (1901), p. 397, notes 1 and 2.

1392, whereas in July of 1393 documents confirm Salutati's statement, as Novati himself indicates (p. 341, n.). In writing to
Loschi Coluccio says that in view of Loschi's negligence in securing a copy of Varro he had asked the Milanese ambassador to
Florence, Ruggieri Cane, about getting one (II, p. 358). Kirner
supposed that Coluccio asked the ambassador in person at the
time the latter was in Florence in September of 1392 (II, p.
387, n.). It seems more likely to me that Coluccio wrote Cane
in July of 1393, shortly before he wrote Loschi. Presumably he
had established friendly personal relations with the ambassador
in September of 1392. Mainardi came to the same conclusion
about the dating of these letters as Kirner [34].

The new dating enables us to get a clearer picture of the
story of Salutati's acquisition of the letters of Cicero. In July of
1392 (II, p. 335) he asks Pasquino what the status is of the
copy of Cicero's letters about which « tu michi spem dederas » (in
the prewar period). Of course Coluccio has in mind the letters
which Petrarch had, i.e., the epistles to Atticus, the only ones he
knew about. In August Coluccio writes in such a way as to
indicate that the manuscript was ready or almost ready to be sent
(II, p. 375). In September he writes that the volume has come
(II, p. 386). He infers that it was copied from a Vercelli codex
and discovers that it contains, not the letters to Atticus, but
another collection (Ad familiares). Presumably Pasquino or Loschi
had said something about a manuscript in Vercelli. Coluccio
goes on to say that there used to be a copy in Verona of the
letters to Atticus and asks Pasquino to get a copy of that as well
(cf. II, p. 397 to Loschi). In July of 1393 (II, p. 340) he is pleased
that Pasquino is having the Verona manuscript copied for him.
Novati realizes that the explicit mention of Verona weakens his
argument for the date, but his explanation is not convincing. Five
days later, in writing to Loschi (II, p. 354) Salutati expresses his
joy at the imminent arrival of the manuscript and repeats the
instructions given to Pasquino to send it by the Florentine ambassadors.

[34] G. Mainardi in Annali della Biblioteca Governativa e Libreria Civica di
Cremona, I (1948; published 1949), p. 82.

Novati is wrong in saying that Coluccio's copy of the Vercelli manuscript of the *Epistolae ad familiares* does not exist; it is Laur. XLIX, 7. The Vercelli manuscript itself also is in that library (XLIX, 9). Coluccio's copy of the Atticus letters is Laur XLIX, 18. See *The Humanism of Coluccio Salutati*, p. 146.

II, pp. 346 ff. and notes. On the poem about Petrarch and the discussion of the Muses see also my edition of Coluccio's *De laboribus Herculis* (Zurich, 1951) I, 9, 15 ff. (p. 45, 10).

II, p. 391, n. 1. See on II, p. 9, n. 1.

II, p. 394. Also in Vat. lat. 1877 and Prague, Univ. III. G. 18.

II, p. 399. For the verse from the Palatine Anthology about the birthplace of Homer, see James Hutton, *The Greek Anthology in Italy to the Year 1800* (Ithaca, 1935), pp. 81-85; Pier Giorgio Ricci in *Rinascimento*, III (1952), p. 159. Dominici, *Lucula Noctis* 10, 87 (Hunt), in quoting the lines follows Boccaccio's text (*Gen.* XIV, 19). In his copy of Dominici Coluccio adds the variant *Piros* for *Pilos*. This shows that Novati was wrong in not accepting the reading *Pyros* of two of his four manuscripts (a third has *Puros*) instead of Pylos [35].

II, p. 400. Also in Prague, Univ. III. G. 18. The Vatican manuscript is numbered 1877, not 1871. An early Italian translation was published by R. Piattoli in *La Rinascita*, VI (1943), p. 182.

II, p. 404. In his note on IV, p. 306, Novati changes his earlier dating of December 25, 1392 (?) to December 25, 1393. Sabbadini dates it January 25, 1394 [36]. In his corrections in IV, p. 617 Novati assigns all the Giovanni da Ravenna correspondence to 1394. Coluccio addresses Giovanni as chancellor in Padua, but Sabbadini shows that Giovanni did not undertake that office until 1393, and Ziliotto believes that this did not happen until the very end of the year, since his predecessor Nicoletto d'Alessio did not die before that time [37].

---

[35] See chapter XII.

[36] *Op. cit.*, p. 74.

[37] B. Ziliotto, « Rime dell'istriano Nicoletto di Alessio », *Archeografo triestino*, Ser. IV. XIV-XV (1948), p. 18.

The letter is a reply to one which Giovanni wrote, according to the manuscripts, on January 4 (IV, p. 305). Coluccio's answer is dated December 25. It does not seem likely that nearly a year elapsed before Coluccio replied to this letter of praise; nothing in his letter implies an apology for delay. Novati changes January 4 to December 4 in Giovanni's letter, while Sabbadini changes Coluccio's December 25 to January 25. The tricky ancient method of dating makes it more plausible that *octavo kalendas ianuarii* is wrong (for *februarii*), since the month in which the letter was written was in that case actually January, rather than that *pridie nonas Iani* is incorrect [38].

II, pp. 411, 437, 470. These letters, also to Giovanni, must now, in the light of the preceding discussion, be dated 1394 instead of 1393.

II, p. 435. Also in Savignano, Biblioteca Comunale 75. See below on III, p. 76.

II, p. 456. As the tradition of this letter (see Novati's note 2) is tied up with the letters just discussed (cf. III, p. 512), the date 1394 is now more probable than 1393. Novati's argument for 1393 is that Coluccio's correspondent Zambeccari had gone to Perugia in June of that year and might have stopped off at Florence. But in his letter Coluccio expresses the wish that Zambeccari might have remained in Florence on Tuesday, the day he left: « die Martis, que te hinc abstulit ». Novati himself says that Zambeccari was back in Bologna on July 24 at the latest [39]. Now Coluccio's letter was written on August 16. His language sounds as if Zambeccari left Florence the immediately preceding Tuesday, not some Tuesday a month or two earlier. Therefore Novati's evidence for the possibility of a visit by Zambeccari to Florence in June or early July of 1393 is not valid for the dating of this letter.

II, p. 480. Novati's date, 1390-96 (?), is narrowed down to before 1395 by G. Mercati, who assigns Simons's translation of

---

[38] To the literature on Giovanni add V. Zaccaria, « Il *Memorandarum rerum liber* di Giovanni di Conversino da Ravenna », *Atti dell'Istituto Veneto*, CVI, Part II, *Scienze Morali e Lettere* (1947-48), p. 221.

[39] We also know he was in Bologna on July 30, 1393, as we have a letter of his of that date (L. Frati, *op. cit.*, p. 54).

Plutarch's *De cohibenda ira* to 1370-78 [40]. But Dean P. Lockwood found a manuscript in Seville containing a dedicatory letter to Cardinal Pietro de' Corsini dated at Avignon January 20, 1373 [41].

III, pp. 3, 6, 20, 41. The facts which Novati presents (pp. 3-4, n. 1) point conclusively, it seems to me, to the date 1392, rather than Novati's 1392-94, for this group of letters to Zambeccari.

III, p. 8, line 12. As Novati says, this is from the *Liber glossarum*, or *Glossarium Ansileubi*, now published in W. Lindsay, *Glossaria Latina*, I (Paris, 1926). This gloss, on p. 282, Ho 64, is based on Isidore, *Etym.* X, 116. See also on III, pp. 158, 590.

III, p. 15. The Macrobius reference should be III, 14, 7.

III, p. 36. Novati's note 2 is confused. Coluccio quoted Juvenal 6, 8, which is an allusion to Catullus 3, 18. Though Juvenal did not mention Catullus' name, Coluccio recognized the allusion, thus revealing that he was familiar with Catullus' poem. Novati's reference to Catullus 14, 13 is completely incorrect.

On the same page Coluccio wrote: « Ridebit et te Veronensis Catullus et dicet: insane, quam in amore castitatem dicis? ». If it were not for the *milieu* in which this is found, it would seem unlikely that Coluccio had in mind 16, 5: « Nam castum esse decet pium poetam ipsum, versiculos nihil necesse est ». « Veronensis » he found in his manuscript of Catullus (Vat. Ottob. lat. 1829).

The word *faleucio*, used by Coluccio on this page in introducing a quotation of nine lines from poem 5, he got from the same manuscript. Coluccio himself added metrical notes in the margins of the earlier poems. Most common is *faleucium endecasillabum*; also used is *endecasillabi faleutici*. In the fifth poem, by an error, he has *faulecii endecasillabi*. In his quotation he cited line 8 as emended by him in his manuscript: « Deinde mi altera da secunda centum ». In line 3 he wrote *reputemus* for *aestimemus*, indicating that he was quoting from memory. So we may infer that he was quoting from memory in mentioning the type of meter: he used the more common form.

---

[40] G. Mercati in *Studi e testi,* 30 (Rome, 1916), Addendum, p. 2; cf. *Bessarione,* 33 (1917), p. 333, n. 3.

[41] *Proceedings of the American Philological Association,* LXIV (1933), p. lxvi.

III, p. 46, line 19. Cf. Seneca, *De vita beata*, 9, 4.

III, p. 58. Also in Prague, Univ. III. G. 18.

III, p. 63, line 23. The reference is to Luscius Lanuvinus, the adversary of Terence. But that does not justify Novati in changing the manuscript reading *Lavinium* to *Lanuvinum*. He himself notes that some ancient texts miscall the man Lavinius. An editor should print the texts of works of the Middle Ages and Renaissance as their authors wrote them, not in accordance with facts established by modern scholarship. Novati does not usually commit this error.

III, p. 65, n. 1. Novati's quotation from Barb. lat. 32 (formerly VIII, 32) of a brief eulogy of Tommaso di ser Rigo is full of errors and queries. Here is a correct copy:

Sermo hic editus a Thoma ser Rigi de Perusio, vigienni quadrienni [42] adolescenti, quem putavit ille, quam primum librum Ethicorum Aristotilis cepisset legere, recitare, sed mors preveniens aliter terinavit [43]. Nam cum divina et humana in divine archano mentis consistant, nec aliter quam [44] ex eadem [45] maxime que in naturalibus cendentia [46] ad generationem et corruptionem per seriem causarum dependent [47], torqueantur, primo iunii MCCCC idem adolescens ad divina evocatus, humana reliquit et superis mixtus quod fide credidit ac tenuit et interdum acuto eius dono Dei ingenio diserte disputavit, clara luce tuetur. Nec mirum, cum a pueritia in hodiernum usque non viderim felix tanto filio pater cum [48] amore illectum pecunie illecebreve alicus [49], non ex ore cadere verbum turpe, non difluere aut labi, uti adolescentibus mos est; quin ymo illam [50] aspernari et voluptates quasque nedum fugere sed abhorrere, nec tantum abhorrere sed detestari. Semper ad aliquid vestigandum utile vel honestum, quod idem est, curam, verba, et opera ponebat. Non modo mores predicabat sed morum in exemplar sese exigebat et totum se studio liberali iugiter vendicabat.

---

[42] I.e., 24 years old.
[43] For *determinavit*?
[44] *Nec aliter quam* seems to mean *nec non*.
[45] I.e., *mente; ex* might well be omitted.
[46] For *tendentia*?
[47] The subject is *(ea) que*.
[48] For *eum*.
[49] For *alicuius*.
[50] Refers to *illecebre*?

From the phrase *felix tanto filio pater*, especially as reinforced by the words I have added from the manuscript, it is clear that the author of this eulogy is not, as Novati thought, some unknown contemporary, but the father himself. In a letter to the father which Coluccio wrote at the time of the son's death (III, p. 400) he used the same phrase of himself and his son Piero, who had died of the plague: *tali filio ... felicem* (p. 401, line 14).

Novati dates the letter in 1395 (?) when Tommaso was 19. But since Coluccio says (p. 66, line 2) that Tommaso has not yet (*nondum*) completed the age of adolescence, which was 25, according to the mediaeval usage which Coluccio, as Novati observes, is here following, I think a time much closer to the end of adolescence is indicated. I should therefore set a date of 1397 or 1398. See too below on III, p. 238.

III, p. 66. The definition of the poet is taken in part from Averroes on Aristotle's *Poetics*. See my edition of Coluccio's *De laboribus Herculis,* I, 2, 1 (p. 10, 5) and *Epist.*, III, pp. 225, 289, etc. But for a discussion of the mediaeval Latin *Poetics* see my forthcoming article in *Estudis Romànics*. The phrase « vis laudandi vituperandique » is used of the orator by Cicero (*Part.* 82; cf. 69, 71).

III, p. 71. On Jean de Montreuil see A. Thomas, « Le nom et la famille de Jehan de Monstereul », *Romania*, XXXVII (1908), pp. 594-602; A. Coville, *Gontier et Pierre Col et l'humanisme en France au temps de Charles VI* (Paris, 1934); A. Coville, *Recherches sur quelques écrivains du XIVe et du XVe siècle* (Paris, 1935).

III, p. 76. The letter of Cardinal Uliari to which this is a reply has been published by A. Campana from a manuscript in Savignano, Biblioteca Comunale 75, in Charles Henderson, Jr., *Classical Mediaeval and Renaissance Studies in Honor of Berthold Louis Ullman* (Rome, 1964), p. 237. The manuscript also contains Salutati's answering letter. Campana makes the attractive suggestion that a ten-line epitaph for the Cardinal that has been preserved to us was composed by Salutati, who wrote similar epitaphs for several others.

III, p. 90, line 18. Cf. on I, p. 206.

III, p. 105. Cammelli says that Cydonius was born

1315-20 at Thessalonica and died in 1400 [51]. The letter printed in
Migne is, contrary to Novati's view, genuine, but the date 1430
for the letter is incorrect. It is attributed to Cydonius in three
manuscripts.

III, p. 108. Loenertz has shown that Novati is wrong in
inferring from this letter that Cydonius and Chrysoloras came
to Venice in 1395, since it can now be proved that this trip took
place in 1390-91 [52]. Loenertz also observes that there is no
reason for Novati's statement (III, p. 106, n., and p. 129, n.)
that Iacopo Angeli da Scarperia accompanied Roberto Rossi
to Venice.

III, p. 119. Cammelli notes that Novati is mistaken (p. 120,
n. 4) in assigning Malpaghini's employment to the year 1396 (it
should be 1397) and therefore in the inferences about Chrysoloras'
and Angeli's movements [53].

III, p. 138, n 1. Novati's assumption that Coluccio's
son Andrea must have held an official position as his father's
assistant is unwarranted. Coluccio says that his son took over
the answering of letters of condolence on the death of Coluccio's
wife. This, of course, was in a purely personal and private
capacity. On the other hand, it is true that Salutati's son
Bonifazio was his *coadiutor* in official matters in 1378 [54].

III, p. 158, line 8. For the gloss from the *Liber glossarum*, see W. M. Lindsay, *Glossaria Latina*, I, p. 157, Cu 217,
based on Isidore, *Diff.*, p. 16, 106 Arevalo. See also on III,
pp. 8, 590.

III, p. 165. Novati's date for this letter is 1395-1400 (?).
On p. 170, line 14, Salutati says that he has been investigating the
problem of Theseus' wishes for forty years. If we date the letter
in 1395, we get back to 1355, the year which perhaps actually
marked the beginning of Coluccio's humanistic interest, as has
been shown in my book on *The Humanism of Coluccio Salutati*.

[51] *Démétrius Cydonès, Correspondance,* ed. G. Cammelli (Paris, 1930),
pp. VI-X.

[52] R. J. Loenertz, « Correspondance de Manuel Calecas ... », *Studi e testi,*
152 (1950), pp. 64, 73, n. 3.

[53] G. Cammelli, *Manuele Crisolora* (Florence, 1941), p. 39, n. 2.

[54] D. Marzi, *La Cancelleria della Repubblica Fiorentina* (Rocca S. Casciano, 1910), p. 139, n. 6.

III, p. 189, lines 19, 26. Novati should have written *Galieni* and *Galienum,* the readings of his manuscript, as his apparatus shows. Novati himself used this spelling in II, p. 234, line 17. So also in my edition of the *De laboribus Herculis,* p. 131, 19.

III, p. 221. The one manuscript containing this letter indicates that it is addressed to « Reverendo in Christo patri d. Iohanni de Sancto Miniate monaco camaldulensi ». Novati vehemently rejects this statement and calls the correspondent an unknown by the name of Giovanni. He toys with the notion that he may have been Giovanni Conversino da Ravenna. But the manuscript is right and Novati is wrong. In his *De laboribus Herculis* III, 31, 2 (p. 344, 6 of my edition) Coluccio quotes from this very letter and says it was addressed to Iohannes ser Duccii, who is none other than Giovanni da San Miniato [55]:

Et sicut ad Iohannem ser Duccii meum scribens memini me dixisse, quid aliud naves significant quam nostram voluntatem? Sicut enim navi per mare ferimur, sic et voluntate in nostras ferimur actiones... Movetur voluntas arbitrii libertate, imo, si pressius respiciamus, incedit; movetur, imo graditur, navis quasi pedibus equali depositione vel interrupta alternatione remorum. Habet navis clavum, cuius regimine quicquid ipsam movet gubernatur; habet voluntas rationem, cuius moderamine dirigitur et salvatur.

Compare with this the words of the letter (p. 230, line 28 ff.):

Navis enim, qua per mare vehimur, nostram significat voluntatem, qua, sicut navi quadam, in nostras ferimur actiones. Et sicuti expanso velorum sinu navis quo ventus impulerit rapitur, sic currens nostra voluntas primis motibus agitatur, remis autem, quasi sue libertatis arbitrio, non fertur sed progreditur et quandoque ipsa sensuum mobilitate... trahitur et portatur. Verum si rationis gubernaculo veluti navis clavo voluntas nostra dirigitur...

But on one point Novati is right: it is clear from the form of Giovanni's name as given in the *De laboribus Herculis* that Giovanni was not yet a monk and that the part of the inscription which gives him that title must be rejected. The date of the letter, which Novati tentatively assigned to 1397, must be 1389 or earlier.

---

[55] Cf. T. F. Rich in *Speculum,* XI (1936), p. 386.

III, p. 221, line 14.   Coluccio attributes the word *queritatus* to « Madaurensis », i.e., Apuleius, but, as Novati notes, the word does not occur in that author but only in Pliny, *Ep.* VI, 20, 14 and Valerius Maximus IX, 2, 1 (also VI, 2, 8).   Coluccio's Apuleius manuscript also contains Pliny and one would like to suppose that this was the origin of the confusion.   Unfortunately, however, the Pliny in this manuscript ends at V, 8.   Could Coluccio have had access to another manuscript containing Apuleius and Pliny?   It is more likely that Coluccio confused Apuleius and Valerius.   Some of the manuscripts of the latter have Coluccio's spelling *queritatus* instead of the generally accepted *quiritatus*.   However, Coluccio's own copy (Vat. lat. 1928) has *quiritatus* at both points.

III, p. 225, line 19.   The Latin version of Alpharabius was printed at Paris in 1638: G. Camerarius, *Alpharabii vetustissimi Aristotilis interpretis opera omnia.*   But it is certain that Salutati is quoting at second hand from Vincent of Beauvais, *Doct.* III, 109 (Douai edition, 1624; also with slight differences, the edition of Rusch and the Venice edition of 1494).   Note the three versions:

> Coluccio: Alpharabius, qui poesim inter partes logice numeravit, adiciens eius proprium esse sermonibus suis, facere auditorem aliquid pulcrum imaginari vel fedum, ut auditor credat et abhorreat vel appetat; quanvis certissime teneat rem ita non esse.

This is partly repeated in IV, p. 231, in this form:

> Quanvis poetice proprium sit... sermonibus suis facere imaginari aliquid pulcrum vel fedum quod non est, ita ut auditor credat et aut abhorreat vel appetat; quanvis etiam certi simus quod non est ita in veritate, tamen exiguntur animi nostri ad horrendum vel appetendum quod imaginantur.

> Vincent: Post artem rhetoricam dicendum restat de poetica, quam et Alpharabius... inter logicae partes ultimam ponit... Idem quoque dicit... quod poetice proprium est, sermonibus suis facere imaginari aliquid pulchrum vel foedum quod non est, ita ut auditor credat et aliquid abhorreat vel appetat, quamvis, cum certum sit non ita esse in veritate, animi tamen audientium eriguntur ad horrendum vel appetendum quod imaginantur.

Alpharabius: De scientia logicae. Elementa autem quibus scientia verificatur quinque sunt, scilicet demonstrativa, tentativa, sophistica, rhetorica, poetica (p. 8). Proprium est autem poeticae sermonibus sensum facere, imaginari pulchrum aliquid et dubium quod non est, ita ut auditor credat et aliquid abhorreat vel appetat; quamvis enim certi sumus quod est ita in natura (p. 10).

The version of Alpharabius in the Paris edition is probably that of John of Seville [56].

Salutati did not make much use of Vincent but preferred to get his quotations at first hand wherever possible. In this case, however, he presumably did not have access to a manuscript of Alpharabius.

III, p. 238. The addressee is Tommaso di ser Rigo, whom we discussed above on III, p. 65. Tommaso had sent an ancient manuscript of Martianus Capella owned by a friend to Coluccio, who now has had it « paulo plus quam congruat ». This can mean anything from several months to several years. At the time of Tommaso's death his father asked for the return of the book. On July 13, 1400, Coluccio apologized to the father for keeping it so long: he had had it for a year or more (III, p. 400). Now the present letter to Tommaso has the date January 24. Coluccio could have received the manuscript in June, 1399, written to Tommaso on January 24, 1400, and thus held the manuscript « a year or more » when he wrote the father on July 13, 1400. Perhaps it is more likely that he received the manuscript in the latter half of 1398 and wrote to Tommaso January 24, 1399. In that case the manuscript would have been in his hands one and a half to two years at the time he wrote to Tommaso's father. Certainly the phrase *annum et ultra* cannot be stretched farther. The letter to Tommaso was therefore written in 1399 or 1400, not 1398.

III, pp. 308, 310. Also in British Museum, Cotton Cleopatra C. 5.

III, p. 351, n. 2. The meager information about Guido di Tommaso is supplemented by Vat. Chigi G. VII. 191, fol. 205, which states that he was ambassador to Charles III of Naples in

---

[56] *Collection of Oriental Writers on Music,* ed. Henry George Farmer, II (Glasgow, 1934), p. 19.

1385 and that he concluded a treaty with the Duke of Milan in 1389. But the latter date is wrong; the correct date (1391) is given by Leonardo Bruni, who names Guido Thommasi as one of three ambassadors sent to negotiate a peace with Gian Galeazzo [57].

III, p. 396. This letter is also in Bologna, Univ. 2845.

III, p. 431. There is frequent allusion to Plato in connection with this idea in De laboribus Herculis: I, 2, 9; III, 31, 9; III, 43, 8; 48; IV, 1, 2, 13; IV, 1, 4, 3; IV, 1, 8, 21; IV, 2, 3, 7. Coluccio's sources seem to have been Plato (Chalcid.), Tim. 41 d; Macrobius, Somn. Scip. I, 11, 10-11; Augustine, Civ. Dei XIII, 19; Myth. Vat. III, 6, 8.

III, p. 501. Novati's date for this letter, 1401 (?), must be rejected. First of all, Novati is inconsistent. In this letter Coluccio says that Malpaghini is perhaps over forty-five years old (p. 510, line 9). On p. 537, n. 2, Novati assumes that Malpaghini was born in 1359. That would date the present letter to 1404 or later. But Sabbadini has shown that Malpaghini was born about 1346 and so dates this letter 1392 or 1393 [58]. Foresti, overlooking or ignoring or minimizing Coluccio's excesseris, makes it 1391 [59].

III, p. 516. This letter too would belong to 1391-93, as it is associated with the preceding.

III, p. 534. In this letter Coluccio recommends Giovanni Malpaghini for a position. Sabbadini determines the birth year of Malpaghini as about 1346 [60]. Interpreting the phrase amodo mature etatis which Coluccio applies to him (p. 537, line 12) as not over forty, he arrives at the date 1386 for this letter. Foresti accepts Novati's date, incomprehensibly rejecting the date 1393 suggested by Massèra, who makes an impressive and convincing presentation of facts and arguments [61]. Massèra's best proof is that Iacopo Allegretti, whose death Coluccio mentions in this let-

[57] Leonardo Bruni, Historiae Florentini populi, ed. E. Santini (Città di Castello, 1926), p. 258, in L. A. Muratori, Rerum Italicarum Scriptores, ed. 2, XIX, 3.

[58] Op. cit., p. 247.

[59] Op. cit., p. 455.

[60] Loc. cit.

[61] A. F. Massèra in Atti della R. Deputazione di storia patria, Romagna, XVI (1926), p. 189.

ter, was still alive in 1391. Giovanni, whom Coluccio is recommending to Carlo Malatesta to take Iacopo's place, had employment as a professor in Florence beginning with October, 1394, and must have known of his coming position by September of that year. Therefore, argues Massèra, the letter (which has the date September 10) was written in 1393. But Massèra's inference that Salutati had already spoken to Malatesta about Malpaghini in the summer of 1393 is inacceptable. Therefore the date of the letter cannot be narrowed down to 1393, but can be set between 1391 and 1393.

III, p. 537, n. 2. Novati's argument that two different persons by the name of Giovanni da Ravenna worked for Petrarch because one was recommended to Petrarch by Pandolfo Malatesta, the other by Donato Albanzani, is generally rejected. As Sabbadini remarks, the one man may have had recommendations from both [62].

III, p. 539. For the date see on IV, p. 170.

III, p. 553. Walser has shown very definitely that Novati's date, October 18, 1401, must be changed to 1402 [63].

III, p. 569. Also in Oxford, Bodl. Misc. 399.

III, p. 585. The date 1401 (?) is corrected to 1402 by Novati himself in his note on p. 586.

III, p. 590, line 17. For the gloss from the *Liber glossarum*, see W. M. Lindsay, *Glossaria Latina*, I, p. 540, St 364, based on Isidore, *Etym*. XII, 7, 42. See also on III, pp. 8, 158.

III, p. 615, n. 1. According to Vat. Chigi G. VII. 191, the last of the Corbinelli brothers was named Filippo, not Piero.

III, pp. 624-627. The information about Ptolemy's *Geography* was no doubt furnished him either by his protégé, Iacopo Angeli da Scarperia, who also gave him information on other Greek texts (III, pp. 522-523 and notes) or by Chrysoloras. Coluccio wrote the present letter in 1403. Angeli finished his translation of Ptolemy's *Geography* three years later [64]. It became very popular and exercised considerable influence, but the name of the translator has been all but forgotten.

[62] *Op. cit.*, p. 243.
[63] E. Walser, *Poggius Florentinus* (Leipzig, 1914), p. 11, n. 2.
[64] For the date see Chapter I, note 28.

When Chrysoloras came to Florence in 1397 to teach Greek, he was handicapped by a lack of texts. One of his students, the rich nobleman Palla Strozzi, remedied the situation. Among other books, he obtained Ptolemy's *Geography*, illustrated (i.e., with maps), in Constantinople, if we can believe Vespasiano da Bisticci, whom there is no reason to discredit in this detail [65].

Chrysoloras too started to translate the *Geography*, but did not get very far. It was only a « particula » according to a letter of Bruni written in 1405 [66]. Angeli also refers to it, in his dedicatory letter to Pope Alexander V, saying that Chrysoloras began a translation (*incipit*). It might be thought that Coluccio obtained his information from this translation, or even that Chrysoloras made it specifically for Coluccio, but against this view is the fact that Coluccio quotes from the third book. Yet the idea of making the translation may have come to Chrysoloras as a result of Coluccio's inquiries for information. It is more likely that Coluccio got his facts from Chrysoloras rather than from Angeli, for the latter says that his teacher preserved the Greek title *Geographia* in his verbatim translation, whereas he, Angeli, changed it to *Cosmographia*. Coluccio uses the title *Geographia*. At any rate, Coluccio apparently has the credit for being the first person in the West to quote from a work that made a great impression during the following century. I have the feeling that it was Coluccio who urged Angeli to make his translation, but of course this is a pure guess.

III, p. 627, n. 3. The inscriptions of Tifernum (Città di Castello) have now been published in *C. I. L.* XI, 2, fasc. 1 (1901). The name of the townsmen is mentioned in 5942, of the town in 5937 and in abbreviated form (*Tif. Tib.*) in 5933 and 5939. 5940 has the name of a woman Tifernia, and this may possibly be the inscription Salutati saw, for it is later reported as in the Duomo (S. Florido), and Salutati states that he saw his *in domibus canonicorum*.

III, p. 634. Also in Oxford, All Souls College 94.

---

[65] Vespasiano da Bisticci, *Vite di uomini illustri del secolo XV* (Florence, 1938), p. 293.

[66] Quoted by G. Cammelli, *Manuele Crisolora* (Florence, 1941), p. 180.

III, p. 653. Also in British Museum, Cotton Cleopatra C. 5.

III, p. 656, n. 1. Novati's suggestion that the Cicero copied by Poggio which Coluccio was awaiting impatiently is Laur. 48, 22 is untenable, for this manuscript was written in 1425 [67]. Accordingly the variants could not have been entered in it by Coluccio. See too B. L. Ullman, *The Origin and Development of Humanistic Script* (Rome, 1960), p. 33.

IV, p. 69. Monfrin has published the dialogue about the schism written by Giovanni da Spoleto and dedicated to Iacopo degli Altoviti [68].

IV, p. 78. Novati dates this letter 1405 (?) but L. Smith on good grounds dates it 1402 (?), or, at the latest, 1403 [69].

IV, p. 97-98, n. 4. Florence, Naz. I. 1. 28, containing Petrarch's *Itinerarium*, did not belong to Salutati; see chapter VII.

IV. p. 106. Novati says that this letter praising Leonardo Bruni to Pope Innocent VII is found in some sixty manuscripts, of which about half are collections of Bruni's letters. Novati uses three and lists twenty-one others. To these may be added Vat. lat. 7283, 8088, 8729, 10506, Chigi I. VIII. 250; Rome, Casanat. C. V. 32 (310) (?); Florence, Laur. Camald. 606, Ricc. 924; Lucca, 1394 A; Ravenna, 227; Gotha, XVI. 38; Prague, Univ. III. G. 18.

IV, p. 123, n. 3. Novati reports that Cristiano da Camerino is completely unknown. The work to which Coluccio refers is found in a Vatican manuscript of the fifteenth century (2847), fols. 229-240. At the end: « Egregii viri magistri Christiani de Camerino super cecatione partium Guelfe et Gebelline et ipsarum obiurgatione liber explicit ».

IV, p. 139, n. 2. This Apuleius manuscript is not in the Laurenziana but in the Nazionale of Florence (I. IX. 39).

IV, p. 157, n. 3. I see no particular reason to think that Ricc. 1222 C, corrected, as Novati says, by Coluccio himself, was the copy made for Leonardo Bruni. The numerous copies of this

---

[67] Walser, *op. cit.*, p. 105. But Walser seems to accept Novati's view on p. 27 (cf. p. 12). The marginal notes are not by Coluccio.

[68] J. Monfrin in *Rivista di storia della Chiesa in Italia*, III (1949), p. 9.

[69] *Op. cit.*, p. 253. See too G. Mainardi, *op. cit.*, p. 82.

collection of letters on the schism attest to the popular demand for these letters. This manuscript was later owned by Guido Magalotti, member of a well-known Florentine family.

IV, p. 170. Also in Vat. Barb. 1813, fols. 11r-12v (ends p. 182, line 12 *prohiberi*) and, apparently, in Berlin, lat. qu. 453, with the title « Confutatio opinionis Iohannis de Angelis » [70].

The defense of liberal studies by Francesco da Fiano (mentioned in n. 1) was composed before October, 1404, according to H. Baron. Da Fiano's important defense has at last been published [71].

IV, p. 197, n. 1, refers to the first line of the page. The reference is to Averroes rather than to Aristotle. See above on III, p. 66.

IV, p. 204, line 26. The word *discolis* is from δύσκολος. Coluccio probably found it in Papias, who defines it as *difficilis, morosus*.

IV, p. 206. On the *Lucula noctis* and the dedication copy presented to Coluccio, see Edmund Hunt, *Iohannis Dominici Lucula Noctis* (Notre Dame, 1940), and below, chapter XII.

IV, p. 231, n. 3. See above on III, p. 225.

IV, p. 270, lines 1, 3. The word *sigli* is for *psili*, ψιλή. The text and meaning have now been cleared up. The text as printed is correct, except that *per* before *ellades* should be omitted, being deleted in the single manuscript that preserves the letter [72].

IV, p. 275. Novati did not include all the letters written to Coluccio in his Appendix containing « Epistole di vari a Coluccio Salutati ». I shall make a few additions based merely on casually obtained information.

Novati includes no letters written to Coluccio by Bernardo da Moglio. One is found in Paris, N. a. l. 1152, fol. 10v. On this and Coluccio's answer see below, chapter XIV.

---

[70] For the date of this letter and other matters connected with it see chapter XI.

[71] H. Baron, *The Crisis of the Early Renaissance* (Princeton, 1955), pp. 405-408. Published by Maria Luisa Plaisant in *Rinascimento*, ser. 2, 1 (1961), p. 119. See too I. Taù, « La 'Difesa della poesia' di Francesco da Fiano », *Archivio italiano per la storia della pietà*, IV (1965).

[72] B. L. Ullman, *The Humanism*, etc., p. 120.

The letter of Antonio dei Baruffaldi which led to the writing of Coluccio's *De verecundia* is found in manuscripts of that work and has been published [73].

Novati himself published two letters of Uberto Decembrio to Coluccio [74].

IV, p. 290. Novati included only four letters of Zambeccari to Salutati; five more are published by L. Frati [75]. One (p. 16, written November 12 or 13, 1389) is certainly an answer to one of Coluccio's (II, p. 214). Novati, IV, p. 290 (=Frati, p. 17), written November 14, is a second reply to Coluccio's letter. Frati, p. 69, is a letter of 1398 not given by Novati. It is a short letter of recommendation for which no reply is extant. Another new letter (Frati, p. 72) written in 1398 or 1399, asks for a copy of *De laboribus Herculis*. One which Frati (p. 73) dates 1398 or 1399 tells of a Lucas de Montelodio who on Coluccio's instructions scolded Zambeccari. This probably has to do with Zambeccari's love affair. Frati suggests that Montelodio is for Montreuil, but that is impossible; for one thing the word *rediens* probably indicates that the man is a Bolognese. A mistake for Monterocho is more likely; *ch* is easily misread as *di*, and confusion of *l* and *r* is, of course, common. A Iohannes de Monterocho was *podestà* at Bologna in 1376. The fifth new letter (Frati, p. 81) is of uncertain date. Frati (p. xxiv) also quotes two lines of verse written by Zambeccari in answer to Coluccio's criticisms of his love affair:

> O vir divine, Cupidinis hostis,
> Cur mecum, saeve, incusas amorem?

IV, p. 293. On the Foligno ms. (C. IX. 18 = 508 Inventario anno 1930; Mazzatinti 41), see M. Faloci-Pulignani, in *Inventari dei manoscritti delle biblioteche d'Italia*, 41 (1930), p. 179; V. Rossi in his edition of Petrarch's *Familiares*, I (Florence, 1933), p. lxxii.

[73] Coluccio Salutati, *De nobilitate legum et medicinae, De verecundia*, ed. E. Garin (Florence, 1947), p. 277.

[74] *Archivio storico lombardo*, Ser. IV, 10 (1908), p. 193.

[75] *Op. cit.*

IV, p. 305. Novati's date of December 4, 1393 (?) is changed to January 4, 1394, by R. Sabbadini; see on II, p. 404. Giovanni's election to the chancellorship of Padua (p. 307, line 6) took place in the summer of 1393. Part of another letter of Giovanni's to Coluccio is printed by Sabbadini (p. 218); its date is Padua, January, 1400.

IV, p. 332, n. 1. The reference is to Cicero, *De or.* II, 261: « ut sementem feceris, ita metes ».

IV, p. 333. The letter to Giovanni da Samminiato is also in Oxford, Bodl. Misc. 399.

IV, p. 333. The date Constantinople, 1396 (?), offered by Novati for Chrysoloras' letter, is changed to Florence, 1397-99 by G. Mercati [76]. For a discussion of Chrysoloras' letters and the manuscripts see below, chapter XIII.

IV, p. 336, n. 1. On Simon of Thebes see G. Mercati in *Studi e testi*, 30 (Rome, 1916), and G. Cammelli, *Démétrius Cydonès, Correspondance*, p. 215.

IV, p. 362. Also in Oxford, Bodl. Misc. 399.

IV, p. 365. Novati prints only three letters of Vergerio to Coluccio. His date of spring, 1405, for this one is changed to 1402 (?) by L. Smith [77]. He also adds three more letters: pp. 53, 62, 64, dated January 31, May 10, and August 18; they are alluded to by Novati on II, p. 278. Smith is inclined to change the August 18 date to February 18, or else to put the last two letters in 1392. His argument is not convincing.

IV, p. 370. Smith (p. 278) dates this autumn of 1405 to spring of 1406; Novati's date is autumn, 1405. The letter was written by Vergerio for the Pope. Vergerio's own personal note, incomplete, is given by Novati on p. 374, n. 2 (Smith, p. 283). If, as Novati suggests and Smith accepts, the letter is unfinished because Coluccio died, it and the preceding must have been written in April or May, 1406.

IV, p. 375. For variants showing revision, see H. Baron, *Leonardo Bruni Aretino* (Leipzig, 1928), p. 317 (X, 5). Baron

---

[76] *Rendiconti dell'Istituto Lombardo,* Ser. II, 51 (1918), p. 232.
[77] *Op. cit.,* p. 257.

(pp. 194 f.) lists seven other letters that Bruni wrote to Coluccio, all published in the edition of Mehus.

IV, p. 387, n. 1.   The date of Coluccio's birth was February 16, not 26.   His protector at Bologna was Giovanni, not Iacopo, de' Pepoli.

IV, p. 446, n. 2.   On Viviano de' Franchi see D. Marzi, *La cancelleria della repubblica fiorentina* (Rocca S. Casciano, 1910), pp. 128 ff.

IV, p. 487.   See on II p. 47.

CHAPTER X

FILIPPO VILLANI'S COPY
OF HIS HISTORY OF FLORENCE

It is well known that a Laurentian manuscript (Ashb. 942) of the first edition of Filippo Villani's *Liber de origine civitatis Florentie et eiusdem famosis civibus* belonged to the author and was corrected by him and by Coluccio Salutati. In his earlier work Novati came to the conclusion that the manuscript was corrected but not copied by Villani [1]. U. Marchesini [2], after comparing it with autograph letters of Villani, argued that Villani copied it. I find his scholarly and thorough paper completely convincing. He is right in saying that two notes attesting to Villani's ownership are by hands differing from each other and from the text. Ordinarily such a note would be autograph, but since the two differ from each other, the one cannot be and the other need not be autograph. We may therefore accept Marchesini's decision that the manuscript was copied by the author. Novati, in his note to *Epist.*, II, p. 47, mentions Marchesini's article without touching on the question of the copyist of the manuscript, but in IV, p. 488, n., he casually accepts it as an autograph of Villani's. Novati and Marchesini identified some of the marginal notes as written by Coluccio Salutati. My own examination of the manuscript convinces me that they were right.

The first item in the manuscript is an unsigned letter which Novati correctly identified as written by Coluccio (*Epist.*, II, p. 47). It emphasizes the importance of orthography, and many of Coluccio's corrections throughout the manuscript are ortho-

---

[1] F. Novati, *La giovinezza di Coluccio Salutati* (Turin, 1888), p. 11, n. 1.
[2] *Archivio storico italiano*, Ser. V, 2 (1888), p. 366.

graphical. It is not, however, the copy that Coluccio sent, as it is in the same hand as the rest of the book, i.e., Villani's. In this letter several lines were erased, in whole or part. Possibly they contained a criticism of the book which Villani decided not to perpetuate. A few corrections on Novati's readings are offered here. The heading was probably not *Responsio* but *Responsive*. 47,8: *micchi.* 10: only *ar* of *arbitror* is now visible, the rest being torn away, but the text may have been complete in Novati's time. The *que* of *tibique* is also missing. 48, 1: only *Ro ... ñ* (of *Rogo tamen*) remains. The spelling was *ortographyam* (not *orthographiam*), with an erasure after the second *o*. 2: only the final *n* of *non* is visible. Of *opus sit elegantissimum* one can make out *o ... t ele ... ssimum*. 3: *pueril ... uinari* is all that can be made out; likewise *sillab ... elementorum*. 5: only the last letter of *pervertat* remains.

Following this letter is one written by Villani to an unnamed correspondent. In Galletti's edition it precedes [3]. Novati and Marchesini believed that it was sent to Salutati and elicited the reply we have just discussed. Novati's failure to include it in Volume IV among the letters addressed to Salutati by various persons does not necessarily indicate that he changed his mind, for he omits others (see above, chapter IX). At the same time certain doubts have developed in my mind. Villani devotes most of his letter to telling of his constant revision of the book, comparing himself to a small boy who kicks over something he has just built. He has finally decided to publish it, he continues, and to get rid of the burden, even though he is not satisfied with it. Then he asks his correspondent to cauterize the book with a knife, if need be, to cure it of its weaknesses. If this is the letter which was sent with the manuscript to Coluccio why did not Villani put it first, before the reply? Perhaps out of modesty. But below the text at the left are the words *responsio So(litarii)*, if I expand the abbreviation correctly. Villani ends the letter with « Tuus Philippus Villanus, velit nolit, solitarius », and the heading of the work itself is « F. V. Solitarii », which seems to indicate

---

[3] *Philippi Villani Liber de civitatis Florentiae famosis civibus,* ed. G. C. Galletti (Florence, 1847).

that he thought of Solitarius almost as a name. Why then *responsio*? Could the letter then be a *second* letter to Coluccio, accompanying the manuscript a second time? This does not seem likely or even possible. Or was the letter addressed to someone else? I believe we should return to the old view that this letter was addressed to a certain Eusebius, as I shall now try to prove, though I do not accept, of course, the old suggestion that Eusebius was the brother of Filippo Villani.

The Ashburnham manuscript has lost its last pages, including the conclusion to Book II and a final letter. At the beginning of the introduction to Book I the text was altered and the name of Eusebius was inserted as the addressee. Novati believed that the name of Eusebius was substituted for that of Coluccio, that it was an honorific appellation for the chancellor. This view was accepted by Marchesini (p. 369) and A. F. Massèra [4]. But why was that name not added in the copy of the two letters at the beginning? In the text of Galletti (based on another Laurentian manuscript, Gadd. 89 inf. 23) the book ends with two letters addressed to Eusebius, a short one called « conclusio opusculi » and a longer « epistola ». Let us now consider the relations of these last two items to the introduction for Book I and the letter at the beginning. Of the four, the last in position was the first to be written. Its introductory words are: « Exegisti saepius et instanter, mi Eusebi, ut quod coeptitaveram opusculum de nostrae urbis origine eiusque famosis civibus insigni viro cuiquam titulatum promulgarem, idque cur non fecerim iam diu iterum exigis importune... Nosti me curis domesticis... occupatum... opus... extrema lima intactum reliqui ». From this it is obvious that the work was not yet in final form. It is also clear that Eusebius had pressed Villani several times, orally or by letter, to dedicate it to someone and to publish it. Villani goes on to say that the work is only in first draft (« Non potui adhuc elimare rudia et scabiosa quae in seriem ferme primam ingenio dictante deduxeram »). Nor has he written any dedicatory prefaces, for hardly anyone cares to be immortalized in the pages of Villani's book: « Cui dabo quod non vult, cum alter iniuriam

[4] *Zeitschrift für romanische Philologie*, XXVII (1903), p. 306.

putet si operi suum nomen indiderit.,,, alter parvi pendat ceu rem ignobilem? ». He asks Eusebius' advice: « Titulos libro dares an illum potius parva insignitum praefatione humilitatem auctoris praeferentem quolibet mallet loci sineres ambulare? ». Then he asks whether he should dedicate it to a member of one of the monastic orders: « Applauderem uni eorum si censeres illi exordia operis dedicari; de quo edoceri cuperem ». He ends by calling attention to the reasons he has given for postponing publication and to Eusebius' offer to defend the work after publication.

The introduction to Book I, next in time of writing, I believe, states that Eusebius' eagerness to have a copy led Villani to publish it. The « conclusio operis », chronologically the third of the four items, indicates that Eusebius had suggested or at least encouraged the writing of the book: « Dixi, ut voluisti, mi frater Eusebi,... et de urbis nostrae principiis et de famosis viris ». He asks Eusebius to correct it. Last in the series, I think, is the letter that comes second in the Ashburnham manuscript, the one supposed to have been written to Coluccio. It was meant to accompany the manuscript in its final form and probably was written in answer to an urgent request by Eusebius.

Except for the matter of correction, Coluccio's brief letter includes none of the matters that Villani in these four douments says that Eusebius had taken up with him. But there is much stronger evidence that Eusebius was not a fanciful name that Villani adopted for Salutati. The contents of the four items are not such as would naturally be addressed to Coluccio. The introduction to Book I mentions the desire of Eusebius to find out about the time of the founding of Florence, what great men it produced, and other such matters. Coluccio's knowledge of these subjects was certainly as great as Villani's, in fact, his supplements to Villani's work (cf. Marchesini, p. 376, etc.) show that his knowledge at some points, at least, was greater and more accurate. Even if we make allowance for flattery, Coluccio could hardly have urged Villani to supply him with information he already possessed. The last letter in the volume speaks of the correspondent's insistence on Villani's completing the book and dedicating it to some outstanding man. Since Salutati was

considered famous enough to have his biography included in
Villani's book it would seem strange that he should be asked to
help Villani decide to whom the book should be dedicated instead
of being himself honored in this way. Villani's suggestion that
a member of one of the religious orders might be a suitable
person to honor and his request that Eusebius indicate such a
person leads one to think that the latter may himself have been
a friar; this would account for Villani's constant use of *frater*
in addressing Eusebius. One possible explanation of the insertion
of Eusebius' name in an erasure is that the monk took that name
on entering the monastery and that Villani knew him before
his adoption of the monastic life.

Salutati's corrections in Villani's manuscript are chiefly or-
thographical and grammatical, but he also corrects or queries
statements of fact. Of these, Marchesini mentions only a few.
Coluccio corrects chronology and adds quotations and information from various authors. Among the more interesting suggestions is one concerning the exile of Dante (Galletti, p. 9).
Where Villani wrote, « pro ingrate patrie monstro », Coluccio
wrote in the margin: « Non placet 'ingrate'; potius dicerem
'sediciose' ». As a loyal Florentine Coluccio refused to label the
whole community as ungrateful, preferring to attribute the exile
to the discord between Blacks and Whites. In the life of Zanobi
da Strada (Galletti, p. 16) Villani speaks of teaching school as
« vili ministerio ». Coluccio suggests « non vili sed tali », evidently because he did not think that teaching should be so vilified.

Of particular interest are Coluccio's corrections in the biography of himself (Galletti, p. 18). Novati has given a careful
collation in IV, pp. 487 ff., on which I can add only a few corrections. 490, 6: Originally Villani wrote N. C. P., then deleted
N and wrote in the margin « Niccolaus cui », etc. The name
Coluccius Pierius was not written out by Villani. 8: The first
n of Stingnani was expunged by Coluccio, then deleted by Villani. 13: *ortu* is not in erasure but has been worked over. 14:
Novati fails to mention Villani's correction of *multis* to *multum,*
a necessary reading which also appears in the second edition. 17:
The underscoring is, I believe, by Villani, not Coluccio. Villani wrote out *cumque*; Coluccio, with characteristic meticulous-

ness, changed *que* (which according to the then current practice
stood for *quae*) to the enclitic form q^3.   18: The correction to
discendis is certainly by Villani, not Coluccio.   491, 5: Surely
Novati is wrong in saying that the sense requires *coaluit* instead
of *coaluerit*.   The verb is in an indirect question.   The second
edition too has *coaluerit*.   15-17: The addition of *constat* and the
changes are the work of Villani.   24: Corrected from *dingnitate*
by Villani.   493, 5: Novati is mistaken here; the manuscript has
mortis, the reading Novati thought should be expected, not *mentis*, the one he gives.   20: Villani added *se* above the line.   23:
Villani added *publici.*

The only one of the few suggestions made by Coluccio in
his own biography that has any significance is the change of
iuris civilis to *notarie* (490, 16).   This makes clear that Coluccio
never attended the school of law at Bologna but only the shorter
notarial course, in which naturally some study of law was
required.

Others have noted that the Codex Gaddianus, which Galletti used as the basis for his text, was copied from the Ashburnham manuscript.   Worth noting are some of the amusing errors
made by the scribe as a result of being confused by the corrections and marginal notes in the autograph manuscript.   In
Book I (not reproduced by Galletti), fol. 6, Villani wrote: « Ea
urbs... prospectat aut longe multo amplius », writing *aut* for
haud, in accordance with his custom and that of the time; Coluccio noted in the margin: « Si 'aut' pro 'non' ponitur, 'haud' per
'h' et 'd' scribatur ».   The Gaddianus incorporates the note in
the text: « prospectat amplius aut longe multo amplius.   Si aut »,
etc.   Similarly on the same page Villani wrote: « triginta sex
milibus annorum maximi celi annum perficere, qui a Platone
annus vertens appellatur ».   Coluccio commented: « Plato dixit
hunc annum esse XV miliorum annorum ».   The Gaddianus
again inserts the note: « perficere qui a Platone Plato dixit... annorum appellatur ».   On fol. 10v Villani wrote « animal... bel-
liger ».   Coluccio added the marginal correction *belligerum* but
in an abbreviation of the last three letters which caused the scribe
of the Gaddianus to take the word as *belligere*.   Where Villani

wrote *Eneapolim* (Galletti, p. 16), Coluccio corrected with the note *Neapoli*.   The Gaddianus has *Enapolim Neapoli*.

It is obvious that the Gaddianus is a poor basis for a text of Villani's first edition.   We need a modern text of both editions of the complete work [5].

[5] An eighteenth-century manuscript containing the Italian version of Villani's life of Coluccio is in the Vatican: Chigi S. 5. 7 (Inv. 3618, No. 10/5).   This is not mentioned by Novati (*Epist.*, IV, p. 495).   For the life of Boccaccio in the Laurentian manuscript see G. Billanovich, *Restauri boccacceschi* (Rome, 1947), pp. 29 ff.

CHAPTER XI

A LETTER OF GIOVANNI DA SAN MINIATO
TO ANGELO CORBINELLI

In studying the progress of humanism in the early Renaissance it is important not to neglect the attacks of the opposition. The most significant onslaught of this sort in the time of Coluccio Salutati was Giovanni Dominici's *Lucula noctis*, which has now been adequately published (see chapter XII). This work was undertaken by Dominici to continue an earlier unsuccessful attempt by Giovanni da San Miniato to undermine the position of Coluccio and his friends. Giovanni's letter to Angelo Corbinelli, Coluccio's young protégé, is extant but has been made known only in a few excerpts in Novati (IV, pp. 170 ff.), Coulon (in his edition of the *Lucula noctis*), and L. Mehus (in *Ambrosii Traversari... Epistolae*, ed. P. Cannetus, Florence, 1759, p. ccxcii). The letter seems to deserve publication in full, but before giving the text it is desirable to clarify the rather involved situation of which it forms part.

In order to explain Coluccio's letter to Giovanni (IV, p. 170) Novati suggested that Giovanni had sent to the Chancellor a copy of his letter to Corbinelli, along with a new letter providing additional arguments. T. F. Rich in *Speculum,* XI (1936), p. 386, showed that this was incorrect and made clear that Giovanni wrote first to Coluccio and then to Corbinelli; he accounted for the second letter by Giovanni's failure to get a reply from Coluccio. Coluccio's opening words to Giovanni, *vidi nuper,* seem to indicate that he saw the original letter to Corbinelli, not a copy sent him by Giovanni, as Novati argued. There is some evidence in the letter to Corbinelli of just what happened. In it Giovanni says that he discussed the subject some time before (*dudum*) with Coluccio but that he remains alone in the field and therefore is the winner. Thus Giovanni cleverly sets out a bait by inferring that Coluccio's silence was an acknowledgment of defeat. He obviously expects that Coluccio will see this letter. Then Giovanni continues by saying that Corbinelli still remains in the field as one willing to take up arms in defense of poetry. So the whole story is this: Giovanni wrote to Coluccio urging him to give up poetry. Coluccio answered this letter quite briefly in *Epist.*, III, 539-543. Giovanni at once wrote again but Coluccio considered it useless to continue the discussion (*Epist.*, IV, p. 175): « Respondi quidem tunc obiectioni tue breviter (i.e., *Epist.*, III, p. 539) fateor, sed solide, sed taliter quod tue responsionis philacteria nichil a me dictum, si recte ponderaveris, commoverunt ». Then nearly five years elapsed (*iam pene lustrum*, p. 174). Giovanni brooded over the situation and finally hit upon the idea of writing Coluccio's protégé, Corbinelli, shrewdly guessing that Coluccio would see the letter.

That Giovanni wrote two letters to Corbinelli was R. Coulon's absurd suggestion (in his edition of Dominici's *Lucula noctis*, Paris, 1908, p. lxiii, n.) on the ground that Coluccio says *litteras tuas* and does not ordinarily use the plural for one letter. Coluccio knew and observed the correct classical usage: a glance through the letters of 1404-06 in Volume IV reveals twenty examples of *litterae* applied to a single letter; for more than one letter he uses *epistolae*. There is one example of *littera* applied to a single epistle. In Volume III there are over forty examples of *litterae* of one letter, some twelve of more than one—but always in an unambiguous context (*duae, tot,* etc.). One or two examples may be interpreted either way. *Littera* occurs eleven times to indicate an epistle.

The dating of Coluccio's reply and of his previous letter to Giovanni (III, p. 539) is complicated. The earlier letter carries the date September 21, without indication of year, the later one is dated January 25, 1406. Because in the second letter Coluccio says that it is almost five years (*lustrum*) since he had had a letter from Giovanni on the subject, Novati in editing Volume III gave the date 1401 to the letter of September 21, but when he came to edit Volume IV he reluctantly—too reluctantly—

began to doubt the date 1406 for the letter of January 25. For after Coluccio wrote this letter these events took place: Dominici had a chance to see the letter and to write his big book in reply, and then Coluccio read the book and started a lengthy answer (IV, pp. 205-240) which was interrupted by his death on May 4, 1406. All this could not have happened in a little over three months; the letter of January 25 must therefore have been written in 1405, if not in 1404. We may establish the chronology as follows: III, p. 539, was written September 21, 1399 (or 1398). Giovanni's lost reply was written soon after January 25, 1400 (or 1399). Shortly before January 25, 1405 (or 1404), Giovanni wrote to Corbinelli. On January 25, 1405 (or 1404), Coluccio wrote IV, p. 170.

I now give the text of Giovanni's letter on the basis of two manuscripts, Florence, Laur. Gadd. 90 sup. 41, 2 (L), and Paris lat. 8573 (P), without, however, reporting variations in spelling.

Angelo Corbinello civi Florentino Dopni Iohannis de Sancto Miniate monaci Camaldulensis epistola exhortatoria ut discedat a lectura poetarum et sacre pagine codicibus innitatur.

Amantissime frater, hance disceptationem quam tecum congressurus nunc obicio, dudum cum viro celeberrimo ser Colucio meo, 5 longis hinc inde succedentibus sermonibus, ventilavi, sed « adhuc sub iudice lis est ». Verum quia ego in campo, ut dici vulgo solet, solus brachio extento, rationibus non evacuatis, remansi, vicisse proculdubio coniecto. Et licet ille sit arte et industria me longe superior, tamen, ubi vis eius succumbit, novi hominem non erubescere superari. Tu 10 vero superes qui aliquibus istius modi poesis blandimentis allectus idcirco in eius amorem exardens imbellia pro ea arma suscipere velle videris. Sed falleris utique, mi Angele, falleris quia umbra et rerum

---

1 I. e., *domini*. This is the heading in L. In P: *Angelo de Corbinellis de Florencia Frater Iohannes de Sancto Miniate ordinis Angelorum Florencie persuasio ut discedat*, etc. 4-10 On the basis of differences between this text and the quotation of it by Coluccio in *Epist.*, IV, p. 174, Oliver, in his review of the first edition of the present book, suggested that Giovanni's letter was not an actual copy of his letter to Corbinelli but a later revision. It does not seem to me that the differences are great enough for that. Coluccio's quotation is found in only two manuscripts. Some of the differences may be due to errors in Novati's text; he says that Coluccio's quotation agrees with Giovanni's letter, which he checked in the two manuscripts I used. In his footnote Novati says that L² has the quotation, in the apparatus he reports that this manuscript omits it. 4 *Dilectissime* P. 6. Horace, *A. P.* 78. 10 *ius* P. 15. Ps. 128, 3-4.

figura, non veritate, non ratione, non auctoritate moveris. Tu modo
15 iuvenili ardore fervescens, uxore forsitan et filiis in circuitu mense tue
sicut novellis olivarum circumdatus, rerum copia et statu publico et
amicorum suffragiis suffultus, pulcrum ducis et acceptabile quicquid
oculis palam arridet. « Gaudes equis canibusque et aprici gramine
campi », delectaris vicinorum honorificentia famulorumque poplitem
20 curvantium, et a cunctis domesticis sive artistis tuis dominus nominari et magister. Conaris circa patrimonii amplitudinem et supellecti-
lis varietatem possessionum augmentum, et circa nanciscende bone
opinionis susurria laboras, et spectabilem te et in populo amabilem
cultu corporis et morum venustate te prebes. Hec licet oculis minime
25 in presentiarum de te videam, argumentum ab his sumo que olim
de tuis vidi, quia in domo tua notior (si ante alia quereres) sum quam
putes. His igitur persuasus tibique plurimum complacens dulcisono
carminum modulamine delectaris. Placet « iudicium Paridis spreteque
iniuria forme », placet et Didonis cum Anna sorore familiare lamentum,
30 et te video in eius iusta morte iniuste dolere. Sed et Augustinus
tandem in se reversus incomparabiliter plangit se in Didonis morte
flevisse. Si illo tu melior (ut te uno iaculo feriam) sis nescio; si verius,
si rationabilius, si sanus sapias, tu ipse iudica. Placent tibi et Buccoli-
corum pastorales confabulationes, licet « non omnes arbusta iuvent
35 humilesque mirice ». Placet Methamorfoseis et Demogorgonis nomen
diis horrendum. Et ut mille huiusmodi monstruosa preteream, placet
Dampnes incestus, Proserpine raptus, Martis Venerisque adulterium,
Minerve lanificia tua, Bachi orgia, Priapi nefanda de celo turbatio,
Europe furtum. Placetne de Amore sive de Sine Titulo Ovidius, de
40 Achille Statius, de Ulixe Homerus? Placetne « bella per Emathios plusquam civilia campos » vel formosa Thebays, qua ego plurimum tuo
ductus errore delectabar? An forsan tragedorum commenta satiro-
rumve censure mordaces placent? Hec omnia non solum vanitas et
vanitas vanitatum sed in ore Christicole pene blasfemie sunt idolo-
45 rumque ignota cultura, que velut monstruosa portenta mentem inqui-
nant, mores dissipant, et si quid boni animo possides huius peste
veneni perimetur. Nam quid non mali tibi suadent hec studia repe-

16 *et* om. P.   18 Horace, *A. P.* 162.   20 *artista* is a skilled workman, member
of one of the *arti.*   20 *Ioh.* 13, 13.   20 *nominari dominus* P.   23 *susurria* for *susurros.*
23 *amabilem in populo* P.   25 *summo* L.   25 *qui* L; perhaps should be *quos.*   26
vidi de tuis P.   28 Virgil, *Aen.* I, 27.   30 Augustine, *Conf.* I, 21.   31 *Didonis
morte* P.   34 Virgil, *Ecl.* 4, 2.   34. *uiuent* L.   36 *huius* L.   37 For *Daphnes?*
38 *tua*] Corbinelli was evidently a wool merchant in the Arte della Lana; cf. *artista*
above and below.   38 *Prinpi* L.   40 Lucan, *Phars.* I, 7.   43 *mordaces censure* P.
43 *Eccl.* 1, 2; 12, 8.   46 *qui* L.   47 *repetita studia* P.   50 I *Cor.* 15, 33.   53 *oblito-*

tita? Si quid pudoris, si quid honestatis, si quid sobrietatis, si quid
iustitie, si quid divine legis inimicum est, illic eligibile et pervium
exhibetur. Si enim « bonos mores corrumpunt colloquia mala »,   50
quid erit ubi omnium proponitur spurcitiarum sentina, scelerum
scola, et omnium instrumenta vitiorum? Tibi utique satis doleo
quod tue indolis nobilitas talibus obrueretur sordibus et, ubi posses
sicut in abrasa carta virtutum depingere formas, huiuscemodi timeo
ne purgamentis resarcias. Nolo nichilominus hec que scribo mea esse   55
adinventicia putes vel sine maiorum auctoritate fuisse compacta. In
sermone quem de filio prodigo Ieronimus condidit sic ait: « Demo-
num cibus sunt carmina poetarum, secularis sapientia. Hec sua omnes
suavitate delectant et, dum aures versibus dulci modulamine curren-
tibus capiunt, animam quoque penetrant et pectoris interna devin-   60
ciunt. Nulla ibi saturitas veritatis, nulla iustitie refectio reperitur ».
Et subdit: « Ne legas philosophos, oratores, poetas, ne in eorum
lectione requiescas. Absit ut de ore Christiani sonet Iuppiter omnipotens et Castor et Hercules, magis portenta quam nomina ». Item
audi non meam sed Boetii vocem, quod tibi nuper sub aliis verbis   65
edidi itidem suis pronuntiare sermonibus. Et id tibi notum satis fore
arbitror: « Quis has scenicas meretriculas ad hunc egrum permisit
accedere, que dolores eius non modo ullis remediis foverent verum
insuper dulcibus alerent venenis ». Et oportune nostro epigramati
subiungit dicens: « Hec sunt enim que infructuosis affectuum spinis   70
uberem fructibus rationis segetem necant. Hominum mentes assuefa-
ciunt morbo, non liberant ». Sed quicquid dixi hic habes pulcerrime
repetitum. Mentem tuam rationis et virtutis bibulam et capacem, si
in hac opinione perseveras, infructuosis et noxiis desideriis extuare
compellent dulcique malignitatis veneno assuefactam faciliter ad que-   75
que vitia flectent. Non ergo me calumpnia arguas: autorem ante
oculos pono, solum dicta recito, non promulgo. Unde reor iam spon-
sioni mee ubertim et dilucide satisfecisse, adeo ut nichil de cetero
contrahiscere valeas. Sed studio huiusmodi et assertionibus veris pro-
vocatus, non necessitate cause exigente, alias tibi subiciam rationes,   80
dicta pariter et exemplum ut, si verbis non credis, vel factis credas.
Ieronimus, tantum ecclesie Dei lumen et specimen, in epistola quam
in laudem virginis ad Eustochium virginem scripsit, se ante tribunal

---

retur P.   55 *refarcias* P.   56 A new word, apparently, formed like *adventicia.*   57
Jerome, *Epist.* 21, 13 (M. 22, 385).   67 Boethius, *Cons.* I, 1, 8-9.   68 For *nullis,* probably an error of Giovanni (cf. Coluccio's criticism of Dominici, *Epist.*, IV, p. 220).
68 *foverent remediis* L.   74 *obnoxiis* L.   78 *me* P.   80 The manuscripts have *al',*
which might be *aliter,* but the sense seems to call for *alias.*   83 *in laudem*] *ad*

iudicis raptum asserit et cum interrogatus quis esset respondit se
85 Christianum fore, improperari sibi audivit: « Ciceronianus, non Christianus es ». Quod utique tolerabilius nomen est quam poeticum.
Unde multotiens corporaliter vapulavit. Quamobrem iuravit: « Si
umquam habuero codices seculares, si legero, te negavi ». Et apostolus: « Videte ne quis vos decipiat per phylosophiam et inanem falla-
90 ciam secundum traditiones hominum, secundum elementa mundi, et
non secundum Christum ». Ne dubites hanc poesim esse muscipulam
diaboli qua miseras animas ad imaginem Dei factas de Christi corpore surripiat, que, dum leni modulatione sonori carminis vanarum-
que fictione fabularum mentem demulcet, a sui rectitudine tramitis
95 false suadela dulcedinis distrahit. Quo fit ut paulatim incipiat homo
sui oblivisci suam salutem postponendo fallaciis divinaque beneficia
atque mirabilia non attendens, sibi thesaurizat iram in iusto iudicio
Dei, tradaturve in reprobum sensum ut sibi amara pro dulcibus, mala
pro bonis, turpitudinem pro honestate propinet. Vellem te originaliter
100 videre que summotenus tetigi quo liquidius ante oculos tuos ex tan-
torum scriptorum testimonio veritas appareret. Profecto si pectus fer-
reum non haberes consilium mutares et amici tui scriptis acquiesceres.
Porro videre videor his obiecturum libros poeticos allegoriis et enig-
matibus fecundos tibi multa naturalia et moralia eleganti modulo
105 prodere, et idcirco tibi licere illis perfrui blandiaris. Quibus in
promptu peremptoria responsio est, ut, si illa queras que moribus
natureve conveniant, laudabilius sit ad fontem accedere quam ex
arentibus rivis exigere pocula venenata. Utique Seneca satius et Aris-
totiles tibi amplius proderunt quam Iunonis et Veneris iurgia vel
110 Herculis imperata mandata vel huiuscemodi enucleare commenta. Sed
cur queris in arenti torrente scientiarum profluvia et ex turpi studio
honestatis culmen ascendere et virtutis? Si mores cupis et rerum
causas nosse multo amplius et securius et compendiosius in sacro
eloquio reperies, unde sine fictione tibi veritas elucebit, que et mo-
115 rum conversionem et vite honestatem et principia rerum, denique
omnium harum rerum conditorem tibi promet. Habes allegorias et
enigmatum figmenta in evangeliis et prophetis luculento sermone

laudem L. 85 *fore Christianum* L. 85 Jerome, *Epist.* 22, 30 (M. 22, 416).
87 *multis* P. 87 *Quamobrem*] *Unde* P. 87 Jerome, *ibid.* 88 *codices habuero* L.
89 *Col.* 2, 8. 89 *fallaciam et hominum traditiones* L (*et* added). 90 *mundi
elementa* L. 90 *et* om. L. 91 *musipulam esse* L. 92 *corpore Christi* P.
96 *oblivisci sui* P. 97 Cf. *Rom.* 2, 5. 97 *iram thesaurizat* L; it should be
thesaurizet. 97-98 *Dei iudicio* L. 99-100 *videre originaliter* P. 102 *mutares
consilium* P. 102 *acquiesceres scriptis* P. 105 *licere tibi* P. 112-113 Virgil,
Georg. II, 490. 117 *luculenti* L. 120 *moralius evangelio* P. 121 Gen. 1, 1.

dispersas. In quibus si mentem libet sacris exercere loquelis ipsam
instruant pariter et oblectent. Si moralia gliscis, quid melius Salo-
mone, quid evangelio moralius? Si naturalia, ab ipso canonum capite   120
incohato lege: « In principio creavit Deus celum et terram ». Si prelia
et opiniones preliorum concupiscit anima tua, habes libros Regum,
Machabeorum et nonnulla in Prophetis inserta. Si ad methaphisicam
et supernaturalia aspirare cupias: « In principio erat verbum » tibi
propino, ubi alta et inaccessibilia hominis apponuntur. Que omnia   125
tibi in litterali cortice patent absque his que intrinsecus latent, que
solum puro corde et mundo oculo consideranda traduntur. Quid hoc
sit vis nosse? Audi psalmistam: « Quam dulcia faucibus meis elo-
quia tua, super mel ori meo ». Homo carnalis, ut ait apostolus, non
percipit que sunt spiritus. Ideo si ad vaniloquia distraharis non mi- 130
rum, cum impossibile sit homini in fluctibus, delitiis, et illecebris
huius seculi obnoxio sapere que Dei sunt. Ceterum sunt et alii mo-
derniores doctorum codices in quibus omnis dicendi ornatus et peritia, servato verborum et sententiarum pondere, reperitur. Quos si
non vidisti, in propatulo sunt. Quorum degustato sapore universus   135
poetarum sermo desipiet. Augustinum dico et Gregorium, Ieronimum
et Bernardum, et infinitos alios quorum fulgor totam illustrat eccle-
siam. Nec sum animo dubius quod nulla de poetis cum eis tibi
videatur facienda collatio; nam que pars potest esse fidelis cum infi-
deli, que « lucis ad tenebras », ut dicit apostolus? Habes igitur patu- 140
lis roboratam auctoritate et exemplo maiorum subnixam. Noli dein-
ceps fabulis et procacibus versibus ingenuitatem tue indolis subicere.
Si fabulas leges fabulas habebis. Laboribus incassum, immo volens
periculo te exponis. Redi itaque ad cor tuum et, illis omissis que
vento animum tuum distentant, si, sacra auri fame postposita et lani- 145
ficio muliercularumque garrulo commercio aliis commisso, laudabili
scientiarum studio mentem exhibere delectat, ad sacri eloquii fontem
accede, hoc sobrio gustu inebriare, qui de anima tua fluenta vite
scaturire faciet et eam non parva oblectatione mulcebit. Vale, mi
Angele, et nominis tui imple significatum. Qui, cum Angelus dicaris, 150
simul re, vita, et moribus Angelus habearis, ut cum ultima dies
defunctionis tue advenerit, ad illorum consortia ducaris in celis quorum nomen, vitam, et opera in hac miseriarum valle sortitus fueris,
quod ille donare dignetur qui est benedictus in secula seculorum. Amen.

124 *Ioh.* 1, 1.   126 *his qui* L.   128 *Ps.* 118, 103.   129 Cf. *Rom.* 8, 5,   130
vaniloqua P.   136 *decipietur* L.   140 2 *Cor.* 6, 14.   140 *igitur] ergo* P.   140
patulis for *patrum?*   145 Cf. Virgil, *Aen.* III, 57.   145 See on vs. 38.   152
illorum in celis ducaris consorcia P.

CHAPTER XII

THE DEDICATION COPY OF GIOVANNI DOMINICI'S
« LUCULA NOCTIS » [1]

In 1933, E. P. Goldschmidt, the well-known London scholar
and bookseller, came to my office to show me a suitcase full of
manuscripts. I told him that the depression had made it impossible for the University to buy manuscripts and that there was
no use in my looking at them. He indicated that it would do
no harm to examine them, which I did. One in particular attracted my attention, as Dr. Goldschmidt was quick to note, for
he suggested leaving the book in my hands for closer examination. I again stated that I had no hope whatever of finding
money to purchase it if it proved to be of interest to me. Nevertheless, the manuscript was left in my hands.

At once I began refreshing my memory about it. It was
the *Lucula noctis* of Giovanni Dominici. I recalled that Coluccio Salutati had written an answer to it and that this answer was
published in Novati's great edition of Coluccio's letters [2]. The
letter is incomplete and Novati rightly decided that Coluccio died
before he finished it and that it was not actually sent to Dominici. As Coluccio died in 1406, Dominici's work was written
shortly before, evidently in 1405. The work is an attack on the
reading of classical literature, and Coluccio's answer is a defense.
The two works belong to the extremely important series of documents dealing with this theme which mark the development of

---

[1] Originally published in *Medievalia et Humanistica*, 1 (1943), p. 109.
[2] *Epistolario di Coluccio Salutati*, ed. F. Novati, IV (Rome, 1905), p. 206.
For Salutati's defense of classical literature see B. L. Ullman, *The Humanism of
Coluccio Salutati* (Padua, 1963), pp. 53 ff.

the early Renaissance. Coluccio contributed several other documents to this series. Dominici and Coluccio were opponents in the struggle, but Dominici dedicated his work to Coluccio and a formal friendship was maintained.

Among the arguments used by Coluccio to refute Dominici was that only by study of the classics could a correct Latinity be achieved. He begins this section of his reply with the wish that all religious might be proficient enough in grammar to avoid barbarisms, solecisms, and other errors [3]. Then he lists some twenty mistakes, most of which, as Novati notes, are found in the *Lucula noctis*. The first of these is « esu quinque prunarum a validis febribus liberatum », where Coluccio remarks that *prunorum* should be used. He refrains from saying that by the eating of five hot coals (*prunarum*) one would be relieved of fever in quite another way than by the eating of plums. Coluccio avoids satire and direct attack and keeps his discussion on a high level of formal politeness.

Novati discovered two manuscripts of the *Lucula noctis* and located most of the errors that Coluccio cites. At that time Coulon's *editio princeps* (of which more later) had not been published.

To return to our manuscript. Naturally I looked at once for the errors of Latinity which Coluccio mentions. In the margin opposite these I regularly found a special mark, varying from an exclamation point to a kind of inverted capital T, consisting of a vertical line, at the bottom of which was a dot or a short horizontal line. The mark occurred not only at these points but at others where mistakes were found. At once a problem arose: is it mere chance that there should be a mark in the margin at all the points where Coluccio criticized the usage? That explanation certainly would not do except as a desperate last resort; coincidences must be explained whenever possible. Did Dominici mark these points after he got Coluccio's letter? But the letter was not sent. Besides, the same marks occur at places on which Coluccio offers no comment. Only one explanation was left: this is the dedication copy which the author sent to

[3] *Ibid.*, p. 217.

Coluccio, and in it Coluccio entered the marks himself and then made a selection of examples when he wrote his letter.

After this exciting decision there came a hunt for traces of Coluccio's handwriting among the corrections and marginal notes. I happened to be thoroughly familiar with his script as I had studied many of the books which he owned for an investigation into his humanistic activity. Several unquestionable examples of his writing were found in the Dominici manuscript.

It is perhaps unnecessary to add that my enthusiasm for the book was such that the money to purchase the manuscript was found. It is now in the Rare Book Room (MS. 831) of the library of the University of Chicago.

The book can be identified with one which was advertised by the Florentine booksellers Franchi and Co. in 1885 [4]. That manuscript is described as being a beautiful one, written on fine parchment, with colored initials; it contained 141 folios. The description fits our manuscript exactly. It is beautifully written in the characteristic formal hand of the early 1400's. The first page is finely illustrated in a floral pattern with five miniature portraits interspersed, besides a portrait in the initial. Stamps on fol. 1 and fol. 141 show that the book was once in the library of the Minutoli Tegrimi family of Lucca, a number of whose manuscripts are now in American libraries. In the catalogue of that library it figures as No. 153 and is described as follows [5]:

DOMINICI Ioannis Cardinalis, Liber qui inscribitur Lucula Noctis. Membr. fogl. Sec. XIV. Nitido codice d'ottima conservazione, colla sua antica coperta in legno e corame.

The *Lucula noctis* was printed for the first time in 1908 on the basis of the two manuscripts known to Novati [6]. This edition

---

[4] Catal. VII, n. 47, quoted by Novati, *op. cit.*, p. 209 n. Between 1885 and 1928 its history is unknown to me. On December 1, 1928, Goldschmidt bought it from Olschki of Florence and listed it in his Cat. XIX, No. 199. He sold it to John. T. Adams of Sheffield on June 18, 1929, and bought it back at a Sotheby sale (Dec. 7, 1931, lot 73). It then appeared in Goldschmidt's list of Mediaeval Literature 5, No. 82 (June, 1932).

[5] *Catalogo dei codici manoscritti posseduti dal nobile signore Conte Eugenio Minutoli Tegrimi in Lucca* (Lucca, 1871), p. 29.

[6] *Beati Iohannis Dominici Cardinalis S. Sixti Lucula Noctis*, ed. Remi Coulon (Paris, 1908). The two manuscripts are: L=Florence, Bibl. Lauren-

is an extremely poor piece of work, partly because the editor made many mistakes in copying, constantly misread the writing, especially the abbreviations, made arbitrary changes, and chiefly followed the late Berlin manuscript, which is an emended copy of the Florence manuscript. Anyone can check these statements by collating with Coulon's text the two pages of the Florence manuscript which he reproduces photographically. The Florence manuscript is independent of, though inferior to, the Chicago codex [7].

The matters of Latin usage, grammar, and spelling which constitute that part of Coluccio's criticism of the *Lucula noctis* which I shall chiefly discuss in the rest of this chapter are far more important and significant than might at first sight appear. The war against mediaevalism was in part fought on this front and the direction that the Renaissance was to take was partly determined by these early forays.

A celebrated instance is the use of the plural *vos* in addressing individuals, a complimentary form of address that has survived in French, English, and in part in Italian. The early humanists were not the first to attack this usage but they were the first to succeed [8]. Petrarch sets himself against it because his beloved Cicero did not employ it. As he writes to one of his

---

ziana, Conv. Soppressi, Lat. 540; and B = Berlin, Staatsbibliothek, Lat. Q. 399. C is the University of Chicago Ms. 831 (PA 57 D 67).

[7] A new edition was prepared at my suggestion and under my direction by my pupil, Bro. Edmund Hunt, and was published under the title *Iohannis Dominici Lucula Noctis* in the « Publications in Mediaeval Studies » of the University of Notre Dame, 1940. It is based on collations of all three manuscripts. Hunt (p. xxv) estimates that there are from five to fifteen errors of all sorts per page in Coulon's edition—and there are 445 pages. He lists thirty-one major deviations (mostly errors) from the Florence manuscript on the two pages which Coulon shows in facsimile. The palaeographical errors (such as reading *quum, unde,* for the abbreviations of *quoniam, verum*) are amazing in any case but extraordinary for the French translator of Steffens' *Lateinische Paläographie,* which Coulon was.

[8] Dr. R. W. Hunt informed me of an interesting example of the twelfth or thirteenth century. Alexander Neckam, in an unpublished sermon (Bodl. ms. Wood empt. 13, fol. 361r) wrote: « Hodie ergo volunt prelati ecclesie ut vobiscetur cum eis, cum numquam Petrus vel aliquis discipulorum dixit Domino, 'vos'. Ait enim Petrus, 'Tu scis, Domine, quia amo te', non dixit, 'vos scitis, Domine, quia amo vos' ». Note that Neckam uses a Biblical example, whereas the humanists quoted classical instances.

correspondents, « I shall address you in the singular because you
are one person, and in this I follow nature and the usage of
the ancients, not the flattery of the moderns ». It is only in
Latin that this movement had any lasting effect, though Coluccio Salutati criticized the vernacular use as well [9].

The spelling of Latin was in a very confused state in Italy
in the fourteenth century and the humanists strove valiantly to
restore it to its classical purity. Coluccio marked all the passages
in his copy of the grammarian Priscian which comment on
spelling. He and other early humanists wrote many letters dealing with problems of orthography. The center of the struggle
was in the words *nihil* and *mihi,* the common mediaeval spellings of which were *nichil* and *michi*. Coluccio discusses the
question in our passage, but it was not until later in the fifteenth
century that the matter was cleared up. To judge from the heat
of the discussion it seems as if the fate of humanity depended
on whether you were a 'nihilist' or a 'nichilist'.

Let us now consider the errors mentioned by Coluccio and
then pass to others which he marked but did not select for comment. *Prunarum* has already been mentioned [10] (Ch. 47, line 67
Hunt ed.). Others are *Geneseos* as ablative [11] (46, 140); *partile
bonum* for *partibile bonum* [12] (3, 29); *fiendum* for *faciendum*
(2, 408; 34, 353; 41, 109; 42, 17, 233; 45, 427; also two
unmarked examples in 4, 10, 19); *deificus* (2, 252, not found by
Novati; also 46, 413); *moderari* as a passive instead of a deponent
(3, 176; cf. 1, 100; 18, 247, the last unmarked; correctly used in
7, 164); *quilibet* of two persons (4, 32); *honos* for *honorem* (7,
23); *cythareda* for *cytharedus* [13] (8, 109 [14]; 15, 21; 18, 154);

---

[9] *Epist.,* II, p. 411.

[10] *Prunas* is correctly used in 13, 77 and 27, 114.

[11] *Genesis* is an ablative in 8, 324 and 11, 21 (both unmarked). *Genesi*
(11, 300; 26, 181; 30, 16), *Genesim* (12, 145), *Geneseos* (26, 151) are correctly used.

[12] Novati did not locate this; *partilia bona* occurs a few lines below (33),
not marked by Coluccio. Other marked examples of *partilis* are in 15, 20; 41,
151; 46, 16; the mark in 15, 20 seems to cover both *partilis* and *cythareda*.
Partiliter in 16, 123 is unmarked; *partibiliter* is used in 45, 135.

[13] *Cytharedorum* is correctly used in 9, 318.

[14] As Coulon notes (p. 135 n.), Novati attributes *citharedus* to Dominici in
this place on the basis of B, failing to note that L has *cythareda* (as does C).

Hortensem for *Hortensium* (8, 175; cf. 2, 33; 24, 123 [15]); *sepe numero* separated or reversed (9, 223, not found by Novati; cf. 2, 30; 46, 207); *humanus genus directiva* (18,20; 36,2 unmarked [16]); *Averoys* (*Averrois*) as an indeclinable noun (22, 104); *proprius* as a comparative (2, 170; 3, 80; 25, 80; 26, 27; 35, 316; 45, 192 [17]); the adverb *propriissime* (35, 310); *ullus* for *nullus* [18] (41, 31, 116); *sine fallo* for *infallibiliter* (42, 40).

Coluccio then criticizes the spellings *micci, niccil, bratium* for *mihi, nihil, bracchium*. Novati observes that there are no instances of these in B or L. Nor are there in C. This would naturally cast suspicion on our identification of C as Coluccio's copy. But a careful reading of Coluccio's words shows that he does not have Dominici in mind at all but is venting his spleen on other *religiosi*: « Et ut ab his nugis abscedam, et que quotidie peccantur in orthographia, in qua quidem re plurimi sunt religiosi, aliqua ex parte contingam, quid est dicere *micci*, vel *niccil*, quid est dicere *bratium?* ». He then attributes this fault to the barbarous French, who do such things as to write *ch* for *c* in words like *chivalier*.

The mistakes on which Coluccio comments occur in both C and L and for the most part in B and are therefore Dominici's errors and not those of scribes. Most of them occur several times. It is possible that a few are slips which Dominici himself would have corrected, as *prunarum* for *prunorum* [19], *honos* for *honorem*. B has eliminated some of the errors in copying L. Dominici himself made no pretense to a knowledge of formal grammar (41, 210 ff.): he has never studied it with a teacher or read the rules or learned Donatus; all he knows is what he has learned from reading pagan and Christian authors.

---

[15] B here has *Hortensium*. Coulon (p. 12 n., 70 n.) says that elsewhere Dominici writes *Hortensius* but cites no instances.

[16] Cf. *anime directivus* 37, 12 (unmarked).

[17] In 11, 387 *proprius* CL *propius* C² (unmarked); in 41, 108 *proprius* C *propius* L (unmarked).

[18] *Nullus* in 40, 40. This error was due to the influence of the vernacular, in which *alcuno* was often used for *nessuno* in Dante and later writers (P. Toynbee, *Dante Studies*, Oxford, 1921, p. 305. This practice has continued in French (*aucun*) and, under certain circumstances, in Spanish (*alguno*).

[19] As already stated, *pruna* is twice correctly used.

Beside the marked passages on which Coluccio comments in his letter there are many other such passages in our manuscript. In some cases we can be certain of Coluccio's intention, in some we can reach a plausible conclusion, in others I at least can find no satisfactory explanation of what was in Coluccio's mind. There is the further complication that some of the errors may be purely scribal and should not be attributed to the author. When C and L disagree (B does not count) this is probably the case; I have therefore marked with an asterisk those readings which are peculiar to C. Where C and L agree the error was presumably Dominici's. In any case our interest is in the humanist's reaction rather than in the ecclesiastic's error.

The surer cases of errors in grammatical forms marked by Coluccio are the following [20]: *auferesis* for *aphaeresi* (Prol., 73); *sapientum* for *sapientium* (2, 3; 34, 116; not marked in 41, 238); *extollissent* (8, 163); *altione* (C) or *alcione* (L) (nom.) for *alcyon* [21] (9, 77); *subtilius* for *subtiliter* (9, 275); **organumque* for *organorumque* (9, 280); *miscunt* for *miscent* (11, 296); **eventium* for *eventuum* (12, 114); *episcoporum trecenti* (20, 91) and *annis septingenti* [22] (29, 185); *multiplicius* for *multipliciter* [23] (22, 161); **teterissimam* (corrected from *tetrissimam*) for *teterrimam* [24] (24, 71); *folleris* as genitive for *follis* (26, 118); **repugnantiis* for *repugnantibus* (27, 263); *necessarius* as a comparative (33, 69; cf. *proprius* above); *farsati* for *farti* or *farsi* [25] (34, 308); *fruebuntur* for *fruentur* (34, 370); *instruisse* for *instruxisse* [26] (36, 377); *ciare* for *ciere* (39, 69); *potentatum* for *potentatuum* (41, 60); *inlecebra* for *inlecebras* [27] (41, 69); * *pinserunt* for *pinxerunt*, though this is really only a matter of spelling, usually not marked by Coluccio (42, 45); **veror* for *vereor* (42, 154); **destini* for *destinari* or

[20] Grammatical errors in proper names are included below.

[21] This is in a quotation from John of Salisbury, some of the manuscripts of which agree with Dominici.

[22] In 43, 216 *trecenti concubinas* does not have the usual mark but there is a cross in the margin. *Septingentis* in 43, 221.

[23] *Multipliciter* is correctly used in 22, 208; 28, 296; 34, 208; 42, 26.

[24] In 29, 169 *tetrissimis* is unmarked; in Prol., 98 *teterrimus* is correctly used.

[25] Unmarked in 11, 367; 28, 54; *farsus* correctly in 36, 485 and 46, 446.

[26] *Haurisse* (*habuisse* L) in 45, 358 is unmarked.

[27] Correct in 42, 225. In 44, 172 *inlecebro* is unmarked.

destrui (L) (43, 12); *suffarsinati* for *suffarcinati* (43, 341); **pollerint* for *polleant* (43, 366); *reperit* for *repererit* (44, 257; correct in 253); *ether* as accusative[28] (45, 50); *estarum* for *extorum* (46, 199); *meniis* for *moenibus* (46, 369); **occidetur* for *occideretur* (47, 21). In 45, 125 the simple language of Boccaccio, *aquam vino miscuisset*, by the aid of Dominici's pen becomes the florid *maritavit laticem Bacco*. Probably it is not so much the rhetoric as the grammar that bothers Coluccio: as *laticem* is masculine the marriage with Bacchus would seem to be slightly irregular.

Not uncommon are confusions of voice, as active for passive (deponent) forms (cf. *moderari* above): *expergiscamus* (19, 41); *mutuemus*, which occurs in classical Latin but is rare[29] (33, 80); other difficulties of voice[30]: *detestari* as passive (17, 116; *detestatos* as passive, used occasionally in classical Latin, Prol., 50[31]); *liqueri* for *liquere* (19, 18); *flui* for *fluere* (22,175); *infamantes* for *infamatos*[32] (39, 115); *inficeret* apparently for *infitiaretur* (42, 109); *protendit* apparently for *protenditur* (46, 271); *impingit* for *impingitur* or *se impingit* (47, 10; this may be a cross).

Syntactical errors include many examples of wrong agreement: *hoc Noctiluca* (a later hand, perhaps Coluccio's, repeats the phrase in the margin: 2, 59[33]); **que sententiam proferetur* (5, 40); *in sui veritatis* for *usui v.* in a quotation (6, 108); *quid ... que* (7, 193); **varium tempestatum forme* for *varie* (9, 86); **quale domum* for *quale demum*, though Coluccio probably thought it a mistake for *qualem domum* (12, 77); *lucem nec vires que* for *quas* (12, 104); *propositionem ... probandum* (13, 123); *corpus cum oculo cecum* for *ceco* (18, 36); *gentes quorum ... legificandas* (18, 41); *disputationes ... littere ... leges ... comparanda* for *comparandae* (19, 122); *genere qui civilis* (21, 158); *hunc errorem ... inrexit* (for *irrepsit*) (21, 170); **ungulas percussa* (23, 121); *eius* (*auri*) *que* (26, 108); *eorum doctrinarum*[34] (28,

---

[28] But the mark here may be a cross.

[29] *Mutuatos* is correctly used as an active participle in 38, 106.

[30] Coluccio himself at an earlier period (1374) used *fruiturum iri* as an active (*Epist.*, I, p. 177, 20).

[31] Correctly used in 6, 99 and 36, 236.

[32] *Infamantes* correctly used in 40, 117.

[33] Unchecked in 47, 206; *hac Noctiluca* correct in 14, 51.

[34] Coluccio misunderstood, for *eorum* may agree with *gentilium*.

26); *singularem ydioma (30, 7); quam for que ... prescribit (32, 112); Cham Noe filium as nominative (38, 114); Porphirianos qui temptavit (40, 170); prospiciendo ista sed prospiciendo (prospicienda L) tantum et ... salutanda for prospicienda ... prospicienda (43, 53); lex ... scissas (43, 223); *non hominis ingenio sed Dei eloquium (43, 324); pulvinaria aut ludi aut processiones aut rituum leges aut nove ferie instituta (47, 90); cerebrum ... invisa (47, 239).

Other syntactical errors are: faciant for faciunt (2, 351); perceptibili for -is (3, 127 [35]); potior with the accusative, sometimes found in classical Latin [36] (9, 134, 148); litteris abdicarunt for (?) l. se a. (9, 132); neque ... invalide for neque ... valide (9, 293); similarly neutrum ... non (34, 230); et urbis et gentibus (12, 156); gustaturus with the genitive (13, 22); acephalum as masc. nom. (19, 79); narrant perhaps for narrabunt (19, 107); propter and the accusative apparently instead of a simple dative with subdere (26, 209); utor with the accusative (30, 63); coram with the accusative (32, 122); perhaps ydolis for ydola (33, 320); infinitive in a quod clause (39, 33); superbie, tumoris, iactantie, immoderataque cupidine glorie tenebantur for superbia, etc. (42, 118).

Vocabulary errors include *repellentem for impellentem (Prol., 60); *derimo for dirimo (Prol., 67); ne dicam quidem for ne dicam (1, 70); sinthasma for syntagma [37] (2, 62); altera for alia (2, 400); *ambigit (ambit L) artes, apparently in sense of 'discuss' or 'include' (3, 146); Hyberas nenias [38] (3, 194); infine for infinite [39] (3, 213); estat (=extat) locutus for est locutus [40] (4, 39); possibly mensuris for metris (5, 64); transfugator in a misquoted passage (8, 29); lepus for lepos or lepor, worthy of a place next to prunarum (8, 298); instruit for dicit (?) (9, 12); helefantinumque barrum for barritum (9, 281; 22, 98); siquidem

---

[35] The mark here may be due to a wrong reference (see below).

[36] Potito triumpho (44, 9) is not marked.

[37] Vel sintagma is added in the margin of C.

[38] This is doubtful. In any case Dominici got it directly or indirectly from Jerome (see C.C.I. Webb's edition of John of Salisbury's Policraticus (Oxford, 1909) I, 13 (p. 55, 7). An unmarked example occurs in 31, 130.

[39] Coluccio corrected to infinite.

[40] Not marked in 6, 56; 39, 136.

for *siquid* (9, 308); *quo* for *quod* [41] (conjunction: 10, 49; 13, 102; 17, 72, 204; 20, 46; 22, 195; 39, 49, 129, 162; 40, 38, 88; 42, 48, 148; 44, 293; pronoun: 9, 32; 32, 10; 41, 129); *pernitior* (*-us*) for *perniciosior* (*-us*) 10, 108; 41, 67); the rare but ancient *violentem* for *violentam* (11, 43); *genethlaicos* for *genethliacos* (11, 175); *inclinat* for *inquinat* (12, 45); *accidentali* for *occidentali* (12, 74); *obgiurgo* for *obiurgo* (13, 112); *resistunt* for *restituunt* (?) (15, 149); *genosophistarum* for *gymnosophistarum* (16, 41); *fundat* for *fundit* (16, 117); *habet* for *potest* (17, 199); *trapertitas* (*trapegitas* L) for *trapezitas* (17, 203); *desperatis* for *disparibus* or *disparatis* in the sense of English 'disparate' (18, 158); *victimarius* and *pervictimarius* for *victima* (18, 241; 28, 238; 47, 31); **populos* for *populum* (19, 74); *fonte Tuliano* (alongside *dyaletica, phisica, poesia*) perhaps for *eloquentia* (20, 127); **qui* for *quid* (20, 129); *labium* for *lingua*, 'language' [42] (21, 17); *tympanistram* for *tympanistam* (26, 67); *dirigit calles* for *dirigit iter* (26, 131); *speculo exemplari* apparently for *imagine* (*Dei*) (26, 201); *satiria* for *satira* (27, 186); *pedota* (a mediaeval Latin and Italian word) for *gubernator* (31, 98); *farmatis* (f. gen.) for *pharmaci* (32, 44); **ploratione* for *prolatione* (32, 69); *quacumque die* in a quotation from the Vulgate, which has *quocumque* (32, 71); *admittentem* for *dicentem* (?) (35, 13); *quid* for *quod* (36, 6); *ostricarum* (based on Italian) for *ostrearum* (38, 204); *completis* for *complexis* (38, 215); *cistarsium* for *cista* [43] (38, 361); *humuccio* (*homucio* L) for *homuncio* (39, 64); *infense* for *indefense* (39, 79); *strumenta, structor* for *instrumenta* [44], *instructor* (39, 98; 40, 179); *stilibio* for *stibio* (41, 246); *utrumque* for *utrumcumque* (42, 36); *tractus* in the sense of 'selection' (42, 208); *quicumque* for *nonnulli* or *plurimi* (43, 111); **ladabilia* for *laudabilia* (43, 211); *ranno* for *rhamno* (44, 106); **vix* for *vis* (44, 242; doubtful, as other instances are unmarked); *paraxitis* for *parasitis* [45] (45, 18); *eufuga*

[41] But others were not marked, e. g., 20, 82; 23, 116; 30, 111; 34, 273; 39, 168, 171; 44, 146; 46, 350. In 15, 27 *quo* (CL) was corrected to *quod* by C².

[42] Unmarked in 21, 34.

[43] Through a misunderstanding of Ovid, *A. A.* II, 609. Cf. Du Cange *s.v. cistarca* and *sitarchia.*

[44] But *instrumentum* is correctly used in 10, 192; 47, 149, etc.

[45] In a quotation from Boccaccio's *Genealogia*, Coluccio's own copy of which (now in the University of Chicago Library) has *parasitis.*

for *aufuga* (45, 172); *filargos* for *philargicos* or *philargyros* (45, 380); *ostium* for *vocabulum* (46, 99); *fabolici* for *fabulatores* (46, 173); *abscisus* for *abscissus* (46, 353); *regere et legificare populos*, apparently in sense of 'make laws for' or 'apply laws to' (46, 403; 18, 42); *auliticas* for *aulicas* [46] (46, 408); *flagore* for *flagrantia* (47, 110); *obstinantur* apparently for *obstantur* (47, 153). In 10, 160 the mark may have been intended for the rare word *polimina* in an Apuleius quotation, a word which may have been unknown and therefore suspect to Coluccio.

Proper names bothered Dominici a great deal, and Coluccio marks many of them: *Methamorum* and *Methaphore* for *Metamorphoseon* (of Ovid) (2, 455; 43, 98); *Aratri* for *Arati* (6, 138); *Sophocli* as genitive (10, 201); *Phisias* for *Phintias* (11, 72); *Platinus* for *Plotinus* [47] (11, 81, 163, 188; 18, 112); *Carnaides* for *Carneades* [48] (11, 83); *Heccite* (C[2] *Hercite* CL) for *Hecate* (11, 138); *Archita* for *Archytas* (11, 236); *Phedronis* for *Phaedonis* (11, 247); *Theophastus* for *Theophrastus*, which Coluccio himself corrected (11, 265); *Esclapium* for *Asclepium* (11, 399); *Sergii Tullii* for *Servii Tullii* (12, 222); *Arpii* for *Arpis* (12, 231); **Nempni* for *Neptuni* (12, 240); *Helydum rota* for *Belidum urna* (13, 38); *Ioachino Florentino* (which would mean 'of Florence') for *Ioachino Florensi* or *de Flore* (14, 43); *Alcimon cum Ysopo* for *Alcmeon cum Aesopo* (16, 34); *Tarsillo* for *Thrasyllo* [49] (31, 101); *Meroes* (nom.) for *Meroe* (33, 98); *Cicerionianos* for *Ciceronianos* [50] (40, 170); *Tusculanorum* for *Tusculanarum* (of Cicero's treatise) (44, 35); *Soddomie* for *Sodome* [51] (44, 126); *Tisbis* (*Cibis* L) for *Thisbes* (44, 214); *Protheosenem* for *Protheum senem* (from Boccaccio, who has *De Protheo sene*) (45, 83); *Mulcebris* as a genitive for *Mulcebri*, *Mulciberi*, or *Mulciberis* (46, 445).

---

[46] The mark here may be a cross.

[47] The name is correctly spelled a number of times, e.g., 11, 123, 132; 34, 191; 39, 28; 40, 61; 41, 237; 42, 211.

[48] But *Carneades* in 11, 46.

[49] There is a character named Thrasyllus in Apuleius, *Met.*, and Dominici refers to this work several times in this passage.

[50] The single mark here seems to refer both to *temptavit* and *Cicerionianos;* the latter word is unmarked in 29, 90, and the correct form is used in 42, 158

[51] *Sodomie* is unmarked in 44, 208.

More important perhaps is Coluccio's attitude towards Dominici's frequent quotations and paraphrases of ancient writers. The difference between the two men in respect to quotations is not only profound but highly significant. Coluccio is the careful humanist of the Renaissance who has a wide knowledge of classical literature and quotes it accurately and directly. Dominici, more mediaeval in outlook, quotes inaccurately, often from memory, and largely at second hand from such encyclopaedic works as those of John of Salisbury and Vincent of Beauvais, works spurned by Coluccio.

Most of Coluccio's own handwriting in his manuscript of the *Lucula* consists of corrections of quotations. In the well-known verses about Homer's birthplace (10, 87) Coluccio writes as variants *Chimis* for *Samos* and *Piros* for *Pilos,* as well as changing *Smirne* to *Smirna.* These are the readings which Coluccio had used[52]. In a paraphrase of Pliny (10, 212) Coluccio writes *Ennii* above *Evinii.* In a quotation from Seneca (23, 36) he writes *relicta* above *et relata* and changes *spolii* to *cum spolio.* Apparently it was he who changed *Macrobius de sonno scipionis* (23, 61) to *somnio.* It is not surprising therefore that he put his mark before 42, 22, where *sonno* is used in reference to the same work. In a quotation from Virgil (40, 73) he adds an omitted *vita;* in one from Cicero (44, 185) he writes *avarior* above *amarior.* He caps the climax in a quotation from Augustine (47, 199), in which Dominici credits Apollo with these words addressed to Pyrrhus: « Dico tibi, Pirre, vincere posse Romanos ». Coluccio writes in the margin the exact words of Augustine: « Aio te eacidem romanos vincere posse ». A splendid instance of the difference between the mediaeval paraphrast and the meticulous humanist.

With this attitude of Coluccio's in mind we can readily believe that some of his critical marks refer to errors of one sort or another in Dominici's many quotations. In 31, 7 the mark may refer to the quotation from Cicero's *De inventione*: « Est enim studium vehemens applicatio animi ad aliquid agendum magna cum voluntate ». Cicero's words are: « Studium est

---

[52] *Epist.,* II, p. 399. Novati wrongly reads *Pylos* with one of his manuscripts as against *Pyros* (*Puros*) of the other three.

autem animi assidua et vehementer ad aliquam rem applicata magna cum voluptate occupatio ». In 36, 319 Dominici refers to Apuleius (*Met.* II, 14) for the man who, on the point of consulting a fortune-teller, heard the latter tell a tale which showed that he could not tell his own fortune; then the prospective customer goes off, quoting in effect, according to Dominici, the words of *Eccli.* xiv, 5: « Qui sibi nequam est, aliis quomodo proterit bonus esse? ». As a matter of fact, the customer goes off without uttering a word. In a paraphrase of Isidore (9, 240) Dominici inserts the statement that the *sortilegi* used the Pythagorean table, and Coluccio's mark seems to be an objection to this untrue insertion. Dominici's statement that Cicero wished for death in order to see his beloved Cato (2, 315) should read that Cato wanted to see his son. Coluccio not only marked this but wrote in the margin « Vide melius librum de Senectute ». Dominici's attribution of a statement to Socrates instead of Anaxagoras (11, 44) is marked; elsewhere Dominici has it right (23, 115). In 11, 55 the mark seems to indicate that in Dominici's brief paraphrase of Valerius Maximus two stories about Xenocrates are confused. Two lines below, Coluccio marked a misunderstanding of the story of Lais and Demosthenes as told by Gellius. A mark at 16, 37 apparently notes a misunderstanding of Augustine: Dominici's « in theatris effigiabant narrata » seems to be based on a wrong interpretation of « fabulosi deorum suorum dedecore », a mistake that Coluccio did not make [53].

Many of the grammatical and vocabulary errors already mentioned are in quotations, and Coluccio may have wished to criticize the textual criticism as well as the usage of his opponent. Other marked mistakes in quotations are *lino* for *limo* (9, 236) and *illo te* for *illoto* (42, 166). In 40, 71 Dominici quotes Virgil indirectly from Augustine with the reading *suscipiunt*. Some of the manuscripts of Augustine have this reading but more have *suspiciunt*; the Virgil manuscripts have *despiciunt* or *dispiciunt*. Probably Coluccio's mark refers to this difference in text.

Wrong references account for some of the marks: *in prologo Recthorice* (of Cicero) should be *Tusc.* V, 5 (7, 209); in 12,

---

[53] *Epist.*, IV, p. 181.

127 Dominici wrongly refers a quotation to the *Tusculans* instead of the *Academica*; a verse attributed to Virgil belongs to Ovid (14, 26); the 'Formo' (*Phormio*) is credited to Cicero instead of Terence (14, 28); Jerome's prologue to the *Psalms* is credited with a passage which is not there (36, 5); Augustine gets credit for a line from Anselm (3, 126). In 9, 256 Dominici says that a knowledge of the doctrines of the Academy, the Stoics, and all the other schools of antiquity is necessary to interpret the book of Ecclesiastes. Coluccio marked this because Dominici should have said Ecclesiasticus [54].

Dominici quotes or paraphrases the *Book of Wisdom* at least fifteen times. In four instances neither author nor work is identified; in one the work is mentioned but not the author; in six the author is mentioned as Solomon but the work is not named [55]. In four instances the author is given as Solomon and the title of the book is given; at two of these (10, 134; 21, 84) Coluccio put his regular mark, at one (47, 11) a mark which may be interpreted in the same way or as a cross, at the fourth (30, 14) there is no mark. It would seem that Coluccio disputed the attribution of the book to Solomon.

But not all the marks call attention to mistakes of the kinds mentioned. Some refer to thoughts, and here we usually cannot tell what comment Coluccio might have made. He marks the etymology *neco-laus* for his own name (Prol., 70), which is a shortened form of Nicoluccio, not only because it is wrong but because he thinks that there is nothing in a name (*Epist.*, IV, 149). The story (from Augustine) that Athens got its name from Minerva (Athena) seems to be marked (39, 92) because Coluccio derived the name of the city from *athanatos* (*De laboribus Herculis*, II, 11, 6). In 22, 99 Coluccio may have objected to the derivation of *animus* from Greek *anemos*.

Coluccio marked Dominici's statement that he had not read of any philosophers ruling nations or of any rulers devoting

[54] Manuscript B correctly has *Ecclesiastici* (by emendation, of course). Dominici and Coluccio probably had in mind *Ecclus.* 39, 1: « Sapientiam omnium antiquorum exquiret sapiens ».

[55] In one of these the quotation follows without separation a quotation from *Ecclesiastes*.

themselves to philosophy (18, 108); presumably Coluccio had examples such as Marcus Aurelius in mind. He also marked the statement (19, 62) that no contemporary had become a philosopher by studying Cicero, Virgil, Livy, Aristotle, and Euclid. He perhaps would have pointed to Petrarch, whom he counts a great philosopher [56]. A mark registers a silent protest against Dominici's claim of all temporal as well as spiritual power for the papacy (1, 98). This was not in accord with Coluccio's ideas or those of other humanists.

Coluccio had no great enthusiasm for John of Salisbury. He rarely quotes him and he considers him greatly inferior to the ancients in style [57]. Perhaps therefore his marking in the *Lucula noctis* of quotations from John may be due to a lack of credence in John's statements. In one (7, 160) there is mention of « Titi pietatem », and Coluccio may have questioned the source of this information, which is not clear to me either. Another is 9, 91, but here it is uncertain whether Coluccio objects to Dominici's rather free quotation of John (which in turn is an unattributed quotation from Vegetius) or to the weather lore mentioned there.

In 15, 148 Dominici, after admitting that books on harmless subjects such as grammar and arithmetic may be read, objects to those which teach a false religion. We can be sure what was in Coluccio's mind in marking this passage. It is implied in his defense of poetry in his reply to Dominici [58] and elsewhere in his allegorical treatment of the labors of Hercules. A similar explanation holds for the mark in 16, 128, where Dominici states that pagan literature dealing with science and theology is to be read only by those who are grounded in the faith [59]. The marks at 33, 222, 238, 241 are on a long quotation from Origenes. The point is that old men rather than young are more suited to the study of philosophy and dialectic. On this question Coluccio

---

[56] *Epist.*, I, p. 178, 27 ff.: « in philosophia ... quantum excessit! ».

[57] *Epist.*, III, p. 83. Novati (II, p. 148) is quite mistaken when he says that Coluccio held John in high esteem and quoted him often.

[58] *Epist.*, IV, p. 233 ff. See, however, above under vocabulary.

[59] In *Epist.*, IV, p. 212 Coluccio says that he and Dominici have no quarrel on this point.

expresses himself in *Epist.*, IV, p. 222 f.: dialectic, he says, is a means for discovering the truth (which is the sole aim of all arts and sciences) and therefore necessary to a Christian, for faith is the highest truth. Therefore dialectic is needed by the young and should not be postponed until faith is established, as Dominici wishes (*ut vis*). Dominici touches on this point a number of times (e.g., in chapter 11), and it is surprising that Coluccio did not employ his mark more often.

In 35, 207 Coluccio marks a quotation from John of Salisbury who says that poets and other writers teach against and destroy the cultivation of virtue. His presumed comment would be that, according to Horace and Aristotle, poets attack vice and praise virtue—for Coluccio makes this comment often in his writings (e.g., *Epist.*, IV, p. 231). Perhaps the mark at 39, 149 is for the statement that poets are not to be believed, though the same statement is unmarked at 39, 56.

Dominici's quotation from Boethius to the effect that the arts were meretricious (19, 65) is marked because Coluccio had answered that argument in a letter to Giovanni da Samminiato (*Epist.*, IV, p. 192). Dominici's « scenicam et obscenam artem poeticam » (45, 13) may have been marked because it suggested to Coluccio Boethius' « scenicas meretriculas (Musas) », but other allusions to this passage are not marked (15, 84; 31, 41; 33, 260).

Dominici's statement that Virgil was not speaking of the Trinity is marked (23, 31) because Coluccio had cited this same verse for the importance of the number three and its bearing on the Trinity (*Epist.*, IV, p. 49); and in his *De laboribus Herculis* (II, 2) he covers the point fully by saying that God inspired pre-Christian poets to utter the truth without their knowing it. Similarly Coluccio put a *Nota* of approval in the margin of 34, 267, where Dominici says that some maintain that persons born before the establishment of the Church were not heretics, while others hold that even the Virgin was conceived in sin. Perhaps because of the inconsistency with this statement Coluccio marks the view of some that Aristotle was a heretic (40, 50). Again Coluccio marks Dominici's quotation (28, 74) from *Colossians* that one should not be deceived by the traps of philosophy because he had answered the same quotation in the letter to

Giovanni da Samminiato (*Epist.*, IV, p. 183) by saying that we must learn about pagan literature so as to avoid the traps. Dominici's quotation of *Genesis* on the creation of Adam and the necessity of his working (32, 25, 32) is marked; in his answer to Dominici (*Epist.*, IV, p. 237) he quotes the same verse to show that the Bible, like pagan poetry, must be interpreted allegorically, not literally. Dominici's distinction between *scelera* described in pagan and Christian literature is condemned with a mark (38, 315). In his reply (p. 235) Coluccio says that people think pagan poetry contains only *fabulae* and *scelera*. But these are found in Christian literature too and both literatures must be interpreted allegorically. Perhaps 41, 248 is marked because Dominici for once treats a pagan story allegorically (« excidium Ylii—altioris hominis partis »), quite in accordance with Coluccio's practice. So too in 31, 91, 99 the marks may refer to the allegorical Circe, Helen, and others. Or did Coluccio disagree with Dominici's interpretation? In 36, 424 Coluccio marked an attack on rhetoric in which the words *omnis splendor orandi* occur; he seems to have had this phrase in mind in his reply (p. 234) when he said that some people think of rhetoric as merely *splendidorum vocabulorum congeriem*.

The proverb *que nova testa capit, inveterata sapit* is twice applied to the education of children by Dominici (20, 45; 44, 150). In the second instance Coluccio put his usual mark; in the first we find the words « non est periculum », perhaps written by Coluccio [60].

The origin of the sign which Coluccio uses is unclear. It may be a variant of the *alogus,* defined by Isidore (I, 21, 27): « Alogus nota ad mendas adhibetur ». But the various shapes of this sign in the manuscripts reported by Lindsay and Arevalo are unlike Coluccio's sign. More likely it is the *ancora inferior,* defined by Isidore (I, 21, 25): « ubi aliquid vilissime vel inconvenientius denuntiatum est ». In the codex Toletanus, as may be seen in the Leiden facsimile, fol. 8r, it has the form of an anchor

---

[60] The only marked passages for which no solution has been offered in the foregoing are: 2, 337; 7, 39; 18, 116; 24, 138; 26, 35; 30, 119; 32, 14, 23; 33, 307; 36, 226; 38, 88; 40, 145; 41, 76; 43, 350.

without the cross-bar[61]. Of the same origin is the treatise *De notis* published by Keil (*GL* VII, p. 533). Here (p. 536, 15) the *ancora inferior* is defined « ad humilius vel inconvenientius quid enuntiatum ». The form is close to that used by Coluccio: an inverted capital T with the transverse member curved upwards at the ends (so too p. 534, 3). The probabilities are that Coluccio got the sign from Isidore and that his manuscript of Isidore had it in the form which he uses.

A theta is found once in the margin of our manuscript, presumably written by Coluccio (22, 23). In the treatise *De notis* (VII, p. 436, 18 K.) the theta represents 'supervacuus', and there is a sentence which is superfluous for the argument in Dominici at this point[62]. There is no such sign in Isidore.

The mark we have been discussing occurs only on the right hand margin. Another mark, in the form of a point, occurs alone or in rows of two or three, and only in the left hand margin[63]. It is obvious that these dots, which run into many hundreds, note wrong or undesirable spellings. Where more than one spelling in a line is noted there are often two or three dots in a row, though one dot may serve for two errors and occasionally two dots arranged vertically seem to refer to one line. My first thought was that Coluccio, who took a keen interest in spelling, was responsible for the dot symbol as for the other symbol. But this cannot be true. In the first place many of the spellings marked were corrected by two or more later correctors and one gets the impression that the man who made the dots worked before any of the correctors, even the technical corrector, or proofreader. In ten cases where C[2] added one or more words in a spelling elsewhere regularly noted by our dotter no dot is found; it might, to be sure, be argued that he paid no attention to marginal additions. But one case of bad spelling by C[2] occurs where he filled a lacuna left by the scribe (46, 185).

---

[61] Similarly in the *editio princeps* (*ca.* 1472, Hain 9270) and the Venice edition of 1483 (Hain 9279).

[62] A list of the *notae* in a manuscript at La Cava has 'theta in amputandis' (Reifferscheid in *Rheinisches Museum*, XXIII, 1868, pp. 128, 130).

[63] Apparent exceptions are due to blotting, e. g., fol. 91v.

There are two dots in the margin but both probably refer to other spellings in that line. On the other hand in three cases (13, 71; 17, 186; 31, 141) the dot is farther out than usual, apparently because a word added in the margin by C² was already there. In the last example the dot (and one in the next line) seem to have been made before the book was bound. In another case (34, 114) there is a dot where nothing seems wrong, but in the next line, whose margin is filled by a word added by C², there is a misspelling. It may be therefore that the dot had to be put higher. But the dot is opposite an abbreviation of the type which the dotter dislikes (*sapie* for *sapientie*), as we shall see, and this may be the explanation [64].

Be that as it may, the dots were put in before Coluccio, for in at least two instances where he corrects a spelling by means of an *r* sign (3, 194 *garrule*; 8, 51 *interpretes*) there is a dot, evidently put in before the correction. If Coluccio had inserted the hundreds of dots he would have corrected more than these few misspellings.

It is as impossible as it would be dull to list all the marked misspellings here, but a few examples and types may be given, partly to make clear that the dot does refer to the spelling. The omission of *h* is marked in many words and occurs over two hundred times, as *ystoria* (24 [65]), *Ieronimus* (60), *pulcer* (18), *scola* (41). Wrongly inserted *h* occurs some eighty times, as in *archanum* (11), *metha-* (19). *Ct* for *tt* appears in *lictera* (30) and *micto* (22). *D* for *t* is found in *capud* (4), *velud* (10), *aud quidquid, -quam* (11). *P* between *m* and *n* occurs in *alumpnus* (4), *contempno* (13), *dampno* (45), *Netumpnus* (2); before *t* in *legiptimus* (4), *scruptor* (8), *volupto* (3), etc. *C* is omitted in *autor*

---

[64] C² was either the author or in close touch with him. In several cases C left a space where the author had failed to look up a reference; these C² filled in. So in 11, 21 he filled in the name of an author; in 28, 29, the source of a cross-reference in a Biblical passage; in 44, 88-9, the exact reference in a citation from Gratian; in 46, 106, the indication that it was a Babylonian king who was referred to in Isaiah.

[65] The figures in parentheses refer to the number of occurrences; all these examples are marked with dots. Of course the many examples overlooked by the dotter are not recorded or counted here.

(11) [66], and other words. *T* for *c* appears in *speties* (6), etc. *X* for *s, ss,* or *ps* occurs in over ten words, as *extimo* (3), *iuxi* (5), *laxus* for *lapsus* (2); the opposite confusion is about as common: *estat* (3), *testus* (1), *tossico* (1). *Y* for *i* is very common: *dya-* (39), *Epycurus* (7), *hystoria* or *ystoria* (36), *Stoycus* (14), *ydolum* (18), *ymago* (12), *ymmo* or *ymo* (48), and a hundred other examples. *I* for *y* is less common: *misterium* (22), *phisicus* (60), and some fifteen scattered cases.

A single consonant where assimilation of a prefix demands two occurs in about thirty words, as *apareo* (3), *irigo* (1). Double for single consonant in the prefix is found chiefly in *addicio* (5). Unassimilated prefixes appear in about twenty words: *inmobilis* (2), *obmitto* (5), etc. Other examples of single for double consonants are: *Apolo* (3), *gramatica* (8), *silogismus* (9), *solers* (11), etc. Double for single consonant: *oppinio* (31), *opportet* (6), *scellus* (5), *Terrentius* (8), *tollero* (7), etc. Other spellings that are marked are *locuntur* for *loquuntur* (6), *secuntur* (4), *cotidie* for *quotidie* (6), *loyca* for *logica* (6), *arismetica* for *arithmetica* (15), *silicet* for *scilicet* (9), *gignasium* (6), *auruspex* (2), various difficulties with *r*, as *intepretor*, etc. (4), *collorarie* (1).

Apparently some of the dots refer to abbreviations that were frowned upon. A clear case is in a passage where the pronoun *quod* is expressed by the symbol properly confined to the conjunction *quod*; a later hand corrected this (34, 63). An abbreviation of the *pre* of *expressis* by *p'* is dotted and corrected (38, 84). Less certain cases are abbreviations of *sapientiam* as *sapiam* with a stroke (5-6), and similarly of *misericordiam* and *penitentiam* (42, 241). Others may be *post'* and *pnt* with a stroke for *possunt* (34, 8; 36, 43), *po'* for *post* (28, 35; 46, 185).

Coluccio put his symbol at some points where the dot had already been used to criticize the same word. The surer cases are *Methamorum* (2, 455); *partile* (3, 29) [67]; *Ortensem* (8, 175), though dotted not for the ending but for the omission of *h*;

---

[66] As Coluccio himself constantly used the spelling *autor* in many manuscripts, the dotting of this spelling is another indication that the dotter was not Coluccio. In this instance he was better than Coluccio.

[67] But no dot at 15, 20; 16, 123; 41, 151; 46, 16.

the other two examples have *h* and are not dotted. Curiously enough the two examples of *fiendum* which Coluccio did not mark are dotted (4, 10, 19) but those which he marked are not. Perhaps Coluccio generally avoided marking words already dotted. *Proprius* seems to be meant by the dot at 2, 170, but none of the other instances of this word are so marked. At 23, 194 and 28, 74 there is a dot for *Coloscenses* but only the second is marked by Coluccio. Other errors which both critics mark are *instruisse* (36, 377); *humuccio* (39, 64); *strumenta* (39, 98); *structor* (40, 179); *ostium* (46, 99); *abscisus* (46, 353).

Chapter XIII

CHRYSOLORAS' TWO LETTERS
TO COLUCCIO SALUTATI

A manuscript of the sixteenth century in The University Library of Leiden (L = Vulc. 95) contains ten letters of Chrysoloras, the Greek scholar who came to Florence at the end of the fourteenth century to teach Greek and who made a notable contribution to the development of Greek studies in that great center of Italian humanism. The fifth letter is incomplete at the beginning and no indication is given of the correspondent for whom it was intended. The sixth letter is addressed to Coluccio Salutati[1]. These two letters are found also in V, a Vatican manuscript (Vat. gr. 1368)[2]. In L the fifth letter comes after the fourth without a break; in V this letter begins on a new gathering, after a speech of Demosthenes which is followed by three blank pages. Novati concluded from the presence of the blank pages that the manuscript once contained the now lost beginning of the fifth letter. This does not follow at all, nor his further conclusion that L was descended from V[3].

Cardinal Mercati decided from a study of the contents of the fragmentary fifth letter that it was written to Salutati in answer to the latter's request for rules about the Greek breathings

---

[1] Published by F. Novati, *Epistolario di Coluccio Salutati*, IV (Rome, 1911), p. 333.

[2] Novati's caution about accepting Fulvio Orsini's assertion that V is an autograph of Chrysoloras is thoroughly justified. Orsini had an instinct for attributing the copying of the books he owned to their authors on little or no evidence. P. de Nolhac, *La bibliothèque de Fulvio Orsini* (Paris, 1887), p. 145, does not question Orsini's attribution.

[3] Cf. G. Mercati, *Rendiconti dell'Istituto Lombardo*, Ser. II, 51 (1918), p. 227; cf. also his note in *Bessarione*, 33 (1917), p. 328.

and that it accompanied a little treatise on the subject, which is also found at the end of Chrysoloras' *Erotemata* [4].

My purpose here is to give further evidence in support of Cardinal Mercati's view; first, a statement of Salutati's indicating that he received this letter; second, manuscript evidence supporting the identification of the recipient as Salutati.

In his *De laboribus Herculis* (IV, 1, 3, 22) Coluccio says that Chrysoloras had informed him that initial epsilon followed by rho takes the smooth breathing except in *Hermes, hercos, hersi,* and *herdo* [5]. This is exactly what Chrysoloras wrote, using the same examples, in the little treatise accompanying the fragmentary letter and repeated in the *Erotemata* [6].

Andres tells us that he saw in the Royal Library of Naples a manuscript containing four letters of Chrysoloras [7]. His description indicates that they are the last four of those in L. Since the same four letters still exist in a Naples manuscript [8] it seems certain that the two manuscripts are one and the same. The manuscript evidently once contained the first six letters, as well as other material [9].

More important conclusions can be drawn from other statements of Andres. He informs us that in 1785 he saw a number of manuscripts in the Royal Library of Naples, many of which

---

[4] Salutati's request is in Novati, *Epist.*, IV, p. 269.

[5] *Colucii Salutati De laboribus Herculis,* ed. B. L. Ullman (Zurich, 1951), pp. 478-479.

[6] My copy of the *Erotemata* is called *Emanuelis Chrysolorae ... Graecae grammaticae institutiones* (Venetiis, 1542). The text and Latin translation are garbled at this point but the examples are not affected.

[7] Juan Andres, *Anecdota Graeca et Latina ex manuscriptis codicibus Bibliothecae Regiae Neapolitanae deprompta,* I (Naples, 1816), p. xlvi.

[8] S. Cyrillus (Cirillo), *Codices Graeci manuscripti Bibliothecae Borbonicae descripti,* II (Naples, 1832), p. 212. Its number is III, A, A, 16 (III, A, 16 in Cyrillus).

[9] The four letters, which cover sixteen leaves (numbered 74-89) in the Naples manuscript, extend over fols. 78r-118v in the Leiden manuscript. Only about thirty-one leaves of the Naples codex would be needed to match fols. 1r-77v of L. Thus some forty-two leaves of the Naples codex were available for other material. The Leiden manuscript has 122 fols., but the last three are blank. Beside the folio numbering it also has a page numbering, which Novati followed (not always correctly), wrongly calling the pages leaves.

were stolen in 1791 and sold abroad (« exteris emtoribus »). Among them apparently was one containing Chrysoloras' two letters to Coluccio Salutati, which Andres could no longer find [10]. Baffius and Rutinellius, according to Andres, had indicated that the manuscript contained Gorgias' *Encomium of Helen*, the two letters of Chrysoloras to Coluccio, and an anonymous work « de praenomine et praepositione » [11]. Of this manuscript, says Andres, only the first and last work remained in the Naples library, and the ten folia containing the missing letters had disappeared, either through carelessness or theft.

The Gorgias and the grammatical treatise are still in Naples, in a manuscript (II, D, 26) described by Cyrillus [12]. On fol. 1 is found a short fragment of Isocrates' *Evagoras*. The *Encomium of Helen* by Gorgias covers fols. 1v-4v and is followed on fol. 4v by a fragment of Isocrates' speech on the same theme. Fols. 5-14 are missing. The treatise Περὶ ἀντωνυμίας (*De pronomine*) begins on. fol. 15, a treatise on the uses of ὡς, followed by a list of words differentiated only by accent or breathing, begins on fol. 31 and ends on fol. 34v.

There is at Oxford a manuscript which can be positively identified as the lost folios 5-14 of the Naples manuscript [13]. It contains the two letters of Chrysoloras to Coluccio on ten leaves numbered 5-14, exactly the folios missing from the Naples manu-

---

[10] *Op. cit.*, pp. xlii, xlvi, lii.

[11] Pasquale Baffi's catalogue of the Greek manuscripts in the Royal Library appeared in J. A. Fabricius, *Bibliotheca Graeca,* ed. 3 by Gottlieb C. Harles, V (Hamburg, 1796), p. 777, no. 38. The two Chrysoloras letters to Coluccio are included. In Vol. IV, p. ix, Harles states that he received Baffi's catalogue in 1793, but Baffi may have made it some years earlier. P. Rutinelli's handwritten *Catalogus codicum manuscriptorum Regiae Bibliothecae Farnesianae,* dated 1747, is in the Naples library; his description of the manuscript reads (fol. 16r): « Gorgiae Leontini, Helenae Encomium et fragmentum Isocratis. Manuelis Chrysolorae epistolae ad Colucium Salutatum. De pronomíne. De prepositione. 4⁰. Chart. ». The rest of the Isocrates was therefore lost before 1747. The present numbering of the folios was introduced after that loss.

[12] Cyrillus, *op. cit.*, II, pp. 69, 104.

[13] Bodl. MS. Gr. Misc. 4 (S. C. 28998); cf. F. Madan, *A Summary Catalogue of Western Manuscripts in the Bodleian Library at Oxford,* V (Oxford, 1905), p. 539.

script [14]. The time when it reached England was not long after it disappeared from Naples, as one can infer from the presence in it of an English bookplate of the early nineteenth century [15]. It was bought by the Bodleian from G. E. Mason in 1870. The fragmentary first letter begins with a colored initial, as does the complete letter that follows. Clearly then it was copied (in the fifteenth century) from a manuscript that was already fragmentary, as were L and V.

Rutinelli, Baffi, and Andres agree in naming Coluccio as the recipient of the fragmentary letter. It seems clear that they obtained this information from the part of the Naples manuscript now in Oxford. For in this the fragment carries a superscription by a second, but early, hand: κολουχιω χαίρειν. The next letter has: τῷ αὐτῷ χαίρειν. Novati was sceptical about Andres' identification of the correspondent as Salutati (Novati does not mention Baffi and Rutinelli, quoted by Andres). He thought that Andres inferred that the letter was addressed to Coluccio because it preceded one that was certainly addressed to him. His scepticism led him to omit this letter in his publication of letters addressed to Salutati. We now know from the Oxford manuscript that the attribution was made much earlier, in the fifteenth century.

[14] Cyrillus' statement that eleven leaves are missing is an obvious error, since he gives fol. 4 as the last before the lacuna and fol. 15 as the first after it. Andres correctly states that the missing leaves number ten. The two manuscripts are of exactly the same size: the Naples manuscript has an outside measurement of 217×147 mm.; the Oxford manuscript, 216×146. Fols. 1-4 of the Naples codex are in a different hand from the rest, and I shall ignore them in the further comparison. On fols. 15-34 (old numbering) the writing space is 133×65 mm.; it is the same in the Oxford manuscript (i. e., fols. 5-14 of the original manuscript). Or if we compare the spacing produced by vertical ruling of Naples, fols. 15-34, and Oxford, we find it is identical: 6, 63, 6, 19, 6. mm. In both manuscripts the number of lines to the page is 23. The gatherings in the Naples manuscript consist of 4 leaves (all that is left of the original gathering of 8 or 10), 10, 10. The ten leaves of the Oxford manuscript fit into this scheme as the second gathering.

[15] Madan (*loc. cit.*) states that the coat of arms is that of Banbury or Flamank. An erasure underneath seems to be that of Thomas (?) Fl(amank). The manuscript was once numbered Canon. Gr. 129, but that number must have been assigned to it late in the nineteenth century, as the highest number in the original Canonici collection was 128.

Cardinal Mercati raises the question whether the treatise on breathing was written expressly for Salutati and then incorporated in the *Erotemata,* or whether it was copied from the larger work for Salutati, or whether the idea itself of writing the *Erotemata* arose out of the various questions asked by Salutati. He quotes a letter of Sabbadini favoring the first view. This would seem to be the most likely explanation, not only because the discussion of breathings is tacked on at the end of the *Erotemata,* where it is not really at home, but because there is a presentation, very brief, to be sure, of breathings at the beginning of the book, right after the discussion of accentuation, where it properly belongs. What is more, the two discussions of the subject begin in identical fashion.

Chapter XIV

ADDITIONS TO SALUTATI'S LETTERS FROM THE TURIN MANUSCRIPT AND CORRESPONDENCE WITH BERNARDO MOGLIO

Among Novati's papers (No. 280 in Box 58) I found a long report on a manuscript in Turin (Univ. Lat. B. 265), containing, among other items, some of Coluccio's letters. It is interesting to note that this report was transmitted to Novati by none other than Professor P. Fedele, later Senator and Minister of Public Instruction, on April 5, 1911. This was four months before the printing of Novati's fourth volume was completed, but no mention of the manuscript occurs in that volume or elsewhere. I have since secured photostats of the Coluccio letters. The correct number of the manuscript is H. III. 38. It is described by Pasini under the number DCCLXXXIV (e. II. 18) as « Monumenta ad historiam saeculi XIII et sequentium spectantia », in which description he is followed in two later lists [1]. This applies to the first 43 folios. Skipping from there Pasini and the others mention only the letters of Petrarch to Cola on fols. 163 ff. Thus the Coluccio letters escaped attention. Gabrielli, however, indicated that the manuscript included various letters of Coluccio [2]. It is strange that Novati over-

---

[1] J. Pasinus, *Codices manuscripti bibliothecae Regii Taurinensis Athenaei* (Turin, 1749), Part II, pp. 257-259; *Rivista di filologia classica*, XXXII (1904), p. 550; G. Mazzatinti and A. Sorbelli, *Inventari dei manoscritti delle biblioteche d'Italia*, XXVIII (Florence, 1922), p. 129.

[2] *Epistolario di Cola di Rienzo*, a cura di Annibale Gabrielli (Rome, 1890), p. xviii, and his « L'epistole di Cola di Rienzo e l'epistolografia medievale », in *Archivio della Società romana di storia patria*, XI (1889), p. 469. K. Burdach, *Vom Mittelalter zur Reformation*, II, 2 (Berlin, 1928), *Briefwechsel des Cola di Rienzo*, by K. Burdach and P. Piur, p. 208, in an eight-page description of the manuscript, merely indicates that it contains letters of Coluccio.

looked this reference. Pasini's date for the collection is fifteenth century; the others say fourteenth and fifteenth. The Coluccio letters seem to me to date from the beginning of fifteenth. As the manuscript was somewhat damaged by water during the Turin fire of 1904 some of the words are illegible or nearly so. The hand changes with the new letter on fol. 148v but reverts on fol. 150r. This manuscript contains exactly the same letters as N^2 except that it omits II, p. 197. But some of the letters are longer in T than in N^2. The presumable explanation is that portions were omitted in the process of editing either by Coluccio or, more likely, by the person responsible for the collection in N^2. This is rather clearly indicated by an omission by N^2 in II, pp. 200-201, the letter which does not occur in T. Furthermore, the order of the letters is not the same in the two manuscripts. In N^2 eight of its twelve private letters are on fols. 43r-48v, one on 60v, three on 133v. In T all eleven private letters are on fols. 142v-152v. To add to the mystery of N^2, Novati adds « n. 431 » after the folio number for II, p. 159, and « n. 447 » after that for II, p. 180. These numbers would seem to indicate a large collection of letters or other items.

The collection must be a copy of one put together originally by Bernardo da Moglio. Two of the four public letters in it are specifically mentioned by Coluccio as being among those which he is sending to Bernardo (II, p. 173), and the other two may well have been included. Of the private letters, two are addressed to Bernardo's father Pietro (I, pp. 3, 164); only one other letter to Pietro is known (I, p. 114). Two are to a fellow citizen of Bernardo, Iacopo Tederisi (de Therisiis); they are II, pp. 159, 162, the only ones addressed to him. He was a colleague of Bernardo's father at the University of Bologna. The only time that Coluccio refers to him is in a letter to Bernardo answering one in which the latter had mentioned Iacopo's death (II, p. 267; cf. p. 283). The other seven letters are addressed to Bernardo, ending with one that Novati thinks was written in 1387-88, but which I believe was written in the latter half of 1390 (see chapter IX on II, p. 192).

Burdach and Piur point out that T is closely related to a

Vienna manuscript which, to judge from its contents, originated in Bologna or Florence, more probably the former. This confirms my suggestion about Bernardo.

T is of interest not only because of the new material it offers but also because it furnishes many corrections in Novati's text, especially in those letters which are found only in N². This in spite of its many errors. The orthography of T is highly Italianized. Assimilation is carried to extremes: *corruttos, exottem, trassit*. Single consonants for double and vice versa occur in almost every line. These and other spellings, such as *ascunditus* (*absconditus*), *malinittas* (*malignitas*), *ac* (*hac*) are omitted in the following report. I also omit a few minor variations of text. The asterisk before a reading indicates my belief that it should be adopted in the text, though I do not necessarily approve the particular spelling of T. Sometimes I put an emendation of mine in parentheses. I follow the order of the letters in the manuscript.

The first private letter in T is II, p. 159, for which it gives a fuller text. Novati depended on N², which indicates merely that the correspondent was named Iacobus, and on a Vatican manuscript containing a letter of Niccolò de' Cesi who, to put it baldly, stole this letter of Coluccio and of course put in the name of his own correspondent. Novati identified Iacobus as Iacopo Tederisi of Bologna. This is now confirmed by T, which has « Magistro Iacobo de Tederisiis de Bononia sacre theologie dignissimo professori ». This amazing identification is one of the many things that make Novati's edition the outstanding work it is.

II, p. 159 (fol. 142v). 16 *Gaspar*. 17 *cuius titulus* om. 160, 3 *et in veram caritatem*. 3-5 are partly illegible. 5 *credat*. 7 *possim*. 7 *sacre*. 8 *est* om. 8 *fuit semper*. 10 *tantum*. 12 *iteratos maiores*. 13 *noluerunt ostendere*. 14 *dicere*. 17 *obscuram maiorem*. 17 *patribus*. 161, 2 *quasulis*. 5 *suam*. 5 *adutitur*. 6 *contrattat*. 7 *iniurius*. 8 *voluerit*. 12 *aurum* om. 22 *igitur*. 23 *addutis*. 26 *properata*. 26 *itaque*. 162, 1 *obveniam*. 2 *belli superant*. 2 *veritate*. 3 *et ut*. 5 *hac atthenus*. 14 *invides*. 14 *datum etc.* om.

It will be noted that T agrees now with N², now with V, and that in most cases it casts a deciding vote.

Between *declamare* and *unum* (p. 162, 8), T has the following long and interesting passage:

Nunc autem ut ad libellum illum veniam, non est Augustini, sicut titulus erat, sed particula quedam ex libris Firmiani Lactantii, qui septem sunt numero, Divinarum Institutionum Adversus Gentes. Quorum primus est de falsa religione, secundus de origine erroris,
5 tertius de vera sapientia, quintus de iustitia, sextus, in quo est ille textus quem paternitas tua requirit, de vero cultu, septimus de vita beata. Autor autem iste Christianus fuit et est proculdubio ille Lactantius de quo noster Aurelius in decimo octavo libro De Civitate Dei affirmat tot Sibillarum oracula ad Christum pertinentia collegisse. De
10 cuius vita, libris, atque statu vide Ieronimum De Viris Illustribus capitulo octogesimo; cuius quidem tibi verba non pono, quia istic facile videre poteris, ut opinor. Quodsi forte illo libello carueris, meum, qualiscumque sit, et alia omnia que apud me sunt ut volueris habebis. Cavenda sunt tamen opera Firmiani. Laborabat enim operi-
15 bus Origenis, de origine anime, de salvatione in fine seculorum, et de statu vite beate et aliis multis in quibus lugenda concisio tanti viri contemptam ex imitatione sola et mentiant. Ut cum attigerit sacras litteras etiam his perspicacissimus videatur, qua . . . . ista etiam vadens in foveam de con . . . . Origenis quod eidem eam ex magistri
20 sui Arnobii disciplina, cui videtur pertinaciter inhesisse, Deo permittente, ne sibi per eloquentie qua nitebat pompam omnia divinarum scripturarum misteria patrasse crederet, arbitror contigisse. Non parum enim sibi visus est in eloquentia placuisse, et forte plus quam virum Christianum deceret. Quorum fides in piscatorum ruditate, non
25 in facundie lenocinio surrexit et crevit. Forsitan et Origeniste magistro suo, quin plenissimus Arnobio, plus quam homini credi debeat fidem dedit, ut qui ex homine putabat se veritatem attigisse, diceret non in homine sed in illa incommutabili veritate a qua cetere veritates sunt, veritatem quam quereret invenire. Quecumque autem causa

1 *bellum.* 2 *lris.* 3 *constitutionum.* 8 *De civ. Dei* XVIII, 23. 10 *vide*] *vitte.* 12 *illo illo.* 13 *qualicumque.* 14 *laboraba.* 15 *orrignis.* The whole passage about Origen and Lactantius is based on Jerome, *Epist.* 84. This includes their heresies, the supposed influence of the former on the latter, the mutilation of Origen, and the word Origenistes. 15 *sarvatione.* 17-19 are partly illegible and unintelligible. 17 perhaps for *contempta.* 17 for *mentiatur?* 19 *originis.* 20 *cui(us).* 20 *inessisse* or *messisse.* 25 *horigeste.* 26 *adnorbio.*

fuerit, cum omnia Dei iudicia sint occulta, lapsus est autor iste plus 30
eloquens quam verax in errores quam plurimos qui possunt a legenti-
bus facile deprendi, ut opuscula sua cautissimos oporteat habere lecto-
res, ne citra nitorem eloquentie, qui certissime sibi familiaris fuit,
quemve etiam in dicendo peritissimus tamquam altissime volans se-
quendum reliquit, ab ipso veritatem Catholicam requiramus. Hec satis. 35
Nunc autem ad textum de quo queris veniam. Est autem illa particula in libro sexto qui de vero cultu supra diximus appellari. Legitur
autem in meo codice in hec verba: « Merito ergo Persius huiusmodi
superstitiones suo more deridet. 'Qua tu', inquit, 'mercede deorum
emeris auriculas pulmone et lactibus unctis?'. Sentiebat videlicet non 40
carne opus esse ad placandum celestium maiestatum, sed mente
sancta, iusto animo, et pectore, ut ipse ait, quod naturali sit honestate
generosum. Hec est religio celestis, non que constat ex rebus », etc.
Que quidem verba non ambigo correctissima fore. In quibus si quid
obscurum tibi visum fuerit propter illius poete quem inducit scabrosi- 45
tatem, consulere potes horum poetarum peritos et videbis, ni fallor,
intentionem autoris, et ego ipse, qui diu poetarum studiis delectatus
sum, si iusseris, rescribam plene quid sentiam.

34 *peritissimis.* 34 *artissime.* 35 *Nec.* 37 *que.* 38 *Inst.* VI, 2, 11. 39
derident. 40 *purmone.* 41 *plantandum.* The Lactantius editions have *placan-
dam celestem maiestatem,* but Brandt reports that one manuscript has *placandum*
(S. Brandt and G. Laubmann, *Lactantii Opera,* in *Corpus scriptorum ecclesiasti-
corum Latinorum,* XIX, Vienna, 1890). 43 *Nec.* 43 *est om.* 43 *et.* 44 *cor-
rectissime.* 45 *hosturunt.*

II, p. 162 (fol. 144v). No heading is preserved for this letter.
Novati had only N² available. 21 *non non.* 22 *te om.* 23 *loqueris.*
23 *hic.* 163, 1 *bene om.* 1 *soloecismo.* 2 *necque enim.* 5 *publicum.* 7 *princeps.* 8 *michi vero nulla.* 11 *simul] *vel.* 12 *numerari.* 16 *eadem.* 16 *videbaris.* 18 *inmuto.* 18 *ut.* 18 *atque.*
20 *nec.* 21 *humilimas.* 22 *qua carateris.* 23 *precellentia.* 24
*unus etenim] *nunc autem.* 27 *cum... patrem, representes* illegible.
28 *quid.* 31 *libere om.* 164, 2 *et in.* 2 *opusculo meo, scilicet in
libro de seculo et religione.* 3 *cossolationem.* 4 *consserim.* 7 *gravis.*
8 *proferi.* 8 *carnalibus* (for *cardinalibus,* a very important difference!) *qui extra sunt istos.* 10 *est om.* 11 *verutatem.* 12 *verittate*
(*veritatis*). 13 *nam] harum.* 13 *minore.* 14 *facis.* 15 *idem* (perhaps
right). 15 *valeas.* 15 *vir] *magister* 17 *an tu] ante.* 19 *lux.* 21 *adorie.*
21 *enim] *quidem.* 23 *extolli.* 25 *protulerit ait.* 26 the reference
should be to Propertius, I, 15, 42. 165, 1 *quun non ossim.* 2 *quam.*
2 *cum tenssero.* 4 *Perssii tex.* 5 *constitutione.* 6 *epertos.* 8 *nosce.*

9 *Perssium.* 10 *voluerit.* 11 *tu secus.* 11 *que* om. 17-20 *et... pretii* om. 20 *meris.* 21 *quasi dicat*] *q. d.* 22 *nuttis.* 23 *favore supermi.* 24 *dixi.* 27 **quicquam.* 28 *audeo,* after which add *Idem in Georgicis*: « Frigidus obstiterit circum precordia sanguis » (*G.* II, 484), *idest ostet. Flacus in Arte Poetica*: « Dixeris egregie » (*A. P.* 47), *idest dices.* 166, 1 *auditore.* 2 *dicit.* 3 *nuttis.* 3-4 *-nium ... signi-* om. 6 *capitulo.* 7 *stillor.* 8 *putabnt.* 11-12 *et ... sentiam* om.

I, p. 164 (fol. 146r). 14 *Mulglo.* 17 *vester.* 165, 3-4 *inclitam ... seve* om. 4 *depositam.* 6 **ignote.* 8 *gaudebamque et.* 12 *trepidus.* 13 **involvat.* 14 *presentiam.* 166, 2 *nosque ... migrans* repeated after *dereliquit.* 3 *neu.* 4 *senes.* 14 *optimaque dies.* 22 *supernos.* 167, 1 *te hoc.* 1 **prestaturum.* 1 *quid.* 3 *liberos.* 4 *suttonius.* 4 *thesauribus.* 6 *ut*] *quod.* 6 *et* om.

I, p. 3 (fol. 146v). 5 *eidem.* 6 *tuus.* 8 *cum valere.* 9 *me.* 10-4, 3 largely illegible. 4 *obtattare* (**obtractare*; cf. above on II, p. 161, 6). 6 **intermissione.* 7 *existo.* 9 **miscere seu inicere.* 9 *movebas.* 10 *dignum quid* om. 10 *cogneris.* 12 *nec.* 17 **derideat.* 18 no lacuna and no need to indicate one if we adopt the reading *derideat.* 19 *respiciamus.* 20 *cum.* 22 *cui.* 23 *que.* 5, 3 **lacrima.* 5 *vive.* 9 *et* om. 10 *cum.* 11 *cum.* 13 *cumque ... diligas* om.

II, p. 141 (fol. 147v). 6 *Bernardo de Muglo.* 8 *necessitate* om. 10 *cius.* 16 *hec* om. 16 *te quidem.* 142, 1 *insensibilibus.* 6-10 om. 12-14 om.

II, p. 180 (fol. 147v). 22-23 *eidem.* 181, 1 *metor.* 2 *designas et migrari.* 2 *quod.* 6 *conversione.* 6-7 **ipsa nos.* 8 *ac refluxus* om. 8 *quod.* 8 *benenittate.* 9 *designat.* 10 *advenerit.* 12-15 largely illegible. 18 second *et* om. 18 *ducimus.* 182, 2 *videamus.* 11 *rissabile.* 14 *feliciter.* 18 *unicumque virtutum.* 20 *supra.* 23 *forte.* 24 *cum affectione* om. 26 *venerari.* 26 *reciperere meruerint.* 183, 1 *perturbaveris.* 4 **quotidie* om. 6 *deformina.* 6 **ducere.* 7 *illum tantum.* 8 *potestet et presentem.* 10 *igitur.* 12 *scio.* 13 *leviter iam ter afflittus non.* 13-15 *Florentie ... Florentinorum* om.

II, p. 192 (fol. 148v). 9 *eidem.* 15-16 *quidem michi.* 18 **ad* om. 21 **non ytalicos fines solum.* 193, 3 **a quibus plerumque male scientibus.* 4 *me oportet.* 5 *explicate.* 7 **dum.* 14 *deputare.*

After *premissis* (15) a long section occurs which is omitted in N², the only manuscript available to Novati.

Ad illa que queris veniam, et prius ad id quod de dissuasionibus ad Ruffinum ne ducat uxorem me discutere petis accedam. Scio enim,

1 *dissuassionibus.*

licet oppositum conere astruere, te mecum plane sentire, virum illum, ut ex scriptis eius apparet, doctissimum, quisquis fuerit (michi quidem incertus est autor), non id velle quod nullus uxorem ducat, sed 5 quod amicus suus Ruffinus abstineat, nec illum ipsum ut omnes mulieres effugiat, sed illam que tunc sibi cum instantia maxima, si bene respicis, intrudebatur. Et videns in illud proclivem, totiens in sue dictionis auspicio, metuens ne deterrentibus non credat sed blandientibus potius acquiescat, repetit ferme contradictorium illud: « Loqui 10 prohibeor, et tacere non possum ». Assumens enim autor ille Ruffini personam, inquit: « Odisti grues, noctuas, et bubones infelicitatis future molestiam precinentes », et ideo dicit ex persona sua: « Loqui prohibeor ». Non enim placet quod tibi veritas astruatur. « Verum », inquit, « ipse liciniam et merulam quasi prosperitatis augurium et 15 Gnatonum blanditias diligis, et ideo quia in hoc longe maius sentio imminere periculum, tacere non possum », et addit: « Quia propinatione melliti fellis trahitur spiritus tuus, hoc est tue deliberationis assensus, loqui prohibeor. Immedicabilis venenationis quam imminere video conscius, tacere non possum », et hoc idem magis declarans 20 addit quod cum inter facundissimos voluptatum suarum persuasores solus sprete veritatis assertor sit, « Loqui prohibeor ». Sed quia quandoque inter mortiferos dulces cantus strepitus admonens profuit, concludit iterum: « Tacere non possum ». Verum quia, splendore nobilitatis ducende coniugis debilitatis obtutibus, non videbat sibi Chime- 25 ram coniungere, subdit identidem: « Loqui prohibeor ». Sed sperans ipsum non aliter quam Ulixem contra Sirenici cantus illecebras et Circea pocula, quorum omnium pestiferam vim prenosceret, virtuosis

---

4 in I, p. 187, which Novati assigns to 1374, Coluccio attributes the letter of Valerius, in which he urges Rufinus not to marry, to Jerome without any question. In II, p. 374, he says the letter was written either by a certain Valerius or by Jerome. Novati dates this 1392. In the present letter Coluccio, without mentioning Jerome, says that he does not know who the author was. This more advanced opinion would seem to indicate a date later than 1392 for this letter. In chapter IX I offered definite proof that it was written after June 16, 1390, not 1387-88, which Novati suggested. It may then have been written as late as 1392-93. 8 *quotiens.* 9 *ditionis.* 10 *contradictoriens* (in correction). 12 the quoted text is a paraphrase, differing considerably from that printed, e. g., in Migne, *P. L.,* XXX, p. 254. 15 for *lusciniam.* All three of the manuscripts used by M. R. James in his edition of Walter Map, *De nugis curialium* (Oxford, 1914), of which the epistle of Valerius is a part, have *luciniam* or *lucinam.* Professor Robert Pratt is preparing a new edition of this work. Of the fifty-three manuscripts thus far collated by him only one (Glasgow, Hunterian 384) has Coluccio's reading *liciniam,* but this manuscript did not belong to Coluccio. 16, 17, 22 *quare.* 18 *spirtus.* 23, 27 *cautus*; cf. Val. 2. 28 *prenoscet*

vinculis obstiturum, adiunxit insuper: « Tacere non possum ». Has
30 igitur inter contrarietates dissuasor ille, sicut retulit, circumscriptus,
inter spem metumque fluctuans, tandem elegit scribere ne videretur
amico qui in interitum pergeret defuisse, et ut ipsum ex personarum
qualitate doceret non universaliter nuptiarum omnium dissuasorem.
Nonne cum incipiens qualitatem sue cause preponderans ad insinua-
35 tionis tortuosos ambitus confugisset, inquit ipsum miserum et seduc-
tum Chimeram petere, in qua scimus meretricum poetas flagitia figu-
rasse? Iam unico verbo, si bene consideres, tota dubitatio dissoluta
est, ut corruptam meretricio mulierem dissuadeat non ducendam.
Nam quamvis pauce sint Lucretie pauceque Sabine, Livie tamen,
40 Semiramides, et Agrippe vel Ispie non omnes sunt. Non igitur quod
personaliter dictum constat universaliter est sumendum. Nec hoc quidem in subsequentibus tacuit adducens Leuchotoen, Appollinis ama-
siam, in exemplum, si tamen mulier fuit que pulcritudine victa Phe-
beios sine querela concubitus passa est. Pro qua perdite dilecta Sul-
45 monensis noster ex recitantis persona plus quam eleganter ad amantem inquit: « Deficis interdum, vitiumque in lumina mentis Tran-
sit ». Nam deperdidit quidem castitatem, imo virginitatem suam. Ob
amantis formam totus ille mitologus sermo institutus est. Hic idem
et in Danae, cui pecunia se prostituenti dicitur Iupiter in imbris
50 aurei formam per tecti culmina depluisse, monstravit. Quid memorem pulcritudinis et nobilitatis fastum, quem in Sulpitio ab uxore
nobili divertenti latenter expressit, quemque nonnullis in locis etiam
expressius pertractavit? Ut omnia ista facile doceant ipsum sensisse
non omnium mulierum sed illius de qua tunc agebatur fugiendum
55 esse coniugium et ipsum eundem Ruffinum ex eo non vult uxorem
ducere quod diu se sacrarum litterarum studio tradidisset, cui dubi-
tabat uxoris illecebras obstituras. Non ergo credas virum illum Cato-
licum unum ex ecclesie sacramentis temere damnavisse, nec hoc sentire quod nulla coniugia contrahantur, ex quo species humana, sublata
60 generatione, depereat aut illegitimis communionibus, sicut de Spar-

29 *obstitutum.* 33 *doceam.* 33 perhaps *se esse* should be supplied with
dissuasorem. 40 for *Agrippine.* 40 who is meant by Ispia is not clear; perhaps
Eppia (Juvenal, VI, 82 ff., where the manuscripts have Ippia). 42 cf. Val. 10. 43
cf. Ovid, *Met.* IV, 233. 46 Ovid, *Met.* IV, 200-201. 48 *Nec.* 49 *Danne*; cf. Val.
25. James' manuscripts have *Danes* (genitive). 50 the manuscript is partly illegible, partly corrupt. It seems to have *al memorem i(n)erore(m).* I interpret
this as *al' memorem*, a gloss on the wrong reading that follows. Another possibility is to take *al* as *alia* and to see in the word after *memorem* a noun in
the accusative (*memorem* or *errorem* will not do). For the thought cf. Ovid,
F. I, 419: « Fastus inest pulchris, sequiturque superbia formam ». 51 *et* om.
51 *faustum.* 51 *suspitio* (cf. Val. 19). 52 *divertentem satenter.*

tanis legimus, coalescat. Sed inquis, imo sicut ad Herennium scribens Cicero Rectoricam non illi soli sed cunctis tradidit, ita et autor ille, licet ad Ruffinum specialiter scriberet, videtur ad eandem coniugii fugam omne genus hominum monuisse. Cave, fili carissime, alia fuit ratio propositumque et intentio istius matrimoniale vinculum dissua- 65 dentis. Ille siquidem sic loquutus est ad Herennium quod omnia que dicebantur ad eum omnibus rectoricam facultatem optantibus conve- nirent. Iste vero considerans amicum suum assentantibus credulum, proclivem in illecebras, ac deceptionibus oportunum, ne a sacrarum litterarum studio ac ordine clericali, quam vitam ex qualitate studii 70 visus fuerat quodammodo profiteri, tractus post delinimenta connu- bialia deviaret, dehortatoria disputatione eundem ab uxore fornicaria, nobili, blanda, atque superba voluit deterrere. Ut videre possis ipsum hanc controversiam non ad vagam incircumscriptamque circumstan- tiis thesim, quod logices est, applicasse, sed ad ypothesim, quod ora- 75 torium est, disceptationem videlicet que est involuta circumstantiis, contraxisse, ni fallor, et tuis obiectionibus consentaneam. Unum ta- men adiciam, quod in conversatione nostra nichil ferme tam validis rationibus affirmatur quod parva circumstantie mutatione, si ratione duceris, non mutetur. Quid enim tam impium quam quod filius ante 80 diem patrios inquirat in annos? Iuste tamen pater occiditur si perti- naciter exitum patrie moliatur, ut quamvis utilius forte sit alicui sin- gulari non nubere, melius tamen sibi consulat ardentis homo libidinis si se curet matrimonio copulare. Ex quo non credas virum illum tante autoritatis ut scribis illam unam partem, fugiendarum scilicet 85 nuptiarum, sic universaliter astruxisse ut cunctos velit a connubiorum sacrimonia prohibere. Hec hactenus.

61 cf. Her. IV, 69. 86 numptiarum. 87 Nec.

P. 193. 15 Nunc ad querelam. 19 ut om. 31 *quam. 194, 1 *et tu. 1 gloriosus. 5 derelinquatur. 9 *subtraxit. 10 *sicque. 14 librum illum. 15 tibi faciam.

After numerari (16) the rest of the letter reads:

Campaldinus filius olim bone memorie magistri Benvenuti de Imola repetit quoddam scriptum super Marciali Capella. Non grave- ris sibi dicere quod illum feci inchoari per quendam scriptorem, quod genus hominum barattancium est, sed me decepit et vix exemplum

1 Campaldinus] see chapter IX. 2 quodam. 2 since both manuscripts have Marciali that should be restored to the text. That name occurs not infrequently in manuscripts of Martianus and in allusions to him. Coluccio uses both forms in his De laboribus Herculis; Martialis is found in I, 9, 15; III, 24, 10; 11; 15; III, 27, 2. 4 vix] iuxta.

5 potui rehabere; et quod non sit sibi grave si ipsum teneam quo
usque scriptorem invenero. Et nichilominus si librum habere desiderat
mox remittam. Si istic reperiretur Donatus speculativus sive, ut aliqui
reputant, compilatio Bartolutii, emas et mittas. Mox enim rehabebis
quantum solveris. Inde libellus etiam speculativus in gramatica repe-
10 ritur qui dicitur methodus. Si habes aut reperire potes fac quod
habeam. Summe quidem gramatice speculatione delector. Etc.

6 *Et et.*   7 In his review of the first edition of this book Billanovich identifies this as the « Donatus Bertolucii)» in a Bologna catalogue of 1460. This may
be Bologna University 2619, the only manuscript known, according to L. Frati
in *Archivium Romanicum,* VIII (1924), p. 317. There it has the title « Flores
veritatis grammatice ».   8 *compilatio*] the expansion of the abbreviation (a reversed
c with a dot after it) is uncertain.   9 *Unde.*

The new part of the letter, a discussion of the meaning of
the epistle of Valerius to Rufinus, was in answer to a letter of
Bernardo which is still extant in a Paris manuscript (N. a. l. 1152),
fol. 10v).   It reads as follows:

Ser Colutio Pieri Cancellario Florentinorum parte Bernardi Muglensis.

Anxia et lugubris est vita scribentis, ni dolorem auferas iam igni-
tum, iam cordis intima penetrantem, adeo ut nequeat Padus, nequeat
5 Danubium, nequeat Occeanus mei animi combustionem extinguere.
Percipis quo me vertam. Tu ille es quem alloquor, care pater, laurea
digne corona, priscis nec vatibus inequalis. Audi, queso: errat nunc
forsitan animus quia michi nunc talis opinio quod garrulitatem meam
frequentatam sepius sapientum more non approbas. Et licet id merito
10 facere possis (meretur enim ipsa ubilibet reprobari), debuisti prius, ut
coniecto, michi imperare silentium quam contra filialem obedientiam
tua paternalis pietas sopiretur. Fuitne lingua effrenis sive maledicax
erga te alicuius de me enuntiativa malitie? Fuine diminutus in aliquo quod misisses? Si sic erravi, fateor; potius imprudentiam argue
15 quam sentisse reputes tibi factum. Valuit errorem mea imprudentia
sepenumero generare. Arguas, dulcis pater, exoro, filialem defectum,
nec erit a me sinistre receptum, imo remanebit potius que prius erat
devotio et obedientia filialis. Adhuc scribam qua filiali devotione sole-
bam. Scriptitabam tibi, bone pater, ut scientie me fama vulgaris ru-
20 dem filium sepius edoceret; edoctum rudes sepe molestant. Parce
queso, rector optime, et licet non habeas, id tamen honoris tibi com-

15 *sentisse* perhaps for *scienter,* with a meaning like that of *sciens,* « deliberately », to contrast with *imprudentiam.*   15 *me.*   20 *molescant.*

petit. Parce queso, divine poeta. Attamen si hoc, ut fateor, tediosa
scriptura tedio tibi fiat, non sic appetit famelicus accipiter escam,
non sic leo iaculo vulneratus firmiter vindictam appetit sitibundus
ulcisci quam cito subticebit lingua scribentis. Si autem tibi inducat 25
aliquale solatium, letor intus et foris. Nunc oro, patere videre parumper nec dedigneris hoc programa perlegere. Exoro nunc licentiam
ampliandi scripture materiam. Queris forsan et merito: « Unde tibi
tanta licentia? ». Respondeo: faciem tuam quavis benignitate fulgen-
tem ipse ego intueor themati licentiam imperantem. Concedis. Pergo 30
confestim, en rem aggredior, horrens igitur primo suffultus peditum
cohortem relinquens equitibus me committam. Attende thematis scrip-
tionem que, licet prima facie debere negligi videatur, non contra-
dictionis pars altera sic requirit; te iudicem exposcit scribendi tanta
facultas. Pridie delectatus legere epistolam Valerii ad Ruffinum, mul- 35
tiplices fui rationes admonitus quibus coniugium relinquatur. Ne tum
sinistre recipias ut putes me frui velle consortio coniugali, absit adhuc.
Quid queram habes. Multiplicia ibi ponit exempla Valerius reproba-
tiva coniugii. At ego, cuius levis est sententia, imo levissimum quod-
comque prolatum breviter, reddor ipsius opinioni contrarius. Rationes 40
annecto nec tum volo procedere per sofismata loycorum. Legent epistolam Valerii forte mille qui videntes documenta ipsius vitam solitariam agent, forsan legent et plures; si publicetur talis epistola,
ad illius verba, bene nosti, mortales hodie minime convertentur. Si
Valeri documenta quilibet sequeretur, iam cito esset in spem me- 45
liori defectum, iam nullus gauderet nuncio filiorum, corrumperentur
species quas voluit Methaphisicus ab eterno fuisse productas, et iam
cito apocopatus esset hic mundus. Instabit quis forsan dicens: « Non
fuit hec epistola edita pro omni hominum cetu ». Audiat ipse respon-
sum non minori ratione: illius nomine edita fuit ut ipse a coniugio 50
exularet quam alterius ab ipso. Quod lucidissime sic deduco: aut
auctor ipsius epistole ipsam edidit illius solo nomine ne in posteros
transcenderet (dogma tale et hoc stare non potest quia auctores tante
fame quante erat ipse Valerius non laborant ad condenda opera ut
unus solus ipsorum scientia potiretur, licet nomine unius solius sua 55
dogmata fabricarent, velut fecit Arpinas ille fecundissimus auctor
ad Gaium Hermenium et ad ipsius unicum natum) aut edidit ipsam
epistolam omnibus in communi, et sic possibile est ut ad ipsum

25 *vulcisci.* 25 *subticebat.* 31 *horreis.* 41 *laycorum.* 41 the two parts
of the sentence give opposing points of view. 44 *Si*] *et.* 45 for *melioris?* 46
corrumparentur. 47 i.e., Aristotle. 52 *ipsam*] *ipsum.* 57 i.e., *Herennium.* 57
natum] he has in mind *De officiis.*

quilibet hominum convertatur. Quia non maiori ratione Ruffinus
60 quam ego; quia stet oppositum. Si maiori ratione ipse quam ego a
copula coniugali desisteret propter monitiones talis epistole, ego magna
ratione desisterem. Tale consequens probat regula primitiva, scilicet
quod comparativum presupponit suum positivum. Instabit iterum:
« Unde est tibi licentia Valerium reprobandi, quem vetusti auctores
65 multipliciter commendarunt? ». Procedit alterum ex duobus: aut erit
superflua epistola Valerii temporibus hodiernis (mores etenim hominum non te latent; hodie impuberes cupiunt uxorari) aut approba-
bitur talis epistola; quod sentio opponentem nullatenus diffiteri. Possibile est ut quilibet hominum audiat talem epistolam. Et si ad ipsam
70 convertantur homines, erit incidere in prelibatum errorem, videlicet
ut de cetero, ut nulli hominum adesset gloria filiorum. Sed hoc noluit
salvator noster, dum inquit: « Crescite et multiplicamini ». Nunc
terrenorum hominum exempla conspicio. Quis ignorat disputantium
doctorem ecclesie coniugem habuisse? Quis eloquentie fontem, licet
75 idem Valerius asserat quod Tullius ab eius consortio deviavit, que,
ut fertur, postea nupsit Sallustio? O quam felix est argumento responsio: nonne constat quanta gloria moveretur Tullius de unico
eius nato, adeo ut eius intuitu addiderit librum Officiorum, quo sub
celo philosoforum nullus liber clarior reperitur, Augustino testante?
80 Excellunt cunctos duos libros philosoforum libri quos fecit tres Tullius
Officiorum. Ni fuisset coniugium, fuisset innominatus hic liber. Sed
post natum habitum Tullius demisit Terentiam quia iam vergens in
senium volebat philosofie studium suum dare. Ergo hac de causa non
debuit Valerius, tanti auctoris salva reverentia, hac levissima ratione
85 coniugium reprobare. Quis diffitebitur poetam theologum fuisse coniugali socia copulatum? Instabit opponens forsan et merito: « Nonne
hi uxorum tedia dimiserunt? ». Fateor, sed inspice tempus. Iam
etate virtutis exacta, temporalia dimittebant. Instabit de Augustino
dicens: « Hic nondum doctrinam omousion predicabat dum uxoris
90 conubia cognoscebat ». Fateor, sed primitus tantam sapientiam doctus

61 *con. ipse des.* 61 *munitiones.* 72 *Gen.* 1, 22. 74 *doctorem*] Augustine
(cf. lines 88, 96). 76 cf. Jerome, *In Iovin.* I, 48. 79 apparently a confusion with
Cicero's *Hortensius* (Augustine, *Conf.* III, 4, 7). 80 *duos*] In his review of
the first edition of the present book in *Speculum,* XXXIII (1958), p. 146, R. P.
Oliver identifies the words « Excellunt ... Officiorum » as a quotation attributed
to Augustine in A. Riese's edition of the *Anthologia Latina* (Leipzig, 1869), No.
785, and cleverly emends *duos* (written II) to *ii,* for *hi,* which is in Riese's
text. Perhaps the scribe was in part influenced by the following *tres.* Billanovich
in his review also identified the quotation. 85 *theologum*] apparently Prosper
(see line 96). 85 for *cum coniugali socia* or *coniugali societate?* 89 i.e., *homou-
sion*; cf. Augustine, *Epist.* 238.

qui non restitit consortio coniugali. Huius saltem non debuit immemor fore Valerius, videlicet, quanto gaudio uniretur Boetius, Philosofia testante primo De Consolatione prosa quarta, dum ipsa Boetius talia proferebat: « Preterea penetral innocens domus ». Quod fuit istud penetral nisi Helphes uxor eiusdem? Reor hoc mecum, bone 95 pater, ut vetustos implectar, Augustinum, Tullium, Boetium, et Prosperum tante auctoritatis fuisse quante Valerius auctor noster. Plures pro hac parte rationes possent adduci, sed scribendi prolixitas plures adiicere me non sinit. Tu, bone pater, termina hoc unum cum Iohanne Virgiliano, egloga prima: omnino votive « respondere velis 100 aut solvere vota, magister ». Tuus Bernardus Muglensis.

91 *cui*. 94 Boethius, *Cons*. I, pr. 4, 40. 96 for *complectar*. 97 *quanto*. 100 Giovanni del Virgilio, *Ecl*. I, 51.

It is difficult to determine how much of the obscurity of this letter is due to the scribe, how much to the author. The latter, who seems not to have been among the best of his father's pupils, certainly is not without blame. When Coluccio speaks of an earlier letter of Bernardo (II, p. 131) as redolent of the father's style he must be more generous than justified in his praise. By comparison, Coluccio's style is limpid and almost classical. The rest of Coluccio's letter is an answer to at least one other of Bernardo's persistent attempts to draw the Florentine chancellor into epistolary discussions.

II, p. 168 (fol. 150r). 16 *eidem*. 18 *astulerut*. 18 *tristitum*. 20 *sincerunt*. 169, 1 *occidere*. 2 *se verius*. 4 *dilacom*. 4 *amovet*. 6 *licentiam*. 9 *sint*] *sicut*. 11 *Flattus*. 13 *et quod et quod*. 15 *dolui te tamen*. 15 *correttum*. 17 *tus*. 19 **Marcialis*; see above on *Epist.*, II, p. 192, 17. 20 **a te missam* om. 20 **per* om. 20 **testaris* om. 170, 3 *nec*. 4 *equidem quod cum*. 5 *nostro*] *meo*. 9 *predicet et*. 11 *contingerit*. 12 **aliqua parte*. 13 *nude*. 14 **est michi f*. 19 **Marone nostro*. 20 *et hic* om. 20 *quisque*. 21 **aut ... aut*. 21 *amores*. 22 **neutri*. 24 *asseristis*. 24 *dicare*. 25 **sacius*. 25-171, 1 *partly illegible*. 26 **est quod* om. 171, 2 *potest*. 3 *si*. 4 *tum per acciones*. 5 *dende*. 11 *quid ob. sed op.* 11 *quodicionis*. 11 *reffellatur* (read *sed op. r. quo dictionis a. refellatur*). 12 *opposite*. 13 *comprobamus* om. 14 **proponere propositis*. 17 *perortare*. 17 *arguta*. 17 **proponere*. 18 *rationem etiam*. 172, 2 **omnium*. 3 *valerent*. 7 *contra* om. 9 *comittem* (read *comitem*). 11 **punctulis et exornacionum*. 13 *illudque quod*] **ius quo* (or read *iusque quo?*). 14 *necessitate fit*. 14 **opportet*. 16 **nullum*. 16 *desertum*.

II, p. 131 (fol. 151v). 10 om. 11 *stili*] *filii.* 12 *mediocrem.* 14 *translaturunt.*

II, p. 130 (fol. 151v). 15 *eidem Bernardo de muglo.* 18 *iudices atque.* 19 *placuerit.* 131, 2 **scribere* om. 2 *adimento*; perhaps this is what Coluccio intended, forming it wrongly from *adimo.* The only other manuscript has *addimento.* 3 **insculpatur versus.* 5 *tercentis.*

Perhaps the most interesting of the new material is a poem on fol. 152r. Although the manuscript gives no clue as to the identity of the person praised in these verses, there can be no doubt that this is the epigram which Coluccio indicated he was sending along with a letter to Pietro da Moglio (*Epist.*, I, p. 5): « nec epigramma leve discipuli dedigneris ». In his note Novati rightly comments that a poetic composition must have accompanied the letter, which, dated 1360-61 by Novati, is one of Coluccio's earliest. The poem does not occur in any of the three other manuscripts which, besides T, contain the letter; even in T it is not associated with the letter. The explanation must be that the poem, including a prose postscript, being on a separate sheet, got separated from the letter. These verses seem to be alluded to by Coluccio in a letter written to Pietro some eight or nine years later (I, p. 114): « iandiu et metris et prosa aures tuas ... importune pulsarim ». The shift from second person singular in the letter and the poem to second person plural in the postscript (*vestra, valete*) is characteristic of Coluccio's early epistles. In I, p. 5 the verse has the singular throughout, the prose has the plural. In IV, p. 619 the plural is used in the first occurrence, the singular thereafter (cf. IV, p. 241).

> Hactenus hec strepuisse satis. Si namque tuarum
> Culmina virtutum aut laudum preconia tentet
> Deficiet calamus. Nec rauca voce canendus
> Seu scribendus eras. Libeat sed parcere falso.
> 5 Nam rerum series devicit sepe loquelam
> Meque rudem fateor tanto nec pondere dicam
> Me equum. Te laudesque tuas quis dicere posset?
> Grandiloqui credam linguam suadere Maronis,
> Nec tibi Romani fulgens facundia Tulli
> Sufficiet laudes dignas. Sed mitis amico

4 *strependus.* 4 *liberat.*

Deprecor indulge. Nam carmine nata voluptas
Suggessit. Credisne meo de pectore lapsa   10
Tempora rethorice quis, te monitore magistro,
Dogma ministrabas sacrum, quid epistola posset,
Quo modo danda salus, quo sint exordia iure
Instituenda modo, qui fit narratio recta,
Poscere quid licitum, et que sit conclusio digna,   15
Denique quid faceret pulcrum et sine sorde politum
Dictamen, que detque sonoros regula cursus,
Et que signari debeat distinctio puncto?
Hec memini quondam te conscendente cathedras
Me monuisse. Michi semper, reverende magister,   20
Hinc innatus amor quem nil delere profecto
Iam poterit, et numquam de pectore cedet.
Attamen oro, pater, te leto assumere vultu
Hoc rude, quodque potes iusta damnare repulsa
Accipe. Sincero precor ut monearis amore   25
Et michi si qua libent iniunge. Valeto.

Hec festino, care pater, qualiaqualia sint, multis circumventus
obstaculis dictavi, imo melius inter labores excerpsi, nec michi data
corrigendi facultas. Vestra tamen prudentia defectum suppleat, tumi-
dum reprimat, artis metrice emendet errores. Valete.

15 *sicut.* 20 *debeat* must be read as dissyllabic. 21 *nemini.* 21 *conscendente*; *te* is apparently both accusative and ablative. 24 a word is missing
after *poterit,* possibly something like *quique.* 25 *vultu(m).* 28 the line is short
but the meaning is complete .Perhaps a word has fallen out, e.g., *tu quaeso* after
libent.

The verses are of interest in showing what topics Pietro
dealt with in his lectures on *ars dictaminis* at Bologna and what
part he played in improving the Latinity of his students. His
achievements here give him a place in the humanistic movement
of the early Renaissance. The words « quid epistola posset »
(vs. 14) recall Gian Galeazzo Visconti's celebrated remark, that
a thousand Florentine horsemen did him less harm that the letters of Coluccio. Salutati's line was prophetic, and Pietro's teaching helped produce the letters which led to Gian Galeazzo's
complaint.

II, p. 173 (fol. 152v). 4-5 om. 6 *sint* om. 9 *Barnabonis.* 10
solum om. 10 **sua.* 11 *quod* om. The letter is signed *tuus Colucius Pyeri.*

On fol. 152v there is a letter without name of writer or correspondent. It could not have been written by Coluccio because he is mentioned in it. The recipient was certainly Pietro da Moglio, to judge from the contents and from its appearing in a collection made by his son Bernardo. Of particular interest is the praise of Coluccio as « princeps moderne facundie » by one who too had studied under Pietro.

Tua, vir generose, ferventissima dilectio quam ad artem dicendi et rectorice suavitatis eloquium ducis, imo qua duceris, de vehementi affectione pertraheris (animi quidem nobilis iudicio meo potissimum decus), etsi dudum primam mentem meam titillaverit atque com-
5 punxerit et quodam velut latenti irritamento calamum concitarit, suppressi tamen atque continui lascivientis et incontinui calami levitatem, id ipsum veritus, ne delectare cupiens fastidio aures delicatas afficerem. Verum dum tecum iterum percontor, tecum alloquor, teque, tua mansuetudine permittente, contero, irrepit animum meum
10 ingens quidam stimulus et iliis meis acutum calcar imprimitur, cuius viribus agor invitus et arceor, nec inscitie mee pudore commonitus nec eximiarum epistolarum quas inter cotidie versaris, ac disertissimorum virorum quorum dictaminibus te ipsum accommodas, ingenti splendore confusus. Scio equidem, orationum mearum tunc imbecil-
15 litas tunc difformitas eo evidentius tibi obstrepet quo gravioribus lepidioribusque egregiorum dictatorum sententiis demulceris. Habes illam ipsam Collucii tui quam tecum paulo ante lustrabam pariterque laudabam (principis, ut ita dixerim, moderne facundie) venustatem, cuius suavitati et maturi sermonis eloquio incultam orationis
20 mee ruditiem inserens. Haud scio an illum magis extulerim an me ipsum, velut quadam oppositorum collatione facta, magis potius deformarim. Hanc enim adversantium naturam esse constat, ut alterum ex alterius inspectu dilucidius demonstretur. « Quid itaque », inquies, « stolide, tuarum ipsarum rationum collatione perplexe? Hanc tibi
25 peperit scribendi libidinem, quam tibi asseris contigisse. Cum ex hac ipsa quam mecum egisti continuari orationem discursitantem non modo non ... aliorum debueris .... verum etiam si prius in

3 *potissimo.* 9 *concreto.* 10 *carcar.* 11 *ne inscitie me.* 14 *quod* perhaps to be supplied after *equidem.* 15 *tibi est obstrepet.* 19 *incurtant.* 20 a new word, for *ruditatem.* 20 *inserens* should be *inserui,* or else *cuius* should be *eius.* He seems to mean that he « inserted » (i. e., by interrupting) his uncouth speech into the refined eloquence of Coluccio. 21 *cadam.* 24 *perplexe* is apparently in the vocative case. 25 *contingisse.* 27-29 partly illegible. 26 *discursitate(m).*

his ex . . . . sumo v . . . . borum equidem scitius nichil . . . . .
. . . . tacuisse. Sed quoniam insto ». Qua putativa opinione per-
ductus delicias animi tui mecum confers et oblectanter volvis meque 30
ipsum ad interiora perquiris, quasi mearum rerum desiderio teneris.
Eo peremptum est ut michi ad hanc rem vinculum quoddam cen-
seam obligationis iniectumque. Quamvis tuam de me ipso extima-
tionem irritam faciat, reprehensibilius tamen videtur, amplexo silen-
tio, aut votorum tuorum urbanitatem quasi surdus non intelligere 35
aut intellecta obmutescendo negligere. Nescio quippe quenam pars
in hac disceptatione tutior provocato, loquine ad mee detectionem
ignavie an tacere ad pertinacis contumacie feritatem. Verum hoc
ipsum indecentius extimavi, arrogans et obstinatus haberi quam in-
scius agnosci. Illud enim moribus vitium, hoc nature facilius ascri- 40
bendum. Quod iterum eo tutius duxi quod, etsi epistola mea tibi
delatu non proficiat, possit tamen responsionis exercitatio te movere.
In quam quidem rem necesse fore nosti animum tuum accommodes
(id enim mecum paulo ante disserebas, nemini posse sine exercitio
artis industria provenire). Ceterum ego non tam picta verba contextas- 45
que artificiose sententias quam ipsum vulgaris et materne lingue,
que catenis ad necessitatem redigitur, imitabo officium. Prohibuerunt
enim externe cure et abstulerunt otia voluptatum. Id continuo dicti-
tans ego non qualiter sed quid animadvertam. Et si saltim res familiaris abesset sarcina, in hanc dicendi artem exercendam et pro- 50
prius comparandam tuo satis abundeque amore pertraherer, sed cohi-
bente graviorum mole non tam voluptati quam necessitati obtempe-
rare oportet. Tu vero, cui latius vivendi arbitrium, cui facultas, cui
perspicax patet ingenium, cui denique nichil deest quod ad optati
explicationem desiderari queat, id magne laudis existimo, ut sapien- 55
tie condimentum suavissimum, ipsam eloquentiam scilicet, studeas
adipisci. Magnis enim in viris feliciter colloquatur res dicendi, quorum manibus magnarum rerum tunc dicendarum, tunc agendarum
negotia committuntur, tenuioribus, quorum ego in numero et tiro,
fructuosa est diebus quidem nostris, quando non tam quid oblectet 60
quam quid proficiat exploratur. Amen.

29 q(uonia)m insto seems fairly clear in the manuscript but gives no
satisfactory sense. As these words come at the bottom of the page, it is
just possible that a line has completely faded below them. 29 perdutus.
30 dilicias dilicias. 31 inteririora. 32 quodam censeant. 34 repreusiblius.
37 me deceptionem. 46 materie. 47 que om. 47 i(n) imitato. 48 dicitans.
49 ego ut non. 50 proprius is the comparative of proprie. 51 pertrahere.
51 inconibente. 53 oporte. 54 obtati. 56 s(cilicet) eloquentiam scilicet.
59 commictitur. 60 fructuosa, sc. res dicendi.

Apparently Coluccio and the unknown writer had been at Bologna and had visited Pietro, probably during the last years of his life, i.e., before 1383. The writer, who seems to have been younger than Coluccio, was probably a notary.

A letter on fol. 153r can definitely be attributed to Coluccio. It is an answer to a request for verses on the death of Marsilio di Santa Sofia. This leading physician of Paduan origin was elected professor of medicine at Florence on June 10, 1388, in the presence of Salutati; his service began October 18, 1389. He was professor at Bologna in 1404-05 [3]. He died at Bologna (as Coluccio's poem shows), presumably in 1405. This then is the date of the letter.

Doctor egregie, frater carissime, vir multe scientie singularissimeque virtutis, magister Laurentius de Prato, me vice sua rogavit quatenus epistolam bone memorie patris tui componere non denegarem. Dulce quidem et lugubre simul officium. Versari siquidem
5 in laudibus tanti viri dulce est, sed lacrimabile reminisci. Amisimus enim, imo premisimus talem virum et tantum qualem et quantum nostri <homines> vix viderunt, cuius memoria, sicut arbitror, in benedictione erit cuiusque virtutem et gloriam nulla posteritas sustinebit. Et ego qualem amisi! . . . . . . in similem non . . . . remansit.
10 Et quem celebrare laudibus nedum sex versiculi sufficiunt sed amplissima volumina non valerent. Sed firmiter teneo possidere perpetem gloriam in celis, extinguibilem famam in terris, qua certitudine sic consolor sicque te velim, frater carissime, consolari, quod placere nobis incipiat quod Deus fecit. Scio quidem quod si totum, presens
15 scilicet et futurum, possemus cum preteritis intueri, nil eorum que Deus fecerit displiceret. Unum oro, cum Deus sciat quali me pater tuus amore dilexerit, quod me non minori caritatis affectu complectaris.

2 I have been unable to identify Lorenzo da Prato. 3 *tua.* 4-9 partly illegible. 7 *homines* is a guess. 9 the word before *in* began with *si* and may have been a miswriting of *similem.* 9 two lines have been rendered completely illegible after *non.* 11 *eum* seems to be missing after *teneo.* 12 should be *inextinguibilem.* 14 *tutum.* 16. *sciat* seems to be badly corrected from *scias.* 17 *affectum.*

[3] Roberto Abbondanza, in *Archivio Storico Italiano,* 117 (1959), p. 99; A. Sorbelli, *Storia della Università di Bologna,* I (Bologna, 1940), p. 262. Marsilio was in Pavia in 1396 (L. Thorndike, *A History of Magic and Experimental Science,* IV, New York, 1934, p. 68), where he was kept by Gian Galeazzo Visconti, who held him in high esteem. For further details see G. Tiraboschi, *Storia della letteratura italiana,* V (Florence, 1807), p. 262.

Ego te fratremque tuum loco patris tui suscipio ea lege, quod cuncta possitis sicut ille si viveret impetrare. Epitaphium manu mea subiunxi, quod obsecro diligentissime caveas ne sculptor illorum vel in 20 minima littera possit errare. Vale. Florentie. Colucius, etc.

> Cui Patavum patriam dedit et cui Sancta Sophia
> Cognomen, proprio nomine Marsilius,
> Gloria doctorum, medicine maximus autor,
> Eximius nullo cum pare philosophus, 25
> Hoc natis tumulo summa pietate sepultus
> Bononiam decorat corpore, mente polum.

20 cf. a similar caution in II, p. 131. 21 *culcus.* 22 *patanum.* 25 *p(at)re.*

A letter on fol. 153v does not reveal the writer or the recipient. As it mentions the sending of a collection of letters of Petrarch and Coluccio, the writer may be Bernardo and the collection he sent something like that in T. The correspondent was a lawyer or notary who was taking up the study of philosophy. Both Petrarch and Coluccio receive high praise, being compared to Cicero.

Quo adhuc conticueram ne te cum litteris affarer, vir generose moribus et prosapia, tunc abductus verecundia ut quid incompictum et verborum et sententiarum falleris offerrem perspicaci ingenio tuo, tum veritus ne forsan arguendus importuna presumptione merito derider et explodirer. Cum nulla occasione tradita teneor, trahe- 5 retur impertinens, quin id ultra, quod foret imbecillius, rusticano tecum sermone prorumperem. Ac nunc ut ad te scribam brevem epistolam, plerisque confirmor, puta, sinceri vultus et venusti eloquii tui equanimitate, presertimque obsequii polliciti satisdatione, et, his vehementius, ea dilectione quam, ubi effigiem tuam conspexi, menti 10 mee confestim et abunde semper iniectam sensi. Accipe itaque cuiuscemodi exquirebas bibliolum hunc, quo quasdam laureati vatis illius Francisci Petrache et facundissimi ac disertissimi viri Colucii Pierii nonnullas cernes epistolas, non dico omnes ex facetissimis earundem, quoniam alias familiares horum tanto lepore fabricatas legimus quan- 15 to pene non modo Demostenis oratoris elegantiam sed ipsum Romane eloquentie speculum Ciceronem exsuperasse videbatur. Ceterum in

1 *tecum cum.* 3 i. e., *phaleris.* 4 *tum*] *tu.* 5 wrong form for *exploderer.* 7 *ad*] *a.* 8 *constitor.* Perhaps a better emendation than *confirmor* can be suggested. 9 *ecanimitate.* 9 *que*] *ne.* 11 *abinde.* 12 *votis.* 14 *non ullas.* 15 *quanto*] *canto.* 16 *modo*] *quod.* 16 *horatoriis.* 17 *speculum*] the letters after *l* are

istis nonne minus arte dicentis potitos et florido philosophantis g<e-
nere> versatos eleganter peracres quod quem scit doctum et illus-
20 trem et quam s . . . . . facultate gravis? Nam cuique manifestum
est . . . . . . quem exquiro seges . . . . <ad> componendam virtutibus
mentem et ad permulcendum et ad instruendum quam est ei philosophia, que dicendi flore et ad fluentiam subgerit. Recte igitur hanc
sacrarum sanctionum studiis copulare satagis, quam vero isti legum
25 professores et compertores amisisse perhibentur. Profecto enim, ut
testantur consultissimorum veterum annales, hinc Foroneus Argivus
et Cretensis Minos, observantissimus legum, Ligurgus, Solon Athe-
niensis, prudentia preditissimus, Quarumdatirus, plenus severitate, et
Locrensis Celencus, equitate integerrimus. Cum insudare legibus sane
30 et vero incassum cuperent, hanc celeberrimam philosophiam interse-
rendam legibus statuerunt. Et identidem ab urbe condita post inclitam Pompoli Nume religionem et post flagitiosum scelus Apii apud
Romanos, Sempronius, Servilius, Cato, Consoonius, Lucius Carsus,
Servius Supplicius, et alii iurisconsulti plurimi magno opere philoso-
35 phiam hanc addiscere capessendis sanctionibus institerunt. Sic recole,
te hos emulari grandi animo enixum, proposito ut celebres philosophorum lares amplectaris, et (quippe recta tua prorsus sententia
est) imitari preclara vestigia predecessorum quorum doctrinis et
exemplis lustramur et admonemur undique. Quocirca et ego hoc
40 illud hortor, vir generose, ut hac gradere, huc proficiscere. Carpsisti
nempe rectum tramitem et ad beatos gaudens properas. Querimus

uncertain; the word is longer, possibly *speculantem* (in abbreviation). 18-21
partly illegible; after *seges* two lines are completely illegible. 18 before
dicentis the scribe seems to have written and deleted *dicendi*. 22 *ad*] *ed*
corrected from *et* (before *permulcendum*). 22 *est ei* is doubtful, being
in correction. 23 *Ruite*. 24 *ceu veruisti*. 27 *certensis*. 27 *solum*. 28 *Quarumdatirus* is an error by scribe or author or partly by each for *Charondas*. Some
manuscripts of Valerius Maximus have *carumde* at VI, 5 Ext. 4; see Kempf's
edition (Berlin, 1854). The story of Charondas, which well illustrates the epistle's
« plenus severitate », follows immediately on that of Zaleucus (see next note).
29 *Celencus* is for *Zaleucus*. One of the manuscripts of Valerius Maximus reads
Calencus at VI, 5, Ext. 3. 30 *in casum*. 31 *condicta*. 32 for *Pompili*. 32
i. e., *Appii*. 33 apparently *servlius* corrected from *serslius*. 33 presumably for
Antonius the orator; *Cosconius* is closer, but no noted jurisconsult by that name
is known. The association with Crassus also favors Antonius. The initial *a*
could be mistaken for the abbreviation for *con*, which the manuscript has. 33
i. e., *Crassus*. 34 for *Sulpicius*. I have kept the misspellings of the names as
they may be what the author wrote. 35 *recule*. 36 *grando*. 36 *celebre*. 41
tramitum. 41 *gades*. I am not too confident about the emendation. 41 *querimus* is probably a wrong emendation; the manuscript has a peculiar abbreviation
of the *q* type (*quam?*), followed by *imo* or *rino*.

quod tuum nobilem animum venustent, quin imo ad astra sublimem ferent et tandem summe felicitatis fruitione perficient. Felix vale, etc.

A letter on fol. 154r conveys the thanks of the writer to a certain Giovanni for sending him a fish. It is written in a grandiloquent style for humorous effect. Curiously enough we have letters of both Petrarch and Salutati on the same theme[4]. As Giovanni is said to be ruling Bologna (« Bononiam frenet habenis ») he may be identified as Giovanni de' Pepoli, who ruled Bologna from 1347-50, or Oleggio (1355-60), or Mangiadori, who became *capitano* in 1376.

Ab equore tue benignitatis ameno tanta largitas effluit ut non solum dignos sed etiam indignos facetia tua feraces efficiat, ac bono multiplici plures faciat opulentos, que ad diversorum animalium fomitem suas glandes emittit et non tantum prodest proprio possessori sed quibuscumque eam profectis salubre parturit alimentum. Ab aula 5 tua, numerose largitatis alumpna, a qua prodeunt bona multos effundentia ramos, venerunt ad me admodum elegantia cete, non decentia me pessumdatum et abiectum ac imparem tantis donis, sed querentia viros precipuos, quibus talia solent tribui. Et cum eorum nares mee gustassent multe suavitatis odorem, obstupui valde et nesciens 10 quis michi indigno hec munera tribuisset, michi lator ait: « Ille heros excipuus et plus quam unus Iohannes in eximia gratia pollens me iussit huc properare celerem et dixit ut tu sui amoris causa satagas hos pisces obedere vel ei quondam morsu lacrimes exinde ». Hec audiens admisi donum letis ulnis assumptum et ego tua dona liguriens 15 infinitis gaudiis circumfusus meditabar obedere, sed maxima letitia non sinebat. Erat autem letitie causa memoria quam habebam benignitatis tue egregie, que suapte natura refulgens sepe suis viribus mea incommoda propulit et ad unguem mea vota peregit. Emersit alia nuper michi causa letitie, quia cum fuerit angustia cetaria, esuriebam 20 admodum nec habebam quo famem propulerem, sed donum tuum adeo vivens mea viscera vegetavit et fecit me lautitia divitem.

1 *bene nigtatis.* 5 for *ad eam?* 6 *alumpna(m).* 9 *principuos.* 12-14 partly illegible. 12 *unus* is uncertain. 12 *eximia*] the manuscript seems to read *exurt(er)a.* 13 *properare* is not entirely clear. 14 *ei ... exinde* is uncertain. 17 *letitie*] *letitia.* 18 *bemingtatis.* 19 *vot.* 20 *angustium cetarium.* 20 *esurgebam.* 22 *adetuirens*; perhaps *adeo virens?* 22 *vegtavit.*

[4] *Fam.* XV, 12; Novati, *Epist.*, II, p. 435.

Hec videns fames hucusque lacrimando profugit et minata est se reversuram et illaturam michi sublestiam. Tunc surrexit ceta tua in
25 illam rigens et dixit: « Si veneris, dira lues, letabor ex animo, quia Iohannes meus habet Molossos opicos, qui morsibus te confugere satagent et tua viscera deserta revolvent et urent ». Hec percipiens mea fames dixit: « Fugiam non reversura magis », et abivit extemplo. Tunc ego tanto bono iocundus et tollens in sidera palmas dixi: « O
30 pater celestis, unde omnis gratia scaturit, demitte rorem pneumatis tui et, queso, gratiam hero meo sublimi, ut ipse, qui est plus quam dimidia pars anime mee, tuo favore circumfluus, sepe possit has et maiores facetias exercere, et urbem Palladis, scilicet gloriosam Bononiam, iustis frenet habenis, ut is maneat in medio semper, polleat
35 eulogio, et cum eius soma parva frigebit, sanctorum tuorum contubernio gaudeat, et quia lingua est hebes ad gratias, tu Deus meus intercede pro me, loco mei sibi inferas de impendio ».

    23 *hucusque* is uncertain.   23 *mimata.*   24 *geta* apparently; if *ceta* is correct, it is wrongly used as a feminine singular.   25 *exanibusi.*   25 *quare.* 28 *fugiant.*   30 *scaturunt.*   32 cf. Horace, *Carm.* I, 3, 8.   34 *manet.*   35 *paria.*

    The last item in the group (fol. 154v) is a sermon on patience written in the form of a letter signed Andreas de Borgatia, i.e., Baragazza. This family was expelled from Bologna in 1306, and their holdings passed into the hands of Taddeo de' Pepoli in 1340[5]. The Bologna connection suggests that the letter was written to Pietro or Bernardo da Moglio.

    [5] Cf. the chronicle of Hieronymus de Bursellis, edited by A. Sorbelli, in Muratori, *Rerum Italicarum Scriptores,* ed. 2, XXIII, 2 (Città di Castello, 1929), pp. 36, 18 and 42, 14.

CHAPTER XV

POGGIO'S MANUSCRIPTS OF LIVY AND OTHER AUTHORS [1]

Subtract two and add three—net change: five. The first purpose of this paper is to remove from the roster two manuscripts of Livy that have been masquerading as Poggio's and to add three others, one of which had not previously been discovered while the other two are unknown in the circles to which such matters are of moment.

Nolhac says that Vat. lat. 3330 and 3331 (containing Livy's third and fourth decades, respectively) were copied by Poggio [2]. Nolhac took his information from notes written on flyleaves of the two manuscripts by Fulvio Orsini: « C. Livio, la terza deca, scritto di mano del Poggio. Ful. Urs. » and « Livio la 4ª Deca, scritto di mano del Poggio. Ful. Urs. ». This is but one instance of many in which Nolhac has uncritically accepted Orsini's unfounded dicta about the previous owners of his manuscripts. No statement of Orsini's can be accepted without verification; therefore Nolhac's book is a very unsafe guide and his work needs to be done over again.

When one examines the two manuscripts he sees at once that they were not written by Poggio, whose handwriting is familiar from facsimiles published by Walser and others. They were both written by the same humanistic hand, which resembles Poggio's only to the extent that any formal humanistic hand of the fifteenth century resembles his. If Poggio copied these manu-

---

[1] Expanded form of an article originally published in *Classical Philology*, XXVIII (1933), p. 282. This chapter is in part superseded by B. L. Ullman, *The Origin and Development of Humanistic Script* (Rome, 1960), pp. 21-57.

[2] Pierre de Nolhac, *La bibliothèque de Fulvio Orsini* (Paris, 1887), p. 194.

scripts he copied thousands of others still in existence. The two are dated: 3331 was written January 3, 1453; 3330 on June 8, 1455. In both there is a coat of arms, in which the initials *I G* occur, overlaid with gold[3]. It should not be impossible to identify the former owner. There is not the slightest indication that Poggio ever owned them[4].

We have finished our problem in subtraction; now for the addition. First let us add two manuscripts to take the places made vacant by the two which we have ousted. They have been easily available to scholars since the publication of Nogara's third volume of the Vatican catalogue[5]. They are Vat. lat. 1849 and 1852, containing the third and fourth decades. The *incipit* of the former is: « T. Livii Patavini historici liber XXI belli punici secundi incipit ». The *explicit* (fol. 182r) reads: « T. Livii Patavini historici preclarissimi liber XXX explicit belli punici secundi lege feliciter liber Poggii ». The *incipit* of 1852 is: « T. Livii ab urbe condita liber incipit XLI de bello Macedonico ». There is no *explicit*, but at the end (fol. 147r), in the same hand but a different ink, are the words « Liber Poggii secret(arii) ». The *incipits* and *explicit* are in capitals, and there are separating points between the words. The two discarded manuscripts, 3330 and 3331, are not even copies of Poggio's manuscripts, as a brief comparison made clear.

There is still another manuscript to add, one heretofore unknown, or rather disguised. It is Vat. lat. 1843, containing the first decade. The *incipit* reads: « T. Livi Patavini historici ab urbe condita liber primus incipit ». The *explicit* (fol. 196v) reads: « T. Livii ab urbe condita liber decimus explicit lege feliciter liber Aurispae secretarii apostolici ». These words are in capitals and are separated by dots as in the other two manuscripts. The name Aurispa is in erasure[6]. That the name

---

[3] Nolhac calls these letters illegible.

[4] In *Classical Review*, XIII (1899), p. 120, n. 1, A. C. Clark vigorously denies that these two manuscripts were copied by Poggio. Facsimile of Vat. lat. 3331 in F. Ehrle and P. Liebaert, *Specimina codicum Latinorum Vaticanorum*, ed. 2 (Berlin, 1927), Pl. 48, « manu Poggii Bracciolini ».

[5] B. Nogara, *Codices Vaticani Latini*, III (Rome, 1912).

[6] So recognized by Sabbadini (*Carteggio di Giovanni Aurispa*, Rome, 1931, p. 184), but not by Nogara.

under it was Poggio, even if it cannot now be made out, is certain by comparison with the other two volumes, for the three were not only written by the same person but were intended to be a uniform set. The writing space in each is 243 by 166 mm.; there are two vertical lines inclosing this space, dividing the 166 mm. into $6+154+6$. The size of the page naturally varies according to the trimming: in 1843 it is 372 by 263; in 1849, 373 by 266; in 1852, 362 by 260. In all three the *incipits* are of the same style. All have marginalia written in Poggio's less formal style.

Not only did Poggio own these three manuscripts, but in my opinion he also copied them. E. Walser[7] lists only five manuscripts as surely copied by Poggio in his calligraphic style. I add the three Livy manuscripts to these five for the following reasons:

1. The handwriting seems to me to be the same (see accompanying plate).

2. We know from a letter of Panormita, to be quoted later, that Poggio copied Livy *manu propria*.

3. The *explicit* in Vat. 1843, containing Poggio's name as owner, seems to be in the same ink and hand as the text. In Vat. 1849 the entire subscription, including Poggio's name, is written in red ink, apparently by the person who copied the manuscript. As it is scarcely likely that a hired scribe entered Poggio's name for him, we conclude that Poggio himself was the scribe (see Pl. 6).

Assuming the correctness of the attribution of the handwriting in these manuscripts to Poggio, let us pass to the question of date. Poggio was apostolic secretary from about 1412 to 1417[8], and again from 1423. Therefore Vat. 1843, the subscription of which, written at the same time as the text, refers to this office, must have been copied between 1412 and 1417 or after 1423. Since the note of ownership in Vat. 1849 does not mention the secretaryship and that in Vat. 1852 was not entered at the time the manuscript was copied, it may be that

---

[7] *Poggius Florentinus* (Leipzig, 1914), p. 317.
[8] *Ibid.*, p. 25, n. 4.

these two volumes were copied before 1412 or between 1417 and 1423. But a later date seems probable for all three, though the evidence, which I shall now submit, is not strong.

In October, 1427, Poggio asks Niccoli for parchment for the transcription of Livy[9], but this refers to the copies of the three known decades made by a scribe in 1428-30[10]. Had Poggio's autograph copies already been made and still been in his possession, he would probably not have taken the trouble to have *Livius ingens* copied again. If the autographs had been sold or otherwise disposed of, he would perhaps have attempted to borrow them for the copying, just as he borrowed, or tried to borrow, for this same purpose the manuscripts of Caesar[11] and Cicero (letters to Atticus)[12] which, copied by himself, he wanted to borrow from their owners, Nicola and Cosimo de' Medici, respectively. Instead he borrows manuscripts of Livy owned by Niccoli and others. It was perhaps after the completion of these copies that Poggio, who constantly complained about the incompetency of scribes, decided to try his hand at copying Livy and produced the three Vatican volumes.

Let us now turn to the further history of Vat. 1843, which passed into the hands of Aurispa. Not recognizing that this manuscript was written or owned by Poggio, Sabbadini thought that it was the book which Aurispa, in a letter written to Panormita in 1447, says was copied by the scribe Francia of Florence[13]. This suggestion must of course now be rejected. The fact that Aurispa did not erase the words *secretarii apostolici* in Vat. 1843 probably indicates that he acquired it in or after 1437, the year in which he was himself made apostolic secretary.

Panormita states in a letter of uncertain date addressed to King Alfonso of Naples that Poggio sold a Livy which he had written with his own hand that he might buy a villa at Florence. This Livy was almost certainly one of the three Vatican manu-

[9] *Poggii Epistolae,* III, 14, 15 (ed. T. Tonelli, I, Florence, 1832, p. 212).
[10] *Ibid.,* 22 (I, p. 223), 27 (p. 264), 38 (p. 285); IV, 17 (p. 340).
[11] *Ibid.,* III, 1 (I, p. 187), written in 1426.
[12] *Ibid.,* II, 22 (I, p. 149), 23 (p. 150), 28 (p. 157), written in 1425.
[13] Sabbadini, *op. cit.,* p. 113, n. 2.

scripts.   Perhaps it was Vat. 1843 and Aurispa was the buyer. Panormita's letter reads:

Significasti mihi nuper ex Florentia extare T. Livii opera venalia, literis pulcherrimis, libri pretium esse CXX aureos. Quare Maiestatem tuam oro, ut Livium, quem Regem librorum appellare consuevimus, emi meo nomine, ac deferri ad nos facias... Sed et illud a prudentia tua scire desidero, uter ego an Poggius melius fecerit: is ut villam Florentiae emeret, Livium vendidit, quem sua manu pulcherrime scripserat; ego ut Livium emam, fundum proscripsi [14].

It seems to be the universal assumption that it was Poggio's manuscript that Panormita bought, or rather intended to buy.   But the use of the past tense *vendidit* indicates that Poggio had already sold although the letter reveals clearly that Panormita had not yet bought.   To be sure, Poggio may have sold to an unknown purchaser from whom Panormita expected to buy, but that is an unnecessary and complicated explanation.   As the story of Poggio's sale apparently was well known, it may have taken place years earlier.   It was some other manuscript that Panormita wanted to buy.   His mention of Florence is of no significance, as it was the great book center of the day.   It is true that the price of the Livy mentioned in the letter (120 florins) agrees with the price paid by Poggio for two of his properties, purchased August 9, 1442 (125 florins), and July 10, 1454 (120 florins), but the very fact that two properties were bought at this price at different times shows that the agreement in figures is a mere coincidence, especially since Poggio made no less than thirty-three purchases of real estate [15], three of them at 100 florins each.

Walser suggests that the money which Poggio derived from the sale of his Livy was used to purchase the property which he bought August 9, 1442 [16].   He does not indicate why he identifies this as the property rather than one of Poggio's

---

[14] *Antonii Bononiae Beccatelli ... Epistolarum libri V* (Venice, 1553), fol. 118.

[15] For the documents, see Walser, *op. cit.*, pp. 329 ff. The agreement in price loses all significance if Panormita bought from an intermediary, who naturally would expect a profit.

[16] *Ibid.*, p. 198, n. 5.

numerous other purchases. It is likely, however, that the purchase was made at about this time or earlier, since Poggio's financial situation was much improved after 1446, as a result of the accession of Nicholas V to the papal throne[17]. No purchases of real estate are recorded between 1442 and 1446[18]. The date 1442 fits well with the suggestion that Vat. 1843 was the manuscript sold by Poggio and that Aurispa was the purchaser, for Aurispa was in Florence between 1439 and 1443 with the church council (as was Poggio), and was particularly active in buying and selling manuscripts during that time[19].

If my interpretation of Panormita's letter is correct, its date is of little consequence for our purpose except as a *terminus ante quem* for the sale of the manuscript. Walser must of course assume the date 1442; Le Gallois dates it 1455 without giving his reasons[20]. Sabbadini is probably right in regarding the words *quem appellare consuevimus* as an allusion to the humanistic circle in which Livy was discussed[21]; in that case we arrive at a date not earlier than 1444-45.

The later history of Vat. 1843 is unknown to me; it is different from that of the other two volumes of Poggio's Livy, for it contains notes by a late fifteenth-century hand which does not appear in them.

In 1444 Panormita wrote to Aurispa that the latter was to procure a Livy from Florence[22]. This is neither the manuscript of Poggio to which Panormita refers in his letter to King Alfonso[23] nor the Poggio manuscript which Aurispa owned (Vat. 1843). Panormita simply means that Aurispa is to get a Livy for copying purposes from the chief book center, Florence. We

---

[17] *Ibid.*, p. 302.

[18] We must, of course, not take Panormita's words « villa » and « Florence » too literally. Any property, either land or house, at or near Florence, can be meant by his rather rhetorical language.

[19] Sabbadini, *op. cit.*, pp. xxi, 97.

[20] Pierre Le Gallois, *Traitté des plus belles bibliothèques de l'Europe* (Paris, 1680), p. 154. He is probably using earlier sources not familiar to me.

[21] In a personal letter to me.

[22] Sabbadini, *op. cit.*, p. 108.

[23] In an earlier work (*Biografia documentata di Giovanni Aurispa,* Noto, 1891, p. 92, n. 3), Sabbadini identified it with Panormita's Poggio manuscript but in his more recent book on Aurispa he rightly omits the suggestion.

can safely conclude, therefore, that Panormita does not figure in our mathematical problem.

Another manuscript owned by Poggio, as the subscription attests, is Laur. 49, 24 (Cicero, *Epist. ad Att.*)[24]. This manuscript too was copied by Poggio, as the writing shows, though O. E. Schmidt denies this[25]. On the other hand, Schmidt is perhaps right in saying that the Berlin rather than the Florence manuscript is the Poggio autograph owned by Cosimo de' Medici. The Florence manuscript has in it the name of Benedetto Martinozi as the owner, which would seem to preclude Cosimo as the owner in 1425, when Poggio requests the loan of Cosimo's manuscript, as we have seen.

While I am confident that the Cicero and Livy manuscripts were copied by Poggio, we must not forget that the identification of handwriting is not always certain. In this case especially it may be true that Poggio succeeded in training a scribe to imitate closely that adaptation of the Carolingian hand of which he may be called the inventor. In that event the Cicero and Livy manuscripts no doubt are the very ones which were copied by one scribe for Poggio between 1425 and 1430[26]. A study of the affiliations of these manuscripts might shed some light on the problem.

Still another manuscript can, I believe, be added to those copied by Poggio—one of peculiar interest. It is a manuscript of Coluccio Salutati's *De verecundia*, corrected by Coluccio himself[27]. The identification is purely on the basis of the

[24] Facsimile in W. Arndt and M. Tangl, *Schrifttafeln zur Erlernung der lateinischen Palaeographie*, ed. 4 (Berlin, 1904), Pl. 30 A.

[25] « Die handschriftliche Überlieferung der Briefe Ciceros », K. Sächsische Gesellschaft der Wissenschaften, Abhandlungen phil.-hist. Classe, X, 4 (1887), p. 353. Walser (*op. cit.*, p. 105, n. 3) also denies that this manuscript was copied by Poggio, maintaining that the writing bears only a superficial resemblance to Poggio's. It seems to me that it resembles the writing of Laur. 48, 22, an unquestioned autograph of Poggio's, more than the latter resembles the Eusebius (Laur. 67, 15), hastily written by Poggio. Did Walser base his judgment of Poggio's calligraphic style on the Eusebius, of which he gives a facsimile?

[26] *Epist.*, IV, 17 (I, p. 340).

[27] I agree on this point with F. Novati, *Epistolario di Coluccio Salutati*, II (Rome, 1893), p. 267. Garin based his text of the *De verecundia* on this manuscript: Coluccio Salutati, *De nobilitate legum et medicinae, De verecundia*, ed. E. Garin (Florence, 1947).

writing. Plate 8 accompanying this chapter shows a correction by Salutati in the third line from the bottom.

Since Coluccio died in 1406 the manuscript must have been copied before that time. We can narrow down the date still more, to the period 1402-1403, for Poggio seems to have worked as a scribe for Coluccio during that period. The chief argument for a still earlier date must be abandoned. Novati identified as Poggio a certain competent scribe mentioned by Coluccio without name, and he dated the letter in which this remark occurs in 1401; Walser accepted this view[28]. But we saw in chapter IX that this date is incorrect, that the letter was written in 1392-93, when Poggio was 12 or 13 years old. On the other hand, in a letter which Novati dates October 18, 1401 (*Epist.*, III, p. 553), but which Walser shows was written in 1402, Coluccio calls the attention of his correspondent to the script (« littere forma ») of the letter, which he tells us Poggio copied. This probably refers to the new humanistic script for which Poggio became famous and would be the first mention of it. At the time Poggio had recently finished his notarial studies. We know nothing of his activities during the following twelve months, but it is likely that he did some copying for Coluccio. To this period I would refer the transcription of the *De verecundia*. Obviously the copying was done in Florence, where Coluccio's master copy was. In the autumn of 1403 Poggio left for Rome, where on at least one occasion soon after his arrival he copied a manuscript for Coluccio, as is made clear by a letter which Coluccio wrote him on December 23, 1403 (*Epist.*, III, p. 653).

The *De verecundia* is in Poggio's fully developed script. It differs from the later examples in having a *g* with a vertical connecting stroke of exaggerated length which he wisely abandoned later. There can be no doubt that Coluccio gave encouragement and wise counsel to the young man in the development of the new script as he did in other things.

A disappointing feature of Walser's book is his failure to make an exhaustive list of manuscripts owned or copied by Poggio. He felt that none of Poggio's writing can be identified

---

[28] Novati, *Epist.*, III, p. 503; Walser, p. 12.

with certainty because the humanist abandoned all personal characteristics in his script (p. 12). This attitude reveals Walser's failure to study Poggio's script intensively more than it does the character of Poggio's writing. To be sure, there are times when one is in doubt about the identification of the script even of a person to whose writing one has given close attention. Yet no script is completely without its idiosyncrasies. Walser also expressed doubt about ownership even when there is a subscription such as « Liber Poggii ». On the other hand, he ventures some suggestions about ownership which are clearly wrong.

It has seemed useful to list books copied or owned by Poggio, although I make no pretense either to completeness or to certainty. More will no doubt be found. The « Inventory » referred to is that made after Poggio's death in 1459 (Walser, p. 418).

I. Manuscripts copied by Poggio.

A) In his formal bookhand.

1. Florence, Laur. Strozz. 96. Copied 1402-1403. Coluccio Salutati, *De verecundia*. See plate in this volume, Ullman, *Origin*, Pl. 13-14.

2. Berlin, Ham. 166. « Scripsit Poggius A. D. MCCCCVIII a Mundi vero Creatione VI Mil. et DCVII ». Cicero, *Epist. ad Att.* Facsimiles in P. Schmiedeberg, *De Asconi codicibus et de Ciceronis scholiis Sangallensibus* (Breslau diss., 1905), H. Sjögren, *Commentationes Tullianae* (Uppsala, 1910), Stanley Morison, « Early Humanistic Script and the First Roman Type », *The Library*, Ser. IV, XXIV (1943), Fig. 11, Ullman, Pl. 15.

3. Florence, Laur. 67, 15. « Hunc librum scripsit Poggius Florentiae summo cum studio ac diligentia diebus XII Romano pontifice residente (*i. m.* Gregorio XII) iterum Senis cum sua curia. Valeas qui legis ». Copied 1408-1409. Eusebius, *De temp.* Inventory 29 « manu poggi ». Facsimile in Walser, Pl. IV, Ullman, Pl. 16.

4. Vat. lat. 3245. Copied during the papacy of John XXIII (1410-15). Cicero, *Acad., Leg.* Inventory 13. Facsimile in Nolhac, *Orsini,* Pl. II, Ullman, Pl. 17.

5. Florence, Laur. 48, 22. « Poggius scripsit », « Scripsit Poggius Romae ». Copied 1425 [29]. Cicero, *Phil., Cat.* Inventory 4. See plate 7 in this volume, Ullman, Pl. 18.

6. Florence, Laur. 50, 31. « Scripsit Poggius secretarius domini Martini Papae V », « Scripsit Poggius Martini Papae V secretarius. Valeas qui legis ». Copied 1425 and later. Cicero, *De or., Par., Brut., Or.* Inventory 5 « manu Poggi ». Facsimile in Stanley Morison, *op. cit.,* Fig. 12, Ullman, Pl. 19.

7. Florence, Riccardiana 499. Cicero, *Verr.* Owned but not signed as copyist by Poggio. Copied in 1425-26. Ullman, Pl. 20.

8. Vat. lat. 2208. Seneca, *Epist.* Owned but not signed as copyist by Poggio. Copied in 1426. Ullman, Pl. 21.

9. Florence, Riccardiana 504. Cicero, *Fin., Am., Sen., Top., Part., Somn. Scip., Acad.* Owned but not signed as copyist by Poggio. Inventory l. Ullman, Pl. 22.

10. Florence, Laur. 49, 24. « Liber Poggii secretarii apostolici ». Cicero, *Att.* See above. Ullman, Pl. 23.

11. Vat. lat. 1843. Livy I-X. See above and plate in this volume, Ullman, Pl. 24.

12. Vat. lat. 1849. Livy XXI-XXX. See above. Ullman, Pl. 25.

13. Vat. lat. 1852. Livy XXXI-XL. See above.

The attribution of Nos. 10-13 has been challenged by Prof. A. S. Dunston, who with unusual courtesy sent me a copy of a paper on the subject which is to be published in *Scriptorium.* I said above that the identification of handwriting is not always certain, but I still think it is likely that Poggio copied these manuscripts. This is not the place to make a detailed reply to Prof. Dunston, for which see the same number of *Scriptorium* [here, Chap. XXVII].

14-17. Four more applicants for recognition as manuscripts copied by Poggio have been seen by me, but I am not yet ready to accept them without further study. They are all in the S. Marco collection of the Laurenziana: 230 (Plautus, first eight plays), 262 (Cicero, *De oratore*), 643 (Augustine, *De libero arbi-*

---

[29] Not copied in 1403. See chapter IX, on Novati, III, p. 656.

trio, Soliloquia, De immortalitate animae, De vera religione),
665 (Augustine, *Contra academicos, De ordine, De trinitate*).
The last three came to S. Marco from Niccolò Niccoli. It is possible that the fourth, which has no flyleaf (on which the provenience
would be indicated) came from the same source. They must
therefore have been copied before Niccoli's death in 1437. They
are, of course, unsigned and can be attributed to Poggio only
on the basis of script and orthography [30]. Characteristic letters
are *g, ct* ligature, *et* ligature, *q*: abbreviation, dotted *y*, and capital
P with a small bowl, which makes the letter seem tall. The
rum abbreviation, however, is narrower than in the signed Poggio manuscripts. *Pre* is regular for *prae* (alone or in compounds),
as in all Poggio manuscripts. The same is true of *Grecus*.
The *ae* diphthong is used in endings as in Poggio's earlier codices.
Coeteri occurs in 262 and 643 and in Poggio's first manuscript;
similarly *coepi* in 230 and 665 is an early Poggio spelling. *Quae,
haec, aetas, quaero* follow the Poggian norm. One strange form
which may raise doubts is *aetiam* spelled with a diphthong (twice
in 262, once in 665); *moetu* (for *metu*) and *aequidem* are found
in 230. But some strange forms are found in the accepted Poggio
too. The adverb *eo* is accented in 665 and in Poggio's Cicero
of 1408. The word divisions *a-utem* and *a-uras* in 665 and
a-uctoritate in 262 are paralleled by *cla-udum* in the Strozzianus
and *a-utem* in the Eusebius of 1408-1409. Poggio usually divides
a word before the *ct* ligature; later he occasionally divides between
c and *t* but keeps the ligaturing stroke. Rarely and apparently only
early does he divide between the two letters without this stroke:
lec-tionis in the Eusebius. An example occurs in S. Marco 665
spec-tacula.

The *De oratore* and the Plautus are probably fairly early.
By 1431 the complete Plautus was available to Poggio. The
De oratore belongs to the *mutili* and was copied before the complete text was made available in 1425. The complete manuscript
was found in 1421 but Poggio did not copy it until 1425. The
two Augustines may have been copied in England, where Poggio

---

[30] I have before me photographs of only single pages of these manuscripts
and notes on only one or two additional pages. See Plate 9 in this volume
for S. Marco 665.

lived from 1418-22, and where, he tells us in 1422 (*Epist.* I, p. 80), he read Augustine and other Church Fathers. Everything considered, I would put this group of manuscripts fairly early, between 1405 and 1415, possibly as late as 1420 for the Augustines.

Dr. Helmut Boese has suggested to me that Poggio may have been the scribe who copied (East) Berlin, Ham. 125, containing Caesar's *Gallic War* and *Civil War,* as well as the *Alexandrine, African,* and *Spanish Wars* attributed to him (Pl. 10). On September 14 and October 23, 1426, Poggio asked Niccolò Niccoli to request Nicola de' Medici to return the *Gallic* and *Civil Wars,* written in Poggio's own hand [31]. A direct appeal to Nicola had brought no reply. Evidently he succeeded in getting the manuscript back, for in the inventory of Poggio's books there is listed « commentaria ceseris (*sic*) de bello civili » [32]. To be sure, this does not prove that the manuscript in the inventory is the one that Poggio transcribed, especially since the inventory does not say it is in Poggio's hand, but the identification of the Hamilton manuscript is perhaps made a little easier [33].

The following characteristics agree with Poggio's, though not of course confined to him: *ae,* not *e,* in case endings; *e* with a cedilla appears at the ends of lines when space is lacking. *Caesar, haec, quae* are regularly used, but at the end of the line one may find *que* with a cedilla or *q* with a line above and a cedilla, and *Cesar* with a cedilla. In compounds the spelling *pre* is regular. *Saepe* and *sepe* both occur. *Coepi, poena,* and *coeteri* are used, as is *Grecus.* All these are found in Poggio's manuscripts, especially in his first two. In his first, Strozzi 96 of 1402-03, he employs the strange form *accoeptus* (for *acceptus*) twice, *suscoepi* twice, *decoeptio* once, *incoepi* twice, though the *o* was expunged by Coluccio or Poggio. The Caesar manuscript has *accoeperit* and *excoepti.* Of all the spellings this is the most significant

---

[31] *Poggii Epistolae,* ed T. de Tonellis, I (Florence, 1832), pp. 187, 195.

[32] Ernst Walser, *Poggius Florentinus* (Leipzig, 1914), p. 420, No. 23. Walser (p. 106, n. 5) says that this item is entered in the margin and suggests that the *Gallic War* was left out because space was lacking.

[33] I asked Dr. Boese to examine an erasure at the bottom of fol. 1r. He was able to make out « Monasterii Clarevallis Mediolani ». This is, however, of no help in tracing the history of the manuscript.

for identifying Poggio as the copyist of the Caesar. On the other hand, the Caesar codex has the spelling *proemium* for *praemium,* which I have not noted in any of the Poggio manuscripts. Then too the unusual *proesidium* is used alongside the regular *presidium.*

The Poggian spelling *nihil* is regular in the Caesar manuscript.

Word division in the Berlin Caesar conforms with Poggio's practice. In a random sampling we find *ca-usa, na-utae, pa-ulo, cu-idam, Su-evos, pa-ucis.* Word division between both recto and verso and verso and recto occurs in the Caesar, as it does in Poggio's early and late manuscripts, but it is avoided in Vat. lat. 3245 (1410-15). An accent mark is used over *a,* as in Laur. 67, 15, copied 1408-09. Word division occurs between *c* and *t* without a ligature, as in Laur. 67, 15: *perfec-tos,* etc.

In the matter of capitals, we find a very interesting situation which seems to confirm the identification of the scribe as Poggio but at a fairly early date, with which the data thus far presented agree. In the first place, the enlarged minuscules and the uncials interspersed with the capitals gradually disappear as the copying of this manuscript proceeds. After Book III of the *Gallic War* the only non-capital that appears is an uncial *h* in the title of Book VIII and one each in those of the *Alexandrine, African,* and *Spanish Wars.* This *h* occurs twice in titles of Strozz. 96, and at least once in the text, as a capital, of Laur. 67, 15 and Vat. lat. 2208.

In the title of Book I of the *Gallic War* capital E occurs seven times, an enlarged minuscule *e* once. In Book II capital E appears four times, enlarged minuscule *e* twice. Strozz. 96 has the uncial *e* several times in titles, Vat. lat. 2208 and 3245 have the large minuscule *e* in the text at the beginning of sentences. An enlarged minuscule *b* is used twice each in the titles of Books I and II. I do not find the latter in the few notes and photographs I have of other Poggio manuscripts. The same is true of the abbreviation for *rum* occurring in the titles of Books I and II.

B) In his less formal hand (*manus velox*).

1. Madrid, Bibl. Nac. 8514 (X, 81). « Poggius Florenti nus ». Copied 1416. Sigebert, Asconius, Valerius Flaccus. Facsimile in Schmiedeberg, *op. cit.,* Ullman, Pl. 27.

2. Vat. lat. 11458. Cicero, *Rab. Post., Rab. perd., Rosc. com., Caec., Leg. agr., Pis.,* etc. Copied in 1417. A. Campana in *Nel cinquantesimo di « Studi e Testi »*, *1900-1950* (Vatican, 1950), p. 79; Cicero, *In Pisonem*, ed. R. G. M. Nisbet (Oxford, 1961), p. xxvi.

II. Manuscripts owned but not written by Poggio.

1. Florence, Laur. 37, 11. « Liber Poggii ». Seneca, *Trag.* Inventory 22.

2. Florence, Laur. 45, 16. Copied 1447. « Liber Poggii Secretarii ». Xenophon, *Cyropaedia*, translated by Poggio. Inventory 92.

3. Florence, Laur. 47, 19. « Liber Poggii Secretarii Apostolici ». Poggio, *In avaritiam, De vera nobilitate, De infelicitate principum, An seni sit uxor ducenda, Contra hypocritas.* Inventory 85.

4. Florence, Laur. 53, 27. « Liber Poggii quem vendidit Ioanni Cosme de Medicis ». Columella.

5. Florence, Laur. 63, 26. « Liber Poggii secretarii summi pontificis quem vendidit Ioanni Cosme » (the last four words were written by the same hand but with different ink). Valerius Maximus.

6. Florence, Laur. 79, 10. Dated 1427. « Liber Poggii secretarii apostolici ». Aristotle, *Ethics*, translated by Bruni. Inventory 67 (?).

7. Florence, Naz. Conv. Soppr. I. V. 42. « Liber Poggii ». Thomas Aquinas on Aristotle's *Physics*. Inventory 72.

8. Vat. lat. 1629. « Liber Poggii secretarii apostolici ». Plautus. Inventory 24.

9. Vat. lat. 1873. Ammianus Marcellinus. Walser, p. 56. Poggio gave the manuscript to Cardinal Colonna.

10. Vat. Ottob. lat. 2035. Cicero, *Epist. Brut., Q. Fr., Oct., Att.* Poggio's notes but no ownership note. Inventory 6.

11. Vat. Urb. lat. 436. Nepos. « Liber Pogii ». Inventory 44.

12. Rome, Biblioteca Nazionale, Vitt. Em. 205. « Liber Poggii Secretarii ». Poggio, *De praestantia Caesaris et Scipionis.* Inventory 82.

13. Madrid, Bibl. Nac. 3678 (M. 31). Copied 1417. Manilius, Statius, *Silvae.* At one time this manuscript was bound with Madrid, X, 81 (see above), but without Sigebert. It has an old list of contents on fol. 1: « Manilii Astronomicon, Statii Papinii Sylvae, Asconius Pedianus in Ciceronem, Valerii Flacci nonnulla » [34]. This combined manuscript is, I suggest, to be identified with Inventory 59: « Astronomicon cum multis aliis in papiro ». The two Madrid manuscripts are made of paper. Copied in 1417.

14. Phillipps 12278, now collection of William H. Robinson Ltd., 16 Pall Mall, London (Catalogue 81, *A Selection of Precious Manuscripts Historic Documents and Rare Books,* 1950, No. 30). Cicero, *Off.* The catalogue's statement that the manuscript was copied by Poggio is based on comparison with a facsimile of his handwriting. Certainly the script is very similar to Poggio's bookhand, but as there are some differences, it may be that the book was copied by a scribe trained by Poggio. The Inventory lists three copies of the *De officiis,* one bound in red, one in black, one in red « manu poggi » (Nos. 9-11). The Robinson manuscript has an old black binding (illustrated in the catalogue) and may therefore have been the one listed as No. 10. Dr. E. P. Goldschmidt, the well-known authority on bindings, kindly informed me that the binding was of the fifteenth century, probably Florentine, pointing out that it has the characteristic roundels which are, or were, gilt. See too his *Gothic and Renaissance Bookbindings,* I (London, 1928), p. 88: « This style of binding with blind stamped knotwork interspersed with gilt roundels was known as peculiarly Florentine, as can be seen from the inventories of the books belonging to the Este at Ferrara, where they are described as 'stampado alla Fiorentina' ».

III. Rejected or Doubtful.

1. Florence, Laur. 35, 21. Lucan. Walser suggests this may be Inventory 53, but this is not likely. It belonged to

---

[34] A. C. Clark's edition of Asconius (Oxford, 1907), p. xviii.

Giorgio Antonio Vespucci (uncle of Amerigo), after whose name we read « nunc vero Baptistae Poggii et am(icorum) ». The book thus seems to have passed from Vespucci directly to Poggio's son Gian Battista without having belonged to Poggio himself. Vespucci, who died in 1514, was presumably a small boy when Poggio died.

2-3. For Vat. lat. 3330 and 3331 see above.

4-5. Walser (pp. 12-13) thought that there might be notes and additions by Poggio in Florence, Laur. Faes. 12-13. He took this suggestion from Novati (*Epist.*, III, pp. 163, 656), who also believed that the manuscripts were owned and annotated by Coluccio. After long study I convinced myself that the books (Augustine, *De civitate Dei*) had no connection with Coluccio. This conclusion weakens the case for Poggio. For Novati's argument in essence was that (1) the books belonged to Salutati, who (2) used Poggio as a copyist several times; (3) the books reveal notes that resemble Poggio's. With the props taken from under the first statement, the second collapses as far as these two manuscripts are concerned. That means that the matter must be determined on the third ground alone. It is possible but not certain that Poggio wrote the notes and additions.

6. A. M. Bandini, *Catalogus codicum latinorum Bibliothecae Mediceae Laurentianae*, I (Florence, 1774), in commenting on Laur. 46, 7 (which he wrongly thought was the manuscript of Quintilian discovered by Poggio in St. Gall) stated that a copy of a complete Quintilian made by Poggio was in London in « bibliotheca Comitis Sunderlandiae ». I have been unable to find a trace of this.

7. S. De Ricci, *Census of Medieval and Renaissance Manuscripts in the United States and Canada*, II (New York, 1937), p. 1887, stated that William M. Clearwater of Tuxedo Park, N. Y., had a Cicero, *De oratore*, which once belonged to H. C. Hoskier, who thought it was a manuscript of Poggio's described in the catalogue of Fulvio Orsini. This is obviously an error [35].

---

[35] For Poggio's hand in papal documents see Karl August Fink, « Poggio-Autographen kurialer Herkunft », in *Miscellanea Archivistica Angelo Mercati* (Città del Vaticano, 1952), p. 129.

Chapter XVI

LEONARDO BRUNI
AND HUMANISTIC HISTORIOGRAPHY [1]

In the introduction to his edition of Leonardo Bruni's *History of the People of Florence*, Santini remarks that general works on Italian historiography and on the Renaissance, such as those of Burckhardt and Voigt, tend to depreciate Renaissance historiography in comparison with that of the Middle Ages and of later periods [2]. In other words, one gets from them the impression that the writing of history reached its all-time low in fifteenth-century Italy. Thus Voigt, writing about the Renaissance, deserts his period and goes into raptures about the mediaeval chronicler Giovanni Villani, and is distinctly cool towards Bruni and other Renaissance historians [3]. This is due in part to the feeling that a chronicle is apparently more factual, in part to the suspicion that the literary finish of the Renaissance is a flashy attire beneath which beats a wicked heart, ready to take advantage of a poor but honest scholar and of the scholar's unsophisticated students. Santini attributes this attitude towards Renaissance historians to a failure to read their books, and in this he is no doubt justified [4]. He observes that, on the other hand, those who study particular historians of that period, go too far in their extravagant praise of these writers, that, for example,

[1] Originally published in *Medievalia et Humanistica,* 4 (1946), p. 45.

[2] In *Rerum Italicarum Scriptores* (the new Muratori), XIX, 3 (Città di Castello, 1914).

[3] Georg Voigt, *Wiederbelebung des classischen Alterthums*, ed. 3, I (Berlin, 1893), pp. 393 ff. The discussion of Villani is comparatively long.

[4] On the other hand, Symonds attributes Foscolo's high praise of Bruni's *History* to a want of familiarity with it (*Renaissance in Italy,* Modern Library ed., I, p. 139, n. 34).

Biondo and Valla have been compared with Vico, Niebuhr, and Mommsen. He explains this opinion by the fact that its proponents have studied only the works they are discussing. Bruni, he holds, has suffered because no one has read him with any care. There is another factor to be considered. Today we like to write our own histories and to go back to original sources for them. The Renaissance historians used our methods, more or less, on source materials; in other words, we may think of them as earlier and less experienced incarnations of ourselves. This is why we prize a fifteenth-century ledger more highly than a fifteenth-century history. We might think of the somewhat analogous situation in textual criticism. We greatly prefer a manuscript of some classical author that was copied by an ignoramus from a fairly old manuscript to one that has behind it the sophistication of fifteenth-century Italian humanism. The former will contain many errors, which we can, however, easily correct. The latter presents a smooth, apparently flawless text because the humanists have, in the course of the tradition, emended the errors to their own taste. They have not always done so correctly but we are often unable to penetrate beneath the seemingly correct text. But this is not merely an analogy; the two phenomena are interrelated. For the humanist's curiosity led him to search far and wide for correct historical data as he did for correct textual readings. In fact, one purpose of seeking correct texts was to achieve historical truth. When Salutati examined twenty manuscripts of Gregory's *Dialogues* in order to find what town was referred to, whether Tifernum, Tibur, or what, he was certainly doing a bit of historical research [5].

In a sense, then, the Renaissance historians *were* precursors of Vico, Niebuhr, and Mommsen. They were modern historians whose technique had not yet been perfected and whose rhetorical form misleads casual readers, among whom I include general writers on historiography. I must admit, however, that in saying this I have Bruni in mind and that other Renaissance

[5] *Epist.*, ed. Novati, III (Rome, 1896), p. 624.

historians are less innocent of the charges that have been heaped upon them.

Santini prepared for his edition in a masterful essay that showed Bruni and, we may say, Renaissance historians in their true light [6]. The few scholars who have read Santini's essay, such as Baron and Ferguson [7], give a sound, though brief, treatment, but the popular writers have followed Fueter, who continued in the footsteps of Burckhardt. Fueter's third edition was published in 1936 but is unchanged from the original edition of 1911, which appeared too early to make use of Santini's essay [8].

Benedetto Croce, in an essay originally published in 1913, admittedly followed Fueter and ignored or showed ignorance of his fellow countryman Santini [9]. Was this the result of being the Germanophile that he called himself in one of his essays? Or did he class Santini among the philologians, a tribe for which his disdain is evident? Croce's condensation of Fueter results in the omission of qualifying statements, and leaves some of Fueter's absurdities in all their stark nudity. Both tend to theorize *in vacuo*, while Santini pores over Bruni's actual words. Still briefer is the treatment in Harry Elmer Barnes, based on Burckhardt or Fueter, and therefore still more absurd the pronouncements [10].

---

[6] Emilio Santini, « Leonardo Bruni Aretino e i suoi 'Historiarum Florentini populi libri XII' », *Annali della R. Scuola Normale Superiore di Pisa,* XXII (1910). In this paper I have dealt lightly with matters covered by Santini and have tried to supplement him by treating of phases which he omitted.

[7] Hans Baron in *Historische Zeitschrift,* 147 (1933), p. 5; W. K. Ferguson in *American Historical Review,* 45 (1939-40), p. 1.

[8] Eduard Fueter, *Geschichte der neueren Historiographie,* ed. 3 (Munich, 1936).

[9] *La Critica,* XI (1913), p. 198; translated in his *Theory and History of Historiography* (London, 1921), p. 224. To be sure, Croce does not deal with individual historians except by way of example, and Bruni is mentioned only once and then in passing. Remigio Sabbadini's brief treatment, in *Il metodo degli umanisti* (Florence, 1922), p. 75, is not up to the usual standard of that master.

[10] Harry Elmer Barnes, *A History of Historical Writing* (Norman, Oklahoma, 1937), pp. 99 ff. Walter Goetz, selecting the favorable remarks that Fueter makes about Renaissance historians, concludes that Renaissance historiography is a blend of ancient and contemporary elements (*Historische Zeitschrift,* 113, 1914, p. 254). It is true that Fueter has some complimentary things to say about the humanists but one has a feeling that they are somehow

Before examining Bruni's historical theory and background and his practice in his only real historical work, the *History of Florence,* let us survey rapidly some of his other excursions into history and biography. They did not penetrate very deep into these regions, for they were hardly more than translations from the Greek, differing little from his acknowledged translations. He started to translate Plutarch's life of Cicero but, finding it unsatisfactory, composed his own *Cicero novus* instead. Plutarch necessarily remained his chief source but he omitted and added from Cicero himself and from other sources. Yet this biography was enough like Plutarch's *Cicero* to cause at least one early printer to substitute it for Plutarch's in an edition of the *Lives* [11]. The *Commentarius de bello Punico* is largely a translation of Polybius, Books I and II, with some omissions. It was intended merely to fill in the account of the First Punic War and of the immediately following events that is missing in Livy. In fact, the Illyrian War and the Gallic War, in a condensed version of Polybius, are represented in at least one edition of Bruni as being taken « from epitome XX », and « from the same epitome », which I take to refer to the lost twentieth book of Livy [12]. Similarly the *De bello Italico adversus Gothos* is regarded as hardly more than a translation of Procopius. In a letter to Ciriaco, Bruni says that it is not a translation but an original work, in the same sense as Livy's, who borrowed from Valerius Antias and Polybius

not really meant; the total impression is that no worse historians ever lived or wrote. J. W. Thompson's *A History of Historical Writing* I (New York, 1942), p. 478, gives a rather good account of Bruni, based on Goetz and Baron; he does not mention Santini. A fairly good report may be found in Paul Joachimsen, *Geschichtsauffassung und Geschichtschreibung in Deutschland unter dem Einfluss des Humanismus* (Leipzig, 1910), p. 19. Excellent, though brief, is the discussion in W. K. Ferguson, *The Renaissance in Historical Thought* (Boston, 1948), pp. 9-11. G. C. Sellery, *The Renaissance, Its Nature and Origin* (Madison, 1950), pp. 152-153, prefers Villani to Bruni. His general attitude is made clear by his use of the phrase « the so-called Italian Renaissance ».

[11] Dorothy M. Robathan in *Classical Philology,* XXVI (1931), p. 93.

[12] So in the edition of 1537. The title page indicates that the period covered is lacking in Livy, but there is no mention of Polybius. Santini, *op. cit.,* p. 23, notes that Bruni's account is incorporated into some editions of Livy. He seems to be in error in denying Bruni's statement that he drew on other writers besides Polybius; I have noticed a few places where Polybius' account is amplified.

but rearranged to suit himself. Why he should bring up this point is not evident, unless it was because of a prick of conscience [13]. He makes no mention of Procopius though he gives Livy's sources. Evidently criticized for concealing his source, he says in another letter that he had merely taken the facts from « him » (even here he does not name Procopius) because he was an eyewitness [14]. The *Commentarium rerum Graecarum* is taken, without credit, from Xenophon's *Hellenica.*

Voigt contends that Bruni had no intention of deceiving in withholding the names of his sources [15]. He even suggests that the manuscripts of Procopius which Bruni used as the basis for his translation lacked the author's name; this seems to me sheer nonsense. A bit of deception is clear in the letter to Ciriaco. In extenuation it may be said that Bruni felt it unjust to give the name of someone else to books which, as far as style was concerned, he had made his own and that, therefore, he felt justified in giving them his name whenever he added material, no matter how slight, from other sources [16]. Then again, he may have felt that the term *commentarius*, « notes », borrowed from Caesar, was so modest that he could afford to be immodest in claiming full credit. Yet in the same letter to Ciriaco he calls the *De bello Italico* a *historia*. In any event, a modern historian imitating Bruni in this respect would be criticized even more than Bruni was by his contemporaries; he would, in fact, be completely ostracized and read out of the profession. But other times, other mores.

Bruni's panegyric on Florence was probably inspired by the one that Salutati worked into his invective against Loschi. Even Salutati, who rose to the defense of his beloved Florence after Loschi's vituperative attack, went to the sources for some of his facts about the history of the city. Bruni was criticized because his panegyric did not stick to facts. Then he wrote a real history of Florence, on which he spent many years. The first book was begun in 1414 or 1415 and finished in 1416; the

---

[13] *Epist.* IX, 5, ed. Mehus (Florence, 1741).
[14] *Epist.* IX, 9.
[15] *Op. cit.*, II, p. 172.
[16] *Epist.* IX, 9.

third appeared in 1420, the sixth in 1429, the ninth in 1439. The twelfth and last remained unfinished at its author's death in 1444.

As an admirer of Petrarch and a disciple of Salutati, Bruni had gone to school to Cicero. From him he learned the importance of style, of dressing up history so as to make it a form of literature. The proper garments for history, according to Cicero, were those of rhetoric, which of course had been designed by and for the public speaker. Though Cicero has left us no historical writing of his own, he repeatedly sets forth his views in his rhetorical works. He held the same opinions about philosophy, and one reason why he wrote his philosophical essays was to show the philosophers, especially the Epicureans, in what garb philosophy should be arrayed [17]. He felt that the uncouth works of Epicurus and his followers were read only by the members of that school, and that other philosophers and the cultivated public avoided them because they derived no pleasure from their perusal, even as today the writings of many of us are read only by our professional brethren.

This lesson Bruni had learned and learned well. Too well, in fact, for in recent years he has usually been charged with writing purely rhetorical exercises, though it is hard to see how anyone who has read the *Florentine History* can make that charge. People are too easily frightened by the word rhetoric, which means nothing more than literary style. Santini, in refuting this charge against Bruni, cites Salvemini as one of the first to recognize, though insufficiently, the historical value of Bruni's work. Bruni's contemporaries, however, held a saner view, for they did not have our modern, especially American, distrust of rhetoric and were able to see the truth beneath its folds. There may be something in Struthers Burt's dictum: « The American, even the American writer, is fearful of words lest, if he use them too well, he be thought undemocratic » [18].

Most interesting is the remark of Barocci, that he did not know whether to give greater praise to Bruni's elegant style or

[17] *Tusc.* II, 6 ff.
[18] *Saturday Review of Literature*, XXVII (Nov. 4, 1944), p. 6.

to his accuracy [19]. That remark would have delighted both Bruni and Cicero, for to them it would have represented the proper balance between two essentials. Similarly, an anonymous contemporary eulogy of Bruni praises his translation of Aristotle as the first that attained a correct interpretation in a becoming style (*decenti elegantia*) [20]. This is, as we saw, exactly what Cicero strove to do. In one of his letters Bruni advises his correspondent to get his knowledge from Aristotle and his literary style from Cicero [21]. In the opening sentence of his *Rerum suo tempore gestarum commentarius* he insists that unless books are written in a luminous style they cannot add vividness to events or perpetuate their memory. As proof of this he states that the history of the past sixty years is less well-known than that of the days of Demosthenes or Cicero. Plato's works, he adds, give a living, breathing image of his time. It is a little unfair of Voigt to quote this passage for his conclusion that Bruni valued style more highly than facts [22]. Also, in complaining that Bruni reports little more than the events of which he was an eyewitness, he forgets that in this book Bruni is writing, not a history, but a *commentarius*, in Caesarian fashion, a notebook setting forth his experiences. It will be remembered that Caesar, according to Cicero's famous remark [23], wrote his *Commentarii* in a plain direct fashion, not as history but as source material to be polished up by a historian, yet he did so excellent a piece of work that he frightened others from attempting the task of dressing up his so-called notes. That Bruni had the Ciceronian passage in mind is, I think, clear from the title of his book, *Rerum suo tempore gestarum commentarius,* apparently based on Cicero's *commentarios rerum suarum,* applied to Caesar's *Commentaries*, and from

[19] Quoted by Santini, *op. cit.*, p. 15.

[20] Laur. 90 sup. 5, as quoted in Santini, *op. cit.*, p. 151. Bruni himself criticizes the earlier translations in the preface to his version of the *Ethics*, and in *Epist.* IV, 22 he concurs in Cicero's judgment about Aristotle's excellent style.

[21] *Epist.* VI, 6. Cf. *De studiis et litteris*: « Nam et litterae sine rerum scientia steriles sunt et inanes, et scientia rerum quamvis ingens, si splendore careat litterarum, abdita quaedam obscuraque videtur », in H. Baron, *Leonardo Bruni Aretino, Humanistisch-philosophische Schriften* (Leipzig, 1928), p. 19; this wording is reminiscent of Cicero, *De or.* I, 48.

[22] *Op. cit.*, II, p. 498.

[23] *Brutus* 262. The *Brutus* had been discovered when Bruni wrote this book.

other similarities [24].   He perhaps hoped that this book might
receive the same praise as Caesar's.   In the work itself he says
that he will not go into detail, for that sort of treatment belongs
to history [25].   When the book was criticized, evidently for omission of details, he said he put in what he knew and considered
worthy of mention, without any thought of preventing anyone
who had more information from writing at greater length.   Commentaries differ from histories, he says, in being shorter and less
detailed, whereas histories are fuller and more carefully done.
Livy, too, in relating the story of the Roman kings (Bruni continues), avoided giving them annalistic treatment and merely
touched the high spots (*rerum summam*).   Polybius, who did
the same, is a higly reputable writer and, says Bruni, « I have
followed his authority » [26].   Incidentally, this tribute to Polybius
should make us hesitate about accepting the facile generalization
that Livy was the idol of Bruni and that Polybius did not come
into his own before Machiavelli.

As I have said, Voigt complains that in his book about the
events of his own time, Bruni gives merely an eyewitness account.
In the letter, already mentioned, about his *De bello Italico* Bruni
says of Procopius that the one good thing about him is that he
participated in the events which he described [27].   Whatever we
may think of Bruni's shortcomings in his book on the events of
his time, we must admit that one who insisted on the importance
of first-hand information cannot have been entirely preoccupied
with stylistic embellishment.

[24] Cf. Bruni's « litterae ... illustres » with Cicero's « illustri brevitate »;
his « Tanta illi clarissimi viri (Cicero, Demosthenes) aetatibus suis lumina infu-
derunt ut ... quasi ante oculos positae discernantur ... Cuius (Platonis) libros
epistolasque dum legimus, quasi picturam quandam illorum temporum viventem
adhuc spirantemque intuemur » with Cicero's « tum videtur (Caesar) tamquam
tabulas bene pictas collocare in bono lumine ».   I quote Bruni in the edition
by Carmine di Pierro in the new Muratori, XIX, 3 (1926), p. 423.

[25] *Ibid.*, p. 457, 14.

[26] *Epist.* IV, 20.   Santini, *op. cit.*, p. 22, wrongly assumes that this letter
(to which he obviously alludes, though, for some reason, he does not cite it)
refers to the *De bello Punico*, being misled by the reference to Polybius.
Bruni's words, « Ego quae scivi, quaeque memoratu digna aestimavi », show
that Bruni has in mind the other book, on the events of his time.

[27] *Epist.* IX, 9.

But to return to Cicero's influence on Bruni the historian. In a famous passage Cicero calls history a witness of the times, the light of truth, the life of memory, the guide of life, and the messenger of the past [28]. Bruni advises the King of Spain to read philosophy and history, which were his own favorites. In recommending history he follows Cicero in calling it the guide of life. He also finds that it furnishes both pleasure and a useful training for the active life [29]. Here too he echoes Ciceronian sentiments [30].

In one of his essays and in his *History* Bruni maintains that one of the functions of history is to serve as a guide in contemporary problems [31]. Thus he wrote his *Commentary on Greek Affairs* so that the dangers that beset the ancient Greek cities might serve as an example to show how wars and quarrels were to be shunned [32]. He maintained that, just as old men are regarded as wise because of all they have experienced, so the right reading of history can produce wisdom [33].

We have noted the compliment paid Bruni by a contemporary who praised the style and correctness of his translation of Aristotle. This correctness corresponds to the truthfulness of history, so that Bruni's histories and his translations may be considered together as different phases of the same activity. He criticized the mediaeval translation of Aristotle's *Ethics* not only for its poor Latin style but for its errors [34]. Of Alfonso de Cartagena, Bishop of Burgos, who though knowing no Greek,

---

[28] *De or.* II, 36.

[29] *Epist.* VII, 6; *magistra vitae* is the expression used by Cicero and Bruni.

[30] In *Fin.* V, 51 Cicero says, « esse utilitatem in historia, non modo voluptatem ». Usefulness is then explained as « gerendi » (cf. *Fin.* I, 25). Bruni says history contributes « tum ad voluptatem animi, tum ad disciplinam agendi ». Compare too the Preface of *De bello Italico adversus Gothos*: « Habet praeterea historiae cognitio voluptatem ... et utilitatem », in Baron, *op. cit.*, p. 148.

[31] *De studiis et litteris*, in Baron, *op. cit.*, p. 13; *Hist. Flor.*, p. 3, 15 (cf. p. 163, 15).

[32] *Epist.* VIII, 3. The same lesson was intended to be drawn, though not explicitly pointed out, from the lack of unity among the Etruscan cities (*Hist. Flor.*, p. 13).

[33] *Hist. Flor.*, p. 3, 16; cf. Introduction to *De bello Italico* in H. Baron, *op. cit.*, p. 147.

[34] *Epist.* IV, 22; X, 26; Preface to his translation of the *Ethics* in Baron, *op. cit.*, p. 76; *De recta interpretatione, ibid.*, p. 91.

preferred the earlier version to Bruni's, he asks: do you prefer it because it is more literary (*elegantior*) or because it is more truthful (*verior*)? [35] He shows by example that it is neither. Nothing can be more illuminating than Alfonso's answer that a translator ought to consider, not what Aristotle says, but what he ought to say [36]. That scholastic view, which in effect canonized the mediaeval translations and interpreted them to suit its purposes, was the very antithesis of the fresh outlook of the Renaissance. The two men were talking about different things: Bruni about a translation of Aristotle, Alfonso about an ecclesiastical document which was more or less based on Aristotle. Just so today many readers of the Vulgate or the King James Version are uninterested in the fact that they contain inaccuracies.

The chief complaint about Bruni's translation of the *Ethics* was his use of *summum bonum* where the earlier translation had *bonum*. That, it can readily be understood, made much difference to the theologians. Even if it is pure chance it is significant that in his defense Bruni uses the phrase « veritatis lux », applied by Cicero to history in a passage familiar to Bruni [37]. Evidently he thought of translations, even of philosophical books, as historical documents. It is not surprising, therefore, that he introduces two historical examples in defense of his translation. Alfonso, knowing no Greek, criticizes Bruni's translation. Suppose (says our author) that he, Bruni, after a careful examination on the spot, should write that a certain church in Bologna is situated on the top of a mountain. A Spaniard who had never been in Bologna would have no right to deny this just because he had read that Bologna is situated on a plain and because the founders of the city would not have built it so dangerously near an overhanging mountain. Even more interesting is his telling of the story about the philosopher who, being an armchair strategist,

---

[35] *Epist.* VII, 4. See A. Birkenmajer, « Der Streit des Alonso von Cartagena mit Leonardo Bruni Aretino », in *Beiträge zur Geschichte der Philosophie des Mittelalters*, XX (1922), p. 129, and E. Franceschini in *Medioevo e Rinascimento, Studi in onore di Bruno Nardi*, I (Florence, 1955), p. 299.

[36] *Epist.* X, 24.

[37] *Epist.* V, 1; Cicero, *De or.* II, 36.

lectured at length on military matters in the presence of Hannibal, who promptly called the fellow crazy [38].

Bruni defends himself against criticism of his *Laudatio urbis Florentinae* by two different arguments. One maintains that the *Laudatio* was a youthful piece, hardly more than a school exercise. The other introduces his often quoted view on truth in history: « History is one thing, panegyric another. History should follow the truth, panegyric goes beyond the truth in its praise » [39]. The two points here made are good Ciceronian doctrine: « Truth is the first law of history », the ancient orator said [40]. As to panegyric being different from history and not subject to its laws, that too is a Ciceronian idea [41]. Ciceronian also is Bruni's often repeated remark about the length of time it takes to write history, though, of course, his own experience told him that [42]. Bruni's emphasis on the causes of wars and other events is derived from Cicero and other ancient writers [43].

Besides getting the theory of historical writing from Cicero and others, Bruni had before his eyes the practice of the ancients, especially of Livy. One of the devices of the ancient historians was the use of fictional speeches attributed to characters in the narrative. This device, so repugnant to the modern scientific historian, was adopted by Bruni and other Renaissance historians and is responsible in large measure for the cloud of suspicion which hangs over them. It should be remembered that even Thucydides made use of this device, and he is, generally speaking, highly regarded. We must think of these speeches as a convention that served a useful purpose. With this medium a

[38] *Epist.* X, 24, taken from Cicero, *De or.* II, 75.

[39] « Aliud est enim historia, aliud laudatio. Historia quidem veritatem sequi debet, laudatio vero multa supra veritatem extollit » (*Epist.* VIII, 4). To a suggestion that he add a supplement to his *Laudatio* to cover the defeat of Pisa he replies that this is more suited to a history (*Epist.* II, 4).

[40] *De or.* II, 62; *Leg.* I, 4-5.

[41] *Att.* I, 19, 10; cf. my « History and Tragedy », in *Transactions of the American Philological Association*, LXXIII (1942), p. 51. *Brut.* 62 was unknown to Bruni at the time of the letter.

[42] *Hist. Flor.*, p. 3, 32 ff.; *Epist.* IV, 4. After spending some thirty years on his history he might well have echoed Cicero's remark that a history cannot be completed in a short time (*Leg.* I, 9).

[43] Cf. *Hist. Flor.*, p. 3, 33 and p. 247, 9 with Cicero, *De or.* II, 63; Polybius, *passim*, etc.

vivid picture could be painted that might be psychologically more true than a mere description. After all, a characterization of an individual in accepted historical form can be quite incorrect. Moreover, the speeches enabled the author to express some of his own ideas more forcefully. As this fact was well-known, no one was deceived. Even Villani and other predecessors of Bruni introduce speeches in the classical fashion, though less extensively [44]. Bruni used this device very skilfully in his *History of Florence* to bring out important points at critical moments.

The direct quotations in the *Florentine History* run from one to 142 lines in Santini's edition. The short ones, of fewer than twenty lines, are of little or no interest for our purpose. There are twenty-four of the longer ones. None is found in Book I, which is a rapid survey of early history.

A group of three speeches clusters around the battle of Montaperti in 1260, Florence's most terrible experience, which almost spelled the doom of that city. First we have the speech of Farinata degli Uberti, a Florentine Ghibelline exile, pointing out to Manfred how important Florence was as the key city in the struggle between the Pope and the Emperor and urging him to attack it. Then, when the people and the popular magistrates of Florence were all in favor of rashly taking the offensive, as they eventually did with fatal results, a more conservative speaker in vain urged caution. Finally, after the defeat, at a meeting of the victors to decide what to do about Florence, when the representatives of Pisa and Siena clamored for its utter destruction, the same Farinata who had made the plea to Manfred, again spoke. Disclaiming any knowledge of the art of rhetoric, he made an eloquent speech which saved the city (pp. 33, 36, 41).

On another occasion a speech is employed to bring out Bruni's sentiments about the Hohenstaufen, especially Frederick Barbarossa, who, he maintained, had no right to the name of Roman emperor and was really another Hannibal (p. 46). The ceaseless and senseless quarrels between Guelphs and Ghibellines lead to a stirring outcry put in the mouth of the Pope: « What childish folly! », he exclaims. « 'A Ghibelline!' you shout, but he is also

[44] Santini, *op. cit.*, p. 77.

a Christian, a citizen, a neighbor, a relative. This one hollow word Ghibelline, the meaning of which no one knows, rouses you to frenzied hatred » (p. 60). The other side is then presented by a Guelph spokesman. But the largest number of speeches, totaling nine, not including those to which they are a reply, revolve about the theme of liberty and democracy.

The classical background and especially the literary form of Bruni and other Renaissance historians have been major points of attack by Fueter and others. Pure imagination, even fantasy, rather than fact plays a large part in Fueter's discussion, at least as far as Bruni is concerned. The performances of the Renaissance historians, he says, were intended to stir the emotions in the same way as a tragedy of Seneca's. As one especially interested in the influence of tragedy on history [45], I should be the first to welcome evidence of such a tendency, but a reading of Bruni's *History of Florence* fails to reveal the slightest indication of such an attempt. As a matter of fact, the material which, to judge from Greek practice, furnished the finest opportunity for writing tragical history, namely the mediaeval miracles, was rigorously excluded by all the Renaissance writers, as Fueter freely admits. I can see no attempt in Bruni to rival rhetorical tragedy, as Fueter charges. The endeavor to give vividness to individuals by putting speeches into their mouths does not, to my mind, constitute such an attempt. Of course, if we use the term loosely, we can say « all the world's a stage ». Nor do I think that Fueter is right in blaming rhetoric for Bruni's omissions of some details. Santini, after exhaustive investigation of details and comparison with Villani and other sources, concludes that classical imitation had little effect on Bruni's historical accuracy. Bruni did precisely the sort of thing that any historian would do, namely, he often omitted what he considered nonessential. Thinking it unimportant to give certain figures exactly, as Villani did, he at times used round numbers. Granting that the single instance that Fueter cites is not an isolated one, it is still true that in scores of places exact figures are given. Furthermore, in one place at least, where Villani gives an exact date and Bruni has refused

[45] See above, note 41.

to commit himself because the facts could not be ascertained with certainty, recent investigations have shown that Villani was wrong[46]. Yet Fueter blames Bruni's suppressions and round numbers on that scapegoat Rhetoric. When Bruni thought them important he gave figures that even Villani omitted, but of that Fueter says nothing. Fueter's criticism, in effect, is that Bruni is writing history, not furnishing source material, as the good Villani did. On the other hand, he finds fault with Bruni for following the annalistic method of his predecessors. Mark you, it is Bruni that he criticizes, not Villani, who can do no wrong. Fueter should have made up his mind whether he wanted to treat Bruni as a chronicler or a historian. If he was a historian the criticism of his annalistic procedure is quite proper but not that of omissions resulting from the historian's judgment, wrong though it may have been, about the relative importance of the data found in his sources. It is obvious that one of the historian's chief functions is to make a selection of his facts, sometimes from an *indigesta moles* of material, using light and shade in the process. He naturally interprets on the basis of his own experience and ideals and those of his time. That is why the history of an epoch must be rewritten from generation to generation. One is almost ashamed to offer these trite observations but they seem particularly fitting here.

In defense of Fueter the retort might be made that Bruni is neither a good chronicler nor a good historian and that Villani is at least the former. But just because the first electric light was inferior to the best gas light it does not follow that gas is a better source of illumination than electricity.

Barnes alleges that the humanists were guided by « the rhetorical canons of Isocrates, Livy, Tacitus, Plutarch and Suetonius, rather than the historical ideals of Thucydides and Polybius ». There are no rhetorical canons in any of these (except in the *Dialogus* of Tacitus, which was scarcely in the writer's mind); Bruni, at least, got his rules from Cicero, who is not mentioned.

One fault attributed to Bruni and other Renaissance historians has been taken altogether too seriously. It is the translation of

---

[46] Santini, *op. cit.*, p. 35.

history from mediaeval to classical Latin. Fueter is so tragic about it that he becomes amusing. He seriously suggests that this procedure almost spelled the deathblow for the scientific treatment of history. This just does not make sense. He says that Bruni becomes obscure through his avoidance of mediaeval words. He makes much of Bruni's use of *adversa factio,* where Villani uses Guelph or Ghibelline, and points out the inconsistency of this practice with the use of the terms Guelph and Ghibelline, for which he cites a single passage in Bruni. But this is misleading. Bruni, writing for foreigners and posterity, at the beginning of his book takes pains not to use the technical terms Guelph and Ghibelline. Later, when the nature of the opposing factions has become clear, he employs the terms, not once, but repeatedly. Naturally he does weed out mediaeval words. He regularly uses *bellum* instead of *guerra,* though he is so faithful to historical accuracy as to preserve *guerra* when he quotes the declaration of war by Gian Galeazzo Visconti (p. 246, 5). But this entire charge against Bruni can be disposed of by pointing out that exactly the same sort of complaint was made by a scholastic theologian against Bruni's translation of Aristotle [47]. Just as he rid his translation of Greek words like *eutrapelia* and *homolochos,* so in his history he banished *guerra* and the like. Do the modern critics wish to be classed with the conservative scholastics who had got so used to the mediaeval Aristotle that they preferred it to Bruni's new and shining model?

Bruni's chief source was the chronicle of Giovanni Villani which he corrected and added to from other sources, especially documents in the archives of Florence. Numerous instances of this may be found in Santini's essay and in the notes to his edition. They put Bruni in an entirely new light as a historian. The mention of Roman ruins and their significance for the early history of Florence (p. 6, 6; p. 24, 26) is a foretaste of that study of archaeology which has contributed so much to our knowledge and interpretation of history.

It is well-known that Bruni and the other historians of the Renaissance secularized history. As already stated, one result was

---

[47] *Epist.* X, 24.

the rejection of miraculous tales and unfounded legends [48]. Bruni did not confine this practice to mediaeval times but in his first book, where he deals with the Etruscans and Romans, he omits or discredits ancient traditions as well. After quoting Virgil to the effect that it was Aeneas who appealed to the Trojans, he says that history, as represented by Livy, is truer than and more remote from the fictions of the poets in assigning this role to Turnus. But the important thing to him was that both versions indicated that the Etruscans flourished before the Trojan War. To those who think that the humanists swallowed all the ancient tales unthinkingly, Bruni's report of the story of Horatius at the bridge must come as a shock. He concludes it by saying: « But greater honor, to tell the truth, is due to the Tiber River: its waters saved the city, which the valor of the Romans could not protect » (p. 11, 5). After a careful study of mediaeval and Renaissance accounts of the origin of Florence, Rubinstein makes this estimate of Bruni: « The chapters dealing with the ancient history of the town are, indeed, a remarkable achievment of the new historical method; on the whole, they stand the test of modern research » [49].

The *post hoc propter hoc* argument is not a safe one and may lead to unsound generalization. Petrarch and Boccaccio had no contact with the political life of their age, asserts Fueter. Accepting this dictum, which is not altogether true, we cannot take the next step with Fueter and admit that therefore they could not be historians, even in the Renaissance sense, and that the writing of history had to wait until Coluccio Salutati and Leonardo Bruni entered upon public careers in Florence. We may grant that one motive of Bruni in writing his *History of Florence* was to publicize his adopted city, as Fueter states, and to put it in a favorable light, but a relatively short book still incomplete after some thirty years' labor can hardly be considered a mere white paper or a press release from the department of public

---

[48] In his Introduction (p. 4) Bruni says he rejects « vulgaribus fabulosisque opinionibus ».

[49] Nicolai Rubinstein, « The Beginnings of Political Thought in Florence », *Iournal of the Warburg Institute*, V (1942), p. 225.

relations.   Moreover, regardless of what may be true of other cities, Florence had, in the eyes not only of its citizens but of others as well, inherited the mantle of ancient Rome.   This doctrine was instilled by Salutati into his pupils, among whom were the historians Bruni and Poggio.   Even earlier we find it in Villani and in Dante's « la bellissima e famosissima figlia di Roma » [50].   The conviction that Florence was the successor of Rome was heightened by the decline of the Eternal City during the Babylonian Captivity and the Great Schism.   The hegemony of Florence in the humanistic movement also contributed to this conviction, as well as the fact that the three great literary masters of modern times, Dante, Petrarch, and Boccaccio, were Florentines, even if two of them lived and died in exile.   It was natural, then, and not just a bit of rhetorical artifice, that Bruni should think of Pisa as a second Carthage, which of course implies that Florence was a second Rome [51].

Bruni at least attempts to be fair in his judgments and not to praise Florentine actions indiscriminately.   Thus he calls the peace that Florence forced on Pisa in 1256 a most unjust one (p. 30, 20); again, he blames both the Pope and the people of Florence for obstinacy when the former tried to settle factional strife in 1273 (p. 64, 3).   He tries to distinguish between conflicting reports and to judge motives.   So he does not deny the possibility that some Florentines asked Charles of Anjou to attack Pisa and Siena but he believes that Charles' real motive in doing so was to blot out all traces of friendliness to the Hohenstaufen (p. 51, 3).   He marvels at the mental processes of a people who in 1329 refused to buy Lucca from the Germans at a bargain price of 80,000 florins and six years later were eager to purchase it from Mastino at four and a half times that price [52].   There are a number of sly digs at the shopkeeper's mentality of the Florentines.   His criticism of unfair legislation is forthright (p. 171,

---

[50] *Convivio* I, 3. Cf. Rubinstein, *ibid.*, p. 198.

[51] P. 3, 10. In *Epist.* II, 4 he states that the Pisan War deserved a separate history, not a supplement in his *Laudatio,* as Niccoli had suggested. In *Hist. Flor.*, p. 285, 26, he has the Milanese envoys of Gian Galeazzo call the Florentines « the new Romans, as they call themselves ».

[52] P. 154, 14 (cf. p. 139, 17; p. 158, 22 ff.).

22). He is vigorous in denouncing the practice of gaining exemption from military service by paying the cost of hiring foreign mercenaries (p. 186, 9). Vespasiano da Bisticci reports Bruni as saying that he praised Florence as much as he could without departing from the truth [53], and this seems to be a fair statement of the case.

In the Introduction to his *Istorie fiorentine* Machiavelli makes what seems to me an astounding remark when he accuses Bruni of having taken little or no account of civil discords and personal enmities and their effects. Apart from Bruni's own statement (p. 78, 46; cf. p. 3, 2) that internal affairs form quite as important a part of history as wars, even a casual reader must be impressed by the amount of space devoted to factional quarrels and internal developments. A check of Book IV shows that twenty-five per cent more space is devoted to internal than to foreign matters, and those internal matters consist almost wholly of quarrels between different groups [54].

Machiavelli goes on to say that, if any lesson is useful to the citizens who govern the republic, it is the one which points out the reasons for hatred and division within the city. Not unlike this is Bruni's remark, in the discussion of the tyranny of the Duke of Athens (p. 163, 15), that it is worth writing about, either for warning citizens or for holding rulers in check. This is, of course, in harmony with his view on the function of history already discussed. Even closer to Machiavelli is his comment on the uprising of the *Ciompi,* that it is a constant lesson to the leaders of the city not to let the mob decide to rush to arms and that these leaders must avoid quarreling, for that leads to popular uprising (p. 224, 30). As a matter of fact, Machiavelli made large use of the data and the ideas in Bruni's book, ap-

---

[53] Quoted by Santini, *op. cit.*, p. 14.

[54] Cf. Santini, *op. cit.*, p. 59. Machiavelli's criticism includes Poggio, to whom it is applicable, according to Santini (p. 108). Bruni obviously had his own *History of Florence* in mind when, in stressing the importance of history, he said: « Est enim decorum cum propriae gentis originem et progressus tum liberorum populorum regumque maximorum et bello et pace res gestas cognoscere » (*De studiis et litteris,* in Baron, *op. cit.*, p. 13). The mention of *liberorum populorum* is of interest for the discussion of liberty below.

parently employing only or chiefly the Italian translation, as is made clear by some of his misunderstandings [55].

It is no more true of historiography than of other activities that the Renaissance marks a sharp break with the Middle Ages or that all humanists were alike.   Much mediaeval thinking persisted—and, for that matter, still persists.   That statement does not necessarily imply a reproach.

Petrarch, perhaps in a moment of aberration, stated that all history is nothing but the praise of Rome [56]. We have seen that Bruni's attitude was a different one.   More important is the difference in their attitudes toward the Middle Ages.   Petrarch ignored them but Bruni, perhaps having no greater liking for them, realized the necessity of bridging the gap between antiquity and his own times and of explaining the course of events. The same motive that led him to sketch the invasion of the barbarians from Alaric to the Lombards caused him later to translate Procopius.   We might say that the translation was incidental to his history.

Bruni's attitude toward the Emperor also was different from that of Petrarch and Salutati, to whom the head of the secular state personified the continuity of the ancient Roman Empire. Bruni is careful to point out not only the gap of three hundred years between Charlemagne and the last Roman emperor but also the differences between the two empires.   The ancient empire, he says, was established by the people during the Republic, and in the last analysis the ancient emperors, tyrants though they were, derived their powers from the people.   On the other hand, Charlemagne was appointed emperor by the pope.   Bruni concludes with these significant words: « It seems to me that it makes a great deal of difference whether the Roman people elect an emperor with the encouragement of the pope, or the pope chooses one without a mandate from the people.   For it is clear that this function belongs to no one as much as to the Roman people » (p. 23, 19).   He admits, to be sure, that the city-states

---

[55] Santini, *op. cit.*, p. 117.

[56] *Opera* (Basel, 1554), p. 1187; cf. Theodor E. Mommsen in *Speculum*, XVII (1942), p. 237.

of Italy, which were left pretty much alone by their German masters, prospered and developed notions of liberty. What Bruni wants is a free choice of an emperor by the people under the benevolent eye of the pope.

In the first book of the *History of Florence* one may discern a five-fold division of history. First, the Roman Republic, which established an empire under free institutions; second, the rule of the emperors, which from the very beginning spelled the decline of the Empire and the loss of liberty. He neatly disposes of the emperors with the epigram: « Verbo quidem legitima potestas, re autem vera dominatio erat » (p. 22, 36). Third, the invasion of the barbarians; fourth, the new empire of Charlemagne and his successors; fifth, the rise of factions in the city-states of Italy about 1250, with which the modern history of Florence begins. This division confirms what was said above about Bruni's attitude toward the Middle Ages. The Roman Empire was already decadent and was responsible for the invasion of the barbarians, which marks what we call the early Middle Ages, once named the Dark Ages. To Bruni these two periods represent the loss of liberty by the people of Italy, first under the heel of their own oppressors, then under that of foreign invaders. The victory of Charlemagne at Pavia removed the heavy Lombard oppression from the necks of the Italians, to use Bruni's own words (p. 22, 21). From then on, liberty begins to make progress in Italy. This neat classification, which has its advantages over the familiar tripartite division into ancient, mediaeval, and modern [57], centers about liberty, its struggles and its achievements. It avoids the sharp break between periods which until a short time ago dominated historical thinking and thus harmonizes fairly well with the recently adopted terms, Carolingian Renaissance and Renaissance of the Twelfth Century. At the beginning of the second book, in summarizing the first, he condenses the five periods into three: the origin and progress of the cities of Tuscany, the decline and fall (« declinatio atque divisio ») of the Roman Empire, and the activities of the factions.

[57] On Petrarch's connection with this periodization and related questions, see Theodor E. Mommsen, *ibid.* Bruni repeats his survey of periods in his life of Petrarch.

Perhaps the most important characteristic of the *History of Florence* has been passed over by critics: its central theme of democratic liberty. This Bruni got, in part at least, from his teacher Salutati, though it was, of course, widespread. It is played up in the relatively long account of the tyranny of the Duke of Athens—liberty lost and regained. He tells his readers that this tyranny and the way it came should be an object lesson to them (pp. 162-167). The popular uprising of the *Ciompi* in 1378 leads Bruni to the reflection that the leading citizens should not allow the people to have control over arms, for they cannot be restrained once they have seized the reins and realize the strength of numbers. But even more dangerous is it to have the leading citizens engage in plots against the constitution, for these cause popular outbreaks (p. 224, 30).

But it is in nine of the long speeches that Bruni's sentiments on liberty and democracy are set forth at greatest length and with most spirit. Of exceptional interest is the speech attributed to Giano della Bella when the Ordinances of Justice were being discussed in 1292. In it Bruni becomes impassioned about the liberty that meant so much to him. Liberty, he has Giano say, depends on fair laws and fair courts (p. 81). Another speech brings out the fact that the government of Florence is truly democratic, in that the magistrates have no legal right to make promises to an exiled faction without the consent of the people [58]. Liberty is the theme of another speech, the liberty not only of the Florentines but of others too (p. 175). As if to balance this, a citizen of Pisa, the traditional enemy of Florence, speaks out, in the name of liberty, against Giovanni Visconti's proposal to Pisa to join him against the Florentines. The speaker states that it is neither honorable nor useful to break the peace with Florence, for Visconti intends to take away the liberty of Pisa as well as that of Florence (p. 180). Liberty is at the core of a speech made before the Emperor by an Arretine who opposes the return of a former tyrant (p. 192). A Florentine speaker, in warning against Gian Galeazzo Visconti and in urging preparedness, harps on the danger to Florentine liberty (p. 242). When, during the war

[58] P. 120. This is a reply to a speech on p. 119.

with Gian Galeazzo, the Bolognese allies of Florence wanted to make peace, the Florentines emphasized the importance of liberty and the danger of slavery (p. 251). As a result, the Bolognese fought harder than ever. Later on, in this same war, a Florentine, upbraiding his fellow citizens for letting nearby cities be brought under the power of the Milanese, repeatedly mentions liberty (p. 276).

I have said that Bruni was indebted in part to Salutati for the emphasis on liberty. During the war with Gregory XI, Salutati, as Chancellor of the Republic, wrote scores of letters to other Italian states; in these he kept hammering away on the idea of liberty and freedom from foreign domination and reminded all his correspondents that it was among Italians that liberty first sprouted[59]. It is not surprising, then, that Bruni devotes his longest speech—142 lines—to this war (p. 211). In it the Florentine spokesman reminds the Pope that lawful government was established for the benefit and utility of the governed. The word liberty occurs but once in this speech but tyrant (tyranny) and slave (slavery) each occurs six times.

Thus long before Hegel, history was to Bruni the history of liberty, and, I suspect, Bruni's definition of liberty might be much closer to that of most of us than is Hegel's.

Closely associated with liberty is virtue. In commenting on the decline of ancient Rome during the Empire, Bruni says that, after liberty gave way before the emperor, virtue too disappeared (p. 14, 18). For previously it was through virtue that the way to office had been open. When the reins of government passed into the hands of single individuals, then virtue and greatness of spirit became suspect. This is obviously Ciceronian language and doctrine, derived in turn from the Stoics[60]. Both thought of participation in civic affairs as the great virtue. Bruni quotes with favor the view of the philosophers, notably the Stoics, that

---

[59] Of these letters 130 are published in Rigacci's edition.

[60] Cf. Bruni's « cessit libertas imperatorio nomini » with Cicero's « libertatem nostram armis tuis cedere » (*Phil.* II, 20). Cicero discusses the four cardinal virtues at length in *Off.* I, 18 ff. He concludes (153) that justice, being applicable to society, is the most important (cf. *Fin.* V, 65-66). Cicero often uses *magnitudo animi* as a synonym or near synonym for *fortitudo,* one of the four virtues. *Magnanimi* should fight for liberty (*Off.* I, 68).

man is an « animale civile » and counts it in Dante's favor that he fought for his country and took part in civic affairs [61].

In 1325 a change was made in the selection of magistrates, from the ballot to the lot (p. 121, 36). Bruni deplores that new method as bringing about a lowering of standards, a snuffing out of the enthusiasm for virtue since men are more circumspect when they have to fight with ballots and risk their reputations. Clearly Bruni is one of those who helped to transmute Ciceronian *virtus* into Machiavelli's *virtù* [62].

While the traditional accounts of Bruni, especially that of Fueter, seem to me to be completely wrong, I do not want to give the impression that he was a perfect historian. His annalistic method, inherited from his sources, is out of harmony with modern practice. There is, from the standpoint of recent trends, an overemphasis on war. The net result is that, despite his supposedly rhetorical tendency, long stretches of his work, especially where he follows Villani, are arid and furnish dull reading. His Latinity is far from perfect. Yet he searched widely for source material, his critical judgment of his sources was sound, he sought for underlying causes, he tried to see events in proper perspective, and he was, therefore, the first modern historian.

[61] *La vita di Dante*, in Baron, *op. cit.*, pp. 54, 68. Cf. the Preface to his translation of Aristotle's *Politics, ibid.*, p. 73, to the effect that man is a weak animal and gains strength and perfection through association with fellow citizens («ex civili societate»). Marsilius of Padua, drawing from the same source, speaks of *civilis virtus* (I, 16, 14). Bruni and Marsilius also hold similar views on the derivation of the imperial power from the people (I, 12, 9; II, 26, 5). These similarities are probably due to Aristotelian and other ancient inspiration rather than borrowing by Bruni from Marsilius.

[62] Cf. Hans Baron, «Cicero and the Roman Civic Spirit in the Middle Ages and the Early Renaissance», *Bulletin of the John Rylands Library*, 22, No. 1 (1938), p. 3; «Das Erwachen des historischen Denkens im Humanismus des Quattrocento», *Historische Zeitschrift*, 147 (1933), p. 5. Machiavelli's *virtù* has been described as the exercise of liberty by F. Ercole, «L'etica di Machiavelli», in *Politica*, VI (1920), p. 12.

CHAPTER XVII

MANUSCRIPTS
OF DUKE HUMPHREY OF GLOUCESTER [1]

Duke Humphrey of Gloucester, brother, son, and uncle of kings, as he styled himself, was a very important figure in introducing Italian humanism into England in the fifteenth century. It has been said that he did for England what Petrarch did for the world, but that is scarcely true, for the fire which he lighted smoldered for a long time, if it did not die out completely. At any rate, Humphrey employed Italian humanists, such as Bruni and Decembrio, to buy books and translate Greek classics for him and was regarded, even in Italy, as a leading patron of literature. He made splendid donations of manuscripts to the University of Oxford. Of these, not one remained there, and, so far as is known, only six or seven have since returned to Oxford; three or four are now in the Bodleian Library; three more are in Oxford colleges. Others have found a home in the British Museum, Bibliothèque Nationale, and elsewhere. Vickers describes twenty-three which without question belonged to Humphrey [2]. At the most, including doubtful examples, he can list twenty-six. Craster accepts one of the doubtful ones as well as one not listed by Vickers. Weiss adds two. In two cases, two manuscripts seem to have been bound together after Humphrey's time. Four more can be added. This would give us a maximum of thirty-six.

---

[1] Originally published in the *English Historical Review,* LII (1937), p. 670. With permission of Longmans, Green & Co. Ltd.

[2] K. H. Vickers, *Humphrey Duke of Gloucester* (London, 1907), pp. 426 ff. See also below.

An addition which can be made to Vickers' list is in some ways of peculiar interest. It is a manuscript of Coluccio Salutati's *De laboribus Herculis*[3] now in the Urbinas collection in the Vatican (lat. 694). How it got there I do not know. On fol. 1r occurs the name, partly erased, of Babington, written in the sixteenth century in the same script as in British Museum, Harl. 647[4]. This Babington is supposed to be a member of the family from Dethick, co. Derby[5]. Also on fol. 1r is an erased inscription which, after close study of the manuscript by ultra-violet light and of a photograph, yielded the letters ... *bien ... dain Gloucestre*. This it was possible to complete as *moun bien mondain* from a statement of Leland to the effect that Humphrey often wrote this motto at the beginning of his books[6]. A photograph made under ultra-violet rays which I received after making this decipherment brings out all the missing letters. Until now no manuscript of Humphrey's has been known in which the motto occurs. Vickers indeed seems somewhat sceptical about Leland's statement and implies that he confused Humphrey and Gilbert Kymer, who is known to have used this motto[7]. The explanation of the coincidence is simply that Kymer, who was Gloucester's physician and confidential assistant, and who was one of the two men who acted for Gloucester in the presentation of 129 volumes to Oxford in 1439, copied his master's motto. It should be added that the script of the motto and of the name in Urb. lat. 694 agrees exactly with that of Humphrey found in his other manuscripts[8].

---

[3] The *editio princeps* of this work is *Colucii Salutati De laboribus Herculis*, ed. B. L. Ullman (Zurich, 1951).

[4] The flourish at the end is especially to be noted. In the Harley manuscript the name is spelled with 'y'.

[5] E. A. Bond, H. Thompson, F. Warner, *Catalogue of Ancient Manuscripts in the British Museum*, II, Latin (London, 1884), p. 69. Dr. R. W. Hunt informed me, on the authority of Prof. Neil Ker, that this Babington was Francis, rector of Lincoln College, Oxford, who died in 1569.

[6] *Ioannis Lelandi Antiquarii de Rebus Britannicis Collectanea*, ed. T. Hearnius, III (Oxford, 1715), p. 58. Reproduced inaccurately by W. D. Macray, *Annals of the Bodleian Library*, ed. 2 (Oxford, 1890), p. 400.

[7] *Op. cit.*, p. 410.

[8] A facsimile of his signature from British Museum, Harl. 1705 is given on Pl. 11 and in Vickers, *op. cit.*, p. 360.

Not only that, but on fol. 179v an erasure of two lines seemed to carry the name of Humphrey as written by himself. The formula usually begins « Cest liure est a moy homfrey duc de gloucestre » in the first line, with the name of the donor in the second, as may be seen in Vickers' facsimile [9]. That apparently was the formula in the Vatican manuscript. I made out, somewhat doubtfully, as follows (the completely invisible letters are in parenthesis): « (C)est l(iure) est a (mo)y h(om)f(re)y (duc de glouce)stre ». The receipt of an ultra-violet light photograph makes certain even the letters I have just characterized as invisible. The rest of the inscription, almost as long as the preceding, is less certain. The first words are probably *du don*, followed by a word of 7-8 letters of which very little can be deciphered. The most likely guess is that it was *maistre*, which Humphrey uses several times at this point in his inscriptions; in fact, there are traces of what may have been *st*. More definite and important are the next two words, which I read as *(and)reu Holes*. The first two letters cannot be made out at all, and there is just enough of the third to say that it might have been *d*. On the other hand, I am confident about *reu*. The second, fourth, and fifth letters of *Holes* are quite clear. The first letter seems to have a different shape from that in the name of Humphrey. Andrew Holes was acquainted with Piero del Monte, who was what might be called Humphrey's humanistic advisor and who helped Humphrey obtain manuscripts [10]. Another mutual friend was Thomas Bekynton [11]. Holes spent thirteen years in Italy, five of them in Florence, where he bought many manuscripts, particularly, we may assume, from Vespasiano da Bisticci, the well-known bookseller, who, perhaps on account of his profitable dealings with Holes, included this Englishman in his famous *Vite di uomini illustri*. Vespasiano tells us that Holes stayed an extra year and a half in Florence to get books copied

[9] Other manuscripts in which it has not been erased are, besides Harl. 1705, British Museum, Royal 5 F. II; 16 G. VI; 19 C. IV; Cotton Nero E. V, Oxford: Bodleian, Duke Humfrey d. 1 (S. C. 2934); Hatton 36 (S. C. 4082); Corpus Christi 243; Paris: Bibliothèque Nationale, lat. 7805. See Pl. 12.

[10] R. Weiss, *Humanism in England During the Fifteenth Century* (Oxford, 1941, 1957), p. 26.

[11] *Ibid.*, p. 73.

for him, and then had to return to England by sea because his collection was too large to transport by land [12]. It seems not unlikely that Holes bought the Coluccio manuscript in Florence and sent or took it to Humphrey.

Savage asked some questions which this gift of Holes to Humphrey can answer in part: « What became of these books [which Holes collected]?—did he collect for his own use?—or was he acting merely for Duke Humfrey or the king—or did he leave them, as it is said, to his Church? » [13]. Since our volume was a gift of Holes to Humphrey, Holes is not likely to have collected his books as agent for the Duke. But Savage's remark was in a way prophetic, in that he saw the possibility of a relationship between Holes' library and that of the Duke.

One other matter of interest is that the manuscript has a tables of contents written in England in the early fifteenth century, probably for Duke Humphrey (fols. 179v-181r). The flyleaf has on it V with an S above it, apparently for *quintus*. The coat of arms on fol. 1r is not Humphrey's but appears to be of the fifteenth century, though the initials E S next to it seem to be a little later. These initials appear also on fol. 181r, obviously entered after the book was bound, as the letters blotted on the preceding page.

The *De laboribus Herculis* was not the only work of Coluccio's owned by Humphrey. Among the books he presented to Oxford in 1439 was a volume of *Epistolae Collusii* [14]. As to how and when he obtained this volume, we might venture a guess

---

[12] Vespasiano da Bisticci, *Vite di uomini illustri* (Florence, 1938), p. 256. Weiss, *op. cit.*, p. 78, assumes that Holes stayed in Florence only the year and a half, but he must have gone there in 1439 or soon after (we know he was there in 1441) and stayed till 1444, a year and a half after the Papal Court left for Rome. Holes' purchase of the Coluccio manuscript perhaps indicates that he had greater humanistic leanings than Weiss is willing to grant. Cf. W. F. Schirmer, *Der englische Frühhumanismus* (Leipzig, 1931), p. 106. Bodleian 247 (S. C. 2443) was once owned by Holes.

[13] Ernest A. Savage, *Old English Libraries* (London, 1911), p. 192.

[14] Henry Anstey, *Munimenta Academica,* Part II (London, 1868), p. 764; also in his *Epistolae Academicae Oxon.,* Part I (Oxford 1898), p. 183. For the spelling *Collusii* compare *Boccasius* in the same list. The same spelling is found in a British Museum manuscript of the letters (Cotton Cleop. C. V), which, however, shows no signs of having belonged to Humphrey. However, its contents are such as to indicate some relation to the Duke's books (see chapter IX).

that Holes purchased it soon after his arrival in Florence or that
Zano Castiglione, bishop of Bayeux, who was commissioned by
Humphrey to buy books for him in Italy, acquired it when he
attended the Council of Florence in 1439. If such was the case,
then Humphrey did not retain the manuscript very long, for
in November of that year the University of Oxford acknowledged
the receipt of this and other manuscripts [15].

Humphrey gave about three hundred books to Oxford in his
lifetime and left all his remaining Latin books to the university
in his will, though it did not actually receive them, despite
numerous attempts to obtain its rights. From the list of books
presented to Oxford, Schirmer drew the inference that Humphrey's humanism was not very deep, for most of the books are
such as might be found in any mediaeval library [16]. But this
inference is scarcely justified, for, in the first place, an examination of other humanistic libraries reveals a large number of mediaeval works. For example, that thoroughgoing humanist, Pico
della Mirandola, owned very many mediaeval books [17]. In the
second place, it is altogether likely that Humphrey reserved for
himself many humanistic manuscripts and gave Oxford those
books which interested him least and those which were most
needed for the university's traditional curriculum. That, in fact,
is clearly indicated by an examination of the donations which
Humphrey made. In 1439 he presented 129 volumes, very few
of which can be called humanistic. There are seventeen volumes
of pagan Latin authors (including such mediaeval favorites as
Priscian), a Plato, six humanistic works (three by Petrarch) [18],

---

[15] In the *Bodleian Quarterly Record*, I (1914-16), p. 131, the three lists
of books given by Humphrey to Oxford are thrown together in one alphabetical
list by Craster, and the items are, as far as possible, identified. John Capgrave's
commentary on Exodus (Oxford, Bodleian, MS. Duke Humfrey b. 1) is a
Humphrey item not in Vickers' list. Furthermore, the identification of Auct.
F. 5. 27 (S. C. 2143) (Bruni's translation of Aristotle's *Politics*) as a Humphrey
book, called doubtful by Vickers, is accepted by Craster.

[16] *Op. cit.*, pp. 56 ff. But cf. Weiss, *op. cit.*, pp. 61 ff.

[17] See the catalogue in Pearl Kibre, *The Library of Pico della Mirandola*
(New York, 1936), and the statement (p. 62) that over a third of the Latin
books were theological, not to mention other mediaeval types of literature.

[18] They are attributed merely to Franciscus in the list and are therefore
not placed with the Petrarch items in *Bodleian Quarterly Record*, I (1914-16),

two of Bruni's translations of Aristotle, Beccaria's translation of Athanasius. A gift of ten books in 1441 includes six volumes of Augustine, one of Rabanus, a Livy, a Seneca concordance, and a book on mathematics. In 1444 Humphrey presented 134 volumes, among which the humanistic books are much more frequent. There are over twenty pagan Latin works, about twenty-five humanistic (seven of Petrarch), eight or more humanistic translations of Plutarch, Aeschines, and Plato. Of all the manuscripts listed in a catalogue made in 1452 of the King's College Library, Cambridge, only one is still there, No. 27. Since this probably belonged to Humphrey, James makes the not unlikely suggestion that some of the others listed may have come from the same source, being those bequeathed to Oxford but not delivered [19]. Henry VI had founded King's College just six years before Humphrey's death and might well have decided to favor it with the Duke's library. James notes the « unusually distinguished character » given to the library by the presence, in the midst of typical mediaeval books, of humanistic translations of Plato (*Phaedrus, Republic*) and Plutarch (lives of Agis and Cleomenes), of Poggio's *De avaritia*, and of classical Latin works (such as Seneca's *Tragedies*, a Renaissance favorite).

Humphrey's requests for books in his correspondence with Candido Decembrio reveal a strong classical and humanistic tendency [20]. Humphrey asks for such books as Celsus, Pliny,

---

p. 133, but the titles and the first word on the second leaf (which the old list gives) make the identification certain. For the *Rerum memorandarum*, Anstey gives as the first word of the second folio *annis,* which is found in the appropriate place in the text of that work (p. 393, edition of 1581), whereas Craster gives *armis.* Similarly for the *De remediis* Anstey gives *exempla,* Craster *extra* or *exempla*; the printed text of the *praefatio* has *exempla.* The entry *Victorius de architectura* (*Mun. Acad.*, p. 771) is an error for Vitruvius. The first words on the second folio are given as *quia et liberationum*; Vitruvius has *que et librationum* (I, 1, 4). Vitruvius is one of the authors that Humphrey requested, as mentioned in the next paragraph.

[19] M. R. James, *A Descriptive Catalogue of the Manuscripts Other than Oriental in the Library of King's College, Cambridge* (Cambridge, 1895), p. 70. See too A. N. L. Munby, in *Transactions of the Cambridge Bibliographical Society,* I (1949-53), p. 280.

[20] *English Historical Review,* XIX (1904), pp. 509 ff.

Apuleius, Varro, Cato, Florus, Cicero, Censorinus, Columella, Vitruvius, Pomponius Mela, Festus, Ptolemy. Over forty books were sent by Decembrio, most of which were probably of the same type.

Existing books which have been identified as Humphrey's but do not figure in the Oxford lists include humanistic translations of Plato (2), Plutarch, and Athanasius (2), two Psalters, a medical treatise, Matthew Paris, a work of Coluccio, an English Bible, an English translation of Palladius, French translations of Livy, Boccaccio, Vegetius, and the Bible, and three other French books. This gives about as high a proportion of humanistic books as could be expected, especially when we note that Humphrey obviously retained some of the non-humanistic books on account of their beautiful illuminations. Six of the non-humanistic books, as well as several of the others, are in this category.

On the whole then, we can say with confidence that Humphrey's collection of perhaps five hundred volumes definitely revealed his humanistic interests and formed a library that any Italian prince of his time would have been glad to own.

One of Humphrey's books was given to him by a person of some interest who has not been properly identified, partly because Vickers misread his name. A Bodleian manuscript (Hatton 36) was given Humphrey by Gulielmus Erardus (Erart), sometimes confused with Gulielmus Evrardus (Evrard). Vickers read the name as Erare. This Erart was one of the judges at the trial of Jeanne d'Arc and one of her most violent opponents [21]. He preached a sermon denouncing her before the assembled people of Rouen. Jeanne stated that her « voices », Sts. Catherine and Margaret, told her to answer Erart boldly, whereupon she called him a false preacher. Champion comments that he was « anglais de coeur ». He was in the employ of the English king as early as 1429, two years before Jeanne's trial. Later he went to England, where he died. In the manuscript he gave Humphrey the latter says (fol. 119v): « Du don Maistre Guillem Errard docteur en theologie chanoyne Nostre

---

[21] P. Champion, *Procès de condamnation de Jeanne d'Arc* (Paris, 1920-21), I, pp. 364 ff., 375, 381, etc.; II, p. 413, n. 498, etc.

Dame de Rouen » [22]. This then is the man whom Vickers calls « an insignificant canon of Rouen » (p. 417)! Erart obtained the canonry in 1432. Another entry in the manuscript (fol. 134v) calls him « chanoyne de Paij », though the last word, which may stand for Paris but which Vickers read as « Ram », is uncertain. Erart became a canon of Notre Dame of Paris in 1434. Perhaps Erart's gift was made between 1432 and 1434, and Humphrey's second inscription was written in 1434 or later, after Erart returned to Paris. The manuscript contains letters of Nicholas de Clamanges, an incipient humanist whom Erart must have known in the University of Paris. One of Clamanges' letters is in fact addressed to Erart.

Another, though lesser, participant in Jeanne's trial was a close friend of Humphrey's and donor of a volume in his patron's collection: Zano Castiglione, bishop of Lisieux, later of Bayeux [23]. He too is called « anglais de coeur » by Champion. Just when he and Humphrey became acquainted, we do not know. Whether Zano's opposition to Jeanne was the cause or result of friendship with the English, notably Humphrey, is uncertain. Schirmer suggested that he may have met Humphrey when he swore allegiance to the English king on January 26, 1431 [24]. Still it is unlikely that Humphrey was in France that year. Zano's letter attacking Jeanne was written May 14 of the same year, and she was burned at the stake on May 30. This may all be pure coincidence, but it suggests some possibilities worth investigating [25].

The following list of volumes belonging to Gloucester is of course based chiefly on Vickers. I have included, wherever possible, that part of Humphrey's ownership inscription which follows the usual « Cest livre... Gloucestre », partly to indicate the nature of the formula as a justification for my reading of the Vatican entry, partly to reveal the names of the donors, on some

[22] *A Summary Catalogue of Western Manuscripts in the Bodleian Library at Oxford*, II, 2 (Oxford, 1937), p. 833.

[23] Champion, *op. cit.*, I, p. 298; II, p. 407, n. 445.

[24] Schirmer, *op. cit.*, p. 29.

[25] Was the John Grey who guarded Jeanne while she was in jail related to the Henry Grey who married Humphrey's daughter in 1437? Probably not.

of whom I have added comments. I have tried to correct Vickers' numerous errors in the inscriptions, in part from my own examination of some of the manuscripts, in part from catalogues.

1. Oxford, Bodleian, Hatton 36 (S. C. 4082). Nicholas de Clamanges, *Epistolae*. For the inscriptions, etc., see above.

2. Oxford, Bodleian, MS Duke Humfrey b. 1 (S. C. 32386) John Capgrave, Commentary on Exodus. Not in Vickers but added by Craster. The *Summary Catalogue* states that the manuscript is in the same hand as Oriel 32, i.e., that of the author, John Capgrave. Both manuscripts have sixteenth-century marginalia by the same hand.

3. Oxford, Bodleian, MS. Duke Humfrey d. 1 (formerly Auct. F. 2. 23) (S. C. 2934). Pliny, *Epistolae*.

4. Oxford, Bodleian, Auct. F. 5. 27 (S. C. 2143). Aristotle, *Politics*, translated into Latin by Leonardo Bruni. Humphrey's ownership is slightly doubtful.

5. Oxford, Corpus Christi 243. Plato *Phaedo* and *Meno,* etc., in Latin. « Du don ... treschier (i.e., tres cher) en Dieu labbe de seint Albon ». The missing word (4-5 letters) was perhaps Jehan. The abbot of St. Albans was the famous Whethamstede.

6. Oxford, Oriel 32. John Capgrave, Commentary on Genesis. « Du don frere Jehan Capgrave quy le me fist presenter a mon manoir de Pensherst jour de lan lan [M]CCCCXXXVIII ».

7. Oxford, Magdalen 37. Ptolemy, *Cosmographia*, Plutarch, *Marius*, translated into Latin by Antonio Pacino, etc. This manuscript seems originally to have consisted of two separate volumes.

8. British Museum, Harl. 33. William of Ockham.

9. British Museum, Harl. 1705. Plato, *Republic*, translated into Latin by Pier Candido Decembrio « Du don P. Candidus secretaire du duc de Mylan ».

10. British Museum, Cotton Nero E. V. Decrees of the Council of Constance. « Lequel jachetay des executeurs maistre Thomas Polton feu eveque de Wurcestre ». Polton died in 1433.

11. British Museum, Royal 2 B. I. Psalms

12. British Museum, Royal 5 F. II. Athanasius, translated into Latin by Antonio Beccaria. « Le quel jai fait translater de grec en latyn par Antoyne de Becaria Veroneys mon serviteur ». Bound with this is another volume of Athanasius. « Le quel je fis translater de grec en latyn par un de mes secretaires Antoyne de Beccara ne de Verone ».

13. British Museum, Royal 14 C. VII. Matthew Paris, *Historia Anglorum.*

14. British Museum, Royal 16 G. VI. *Chroniques de France.* « Du don les exsecuteurs le seigneur de Faunhope ». Vickers' number, 15 G. VI, is an error. The donor is identified as Sir John Chandos, who was lord of the manor of Fownhope and who died in 1428, by G. F. Warner and J. P. Gilson, *Catalogue of Western Manuscripts in the Old Royal and King's Collections,* II (London, 1921), p. 212.

15. British Museum, Royal 19 C. IV. *Le Songe du Vergier.*

16. British Museum, Egerton 617-618. Bible. Ownership doubtful.

17. British Museum, Sloane 248. Albucasis, *Antidotarium.*

18. British Museum, Add. 39810. Psalter. When Vickers wrote his book this manuscript belonged to Henry Yates Thompson, 58.

19. London, Sion College, Arc. L. 40. 2-L. 26. Doubtful (R. Weiss, *Humanism in England During the Fifteenth Century,* Oxford, 1957, p. 188). I found no reference to this manuscript in Guil. Reading, *Bibliothecae Cleri Londinensis in Collegio Sionensi Catalogus* (London, 1724). Nor was there any in Syon monastery, though Mary Bateson, *Catalogue of the Library of Syon Monastery* (Cambridge, 1898), p. XVI, says: « The absence of Humphrey of Gloucester [from the names of donors] is surprising, as he was interested in the house ». The catalogue was made in the sixteenth century.

20. Wentworth-Woodhouse, Z. i. 32. Palladius, in English. Dr. R. W. Hunt informed me that the Bodleian Library has a complete photostat (Arch. F. d. 1; Summary Catalogue 31502). Humphrey received the manuscript between 1439 and 1446.

21. Cambridge, University Library Ee. 2, 17. Aegidius Romanus, *De regimine principum* (fragment), Vegetius, both in French. « Du don mess Robert Roos chevalier mon cousin ».

22. Cambridge, King's College 27. Athanasius, translated into Latin by A. Beccaria. Ownership somewhat doubtful.

23. Paris, Bibliothèque Nationale, lat. 7805. *Panegyrici Latini*, including Pliny's *Panegyric*, which Weiss, *op. cit.*, p. 63, listed as a separate manuscript.

24. Paris, Bibliothèque Nationale, lat. 8537. Cicero, *Epistolae ad Brutum, Q. fratrem, Atticum* (not the *Ad familiares*, as Weiss [*op. cit.*, p. 62] and Craster say). It is presumably the *Ad Quintum fratrem* mentioned in the list of Humphrey's gifts to Oxford. « Du don Reverend piere en Dieu Zanon eveque de Bayeux ». Zano Castiglione became bishop of Bayeux in 1432.

25. Paris, Bibliothèque Nationale, lat. 10209. Petrarch, *De remediis utriusque fortunae*. Copied in 1432. In the line after Humphrey's inscription all that can be made out are the last letters: 'bucy' (R. Weiss in *Bodleian Library Record*, V, 1955, p. 123).

26. Paris, Bibliothèque Nationale, fr. 2. Bible, in French. Given by Sir John Stanley.

27. Paris, Bibliothèque Nationale, fr. 12421. Boccaccio, *Decameron*, in French. « Du don mon tres chier cousin le conte de Warewic ».

28. Paris, Bibliothèque Nationale, fr. 12583. *Le Roman de Renard*.

29. Paris, Bibliothèque de Ste. Geneviève, fr. 777. Livy, in French.

30. Stonyhurst College. Henry of Lancaster, *Livre des Seintes Medicines*. « Du don du baron de Carew ». This manuscript is not listed by Vickers; see E. J. Arnould, *Bulletin of the Rylands Library*, 21 (1937), p. 352 and his edition, Oxford, 1940 (Anglo-Norman Texts, II), p. ix. Carew died in 1429.

31. London, College of Arms, Arundel 12. Frulovisi, *Vita Henrici Quinti*. Weiss, *op. cit.*, p. 65, n. 6, suggests this

as a probable Humphrey manuscript. William Henry Black, in his privately printed *Catalogue of the Arundel Manuscripts in the Library of the College of Arms* (London, 1829), states that the manuscript bears the coat of arms of the Duke.

32. Brussels, Bibliothèque Royale, MS 9627-8. French Arthurian romances: *Queste del Saint Graal* and *Mort Artus.* Ca. 1300. Erased ownership mark on fol. 157v (*Bodleian Library Record*, IV, 1952-3, p. 124).

33. Leiden, University Library, MS Scal. Hebr. 8. Hebrew psalter. Twelfth century (G. I. Lieftinck, in *Transactions of the Cambridge Bibliographical Society*, II, 1955, p. 97.

34. Rome, Vatican, Urb. lat. 694. See above.

CHAPTER XVIII

MANUSCRIPTS OF NICHOLAS OF CUES [1]

Cardinal Nicholas of Cues (1401-64) is best known as church-man and philosopher, but he came into contact with the Renaissance movement while a student of law in Padua and made the personal acquaintance of a number of leading Italian humanists, especially at the Council of Basel [2]. Before that he had become famous, if not notorious, to all humanists by his discoveries and supposed discoveries of manuscripts of Latin authors. Great excitement was caused by the announcement made to the humanistic world in 1426 by the famous Guarino that Nicholas had found eight hundred very old manuscripts in Cologne. These were said to include the complete *De re publica* of Cicero, Pliny's history of the German wars, and a complete Gellius. The first turned out to be the well-known sixth book, *Somnium Scipionis,* the Pliny was the usual *Natural History*, and the Gellius was like all the others. Nicholas so far turned out to be as disappointing as his countryman who asserted that he had found a complete Livy. But Nicholas won his humanistic spurs when he produced a manuscript of Plautus containing twelve plays not previously known. By this find he took his place among the great discoverers of the age. He accumulated a large library, which he left to the « hospital » (an old man's home) which he founded at Cues. Some 270 of them are still there [3]. To this

---

[1] Originally published in *Speculum,* XIII (1938), p. 194.

[2] Perhaps the best general account of Nicholas is that by Edmond Vansteenberghe, *Le Cardinal Nicholas de Cues* (Paris, 1920). The best discussion of his books is in R. Sabbadini, *Le scoperte dei codici latini e greci ne' secoli XIV e XV*, I (Florence, 1905), pp. 109 ff., and II (1914), pp. 16 ff.

[3] This is the estimate of J. Marx, *Verzeichnis der Handschriften-Sammlung des Hospitals zu Cues* (Trier, 1905), p. vii. Not all of the 314 Cues manuscripts

number Sabbadini adds eleven now at Brussels, two in the Vatican, twenty-two in the British Museum[4]. In a valuable article, Lehmann reports a total of twenty-five in the British Museum[5]; he overlooks Sabaddini's account and states that the largest number previously mentioned was fifteen, given by Weinberger. It is my purpose to add ten more to the list and thus to bring the number up to thirty-five.

Harl. 2497. I have not myself seen this manuscript, but Miss Johnson[6] states that it was formerly the property of the hospital of St. Nicholas of Cues. It is a fifteenth-century paper manuscript of Pliny's *Letters*, a work not now represented in the library of Cues.

Harl. 2652. On fol. 1: « liber hospit. sancti Ni... ». Contains Plato (Chalcidius), *Timaeus*; Macrobius, *In somnium Scipionis*. Perhaps this is the copy of the latter mentioned by Poggio which Sabbadini listed among the missing (II, p. 27). Twelfth century.

Harl. 2724. The identification of this as a Nicholas manuscript depends on the statement in Wanley's diary[7]: « quondam peculium Nicolai Cardinalis Cusani », and again: « Hic codex olim peculium Nicolai Cardinalis Cusani ». There is no sign left now in the manuscript of Nicholas' ownership, but a strip 50 mm. high has been cut from the bottom of fol. 1, and this perhaps contained the ownership mark. There is, too, an erasure

were in the library of the Cardinal: 67 are certainly from that source. In his review of the first edition of the present book (*Scriptorium*, X, 1956, p. 333), Masai mentions only 37. He was misled by the « Index codicum qui olim fuerunt Nicolai de Cusa » in the edition of Nicholas' *De pace fidei* by R. Klibansky and H. Bascour (*Mediaeval and Renaissance Studies, Supplement* III, 1956). This Index does not list *all* the manuscripts of Nicholas but only those mentioned in the notes of this edition.

[4] *Op. cit.*, II, p. 26. The B. M. number 3478 is an error for 3487. In I, p. 112, n. 27, Sabbadini mentions Harl. 2773; thus he really refers to twenty-three.

[5] *Sitzungsberichte der Bayerischen Akademie der Wissenschaften, Phil.-hist. Abt.*, 1930, 2, p. 20.

[6] *Classical Philology*, VII (1912), p. 70, n. 8.

[7] British Museum Lansdowne 772, fol. 11, No. 63. Under date of 18 January, 1723/4 Wanley states that the manuscripts in the list just quoted were purchased, and that in each this date will be entered. This date is found in Harl. 2724 and 2728 and confirms the identification of them with Nos. 63 and 71 in the list. These seem to be the only Nicholas items in the list; others are found in a list given under date of 24 August, 1723.

of some sort on fol. 1. The manuscript (136 fols., s. XII) contains Horace fols. 2r-130r) in the order *Carm., A. P., Epod., C. S., Epist., Serm.* Fols 1 v, 131 v have definitions of Greek words; fol. 130r a life of Horace; fol. 130v names of the Furies, etc.; fols. 132r-135v (different hand) life of Horace, etc. A gathering is missing after fol. 25. There is no Horace in the present Cues library.

Harl. 2728. This too owes its identification as a Nicholas manuscript to Wanley's diary (No. 71): « olim peculium Nicolai Cardinalis Cusani ». There is now no trace of this ownership; perhaps it has been carefully erased. The manuscript (152 fols., s. X/XI) contains Lucan with a commentary, written in several hands, with some old characteristics, such as the *rt* ligature. There is no Lucan now in the Cues library. A note in Wanley's diary for 17 June, 1723, shows that Bentley borrowed this manuscript and returned it on June 22.

Harl. 2738. On the bottom of fol. 1r: « liber hospitalis sancti Nicolai prope Cusam ». Fols. 49, s. XIII. Fols. 1 and 49 contain examples of logic; fols. 2r-48v contain Ovid's *Fasti*. On fol. 48v appears the note: « Fulco de Corbeia debet 1 s pro ordine t. Liber Iohannis ». Nicholas refers to Ovid's *Fasti* (Vansteenberghe, p. 238). There is no Ovid now in the Cues library.

Harl. 4241. At the bottom of flyleaf 2: « liber hospitalis sancti Nicolai prope Cusam Treverensis diocesis d(ono?) Car(dinalis?) ». The last word is abbreviated Car¹'. Parchment manuscript of the fifteenth century in a German imitation of Italian humanistic script (88 fols.). Contains Latin translation of Aristotle's *Metaphysics*. There are three copies of this work in the present Cues library (182, 183, 184).

Harl. 5098. On fol. 1: « liber hospitalis sancti Nicolai prope Cusam ». Thirteenth-century French script (70 fols). Contains *Theorica pantegni*, translated by Constantinus Africanus. This work occurs in Cues 310.

Harl. 5588. Lehmann includes this manuscript in the list which he quotes from Weinberger but does not give it in his own list[8]. It is a paper manuscript of the thirteenth century

---

[8] Sabbadini, *op. cit.*, II, p. 26, n. 132, also mentions it.

containing *N. T., Acts*, and *Epistles*, in Greek. It contains (according to the catalogue) the library entry: « Liber hospitalis de Cusa Treverensis diocesis R^{mi} ».

Add. 19952. On fol. 1: « Iste liber est domini Nicolai de Cusa ». To this was added in different ink but apparently by the same hand: « dyocesis Treverensis qui postea factus est cardinalis tituli sancti Petri ad vincula Rome ». Apparently the same hand wrote some Latin-German glosses on this page: « Afflatorium dicitur eyn blaesbalg, id est follis. Labrum dicitur eyne wanne ad purgandum ». On fol. 1 v: « Liber magistri Theodori de Xanctis cancellarii Leodiensis ». A note on a flyleaf (by Madden) indicates that the manuscript was purchased of Dr. Henry Wolff 12 August, 1854. Paper manuscript written in 1445 (not 1472 as in catalogue), containing Marco Polo's *De condicionibus et consuetudinibus orientalium regionum* translated into Latin by Franciscus Pipinus of Bologna (fols. 2r-84v), *noticia de Machometo ... Alcoran ... a fratre G. Anconitani conventus* to the Archdeacon of Liège (fols. 85r-98v), *Tractatus de Talmut* (fols. 99r-111r). On fol. 84v is the subscription: « Ffinitum per me Iohannem de Cusa (*not* Cusera, *as in catalogue*) anno 1445, ipso die Silvestri que est ultima Decembris hora vesperarum V Confluentie ». For this scribe see Cues 12 and 58 as described by Marx. The rest of the manuscript is in a different hand. It may be that this manuscript never was in the hospital at Cues (it lacks the usual library mark) and that it was given to Theodore of Xanten by Nicholas, for the former was a contemporary of Nicholas and became rector of an institute founded by the Cardinal [9].

To be added to this list is Harl. 2668, a twelfth-century manuscript of Virgil's *Eclogues, Georgics*, part of the *Aeneid, Carmina Vergiliana* [10]. On fol. 1: « Liber hospitalis sancti N[icola]i prope Cusam ».

I add a few corrections and supplements to Lehmann's notes.

Harl. 1347. The first part of this fifteenth-century manuscript contains Traversari's translation of Diogenes Laertius.

[9] Vansteenberghe, *op. cit.,* pp. 459-460.

[10] H. Thoma, in *Beiträge zur Geschichte der deutschen Sprache und Literatur,* 73 (1951), p. 256.

This ends on fol. 205v. Lehmann does not note that the hand and the subject matter change completely on fol. 206. The following pages to fol. 296 are ruled for double columns, but only the left columns are written in. On fol. 296 is the subscription: « Ex archetypo reverendi patris domini Petri Balbi episcopi Iohannes Andreas episcopus Acciensis descripsit in castroplaebis dicionis Perusinae fideliter VIII. mensis Decembris MCCCCLXII ». Lehmann and Vansteenberghe [11] wrongly assume that this subscription refers to the Diogenes. Instead it refers to the unidentified sermons on fols. 206-296 [12]. Of these I have been able to identify only one: on fol. 275v a sermon is attributed to John Chrysostom. This is one of the *spuria* given by Migne, *Patr. Gr.*, LII, p. 813, though in a different Latin version. It would seem that all the sermons are translations from the Greek and that the right-hand columns on each page were left blank for the Greek text.

Harl. 3698. The subscription is not quite accurately given by Lehmann:

Expletus est liber. Benedictus deus in secula seculorum. Dum possum dicere 'hoc opo (*sic for* opus) exegi quod nec ionis (*sic for* Iovis) ira nec ignes nec ferrum nec edax poterit abholere vetustas'. Fuit scriptus iste liber anno incarnacionis domini MCCCIIII die sancte Agathee virginis. Hunc qui scribebat Henricus (*in erasure*) nomen habebat de Almania studio medicine vacans (*this word is expunged*) vacans in precl'ari (*sic*) studio Montis Pestulani (*sic*) socius bonus et fidelis. Deo gracias. Amen.

The errors in the subscription show that it was copied from another manuscript. The date 1304 is clearly the date of composition of the work [13]. Lehmann notes that the first part of the subscription (to *virginis*) occurs also in Cues 304.

Harl. 3745. At the end (fol. 190v): « Iste liber pertinet magistro Petro Rodmullir » (*sic,* not « Rodmiller »). The last

---

[11] *Op. cit.,* p. 274, n. 4, p. 438.

[12] Lehmann refers to these in the phrase « einige Homilien » without indicating where they appear in the manuscript.

[13] Cf. J. Destrez, *La Pecia* (Paris, 1935), p. 95, who indicates that the work was begun by Bernard in 1303 and finished soon after.

three words were deleted and the following added: « Nicolaus de Cusa qui emit a magistro fabrice in Lorch istum et alios plures libros in medicina et in artibus que fuerunt illius magistri Petri Rodmullir plebani ibidem pro 80 (*sic*) florenis Rinensibus 1449 » (Lehmann omits the date). Lehmann points out that Cues 294, 307, 308 belonged to the same Rodmullir. They are all medical treatises.

Harl. 5402. A date has been added on fol. 104v: «1421 mense septembris ».

Harl. 5792. This manuscript is called French by Lehmann, Italian or French by E. A. Lowe (*Codices Latini Antiquiores*, II, Oxford, 1935, No. 203). The former dates it « saec. VII ex. », the latter « saec. VII-VIII ». My notes call it « VII? ». Lowe does not mention the presence of the pseudo-Ciceronian *Synonyma* (fols. 260r-272r). The best description of this celebrated manuscript is still that given by G. Goetz in *Corpus Glossariorum Latinorum*, II (Leipzig, 1888), pp. xx ff., though there are a few minor errors.

A list of all the Cues manuscripts thus far brought to light in the British Museum follows: Harl. 1347, 2497, 2620, 2637, 2652, 2668, 2672, 2674, 2724, 2728, 2738, 2773, 3063, 3092, 3261, 3487, 3698, 3702, 3710, 3729, 3734, 3744, 3745, 3748, 3757, 3934, 3992, 4241, 5098, 5402, 5576, 5588, 5692, 5792, Add. 19952. This is a total of thirty-five, as against Lehmann's twenty-five. Though all come from the Cues library (except possibly Add. 19952), some may not have belonged to Nicholas. We can be sure of Harl. 1347, 2724, 2728, 3063, 3092, 3261, 3702, 3710, 3745, 5692, Add. 19952, and we have no reason for rejecting any of the rest.

It seems desirable to list briefly the other known Cues manuscripts besides those listed in Marx' catalogue. I have depended chiefly on Sabbadini, Thomas, and the Brussels catalogue [14]: Brussels 3819-20 (Cat. 2499), 3897-3919 [15], 3920-23,

---

[14] J. van den Gheyn, *Catalogue des manuscrits de la bibliothèque royale de Belgique* (Brussels, 1901-1936), still incomplete; Paul Thomas, *Catalogue des manuscrits de classiques latins* (Gand, 1896).

[15] Given to the hospital by Io. Incus (not Iucus, as in the catalogue,

5092-94 [16], 7882 [17], 8873-77 [18], 9142-45 [19], 9581-95 [20], 9799
9809, 10054-56, 10615-729, 11196-97; Vat. gr. 358, Vat.
lat. 3870.

In addition to these, which bear some statement that
they belonged to Nicholas or to the hospital at Cues, Klibansky-
Bascour list a number of manuscripts which they identify as
Nicholas' by the handwriting of either the text or the notes.
I can neither deny nor confirm that they are right, as I have
not seen the manuscripts nor have I found any detailed analysis
of the writing. The editors are no doubt right about the manuscripts containing Nicholas' own works, as most or all of them
apparently have in them « vidi N. car. etc. ». In the following
list I have placed (N) after the manuscripts that contain Nicholas'
works: Strasbourg, Univ. 84; Brussels 271; Ehrenbreitstein,
Capucin monastery 1; Lobcovic (Prague), 249; London, B. M.
Add. 11035; Munich, Staatsbibl. lat. 23434; Salamanca, Univ.
19 (N); Treves, Civ. 1205/503 (N); Vat. lat. 1245 (N), 3074,
3908 (N). J. Koch adds Vat. lat. 1244 (N) [21].

Well over three hundred of the Cardinal's manuscripts are
known, but he must have had a much larger library. Sabbadini
observes that of fifteen manuscripts of Nicholas mentioned in
contemporary letters, only three have been identified. Of the
many Greek manuscripts which Nicholas acquired at Constanti
nople and elsewhere, only seven have been located. Vansteenberghe points out that Nicholas left many of his books with
friends at Ferrara and that these disappeared [22]. Hardly any of

---

3095) in the sixteenth century and therefore did not belong to Nicholas. The same
donor gave Cues 13 and 110 (see Marx).

[16] Thomas gives no indication of Cues origin; this is therefore doubtful.

[17] Cat. 3188, *Vitae sanctorum* (*s.* XI); once belonged to Joh. Breddendych.

[18] Van den Gheyn (Cat. 3218) gives no indication of Cues origin; it is
therefore doubtful.

[19] Belonged to Nicolas but was never in the hospital.

[20] Labeled (Cues?) by Thomas. The only Cues indication is a « copie moderne », on fols. 168-170, of the *Interrogatio domni Caroli, ex manuscripto Cusano
vetustissimo.* As this work occurs earlier in the old part of the manuscript,
it presumably was the *manuscriptum Cusanum vetustissimum.*

[21] *Sitzungsberichte der Heidelberger Akademie der Wissenschaften* (1936-37),
2, pp. 11-13.

[22] *Op. cit.*, p. 24.

his classical Latin manuscripts are left at Cues. Of the thirty-five Cues manuscripts in the British Museum at least eight can be called classical. Obviously the classical manuscripts were particularly attractive to the buyers who came to Cues, and we may expect that others will turn up, especially in England. On the other hand, there may be more non-classical Cues manuscripts in Brussels. Most of those listed were discovered from Thomas' catalogue of the classical Latin manuscripts in Brussels. Nearly all of these came to that library from the Bollandists. One would expect to find more nonclassical manuscripts (especially, of course, lives of the saints) among the Brussels manuscripts which came from Cues via the Bollandists [23].

[23] In *Forschungen und Fortschritte*, 29 (1955), p. 318, n. 12, K. Manitius casually mentions that there is a Cusanus in Leiden, but he gives no library number. Perhaps he was thinking of Sabbadini's remark in *Le scoperte dei codici latini e greci ne' secoli XIV e XV* (Florence, 1905), p. 113, n. 32, that Nicholas' copy of *Itinerarium Antonini* is recalled by the entry in *Catalogus bibl. publ. Universit. Lugduno-Batavae* (1716), p. 387, which describes a book made in 1615 containing readings from Nicholas' manuscript. In his second volume (1914), p. 27. Sabbadini says that Nicholas' manuscript of this work has disappeared.

CHAPTER XIX

THE DEDICATION COPY OF POMPONIO LETO'S EDITION OF SALLUST AND THE « VITA » OF SALLUST

A number of fifteenth and sixteenth-century editions of Sallust are based on the recension of Pomponio Leto. The first seems to be that printed by Silber at Rome in 1490 (Hain 14217). It includes a dedicatory letter of Leto to his friend Agostino Maffei and a short unsigned biography of the historian. This edition has both a humanistic and a more narrowly classical interest [1].

The editions begin with the letter to Maffei, continue with Sallust's *Catiline, Jugurtha,* and the fragments « ex libris historiarum », and end with the *Vita* of Sallust. Exactly the same contents are found in a neatly written Vatican manuscript, Ottob. lat. 2989, a parchment codex of the fifteenth century. A flyleaf (fol. 146) carries this note: « Reverendissimi et illustrissimi domini B. Cardinalis Maphei ».

Bernardino Maffei, who became a cardinal in 1547, was the great-grandson of Benedetto, the brother of Agostino. The two brothers had come to Rome from Verona in or before 1473 [2]. Agostino started a museum and a library, which passed to the descendants of his brother Benedetto. It therefore seems probable that the volume of Sallust owned by Cardinal Bernardino came

---

[1] Letters of Prof. A. Campana and M. José Ruysschaert to Dr. Curt F. Bühler of the Pierpont Morgan Library indicate that a Vatican copy of this edition (Ross. 441) has marginal notes by Leto, and that the notes in a Morgan copy of the same edition were transcribed from the Vatican copy. M. Ruysschaert wrote me that he knew of another Sallust edition with Leto notes about which he was planning an article.

[2] Benedetto married and bought a house at Rome in that year, according to Scipione Maffei, *Verona illustrata*, Part II (Milan, 1825), pp. 261 ff.

to him from Agostino. In that case the manuscript was the dedication copy presented to Agostino by Leto. The book has the appearance of being just such a copy. Though I made no study of the matter when I examined the manuscript, the writing did not impress me as Leto's, as I recalled it from other manuscripts. It may be possible to identify it as that of one of Leto's copyists. A note on the flyleaf reads: « Emendatus a Pomponio Laeto ». This does not mean that this particular copy was corrected by Leto but merely repeats what Leto says in his letter, that he has emended the corrupt text of Sallust. The early editions repeat this in the phrase « Romae per Pomponium emendata ». In any event, I am convinced that this is the manuscript which Leto presented to Agostino [3]. Leto obtained his copy of the fragments of Sallust's *Histories* directly or indirectly from the celebrated codex Vat. lat. 3864, which came from Corbie [4].

So much for the humanistic side; now for the classical [5]. The *Vita* at the end of the volume in the manuscript and the printed editions has, I suppose, generally been regarded as Leto's,

[3] The manuscript is not mentioned by P. de Nolhac, *La Bibliothèque de Fulvio Orsini* (Paris, 1887), V. Zabughin, *Giulio Pomponio Leto* (Rome, 1909-12), or G. Muzzioli, in *Italia Medioevale e Umanistica,* II (1959), p. 337. Zabughin speaks of an undated edition of Sallust, containing the letter to Maffei, printed at Brescia by Antonio Moretti before the Rome edition of 1490 (II, pp. 61, 66). Zabughin obviously did not see the edition but took the information from Naeke, who in turn falsely interpreted the statement in Leto's letter to Maffei, that he had permitted Antonio Moretti of Brescia to hand the manuscript to his printers (A. F. Naeke, *Opuscula Philologica*, I, Bonn, 1842, pp. 122, 140). In his elaborate index of printers of incunabula, added to W. A. Copinger's *Supplement to Hain's Repertorium Bibliographicum,* II (London, 1902), K. Burger mentions Moretti only once: a book (not Sallust) was printed at Venice in 1500 by Iohannes Hamman « expensis Antonii Moretti ».

[4] Its earlier history is set forth by me in *Philological Quarterly*, I (1922), p. 17; its appearance in Italy in the fifteenth century is discussed by R. Sabbadini in *Bollettino di Filologia Classica,* XXVIII (1922), p. 172. Sabbadini notes that Leto had a copy of the speeches in the *Histories* as early as 1484 in another Vatican manuscript, 3415. According to Zabughin (*op. cit.,* II, p. 112), this manuscript was copied by pupils of Leto. Actually the date is that of the students' notes on Leto's lectures, which occupy most of the manuscript. Zabughin does not mention the Sallust excerpts.

[5] I am indebted to my colleague Walter Allen, Jr., for calling my attention to the problem posed by the *Vita* of Sallust in Leto's edition.

as undoubtedly it is. I am sure too that Leto had no intention of passing the biography off as ancient or of concealing his own authorship. The fact that it occurs in the dedication copy and that there is no indication that it came from any other source than the editor's study seems sufficient proof. But there is some danger that scholars may be led into thinking that this is an ancient biography and into making unwarranted assumptions and assertions. The reason for this fear is this: in the eleventh edition of the *Jugurtha* by R. Jacobs and H. Wirz (Berlin, 1922), A. Kurfess added the Leto *Vita* under the title « Eine Sallustvita » with this introduction:

In der Sallustausgabe des Pomponius Laetus d. h. Ed. Romana vom Jahre 1490, wie die Subscriptio zeigt, findet sich folgende Sallustvita, die es vielleicht verdient, einem grösseren Kreise bekannt gemacht zu werden. Ich gebe gleich unter dem Text die in Betracht kommenden Parallelstellen, soweit sie sich mir bei genauerem Nachforschen ergeben haben, natürlich, ohne den Anspruch auf Vollständigkeit zu erheben.

At the end he sums up:

An sich bringt sie wenig Neues. Es ist dieselbe Art zu kompilieren und kombinieren, wie wir es an anderen Viten gewohnt sind. Die erste Hälfte ist in ihrem Stil nicht uninteressant. Vielleicht geht sie auf eine alte Sallustvita zurück, aus der auch der Deklamator der Invektive sein Material geholt haben mag.

Apparently it did not occur to Kurfess that Leto, a good Latinist, might have been the author. The similarity between the *Invectives* and the *Vita* is due to Leto's drawing on the former. Kurfess even deletes one line as being a gloss! This honor makes a classic out of the *Vita*. It is a *reductio ad absurdum* of the practice of labeling every parenthesis or explanation as a gloss, a nineteenth-century fad, or philology of despair, which it is high time to abandon.

Before proceeding further, it will be useful to print the *Vita* as it is given in the Ottobonianus, though I have modernized the punctuation.

C. CRISPI SALLUSTI VITA

Crispus Sallustius genus ex Amiterno Sabinorum ducit, C. Sallustio patre genitus. Ex liberalibus artibus in quibus educatus erat preter eruditionem nihil accepit: omnibus voluptatibus turpissime indulsit, paternam domum vendidit ut crimine adulterii se redimeret.
5 Ex questura et tribunatu nullam laudem est adsecutus: favente C. Caesare pretor Aphricam sortitus, provinciam expilavit et exhausit tantumque inde pecuniarum reportavit ut amenissimos hortos sub Quirinale extra pomerium ad Collinam portam titulo sui nominis, empto loco, habuerit atque adornaverit, non vulgares illius seculi et poste-
10 rorum etatibus delitias atque secessum, usque ad exactam etatem libidinis avidus et potens. In amicitia varius et inconstans, sepius tamen livido dente momordit.   Habitus est ore improbo et animo inverecundo.   Manis Pompei Magni, existimans hac via se Caesari gratiorem fore, lacerare ausus est.   Unde in Sallustium Laeneus, Pompei
15 libertus, scripsit moresque eius sigillatim paucis vocabulis expressit, nebulonem, lurconem, popinionem, et lastaurum appellans. Vox postrema indicat fuisse hominem validae libidinis.   Scripsit stilo non abhorrente a veteribus. Extant coniuratio Catilinae et bellum Iugurtinum et quedam contiones e libris bellorum civilium.   Ut secreta ini-
20 mici fidelius intelligeret, Terentiam a Cicerone repudiatam duxit uxorem, quae tertio nupsit Messale Corvino.

It should be noted that the manuscript does not have the errors found in the 1490 edition.   It correctly has *contiones* (line 19), *intelligeret* (20), *uxorem* (20), after which it omits *et*.   It has *adornaverit* (9), which Kurfess unnecessarily wants to change to *adamaverit*.   Kurfess finds the expression *delicias atque secessum*, applied to Sallust's famous gardens, strange (« auffallend »). But Pliny has: « Quid agit Comum, tuaeque meaeque deliciae », and « in alto secessu » in the same letter (*Ep.* I, 3, 1, 3), and that was probably Leto's source.

It did not take long for Kurfess' timid little puff of wind to become a strong confident hurricane. O. Gebhardt referred to the *Vita* published by Kurfess as a hitherto unknown biography of Sallust [6].   He thought that one sentence in the *Vita* could be regarded without hesitation as genuine tradition, hardly as an

[6] *Philologische Wochenschrift,* 43 (1923) p. 789.

invention of Renaissance scholarship. The sentence is in line 13. But the next sentence begins with *Unde*, which shows that the two sentences are closely connected. What follows is clearly taken from Suetonius, *De grammaticis* 15, where it is stated that after the death of his patron Pompey, Lenaeus supported himself by teaching school. When Sallust attacked the dead Pompey, Lenaeus replied in a vituperative satire. Leto said the same thing but in different language. He even used the same word as Suetonius, *lacerare*, but made Sallust rather than Lenaeus its subject.

Gebhardt, assuming that the *Vita* was ancient, thought it might have been the work of Asconius. Even our most authoritative history of literature, by Schanz-Hosius, fails to reject the antiquity of the *Vita*, or to attribute it to Leto, contenting itself with saying that the *Vita* scarcely goes back to Asconius, as Gebhardt had suggested[7]. Ernout remarks that the *Vita* contains nothing new and is drawn uncritically from various existing sources but does not definitely pronounce it modern[8]. I have seen no more specific rejection of the biography. Schindler assumes that its author was Leto, but as he does not mention Kurfess, he may have been blissfully unaware of the latter's and Gebhardt's disturbing suggestions[9].

The parallels that Kurfess cites indicate where Leto found most of his material, but a few points remain to be discussed. The *Vita* says that Sallust was « C. Sallustio patre genitus ». The prenomen of the historian's father is, apparently, not mentioned in any ancient source. This is probably a pure inference on Leto's part. Another possibility is that Leto saw the bust of Sallust now generally regarded as spurious which is (or was) in Leningrad (207). This bust, which was once in the Campana collection and which is said to have been found near the Gardens of Sallust, carries the inscription « C. Sal. C. », the last letter of which may have been interpreted as « C. (f.) » instead of

---

[7] M. Schanz, *Geschichte der römischen Literatur*, ed. 4 by C. Hosius, I, 1 (Munich, 1927), p. 362.

[8] *Salluste*, ed. A. Ernout (Paris, 1947), p. 7, n. 2. He is followed by E. Bolaffi, *Sallustio* (Rome, 1949), p. 21, n. 1.

[9] F. Schindler, « Untersuchungen zur Geschichte des Sallustbildes », *Breslauer Abhandlungen zur Altertumswissenschaft*, 1939, Heft 1, p. 10

« C(rispus) ». Even if it is not ancient could it have existed in Leto's time? [10]. Sallust's origin in Sabine Amiternum is mentioned by Jerome in his translation of Eusebius' *Chronicle*. His training in « liberalibus artibus » may be inferred from his own statement in *Cat.* 4, 2.

For Sallust's self-indulgence (lines 3-4) compare the pseudo-Ciceronian *Inv. in Sall.* 13-14: « postea quam immensae gulae quaestus sufficere non potuit... cupiditatibus infinitis efferebaris... Domum paternam, vivo patre, turpissime venalem habuit vendidit ». Such is the reading of nine out of ten of the manuscripts cited by Kurfess in his edition (Leipzig, 1950). The tenth manuscript omits *vendidit,* which Kurfess properly brackets. Leto, obviously using a text like that of most of the manuscripts, omitted the other of the two synonymous expressions. But the sale of the house is not specifically connected in any of our sources with the charge of adultery. The *Invective* mentions Sallust's confession of adultery some fourteen lines after telling of the sale of the house (15). The payment of money to escape the charge of adultery is mentioned by Gellius (XVII, 18). The combination of the two, i.e., the assumption that the sale of the house was due to the necessity of buying himself off from punishment, I attribute to Leto. Between the two passages in the *Invective* (15), Sallust's quaestorship is mentioned, which is the next point brought up in the *Vita* (line 5). But it is the second quaestorship that Leto seems to have had in mind in saying that it gained him no glory; this is described in *Inv. in Sall.* 17 as follows: « quem honorem ita gessit ut nihil in eo non venale habuerit », etc. [11]. Of the tribunate Leto could have gained an unfavorable opinion from Asconius' commentary on Cicero's *Pro Milone* (p. 37 Clark, etc.). Sallust's pillaging of the province of Africa while praetor (lines 6-7) is known from *Inv. in Sall.* 19: « praetor ... provinciam vastavit ... hoc Africam interiorem ob-

---

[10] This possibility is not discussed by J.J. Bernouilli, *Roemische Ikonographie,* I (Stuttgart, 1882), p. 201.

[11] Only the *Invective* indicates that Sallust started his new career by repeating the quaestorship; Dio Cassius says it was the praetorship. T. R. S. Broughton points out that the quaestorship is more likely (*Transactions of the American Philological Association,* 79, 1948, p. 77, n. 2).

tinente. Unde tantum hic exhausit quantum potuit aut fide no-
minum traici aut in naves contrudi... Repente tamquam somno
beatus hortos pretiosissimos, villam Tiburti C. Caesaris, reliquas
possessiones paraveris ». Note the identical use of *exhausit* and
of *tantum*. The part played by Caesar (line 5) may be inferred
from this same passage as well as from *Bellum Africanum* 8, 3
and 34, 1.

Then suddenly Leto departs from his chief source, which he
has so drastically abbreviated, and gives more details about the
famous gardens of Sallust than the *Invective* does. That they
were near the Porta Collina may be gathered from Tacitus (*Hist.*
III, 82). That they were named the *Horti Sallustiani* (Leto says
« titulo sui nominis ») is known from the same source and others.
That they were a pleasant retreat not only for Sallust but for
later generations is attested by Dio Cassius LXVI, 10, Scriptores
Historiae Augustae, *Aurel.* 49, etc., and was in fact personally
known by Leto, who was somewhat of an expert on the topog-
raphy of Rome. His *De Romanae Urbis vetustate* is a brief
outline of the existing remains of the ancient city [12]. It contains
the following statement about the gardens: « Intrinsecus a porta
Collina a sinistris est vallis longa ubi fuerunt horti Salustiani
circundati pulcherrimis aedificiis, qui fuerunt non modo morum
sedent propter sumptum et ornatum aedificiorum satis amaeni, et
aquae subterraneae manu factae irrigabant hortos » [13]. Compare
satis amaeni with *amenissimos* in the *Vita, ornatum aedificiorum*
with *adornaverit*. Location near the Porta Collina and below the
Quirinal is mentioned in both [14]. We might almost say that the
topographical information in the *Vita* proves that Leto was its
author.

The *Vita* calls Sallust « in amicitia varius et inconstans »

---

[12] I quote from the edition of 1510 (Rome).

[13] It is simple to emend *sedent* to *sed etiam*; *moru(m)* may be emended
to an adjective such as *magni*.

[14] Leto states that the Porta Collina is on the Quirinal. Therefore when
he say that the gardens of Sallust are in a valley inside the Porta Collina he
means that they are *sub Quirinale*, as the *Vita* puts it. He also says that this
gate for a long time was the outermost gate of Rome, and that the wall (i. e.,
the Servian Wall) extended only a short distance to the west. This shows that
he realized that the gardens were *extra pomerium*, as the *Vita* has it.

(line 11). As this precedes the story of his attack on Pompey,
we may assume that Leto supposed that this incident indicated
that Sallust had previously been on friendly terms with Pompey.
As indicated above, the attack on Pompey and Lenaeus' reply
were taken from Suetonius. The explanation of *lastaurus* (line
16), bracketed by Kurfess as a gloss, was quite to be expected of
Leto, expounder and editor of Varro's *De lingua Latina*. Finally,
the reference to Terentia was taken from Jerome (*In Iovin.* I, 48).

In conclusion let me quote Nolhac's remarks about Leto,
based on a study of his notes and manuscripts:

> On est surpris, en étudiant la bibliothèque manuscrite du grand
> humaniste romain, de l'abondance et de la variété de son érudition...
> Rien n'y manque de ce qui peut éclairer le texte: arguments, remar-
> ques de grammaire et de rhétorique... Ajoutons des rapprochements
> historiques ou littéraires... Les allusions aux institutions, à la topo-
> graphie antique de Rome et de l'Italie sont l'objet de scholies fort
> étudiées [15].

[15] *Op. cit.*, p. 205.

CHAPTER XX

CODICES MAFFEIANI

Two families named Maffei produced important scholars and collectors of manuscripts, one from Volterra, the other from Verona [1]. Studies of their book collections should be made [2]. In the meantime a few random notes may not be without interest.

The best known scholar in the Volterra branch was Raffaele (1451-1522), who edited various authors, translated Greek works into Latin, and wrote other books. Apparently one of the most active collectors in this family was a brother of Raffaele, Mario, who became bishop of Aquino in 1516 and of Cavaillon in 1527. He died in 1537. The following manuscripts of his are in the British Museum [3]:

1. Burney 68. Parchment, s. XV, Aristotle, *Secreta secretorum*. The flyleaf has the notes « Olim Maffeianus » and « Bibliothèque de la Chevalière D'Eon ».

2. Burney 74. Parchment, s. XV, Bruni's translations of Demosthenes, Aeschines, and Plato's *Epistles*. « Olim Maffeianus ». « Bibliothèque de la Chevalière d'Eon ».

3. Burney 158. Parchment, s. XV, Cicero, *Verrines*. Traces of Maffei ownership note, as in Burney 214. Maffei (of Volterra) arms, forequarters of a stag, or on azure. « Duke of Grafton 1785 ». Askew sale.

---

[1] The Verona family came from Volterra; cf., e.g., V. Spreti, *Enciclopedia storico-nobiliare italiana,* IV (Milan, 1931), p. 203.

[2] This has now been done with the utmost thoroughness by José Ruysschaert in *La Bibliofilia,* 60 (1958), p. 306. He lists 69 items belonging to the Volterra branch, 51 belonging to the Maffei of Rome.

[3] A printed book with many of his marginal notes was for sale by H. P. Kraus of New York in 1963: « Baptistae Fulgosi de dictis factisque memorabilibus collectanea », Milan, 1509. It came from the library of Prince Liechtenstein.

4. Burney 160. Parchment, *s.* XII, Cicero, *De oratore.* Erasure, perhaps of ownership note, on fol. 1, top. Maffei arms. Fol. 167v: « Marius Maffeus Volaterranus ».

5. Burney 161. Parchment, *s.* XII, Cicero, *De inventione, Ad Herennium.* Erasure, perhaps of ownership note, on fol. 3, top, and on fol. 98. Maffei arms. « Bibliothèque de la Chevalière d'Eon ».

6. Burney 170. Parchment, *s.* XV, Dictys. « Olim Maffeianus ». « Bibliothèque de la Chevalière d'Eon ».

7. Burney 174. Parchment, *s.* XV, Gellius. Maffei arms in a border, which seems to indicate that the manuscript was written for Maffei. « Duke of Grafton 1785 ». Askew sale.

8. Burney 214. Parchment, *s.* XV, Orosius. Copied at Basel in 1434 by Francesco di Marerio, bishop of Brescia. Fol. 4: « De figli et eredi di messer Mario Maffei ».

9. Burney 221. Parchment, *s.* XV, Ovid, *Fasti.* Fol. 2, top, erasure, apparently of Maffei ownership note, over which « Duke of Grafton 1785 ». Maffei arms.

10. Burney 238. Parchment, *s.* XIII, Commentary on Priscian. « Olim Maffeianus ». « Bibliothèque de la Chevalière d'Eon ».

11. Burney 259. Parchment, *s.* XV, Suetonius. Fol. 1, top, erasure of Maffei ownership note. Maffei arms.

12. Add. 21241. Parchment, *s.* XIII, Lucan. Fol. 1: « Olim clarissimi Maffei ». Flyleaf: « Purchased of E. Trop of Paris, 8 Mar. 1856 ».

13. Add. 23777. Parchment, *s.* XV, Pliny, *Epistles.* Maffei arms. Written for Maffei. Payne sale, Sotheby 21 June 1860, lot 297.

14. Add. 24894. Parchment, *s.* XV, Asconius. Fol. 3, top, erasure of Maffei ownership note. Maffei arms. I. Mitford, 1817. Purchased of Messrs. Boone 14 June 1862 (formerly Askew's).

The entry « olim Maffeianus » in some of the Burney manuscripts was made in the eighteenth century when they were in the library of the Chevalière d'Eon. It may be that they were obtained by Eon from a member of the Maffei family. There is a curious tale about Eon. Actually this was the Chevalier d'Eon, a successful diplomat and soldier, who fell into disgrace while on a mission to London. On his return to France in 1777 he was forced by the king to wear women's clothes. It was then that he began to call himself « La Chevalière d'Eon ». In 1783 he returned to London, where he died in poverty in 1810 [4]. The entries in the Burney manuscripts must then have been made between 1777 and 1783.

The most active collectors in the Verona branch were Agostino and the descendants of his brother Benedetto. The two came to Rome with a third brother in 1473 or earlier, as stated in the preceding chapter. We really should therefore speak of them and their descendants as the Maffei of Rome, but contemporaries even of the later generations continue to mention their Veronese origin. At a much later time the Verona family produced the celebrated Scipione Maffei, author of *Verona illustrata* and many other works. But it is the Roman branch that will engage our attention in the rest of this chapter.

Agostino started a museum and library in Rome, which passed to his brother's family. He was a patron of several scholars during the end of the fifteenth century and the beginning of the sixteenth. Leto's dedication of his Sallust to him was mentioned in the last chapter. In the same year as the Sallust (1490) an edition of Cicero's letters to Atticus appeared (Hain 5216), edited by Bartolomeo Saliceto and Lodovico Regio. This too is dedicated to Agostino Maffei. The editors made use of a manuscript in Maffei's collection. The volume also contains a short poem by Pomponio Leto addressed to Maffei. According to Nolhac, the manuscript copy presented to Maffei is Vat. lat. 3250 [5]. Another manuscript of Agostino's is Ottob. lat. 1937.

Benedetto too had something to do with an edition of Cicero's letters. Hain 5222 is Cicero's *Familiares,* published in Rome in 1483. It opens with a prefatory letter: « Benedictus Maffeus maioris praesidentiae Abbreviator apostolicus Iohanni Schoemberger de Ruitlingen Constantiensis diocesis librorum impressori

---

[4] *Biographie universelle,* nouvelle édition, XII (Paris, 1855), p. 500.
[5] Pierre de Nolhac, *La bibliothèque de Fulvio Orsini* (Paris, 1887), p. 231.

in urbe commoranti Salutem dicit ». I have not seen this volume. One manuscript that belonged to Benedetto is Ottob. lat. 1995. Benedetto's son Achille and grandson Girolamo seem not to have had a major role in increasing the collection, which they carefully preserved. But two of Girolamo's four sons, the great-grandsons of Benedetto, seem to have been more active, for they and their manuscripts are mentioned by contemporaries. The collection seems to have been kept intact in the house in which it had been for a hundred years. Among existing Maffei manuscripts are Ottob. lat. 1209, 1368, 1557, 1560, 1785, 1954. Others were individually owned, or at least are associated with one or another of Girolamo's sons. Marco Antonio, who became a cardinal in 1570, owned Ottob. lat. 389 [6]. Achille and Bernardino took a greater interest in the ancestral library. Scipio Maffei tells about Achille's museum of antiquities, including inscriptions, and his library, stating that it contained good manuscripts of Varro, Festus, the philosophical works of Cicero (used by Paolo Manuzio), and Catullus (used by Achilles Statius) [7]. This last, a manuscript of peculiar interest, can be identified.

The Maffeianus of Catullus

In his edition of Catullus, published by Aldus in 1566, Achilles Statius quoted seven manuscripts: two Patavini, a Vaticanus, one of Basilio Zanchi, one of Pope Marcellus II, one of Achille Maffei, and one of his own. Four of these have been identified [8]. The Vaticanus, though cited only once, can be identified as Vat.

---

[6] Ruysschaert (p. 309, n. 2) denies this on grounds that I cannot follow. It is a work dedicated to Cardinal Marco Antonio Maffei. But because (if I interpret Ruysschaert correctly) in another copy the same work is dedicated to someone else, Ruysschaert does not believe that Ottob. lat. 389 belonged to Marco Antonio. It seems to me that the two different dedications strengthen rather than weaken my case. I venture to suggest that these two copies are the only ones in existence.

[7] Scipione Maffei, *Verona Illustrata*, Part II (Milan, 1825), p. 272.

[8] B. L. Ullman, *The Identification of the Manuscripts of Catullus Cited in Statius' Edition of 1566* (Chicago, 1908), which see for further details. G. B. Pighi, accepting my conclusions, has reprinted the readings from Statius' edition, adding Statius' emendations as well as readings from some of the old editions (G. B. Pighi in *Humanitas*, III, 1950).

lat. 1608, which was written for Sixtus IV in 1479, as an account book of that pope indicates. It also appears in an inventory and a catalogue of the Vatican made about 1550 (Vat. lat. 3967, 3946). Marcellus II's manuscript is Ottob. lat. 1550. One of the Patavini can be identified from its readings as Padua, Capit. C. 77; the other has disappeared. The codex Zanchi, belonging to Basilio Zanchi, who died in Rome in 1558, has not been identified[9], nor has Statius' own. That brings us to Achille Maffei's manuscript. It can be identified only on internal evidence, i.e., from the many readings which Statius cites. We note a remarkable combination of old and recent readings, which suggests an old manuscript corrected by a *manus recens*. We have three manuscripts of the fourteenth century: O (Oxford, Bodl. Canon. class. lat. 30), G (Paris, Bibl. Nat. lat. 14137), R (Vat. Ottob. lat. 1829). The reading of the Maffeianus in 106, 1, *ipse*, eliminates O and G, which have *esse*. Many of the fifteenth-century manuscripts are eliminated by some readings. I have collations of practically every extant manuscript of Catullus—well over a hundred. In 66, 54 Statius reports that the Maffei codex had *asineos* with *al' arsinoes* written above. In this form (with the variant written above, not in the margin) that is the reading only of R and Venice, lat. cl. XII, 80, and the latter is eliminated by the following readings. In 2, 6 Maffei's manuscript is reported as having *Rarum*. R has *Karum* but so written as to be easily read as *Rarum*. A correction in R of *amaret* to *a mari* at 4, 23 can easily be mistaken for *a mare*, which is reported for the Maffeianus. Thus we must conclude that the Maffeianus was R (Ottob. lat. 1829). A minor point is that in his edition of Tibullus Statius makes no mention of a Maffeianus. Therefore Maffei's manuscript was not one of the many which include both Catullus and Tibullus, and R contains only Catullus. It once belonged to Coluccio Salutati (see also chapter VIII).

Achille's brother Bernardino was born in 1514 and made cardinal in 1549. Scipione Maffei says that he wrote a commentary on Cicero's letters, but I have found no confirmation of

---

[9] Nolhac (*op. cit.*, p. 258) mentions a copy of the 1502 Aldine with notes by Zanchi.

this statement. Bernardino owned Ottob. lat. 1141 and a manuscript of Cicero's *Philippics* which can be identified.

The Codex Maffeianus of Cicero's *Philippics* [10]

In his *Emendationes in Philippicas Ciceronis,* first printed at
Venice in 1542, Hieronymus Ferrarius quotes several manuscripts [11]. The one which he cites most frequently for the orations which it included (I-IV), and which he considers the most
valuable, was the Colotianus (belonging to Angelo Colocci). He
says of it: « is liber ex omnibus minime mendosus est » (II, 1)
and « cui ex omnibus maximam fidem habeo » (III, 17). Of its
age he remarks: « Liber Col. et alter non minoris vetustatis » (II,
21) and « non mediocris vetustatis est » (II, 50). The manuscript
has not been identified but Clark speaks of a *familia Colotiana,*
consisting of manuscripts as old as the twelfth century. He
rates this family next to the best manuscript [12].

Next in favor with Ferrarius, as shown by the frequency
of his quotations and by his comments, is the Langobardicus. This
has been identified by Clark as Vat. lat. 3227, written in a Beneventan script of the twelfth century. The manuscript came into
Ferrarius' hands through the kindness of Cardinal Marcello Cervini (VIII, 21), who became Pope Marcellus II in 1555.

A third manuscript which appears frequently in Ferrarius'
notes is the Codex Scalae, which belonged to Iohannes Scala (X,
15). Clark has identified this as Vat. lat. 3228, of the tenth
century [13].

Another manuscript mentioned rather frequently by Ferrarius is called Gad. This is probably to be expanded into Gaddianus and to be referred to some member of the well-known Gaddi

---

[10] Originally published in *Classical Philology,* XXX (1935), p. 161.

[11] I have used the apparently correct and complete reprint given by *In
omnes M. Tullii Ciceronis orationes ... enarrationes,* Vol. II: *Lucubrationes in
M.T. Ciceronis orationes* (Basel, 1553).

[12] A. C. Clark in the second edition of the *Philippics* (« Oxford Classical
Texts ») and in *Classical Review,* XIV (1900), p. 40.

[13] In the (undated and unpaged) Preface to his edition, Clark several times
wrongly numbers these two manuscripts 3327 and 3328; the correct numbering
is given in the *Sigla* preceding the text.

family of Florence, many of whose manuscripts are now in the Laurentian and National libraries of that city. Some of the manuscripts of Giovanni Gaddi came into the hands of Fulvio Orsini and are now in the Vatican. Orsini was in touch with Niccolò Gaddi [14].

Besides these four manuscripts, others are mentioned less frequently by Ferrarius. If we consider the respectable age of at least three of the four, we wonder whether another, called the Maffeianus and as yet unidentified, was also an early one, especially since in the two passages in which Ferrarius mentions it [15] editors accept an emendation of his supported by Maffei's manuscript. His note on the first reads:

Sic l(iber) Lang(obardicus): ... *conversione et perturbationum rerum*. Ego sic: ... *conversione et perturbatione omnium rerum*, ut illud pro Flacco [94]: ... *conversione rerum ac perturbatione*... Sententiam meam Bernardini Maphaei liber approbavit.

Bernardino enriched the library which he and his brothers inherited from their ancestors:

Eius mihi copiam fecit Achilles Maffeus antiquitatis omnis peritissimus. Quem [librum] in antiqua et vetustorum codicum refertissima avita bibliotheca invenit; quam a maioribus inchoatam vir optimus idemque doctissimus Bernardinus Cardinalis mirum in modum locupletaverat [16].

Noting the mention of Maffei by Ferrarius, I asked myself this question: if Achille's Catullus was in the Ottoboni collection of the Vatican, would his brother's Cicero be in the same collection? To answer this I looked over the six manuscripts of the *Philippics* in the Ottoboni collection. In quite proper dramatic manner it was the last one to be examined, No. 1992, a manuscript of the fifteenth century like the rest, that yielded the sought-for evidence: on fol. 1r there is a coat of arms with the name *Mafeorum*. This is repeated on fol. 96r in the form

---

[14] Nolhac, *op. cit.*, pp. 216-17.

[15] *Phil.* XI, 27; VIII, 28.

[16] O. Panvinio, *Fasti et Triumphi* (Venice, 1557), quoted by A. Ronchini in *Atti e Memorie della R. Deputazione di storia patria per le provincie Modenesi e Parmensi*, VII (1874), p. 336.

Mafaeorum. Furthermore, this is the only one of the six manuscripts which at *Phil.* XI, 27 has in the first hand a reading ap-
proximating that of Ferrarius, supported, as he says, by the Maffeianus. It has *concursatione ac perturbatione omnium rerum.*
Ferrarius' reading is *conversione et perturbatione omnium rerum.*
Most manuscripts have *concursatione* (or *concursione*) *perturbationum rerum.* This is true also of the five other Ottoboni manuscripts except that 1662 has *eversione,* 1528 omits *rerum,* and a
second hand in 1577 added *ac* and *omnium,* without, however,
changing *perturbationum.*

Editors give chief or entire credit for the accepted reading
to the Maffei manuscript [17], but it is now evident just where
credit is due: *conversione et* was from the Langobardicus; *Flacc.*
94 confirmed this and suggested *perturbatione*; *omnium* was apparently Ferrarius' emendation; later an examination of the Maffeianus confirmed both *perturbatione* and *omnium.* Probably
this reading of the Maffeianus is due to fifteenth-century emendation rather than tradition, but this question cannot be decided
until the manuscripts of that century are studied. The reading
conversione et should be credited to Vat. 3227 (Langobardicus)
rather than to Ferrarius (if the latter's report is correct); Clark,
who gives some readings of this manuscript, does not cite it at
this point.

The only other reference to the Maffeianus that I have noted
is at VIII, 28: « Lang. pro *hi, hic.* Nonnulli, *et se. Hi se,* alii.
Ego, *usi* correxeram. Opinionem meam Bernardini Maffaei liber
approbavit ». Here one sees clearly that the emendation preceded
the examination of the manuscript. But unfortunately Ottob.
1992 (the Maffei manuscript) does not have *usi* but *sed* [18]. This,
of course, makes its identification as Bernardino Maffei's dubious,
but I am inclined to think that there is some confusion about
Ferrarius' report. We must remember the positive evidence of
the coat of arms. It is possible, of course, that there were two
manuscripts of the *Philippics* in the hands of the various members of the Maffei family, but the striking reading at XI, 27 tends

---

[17] Clark credits it to Codd. Ferrarii.
[18] So do 1577 and 2842 (corrected from *se*); 1528 and 1787 have *ii se*; 1662
has *hic.*

to show that Ottob. 1992 is the particular Maffei manuscript (if there was ever more than one) which Ferrarius cites. That Ferrarius makes mistakes is shown in his comment on XIV, 9. He states that all his manuscripts lack *cum dedecore,* but, according to Clark, both *s* (Codex Scalae) and *v* (Langobardicus) have it. Perhaps some of the differences between *c* and the Colotianus noted by Clark [19] are due to confusion or other forms of error on Ferrarius' part.

In any case this much is true: my reasoning that the Maffei Cicero should be in the same library and collection as the Maffei Catullus proved to be right. It follows that the converse is true and that we now have external as well as internal evidence that the Catullus manuscript Ottob. 1829 belonged to Maffei.

It has already been stated that Ferrarius obtained the Lango bardicus through the kindness of Cardinal Marcello Cervini. Another manuscript which Ferrarius cites belonged to the Cardinal himself (II, 48; III, 23; VII, 3). The Cardinal also owned Catullus and Tibullus manuscripts quoted by Statius. The former, as stated above, is now Ottoboni 1550; the latter is Ottoboni 1369 (see Chapter XXIII). The Cardinal's library was, in fact, the nucleus of that collection. Therefore it is natural to assume that his Cicero manuscript is there too.

The readings of the six Ottoboni manuscripts in the three passages just mentioned enable us to identify Marcellus' manuscript with a fair degree of certainty. On II, 48 Ferrarius approves the reading *religionem* of Cardinal Marcello's manuscript as against the vulgate *religiones.* Of the six Ottoboni manuscripts only 1577 has *religionem*; the others have *religiones* [20]. On III, 23 Ferrarius approves the reading *Tiberium* of the Cardinal's manuscript instead of *Tyberinum.* Ottob. 1577 is one of the three Ottoboni manuscripts which have *Tiberium* [21]. On VII, 3

---

[19] *Classical Review,* XIV (1900), pp. 41-42.

[20] Ottob. 1662 has a correction, from or to *s,* but in any case it cannot be read as *religionem* now.

[21] The others are 1787 and 1992 (Maffeianus). The fact that Ferrarius does not quote the Maffeianus for this and the following readings shows that he had only a few readings from it. The other Ottoboni manuscripts have *Tiberinum* in various spellings.

Ferrarius reports that in place of the vulgate *providi cives et* the Cardinal's manuscript reads *p. r. vindicius esset hi*. This reading is found in three Ottoboni manuscripts: 1577, 1992, and 2842, though in the last there has been a correction[22].

The last of the manuscripts which Ferrarius cites by name is one brought to him by Paulus Ricardus; it was not an old one (VIII, 21).

Ferrarius makes a distinction between old and recent manuscripts and printed editions—a distinction which not all of his contemporaries observe. By recent manuscripts he presumably means those written in the fifteenth century. Just how many manuscripts Ferrarius consulted regularly or occasionally is not certain. In one place (IX, 3) he states that four old manuscripts have the reading *morti*. This is in addition to the Colotianus which did not extend this far. Apparently, then, he had seen at least one manuscript older than the fifteenth century besides the Colotianus, Langobardicus, Codex Scalae, and Gaddianus. On I, 34 Ferrarius reports that five manuscripts, including the Langobardicus, omit a clause, while many others, including the Colotianus, have it. Here old and new manuscripts are not distinguished, except that it is implied that the two which are named are older and better. On XIV, 20 Ferrarius attributes the reading *invigilasse* to five *veteres,* including the Langobardicus. If he is using *veteres* as carefully here as he does sometimes, he consulted six manuscripts older than the fifteenth century, since the defective Colotianus must be added to the five.

[22] I owe the readings on these three passages to the kindness of Mgr. (now Cardinal) E. Tisserant and Miss Dorothy M. Schullian, formerly fellow of the American Academy in Rome.

CHAPTER XXI

JOSEPH LANG AND HIS ANTHOLOGIES [1]

Joseph Lang (Langius, Lange) was born at Kaisersberg, in Alsace, about 1570 [2]. He studied and taught in Strasbourg, then in 1604 he took a position at Freiburg i. Br. as professor of rhetoric, later teaching Greek and mathematics. He died in 1615.

In 1596 Lang published his *Adagia,* a collection of Latin and German proverbs based on earlier collections, as he himself tells us. About 1598 he got out his *Loci communes sive florilegium rerum et materiarum selectarum,* etc. [3]. This octavo edition

---

[1] Originally published in *Festschrift for John G. Kunstmann* (Chapel Hill, 1959).

[2] I take most of my data about him from the *Allgemeine Deutsche Biographie,* 17 (1883), p. 602, article by J. Franck. I am indebted to Prof. Archer Taylor for some bibliographical details.

[3] According to Franck the title page gives no date, but Lang's *Epistola nuncupatoria* is dated 1598. But the copy that Franck describes was printed by " Iosiae Rihelii haeredes ", and Rihel was alive until 1609. The Folger Shakespeare Library (Washington, D. C.) has a copy with the date 1598 on the title page but with the publisher's name as "Iosiae Rihelii haeredes." The simplest explanation is that the date is incorrect, merely repeated from the first edition. Franck also states that the title *Anthologia sive florilegium* began to be used in 1645, but this is an error for 1605, as shown by the biography of Rihel in the *Allgemeine Deutsche Biographie.* The British Museum catalogue lists a 1631 copy with the new title. Two editions are available to me, both unfortunately lacking the title page. In both the *Epistola* gives the date 1598. There is a title at the top of fol. 1 (after the front matter) reading *Anthologia seu florilegium,* etc. The total number of numbered leaves in each is the same as that of the supposed first edition (639). The two copies (one mine, one in the University of North Carolina Library) have the same woodcuts and were evidently put out by the same printer, presumably Rihel, but there are minor typographical differences. My copy has errors not in the other copy. The University copy has on its spine "Loci Communes Sive Florilegium 1625" in ink, but it is uncertain whether this is correct. This title may have been taken from the *Epistola,*

was printed in Strasbourg by Iosias Rihelius (Rihel, Richel).
The work immediately became popular and was reprinted a
number of times. The editions of 1605, 1613, 1615, 1621, 1622,
1624, 1625, 1631 were printed in Strasbourg by Rihel or his
successors with his types. Franck does not include the 1615,
1622, and 1625 editions; the first is mentioned by Michaud
(*Biographie Universelle*), who may, of course, be in error, the
second is in the Princeton University Library (verified), the
third is in the Bibliothèque Nationale catalogue. There may be
still other editions; on the other hand, some of those listed may
possibly be "ghosts," and some may merely have new title pages.
Glaser printed an edition at Strasbourg in 1655. Lang mentions
a Philip Glaser as son-in-law of Rihel. It may well be that the
printer Glaser was a relative who continued Rihel's business.
In a Strasbourg edition of 1662 (which seems to be a copy of
the 1655 edition), the printer Iosias Staedel warns against a
reprint by his partner Wilhelm Christian Glaser. Other Strasbourg editions are dated 1674 and 1690. About Lang's similar
later work, always published in folio, something will be said
below.

It is with the original octavo work and its sources that this
chapter is primarily concerned. The book consists of a large number of Latin quotations arranged according to topics, beginning
with *Abstinentia* and ending with *Zelus*. The author, work, and
book of each citation are given. Within each topic, the quotations
are grouped in nine classifications according to origin: Bible,
Church Fathers, poets, philosophers, sayings (*apophthegmata*),
similes (*similitudines*), *exempla sacra* (or *Biblica*), *exempla profana,*
and *hieroglyphica* (emblems), in this order, but not all are

which speaks of the book as "Loci communes sive florilegium." Similarly
my copy has a title page supplied in ink: *Anthologia sive florilegium rerum,
et materiar. . . . Argentorati,* but again it cannot be proved that this was
what the original title page had. Franck considers Krebs' statement that
there was a 1596 edition more than doubtful. Krebs' error may be due to
the fact that the front matter contains a Greek epigram by Henricus Stephanus
(Estienne) about Lang, written in 1596 while he was visiting Lang in
Strasbourg. Probably Lang showed his guest the manuscript on which he was
working. Or perhaps Krebs confused the *Adagia* (published in 1596) with the
Loci communes.

represented under each topic. At times, indeed, only one class is quoted under a given topic. The purpose of the book was to instruct the young. Lang makes clear in his preface that his big contribution was the combination of the nine types of quotation in one volume. He recalls that in his school days there were separate collections of *sententiae* of philosophers and orators, "flores et versus gnomologici poetarum a diversis collecti", separate volumes of quotations from the Bible and from the Church Fathers by a certain (*quendam*) Thomas Hibernicus, etc.

It is my purpose to show from what main sources Lang drew some of his materials. Actually it might have been inferred from the above what they were. First of all, he used Thomas Hibernicus, *Manipulus florum,* from which he not only took his quotations from the Bible and the Church Fathers but also the very arrangement of material, beginning with *Abstinentia* and going down the list. He omitted some of Thomas' classifications, changed the titles of others, and added a large number, perhaps chiefly from some of his other sources.

First, however, we must say something about Thomas' life and work. His real name seems to have been Palmer or Palmerston. Born in the thirteenth century, he took a degree at the Sorbonne about 1306 [4]. Among his writings, or rather those attributed to him, was a work called *Tabula originalium sive manipulus florum*, consisting of two parts, one containing quotations from the Bible ("Flores Biblici") the other from the Church Fathers and others ("Flores doctorum"), arranged by general topics. It is now thought that John Waleys did most of the work and Thomas merely finished it, in 1306. The book was popular, as indicated by the number of surviving manuscripts [5].

---

[4] *Dictionary of National Biography,* 19, p. 654; L. Delisle, *Le Cabinet des Manuscrits de la Bibliothèque Nationale,* II (Paris, 1874), p. 176.

[5] Without any attempt to achieve completeness I know of over sixty, many supplied to me by Prof. R. H. Rouse, who has listed over a hundred. Thomas left some of his books to the Sorbonne: L. Delisle, *Le Cabinet des Manuscrits de la Bibliothèque Nationale,* II (Paris, 1874), p. 176. One of these, now Paris, B. N. lat. 15986, contains the *Manipulus florum.* It should be the best manuscript, but Prof. Rouse tells me that it omits words and has other errors. He discovered that the order of authors quoted is based on the order in the Sorbonne Library catalogue.

The part containing the *Flores doctorum* was printed many times under such titles as *Manipulus florum seu sententiae Patrum* and *Flores doctorum pene omnium, tam Graecorum, quam Latinorum, qui tum in theologia, tum in philosophia hactenus claruerunt*: 1483, ca. 1494, 1550, 1555, 1556, 1558, 1563, 1564, 1567, 1568, 1575, 1576, 1579, 1580, 1614, 1622, 1664, 1669 (*bis*), 1678, 1699, 1858, 1887 [6]. None of these seem to include the Biblical quotations. Separate editions of the *Flores Bibliorum* were published in 1567, 1568, 1572, 1574, 1699.

In compiling his work Lang seems to have started with the Biblical part of Thomas' book [7] and then proceeded to the other. The justification for this view is that, though under the various subject headings not all of the nine classes of quotations are always given, Biblical quotations if given come first; if there are none, the *Sententiae Patrum* have first place.

To give an idea of the extent to which Lang borrowed from Thomas, let us examine the first subject head, *Abstinentia*. Under *Sententiae Patrum,* there are seventeen quotations identical with those in Thomas. Also, they come in the same order except that one from Prosper is put earlier without author's name. Seventeen quotations in Thomas (including one group of five and one of ten at the end) are omitted by Lang. Three quotations are added in Lang which are not in Thomas. It should be added that I have not counted two quotations in later editions of Thomas that are marked with an asterisk to show that they are additions to the author's work. They are not in the 1483 and 1563 editions nor in the two manuscripts examined by me [8]. The printer of the 1606 edition, Bernardus Gualtheri, gives the impression in his preface that he was the one who introduced

---

[6] I have the 1699 edition and have seen the editions of 1483, 1563, 1575, and 1606. My list includes those given by P. Glorieux, *Répertoire des Maîtres en Théologie de Paris*, II (1933), p. 118. T. Georgi, *Allgemeines Europäisches Bücher-Lexicon* (1742), lists an edition of 1536 (Vienna, Krauss), but this is an error, as no printer of that name operated in Vienna at that time. There were two issues of the 1483 edition, as Curt F. Bühler showed in *Gutenberg - Jahrbuch,* 1953, p. 69.

[7] I have been unable to consult a copy of this book and therefore my statement that Lang used it is purely a guess.

[8] I am indebted to Professor Robert Pratt for lending me his microfilms of Cambridge, Peterhouse 163, 164.

them, but they are in the 1575 edition. Examination of more editions is needed to determine when they were added.

Two or three additional illustrations will clinch the point about Lang's borrowing. Under *Ira,* Thomas gives fifty-one passages, not including four marked with an asterisk. Lang has twelve of these, in Thomas' order, from the beginning of Thomas' selection. Under *Sapientia* Thomas has forty-four quotations, not counting two that are marked with an asterisk. Lang has fifteen of these, in the same order. The omitted ones are mostly from the end of the section. Under *Voluntas* Thomas furnishes thirty quotations, of which thirteen are represented in Lang, in the order followed by Thomas [9].

Lang's poetical quotations are easily traced: they come directly from the *Illustrium poetarum flores* of Octavianus Mirandula (Fioravanti). This anthologist from the town of Mirandola was a canon regular of the Lateran, as he calls himself in a letter about his book addressed to the apostolic protonotary Ottaviano Arcimboldi. What seems to have been the first edition of the *Flores* was called *Viridarium illustrium poetarum* and was published at Venice in 1507, Lyons in 1512, Paris in 1513, and Hagenau in 1517 [10]. The first edition under the new title, *Illustrium poetarum flores*, seems to be that of Strasbourg, 1538. The title page reads: « Illustrium poetarum flores per Octavianum Mirandulam collecti et a studioso quodam in locos communes digesti ac castigati. Cum indice locupletissimo ». This leads one to think that the *Flores* differs from the *Viridarium* only in the rearrangement of the quotations by topics (*loci communes*) and that by this time Ottaviano was no longer living. The rearrangement by the anonymous scholar was clearly intended to produce

[9] M. Iacobus Thomasius includes Lang in his book on plagiarism (*Dissertatio philosophica de plagio litterario,* 1692), merely to prevent an incautious reader of Dieterich from concluding that he was a plagiarist; actually Dieterich and Thomasius criticize Thomas for plagiarism and carelessness, Lang only for trusting Thomas, whose use he acknowledges in his preface. The main point for us is the early recognition that Lang drew on Thomas for the *Sententiae Patrum.*

[10] My list of editions, based chiefly on the catalogues of the British Museum and the Bibliothèque Nationale, is probably incomplete. I have the edition of 1590, Lyons, Sybil a Porta, listed in neither catalogue, and have seen that of 1564.

a verse counterpart to Thomas' *Flores doctorum*. They both begin with a list of authors excerpted, the quotations are placed under subject heads that are arranged alphabetically and that in part agree, and each of the two books ends with an *Index locorum communium*. The 1538, 1544, and (probably) 1549 editions were published by Wendelin Rihel of Strasbourg and those of 1559 and 1567 by his son Iosias, who also printed the first and other editions of Lang. Other editions of the *Flores* appeared in 1539, 1553, 1559 (Lugdunum), 1564, 1565, 1566, 1568, 1574, 1576 (*bis*), 1579, 1582, 1583, 1585, 1586 (*bis*), 1588, 1590, 1598, 1599, 1616, 1653, 1834. Probably there are several more. Obviously a popular and influential book, presumably used largely in the schools, like other anthologies [11].

The editions of Mirandola have an endorsement by Filippo Beroaldo, no doubt the elder and better known Beroaldo, who died in 1505, rather than his nephew, who lived until 1518. I do not know whether this endorsement occurs in the first edition; the catalogue of the Bibliothèque Nationale mentions it first for the edition of 1538. The Ottaviano Arcimboldi addressed in Ottaviano Mirandola's letter is presumably the archbishop of Milan; he died about 1503, before entering upon his office; Tiraboschi plausibly argues that there must have been an edition before Arcimboldi was named archbishop, as Mirandola still calls him a protonotary [12]. The Iacopo Antonio Balbi of Piacenza who wrote a poem praising Ottaviano Mirandola, quoted in the front matter of some editions, is unknown to me.

How closely Lang followed Mirandola may be seen from a few examples. Under *Abstinentia* Mirandola gives seven quotations, all of which are repeated in the same order by Lang, who added one after the first and two at the end. These last are from

---

[11] I can mention two such poetical anthologies. One is called *Sententiae illustriores ex antiquorum poetarum principibus selectae* and was published by the Jesuits of Bourges in 1667. It bears no resemblance to Mirandola or Lang. The other is *Sententiae veterum poetarum per locos communes digestae,* by Georgius Maior (Maier). This is much closer to Mirandola and Lang but was not the latter's source. The quotations are arranged topically (*per locos communes*), to be sure, but in a haphazard fashion, not alphabetically, and they are quite different from those of Mirandola and Lang. Many editions were published, beginning in 1534.

[12] G. Tiraboschi, *Biblioteca Modenese,* III (1783), p. 211.

Menander, in Greek with Latin translation. After a quotation from Ovid, Mirandola gives another with the heading « Et infra ». Lang does the same. Other examples are more clearly represented in tabular form:

Mirandola	Lang
	Admiratio 1
	Admonitio 3 ("Ex Comicis Graecis")
De adolescentia 9	Adolescentia 20 (including M.'s in order)
De adversitate 37	Adversitas 24 (19 from M. in order, 5 new at end)
De adulatione 3	Adulatio 3 (from M.)
De adulterio 5	Adulterium 3 (from M.)
De morbis 8	Aegritudo, morbus 14 (8 from M., 6 added at end)
	Aemulatio 1
De aetatibus 27	Aetas, aevitas 4 (from M.)
De afflictione 22	Afflictio 17 (19)[13] (all from M. in order, 5 omitted)
De nobilitate 15	Nobilitas 12 (all from M. in order; first and last three omitted and one, "Ex Comicis Graecis", added)

It will be noted that several of Lang's additions are from the Greek comic poets, in Greek with Latin translation. It is easy to surmise that Lang took these from the book of his friend and guest, as noted above, Henri Estienne (Stephanus), which is entitled *Comicorum Graecorum sententiae, Latinis versibus ab Henrico Stephano redditae*, Paris, 1569. All of the above cita-

---

[13] Lang breaks up the first quotation into three. Mirandola quotes Ovid, *Met.*, then *Fast.*, then *Fast.* again with the heading *Et infra*. Lang omits the first *Fast.* citation but leaves the heading *Et infra* for the second, making it appear that this is from *Met.* This example alone is sufficient to prove that Lang drew on Mirandola.

tions agree with Estienne's Latin version, except the first, which may have been taken from Erasmus.

The *Sententiae philosophorum* were taken almost entirely from Cicero and Seneca. An examination of nearly a third of the volume reveals about four hundred quotations from Cicero, about one hundred and eighty from Seneca, and the rest from Valerius Maximus (5), Vegetius (2), Gellius (1), Solon (1), Solinus (1). The Ciceronian passages are largely from the philosophical works, but the orations, letters, and rhetorical books are well represented. Thomas Hibernicus included several « authores humanitatis » after the Church Fathers, notably Seneca. It is from this source that Lang drew practically all his Senecan material, as well as that from Valerius and the other rarely cited authors. This is assured by the order of the quotations and by other indications. Sixteen of Lang's Ciceronian passages are in Thomas, but all but one are starred, that is, were added in the sixteenth century. Lang's source for Cicero can definitely be identified either as *Ciceronis ac Demosthenis sententiae selectae*, put together by Petrus Lagnerius (1564, etc.) or a closely related work. Under *Deus* the first eight passages in Lagnerius and Lang are identical and in the same order. There is also another run of seven. Lagnerius has many more quotations than Lang. Under *Servitus* both have the same eight passages, and only these, in the same order; under *Exilium* they have the same seven. They agree in the form of the reference, e.g., « Cicero Paradoxa penult. », the next to the last (fifth) paradox.

The *Apophthegmata* seem to have been put together by Lang from several sources. One naturally thinks of Erasmus' work by that title (1531, etc.). In fact, Erasmus is quoted frequently. This very circumstance shows that Erasmus is not his only source. If Erasmus were not mentioned at all he might be thought of as the sole source, though an insurmountable objection is that Erasmus does not give references for his ancient quotations and Lang does, when Erasmus is not given credit. In about one-third of the book, Erasmus is quoted about 75 times, Plutarch over 100, Diogenes Laertius about 60, Stobaeus about 65, Antonius Melissa 25, Maximus Confessor 35. Lang could have read Plutarch in the volume edited and published, with Latin translations, by his friend H. Estienne (Geneva, 1572)[14]. He did not use Laertius in the volume edited and published by Estienne at Paris in 1570, as the translations differ. Stobaeus, Antonius Melissa, and Maximus Confessor were printed together, with Latin translations, at Frankfurt in 1581, and we may be sure that this is the ultimate, though not necessarily the immediate, source that Lang used for these three authors. Brusonio is quoted over forty times, apparently indirectly from his *Facetiarum exemplorumque libri* (1518, etc.). Less often quoted (nine times) is Aelian's *Varia historia*, perhaps from Gesner's edition of 1556, or the Lyons edition of 1587, or the *Exempla virtutum et vitiorum* of J. Herold (Basel, 1555, etc.). Philostratus, *De vitis sophistarum,* is quoted five times, either from the Strasbourg edition of 1516 or the Basel edition of 1563.

But while Lang may have consulted the ancient authors in the editions mentioned, it is clear that he took at least part and probably all of his material at second hand. He did not use Lagnerius in this part of his book. In his preface, Lang speaks of the « volumina item apophthegmatum et similium ab Erasmo et Lycosthene inchoata, locupletata post et digesta per Theodorum Zuingerum, cuius etiam incomparabilis viri industria locupletissimam exemplorum penum, opus illud nobile, quod Theatrum vitae humanae inscribitur nobis exhibuit ». Erasmus has already been mentioned, Lycosthenes and his son-in-law Zwinger must be considered. The former's innovation was to arrange Erasmus' selections by *loci communes* (Paris, 1564). T. Zwinger revised Lycosthenes' work under the title *Theatrum humanae vitae* (Basel, 1555, etc.). An examination of Lycosthenes shows that Lang took some of his passages from him or his reviser Zwinger. Lycosthenes' *loci communes* often agree with Lang's. Under each the passages generally succeed one another in the chronological order of the persons who are subjects of the stories. Under *Abstinentia* Lycosthenes has twenty-two passages, only

---

[14] He did not use *Apophthegmata Graeca regum ... ex Plutarcho et Diogene Laertio cum Latina interpretatione* (H. Stephanus, 1568), for the Latin translation by Raphael Regius (Regio) differs from that quoted by Lang, nor Regio's translation of Plutarch (1508). An occasional passage was taken from Thomas Hibernicus, such as the remark of Fabius Verrucosus under *Beneficentia.*

two of which (Stobaeus and Plutarch's *Aristides*) were used by Lang. Under *Abusus,* Lang gives two passages, both taken from Lycostenes' five.   The first is attributed by both in the same words: « Erasmus libro septimo Apophthegmatum ex Gellii libro 17, cap. 19 ».   This makes clear that Lang borrowed from his predecessor.   Under *Admonitio* Lang has five apothegms, all among Lycosthenes' seven.   Under *Adulatio* seventeen out of eighteen passages in Lang are in Lycosthenes' longer collection. Here as elsewhere Lang often cuts the quotation down.   A passage about Antisthenes ends with these words in both: « Laertius libro 6, cap. 1, Brusonius libro 1, cap. 7.   Hoc alii Diogeni adscribunt ».   This too shows where Lang found the passage. On the other hand, there are indications that Lang did not draw directly on Lycosthenes, but on an intermediary, such as Zwinger. Under *Aerarium* Lycosthenes fails to give an attribution to an apophthegm of Trajan's but Lang gives credit to « Lang. in Nicephori annotationibus ».   He may have taken this direct from Johann Lang's translation of Nicephorus (1560, etc.), but it is more likely he depended on Zwinger.   Probably Lang obtained from Lycosthenes-Zwinger all his quotations of Stobaeus, Erasmus, Plutarch, Laertius, Brusonio, and the other authors mentioned above.   In the *exempla profana* Lang sometimes quotes Zwinger by name.

Lang's remark about Erasmus' *apophthegmata* and *similia* was quoted above.   The *similia,* or *similitudines,* are similes. Erasmus' *Parabolae sive similia* was published in 1512 at Strasbourg and was used by Lang, at least indirectly.   In his preface Erasmus states that in the case of Plutarch and Seneca he merely picked and shortened the passages, whereas he made up the simile himself in passages taken from Aristotle and Pliny. For example, in Seneca, *Epist.* 50, 6 the comparison between the flexibility of oak wood and the soul is already made, and Erasmus quotes it almost literally.   On the other hand, Pliny merely reports (37, 98, 194) that some gems become more brilliant when steeped in vinegar, others when treated with honey, but Erasmus adds a comparison with human beings, some of whom are improved by sharp scolding, others by mild admonitions.

Lang's quotations in the *Similitudines* are of two kinds.   In the one, he gives merely the author's name; in the other, a more exact reference. Most of the former go back to Erasmus, whose plan was to give the similes by authors and works without identifying them more precisely. He began his book with « ex Plutarchi moralibus ». Most of these are also in Lang, distributed according to topics and ascribed merely to Plutarch. Of the first sixty, not over eight at the most are missing in Lang; those used are in identical language. This, of course, identifies the ultimate source as Erasmus, as he made the translation and adaptation. In about a third of Lang's book, the ascriptions in the *Similitudines* are about as follows: Plutarch 210, Erasmus 65, Seneca 40, Pliny (*N. H.*) 25, others 6. Erasmus specifies at least « in Moralibus » for his Plutarch citations, Lang omits this. Lycosthenes' *Parabolae* (1575, etc.) (probably in Zwinger's revision, not seen by me) is clearly the intermediary between Erasmus and Lang. It contains more of the Erasmus material than is found in Lang. The material is classified as in Lang and the order is often the same.

In the second class of Lang's citations, the references are given, indicating that these were not derived from Erasmus but from a different ultimate source. In a third of the volume, they run about as follows: Pliny 65, Seneca and Cicero 25, Plutarch 1, others 8. The immediate source is Lycosthenes, as is shown by the fact that under *Ars* both he and Lang quote Pliny, giving both book and chapter, and under *Avaritia* one passage from Cicero, and five from Pliny are identified in the same language. In one case the reference is to both Pliny and Herodotus, in another to Pliny and Aristotle.

Valerius Maximus is mentioned by Lang in his preface, but it is quite clear that he was not a main source for Lang's *exempla profana*. In ten topics common to Valerius and Lang, eight are without mention of Valerius, one has one quotation and one has two quotations from Valerius. Either Lang selected his own *Exempla profana* from ancient and later literature or used a contemporary intermediary. Also mentioned in the preface is Marcus Antonius Sabellicus (Coccius). As in the case of Valerius Maximus, it is clear that Lang in his *Exempla profana* took only a few passages from Sabellico; he cites two works, *Rapsodiae* (*Enneades*), published in 1498-1504, and an unnamed book which is probably the *Exemplorum libri decem* (Strasbourg and Paris, 1509; Basel, 1541). *Rapsodiae* and *Exempla* appeared together at Basel in 1538. Lang's quotations from the untitled book are from books 1-10; i.e., within the number of books of the *Exempla.*

The preface also speaks of Ioannes Baptista Campofulgosus. This is Battista Fregoso, author of *De dictis factisque memorabilibus,* written originally in Italian and translated into Latin by C. Gilinus. It was published in 1509, 1518, 1541, 1555, 1565, 1578, 1587, and 1604. If it is safe to judge from the British Museum catalogue, only the 1555 edition of Based by Herold has the name Campofrugosus and would therefore be the edition that Lang presumably used, though in the text he also calls him Frugosius. A book of Ravisius Textor (Tixier) also appears in the preface. This is the *Officina,* for a quotation in Lang from Ravisius among the *Exempla profana* under the heading *Apostata* is found on fol. 18v of the Venice 1584 edition of Textor. Similarly Lang's quotation under *Astutia* is from Textor fol. 71. Marullus Spalatensis too is occasionally quoted in the *Exempla profana.* Marco Marulo (Marulić) was born at Spalato (Split) in 1450 and died in 1524. Lang probably drew on his *De institutione bene beateque vivendi,* first printed in 1506. The Basel edition of 1513 has the title *De religiose vivendi institutione per exempla ex veteri novoque testamento collecta; ex autoribus quoque divi Hieronymi, Gregorii, Eusebii,* etc. The Antwerp edition of 1577 has the title *Dictorum factorumque memorabilium libri sex; sive de bene,* etc. Other editions are of 1531, 1555, and 1586. This must be the work referred to by Lang. But he probably found the quotations from Fregoso, Sabellico, and Marulo in Herold's book of *Exempla,* which is simply a collection of editions of these and other writers.

About the origin of the *Hieroglyphica,* the last of the nine classifications, there is no doubt whatever. Nearly all are marked as taken from Piero Valeriano's *Hieroglyphica sive de sacris Aegyptiorum,* first published in 1556. In five instances the attribution is to « eruditus quidam libro 1 (*or* 2) hieroglyphicarum », but one of these is fuller (*s. v. Mercator*): « Pier. Val. lib. 2 Erud. cuiusdam hierogl. p. 570. F. ». In many editions of Valeriano, his work is followed by two books attributed in the earlier editions to C. A. Curio. In later issues the title reads « . . . duo alii ab eruditissimo viro sunt annexi ». In the British Museum catalogue the earliest edition with this title is that printed at Lyons in 1602. One quotation is not attributed, but this is an oversight, for it comes from Valeriano. Just one citation seems at first sight to be independent: under *Ignorantia* Lang cites Hesychius and states that confirmation is to be found in N. T., Acts 9, but this too is from Valeriano. Thus the case stands at 100 per cent use of Valeriano in Lang's *Hieroglyphica*.

At the end of the volume Lang added an index of fables, emblems, and symbols prepared by a young student, Ioannes Philius. These were based on Joachim Camerarius, *Fabellae Aesopicae*, and the *Emblemata* of Alciati and of Camerarius the Younger.

One of Lang's predecessors in producing classified anthologies was Dominicus Nan(n)us Mirabellius, whose very popular *Poly·anthea* was first published in 1503 [15]. In 1574, apparently, the printer Maternus Cholinus of Cologne got out an edition in which he combined with Nani's work the *Flores celebriorum sententiarum* of Bartholomeus Amantius, originally published in 1556. Later still the *Sententiarum opus absolutissimum* of Franciscus Tortius (1560, 1580) was integrated with it [16]. In 1604 Lang published a revision under the title *Nova Polyanthea* (Lyons, Zetzner) [17]. Like the original Nani, this was printed in folio, as were successive editions and revisions.

Nani too made use of Thomas Hibernicus, though sparingly. Under *Abstinentia* fifteen of his quotations from the Fathers are among Thomas'. In the octavo edition only eight of Lang's

---

[15] Reprinted 1507, 1508, 1512, 1513, 1514, 1517, 1522, 1539, 1556, 1565, 1592.

[16] I have examined the edition of 1574, printed by Cholinus. His preface is dated 1574, but there are reports of an edition of his in 1567. Other editions are 1575, 1576 (Cologne and Dillingen), 1585, 1599, 1600 (Lyons and Geneva), 1604, 1612, 1645. The addition of Tortius seems to have been made in the edition of 1585, for which Cholinus wrote a new preface.

[17] A Geneva edition of 1600 is listed by J. G. T. Graesse, *Trésor*, IV (Leipzig, 1900), P. Bayle, *Dictionaire Historique et Critique*, II (Rotterdam, 1697), p. 282, *Biographie Universelle Ancienne et Moderne* (Michaud), 23 (Paris, 1854), p. 167, and *Nouvelle Biographie Générale*, 29 (Paris, 1859), p. 389. This must be the edition of Nani (before revision by Lang) which we know was published in Geneva in 1600.

seventeen from Thomas are identical with Nani's. I see in this Lang's independence of Nani. In the *Nova Polyanthea* nearly all of Thomas' passages are cited, almost four times as many as Nani gives, and some are in the same order as in Thomas. In other words, in his new work Lang integrated his old work with Nani, subtracting some passages from both, adding others from other sources, including Thomas. Under *Ira* Nani has some thirty passages taken from Thomas. Lang in his octavo volume has twelve, six of which are in Nani. The folio editions have twenty-two, all in Nani. Under *Sapientia* Nani gives eight of Thomas' quotations. In his octavo edition Lang has fifteen, only four of which are in Nani. The folio editions have twenty-two (and none from any other source). Of these seven are in Nani, twelve in Lang's octavo edition. Obviously in the folio editions Lang resorted directly to Thomas. Under *Voluntas* Nani quotes ten of Thomas' examples. Of these, three are among the thirteen from that source in Lang's *Loci communes*. The *Nova Polyanthea* has twelve of Thomas' passages. Seven of these are in Nani, five others in the *Loci* [18].

Nani's book was first published about the same time as Mirandola's but neither drew from the other. In his *Loci* Lang seems not to have used Nani, in the *Nova Polyanthea* he generally follows his earlier selections from Mirandola with those from Nani. In his revision of Nani's book Lang introduced the emblems and fables which he merely indexed in his own *Loci*. He also drew on his first book, the *Adagia,* and added proverbs to his now huge collection of material.

A brief survey of the revisions of the *Nova Polyanthea* may help clarify a confused situation [19]. In 1607 Lang got out a new edition under the same title but with a new dedicatory letter. This (or the preceding) was reissued in 1608, 1611 (Frankfurt and Lyons), 1612, 1626, 1681. In 1613 Lang produced a revision

---

[18] Another collection, called *Pharetra doctorum et philosophorum* (ca. 1472) agrees with Nani and Lang only where they have passages taken from Thomas. This of course means that neither Nani nor Lang were influenced by *Pharetra* but that it too drew on Thomas.

[19] Books such as Graesse's *Trésor* confuse the various editions and titles. Only an examination of a large number of copies in various libraries can straighten out matters completely.

under the title *Novissima Polyanthea*, with a new preface (Frankfurt and Lyons). In this edition additions were made in the preliminary definitions by Franciscus Sylvius Insulanus, who quotes an *Etymologicon trilingue* of 1607. This was reprinted in 1616 and 1617. In March of 1615, a month before his last illness, Lang wrote a preface for his last edition, entitled *Polyanthea novissimarum novissima* [20]. But the end was not yet. In 1619, four years after Lang's death, his Frankfurt publisher issued a revision under the title, *Florilegium magnum*. This was reprinted in 1620, 1621, 1624, 1625, 1626, 1628, 1639, 1645, 1648, 1659, 1669, 1681.

In some editions of Thomas' *Flores doctorum* a dedicatory epistle of Bernardus Gualtheri to Gualtherus Xylander (dated Cologne, 1606) states that Thomas' book had strengthened the « orthodox religion of our fathers » and that not only those who were in agreement with the writer in religious matters but « the enemies of our religion » had recognized that fact, for the latter had for a long time been printing and reprinting this work. But, he laments, they had printed it in mutilated, depraved form, loaded down with spurious additions, as one might expect from a Calvinist shop. The result is no longer Thomas but the spirit of Calvin, not flowers (of an anthology) but poison. Then he notes some of the changes made. Under *Antichristus* those passages have been omitted which show that the pope is the true head of the Church, under *Confessio* all reference to confession to a priest is deleted, under *Ecclesia* quotations favoring the Roman Church have disappeared, under *Eucharistia* everything is changed, under *Maria* all the passages about the Virgin that Thomas had cited are omitted and instead some misleading quotations from Epiphanius are introduced. And so on. Wondering which edition of Thomas was in the mind of the writer, I con-

---

[20] I have seen no reference to an edition of 1615, but, to judge from the date of the preface, one must have come out then or the next year. Lang's letter and the new title appear in a Venice edition of 1630. The printer was Paulus Guerilius. In his letter Lang mentions as his printer Ioannes Guerilius (presumably the father of Paul), who published the edition of 1607. The 1615 letter may have been merely a revision of one of earlier date. The 1607 edition has a preface by Ioannes Suentius (Svarz), in which he uses language similar to Lang's of 1615.

sulted the *Index librorum prohibitorum* and found it mentioned in the *Index* (editions of 1758, etc. down to 1948) as the one published by Iacobus Stoer at Geneva in 1596. The 1841 *Index* says it was prohibited (in 1642) because it was falsified in many places by this heretical printer.

This raises a question about Nani and Lang. Nani's book was not put on the *Index*, but Lang's revision of it in the *Novissima Polyanthea* was prohibited in 1626 and 1627 and still appears in the *Index* (1758, etc., 1948). His earlier work escaped. Lang was born a Protestant but became a Catholic in 1603 or 1604. His first printer, Josias Rihel, was a Protestant and perhaps was responsible through his son-in-law, Philip Glaser, for persuading Lang to undertake the *Loci communes*. Rihel's father Wendelin too was a printer, whose first book was Luther's translation of the Bible. Henri Estienne, who was a guest of Lang's and wrote a Greek poem in praise of his *Loci communes*, was a Protestant. In the preface to the *Nova Polyanthea* of 1607 Suentius says that he cleansed the volume of some things that might offend Catholic ears.

Lang's *Loci communes* seems to have followed the « Calvinized » Thomas in avoidance of Catholic dogma. If we consider the criticism of Bernardus Gualtheri of the Calvinistic edition of Thomas, we find that Lang completely omits the topics *Antichristus, Eucharistia*, and *Maria*. Under *Confessio* Lang gives six of Thomas' twenty-five quotations from the Fathers; not included are the two that specifically mention priest or confessor. Under *Ecclesia* Lang has nineteen quotations (including six starred items) of Thomas' thirty, plus three not in Thomas. Not included is the example omitted in the « Calvinized » Thomas, according to the complaint of Bernardus, a quotation from Peter of Ravenna (Chrysologus) that favors the Roman Church by saying that all churches in the world owe to it what the branches of a tree owe to the trunk, etc.

Nani, on the other hand, gives the topics *Antichristus, Eucharistia*, and *Maria*, with many selections taken from Thomas, includes the two under *Confessio* that mention priest and confessor, but omits the one from Peter of Ravenna about the Church at Rome. Lang's various revisions of Nani's *Polyanthea* contain the topics *Antichristus, Eucharistia*, and *Virgo Maria*. They omit Thomas' quotation about priests receiving confession, but add a different one. The quotation from Peter of Ravenna about the Roman Church is not included. Lang had become a Catholic by the time he made his revisions of Nani.

In his preface to the *Loci communes* Lang spoke of Zwinger's *Theatrum humanae vitae* as a noble work, an extremely rich storehouse of examples, by a man without a peer. This work was still in the *Index* as late as 1841. In the *Index expurgatorius*, published in 1607 and 1608, over twenty pages are devoted to deletions and changes in the 1586 Basel edition of the *Theatrum* to make it acceptable. Some of Erasmus' works were on the *Index* as late as 1847 but not those used by Lang.

The great popularity of the anthologies discussed in this chapter, those by Thomas, Nani, Mirandola, and Lang, give some idea of the influence they must have had on the education and literature of the sixteenth and seventeenth centuries, especially in Germany. Many an allusion to or imitation of Plutarch or Pliny may indicate borrowing from Lang or Nani, as today (to use an Erasmian *parabola*) a quotation from Shakespeare or Dante may merely reveal familiarity with Bartlett or Hoyt.

Chapter XXII

PONTANO'S HANDWRITING
AND THE LEIDEN MANUSCRIPT OF TACITUS
AND SUETONIUS [1]

« The Leiden manuscript is known not to be in the hand of Pontanus but is a copy of his manuscript, and the notes are copied as well by the scribe of the manuscript » [2]. This categorical statement, the latest in a long series of the same intent, I wish to challenge and to assert once more that the Leidensis was copied from beginning to end, marginal notes included, by the celebrated humanist Giovanni (Gioviano) Pontano. I say « once more » because I said it once before in a communication published by William Peterson many years ago [3].

Those who over the years have taken the same view as Mendell have done so partly on philological grounds, i.e., on the basis of an examination of the readings of the manuscript in relation to those of other manuscripts, partly on the *auctoritas* of their predecessors. They have chosen to ignore or have misinterpreted the palaeographical evidence. Since 1907, when Wissowa published a facsimile of the Leiden codex (Periz. 4°. 21) and pronounced it a copy of Pontano's manuscript, most scholars have accepted this view.

The Leiden manuscript contains Tacitus' *Dialogus* and *Germania*, and Suetonius' *De grammaticis et rhetoribus*. What is there to show that Pontano copied the Leiden manuscript?

---

[1] Originally published in *Italia Medioevale e Umanistica*, II (1959), p. 309.
[2] C. W. Mendell, *Tacitus* (New Haven, 1957), p. 251.
[3] Peterson, in *American Journal of Philology*, XXXIV (1913), p. 13, n. 1

Nothing but his explicit statement in the manuscript that he did. On fol. 1 v we find (Pl. 14): « Hos libellos Iovianus Pontanus excripsit nuper adinventos et in lucem relatos ab Enoc Asculano quamquam satis mendosos. MCCCCLX Martio mense ». On fol. 47v (Pl. 13): « C. Suetonius scripsit de viris illustribus, cuius exemplum secutus Hieronymus ipse quoque libellum de scriptoribus Christianis edidit. Nuper etiam Bartholomeus Facius familiaris noster de viris illustribus temporis sui libros composuit. Qui ne hos Suetonii illustres viros videre posset mors immatura effecit. Paulo enim post eius mortem in lucem redierunt cum multos annos desiderati a doctis hominibus essent. Temporibus enim Nicolai quinti pontificis maximi Enoc Asculanus in Galliam et inde in Germaniam profectus conquirendorum librorum gratia, hos quamquam mendosos et imperfectos ad nos retulit. Cui sic habenda est gratia ut male imprecandum est Sicconio Polentono Patavino, qui cum eam partem quae est de oratoribus ac poetis adinvenisset, ita suppressit ut ne unquam in lucem venire posset. Quam ego cum Patavii perquirerem, tandem reperi eam ab illo fuisse combustam; ipsumque arrogantia ac temeritate impulsum de vitis illustrium scriptorum loquacissime pariter et ineptissime scripsisse. Iovianus Pontanus Umber excripsit ».

Perhaps the best way to proceed is to summarize the discussion to date. Apparently the Leiden manuscript was first used in the edition of the three items by L. Tross in 1841. He accepted the Pontano ascription without question. So did Hans F. Massmann in his edition of the *Germania* (Quedlinburg, 1847; the preface is dated 1845). He did not accept Pontano's sensational story about Sicco Polenton's plagiarism of Suetonius (p. 187). Actually he made Pontano's tale worse than it is by asserting that Pontano made the charge during the lifetime of Polenton, for he gives the date of the latter's death as 1463 when it actually took place ca. 1447. About the same time Ritschl attacked the credibility of the story, which is now completely deflated[4]. Later Pontano was charged with making

---

[4] F. Ritschl, *Parergon Plautinorum Terentianorumque*, I (Leipzig, 1845), p. 628; *Sicconis Polentoni Scriptorum Illustrium Latinae Linguae Libri XVIII*, ed. B. L. Ullman (Rome, 1928), p. xiii.

up the story out of whole cloth. Though this point seems to have no bearing on our primary purpose, it has served to discredit the Pontano note and the Leiden codex in general, just as a man brought to trial on a criminal charge suffers from any previous difficulties he has had, any unfortunate associations, etc. Perhaps Pontano lied but I do not think so. He had heard the rumor about Sicco and had taken the trouble (if his detractors are willing to grant that he did not invent even this to make his remark more plausible) to ask about it when in Padua [5]. How did the rumor start in the first place? Fifteenth-century scholars knew from Jerome's De viris illustribus, from Isidore, and from other sources that Suetonius had written a book De viris illustribus. Thus Polenton cites this work on p. 42, 1 (from Isidore) and p. 227, 24 (from a manuscript of Pliny, N. H.). Whether anyone had inferred that the De grammaticis et rhetoribus was part of the larger work before Pontano did so in the Leiden manuscript I do not know but it seems likely. The existence of a manuscript of the De grammaticis became known to Poggio in 1425. He spread the news far and wide. In 1426 Panormita informed Guarino in Verona [6]. In 1432 Nicholas of Cues had a copy, apparently entitled De viris illustribus [7]. So when in 1437 Polenton, imitating Suetonius, entitled his book Scriptorum illustrium Latinae linguae libri, what was more natural than the spreading of the rumor that Polenton had used a copy of Suetonius' eagerly desired volume?

Massmann assumed that Pontano made his copy from Enoch's manuscript; that interpretation is not necessarily justified by Pontano's words « libellos... excripsit nuper adinventos ». He devoted much space to arguing that Pontano was the copyist. He took the trouble to look in the library at Munich (at whose University he was professor until 1842) for manuscripts which had Pontano's name in them as scribe or owner. He found

---

[5] He presumably was in Padua in 1451 on his way to Venice. E. Pèrcopo, Vita di Giovanni Pontano (Naples, 1938), p. 12, came to the same conclusion for entirely different reasons.

[6] R. Sabbadini, Le scoperte dei codici latini e greci ne' secoli XIV e XV (Florence, 1905), p. 108.

[7] Sabbadini, Le scoperte ..., II (Florence, 1914), pp. 18, 25-26.

three (lat. 234, 802, 822). He even gave facsimiles of these and the Leiden codex to support his case. Why doth he protest so much? He would hardly have gone into such detail unless suspicion had been cast upon the genuineness of Pontano's hand-writing in the Leiden manuscript. So far as I know, no one had questioned this attribution in print. That did not happen until 1852, when J. Geel published his *Catalogus librorum manu-scriptorum* of the Leiden collection. Was Massmann tilting at windmills, as readers of his book immediately after its appear-ance may have wondered, or was he a seer who could foresee the future? The answer to this double question can, I think, be surmised. Massmann tells us that he was not satisfied with Tross' reports of the manuscript and so through the kindness of the learned and obliging Geel made a new copy [8]. My guess is that during their correspondence Geel expressed the opinion that Pontano did not copy the manuscript, an opinion that he later put in print in his catalogue. Massmann found himself in a predicament. He was greatly indebted to Geel for his assistance but he could not accept Geel's view about the copying. His solution of this delicate problem in good manners was to refute Geel's argument in great detail — but without mentioning Geel's name.

Massmann's presentation and his good facsimiles, even though lithographs, should have made this chapter unnecessary. But in the main, his views were not accepted. Unfortunately he made the impossible suggestion that Pontano was trying to reproduce the script of his exemplar; as evidence of this he relied on the long *r* used throughout the Leiden codex. Without mentioning Massmann's name, Lachmann criticized this view in his commentary on Lucretius (1850, p. 10). Now since

---

[8] Massmann, p. x. Thinking that correspondence between Massmann and Geel might exist in the Leiden library, I asked Dr. Lieftinck, the manuscript librarian, who promptly and courteously sent me microfilms of some of Massmann's letters to Geel of the years 1841 and 1842 (now catalogued as B. P. L. 2426). Though Massmann discusses the Tacitus in these, he takes it for granted that Pontano copied the manuscript and does not feel the need of argument. Thus my hypothesis may be wrong. Geel's replies may be somewhere in Germany in Massmann's *Nachlass*. In his letters Massmann deals primarily with the sending of the Tacitus to Munich for his use.

Lachmann has been misunderstood, it seems desirable to examine his argument more closely. In describing the unique importance and sufficiency of the *oblongus* and *quadratus,* the two oldest manuscripts of Lucretius, he remarked that if the scribes of these two manuscripts had imitated the writing of their common exemplar stroke for stroke, as faithfully as Foggini made a copy of the Medicean manuscript of Virgil, all that would be necessary in an edition such as Lachmann's would be to note their few individual errors. For such a copy would reveal what was written by a second hand in the exemplar, what was added in the margins and between lines, what was erased, etc. Foggini had published a « diplomatic » copy of the Medicean Virgil in 1741, reproducing the capital letters of that codex. Today we would publish a photographic facsimile, like that of the Leiden Tacitus. Lachmann went on to say that scribes did not make faithful facsimiles of their exemplars, reproducing script, corrections, variants, etc.; then he added: « Neque Iohannem Iovianum Pontanum unum Taciti libellum tam superstitiosa sedulitate transcripsisse ullus homo suspicari potuit, nisi insigniter perversus ». The man who was *insigniter perversus* was Massmann. The word *tam* refers to the preceding discussion. All that Lachmann meant (and he was, of course, quite right) was that scribes did not make such copies.

A. Reifferscheid in his edition of Suetonius' *Reliquiae* (1860, p. 413) argued that all the manuscripts of Suetonius' *De grammaticis* were copied by « Itali », i.e., Italian humanists, and that these did not make faithful copies letter for letter as we do but emended the texts, as they thought, but actually interpolated, as we would put it. Therefore, he continued, it is hardly believable that Massmann and Ritter « superstitiose Pontani auctoritati ... se addixisse ». Then he quoted the sentence of Lachmann given above, thus showing that he had completely misunderstood him.

There is a further point: Reifferscheid, like many other scholars, made the mistake of assuming that a humanist like Pontano would emend as he copied. This widespread error overlooks the fact that a scribe, no matter how learned, almost becomes a machine when copying. His attention is absorbed in writing legibly, and even so his mind is apt to wander. I am sure that we have all had this experience ourselves. If the text of the Leidensis, before correction, contains Pontanian emendations, these had been previously entered in the exemplar.

Reifferscheid also quoted Geel to the effect that the manuscript was not Pontano's copy but a copy of it. He then discussed its close relation to Vat. lat. 1862. In an addendum (p. xv) Reifferscheid, after examining the manuscript, adduced palaeographical grounds against the identification of the scribe as Pontano. These will be taken up later. Meanwhile C. L. Roth in his edition of Suetonius (1857, p. LXV, n. 47) accepted the ascription to Pontano. In his edition of the *Dialogus* A. Michaelis (1858, p. XI) agreed with Geel and Reifferscheid; so did F. Scheuer [9].

The next object of attack in Pontano's note was his statement that Enoch of Ascoli brought back the Suetonius and Tacitus. Voigt questioned this because some contemporary statements say that Enoch returned from Germany with few works of importance, Tacitus and Suetonius not being included among those mentioned [10]. Voigt suggested that Pontano's mistake was due to his living in Naples, thus being out of touch with literary developments, which centered in Florence. This too was the explanation of his being hoaxed in Padua, added Voigt.

In his edition of Tacitus' *Dialogus* (Oxford, 1893) W. Peterson adopted the view of his predecessors that the Leiden manuscript was not copied by Pontano (pp. LXX, LXXV) but he did not challenge the statement about Enoch. The next year A. Gudeman came out with his edition of the *Dialogus* (Boston, 1894). He accepted Voigt's argument about Enoch and Geel's about the Leiden codex being a copy of Pontano's (pp. CXX, CXXIII). He added a new argument: that Pontano would not have abstained from emendations [11]. But these he must have entered in the

---

[9] *Breslauer Philologische Abhandlungen*, VI, 1 (1891), p. 5.

[10] G. Voigt, *Die Wiederbelebung des classischen Alterthums*, ed. 3, I (Berlin, 1893), p. 255, n. 3. The point was already made by Voigt in his second edition (1880), I, p. 257, n. 4.

[11] He quoted Lachmann and Reifferscheid for this view, showing that, like the latter, he misunderstood Lachmann, whom he obviously quoted at second hand from Reifferscheid.

exemplar before producing his de luxe copy. Besides, he did make some corrections after completing his copy. It might also be pointed out that the Wolfenbüttel Tibullus, written in the same hand as the Leiden Tacitus, is so full of supposedly correct readings (emendations by Pontano and others) that it reads like a printed text. By its « excellence » it fooled Baehrens and other scholars for many years.

In his edition of the *Germania* (Oxford, 1894), H. Furneaux is much confused (p. 2): « 'Leidensis'..., also called 'Pontanus' [*sic*] ... now found to be not the actual copy taken by Pontanus, but one from it by Geelius ». Incredible though it may be, Furneaux seems to say that Geel copied the Leiden codex!

In his dissertation Wünsch had rejected Voigt's argument against Enoch, but in an article written four years later he changed his mind [12]. In this article he added a new argument, one that could have been foretold: Pontano's statement about Polenton was false, *ergo* his report about Enoch was false. Once a liar (if he was a liar and not, as Voigt thought, an innocent victim guilty only of *naiveté*), always a liar. But later Wünsch once again changed his mind and defended the Enoch story most vigorously. It would be excessive skepticism, he said, to find no support in Pontano's note for Enoch's discovery [13]. In 1898 M. Lehnerdt took issue with Voigt and Wünsch (his *Hermes* article) on the basis of facts brought to light in letters of Carlo de' Medici published by Rossi [14]. On December 10, 1457, Carlo reported that Enoch had died without disposing of his books. Listed are Apicius, Porphyrio, and Suetonius, *De viris illustribus*. This Lehnerdt supposed to be the *De grammaticis* (a view later challenged, as we shall see). The absence of Tacitus' minor works he explained as due to their being in the same volume as Suetonius, which came first. More will be said on this point below.

[12] R. Wünsch, *De Taciti Germaniae codicibus Germanicis* (Marburg, 1893), p. 1; *Hermes*, XXXII (1897), p. 58.
[13] In a review of Annibaldi in *Berliner Philologische Wochenschrift*, 27 (1907), p. 1028.
[14] *Hermes*, XXXIII (1898), p. 499; V. Rossi, *Accademia dei Lincei, Rendiconti, Cl. di sc. mor.*, s. V, II (1893), p. 128.

In 1898 Müllenhoff accepted the Enoch story but not the copying of the Leidensis by Pontano [15]. He too misunderstood the now famous sentence in Lachmann, evidently taking it at second hand from Reifferscheid [16].

In 1905 Sabbadini wrote in his *Scoperte* (p. 141) that the minor works of Tacitus and Suetonius, *De grammaticis*, were brought from Hersfeld by Enoch and stated without hesitation that Pontano owned the Leidensis (p. 148, n. 40). He held to this opinion in 1914 in his second volume (p. 254) [17]. But in 1905 Wissowa struck the hardest blow at the view that Pontano copied the Leiden codex, and two years later he struck again in the introduction to the facsimile of the manuscript [18]. To be sure, he disagreed with Voigt about the Enoch story and he objected at some length and with much vehemence to the downgrading of the Leidensis, especially by Sepp, who had argued that it was a copy of Vat. lat. 1862. He took a middle ground between those who, like Massmann, placed too high a value on it and those who wanted to disregard it entirely as valueless. Wissowa too quoted Lachmann, apparently at second hand from Reifferscheid, for he misunderstood him in exactly the same way: « Dass Pontanus durchweg nur den Text der Vorlage X weitergegeben und sich selbständiger Eingriffe ganz enthalten habe, wird niemand glauben, der den Brauch der Zeit kennt—Lachmann zum Lucrez S. 10 hat darüber ein kräftiges Wort gesagt ». Similarly in the facsimile volume (p. xx). It is because of Wissowa's influence that I devoted so much space above to Reifferscheid's misunderstanding of Lachmann, repeat-

---

[15] K. Müllenhoff, *Deutsche Altertumskunde*, IV (Berlin, 1898), pp. 61, 64, 67.

[16] On p. 63, after mentioning Tagmann on abbreviations in the archetype. Müllenhoff stated that Lachmann on p. 93 of his Lucretius criticized Massmann and Kritz (on Velleius) for their impossible assumptions about abbreviations. I find no such statement in Lachmann. Nor was R. Tagmann, *De Taciti Germaniae apparatu critico* (Breslau, 1847), his source.

[17] Also in his *Storia e critica di testi latini* (Catania, 1914), pp. 263 ff.

[18] G. Wissowa, *Zur Beurteilung der Leidener Germania-Handschrift*, in *Festschrift zum 25jährigen Stiftungsfest des historisch-philologischen Vereines der Universität München* (Munich, 1905), p. 1; *Taciti Dialogus de oratoribus et Germania, Suetonii de viris illustribus fragmentum* (Leiden, 1907; *Codices Graeci et Latini photographice depicti*, Suppl. IV). A. Schoenemann in his dissertation, *De Taciti Germaniae codicibus capita duo* (Halle, 1910), follows his teacher Wissowa.

ed by Müllenhoff, Gudeman, Wissowa, and probably others. This should be a lesson to those who quote at second hand, but it probably will not have any effect.

In the meantime a sensation was caused by the finding of a manuscript at Iesi containing the *Agricola* and *Germania* in which part of the *Agricola* is of the ninth century. This culminated in the publications of Annibaldi [19]. Scholars were unanimous in calling the older part of this manuscript the Hersfeldensis.

In 1913 the *Commentarium* of Niccolò Niccoli was published [20]. The first part of it is a list of books that Niccoli knew were in German libraries and of which he wanted copies. The list is referred to in 1431 but was put together several years earlier. Among the manuscripts listed at Hersfeld is one containing Tacitus, *Germania, Agricola, Dialogus,* Suetonius, *De grammaticis,* in that order. We knew before that these works had been discovered, as Panormita tells us in a letter of 1426, but we did not know with certainty that they were together in one volume [21]. The detailed description of the manuscript in Niccoli's *Commentarium* is very similar to that given by Pier Candido Decembrio of a manuscript he saw at Rome in 1455. It was in this year that Enoch returned to Rome with manuscripts from Germany. It is a fair conclusion that Enoch had brought the Tacitus manuscript, as Pontano stated. An immediate result of all the new facts led Gudeman to reverse his position and to accept Pontano's statement about Enoch [22]. But he maintained that the Leidensis was not copied by Pontano.

[19] C. Annibaldi, *L'Agricola e la Germania di Cornelio Tacito nel MS. latino n. 8 della biblioteca del Conte G. Balleani in Iesi* (Città di Castello, 1907); *La Germania di Cornelio Tacito,...* (Leipzig, 1910). Earlier Annibaldi had referred to the manuscript in *Atti del Congresso internazionale di scienze storiche,* II (Rome, 1905), p. 227.

[20] In Catalogue XII of the booksellers T. De Marinis & Co.; reprinted by Sabbadini, *Storia...,* p. 1. The best edition is that of Rodney P. Robinson, *Classical Philology,* XVI (1921), p. 251. N. Rubinstein published a similar document by Poggio's son Iacopo in the first volume of *Italia Medioevale e Umanistica* (1958), p. 383. He gives evidence to show that the two documents are independent of each other, both being based on Poggio's notes.

[21] Sabbadini, *Storia...,* p. 270, originally published in 1899.

[22] *Dialogus,* ed. 2 (Leipzig, 1914), pp. 112, 116. In his edition of the *Germania* (Berlin, 1916), Gudeman had little to say about the manuscripts. The Leidensis was still considered a copy of Pontano's manuscript.

In 1922 Robinson came out strongly against the then prevailing belief that Enoch had brought the Herfeldensis to Rome, calling it a superstition[23]. He repeated his views in detail in his edition of the *Germania* (1935, p. 351) because he felt that his earlier presentation might not have come to the attention of scholars. He could cite only Voigt on his side, as Wünsch had abandoned his former position. He discredited Pontano's specific statement—the only one that we have—on the ground that other sources of information (Aurispa, Carlo de' Medici) make no mention of Tacitus in their list of Enoch's finds. Surely Tacitus would have been included, argued Robinson (as others had before him), as being of much greater consequence than any of those reported, such as Apicius and Porphyrio's commentary on Horace. Robinson was not satisfied with the various explanations offered. Enoch returned to Rome in 1455 after the death of his patron Nicholas V. He tried desperately to find another patron (such as King Alfonso of Naples) to buy his manuscripts at a good price. Robinson argued that Enoch would have mentioned his biggest prize, the Tacitus, if it had been in his possession. That is a natural supposition, yet he might have done just the opposite, suppressing the news of his best find, thus hoping to whet the appetites of potential buyers by a bit of mystery. He did not allow anyone to make copies of his books. Another point to be made against Robinson is that Carlo de' Medici in his letter was for some reason minimizing the importance of Enoch's collection. He may not have liked Enoch's personality or the high price he was demanding or his secretiveness. One strong argument in favor of Enoch has been that Enoch returned from Germany in 1455 and that Decembrio saw an old Tacitus that same year. Robinson explained this as coincidence, but scholars do not like to resort to coincidence as an explanation. Usually there is a relationship between coincident facts. In the earlier work Robinson asserted that the Enoch story told by Pontano was untrue because the latter's statement about Sicco was a lie (*mendacium*). Once a liar always a liar, as I said before. This

[23] Rodney P. Robinson, *De fragmenti Suetoniani De grammaticis et rhetoribus codicum nexu et fide* (Urbana, 1922), p. 19

statement Robinson toned down later. He suggested that Pontano had heard that Enoch brought back Suetonius' *De viris illustribus* (as Carlo tells us) and that when he (Pontano) found a manuscript of *De grammaticis* along with Tacitus he assumed that this was the one that Enoch had found. It must be admitted, however, that Robinson may have had a point about « Suetonius De viris illustribus », in thinking that it might have been the pseudo-Victor work, often attributed also to Pliny. He cited a manuscript of the Duke of Marlborough in which Suetonius is credited with this treatise. Early incunabula (Hain 2133, about 1475; 2132, about 1484) and later editions attribute it to Suetonius. But the work was so well known under the name of Pliny that it could scarcely have deceived anyone. It is found under Pliny's name along with the *De grammaticis* in two manuscripts (Copenhagen, Vat. lat. 4498). The failure of Poggio's son Iacopo to mention Enoch in the manuscript list recently published by Rubinstein could be used as an argument against Enoch, but Rubinstein satisfactorily disposed of that possibility, as he did of Iacopo's statement that Tacitus and Suetonius came to Italy through the efforts of Pius II.

Certain evidence can be adduced in favor of Enoch which, as far as I know, no one has fully exploited [24]. Among the works that Enoch certainly brought back were Porphyrio and Apicius, besides Suetonius, *De viris illustribus*. Two manuscripts of *De grammaticis, Dialogus, Germania,* also contain Porphyrio (Vat. lat. 1518, Ottob. lat. 1434) [25]. One manuscript of the *Germania* contains Apicius (Laur. 73, 20) and another manuscript once contained both (Pesaro, now lost). We know from Niccoli's *Commentarium* that Apicius was at Fulda. Other manuscripts show no such connection with Enoch, but as they include authors listed by Niccoli, they may have been among those that Enoch brought back. Thus Frontinus, *De aquis*, was at Hersfeld. This we find combined with Suetonius, *Agricola, Dialogus, Germania* in Vat lat. 4498. Hyginus, *Astrologia*, listed by Niccoli as at Fulda, is

---

[24] Mendell, *Tacitus*, p. 253, hinted at it but did not develop it.
[25] The second was discovered by Dorothy M. Robathan, *American Journal of Philology*, LXXI (1950), p. 225.

coupled with the *Germania* in Ottob. lat. 1795. Possibly the gromatic material in Vat. lat. 4498 (Nipsus, etc.) bears a relation to two gromatic manuscripts that Niccoli listed at Fulda.

At this point some observations on the manuscripts of Tacitus and Suetonius may be in order. The *Agricola* is found with the other three items of the Hersfeld codex as described by Niccoli in only one manuscript (Vat. lat. 4498, already mentioned), and in this the order of the treatises is different. Only three other manuscripts of this work are known, the Iesi manuscript, containing part of the original Hersfeldensis (with a fifteenth-century copy of the *Germania*), a Toledo manuscript which is said to be a direct copy of the Iesi book [26], and the *Agricola* alone copied by Pomponio Leto (Vat. lat. 3429). It seems quite obvious that the *Agricola* was removed from the Hersfeldensis at a relatively early date, as several scholars have observed. One wonders whether the fifteenth-century supplements to the Iesi *Agricola* were not added from a manuscript of the same century, not from the Hersfeldensis [27]. It would seem certain, as many think, that the Iesi *Germania* was not copied from the Hersfeld manuscript. The *Germania* is found without *Dialogus* and Suetonius in seventeen manuscripts [28]. The contents and their order in the other manuscripts should furnish a clue as to their relationships [29]. *Germania* and *Dialogus* are together in that order in Vat. lat. 2964, Vienna 49, and Baltimore, Walters Art Gallery 466 [30]. Suetonius and

---

[26] Annibaldi, *L'Agricola e la Germania ...*, supported by Robinson, *Germania*, p. 206.

[27] In spite of those who claim that the first part was copied from missing leaves of the Hersfeldensis, this part (ending fol. 55v) does not fit exactly with the second (fol. 56r), for there is a repetition of the word *munia* and furthermore the preceding words are in erasure, not "leggermente abrasa", as Annibaldi said. This is clear from Till's reproduction (for which see below). The manuscript needs careful re-examination at this point. Likewise the disagreement in colophon between the late copy (« De vita et moribus ») and the traces of the original (« De vita ») needs to be explained. I am unwilling to concede that the late copyist (Guarnieri?) changed this in copying.

[28] The fullest list of manuscripts is in Robinson, *Germania*, pp. 79 ff. and in Mendell, *Tacitus*, pp. 256 ff.

[29] C. W. Mendell has done something with this but not in a complete fashion (*American Journal of Philology*, LVI, 1935, p. 113).

[30] This manuscript is listed only by Mendell and has not been discussed in detail by anyone.

Dialogus, in that order, occur in six manuscripts [31], Suetonius, without the other two, in seven. In the manuscripts containing all three items, the order of the Hersfeldensis (*G., D., S.*) is found only in Vienna 711. The *G., D.* manuscripts may represent a subgroup, shortened by the omission of *S.* The order *D.,G.,S.* of the Leidensis occurs also in Naples XIV, *C,* 21. *G., S., D.* is the order in Vat. lat. 1862; *S., D., G.,* in Venice XIV, 1. These two could represent the *S., D.* combination (noted above in six manuscripts) with the addition of the *Germania.*

Groupings of other contents may also throw light on the confused stemma of the *Germania.* Thus Harl. 1895, Cesena XVII, 2, 1-2, and Paris, N. a. l. 1180 offer Pomponius Mela and the *Germania,* but Robinson's stemma shows no close connection. Is the stemma wrong? I raise the question without attempting to answer it. Mela occurs with Suetonius and the *Dialogus* in Ottob. lat. 1455, but this may be due to chance. Angelica 1172, Laur. 73, 20, Ricc. 158, Madrid 10037, and the lost Pesaro manuscript contain, besides the *Germania,* Francesco Aretino's translation of pseudo-Diogenes with a dedicatory poem and an elegy to Pius II. Robinson's stemma shows the first four in fairly close relationship; perhaps it should be still closer.

Whether the presence of the dedicatory poem to Pius II in these five manuscripts indicates a direct connection with the Pope, as has been suggested, is a bit doubtful [32]. Another manuscript has a definite connection with him: Venice, XIV, 1. The first part contains Pius II material, followed by *S., D., G.* This second part was copied at Bologna in 1464 for the well-known Paduan Giovanni Marcanova, as was the latter part of the Pius II material, according to a colophon on fol. 116 [33]. Ottob. lat. 1455 (*S., D.*), though it has a work of Pius II, contains several other humanistic works so that no connection with the Pope can be established.

---

[31] Robinson, *De fragmenti* ..., p. 29.

[32] Wünsch (*De Taciti* ..., pp. 82, 121; *Hermes,* p. 56) pointed out the Pius II thread binding together various manuscripts. Pius II had read the *Germania* as early as 1458 (Lehnerdt, *op. cit.,* p. 502).

[33] So Massmann, p. 20. Others make no mention of such a colophon within the Aeneas Silvius selections, but Dr. Giorgio E. Ferrari kindly confirmed it and called attention to a similar statement on fol. 1, together with Marcanova's coat of arms, which Wünsch had wrongly attributed to Pius II.

Furthermore, it does not contain the *Germania,* which appears in all the other manuscripts mentioned above and in which he had a special interest. Wünsch added the Stuttgart manuscript to the group because it contains an extension to Benvenuto da Imola's *Liber Augustalis* made by Aeneas Silvius for the years 1440-1457 [34]. The manuscript has a marginal note reading: « Addidit sequens Eneas Senensis » [35]. Robinson gave this manuscript a status independent of the others. Lehnerdt added Vienna 711 to the Pius II group because it was written (in 1466) for the Bishop of Trent, a friend of the Pope. This manuscript is, as noted above, the only one that preserves the order of the Hersfeldensis, though omitting the *Agricola.* Robinson noted this and called this the only manuscript of the *Germania* which has independent value (p. 153).

The Stuttgart codex sends our thoughts into other, rather interesting, channels. It contains Pier Candido Decembrio's *Compendium historiae Romanae* [36]. Now Decembrio is the man who gave us an excellent description of the Hersfeldensis which he saw at Rome in 1455. In 1456 he went to Naples as secretary of King Alfonso and stayed till late in 1459. Whether the presence of his work in the Stuttgart codex has any significance or not, the fact remains that Decembrio may have told Pontano about the Hersfeldensis and its discoverer Enoch, as they were together in Naples for over three years. Decembrio left Naples only a few months before Pontano wrote the date 1460 in the Leidensis.

A timetable may be put together as follows:

March, 1455.   Death of Nicholas V.

Autumn, 1455.   Enoch returns to Rome with the Hersfeldensis.

---

[34] It is not stated who made the additions preceding 1440. Benvenuto died in 1390.

[35] Wünsch (diss.), p. 121.

[36] Apparently composed in 1442 and dedicated to Alfonso, who had just captured Naples (L. Bertalot, *Zentralblatt für Bibliothekswesen,* XXVIII, 1911, p. 93), but V. Zaccaria suggested a date around 1450 (*Rinascimento,* VII, 1956, p. 29). The Stuttgart manuscript has an early statement about the *Compendium*: « Scripsit nostro tempore Neapoli ». This seems to be an error.

Autumn, 1455. Decembrio sees Hersfeldensis in Rome.

November-December, 1455. Panormita (in Naples) writes Aurispa (in Rome) to bring Apicius, etc. (among Enoch's finds).

December 13, 1455, Aurispa replies.

March 13, 1456, etc. Carlo de' Medici writes his brother Giovanni about Enoch's manuscripts.

August 28, 1457. Aurispa writes that he saw Enoch a few days earlier.

November, 1457. Suetonius not yet available at Fazio's death but becomes so « paulo post » (Pontano).

December 10, 1457. Carlo reports Enoch's return to Ascoli and subsequent death. Reports that Aeneas Silvius had made inquiries about Enoch's manuscripts and later had written to Ascoli.

January 13, 1458. Carlo writes that Enoch manuscripts not yet available.

February 1, 1458. Aeneas by this time has read the *Germania*.

March, 1460. Pontano copies Leidensis.

The probability is therefore that the *Agricola* had been removed and sold between January, 1456, and December, 1457. Aeneas obtained a copy or the original of the rest of the manuscript before January, 1458. It is possible that the multiplication of copies was due to Aeneas' liberality in allowing them to be made. All the dated manuscripts belong to the year 1460 (Leidensis) and later (1464, 1466, 1471, 1474, 1476, 1502).

A possible inference may be drawn from Pontano's statement in the Leidensis. Bartolomeo Fazio came to Naples in 1444 and lived there the rest of his life. He was working on the tenth and last book of his *De viris illustribus* in 1455 [37]. Did he and Pontano get word of the discovery of Suetonius immediately after Enoch's arrival in Rome or at least after Decembrio's arrival in Naples and did they try to get a copy? Did Fazio die before Pontano received (*priusquam accepit*) a copy or before he

---

[37] Voigt, *Die Wiederbelebung...*, I, p. 489, n. 2.

could receive it (*priusquam acciperet*)? I admit at once that my inference that Pontano was trying to get a copy before Fazio's death is not a necessary one, but perhaps it is possible.

For years scholars, Italian and foreign, knocked at Count Balleani's door in order to study the Iesi manuscript, only to be turned away. But in 1939 Rudolph Till succeeded. He and Paul Lehmann not only were allowed to study the manuscript at their leisure in Rome but Till was even able to publish a photographic reproduction, for which we are most grateful. This he did through the persuasiveness of Heinrich Himmler: *Nihil dico amplius* [38]. Till followed Robinson and Mendell in rejecting the Enoch story [39]. One difficulty in accepting the old part of the Iesi manuscript as the Hersfeldensis, one that seems to have gone unnoticed until Lehmann mentioned it, is that the manuscript starts out with Dictys Cretensis, not included by Niccoli in his description of the Hersfeld codex or by others. Robinson believed that one of the Dictys scribes entered marginal notes in the *Agricola*. Lehmann in denying this made it possible to assume that the Dictys was combined with the *Agricola* after the latter was torn away from its fellows in the Hersfeld book. But if the two were together from the beginning the Iesi manuscript is hardly likely to have been the Hersfeldensis.

In 1949 and 1950 Perret reviewed the entire situation [40]. Though basing his work chiefly on Robinson's edition, which

---

[38] Rudolf Till, *Handschriftliche Untersuchungen zu Tacitus Agricola und Germania* (Berlin, 1943).

[39] Mendell, *A. J. P., loc. cit.* He thought that two or even three manuscripts, at least of the *Germania*, were brought down from Germany. Robinson (p. XII) rejected this idea, though, of course, welcoming the expulsion of Enoch from the Tacitus story. On one point Mendell was surely mistaken, that Frontinus may have been in the same Hersfeld manuscript as Tacitus. The *Commentarium* of Niccoli ties together the three Tacitus treatises and Suetonius with the repeated phrase « Item in eodem codice ». No such phrase occurs after Frontinus. Niccoli's statement is now confirmed by the document of Poggio's son Iacopo, published by Rubinstein, *op. cit.*

[40] J. Perret, edition of *Tacite, La Germanie,* Paris, Budé series, 1949; *Recherches sur le texte de la « Germanie »* (Paris, 1950). L. Pralle, *Die Wiederentdeckung des Tacitus* (Fulda, 1952), piling one unconvincing hypothesis on another, concluded that Poggio received the Tacitus from a Hersfeld monk in 1427, and that this monk got it from Fulda. Pralle's sole concern is to exalt Fulda; it is not worth while to refute him in detail. Rubinstein, *op. cit.*, has some telling arguments against Pralle's assertions.

he rightly praised highly, he could not go along with Robinson on the Enoch story, which he defended in a detailed discussion. He explained the absence of contemporary testimony on the finding of Tacitus by Enoch by the supposition that Enoch went to Hersfeld first and sent back the Tacitus to Nicholas V, probably in 1452-53. There are, however, several objections to this hypothesis. First of all it would destroy, or at least greatly weaken, the chief support of Pontano's statement, the coincidence of date of Enoch's return in 1455 with that of Decembrio's examination of the Hersfeldensis, a coincidence which Perret himself accepted as valid evidence. One cannot eat his cake and have it too. Also, if Enoch went to Hersfeld early in his wanderings, he is likely to have gone to near-by Fulda at the same time, and it was at Fulda that he found the Apicius which he is said to have brought back with him. Niccoli tells us that Apicius was at Fulda. Finally, it might be argued that a humanist such as Nicholas V would have allowed other humanists to read and copy the new find. As we saw, Aeneas Silvius was trying to get copies of some of Enoch's manuscripts in the last months of 1457 and he had read the *Germania* early in 1458; it would seem that the *Germania* is what he succeeded in getting from Enoch's heirs. To be sure, Perret suggested that Aeneas may have seen the *Germania* as early as August, 1457, but his argument is not convincing. We can be sure that if Nicholas V had Tacitus, his friend Aeneas, whom he made Cardinal in 1456, would have had access to it.

Perret made the interesting observation that the reconciliation of the Papacy with the Aragonese dynasty of Naples coincided in time with Pontano's date in the Leidensis (1460), that is, Pontano was able to get a Tacitus to copy only after this reconciliation had taken place. Perret followed Wissowa in calling the Leidensis a copy of Pontano's manuscript. He noted the close relationship of the manuscripts containing Francesco Aretino (mentioned above) and added to the group the Cesena and Urbinas codices on the basis of their readings as shown in Robinson's stemma. He noted that in 1460 Pius II tried to reconcile the Sforza of Pesaro, the Malatesta of Cesena, and the Duke of Urbino, and he was tempted to see in that circumstance the explanation of why there were *Germania* manuscripts at Pesaro, Cesena, and Urbino (Urb. lat. 412) [41]. In any case he thought that the archetype of the five families worked out by Robinson was Aeneas' copy of the Hersfeldensis. Aeneas, he observed, had a special interest in Germany, in education, and in rhetoric (*Germ., Dial.,* Suetonius) but not in England (*Agricola*).

The uncertainty about the script of the Leidensis is highlighted by the somewhat conflicting statements of Lenchantin de Gubernatis in his edition of 1949. In the *Dialogus* (Paravia series, p. v) he said that it is regarded as Pontano's by those who rely on the inscription on fol. IV but countered with the statement: « At cum codicis scriptura a Pontani prorsus differat, de aliquo librario cogitandum est a Pontano mercede conducto ». In the *Germania* (p. VI) he took a neutral position, saying that it is uncertain whether the manuscript was copied by Pontano or an unknown scribe, the inscription favoring the former, the script the latter. In his edition of the *Agricola* he implied that Pontano wrote the note about Enoch.

Mendell gathered together his various studies in a book published in 1957, a quotation from which has served as the *incipit* of the present paper. He accepted the Enoch story but assumed that a second Tacitus had previously been brought from Germany.

Thus it may be said that the Enoch story is generally accepted but the ascription of the writing of the Leidensis to Pontano is almost universally rejected.

It is high time to discuss the handwriting of the Leiden manuscript. It has been discussed too much by scholars not familiar with palaeography or at least not with fifteenth-century Italian palaeography. To give one example of Wissowa's weakness in this respect, he considered the practice of putting a small *o* above a vocative *a* « rationem satis singularem ». On the contrary, it is extremely common; I have seen it in scores of manuscripts.

---

[41] This Vatican manuscript can easily be identified from its varied contents with the one described in a catalogue of the Duke of Urbino's library made before 1482. This catalogue was published in *Giornale storico degli archivi toscani* (Florence, 1857), VII, p. 54, No. 250.

For over one hundred years, ever since Geel's catalogue of 1852, it has been repeated that Pontano did not copy the Leidensis. I have stood practically alone [42]; in fact I can only recall one man who supported my position, but that one man, Remigio Sabbadini, is worth a host of others [43]. He wrote: « G. Wissowa ... lo crede apografo del cod. Pontaniano; ma io sono di contrario avviso », and referred to my note in Peterson's article.

The very inconsistencies of the opponents of Pontano tell against them. Some say the Leidensis was copied by a hired scribe; others, such as Wissowa, reject this in favor of a scholar member of Pontano's academy. Then there is difference of opinion about the two notes signed by Pontano. Reifferscheid thought that they were not written by the text hand, Wissowa denied this, and rightly so.

Here is a portrait of the copyist of the Leidensis as described by Wissowa. He is no ordinary copyist but a scholar, a member of Pontano's academy. He emends as he copies (which, as I said above, not even scholarly scribes are apt to do very often), he frequently preserves the peculiarities of Pontano's orthography with amazing fidelity (*haerba, sullimis,* etc.), he copies Pontano's signature and date. It is true that such copying sometimes happens, but is there enough evidence to make it likely in this particular case? All in all, the description of this member of the Pontanian academy fits no one so well as Pontano himself.

One of the things that first aroused suspicion was the note on fol. 47v. Geel stated in 1852 that the errors and erasures in this note show that Pontano did not copy the book. The phrase « eam partem que est » is added above the line (for the text see the beginning of this article and Pl. 13). The scribe also originally wrote an *est* which had to be deleted. To me the changes indicate that it was Pontano who wrote the note, making it up as he went along, and not a scribe who made mistakes. Pontano

---

[42] In the note in Peterson's article, already cited; also my *Ancient Writing* (New York, 1923), p. 141. See Pl. 13-28.

[43] *Le scoperte,* II, p. 254, n. 1. B. Sepp accepted Massmann's statement in a brief footnote in *Philologus,* 62 (1903), p. 292, n. 1. E. Chatelain, *Paléographie des classiques latins* (Paris, 1884-1900), II, p. 15, also accepted it without discussion. Rubinstein, *op. cit.,* quotes my view with seeming approval.

first wrote: « qui [Polenton] cum de oratoribus ac poetis est inven » as if he were going to say « inventus liber ». He then deleted *est* and changed to *invenisset librum* (or some such word). As neither form was entirely accurate, he corrected to « qui cum eam partem que est de ... adinvenisset », erasing the last word (*librum*?); *ad* was added to *invenisset* to fill the space in part. This is much simpler than to try to explain how a scribe came to omit words, to repeat *est*, etc.   Earlier in the note the *A* of *Asculanus* was expunged and a Beneventan *e* (therefore made by the scribe, Pontano) was written above it, to make it *Esculanus* (not *Aesculanus*, as Wissowa said).   The same change was made on fol. 1 v (Pl. 14); in both cases the *e* was later erased.   This is a clear instance, not of a correction of an error by a scribe, but of a change of mind by an author.   The spellings *Esculanus* and *Aesculanus* are common variants, as one can see from the *Thesaurus Linguae Latinae*. If, for example, Pontano had been reading Gellius, the chances are that he would have found *Esculanus* in his copy.   Poggio used this form in writing of Enoch [44].   So too the change of « habendae sunt gratiae » to « habenda est gratia » is the author's correction.

Let us come to grips with the specifically palaeographical problem. It seems not to be realized among Tacitus scholars that a scribe may change his style from time to time and especially that he may use two or three styles at the same time for different purposes, just as a printer today has at his command at least several different fonts of types. It is a familiar fact that Petrarch wrote both in a formal Gothic book hand and in a cursive style. A more appropriate example is Poggio. It is my belief that Poggio was the inventor of humanistic script [45]. One of the essential features of this script was the abandonment of uncial *d* and round final *s* in favor of minuscule *d* and long *s* respectively. In the same way Pontano was experimenting with two new letters, a long *r* and a broken *e* in imitation of « Beneventan » (i.e., South Italian) script.   Perhaps he thought that Naples deserved a script of its own, based in part on that of near-by Monte Cas-

---

[44] Quoted by Perret, *Recherches*..., p. 139, n. 2.

[45] I have developed this view at length in a book called *The Origin and Development of Humanistic Script* (Rome, 1960). See too Chapter XV above.

sino, and that the Florentine script should not have a monopoly. For Naples was full of Florentine scribes and others who had been trained in the beautiful Florentine script. They had been busy copying fine manuscripts for Alfonso and Ferdinand [46].

Now scholars have argued that Pontano was not the scribe of the Leidensis because of the long *r* and broken *e*, not found in other autographs and signatures of Pontano. This experimental script was apparently confined to the year 1460 and perhaps only to a month or two in that year. Furthermore, it was the formal text script not always employed in marginalia and other less formal writing. In the same way Poggio used a mixture of Gothic and humanistic in his marginal notes, occasionally including uncial *d* and round final *s*. Pontano did exactly the same sort of thing. In the note on fol. 1 v (which Wissowa accepts as done by the scribe) the *e* is always Beneventan, but the *r* is definitely long as in Beneventan in only two instances, definitely short in *martio* and intermediate in *excripsit*. In the long note on fol. 47v there are several instances of Beneventan *e* and *r* but for the most part these letters have the ordinary form. In other respects the writing of the note and the text is alike, as may be seen in Pl. 13. The general cast is the same, both have long ascenders and descenders, that typical letter *g* is identical, as is the *s*.

Actually even in the text the Beneventan *e* at times yields to the ordinary minuscule *e*. On fol. 57v there are seventeen instances of the latter, over sixteen per cent of the total. Even so I have included every intermediate and doubtful form among the Beneventan examples. On fol. 47v (Pl. 13) there are several examples (last line, *disseruit, exemplo*); on fol. 2r (Pl. 15) it occurs in *ingeniis, autem*, etc. Short *r* is much less common but can be found: fol. 9r, line 2 *eorum*, fol. 12r, line 21 *nostrorum*, fol. 47v, line 1 *illustribus*, fol 2r (Pl. 15) *temporum*. In some

---

[46] To be seen in the splendid volumes of T. De Marinis, *La biblioteca napoletana dei re d'Aragona* (Milan, 1947-52). In view of the discovery that there once was an *Agricola* at Monte Cassino and the suggestion that a *Germania* too was there (Mendell, *Tacitus*, p. 283) it is surprising that no one has suggested that the Beneventan *e* and *r* in the Leidensis were copied from the Monte Cassino manuscript. I mention this, not as a possibility, but as a warning to some ingenious scholar!

cases a tick was added to lengthen a short *r*: fol. 56r, line 8 *sectatores*.

Wissowa accepted as the scribe's the marginal note on fol. 59v: « Amplius repertum non est adhuc; desunt rhetores xi ». The first two *e*'s are Beneventan, the last three are not; two *r*'s are long, one is not. Wissowa also accepted various interlinear variants and corrections as the handiwork of the original scribe. Let us consider only those he mentions. In Suet. 13 (fol. 52v) the suprascript *herosnametra* has one long and one short *r*. In *Germ.* 26 (fol. 39v) the *r* of *labore* is long, as is that of *armantur* in *Germ.* 38 (fol. 43v). In other words, the absence of Beneventan characteristics proves nothing, for the text hand does occasionally omit them in marginal notes.

Wissowa distinguished a second hand which entered marginal summaries, index, parallel passages, etc. To me it seems that these were entered by the scribe Pontano. I think that this would be clear to anyone not overawed by the authority and positiveness of Tacitean scholars of the last hundred years. On fol. 4v *Marc*(*ellus*) has the Beneventan *r*. On fol. 8r the first *e* of *elegia* is the broken Beneventan. On fol. 4r the first *e* of *eloquentiae* is a borderline case, like the last *e* of *necessitates* in the adjoining text, and two other *e*'s are regular. On fol. 4v the first *e* of the same word is definitely Beneventan, the other two are not. In *litterator* on fol. 49r one *r* is short, the other long. On the previous page both are short. This letter is long in *apparitura* and *laceravit* on fol. 50v, *gibber* on fol. 51r, *calator* and *liberaliter* on fol. 52v, *uxor* on fol. 54r, *polyhistor* on fol. 54v, *Curio* on fol. 56v.

In *Germ.* 25 the last five lines are misplaced at the end of 26 in L and its close relative V. What Robinson calls «a later hand » added the lines at the bottom of fol. 39r with insertion marks at the proper point [47]. Wissowa did not refer to the addition, but it seems to me to be in Pontano's less formal hand, like the marginalia I have been listing. The *r* is usually short

---

[47] The extent of the downgrading of the LV family is indicated by the silence of Robinson's and Perret's apparatus on the omission; Robinson mentioned it in discussing manuscript relations (p. 196).

but is long in *raro* and *libertatis*, slightly lengthened in *liberti*. Except for *e* and *r* the script is very much like that of the text, as may be judged from its graceful sweeping character, its long letters, its characteristic *v* and *g*, and even its Pontanian spelling (*coeteros*).

Wissowa detected a third marginal hand in a note on fol. 46v referring to the visit of a certain Alexander Soltan of Lithuania to Naples. Wissowa was able to date this note as of the year 1476. He suggested that either the writer of the note or Pontano heard Soltan talking about the matter in question. This is almost an admission that Pontano wrote the note, as I am sure that he did.

Wissowa made a distinction between the first two correctors (B^1 and B^2 he calls them) on the basis of the paler ink and thicker pen used by B^2. This difference can be explained just as well by supposing that Pontano entered his notes at various times, a situation one meets very frequently in manuscripts. The hand that he called B^2 cites Tacitus' *Histories*, Catullus, and Ovid, knows Greek and emends frequently. A good description of Pontano, to my thinking. B^1, as Wissowa calls him, wrote a note on fol. 10r: « quod ad curiales et aulicos principum totum pertinere videtur ». Wissowa made the interesting comment that one can recognize in the author of this remark a person at the royal court of Naples. Whom does this fit better than Pontano? [48]

It was Wissowa, I believe, who first made mention of the facsimile of Pontano's handwriting in Soldati's edition of the humanist's poems [49] and proclaimed that now all doubt was removed that Pontano did not copy the Leidensis. One might quibble with him and ask, if it was already certain that the script was « toto caelo diversa » from the examples that Massmann gave, how any doubt remained to be removed. Many scholars have since echoed Wissowa. An amusing instance is

---

[48] The dissertation, already cited, of A. Schoenemann, a pupil of Wissowa's, discusses the correcting hands in the Leidensis but adds nothing new for my purpose.

[49] *Pontani Carmina*, ed. B. Soldati, II (Florence, 1902), frontispiece.

that of Gudeman. He wrote me after Peterson's article appeared to ask why I thought Pontano was the copyist of the Leidensis. I gave him some of my reasons, not mentioning Soldati as there was no occasion to do so. When he published his edition of the *Dialogus* (1914) he said my reasons were invalid because I was not familiar with Soldati's work![50] One reference to Soldati settles the matter, apparently. But consider that the autograph of Pontano's *De stellis* (Vat. lat. 2837) was made nearly thirty years after the Leidensis and is the author's first draft, on paper, with many corrections, in cursive script[51]. The Leidensis is written in a handsome formal script on parchment. Even so the marginal material is not so very different in script from the later less formal writing. The presence or absence of the Beneventan letters is no final proof for or against Pontano as the scribe. The two pages of Vat. lat. 2837 that have been published in facsimile reveal a final straight *s* except for a small number of examples of round *s* at the end of the line. On the other hand, two pages of Vienna 3413 show a reversed situation: round *s* is always found except in two examples in the margin. Shall we say then that these two manuscripts (only some ten years apart) were not written by the same man?

One thing scholars have either ignored entirely or passed over lightly, the autograph signatures in the Munich manuscripts reproduced by Massmann. They certainly do not resemble the later autographs any more than the marginal notes in the Leidensis do. Are they forgeries then? Hardly. Which re-

---

[50] P. 116, n. 3. As a matter of fact, I was acquainted with Soldati's edition and had referred to it in an article in *Classical Philology*, VI (1911), p. 299. It is obvious that Gudeman did not himself consult Soldati but took his information from Wissowa and Sabbadini, as the form of the reference shows: « Soldati . . . S. XXII. XXX). Sabbadini has « I p. XXII; XXX », which should be XXII-XXX. This covers the description of the manuscripts only; the facsimile in Vol. II was not mentioned by Gudeman. Incidentally Sabbadini credited Pontano with the ownership of the Leidensis, a fact that Gudeman ignored.

[51] A facsimile of part of the same page and of Vat. Lat. 2838 on Pl. 16, 17. The *Enciclopedia Italiana, s. v.* Pontano, gives a reduced facsimile of fol. 25 of Vat. lat. 2837. Facsimiles of another Pontano autograph (Vienna 3413, fols. 194v and 197v) are in the *De sermone*, ed. S. Lupi and A. Risicato (Lugano, 1953). The manuscript was copied in 1499 and was worked over by Pontano until his death in 1502.

calls that, whereas other scholars call the Pontano signature in the Leidensis merely faithful copying, Pèrcopo maintained it was « falsificata, ma con poca abilità » because it is unlike other contemporary autographs[52]. What had been thought merely innocent fidelity now becomes clumsy forgery. The signature of the Leiden codex seems to me to be identical with those in Vat. Barb. lat. 146 and the Munich manuscripts (Pl. 20-22). Note especially the capital P with the long serif at the bottom. Even the *Pontani* of the late Vatican manuscript (Pl. 16) is similar. This P appears in the text of the Leidensis as well. But of course the closest resemblance of the Munich autographs is to the less formal script of the marginal notes of the Leidensis, where the artificial *e* and *r* do not tend to disguise the script. The last word *sunt* in the addition on fol. 39r is very much like the last word in Pl. 22, with the capital T and its long curving cross stroke. The capital F of the Munich autographs is like the one used five times on fol. 30r. The *g* and *s* of the Leiden text are like those of the autographs.

Chatelain compared the script of a manuscript of Tibullus at Wolfenbüttel (Aug. 82, 6 fol.) with that of the Leidensis[53], but it was Wissowa who first stated that they were copied by the same person. This view has not been questioned, nor indeed could it be, for the writing is identical. The marginal notes too are like those in the Leidensis in script and content. Wissowa thought that one of the marginal hands in the Leidensis (which he called the « glossator ») was the same as that in the Tibullus, with which I agree, since I believe that Pontano wrote the notes (at different times) as well as the text. For good measure, I would also include the second hand (the « corrector »). Actually four of the notes in the Tibullus are signed Pont(anus) and yet this claim has regularly been rejected. They are on I, 7, 18 (fol. 11r), I, 8, 51 (fols. 12v and 13r, with two signatures), III, 5, 24 (fol. 28r), and IV, 5, 4 (fol. 36r). Leo assigned them to two different correctors, which is incredible.

---

[52] *Vita di Giovanni Pontano*, p. 126.
[53] Chatelain, *Paléographie . . .*, II, p. 4 and Plate CV. The manuscript is reproduced in the same Leiden series as the Tacitus (Vol. XIV), with a preface by F. Leo, who depended almost entirely on Wissowa in matters of script.

They were done by Pontano at different times, as the difference in ink shows. Then too we should consider the added lines. At certain points where lines are obviously missing humanist scholars vied to supply them, men such as Thomas Seneca and Aurispa. In G (the Wolfenbüttel manuscript) lines were added at I, 2, 26; 10, 25 (four lines); II, 3, 16; 78; III, 4, 65. Francesco Pucci, a friend of Pontano, has left us some notes attributing these lines to Pontano[54]. That is not all. At I, 5, 33 G has *assecula* and above it *i(d est) ancilla*. Pucci has « hunc asserula ita legebat Pont. i(d est) ancilla ». Pucci misread G. At I, 10, 33 *arcessere* is the text reading of G, which Pucci attributes to Pontano. At III, 1 Pucci paraphrases Pontano's note in G indicating that Neaera is not mentioned by Ovid. At III, 1, 20 G has *An maneam*, with which Pucci credits Pontano. Similarly II, 6, 45, III, 2, 5, and 3, 20. This seems to mean that Pucci used G and recognized the writing as Pontano's[55].

Other marginalia in G are found in Pucci's notes, though not attributed to Pontano: I, 1, 43 « Parva satis mensa est »; I, 4, 73 the quotation from Horace; I, 5, 28 *Sp.* in margin, apparently in reference to the word *spicas*; I, 7, 57 the note « Messala vias has constravit silice », though in a changed word order; I, 9, 25 « absque supplicio »; III, 5, 17 note on Ovid's birth; IV, 1, 70 the note « fato, casu, aut genitura morimur » is lengthened to « Tergeminae Mortis an propter tres Parcas an quia fato, casu, aut natura morimur », etc. Pucci's notes are dated 1502, the very year in which Pontano died. Obviously Pontano's manuscripts were made available at his death to his old friend.

Leo claimed two correcting hands in G, one of which Wissowa identified with the text hand. I would of course say that

---

[54] The various printed editions with manuscript notes taken from Pucci were discussed by F. Calonghi, *Marginalia* (Genoa, 1921). There are others missed by Calonghi. The present home of the copy made by Pier Vettori, which Calonghi could not locate, is Munich, Staatsbibl. 2 Inc. c. a. 1120. Vettori also owned two of the Munich manuscripts containing Pontano autographs. Did he get them from Pucci? On Pucci see M. Santoro, *Uno scolaro del Poliziano a Napoli: Francesco Pucci* (Naples, 1948).

[55] I have quoted from the Riccardiana and Munich copies. Leo used a Göttingen copy which quotes Pucci at second hand. Hence some of Leo's conclusions are wrong.

all three belong to Pontano, working at different times with different ink and pen. The « tres viros academiae Pontanianae », as Leo called the scribe and the two correctors, are but one man in three guises—the head of the Pontanian academy himself.

Years ago I discovered a third manuscript written in the same hand, i.e., by Pontano. It is a parchment Propertius of the Berlin library (at present in the Tübingen university library), lat. fol. 500 (see Pl. 23-28). It is dated at the end « MCCCCLX Martio mense Neapoli », in other words, in the same month and year as the Leidensis. It gives us the further information that it was copied at Naples, where Pontano was living. We have a list of books presented by Pontano's daughter Eugenia to the Church of S. Domenico at Naples [56]. In it we find among the parchment books « Propercium manu Pontani ». Can anyone doubt that this is the Berlin codex or that this contemporary statement that Pontano did the copying is correct? This evidence alone should be sufficient to settle the argument about the Leidensis. I have only a few readings from this manuscript but one shows the same agreement with Pucci notes as the Tibullus. At IV, 6, 8 the manuscript has *cadis* with (*ve*)*l modis* above it (see Pl. 28). That is exactly what the Pucci notes give.

Other evidence may be found in the facsimiles here given and in those of the Tacitus and Tibullus manuscripts. The Madrid manuscript of Pontano's *De divinis laudibus*, rightly called the autograph dedication copy by Soldati, is very similar in script to the Leidensis except for the absence of the Beneventan letters (Pl. 18). Note especially the *g* and *s*. Large and small capitals are used together in the name Pontanus as in the Leidensis (Pl. 13; 18). This manuscript is close in date to the Tacitus. Another general similarity among Pontano's manuscripts is to be seen in the dot and line flourishes. In the Tibullus two dots and a wavy line occur frequently at the end of poems and after marginal notes (fol. 24r). These are found often in the Tacitus (Pl. 13, margin), in the Madrid manuscript (Pl. 19), and in

---

[56] G. Filangieri, *Documenti per la storia, le arti e le industrie delle provincie napoletane*, III (Naples, 1885), p. 50; also in Pèrcopo, *Vita di Giovanni Pontano*.

the Propertius (Pl. 23). The combination of dots and lines in the Madrid codex (Pl. 18) is similar to that on fol 47r of the Leidensis. A mark consisting of three dots and a wavy line beneath them is used below notes and to mark passages in the Tacitus (fols. 12r, 12v, etc.), the Tibullus (especially fol. 12r), the Propertius (Pl. 23), and the Madrid manuscript (Pl. 19). Other similarities are in the abbreviation stroke and the enclitic *que* [57].

On this presentation and especially on the facsimiles I rest my case. The fact that Pontano copied the Leidensis has no bearing on its value for the text. It must have been copied from a manuscript thoroughly corrected by Pontano and may have as little value for the text of Tacitus as the Guelferbytanus has for that of Tibullus. The matter is of importance for the activity of a great humanist and for the history of palaeography.

---

[57] Other examples of Pontano's writing in text or margin may be seen in Soldati's edition and in W. H. Bond, in *Studies in Bibliography*, 8 (1956), p. 147. A note in British Museum, Add. 12027 (Pontano, *De prudentia*) reads: « Pontani manu opus conscriptum ». Bond's plates show that he is right in denying that Pontano copied the manuscript, but Bond believes that Pontano contributed some of the notes in it. For other Pontano notes see my discussion of « Pontano's Marginalia in Berlin, Hamilton 471 » in the book by Franco Munari, *Il codice Berol. Hamiltonensis 471 di Ovidio* (Rome, 1965), p. 65 [here, Chapter XXVIII]. In *Musée Belge*, XIII (1909), p. 80, Th. Simar made the utterly nonsensical suggestion that Vat. lat. 1612 and Barb. viii. 58 were copied by Pontano. I refuted this in *Classical Philology*, VI (1911), p. 298.

CHAPTER XXIII

ACHILLES STATIUS' MANUSCRIPTS OF TIBULLUS [1]

Achilles Estaço (1524-1581), who Latinized his name as Achilles Statius, was a Portuguese who got his education in Evora, Coimbra, Louvain, Paris, and Padua. He went to Rome and became the librarian of Cardinal Guido Ascanio Sforza and later secretary of Pope Pius V [2]. In 1566 he published an edition of Catullus in which he gives readings from a number of manuscripts. Many of these I was able to identify [3]. The most interesting of these was the Maffeianus of Achille Maffei. This turned out to be the famous manuscript R (Vat. Ottob. lat. 1829), rediscovered by William Gardner Hale (see above, p. 376).

In 1567 Statius published his Tibullus (Venice, Manutius). Again he cites a number of manuscripts and old books. The eight to which he gives names are: *Vaticanus, Florentinus, liber Marcelli, mei* (two), *liber Sfortiae, liber Colotii, Patavinus*. This is one more than those quoted by name in the edition of Catullus. Although some sixty of the 180 Tibullus manuscripts known to me also contain Catullus, none of Statius' identifiable manuscripts of either author contains the other. The manuscripts with the same name in both editions are *Vaticanus, liber Marcelli, Patavinus, meus*. The first two have been identified in the case of both authors; but in both the names represent different manuscripts. Since the chances of a Tibullus being combined with a Catullus

---

[1] Originally published in *Didascaliae, Studies in Honor of Anselm M. Albareda* (New York, 1961), p. 451.

[2] The most recent account of Statius is by J. Gomes Branco, in "Relazioni storiche fra l'Italia e il Portogallo", *Accademia d'Italia* (Rome, 1940) p. 135.

[3] Berthold Louis Ullman, *The Identification of the Manuscripts of Catullus Cited in Statius' Edition of 1566* (Chicago, 1908). See also Ioannes Baptista Pighi, "Achillis Statiii lectiones atque emendationes Catullianae", in *Humanitas* (Coimbra), III (1950), p. 37.

are 1 in 3 (sixty out of 180 existing codices), the odds are in favor of the *Patavinus* and one of the *mei* containing both authors.

Let us start with the Vaticanus, which I identify as Vat. lat. 1609. In the following list, the reading attributed by Statius to the Vaticanus is that of Vat. lat. 1609 unless otherwise indicated.

I, 1, 12   In veteri libro Guidonis Ascanii Sfortiae Cardinalis, et Vaticano altero Florea, non Florida legitur.   In eodem tamen libro post, illo in versu [I, 2, 14], Cum posti florida serta darem, nihil est immutatum. [Florea *Vat.* al' Florida *i. m. Vat.*[1]].

I, 2, 32   Tacitura.

I, 2, 37   Si quid, non, Si quis.

I, 2, 42   pro Pollicita, Sollicita.

I, 2, 63   non, Ut, sed, Ego.

I, 3, 33   Ac, non, At, et in extremo margine, pro Ac, Fac. [At *Vat.* vel fac *i. m. Vat.*[1]].

I, 3, 34   Tura sic scriptum erat, ut aspirationis quidem abesset nota, supra tamen vocalem ipsam V. Asperi nota spiritus esset haec.

I, 4, 48   Atteruisse vero in omnibus libris erat. nec enim nulli sunt, qui malint, Attenuasse. et erat id scriptum in Vaticani libri margine. [atteruisse *Vat.* attenuasse *i. m. Vat.*[2]].

I, 4, 59   Iam tu, qui Venerem] Ita etiam in Vaticano, sed emendatum supra, At tibi. [Iam tua *Vat.* vel tibi *sscr. Vat.* tua *in* tu *corr. Vat.*[2]].

I, 5, 12   Pertimuisset.

I, 5, 24   non Candida, sed Pinguia.

I, 5, 61   Pro, Tibi, Nam, legebam. [nam *Vat.* vel tibi *sscr. Vat.*].

I, 5, 69   Pro, Nunc es, erat in Vaticano scriptum, Vinces. [vinces *Vat.* nunc es *i. m. Vat.*[2]].

I, 5, 74   Excreat ipse fores.

I, 6, 73   non, Iste, sed Ipse.

I, 7, 12   Carnoti.

I, 7, 21   Cum scindit. [quom scindit *Vat.*].

I, 7, 27   non Proles, sed Pubes.

I, 7, 42   pro Compede, Cuspide. [cuspide *Vat.* compede *i. m. Vat.*[2]].

I, 7, 61   Te canet.

I, 8, 4   Vaticanus liber duplicem ostendit lectionem. est enim etiam illic, Exprimit eventus. [Exprimit *Vat.* vel praecinit *sscr. Vat.*[1]].

I, 8, 12   Vaticanus liber illam quoque lectionem prae se fert, ut pro Subsecuisse, Supposuisse etiam legi possit. [supposuisse *exp. et* subsecuisse *sscr. Vat.*[1]].

I, 8, 33   Huic tu candentes] In Vaticano praeter hanc, illa etiam lectio, Huius candentes. [Huic tu candentes *Vat.* vel huius candentes *sscr. Vat.*[1]].

I, 8, 51   non illi sontica caussa est] In Vaticano etiam, Sartica. [scutica *Vat.* sontica *i. m. Vat.*[2]].

I, 8, 64   non Modis, sed Malis.

I, 8, 73   Lacrimas, non Lacrimis.

I, 9, 35   Placet Vaticani libri lectio, Sidera caelo Lucere. [caelo *Vat.* vel i *sscr. Vat.*[1]].

I, 9, 36   non Esse, sed Ire legebatur. [esse *Vat.* vel ire *sscr. Vat.*[1]].

I, 9, 39   Quid dicam, quod, ut ipse, fores in amore puellae.

I, 9, 60   non Vel, sed Quam. [vel *Vat.*].

I, 9, 81   Veneri ipsa merenti.

I, 10, 17   Nec pudeat.

I, 10, 19   Tunc...] Vaticanus liber illam etiam lectionem prae se ferebat, Sic melius tenuere fidem. [Sic *Vat.* vel tunc *sscr. Vat.*[1]].

I, 10, 23   Compos voti.

I, 10, 31   non Potanti, sed Pacanti.

I, 10, 60   non E, sed Et.

I, 10, 62   Sit satis, ornatus dissoluisse comae. In aliis, Ornatus dissoluisse comis. [comae *Vat.* vel comis *sscr. Vat.*[1]].

I, 10, 68   Praefluat.

II, 1, 12   Non Externa, sed Hesterna.

II, 1, 18   pro Limitibus, Liminibus. [Liminibus *Vat.* vel ti *sscr. Vat.*[1]].

II, 1, 35   Nunc ades.

II, 1, 36   non Gratia, sed Gloria.

II, 1, 56   Ab arte, non Ab urbe.

II, 2, 5   Adsit genius. [genius adsit *Vat.*].

II, 2, 7   Illius puro.

II, 2, 9   Cornute, non Cherinte. [Cornute *Vat.* cherinthe *i. m. Vat.*[2]].

II,	3, 2		Sed in Vaticano, etiam hoc modo, Ferreus est heu heu si quis. [si quis *Vat.* vel quisquis *sscr. Vat.*[1]].
II,	3, 14a		Depellere, non Expellere.
II,	3, 25		Si quis.
II,	3, 41		Placet legere Osidere ut est in Vaticano, non Obsistere. [obsidere *Vat.*].
II,	3, 59		Legendum, ut in Florentino, Quem, non Quo. In Vaticano etiam, Quam: quod mutandum in Quem. [quae *Vat.* quem *sscr. Vat.*[2] al' Nota loquor regnum ipse tenet quam saepe coegit *Vat.*[1]].
II,	3, 70		Quid nocuit, sulcos non habuisse satos]. In Vaticano etiam hoc modo legitur, Quis docuit, sulcos nos habuisse satos. [Quid *Vat.* Quis *Vat.*[1] nos *Vat.* non *Vat.*[1]].
II,	4, 29		Stimulos, non Caussas. [stimulos *Vat.* vel causas *sscr. Vat.*[1]].
II,	4, 31		sensit.
II,	4, 39		Vinctos, non, Victos. [victos *Vat.* vinctos *Vat.*[2]].
II,	5, 63		Laurus.
II,	5, 66		Fuscas, non Fusas.
II,	5, 68		Grataque quod monuit.
II,	5, 72		In Vaticano in margine pro Multus et, Plurimus. [Multus et *Vat.* Plurimus *i. m. Vat.*[2]].
II,	5, 110		non Cum, sed Tum.
II,	5, 115		Et Messallinum. [Et Messalinum *Vat.*].
II,	5, 116		Geret, non Feret.
II,	5, 118		non, Canet, sed, Canat.
II,	6, 6		Et verum erronem.
II,	6, 20		Et semper cras fore ait melius.
II,	6, 39		Sagitta.
III,	1, 11		Protexat.
III,	1, 18		Sicut erit.
III,	1, 20		E toto. [toto an *Vat.* e toto *Vat.*[2]].
III,	2, 5		Non hoc nostro patiemur Ingenio.
III,	2, 13		Veniat.
III,	2, 19		non, Collecta, sed, Perfusa.
III,	3, 7		Sociarent. [sociarent *ex* sotiarent *corr. Vat.*].
III,	3, 9		Tunc, cum praemensae...] Tum, cum permensae. [Tunc quom p. *Vat.*].

III,	4, 9	Sunt, qui pro Omnia, legant, Omina. In Vaticano, Et tantum metuens hominum genus, omnia noctis. [omina *Vat.*].
III,	4, 11	Monenti.
III,	4, 21	Somno.
III,	4, 26	Fuit, non, Videt.
III,	4, 49	Excipe.
III,	4, 65	Fera bella.
III,	4, 83	Non ego crediderim.
III,	4, 87	Nec consanguinea.
III,	4, 89	Succincta, non, submixta.
III,	4, 93	Ante omnes alias.
III,	5, 1	etiam pro, Fontibus legebatur, Montibus. [fontibus *Vat.* vel mon *sscr. Vat.*[1]].
III,	5, 4	non, Humus, sed, Hiems.
III,	5, 11	Sacrilegos aegros.
III,	5, 13	non, Linguae, sed, Mentis.
III,	5, 20	Laedere, non, Vellere.
III,	5, 27	Torrear.
III,	6, 11	Recuset.
III,	6, 15	Et fulvos ille leones.
III,	6, 30	Non, Tua, sed, Tibi.
III,	6, 59	Nostrae fugiat.
IV,	1, 5	Praeter te.
IV,	1, 9	Detulit in cunctis Baccho iucundior hospes.
IV,	1, 13	Fastigia.
IV,	1, 18	Dictat, non, Dicat.
IV,	1, 19	In immensum descenderet aera.
IV,	1, 27	Nec tanto careat mihi pondere charta.
IV,	1, 30	Quidquam, non Quid qua. [quicquam *Vat.* vel quid qua *sscr. Vat.*[1]].
IV,	1, 32	Futurus.
IV,	1, 33	Captet, non, Capiet.
IV,	1, 36	Iuncto pede.
IV,	1, 43	Onus surgit.
IV,	1, 45	Nam, seu divisi premat inconstantia vulgi.
IV,	1, 64	Arces, non, Oras.
IV,	1, 84	Vernos.
IV,	1, 91	At quis equum.
IV,	1, 94	Turno brevius.
IV,	1, 95	Per via seu dextra.

IV, 1, 97   Amplior.

IV, 1, 98   Venient.

IV, 1, 99   Parent.

IV, 1, 110   Testis et Arpinis, et pauper natus in armis.

IV, 1, 112b   Famae. [phamae *Vat.*].

IV, 1, 115   Validusque.

IV, 1, 122   Artis, non, Anni.

IV, 1, 127   Nulla haec aerias.

IV, 1, 139   Terreno.

IV, 1, 146   Magistros. [magīos = maginos *Vat.*].

IV, 1, 152   Toto disponitur orbe.

IV, 1, 157   super egerit. [superegerit *Vat.*].

IV, 1, 173   Confunditur, non, Confinditur.

IV, 1, 174   Exurgitat.

IV, 1, 189   Accitus.

IV, 1, 197   Dum quodcumque. [Dum quidcumque *Vat.*].

IV, 1, 202   Summo vel inerret in ore.

IV, 1, 208   Tardus.

IV, 4, 12   versus illi, Nil opus est fletu et, Si quando fuerit, le-
               guntur post versum, Corpore servato.

IV, 5, 9   Mane, veni. [geni *Vat.* veni *Vat.*[2]].

IV, 5, 16   Quae soluisse.

IV, 6, 5   Orandi.

IV, 6, 14   Sic, non, Sit.

IV, 8, 3   Puellae, non, Puellis.

IV, 8, 6   Tuae, non, Viae.

IV, 8, 7   His. [His *Vat.* c sscr. *Vat.*[2]].

IV, 9, 2   Non sinet esse tuo.

IV, 10, 2   Permittas.

IV, 10, 6   Ne credam ignoto maxima caussa toro. [Nec c. i. m.
               causa thoro *Vat.*].

IV, 13, 17   Cedo, non, Credo.

IV, 13, 23   Confidam, non, considam. [confidam *in* considam *corr.*
               Vat.].

In the first passage, and only there, Statius seems to mention
two Vatican manuscripts. His expression 'et Vaticano altero' was,
I believe, careless writing for "et in altero, id est, Vaticano". In
IV, 13, 23 he made out the original reading before correction (cf.
II, 3, 70). When the Vaticanus offers a text reading and a mar-
ginal variant, Statius' method of reporting varies: he may give both

readings (I, 3, 33, etc.) or that of the text alone (I, 1, 12, etc.), or the variant alone (I, 7, 42). This can mislead the reader, as in I, 9, 36, where he says 'In Vaticano non Esse, sed Ire legebatur'. Actually *esse* is the text reading and *ire* the marginal variant. All these peculiarities are to be explained by the fact that Statius, like other scholars of the period, was not giving a collation but was selecting readings which he thought might be correct. That explanation also accounts for the fact that he by no means cites all the readings in his manuscript which differ from his text. Silence on his part proves absolutely nothing about the readings of his manuscripts. It should be noted that he usually pays no attention to spelling, e.g., IV, 1, 30, where Statius reports *quidquam* and the manuscript has *quicquam* (cf. I, 7, 21; II, 5, 115; IV, 1, 112b).

By being a bit charitable, we can explain some of Statius' errors as misprints (I, 8, 51; II, 2, 5; 3, 41; III, 4, 9). The wording of the statement in I, 8, 51 points to a misprint: "sontica caussa est] In Vaticano etiam, Sartica. In uno meo, Rustica. In alio, Scutica. quae sunt omnia vitiosa. Legendum itaque Sontica". Note *etiam*.

Statius' report of *magistros* (IV, 1, 146) where the Vaticanus has *magīos* (for *Maginos*) is a palaeographical error on Statius' part. The abbreviation for *magistros* is *magīros*. Other errors seem to be slips on his part (I, 9, 60; II, 2, 5).

One type of inaccuracy in Statius' reports is common to scholars of the period. When he cites the reading of a phrase it does not follow that every word in that phrase agrees with the manuscript. Thus in III, 3, 9 the incorrect report *tum* is due to his not being interested in that word but only in *permensae* (instead of *praemensae*); cf. IV, 1, 197.

The manuscript which Statius calls that of Marcellus Pontifex Maximus or Marcellus Cervinus Pontifex Maximus is easily identified. Cardinal Marcello Cervini became Pope Marcellus in 1555 but died three weeks after his succession. His manuscripts passed first to Cardinal Sirleto and eventually became part of the Ottoboni collection of the Vatican, and his Tibullus is Ottob. lat. 1369. Here are the readings quoted by Statius with differences noted within square brackets.

I,	2, 37	Si quid, non, Si quis.
I,	4, 59	Superne emendatum, At tu qui [Iam tua qui *Ottob.* At tu qui *sscr. Ottob.*²].
I,	4, 79	Canentem.
I,	5, 24	Non Candida, sed Pinguia.
I,	5, 74	Excreat ipse fores.
I,	5, 76	Pro Nat, Iam. Sit etiam fortasse haec sententia, Lubricus amor est, atque instabilis, et paullo momento mutabilis, ut in aqua linter levi aura huc vel illuc impellitur. [nam *Ottob.*].
I,	6, 73	Non, Iste, sed Ipse.
III,	5, 11	Sacrilegos aegros (*i. e.*, sacrilegos templis admovimus aegros).
IV,	1, 9	Tres.
IV,	1, 18	Dictat, non, Dicat.
IV,	1, 30	Quidquam, non Quid qua. [quicquam *Ottob.*].
IV,	1, 68	Mediis discurreret undis.
IV,	1, 72	Rabidas.
IV,	1, 78	Miseri, non Misero.
IV,	1, 86	Educat, non, Erumpat.
IV,	1, 94	Turno brevius.
IV,	1, 152	Toto disponitur orbe.
IV,	1, 157	Super egerit. [superegerit *Ottob.*].
IV,	1, 161	Exurgit.
IV,	1, 173	Confunditur, non, Confinditur.
IV,	4, 21	Versus ille, Nil opus est fletu, et, Si quando fuerit, leguntur post versum, Corpore servato.
IV,	5, 9	Mane, veni.
IV,	6, 14	Sic, non, Sit.
IV,	6, 16	Iam sibi.
IV,	7, 8	Me legat advenio.
IV,	10, 2	Permittas.

Most of the readings are not striking, but I, 4, 59 convinces me that the identification is correct. In I, 5, 76 there is a misprint, as Statius' discussion shows.

The manuscript which Statius generally calls Florentinus is more specifically named 'libro qui est Florentiae in S. Laurentii' (I, 3, 89; cf. I, 4, 79; I, 7, 42). We can easily identify the manuscript as Laur. 33, 11. But Statius did not himself examine the manuscript, for in his first citations he says *esse aiunt* (I, 4,

83; I, 7, 42), *esse adfirmant* (I, 4, 79; I, 5, 11), *testantur esse* (I, 5, 13), *fuisse intellego* (I, 5, 33). The very first citation reads: "In veteri libro, qui est Florentiae in S. Laurentii, erat, Ne quisquam". The word *erat* for *est* seems *to imply*: "erat quando quidam pro me codicem inspexit".

I,	3,	89	Ne quisquam.
I,	4,	79	Canentem.
I,	4,	83	Turpis, non Turbis.
I,	5,	11	Ipse ego te circum.
I,	5,	13	Ipse ego curavi.
I,	5,	33	Huic. [Hunc *Flor.*].
I,	6,	31	Nec iam me.
I,	7,	42	pro Compede, Cuspide.
I,	7,	44	Levis, et aptus amor. [et levis aptus amor *Flor.*].
I,	8,	6	Perdocuit Marathum non sine vulneribus. [Marathum *Flor.* al' multis *i. m. Flor.*[1] vulneribus *Flor.* vel verbe sscr. *Flor.*[1]].
I,	8,	10	Saepe et mutatas.
I,	8,	15	Ipsa. [Illa *Flor.*].
I,	8,	35	non, Concumbere, sed, Succumbere.
I,	8,	60	Et sonitu nullo.
I,	8,	61	Quid prosunt artes. [Quid possunt artes *Flor.*].
I,	8,	73	Lacrimas, non Lacrimis.
I,	9,	1	Amantes. [amores *Flor.*].
I,	9,	9	Parentia per freta.
I,	9,	36	Fulminis, non Fluminis.
I,	9,	53	Qui donis puerum.
I,	9,	61	Ferant, non, Ferunt.
I,	9,	68	Et tenues.
I,	10,	37	Illic percussisque genis, ruptoque capillo.
I,	10,	46	Non Curva, sed Panda. [panda *Flor.* al' curva *i. m. Flor.*[1]].
I,	10,	56	Convaluisse.
I,	10,	62	Sit satis, ornatus dissoluisse comae.
I,	10,	68	Profluat.
II,	1,	18	Tollite, non Pellite.
II,	1,	54	Diceret, non Duceret.
II,	1,	67	Ipse interque greges.

II,   1, 89-90 sic leguntur hi versus, Postque venit tacitus, nigris circun-
               datus alis Somnus, et incerto somnia vana pede.
               [fulvis *Flor.* vel nigris *Flor.*[1] nigra *Flor.* vel vana
               Flor.[1]].

II,   2, 7   Illius puro.

II,   2, 9   Cornute, non Cherinthe.

II,   2, 21   Hic, non, Huc. [Haec *Flor.*].

II,   3, 8   non Serenda, sed Colenda.

II,   3, 31   pro Sua, Nunc.

II,   3, 36   Non Operata, sed Adoperta.

II,   3, 48   Testa, pro, Terra. [terra *Flor.* testa *i. m. Flor.*[1]].

II,   3, 59   Quem, non Quo.

II,   4, 10   Ira, non, Unda.

II,   4, 15   Si nil prodestis.

II,   4, 36   Ille, non, Ipse.

II,   5, 30   sacra] Farta. in uno meo, Facta. [facta *Flor.* sacra *i. m.*
               Flor.[1]].

II,   5, 58   Quaqua, non, Qua sua [Qua qua *Flor.* sua *i. m. Flor.*[1]].

II,   5, 64   Noscar, pro Vescar. [Noscat *Flor.*].

II,   5, 69   Non Quasque, sed, Quotque. [Quotque (t *in ras.*) *Flor.*
               al' Quasque *i. m. Flor.*[1]].

II,   5, 72   In Terris, non, In Terras.

II,   5, 92   non, Compressis, sed, Comprensis.

II,   5, 98   Stabit et ante calix [Stabit et ipse calix *Flor.*].

II,   5, 99   Aut, non, At.

II,   5, 109   At mihi.

II,   5, 111   Usque cano.

II,   5, 116   Ferent.

II,   5, 120   non, Pater, sed, Parens.

II,   6, 7   Parcis.

II,   6, 8   Levi galea.

II,   6, 20   Et fore cras semper ait melius.

II,   6, 28   Bella puella.

III, 1, 19   Referet.

III, 1, 20   An maneam.

III, 1, 21   Meritam, non Nympham.

III, 2, 26   Carmen in ossa.

III, 2, 27   Casum, non, Caussam.

III, 4, 11   Monenti.

III, 4, 17   non, Emersa, sed Dimensa.

III, 5, 10   Non umquam.

III, 5, 13   non, Linguae, sed, Mentis.

III,   6, 2   Geras.
III,   6, 7   Dirum, non, Durum.
III,   6, 8   Fluxerit, non, Fulserit. [Fluxerit *Flor. in* Fulserit *leviter*
                 corr. Flor.[1]].
III,   6, 13   Feroces, non, Ferocem.
III,   6, 37   Quid loquor.
III,   6, 43   Sic moneo.
IV,   1, 1   Tua.
IV,   1, 43   Utrumque. [Utrunque *Flor.*].
IV,   1, 55   Non valuit tempus coeptos convertere cursus. [Non
                 valuit Cyclops tempus convertere cursus *Flor.*].
IV,   1, 66   Sive supra terras. [Seu supra terras *Flor.*].
IV,   1, 91   pro, Ve, Ne.
IV,   1, 93   Passu.
IV,   1, 100   Non defit.
IV,   1, 108   Iapidiae.
IV,   1, 110   Testis et Alpinis est pauper natus in armis.
IV,   1, 113   Revocaverat.
IV,   1, 123   Tum Sol.
IV,   1, 133   Abditus.
IV,   1, 139   Threicio.
IV,   1, 146   Maginos.
IV,   1, 157   Quippe ubi.
IV,   1, 161   Exurgit.
IV,   1, 197   Dum quodcumque. [Dum quodcunque *Flor.*].
IV,   1, 206   Figura.
IV,   1, 211   Nomina, non, Carmina.
IV,   2, 3   Hoc Venus ignoscet] in Florentino, Sed Venus. [Hoc
                 Venus *Flor.*].
IV,   5, 16   Nos soluisse.
IV,   6, 5   Orandi.
IV,   6, 7   Ne nox. [ne nos *Flor.*].
IV,   6, 15   Quod optet.
IV,   6, 16   Iam sibi.
IV,   6, 19   Sic iuveni grata est? veniet, etc.
IV,   7, 1   Pudore.
IV,   8, 3   Puellae, non, Puellis.
IV,   8, 8   Quoniam, non, Quamvis.
IV,   10, 2   Permittas.
IV,   13, 1   non Titulis, sed, Nobis.
IV,   13, 16   Est mihi.
IV,   14, 3   Ficta, non, Facta.

The large number of agreements, some in unusual readings, is the chief reason for identifying Laur. 33, 11 as the Florentinus. Among the more unusual readings are: I, 9, 9; 10, 37; II, 3, 31; 4, 10; 15; III, 2, 26; 5, 10; IV, 1, 110; 6, 16; 14, 3. Apart from this, perhaps the most convincing evidence is furnished by II, 1, 89-90 and II, 3, 48. It must be admitted, however, that there are some readings which oppose this identification: I, 5, 33; 7, 44; 8, 15; 61; 9, 1; II, 2, 21; 5, 30; 64; 98; IV, 1, 55; 66; 2, 3; 6, 7. These may be due to confusion on the part of Statius or his source, for, as stated above, Statius did not himself examine this manuscript.

Statius had two manuscripts of his own which he quotes under the term « meus ». This designation does not have the broad sense of « one of the manuscripts which I quote », for he frequently makes such statements as: « in uno meo et Florentino » (I, 8, 61), « in Vaticano et uno meo » (I, 7, 21), « in meis, item in Vaticano et Florentino » (I, 8, 73).

One of the two « mei » I can positively identify as British Museum, Burney 268, the other I have not located. All the readings of the « mei » are given below. When the Burney manuscript agrees, no comment is made; when it differs, its reading is given in square brackets. It is to be understood that Statius says « in uno meo » or the like unless otherwise stated.

I, 2, 79	Non Veneris magnae] parum, multumve, deficit certe hoc loco aliquid. Sic enim video. . . , et meo quodam veteri libro admoneor, ut id putem.
I, 4, 40	In meo quodam etiam, Cedas.
I, 4, 44	in meo enim quodam libro aperte sic est, Annuntiet. [admittat *Burn.*].
I, 4, 48	in quodam etiam meo, Opera. [operi *Burn.*].
I, 4, 69	Impleat. [expleat *Burn.*].
I, 4, 83	Turpis, non Turbis.
I, 7, 12	in II meis, Carnoti.
I, 7, 21	Cum scindit. [cum findit *Burn.*].
I, 7, 27	in. . . duobus meis veteribus, non Proles, sed Pubes.
I, 7, 42	pro Compede, Cuspide.

I, 7, 61   E, non legitur, non etiam in II meis.

I, 7, 63   Celebrata.

I, 8, 11   non Comas, sed Genas.

I, 8, 21   Deducere lumina. [lunam deducere *Burn.*].

I, 8, 32   Hispida. [aspera *Burn.*].

I, 8, 51   in uno meo, Rustica. In alio, Scutica. [rustica
                  Burn.].

I, 8, 61   Quid prosunt artes] sic in uno meo. [Quid
                  possunt artes *Burn.*].

I, 8, 73   in meis... Lacrimas, non Lacrimis.

I, 9, 25   Ipse Deus tacito permisit lena magistro. [pre-
                  misit *Burn.*].

I, 9, 60   non Vel, sed Quam.

I, 9, 63   Illa queat nullam melius consumere noctem]
                  sic in uno meo.

I, 9, 67   Putes.

I, 9, 80   In duobus meis, Et geret in regno bella su-
                  perba tuo.

I, 10, 62   in... duobus meis, Sit satis, ornatus dissoluisse
                  comae.

II, 1, 22   in meis, Ingeret.

II, 1, 35   Nunc ades.

II, 1, 56   item in duobus meis, Ab arte, non Ab urbe.

II, 2, 7   Illius puro. [Ilius e puro *Burn.*].

II, 2, 9   Cornute, non Cherinthe. [Cherinte *Burn.*].

II, 2, 17   Trepidantibus, non Strepitantibus.

II, 2, 21   Hic, non, Huc. [Huc *Burn.*].

II, 3, 14a   Sed ponam hos versus eo, quo leguntur, ordine
                  in scriptis libris... In uno meo, Ipse
                  Deus, etc. Creditur ad mulctram, etc. Et
                  miscere, etc. Et potum, etc. In altero meo,.
                  Ipse Deus, Creditur ad mulctram, Et po-
                  tum, Et miscere, Lacteus. [Ipse deus, Cre-
                  ditur ad multam, Et miscere, Et potum
                  Burn.].

II, 3, 75   A pereant artes, et mollia iura colendi. Horrida
                  villosa corpora veste tegant. Nunc si clausa
                  mea est, si copia rara videndi, Heu mise-
                  ram, laxam quid iuvat esse togam. Ducite
                  ad imperium dominae, sulcabimus agros:
                  Non ego me vinclis, verberibusque nego.
                  [lassa quidem iuvat *Burn.*].

II,	4,	18	Recurris. [recuris *Burn.*].
II,	4,	43	Venit.
II,	5,	27	Umbra.
II,	5,	30	Facta. [sacra *Burn.*].
II,	5,	39	in uno meo, veterum consuetudine, scriptum, Inpiger [*i.e., pro* impiger].
II,	5,	70	Pertuleritque. [perlueritque *Burn.*].
II,	5,	71	Haec, in meis, non Hae. [Hee *Burn.*].
II,	5,	73	in meis. . . Crepitantia. [crapitentia *Burn.*],
II,	5,	81	Et succensa. [Ut succensa *Burn.*].
II,	5,	82	In Sfortiaco, ac duobus meis, non Eat, sed Erit.
II,	5,	111	in Sfortiae libro, Florentino, ac duobus meis, Usque cano.
II,	5,	116	Gerent.
II,	6,	20	Et fore cras semper ait melius. In altero item meo et Vaticano, Et semper cras fore ait melius. [Et semper cras fore ut melius *Burn.*].
II,	6,	41	Desine.
II,	6,	49	Saepe, ubi nox mihi promissa est. [S. u. n. promissa mihi est *Burn.*].
III,	2,	8	Tot mala perpessae tot superesse meae] sic in uno meo. [supesse *Burn.*].
III,	2,	13	in Vaticano ac duobus meis, Veniat. [venit *Burn.*].
III,	2,	19	in Vaticano, non, Collecta, sed, Perfusa, ut in uno meo. [colleta *Burn.*].
III,	2,	24	Pinguis et Assyria. [p. et asiria *Burn.*].
III,	3,	9	in Vaticano, Tum, cum, permensae, itaque in uno meo. In altero, Tunc, cum permenso defunctus tempore lucis. [Tunc cum premenso defuntus t. l. *Burn.*].
III,	4,	9	In duobus meis, Et natum in curas hominum genus, omnia noctis.
III,	4,	22	in Sfortiae libro, et duobus meis, Fessa, non, Sera.
III,	4,	47	Quicumque, non, Aevique. [Evique *Burn.*].
III,	4,	50	Quidque. [Quid ve *Burn.*].
III,	4,	65	Fera bella. [fera verba *Burn.*].
III,	4.	83	Non ego crediderim. [Nec tibi c. *Burn.*].
III,	4,	87	Nec consanguinea. [Nec canis anguinea *Burn.*].

III,	4, 89	Succincta, non, Submixta. [sub mista *Burn.*].
III,	5, 11	Nec nos sacrilegos templis admovimus ignes] sic omnino in uno meo. In altero..., Nec nos sacrilegis templis admovimus aegros. [Nec nos sacrilegis t. amovimus egros *Burn.*].
III,	5, 13	non Linguae, sed Mentis. [lingue *Burn.*].
III,	5, 32	Volent, non, Velint. [velint *Burn.*].
III,	6, 11	At, si quis. [Aut siquis *Burn.*].
III,	6, 15	Et fulvos ille leones. [et fulvas ille leenas *Burn.*].
III,	6, 17	Et maiora valet.
III,	6, 21	Nam venit.
III,	6, 23	Quales is poenas.
III,	6, 32	Post multas.
III,	6, 59	Non te si nostrae fugiat. [Non te si nostre capiant *Burn.*].
IV,	12, 2 (*post* III, 6)	in duobus meis, Ac videor.
IV,	1, 9	in duobus meis, Res, non Cres.
IV,	1, 22	Hinc, non, Huic. [Hic *Burn.*].
IV,	1, 30	Quidquam, non Quid qua. [quicquam *Burn.*].
IV,	1, 32	in meis, Futurus. [futuros *Burn.*].
IV,	1, 66	Seu supra terras. [Sive supra dies *Burn.*].
IV,	1, 94	non, Brevius, sed, Levius.
IV,	1, 110	In uno meo, Testis et Arapinis, et pauper natus in armis. In altero, Testis et Arpinis, et pauper natus in arvis. [Testis et Arapinis, et p. n. in armis *Burn.*].
IV,	1, 112a	Famae.
IV,	1, 115	Validusque. [validisque *Burn.*].
IV,	1, 139	Tetereo tellus. [te tereo t. *Burn.*].
IV,	1, 142	In duobus meis, Caristia.
IV,	1, 146	Magistros.
IV,	1, 157	Quippe ubi non umquam Titan superegerit ortus. [Q. u. n. u. T. super ingerit o. *Burn.*].
IV,	1, 161	in meis..., Exurgit.
IV,	1, 165	Rigentem. [rigentes *Burn.*].
IV,	1, 173	in... duobus meis, Confunditur, non, Confinditur.
IV,	1, 174	Consurgunt. [exurgunt *Burn.*].
IV,	1, 189	Accitus. [accitos *Burn.*].

IV, 1, 195	Densis solus consistere. [D. s. obsistere *Burn.*].
IV, 1, 197	In meis, Sum quodcumque tuus, nostri, etc.
IV, 1, 206	Figura. [figuram *Burn.*].
IV, 1, 210	in meis, In quaecumque.
IV, 5, 9	in. . . utroque meo, Mane, veni.
IV, 5, 13	in utroque meo. . . , Nec tu sis.
IV, 5, 16	in utroque meo. . . , Nos soluisse.
IV, 6, 5	Orandi. [ornandi *Burn.*].
IV, 6, 7	Ne nox. [ne nos *Burn.*].
IV, 7, 1	Pudore. [pudori *Burn.*].
IV, 7, 8	In duobus meis. . . , Me legat advenio.
IV, 8, 3	Puellae, non, Puellis.
IV, 13, 1	in utroque meo. . . , non Titulis, sed, Nobis.
IV, 13, 16	in. . . duobus meis, Est mihi.
IV, 13, 17	Cedo, non, Credo.
IV, 13, 23	Confidam, non, Considam. [considam *Burn.*].
Epit. Tib. 1	Me quoque.

In uno meo extremum erat Epigramma, quod in lusibus in Priapum legitur, Villicus aerari quondam, nunc cultor agelli. In quo eadem omnia, praeterquam in ultimo versu, Hunc tu, sed taceo, scis puto, quod sequitur. In vulgatis enim legitur, Hunc tu, sed tento. Sunt autem versus ipsi [*sic*] Tibullo, elegantissimo poeta, digni.

The large number of agreements is an argument for identification, but the agreement in less common readings is a better one (II, 3, 14; 4, 18; 43; 5, 39; 116; 6, 41; III, 2, 8; IV, 1, 110; *Epit. Tib.* 1). But the clinching argument is furnished by the *Vilicus* poem. This poem was discovered in an inscription in the fifteenth century and found its way into epigraphical collections. It occurs in such a collection in Vat. lat. 6875; this manuscript contains several literary works as well, including Tibullus, but in a different hand. Cesena 29. 19 sin. also contains the poem in a collection of epigrams and epitaphs, ancient and modern, following Theophrastus, Catullus, Virgil's *Moretum*, and Tibullus. The Burney manuscript is the only one containing Tibullus alone, followed by the *Vilicus* poem in the same hand. It is untitled, and thus one might infer, as Statius did, that it was composed by Tibullus. I have seen or had reports on almost all the Tibullus manuscripts known to me (about 180), and the Burney codex is the only one that fits Statius' description of his « meus ». I shall have more to say about the *Vilicus* poem at another time, in connection with Scaliger's lost Fragmentum, which also contained it and another of the Priapea.

This concludes the list of Statius' manuscripts that I have been able to identify. The Patavinus is cited only three times:

II, 3, 14   post versum, Ipse Deus solitus, sequitur, Et potum
                 fessas: deinde, Et miscere: post, Lacteus et mixtus.
IV, 1, 9   Tres.
IV, 7, 8   Me legat advenio.

It seems likely that Statius was already interested in Catullus and Tibullus while at Padua and jotted down readings from the Paduan manuscripts of these authors.

Statius cites a manuscript of Cardinal Guido Ascanio Sforza some 155 times. As was stated at the beginning of this chapter, Statius was for a time the Cardinal's librarian, and so had access to his books. The Cardinal died in 1564. As I have been unable to identify this manuscript, it seems unnecessary to give its readings here [4].

Statius also quotes from a manuscript of Angelo Colocci, bishop of Nocera, who lived in Rome. As he died in 1549, eight years before Statius arrived in Italy, it is not surprising that Statius cites Colocci's Tibullus at second hand. In almost all of the twenty citations of this manuscript Statius says of its readings « fuisse aiunt », « fuisse intellego », « fuisse dicunt », « fuisse adfirmant », « fuisse testantur », « fuisse autumant », « fuisse confirmant », revealing a nice variation of synonyms. Who « they » were is not clear.

---

[4] Pierre de Nolhac, *La bibliothèque de Fulvio Orsini* (Paris, 1887), p. 79, states that Vat. lat. 3958, fol. 103, has an inventory of the Cardinal's library. Actually only the Greek books are listed. Some of his books are now in the Biblioteca Angelica, Rome, but the Tibullus is not one of them. About the dispersion of the library of Sforza see G. Mercati, *Note per la storia di alcune Biblioteche Romane nei secoli XVI-XIX* (Città del Vaticano, Biblioteca Ap. Vaticana, 1952; Studi e Testi 164), pp. 15-29; 58-67 and *passim*.

After Colocci's death his library passed to the Vatican. A catalogue of his books was made in 1558 apparently at the time of its final incorporation into that library, though we know it was stored there several years earlier[5]. Two Tibullus manuscripts are listed in that catalogue[6]; one is a paper manuscript in Capsa 6, No. 70, the other is in Capsa 9, No. 4. The Tibullus manuscript Vat. Lat. 1610 has been in the Vatican at least since 1595, as it appears in a Vatican catalogue of that year[7]. This is probably the first of the two manuscripts in the Colocci catalogue[8]. At any rate, it is not the one to which Statius referred. That manuscript has disappeared but has left some traces, as we shall now see.

Several printed editions of Catullus, Tibullus, Propertius in the Vatican library contain manuscript readings in the margins, attributed to Colocci or his manuscript. All are listed in the inventory of Fulvio Orsini's library (printed in Nolhac, *op. cit.*), in the section headed « Nota de libri latini stampati che sono tocchi di mano di huomini dotti » (p. 381).

1. Aldine III, 20 (formerly A. 16). Orsini 12: « con emendationi del Colotio e di Basilio Zancho ». Aldine edition of 1502. Inside the book Orsini wrote: « Catull. Tibull. Propert. con emendationi de Colotio, e di Basilio Zancho ». The marginalia are in two hands; the first uses a reference mark (line and dot) or *vel* for the variant, the second (that of Colocci) underlines the text word.

2. R. I. V. 2238. Orsini 11: « con emendationi del Pontano e del Colotio ». Nolhac did not see this volume and confused Orsini No. 11 with a missing 1486 edition. J. Ruysschaert pointed out the error[9]. Edition of Gryphius, Lyons, 1534. Inside

---

[5] S. Lattès, « Recherches sur la bibliothèque d'Angelo Colocci », *Mélanges d'archéologie et d'histoire*, 48 (1931), p. 308.

[6] The catalogue is in Vat. lat. 3958, fol. 184.

[7] Vat. lat. 6958, fol. 124.

[8] Lattès definitely credits it to Colocci, on what basis I do not know.

[9] *Bulletin de l'Institut historique belge de Rome*, 23 (1944-46), p. 139. I am indebted to Monsignor Ruysschaert for this and other references.

the volume Orsini wrote: « Catullo, Tibullo, e Propertio con emendationi del Pontano, e del Colotio ». Variants signed *v. c.* or *Col.* or both.

3. Aldine III, 19 (formerly A. 15). Orsini 51: « emendato ». Aldine of 1502. Orsini wrote his name in the volume but made no comment on the annotator. Some notes are attributed to *v. c.* (*vetus codex*) others to *p.* or *Pont.* (Pontanus), but Colocci is not mentioned.

4. Incun. III, 18 (formerly 73). Orsini 15: « di stampa vecchia, con scholii del Colotio ». Venice edition of 1472 (Hain 4758). In the book Orsini wrote: « Catullo, Tibullo, et Propertio, di stampa vecchia con scholii del Colotio ». The notes are few and consist of explanations and parallel passages. The book is therefore of no value for our present purpose [10].

In the following I give the readings of the Colotianus as reported by Statius, followed by the marginal readings in the editions just described, retaining my numbering to designate them. By 1 I mean the first of the marginal hands in Aldine III, 20 presumably that of Zanchi if Orsini was right; 1ᶜ is the second hand, i.e., Colocci. If the number is given (1, 1ᶜ, 2, 3) without a reading, it agrees with Statius' report. The words and letters given in parentheses after the number are those found in the margins of the editions indicated.

I,	1, 14	agricolam. [1ᶜ, 2 (v. c. Col.), 3 (p.)].
I,	3, 49	nunc. [1ᶜ, 2 (Col.)].
I,	3, 63	hic. [1ᶜ, 2 (Col.)].
I,	4, 28	it. [1ᶜ, 2].
I,	4, 43	picea. [1ᶜ, 2 (v. c. Col.)].
I,	4, 55	mox. [vel mox 1, 2 (v. Col.)].

[10] Other annotated editions in Orsini's list are: N. 10 = II. 200 (formerly 502), Brescia, 1486 (Hain 4761), of which Orsini says: « Catullo et Tibullo, con commento, di stampa vecchia, con scholii di mano di Pontano ». I doubt Orsini's statement; I do not think the notes are in Pontano's hand nor that they emanated from him. The notes are explanatory rather than emendations or manuscript readings. No. 54=R. I. V. 2243. No. 59=Aldine III, 7 (formerly A. 7, for which Nolhac has A. 10). No. 103=Incun. III, 15 (formerly 73) 1472 (Hain 4758, but a different copy from the one mentioned above).

I, 4, 69   explicet. [vel explicet 1, 2 (Col.)].
I, 4, 80   diludat. [vel diludat 1, deludat 2 (Col.)].
I, 4, 83   turpis. [2 (v. c.)].
I, 5, 23   et. [1°, 2].
I, 5, 30   At iuvet. [At 1°, vel adiuvet 1, At 2, (v. c. Col.) adiuvat 2 (v. c. Col.)].
I, 5, 33   huic. [huic vel hunc 1°, 2 (v. Col.) hunc 3 (Pont.)].
I, 5, 60   amans. [vel amans 1, 2 (v. Col.)].
I, 5, 75   nescis. [vel nescis 1, 2 (Col.)].
I, 6, 8   nam sic et. [vel nam sic et 1, 2 (Col.)].
I, 6, 11   ut. [1, 2 (Col. v. c.), 3].
I, 6, 80   textaque.
I, 6, 80   dente parat. [texta 1°, texta parat 2 (v. c. Col.) ducta videlicet fila 2 (v. c.), ducta putat 3 (v. c.)].
I, 7, 40   laetitiae. [2 (v. c.), tristitiae 2 (v. c.].
II, 3, 45   intus. [1°, 2 (Col.)].
IV, 1, 91   artato. [arctato 1°, 2 (Col.)].

First of all it is clear that No. 3 has no connection with Colocci. Of the other two No. 1 presents a more faithful picture of the Colotianus, as was to be expected of notes said to have been written by Colocci himself.

At II, 3, 45 Statius says « in uno Colotii ». As we have seen, Colocci had at least two manuscripts of Tibullus, but in this passage the reading is the same as found in the printed editions with Colocci notes.

Except for one passage, Statius ends his Colocci notes at II, 3, 45. It might be thought that the Colocci manuscript was incomplete, especially since the last citation is introduced by Statius in a different manner: « Colotium legisse adfirmant in veteri libro ». But the printed editions No. 1 and 2 give Colocci readings throughout the work. Either Statius' source of information dried up or—perhaps more likely—he got tired of quoting the Colotianus. There is a considerable gap before the next to the last quotation.

It was common practice for fifteenth-century scholars to copy or have copied in their printed editions the notes (emendations, variants, interpretations) of well-known scholars. There are probably in existence other editions of Tibullus with Colocci notes, just as there are a number containing those of Pontano via Francesco Pucci [11].

I have not tried to identify the many references to *vetus liber, omnes veteres,* etc., in Statius. In some cases these probably include the manuscripts he at other times names specifically, in others he is presumably drawing on earlier editions. None of his manuscripts is of any importance for the text, though some of the readings may be of interest as emendations.

[11] Cf. F. Calonghi, *Marginalia* (Genoa, 1921) and Chapter XXII, n. 5A, of this book.

Chapter XXIV

ABECEDARIA AND THEIR PURPOSE[1]

A manuscript in the possession of Mr. A. N. L. Munby is the occasion for this chapter. Written in a neat humanistic cursive by a certain Iacobus Panigallius about 1440-60, it contains two alphabets, one majuscule, the other minuscule. As there seem to be no parallels for just this type of abecedarium in fifteenth-century Italy, Mr. Munby asked me to write it up[2]. To judge from the white-vine decoration as well as the script, it was probably written in Florence.

Why did people produce such alphabets? The reason was not always the same. It might be to aid in learning to write either one's own language or another in a different alphabet, or to learn to write in a specified manner, or to teach how to write, or to analyse writing, or to devise means for improving it, or to show one's writing wares.

The oldest abecedaria known to me are those from ancient Etruria, beginning with the Marsiliana alphabet of about 700 B.C.[3] This is cut into the raised ivory rim of a tiny wax tablet, only 9×5 cm. in size. Its purpose is obvious: to serve as a reminder to a writer not too well versed in the new and little known art of writing. In this art adults were

---

[1] Originally published in the *Transactions of the Cambridge Bibliographical Society*, III (1961), p. 181.

[2] I have found no trace of the scribe Panigallius, though, to be sure, I have not made a very thorough search.

[3] This and the following abecedaria are described by Giulio Buonamici, *Epigrafia etrusca* (Florence, 1932), pp. 101 ff., and illustrated in figs. 1-8. The present article deals with abecedaria in Greek and Roman script. The earliest of them all is in the Ras Shamra cuneiform alphabet of the fourteenth century B. C. 'C. Virolleaud in *Acad. des Insc., Comptes-Rendus*, 1950, p. 71).

at that time like children today: they had to learn their letters before they could read or write.

The other early Etruscan abecedaria are, with one exception, on vases and date from the seventh century B.C. The Viterbo vase, in the shape of a cock, is only 8.5 cm. high, without cover, and 5 cm. wide. It has been suggested that it was an ink-pot. In that case its alphabet might well have had the same purpose as that on the Marsiliana tablet. A vase from Caere looks like a short tapering wine bottle, some 14 cm. high. This bottle too is thought to have contained a writing fluid. The Formello vase is a small two-handled amphora, 17 cm. high. It has on it two abecedaria, besides several short inscriptions. At Colle a tomb has an alphabet on its walls. What its purpose was is not certain. The Narce alphabet is on a small chalice, 11×13 cm. Its shape and the upside-down position of the alphabet preclude the possibility of its having been an ink-bottle. Finally, a large amphora from Leprignano carries an alphabet. Four other alphabets of a somewhat later date are described by Buonamici.

The earliest Greek example has been attributed to the eighth century B.C., though some would put it later[4]. It is on a bowl from Mt Hymettus and includes only the first three letters of the alphabet; it never had more. Incised after the bowl was fired, it apparently was the result of idle scratching. The bowl belongs to the Geometric period, and its dating depends on our dating of that era. Fragments of two Greek abecedaria, one Corinthian of the sixth century B.C. and one Ionic of the fifth century are mentioned by Roberts[5]. Others have been described, including a stone with twenty-four alphabets on it![6] The plausible suggestion has been made that the stonecutter was practising his art on a discarded piece of stone. A lamp from Pompeii shows an old man holding a roll on which the first six letters of the Greek alphabet appear. The suggestion that he was a schoolmaster seems reasonable. Over fifty ABC's, most of them incomplete, were scratched on the walls of Pompeii. Those which are nearer the

[4] Carl Blegen in *American Journal of Archaeology*, XXXVIII (1934), pp. 15-17.
[5] E. S. Roberts, *An Introduction to Greek Epigraphy*, Part I (Cambridge, 1887), p. 19.
[6] E. Kalinka in *Mitt. dtsch. arch. Inst., athen. Abt.* XVII (1892), p. 101.

ground were evidently done by schoolboys displaying their newly learned art. I suppose that by careful measurements one might establish their several approximate ages!

Sometimes alphabets seem to have served a purely decorative purpose, as they still do. It has been maintained that they were employed in witchcraft or in mystical religions[7]. They occur in Christian inscriptions too.

The next abecedaria I know anything about date from the fourth or fifth century A.D.[8]. They appear on a papyrus found in Egypt. Their purpose was obvious: to teach two Latin alphabets to the Greek-reading and Greek-writing people of Egypt. The one alphabet is in rustic capitals, the other in a semi-formalized cursive minuscule. They establish the fact that both alphabets were in use at the same time for different purposes. One might compare the learning of printed and script alphabets in modern languages. In the rustic capital abecedarium Z is followed by TH, PH, CH, PS, to represent the four Greek characters not found in the Latin alphabet. Following these come AE and OE, the two Latin diphthongs that are spelled differently from the Greek.

If any alphabets have survived the early Middle Ages they are unknown to me. From the later Middle Ages we have some indications of the activity of writing-teachers, but no model alphabets of theirs seem to have survived. Thus Hugo Spechtshart (born c. 1285) has left us a writing manual but apparently no alphabets[9]. Nor does Hagen, in his advertisement of his school, give any (c. 1400), though he does illustrate in continuous text the various scripts he is prepared to teach. After 1432 a certain Gotzkircher put together a commonplace book in which he included *alphabeta variarum nationum*. This is not in any sense a series

---

[7] A. Dieterich in *Rhein. Mus.* LVI (1901), p. 77, and elsewhere argues for witchraft; C. Huelsen in *Mitt. dtsch. arch. Inst., röm. Abt.* XVIII (1903), p. 73, opposes but accepts religious practices in some instances. F. Dornseiff, *Das Alphabet in Mystik und Magie,* 2nd ed. (Leipzig, 1925), goes all out for magic. He lists later Greek and Latin abecedaria.

[8] Published by H. J. M. Milne in *Greek Shorthand Manuals* (London, 1934), p. 70 and Pl. IX. I called attention to their importance and elucidated some matters of reading and interpretation in *American Journal of Philology,* LVI (1935), p. 147.

[9] S. H. Steinberg in *The Library,* ser. 4, XXI (1941), p. 264. In what follows I have depended chiefly on the same writer's excellent article on writing-masters in *The Library,* ser. 4, XXII (1942), p. 1.

of model alphabets for perfection in the art of writing but a group of alphabets used in different languages, whose purpose it was to teach these languages. They include Latin (presumably as a basis for comparison), Croatian, Chaldean, Bosnian, Russian, Hebrew, Egyptian, and Greek [10]. The first alphabet for teaching writing in a familiar language, as far as I know, is that of Benedict Schwerczer of Passau in 1466 [11]. The Gothic capitals are represented by single letters from A to Z. In the minuscule alphabet the ordinary vowels precede the consonants and those that have an *umlaut* follow.

Paris MS. Lat. 8685 of the middle of the fifteenth century is the work of a writing-master. It contains an alphabet in which the various letters are followed by *m* to show how they should be combined [12].

An Augsburg manuscript of 1481 gives a minuscule alphabet beginning with a capital A [13]. Alternative forms are written above several letters, but the round *r* and *s* are put next to the regular forms. After *z* comes *tz*.

In Italy we find alphabets of the fifteenth century but they are in no way comparable to those of Panigallius. They consist of capital alphabets analysed and improved geometrically, not intended as samples for ordinary writing but designed chiefly for monuments. We find such names as Mantegna, Feliciano, Leonardo da Vinci, Damiano da Moile, and Luca de Pacioli engaged in this sort of activity [14].

In Magdalene College, Cambridge, in the collection of Samuel Pepys, there is a copybook (2891), dated by Pepys about 1400 (confirmed by James), which contains minuscule and majuscule

[10] P. Lehmann in *Festschrift für Georg Leidinger* (Munich, 1930), p. 157. Similar in its purpose is an entry in a manuscript in the Pierpont Morgan Library, New York (M.A. 812) of the latter part of the fifteenth century, perhaps copied by Giorgio Antonio Vespucci, uncle of Amerigo. It gives the forms of the letters in Old Attic, followed by the Panhellenic alphabet.

[11] Steinberg, *op. cit.*, Pl. IV.

[12] L. Delisle in *Journal des Savants* (1899), p. 58. Montpellier 512 seems to contain only large capitals for initials, to judge from Delisle's description.

[13] Steinberg, *op. cit.*, Pl. VI.

[14] Cf. Stanley Morison in Ambrose Heal, *The English Writing-Masters and their Copy-Books 1570-1800* (Cambridge, 1931), p. XXV, and his *Fra Luca de Pacioli* (New York, 1933), etc.

alphabets [15]. James describes them as follows: « P. 1. The Alphabet ending z÷est amen. Two forms of *a, r, s.* Then the alphabet a-z written as one word... P. 2. Alphabets a-z÷est. Two forms of *a, r, s.* As on p. 1, but larger... P. 3. Alphabet in Gothic capitals. Two forms for each letter (3 for s): goes down to V ». There are also colored capitals.

The next abecedarium known to me is the one that is the excuse for the present chapter. It is found in a manuscript of Basil, *De legendis antiquorum libris oratio* and Aristotle's *Oeconomicus,* both translated by Leonardo Bruni, and a work entitled *Officia et dignitates Romanae,* sometimes attributed to Bruni. Thus the contents tend to confirm the attribution of the volume to Florence, since Bruni lived in that city.

One of the two alphabets is in capitals, the other in minuscules, like the alphabets on papyrus of a thousand years earlier. But there are interesting differences which make clear the purpose of these alphabets. In many cases, two, three, and even four examples of the same letter are given. Each of the capitals is represented twice except F and G (three times) and Z (four times). There seem to be no intentional differences in D, E, L, N, O, T, X. One A has a serif at the top, the other has not. One B and one C are a little fatter, but this may be unintended. The first F has a long top stroke projecting to the left. The second has a top stroke that ends in a semicircle, a form common in humanistic script, especially in Florence. The first G curls inward, like the figure 6, the second has the usual inscriptional form. Both were used by Poggio, the inventor of humanistic script. The third has a squared shape. H has not only the regular capital form but also an enlarged version of the minuscule *h.* One I comes to a sharp point slightly below the line. One K has a curling tail, as does one of the Q's. In one M the two middle strokes come down to the line of writing. One P turns to the left slightly below the line. One R has a longer tail. The lower part of one S is fatter. One V

---

[15] I am indebted to Mr. James Wells of the Newberry Library for calling the manuscript to my attention. He tells me that Graham Pollard is at work on it. The book is described by M. R. James in *Bibliotheca Pepysiana,* Part III (London, 1923), p. 122. James thought it might be unique (p. viii).

has a serif at the top of the second stroke. One Y curls to the left a little more than the other does. The first Z has finials at beginning and end; the second has a top stroke extending to the left and a bottom stroke extending to the right. The fourth Z is an enlarged form of an old minuscule *z*, like a *c* with a cedilla. It may well be that not all the differences indicated are significant. One Z was probably added to fill out the fourth line, which is spaced out for the same reason, containing only eleven characters as compared with thirteen in each of the first three lines.

The minuscules are arranged in three lines. They start with a capital A, presumably because the scribe, deliberately or unconsciously, followed the usual custom at the beginning of a sentence. All letters occur twice except *h, s, z*, of which three examples are given. Apparently no significant differences are found in *b, c, d, e, g, l, o, p, q, t, u, x, y*. The first *f* is a little longer than the second. The first *h* ends a little below the line. The first *i* is normal, the second is long, as used in *ii*. The first *k* has a loop, the second merely a slanting line. The letters *m* and *n* are represented by two forms, one with a straight final shaft, one with a turned-up join. The second *r* has its second stroke starting from the line of writing. The two examples of long *s* are alike, but the third *s* is round, for use at the end of a word. The first *z* is in the minuscule form, the other two are smaller versions of the capital, one a little wider than the other. The last letter is followed by two different forms of ampersand and by abbreviations of *con* (or *-us*; the same sign is used for both in the text) and *-rum*. The first line has seventeen characters but the initial capital A takes the space of two; the second line has eighteen, the third, to *z*, has fourteen. It is obvious that the two ampersands and the two abbreviations were added to fill the line. It may be pointed out that practically all the forms occur in the text (I have not noted a *k* or a *z*). But in the text some additional forms turn up that are not in the alphabets: a minuscule *v*, a different *x*, and an ampersand lying on its back. The capitals especially show freer forms occasionally: an uncial E and an epsilon and at least six more varieties of V.

What then was the purpose of these two apparently unique alphabets? It seems that the scribe was exhibiting his wares, indeed I should say that this was his obvious purpose. Here were the letter styles he was prepared to furnish a prospective client. Where did he get the idea? Presumably his writing-teacher had furnished him with alphabets to follow. His purpose was not the same as that of the German and other writing-masters: he was available not to teach writing, but to execute commissions to copy books. Yet there is of course a close affinity between the teacher of writing and the pupil who learns to write for a living.

Knowing that in some cases he would have to give two specimens (as in long and short *i,* long *s* and final round *s*), Panigallius apparently decided for the sake of balance to give two examples of each letter, whether they differed or not. Though I say that it was he who made this decision, it is quite possible, even likely, that he was merely following previous practice.

Except for short runs of letters found in *probationes pennae* I cannot recall any other Italian abecedaria before the sixteenth century, when the writing-masters began to give samples of their wares. The first was Ludovico Arrighi in his *La Operina* of 1522 [16]. Like Panigallius, he offers a majuscule and a minuscule alphabet. For the capitals he presents two or more quite different examples of every letter. There are three kinds of A, P, T, X, four of M and V. He ends with ampersand and *etc.* Like Panigallius, he begins the minuscule series with a capital A. Only one example of each letter is given, except that he affords two *x*'s and intersperses *m*'s at various points to show how they join: before *f, g, h,* and each of the *x*'s. Apparently this was an old practice, as it was used in the preceding century in France, as noted above. At the end he puts *etc.* In the next year he exhibits two examples of most of the capitals, but only one of K, O, Y, Z, and three of V and ampersand [17], as well as two of the abbreviation *-rum.* The minuscules are generally represented by a single sample, but there are two *e*'s, *g*'s, and *s*'s. In 1524 G. A. Tagliente begins two minuscule series with

[16] Alfred Fairbank and Berthold Wolpe, *Renaissance Handwriting* (London, 1960), fig. 57.
[17] *Ibid.,* fig. 59.

a capital A and generally shows only one form of each letter [18].   He
ends with ampersand.   In the revision of 1525 Tagliente illustrates
a number of alphabets by two or more examples of each letter [19].
Some of these do not differ from each other, in which respect
he resembles Panigallius.   Like Panigallius again, he sometimes
gives two forms of *m* and *n,* with and without join.

It is obvious, I think, that the sixteenth-century teachers of
script followed the practice of their predecessors of the preceding
century as exemplified by Panigallius.   Not that his manuscript is
likely to have been known to the later writing-masters; rather,
there must have been many other such alphabets in circulation for
the use of students.   The persistence of ampersand, still sometimes used, is a tie that binds the Panigallius alphabets to those
of Arrighi and his successors.   So is the *-rum* abbreviation, as
well as the double set of letters.   Mr. Munby's manuscript seems
to be a unique example of a scribe exhibiting his wares for
prospective clients.   It is, however, closely related to the writing-
manuals and advertisements of earlier and later writing-teachers.
Perhaps the present study will stimulate others to find additional
parallels.

A further note of interest in connection with this manuscript.
On a fly-leaf a hand of the eighteenth century (after 1754) wrote
that the manuscript had been owned by Cardinal Juan de
Torquemada (Turrecremata; 1388-1468).   This is not the famous
inquisitor but his uncle.   He was present at the Council of
Constance, where he could have met Poggio, whose humanistic
script was already being widely used.   Later the Cardinal attended
the Council of Florence (1438-45) and there he could have picked
up the Panigallius, if I am right in thinking it was written in
Florence.   Torquemada was responsible for bringing Schweynheym
and Pannartz from Germany to Subiaco to print the first book
ever printed in Italy.   Possibly the Panigallius volume and its
alphabet had something to do with his interest in the new art of
printing.   After the Cardinal's death his library passed to a

---

[18] Fairbank and Wolpe, *Renaissance Handwriting,* fig. 65 *b.*
[19] See the facsimile in *Opera di Giovanniantonio Tagliente,* edited by James
M. Wells (Chicago, 1952).   Probably some of these features are in the 1524 edition,
which I know only in the one page reproduced in Fairbank and Wolpe.

nephew, who took it to Spain and left it in the Dominican friary at Valladolid, to which his uncle had belonged. In the eighteenth century the manuscript reached the library of Rafael Floranes, who I suspect is the author of the note on the flyleaf. Floranes was sufficiently involved in handwriting to achieve a place in E. Cotarelo, *Diccionario biográfico y bibliográfico de Calígrafos Españoles* (Madrid, 1914). Floranes' views on teaching a single style of writing were quoted by Servidori and through him affected Palomares, two of Spain's best-known writing-teachers, whose writing-specimens are found in modern works on Spanish calligraphy. It is idle to speculate whether Floranes was influenced by the handsome and fluent script of Panigallius.

Chapter XXV

COLUCCIO SALUTATI ON MONARCHY [1]

Vatican manuscript Capponi 147, copied on paper, contains first drafts of letters, chiefly official, and a few other items composed by Coluccio Salutati from 1375 on. Some are Coluccio's autographs, others were copied by his assistants. Most of them have corrections that only an author would make in revising a first draft. This is true not only of the Coluccio autographs but also of most of those copied by others. The letters that have no corrections such as an author would make in revising are for the most part very short, from two to ten lines long. A few are fair copies of letters written by others, such as a letter (p. 95) of Pope Boniface IX to the bishop of Florence. Another fair copy is of an address made by Coluccio in behalf of his colleagues and the commune of Florence to representatives of the King of France.

The subject of the present paper is an unpublished document on pp. 39-43 which presents in two parts arguments for kingship by succession and by election. This is a Coluccio autograph, with many of his corrections, some made as he was writing this first draft, others made later [2].

Mehus mentions the treatise in 1759, when he was living in Florence [3]. At that time the manuscript was already in the

---

[1] Originally published in *Mélanges Eugène Tisserant*, V (1964; *Studi e Testi*, 235), p. 401.

[2] The treatise is mentioned in B. L. Ullman, *The Humanism of Coluccio Salutati* (Padua, 1963), pp. 29, 34, 35, 205, 276. F. Novati, *Epistolario di Coluccio Salutati*, IV (Rome 1911), p. 609, gives a collation of this manuscript for the important private letter to Carlo di Durazzo, which he had published in II, p. 11 on the basis of a seventeenth-century copy (Florence, Marucelliana C 89)

[3] L. Mehus in Vol. I of *Traversarii Ambrosii ... epistolae*, ed. by P. Cannetus Florence, 1759), pp. 301-302. He mentions also the speech made by

Vatican. The Capponi collection was made by Alessandro Gre-gorio Capponi of Rome, by whose will of 1745 it was left to the Vatican. He died in 1746 and in that year the collection was transferred to the Vatican. Our manuscript was in Florence in 1734, as we know from three letters written in that year by Salvino Salvini to Alessandro Capponi. In the first two he urges Capponi to buy it, as it is an autograph. Capponi took the advice, for in his last letter Salvini says that Capponi's offer had been accepted [4]. Unfortunately he does not name the seller.

Before discussing the treatise I will give the text as it is in the Capponi manuscript [5].

Quod melius sit regnum successivum quam electivum.

Non sine causa ab omnibus gentibus receptum est omnia ferme regna transire in posteros. Optimum enim est dominium quod rex putat ad se non brevi vitae sue tempore sed etiam postquam decesserit
5 pertinere. Edificamus domos, plantamus vineas, et colimus atque inse-rimus arbores, quas ad nos cognoscimus non spectare, cogitantes illas in posteros transituras; in quibus etiam quandoque non filiis sed pronepotibus consulimus nostris. Que momentanea sunt, fixe diligi nequeunt; mansura constantiore mente et propensiore animo diliguntur.
10 Conatur rex, cui filius regni futurus est heres, ut liberis amorem civium derelinquat, ut tutum illud et certum dimittat parvulo, et in grandem natu, si forte sibi sit, transferat. Qui eligitur in diem cogitat, sibi soli providet. Qui vero per successionem fit paternos ampliat fines, cives honorat suos, et non sibi soli sed filiis accumulatis meritis
15 obnoxios facit. Semper angitur semperque formidat ne quid lubricum,

1 electivum *post* regnum *del.*   2 a maioribus *del. et* ab omnibus gen-tibus *sscr.*   4 vita *in* vitae *corr. et* sue *sscr.*   5 *Cf. Cic. De sen.* 24   6 lati et *del. et* quas ... spectare *i. m. add.*   7 *ex* per transitus *corr.*   7 etiam ... sed *sscr.*   11 relinquant *del. et* dimittat *sscr.*   12 *ex* grantem *corr.*   14 soli *sscr.*

Coluccio to Cardinal Philippe d'Alençon and the letter to Carlo di Durazzo. He does not say where he saw the manuscript.

[4] The letters of Salvini are in Cappon. 279, fols. 9, 20, 36. They are dated January 12, 26, and February 9, 1733 (Florentine style; 1734). See also G. Salvo Cozzo, *I codici capponiani della Biblioteca Vaticana* (Rome, 1897).

[5] The seventeenth-century copy of the Capponi manuscript in the Maru-celliana of Florence (C 89) once belonged to Alessandro Segni. It is the only other manuscript that contains the treatise on monarchy, as far as I know.

ne quid periculosum filiis suis relinquat, ne maiorum suorum virtus aliquando in semet desideretur. Habet ante oculos maiorum exempla, nititur ipsis se inferiorem non ostendere. Eneas etenim, ut inquit Maro, « Ascanium fusis circum complectitur armis Summaque per galeam delibans oscula fatur: 'Disce, puer, virtutem ex me verumque laborem, Fortunam ex aliis' ». Dum enim rex natus maiorum virtutes superare cogitat exemplumque filiis dare, maximis hinc inde stimulis agitur ad virtutem. Noverunt reges fortissimam regni ac munitissimam arcem fore dilectionem civium. Sic conatur igitur rex nativus ut ametur, sic metuit ne in filio sit paterna memoria vel leviter odiosa. Hoc ipse deus omnipotens manifesto nobis ostendit exemplo. Regnum etenim David et Salomonis instituens ex successione voluit, non ex civium suffragiis propagari. An melius est civibus de regis electione pendere quam habere fixum qui sibi debeat imperare? Nonne scimus quot et quante seditiones quotque bella civilia nata sunt propter principum electiones? Nonne videmus quotidie, quotiens principes eliguntur, in potentiorem magis quam in optimum consentire suffragia, multaque per ambitionem et largitiones inhonestissimas magis quam virtutibus obtineri? Denique regere populos ars est non vilis, non abiecta, sed honorabilis et sublimis. Hanc filii in regia domo discunt. Nutriuntur in maiestate principatus, in oculis civium, in frequentia famulatus, inter alta negocia. Cumque quicquid agant latere non possit, habent ad virtutem quandam quodammodo necessitatem indictam. Non potest ignorare conditiones civium suorum, nec eius mores queunt a subditis ignorari. Cognoscit oves suas, et cognoscunt ipsum suae. Naturalia accidentalibus diviniora sunt. Non ex armento tuo velis pullum eligere vel habere, sed ex quocumque potius armento optimum. Gratior tamen est in septis natus tuis, si bonus sit, quam aeque bonus emptitius, minusque periculosus si malus fuerit. Refractus est actus de servo dominum fieri. Novit servus quid sibi, non quid omnibus grave sit. Novit autem dominus et iubet quid deceat imperare, non quid subditorum plerumque sibi remitti velit ignavia. Sed regnum quandoque pervenit ad puerum. Interim quasi quodam interregno populi rege carent, quem oportuno tempore recipiunt. Honorabile fateor scire regere. Hoc autem plenius addiscitur imperando quam serviendo. Qualia sint servorum imperia cum evadunt in dominos docuit olim Tyrus,

17 aliquando] do in corr.   19 Verg. Aen. XII, 433-436.   24 igitur agit quod dilig post Sic statim del.   25 pater odio post sit statim del.   26 nos post Hoc statim del.   27 Cf. III Reg. 9, 5   29 fixum] f in corr.   29 qui ex quis corr.   32 in post quam sscr.   38 u (?) post ad del.   38 ex virtud corr. 38 ras. i. m.   46 et iubet sscr.   49 et del. et quem sscr.   50 addiscitur statim ex adi corr.   51 dominia post servorum del et imperia sscr.

docuit et in Italia, luxuria effeminante Vulsinum. Non pudet aliquem regie proli subesse. Felicius valere videmus regna quibus reges prosunt quam Italiam cui dominatur imperium.

55   Extra controversiam habet utrumque regnum perfectiones et utilitates suas, quae omnes in domino nostro Romanorum rege conveniunt, ut fateri oporteat quod dignitate perfectissimus sit omnium principum orbis terre.

Pars Altera

60   Quod regnum melius sit electivum quam successivum

Expedit rei publice non hominem hunc, non genus hoc, sed virum optimum dominari. Nec si aliquem qui armentum habeat interroges velitne ex armento suo pullum an ex quocumque grege optimum pullum habere, invenias aliquem qui non potius optimum ex alio quam ex suo
65   minus bonum velit. Ceterum si tibi proponatur quid maius, an de uno grege solum pullum qualis a natura sit productus possidere an tibi undecumque volueris eligere, nonne malis quanto latius fieri potest eligendi tibi propositam facultatem? Proinde quid magis corrumpit mores quam principem vivere, quam legibus esse solutum, quam omnia sine metu et
70   sine pudore gerere? Virtuosum oportet regem esse, non fieri; difficile intra licentiam regiam virtus discitur. Nescit dominari nisi qui experiendo didicerit quid sibi velint subditi a maioribus imperari. Ideo rata est erga patres filiorum benivolentia et in ipsos patris imperium et autoritas, quia, dum se filios agerent, edocti sunt quid conveniat parentes a
75   filiis expectare. Melius et maioris libertatis est imperium tradere quam suscipere. Vernacularum est servos nasci, ingenuorum liberos. Et quantum prestrigium est regimen quod ad subditorum utilitatem referri debet puero contingere qui nec sua possit nec aliena commoda procurare? Beatissimas affirmavit Plato res publicas quarum rectores sapientes
80   essent aut studere sapientiae contigisset. Et tu michi vis puerum recens natum prepositum fore, qui adhuc in cunis vagiat, quemve ut ydolum et statuam quandam adorent subditi, qui, ut inquit scriptura, oculos

---

52 in Italia *sic*   52 Cf. *Val. Max.* IX, 1, *Ext.* 2   53 imperia *del. et* regna *statim scr.*   57 ut ... dignitate *i. m. add.*   57 *ex* opporteat *corr.*   59 Pars Altera *postea add.*   62 armentum] e *in corr.*   63 proprio *ante* suo *del.*   63 grege *ex* h(abe)re *corr.*   63 optimum *i. m. add.*   63 genitum *post* optimum *del.*   64 habere *post* pullum *sscr.*   64 *ex* invenies *corr.*   64 ex alio ... bonum *i. m. add.*   65 quam suum *post* bonum *del.*   65 tuo *del. et* uno *sscr.*   66 eligere *post* pullum *del.*   70 Virtuosum ... discitur *i. m. add.*   73 patres filiorum *in ras.*   73 *ras. i. m.*   73 et ... patris *i. m. add.*   74 filios *post* se *del.* patres pro filiis *i. m. add. et del.* filios *i. m. add.*   74 patres *del. et* parentes *sscr.*   77 pro *prestigium*   79 Cf. *Plat. apud Cic. Ep. Q. Fr.* I, 1, 29   82 q(uan)d *in* qua(n)dam *statim corr.*   82 Cf. *Nov. Test. Marc.* 8, 18

habeat et non videat, aures habeat et non intelligat, pedes habeat et
non ambulet, manus habeat et nichil operetur. Denuo aut honorem vel
utilitatem regnantium querimus aut, ut ita dixerim, regnatorum. Et   85
de hoc quidem satis. Sed si illud aspicias, nonne utilius et honorabilius
est regi ob virtutem eligi quam regem nasci? Nonne melius regendi
scientiam habere quam regere? At numquam hoc sciet nisi gradatim
ascenderit. Non ad superbiam, non ad inanem gloriam institutum est
ut regum thronus maneat in sublimi, sed ut scirent illuc ascensuri rem   90
arduam se aggredi et laboriosam fore et multis ante meritis acquirendam
illam super alios prelaturam, et ut cum illic sint, pudeat eos siquis
forte melior infra ipsos sedeat. Non enim imperare bonis sed bonum
esse gloriosum est et honorabile. Si optimus regnum teneat, neminem
subesse pudet, neminem regnantium in aliquo se minorem subdito   95
fateri, quod extremi pudoris est, oportet. Nulla permittit ratio maioribus minora preponi nec melioribus bona, nedum ut in hoc sepe
contingit preesse bonis mala. Denique eligentes cum agant ex proposito minus errare possunt. Sed natura producens non regem intendit
sed hominem. Sed optime gubernatur maiorique cum amore possidetur   100
quod transiturum est in posteros. Iam michi malignitatem obicis
presidentis, sed si par sit bonitas, quantum ad hoc nulla erit differentia;
si par malignitas, nulla in altero prerogativa. Uterque suo tempore
ferendus est. Hoc interest, quod qui electus est minus sibi licere putat
quam cui avitum regnum obvenit. Et quot et quantos videmus   105
maiorum suorum dissipare patrimonia, cum ferme nullos aspiciamus
a se quesita dispergere! Sed inquis: « Errare possunt eligentes et
improbum pro virtuoso preponere ». Fateor. Frequentius tamen contingit paternas in filio non apparere virtutes quam eligentes errare.
Cuius rei meticulosus pater Micissa, cum naturales alloqueretur filios,   110
monuit ut conarentur se meliores vel equales esse Iugurthae, quem in
filium adoptatum heredem aequaliter dimittebat, rationem adiciens ne
meliores sumpsisse videretur liberos quam genuisse. Nec illum fefellit
suspicio: Hyensale quidem et Adherbale clarior atque prestantior

84 honorem vel *i. m. add.* 85 dominantium *del. et* regnantium *sscr.* 85 Et ...
satis *i. m. add.* 86 Si *in* Sed si *corr.* 87 ob ... melius *i. m. add.* 87 regere
scire *del. et* regendi scientiam habere *i. m. add.* 91 illam acquirere prelaturam *post* meritis *statim del.* 92 eos *ex* ipsos *corr.* 95 neminem *post* pudet
ex nemo *corr.* 96 q *post* fateri *del.* 97 nec ... mala *i. m. add.* 99 minus
... hominem *i. m. add.* 106 vide *ante* aspiciamus *statim del.* 107 Sed *ante*
Errare *del.* 107 errantes *ante* eligentes *statim del.* 109 non *ante* non *del.*
110 *Cf.* Sall. *Iug.* 10, 8 111 esse *del. et* vel equales esse *i. m. add.* 111 Iu-
gurta *in* Iugurthae *statim corr.* 113 elegisse *del. et* sumpsisse *sscr.* 113 quam
f *del. et* liberos quam *statim add.*

115 Iugurtha evasit. Sed inquies Deum et astrorum vim et ipsam rationem
ordinis universi hunc a nativitate in regnum ordinare, cuius quidem
providentia errare non potest. Et de Deo quidem et universi ordine
fateor. Sed sit aequaliter de omnibus ut asseritur. Nonne Dei providentia et universi quem allegas ordo et ipsa vis astrorum aequaliter
120 nativitates et electiones aspicit et disponit? Ut in hoc neutrius condicio
melior dici possit. Nos autem nunc de inferioribus causis, non de his
sublimibus disputamus. Sed omnium regnorum principia damnas, quae
videmus ex successione transferri. Verum tamen imperium, quod
quidem regnum regnorum est, per electionem institui maiores voluere.
125 Ut potius hinc deceat, quod maius est, quam a minoribus exemplum
et rationem duci. Quod si minor in regibus cura sumpta est, cum iure
debeant imperio subiacere et imperatoris sit reges deponere regnaque
transferre, neminem convenit admirari. Et ipsum regum exordium ab
electione, non a nativitate principium habuit. Subcessionem introduxit
130 ambitio atque potentia. Sed in electionibus plus potentia, plus fortis
ambitio, plus plerunque gratia potest quam virtus. At non decet
electivam damnare viam ob imprudentiam vel turpitudinem eligentium,
sicut nec aliquam artium ob inscitiam vel malignitatem artificum. Sed
ordinavit Deus, qui quidem optima semper facit, in semine David pueri
135 sui sceptrum non cessare super Israel donec veniret qui salvaret
populum suum: nec dubium quin si electivum regnum melius foret
quam per successionem, ipsum ordinasset electione, non successione
transire. Sed qui hec dicit non reminiscitur Deum iratum insaniae
populi sui, iudicibus sublatis, regem illi populo consensisse, non hoc
140 in populi sublevationem sed in penam et onus instituendo. Quid
autem obicis michi ob electionem seditiones et bella civilia, cum etiam
soleant consanguinea atque fraterna et plusquam civilia bella inter
eiusdem sanguinis principes obvenire? Felicius valent subditi regum
quam Italia cui dominatur imperium. Nam illa reguntur, hec pro
145 derelicta habetur, sed quando recta fuit super omnia regna tenuit
principatum.

116 hunc *ex* hos *corr.* 120 et disponit *i. m. add.* 120 *ex* conditio *corr.*
121 adeo *post* his *del.* 123 tamen *sscr.* 123 quod et summus pon *post*
imperium *statim del.* 125 quam *ante* quod *del.* 125 q *post* quod *del.*
126 *ex* ratio *corr.* 128 Et ipsum ... potentia *i. m. add.* 130 quam vi quod
plus potentia *statim del.* 132 electorem *del. et* eligentium *i. m. add.* 134 ex
del. et in *sscr.* 134 *ex* Davit *corr.* 135 sui *sscr.* 135 stare *del. et* non
cessare *i. m. add.* 136 quod *del. et* quin *sscr.* 137 foret per electionem
ordinaturus *in* ordinasset electione non successione transire *corr.* 138 insaniae populi sui *i. m. add.* 139 explosis revoca *post* iudicibus *statim del.*
140 in *ante* penam *sscr.* 141 illa *post* cum *del.* 142 consanguinea ... bella
i. m. add. 144 illa *sic pro* illi.

As to the date of composition of this little treatise, all we can say is that the letters found together with it are dated from 1375 to 1404. The years that have the greatest number of dated letters are 1382, 1386, 1387, 1390-93. Our treatise follows a letter of 1383 and precedes several of 1391. The leaves have been badly disarranged, as traces of an old pagination show. Thus new p. 95 is old p. 1, new p. 1 is old p. 92, new p. 33 is old p. 82, new p. 428 is old p. 31, etc. But even in the old paging the letters are not in a strict chronological order. The best guess (and it is only a guess) is that the treatise was written between 1383 and 1390. Coluccio's letter to Carlo di Durazzo, which belongs to the literature on the education of princes, was written in 1381, and our treatise may have been written in the same decade. But the *De tyranno,* also dealing with government, was not written until 1400.

In the thirteenth and fourteenth centuries the discussion of the organization of government was a favorite topic. In part it arose out of the relations of Church and State, and in part out of the desires of Italians to make over the Holy Roman Empire, or, to put it another way, to mold the Emperor nearer to their hearts' desire. Some of the treatises dealt specifically with the training of princes, and even in these as well as in the more general types, the question of hereditary versus elective monarchy might find a place[6]. The discussion began with Aristotle[7], and the whole question of political organization centered largely around him in the thirteenth century, the period of his greatest popularity.

In his *De regimine principum* (ca. 1265) Thomas Aquinas does not discuss the question with which we are concerned here. Some of his disciples, however, did. One was Aegidius Colonna.

---

[6] For a survey of works on the training of princes see Lester K. Born, « The Perfect Prince: a Study in Thirteenth and Fourteenth-Century Ideals », *Speculum,* III (1928), p. 470.

[7] *Pol.* III, 15 (1286 b 22). There is also the commentary by Petrus de Alvernia, attributed to Thomas Aquinas, published in the Parma edition of Thomas, vol. XXI, p. 495 (III, Lectio XIV).

Of all the predecessors of Coluccio on the theme of the monarch, Aegidius Colonna, in his *De regimine principum* (ca. 1287), might seem on *a priori* grounds to have influenced him most. For Coluccio had two copies of it in his library: Florence, Laur. S. Croce XVI, sin. 11 and Vat. lat. 770 [8]. Presumably Coluccio read the work, or part of it, but neither of these manuscripts contains any notes by him. Besides, there is no resemblance between Aegidius and Coluccio. The former favors hereditary monarchy, challenging the view of some that election is preferable. Superficially, he says, that would be true, as it would seem to be based on deliberate choice (*arte*) rather than chance (*sorte*), for one does not know how the heir will turn out [9]. He answers that argument from three points of view, that of the ruler, the heir, and the people. The king will be a better ruler if the kingdom is really his own, which he can leave to his son. This argument reappears in later discussions, including Coluccio's, though differently phrased; it was common property, based on Aristotle. Just as the characters (*mores*) of newly rich generally become worse than the characters of those used to wealth, so the rulers who have just come to power deteriorate, becoming tyrants, puffed up with their own importance. Not so with the men who inherit a kingdom. As for the people, custom is second nature; therefore they will obey the son as they did the father. Election leads to civil war, a point that Coluccio mentions. In spite of these similarities the treatments are so different that there is nothing to indicate that Coluccio had read the manuscripts of Aegidius which he owned.

In his *De monarchia* (before 1321) Dante deals with the

---

[8] B. L. Ullman, *The Humanism of Coluccio Salutati,* pp. 167 and 180.

[9] *De regimine principum* III, II, 5. I have used the Rome edition of 1556. The contrast between *ars* and *sors* goes back to Thomas Aquinas, *De regimine principum* IV, 20: « quantum ad electionem, ut non arte vel sortialiter ». In view of the fact that Thomas here is in the midst of discussing Aristotle's *Politics,* it may be that he had 1273 a 18 in mind: « (Chalcedonii) oligarchicum; quod autem sine pretio et non sortiales aristocraticum ponendum » (translation of Guilelmus de Moerbeke in F. Susemihl's edition of Aristotle's *Politics,* Leipzig, 1872). For others who argued for monarchy by succession see Alan Gewirth, *Marsilius of Padua,* I (New York, 1951), p. 244, n. 58.

relation of the Empire to the Papacy but does not take up the question with which Coluccio is concerned in his treatise.

Marsilius of Padua, in his *Defensor pacis* (1324), comes closer to Coluccio than anyone else. The title of I, 16 reads [10]:

« An magis expediat politiae monarcham quemlibet per novam electionem singillatim sumere, vel aliquem quendam solum eligere cum omni posteritate sua, quam generis successionem vocare solent ».

Marsilius, like Coluccio, gives both sides, first arguing for succession (I, 16, 1-10), then coming out strongly for election (11-25), though Coluccio with his two titles contrasts the two parts more sharply.

Yet in spite of the similarity, it is not certain that Coluccio knew or used Marsilius. The arguments in the two works are often quite different, and so is the form in which they are clothed. In the part favoring succession Coluccio says: « Ab omnibus gentibus receptum est omnia ferme regna transire in posteros ». Marsilius says (9): « Rursus, quo plures et in pluribus regionibus ac populis et pluri tempore perfectior est modus assumendi monarcham; quoniam qui magis naturalis, magis perfectus; magis naturale autem quod in pluribus est ». The monarch strives, says Coluccio, « ne maiorum suorum virtus aliquando in semet desideretur », and cites Aeneas' advice to his son: « Disce, puer, virtutem ex me verumque laborem ». Marsilius (3) remarks that some one family may so excel other citizens in virtue that they deserve to rule forever. Also (4): « tales ad virtutem magis inclinantur quoniam ex strenuis parentibus prodeunt magis ». The hereditary monarch feels, says Coluccio, that his « dominium ... ad se non brevi vitae sue tempore sed etiam postquam decesserit pertinere ». Marsilius (1) remarks that « monarcha succedens ex genere rem publicam magis curabit, tamquam sibi quasi propriam et hereditariam ».

The closest parallel between the two writers is in the

---

[10] Edited by C. W. Previté-Orton (Cambridge, 1928).

argument that elections produce civil wars. Marsilius is quite specific (5): « dubium est in seditionem universam deducere politiam, quemadmodum monstrat experientia in electione nova principis Romanorum ». He is alluding to the war between Louis IV of Bavaria and Frederick of Austria, who were fighting for the emperorship. Coluccio is obviously referring to the same events, though he is not specific: « nonne scimus quot et quante seditiones quotque bella civilia nata sunt propter principum electiones? Nonne videmus ... multaque per ambitionem et largitiones inhonestissimas magis quam virtutibus obtineri? » At the end Coluccio defends election: « Quid autem obicis michi ob electionem seditiones et bella civilia, cum etiam soleant consanguinea atque fraterna et plusquam civilia bella inter eiusdem sanguinis principes obvenire? » Marsilius presents the view (of others) that a hereditary monarch « subditorum ambitionem, ... atque seditionis concitationem videtur auferre ». He answers this in 21: « Attendentes enim civium plurimi super se monarchizare frequenter minus dignos secundum virtutem ... iuste seditionem movebunt ».

Coluccio's statement, « nec eius mores queunt a subditis ignorari », is matched by Marsilius' (6): « Facilius autem est unici mores [11] nosse quam plurium ».

In defending election Coluccio asks: « Nonne utilius et honorabilius est regi ob virtutem eligi quam regem nasci? Nonne melius regendi scientiam habere quam regere?» Marsilius (18) remarks: « Non solum inclinatum ad prudentiam et virtutem, qualem dat natalis successio, verum etiam iam perfectum et actualiter operantem secundum virtutem ». Coluccio refutes the objection made by an advocate of succession: « Errare possunt eligentes et improbum pro virtuoso preponere ». Marsilius (5) mentions the « difficultas habendi studiosos electores ». Both point out that the founder of a hereditary monarchy was chosen by election.

In contrast with Marsilius' crabbed Latin, Coluccio's sounds almost classical. Marsilius quotes copiously from Aristotle (over twenty-five times) and once from Cicero. Coluccio introduces

---

[11] The *editio princeps* and one of the manuscripts have *morem*.

Virgil, Plato (via Cicero), the Bible, Valerius Maximus, Cicero, and Sallust.

In speaking of the Emperor as the King of the Romans Coluccio is alluding to the « election » of the emperor by the people of Rome. Marsilius was responsible for the coronation of Louis IV by the Romans. According to Leicht he may have been influenced by Mussato's account of the coronation of Henry VII [12].

In a detailed study Ercole found some close resemblances between the treatise *De tyrannia* of Bartolus of Sassoferrato and Coluccio's *De tyranno,* but concluded that Coluccio had not borrowed from his predecessor. In fact, he emphasized the differences between the two [13]. In the same way, there seem to be no indications of any dependence of Coluccio in his treatise about monarchy on Bartolus' very brief statement in *De regimine civitatis* (written before 1357). He favored election for the Empire, calling it *magis divinum,* but succession for the lesser kingdoms [14].

Coluccio uses the expression *legibus solutus* of the ruler. It was widely current in his time and goes back to *Dig.* I, 3, 31, quoting Ulpian. Esmein says that few texts exercised a more profound influence on the development of public law in certain European countries [15]. The phrase *legibus solutus* actually goes back to the Roman Republic, occurring as early as Lucilius (48). Pompey was freed from the operation of election laws; he was elected consul at the age of 36 (instead of 43) and had not previously served as praetor [16].

---

[12] Pier Silverio Leicht, *Le funzioni elettive del popolo romano e la dottrina di Marsilio da Padova,* in *Marsilio da Padova,* by Aldo Checchini and Norberto Bobbio (Padua, 1942), p. 42.

[13] Francesco Ercole, *Tractatus de Tyranno von Coluccio Salutati* (Berlin, 1914), pp. 105-149. An Italian version is in Ercole's *Da Bartolo all'Althusio* (Florence, 1932), pp. 313-358.

[14] Bartolus, *Consilia, Quaestiones et Tractatus* (Venice, 1575), fol. 153, N. 23.

[15] A. Esmein, *La maxime « Princeps legibus solutus est » dans l'ancien droit public français,* in Paul Vinogradoff, *Essays in Legal History* (Oxford, 1913), p. 201.

[16] Cicero, *De imp. Cn. Pompei* 62. Curiously, Esmein does not mention the practice during the Republic.

The phrase *naturalia accidentalibus diviniora sunt* in Coluccio sounds Aristotelian and perhaps goes back to one of the Aristotelians of the thirteenth or fourteenth centuries. The allusion to astrology is also characteristic of the period.

So it appears that Coluccio did not depend directly on any of the predecessors I have mentioned. He probably had at some time read one or more of them or similar works, especially Aegidius and Marsilius. Even more likely is that he took part in discussions of the matter with colleagues, disciples, and others. The relation of the city-state Florence to the Empire and the Papacy must have been frequently discussed. Coluccio, in effect the foreign minister of Florence, must have played an important part in such discussions, as well as in determining policy.

At the end of the first part of his treatise, Coluccio, in arguing, contrary to his own belief, for hereditary monarchy, remarks that kingdoms which have (hereditary) kings are better off than Italy, dominated by the Empire. Whether in the depth of his heart he believed this or not, he at once takes it back in the curious sentence that separates the two parts. For he hastily adds that it is incontrovertible that both kinds of kingdom (elective and hereditary) have their good qualities, all of which are to be found in our lord the King of the Romans, so that one must admit that he is the best of all the rulers in the world. The King of the Romans is, as already noted, the Emperor. Yet, in spite of this statement, at the very end of the treatise Coluccio repeats what he had said at the close of the first part, that kingdoms are better off than Italy, which is dominated by the Empire. The last sentence of the treatise furnishes the key to his contradictory statements. Kingdoms are better off because they have rulers, Italy is abandoned by the Emperor. When Italy had a ruler (i.e., in antiquity), it had power over all kingdoms. What Coluccio means to say, but not too loudly or clearly, is that he would like to see the ancient Roman Empire restored, with its capital in Italy and its ruler an Italian. If this is impossible, he is willing to have the present Empire, with its German Emperor, continue, provided that the Emperor showed some interest in Italy and really ruled it. His views

were similar to Petrarch's [17]. One cannot help thinking of the
fable of the frogs, who begged Jupiter to send them a king
but were not satisfied with the one he sent, the do-nothing
log. It is too late to warn Coluccio that a *fainéant* king is
preferable to a snake in the grass, the frogs' second king [18].

[17] See B. L. Ullman, *The Humanism of Coluccio Salutati,* p. 78.
[18] I am gratly indebted to Professor Ernst Kantorowicz for several valuable
suggestions and for making available to me a copy of Bartolus' *De regimine
civitatis.* He wrote me just before his sudden and untimely death, which
brought great sadness not only to his friends but to all scholars who were
familiar with his scholarly work.

Chapter XXVI

COLUCCIO SALUTATI ED I CLASSICI LATINI [1]

I nomi di Petrarca e di Boccaccio sono noti a tutti dal *Canzoniere* e dal *Decamerone*. Il nome di Coluccio Salutati è, invece, noto a ben pochi, anche qui a Firenze, se non mi sbaglio, perché non ci ha lasciato alcuna opera di alta importanza letteraria. Petrarca e Boccaccio sono rinomati anche come umanisti, come risuscitatori, cioè, degli studi classici. Quanto a Petrarca, questa fama è certo meritoria, ché egli ebbe un posto unico come fondatore, o, forse meglio, come propagatore del nuovo movimento umanistico; quanto a Boccaccio, la sua reputazione in questo campo è molto meno giustificata. A mio parere, Coluccio come umanista è molto più importante di Boccaccio, ma la mancanza di lustro letterario ha diminuito la sua gloria umanistica. Non vorrei denigrare il buon Boccaccio, ma piuttosto mettere Coluccio al posto d'onore che è suo di diritto. Mise insieme, per esempio, una grande biblioteca composta di centinaia di volumi, dei quali oltre un centinaio sono tuttora esistenti. Molti altri sono citati nei suoi scritti, numerosi anche se non di gran merito letterario. Di più, come vedremo, le sue copie di parecchi autori classici servirono di base per il loro studio e la loro diffusione. Inoltre Coluccio fu il patrono, la guida, il maestro, sebbene non nel vero senso della parola, di umanisti egregi quali Poggio, Niccoli, Bruni, Loschi, Vergerio, ed altri, cioè fu il fondatore del circolo fiorentino che dominò il Rinascimento nel quattrocento e che servì ai Medici nel loro programma di

---

[1] *Il Mondo Antico nel Rinascimento* (*Atti del V Convegno Internazionale di Studi sul Rinascimento*, 1956), 1958, p. 41. Questa comunicazione è un brevissimo riassunto di parte di un libro che ho scritto su Coluccio Salutati e l'Umanesimo: *The Humanism of Coluccio Salutati* (Padova, 1963).

far di Firenze il centro culturale del mondo. Per trentadue anni mantenne il posto di principe del movimento umanistico, dalla morte del Petrarca nel 1374 alla propria nel 1406. Come disse il Novati, la battaglia più strenua combattuta per il ravvivamento degli studi classici nel tardo trecento, un'epoca decisiva, fu quella che sostenne e vinse Coluccio Salutati. Grazie a lui il nuovo movimento andò avanti a passi da gigante nel sentiero aperto dal Petrarca, iniziando il rapporto intimo fra la letteratura e la politica a cui l'umanesimo d'allora in poi diede sanzione.

All'università di Bologna Coluccio fu allievo di Pietro da Moglio, amico e corrispondente del Petrarca, da cui Coluccio imparò ad apprezzare i classici antichi. Rimase ammiratore e corrispondente del maestro. Dopo la morte di quest'ultimo, su richiesta di Bernardo, figlio di Pietro, scrisse un epitaffio in versi. Con Bernardo mantenne l'amicizia fino alla morte. Versi indirizzati da Coluccio a Pietro, ultimamente pubblicati, rendono più chiara l'attività di Pietro nel campo della retorica e lo elevano nella scala degli umanisti primi. Incoraggiato da lui, Coluccio sembra aver sviluppato interesse per Cicerone, Virgilio, Seneca, e Petrarca, e forse anche l'idea di scrivere versi.

Coluccio fu impressionato dal Petrarca, nonostante che i due mai s'incontrassero né vi sia stato scambio di molte lettere. Ma la lettura degli scritti latini del Petrarca stimolò in Coluccio il desiderio di emulare il grande uomo del giorno, e di leggere gli scrittori antichi da lui citati. Non vi è nessuna indicazione di lettere scambiate tra i due umanisti prima del trecentosessanta, quando già gli interessi di Coluccio avevano preso una piega definitiva.

La prima lettera del Salutati al Boccaccio è del 1367, ma il tono d'intimità di questa suggerisce un'amicizia di parecchi anni. Forse Coluccio, visitando Firenze durante i quindici anni precedenti, incontrò il Boccaccio. Non furono le pubblicazioni del Boccaccio che attrassero Coluccio dal milletrecentocinquanta al sessanta, visto che in quella decade il Boccaccio non pubblicò nulla in lingua latina; il *Decamerone* ed altri scritti italiani non avevano importanza agli occhi di Coluccio. Ma nel 1350 circa il Boccaccio cominciò il *Genealogia deorum* e questo libro fu certo un soggetto d'interesse comune. Forse l'ammirazione straordina ria che il Boccaccio concepì per il Petrarca influenzò il suo gio· vane amico. Se si può giudicare dalla loro pratica nei seguenti anni, la loro conversazione si basava unicamente sul Petrarca.

Fra le prime delle epistole del Salutati ve ne sono due, probabilmente scritte dal cinquanta al sessanta, a Francesco Nelli, un altro corrispondente entusiasta del Petrarca. In una Coluccio chiama Petrarca e Nelli i suoi sicuri rifugi; nell'altra chiede copie di qualsiasi opera del Petrarca. Malgrado le molte richieste, pare che non ricevesse da lui nessuno scritto petrarchesco tranne parecchie epistole.

Anche Dante fece impressione sul nostro umanista, ma non si sa quando tale impressione sia sorta per la prima volta. Prima di lasciare Firenze per stabilirsi a Napoli nel 1352, Zanobi da Strada tenne una conferenza su Virgilio. Pare che questa conferenza abbia colpito il giovane Coluccio.

Certo è che il Novati ha torto di suggerire che il Salutati fosse un socio del circolo fiorentino (o Accademia Petrarchesca, come la chiama il Cochin); tale circolo si adunava di tanto in tanto dal Nelli e forse altrove per parlare del proprio idolo, Petrarca. Secondo il Nelli i soci di questo gruppo furono Francesco Bruni, Forese Donati, Lapo da Castiglionchio, Zanobi da Strada, e Boccaccio. Il nome di Coluccio non si trova mai nelle trenta epistole di Nelli. Soltanto dodici anni dopo la morte del Nelli nel 1363 il Salutati venne ad abitare a Firenze. Perciò non poté essere presente a molte adunanze dell'Accademia. In ogni caso è chiarissimo che di tutti i contemporanei, e quasi contemporanei, il Petrarca per mezzo dei suoi scritti fu quello che più incoraggiò il suo giovane seguace nello studio della letteratura antica. Si vede però che anche prima di sentire l'influenza del Petrarca, fece i primi passi, o da sé o sotto l'ispirazione di Pietro da Moglio.

Non dirò di più delle influenze contemporanee sugli inte· ressi di Coluccio. Quando questi interessi furono sviluppati e Coluccio cominciò a leggere la letteratura antica, l'incendio si estese, e più libri leggeva più desiderava trovarne. Un passo di non poca importanza nella carriera umanistica di Coluccio fu l'acquisto nel 1355 di una copia della grammatica di Prisciano, la quale esiste tuttora. E' piena di sue postille. Sembra che la sua preoccupazione dell'ortografia derivasse da quest'opera. In una epistola scritta nel giugno del 1391 dice che si è occupato di ortografia per 35 anni, cioè dal 1356. Questa data è così vicina a quella dell'acquisto del Prisciano che pare certo ch'egli si riferisca all'inizio della sua conoscenza col grammatico antico, e che questo sia il « significato particolare » che il Novati non poteva spiegare. In un'altra lettera, di data ignota, il Salutati ci dice d'essersi dedicato a questioni ortografiche per 46 anni.

Ma il Prisciano non servì soltanto allo scopo di istruire Coluccio nella grammatica, come servì a migliaia prima di lui, e di dargli interesse per l'ortografia durante la sua vita, ma anche gli fece conoscere i nomi di ventine di scrittori antichi, i quali copiò scrupolosamente ai margini del libro. Si può ben immaginare che questi nomi lo stimolassero a cercare codici degli autori elencati.

Una postilla nel Prisciano ci insegna che allo stesso tempo Coluccio acquistò codici di Virgilio, Lucano, ed Orazio, i quali disgraziatamente non sono riuscito a trovare. E' chiaro che questi libri, indispensabili alla biblioteca di un umanista, furono probabilmente fra i suoi primi acquisti. Virgilio è restato uno dei suoi autori preferiti. Un altro era Ovidio nelle *Metamorfosi*. Di questo dice: « Gli devo molto, perché in lui avevo una porta, per così dire, e un maestro, quando la mia passione per tali studi si accese, come per ispirazione divina, alla fine della mia adolescenza. Benché non avessi nessuno con cui consigliarmi e non udissi alcuno discutere la cosa, dopo che Ovidio mi capitò tra le mani, spontaneamente lessi tutti i poeti e per dono divino, per così dire, li capii ». Altrove chiama Ovidio chiave alla poesia e suo illuminatore.

Probabilmente l'acquisto di Ovidio avvenne prima di quello di Prisciano, Orazio, Virgilio, e Lucano, e condusse all'acquisto di questi altri poeti. Così abbiamo il diritto di dire che Ovidio aprì a Coluccio prospettive della gloriosa rinascita non ancora giunta, e che, simile ad una porta, Ovidio aprì il futuro per mezzo del passato.

Nel 1357 Coluccio comprò i *Fasti* d'Ovidio in una libreria fiorentina. Dalle epistole al Nelli, si sa che in questa decade lesse anche Valerio Massimo, la *Consolazione* di Boezio, e le epistole di Seneca a Lucilio. Certo lesse molto di più durante gli anni in cui non fu tanto occupato negli uffizi notarili. Si può immaginarlo importunare gli amici per il prestito di libri, e spendere tutto ciò che risparmiava per aumentare la sua biblioteca.

Ora esaminiamo brevemente alcuni degli scrittori conosciuti da Coluccio. Abbiamo già fatto menzione delle tragedie di Seneca. La rinascita d'interesse per le tragedie si deve attribuire ad Albertino Mussato ed al suo circolo padovano, come hanno ben mostrato il Franceschini ed altri. Si può dimostrare che l'interesse di Coluccio per le tragedie derivò da Mussato in qualche modo, forse per mezzo di Pietro da Moglio quando Coluccio studiò a Bologna, visto che nel suo codice dei drammi di Seneca, ch'egli stesso copiò, aggiunse l'*Ecerinis* di Mussato. Un segno del suo interesse particolare per le tragedie è il fatto che questo è il solo manoscritto letterario ancora esistente copiato di sua mano: « Colucius Pyerius manu propria scripsi », orgogliosamente aggiunge alla fine del codice. Evidentemente un lavoro d'amore, il libro fu copiato prima del 1375, quando Coluccio divenne cancelliere di Firenze, un titolo che in seguito aggiunse sempre al suo nome. Di più, furono le tragedie di Seneca, particolarmente quella di Ercole pazzo, che lo indussero a comporre il suo *magnum opus, De laboribus Herculis*.

Interessante e importante è la storia ben nota della scoperta e diffusione delle *Epistole* di Cicerone, nelle quali Coluccio ebbe parte principale. Vedendo citazioni delle *Epistole* di Cicerone nelle lettere di Petrarca, desiderò acquistare una copia di tutto il codice. Nel 1375 scrisse ad un corrispondente in Verona, dove il Petrarca aveva ottenuto la sua copia, ma senza riuscirvi. Poco dopo il 1387 o '88, quando Gian Galeazzo Visconti di Milano conquistò Verona e Padova e portò via molti manoscritti, Coluccio si rivolse a Pasquino de' Capelli, Cancelliere di Milano, pensando evidentemente che o il codice veronese o la copia di Petrarca (che era restata a Padova dopo la morte del poeta) fossero a Milano. Poi scoppiata la guerra tra Firenze e Milano, non fu prima del 1392 che Pasquino gli spedì un manoscritto. Il Salutati si accorse che la raccolta differiva da quella di Petrarca, cioè comprendeva le *Epistolae Familiares*, non le *Epistolae ad Atticum,* la sola raccolta conosciuta dal Petrarca. Coluccio scrisse a Pasquino ancora una volta e finalmente ricevette una copia anche di queste lettere. Così poté vantarsi di avere tutt'e due le raccolte, anziché la sola posseduta dal Petrarca. Nei due codici si trovano molte postille di mano di Coluccio. Più tardi, non si sa quando, l'originale delle *Familiares* arrivò a Firenze da Vercelli, ma non fu mai nella collezione del Salutati. Gli umanisti si servirono di tutt'e tre. La copia delle *Epistolae ad Atticum* posseduta dal Petrarca e l'originale veronese sono spariti. Così il contributo di Coluccio allo studio della corrispondenza di Cicerone fu molto grande, sebbene non si possa calcolarlo.

Nel 1380 Coluccio riuscì ad ottenere una copia del Properzio di Petrarca. Questa copia fu quasi il solo manoscritto di quell'autore conosciuto dagli umanisti, perché la copia di Petrarca sparì. La sua copia di Catullo, la quale ottenne a Verona nel 1375, divenne la base principale dei testi studiati dagli umanisti ed imitati dai poeti. Dove trovò il suo Tibullo non si sa, ma fu il testo fondamentale usato dai suoi successori. Tutti e tre i manoscritti esistono ancora e portano molte tracce delle sue correzioni e dei suoi commenti, benché nelle sue opere non li citi spesso. Questi autori presentati alla conoscenza dei circoli umanistici da Coluccio, divennero molto popolari nel quattrocento, come si vede non soltanto dal gran numero di manoscritti che esistono ancora, ma dalle imitazioni del Panormita, Filelfo, Poliziano, Pontano, Strozzi, ed altri. Molti manoscritti delle epistole di Plinio sono copie del suo testo, altri sono discesi dal testo guariniano. Quanta fosse l'influenza di Coluccio nel render popolari altri testi classici, non sappiamo.

Nessun segno di studio si trova nel Plauto di Coluccio, ma è possibile che ne possedesse un'altra copia, visto che esistono due o più copie sue di altri autori. L'*Amphitruo* è citata spesso nel *De laboribus Herculis*. Il suo Terenzio è sparito, ma lo cita abbastanza spesso. Oltre le epistole abbiamo soltanto due dei manoscritti di Cicerone, e questi sono fittamente postillati. Molte citazioni, specialmente dalle opere filosofiche, si trovano negli scritti di Coluccio. Nessuno dei suoi manoscritti di Cesare e di

Sallustio è stato trovato, e scarse sono le citazioni. D'altra parte Orazio e Virgilio sono citati molte volte, specialmente l'*Eneide*. Di Ovidio abbiamo la copia sua dei poemi elegiaci, piena di postille di sua mano, ed il suo *Fasti* ottenuto già nel 1357. Poche sono le postille, sebbene Coluccio citi questo poema assai spesso. Disgraziatamente il suo *Metamorfosi* non esiste più, un libro che egli cita copiosamente, particolarmente nel *De laboribus Herculis,* e che molto lo influenzò. Livio è citato poco e il codice di Coluccio non si trova. Il suo Valerio Massimo esiste ancora, ma è postillato soltanto al principio. Probabilmente ebbe un secondo manoscritto. Se si giudica dalle citazioni, Valerio fu molto letto da Coluccio. Di Seneca il Vecchio abbiamo un manoscritto scarsamente postillato e poche sono le citazioni. Seneca il Giovane è adoperato spesso. Delle tragedie abbiamo già parlato. Quanto agli scritti in prosa, tre dei quattro codici posseduti da Coluccio sono bene postillati; le citazioni sono assai frequenti. Lucano, Persio, e Stazio sono citati spesso, ma i suoi codici sono perduti. Marziale è appena menzionato. Dalle numerose citazioni di Plinio il Vecchio si può indovinare che Coluccio lo trovò molto utile. Abbiamo una parte del suo manoscritto che rivela molte postille. Abbiamo già parlato di Plinio il Giovane. Poche sono le postille nel codice di Coluccio e poche le citazioni nelle opere. Cita Quintiliano ogni tanto. Tacito non l'ha conosciuto, nonostante la scoperta di Boccaccio. Giovenale e Gellio sono citati abbastanza spesso, ma i suoi manoscritti non ci sono più. Svetonio non è molto citato. Il Floro di Coluccio esiste ancora, ben postillato, ma le citazioni sono scarse. Abbiamo due dei suoi codici di Apuleio, uno ben postillato, l'altro no. Le citazioni sono relativamente poche. I due manoscritti di Solino posseduti da Coluccio portano poche note, neppure le citazioni sono numerose. Secondo le postille del suo codice e le citazioni, Macrobio gli fu utilissimo.

Quanto alle traduzioni dal greco, abbiamo le copie possedute da Coluccio del *Timeo* e del *Fedone* di Platone, questo postillato, quello no. Le citazioni non sono considerevoli. Restano quattro dei suoi manoscritti di Aristotele, quasi senza postille. Le citazioni dalle opere singole sono poche, sebbene il totale sia abbastanza grande.

Coluccio adoperò molto i commentatori antichi, come mostrano i suoi codici di Fulgenzio e del commento a Germanico, e le citazioni di questi e di Servio e Lattanzio Placido.

Si vede una differenza enorme fra gli autori classici e gli scrittori patristici e medievali nell'uso di Coluccio. Non meno di dieci copie d'Agostino possedute da Coluccio ci restano, ma una sola è postillata copiosamente. E' facile indovinare quale: il *De civitate Dei,* ove si trovano tante allusioni alla letteratura e ad altre cose antiche. La copia dei *Varia* di Cassiodoro ha molte note marginali; quest'opera influenzò gli epistolografi del trecento, il Salutati compreso.

Che ne è del gran numero di testi classici posseduti da Coluccio che non esistono più? Forse molti furon tanto ricercati che andarono distrutti per il troppo uso. Niccolò Niccoli ne acquistò molti e li lasciò a S. Marco. Di questi la maggior parte esistono ancora. Ma pare che quelli acquistati da altri umanisti fossero meno fortunati. Sono precisamente i testi classici che gli umanisti desideravano avere.

Per riassumere, mediante Coluccio gli umanisti del suo circolo fiorentino ed altri fecero la conoscenza delle epistole di Cicerone e delle poesie di Catullo, Tibullo, Properzio. Non è improbabile che senza di lui alcuni di questi libri sarebbero andati perduti. Comunque, lo studio di questi autori negli anni seguenti si accentrò sui suoi manoscritti. Allo stesso modo la sua copia di Plinio il Giovane ebbe una parte importante. Non senza ragione si può congetturare che altri suoi codici fossero studiati e copiati, allorché furono nella biblioteca del generoso Niccoli e poi in quella di San Marco.

Fra gli autori preferiti da Coluccio si possono includere i nomi di Cicerone, Virgilio, Ovidio, e Seneca, ed il suo entusiasmo per essi ispirò senza dubbio gli umanisti chiarissimi che furono i suoi discepoli. In questo modo indiretto (anziché per i suoi scritti) e per mezzo della sua bella biblioteca lasciò una incalcolabile impronta sul Rinascimento.

CHAPTER XXVII

POGGIOS' MANUSCRIPTS OF LIVY [1]

The generosity and courtesy of Professor A. J. Dunston in
sending me long before its publication a copy of his paper on the
Vatican manuscripts of Livy which I had suggested were copied
by Poggio makes me reluctant to take issue with him. But I
must present my arguments and let the reader decide which of
us is right. In his paper, published in this number of *Scriptorium*,
Dunston very acutely found a weak spot in my armor and thrust
his lance unerringly at that spot. Yet, in my opinion, the thrust
was not fatal; hence this article.

In an earlier version of my views I was more cautious than
in my later statement about the identity of the scribe of the three
manuscripts (Vat. lat. 1843, 1849, 1852) [2]. Let me say at once
that it is certain from ownership notes in all three manuscripts
that they belonged to Poggio. The lesser caution in my later
presentation was partly due to condensation but chiefly because
I felt that I was on safer ground. Perhaps my chief argument
is that the words « Liber Poggi » at the end of Vat. lat. 1849
are written in red ink by the scribe who wrote the colophon in
the same shade of red. I cannot believe that one of Poggio's
well-trained scribes (to whom Dunston credits the three volumes)
would write his master's name for him in a hand just like
the master's. I have seen secretaries imitate the signature of
their employers in a fashion that would pass the scrutiny of a
bank teller, but I do not believe that the analogy is sound. To
be sure, I have seen a number of manuscripts in which an *ignorant*

---

[1] [*Scriptorium*, XIX (1965), pp. 71-76, after the paper of A. J. Dunston,
« The hand of Poggio » (pp. 63-70)].

[2] *Studies in the Italian Renaissance* (Rome, 1955), p. 313 [here, Chap. XV]

scribe copied an ownership claim along with the rest of the manuscript. As it happens, we have four examples in the case of Poggio himself. Vat. lat. 11458 is a rough draft made by Poggio in 1417 of some of the orations of Cicero that he had discovered. At the end he wrote: « Has septem M. Tullii orationes... Poggius Florentinus... cum latentes comperisset in squalore et sordibus, in lucem solus extulit... » Laur. Conv. Soppr. 13 contains the same statement about the discovery, thus leading Bandini to say that Poggio copied this manuscript, which he certainly did not. At the end of Urb. lat. 327 we find: « Scripsit Poggius Florentinus hunc librum Constantie ». If the scribe had stopped there the writing would have been claimed as Poggio's by some scholars. But the copyist went on to say: « Hec verba ex originali Poggi sumpta ». But the best example is Munich, Clm 69, containing Celsus, with this subscription in the hand of the scribe: « Liber Pogii secretarii apostolici explicit ». The scribe was definitely not Poggio, nor was he the owner of the manuscript. The whole book, subscription and all, was copied from Poggio's now lost codex, listed in the inventory of his library as No. 28 [3]. A similar example is that of Rome, Bibl. Naz., Vitt. Em. 205, which has « Liber Poggi secretar. », not written by Poggio and presumably copied from his manuscript, which is No. 82 in the inventory [4].

Such statements as the last two are, I think, to be explained as ignorant copying of the exemplars. If it is admitted that Vat. lat. 1849 belonged to Poggio (so far as I know, no one has denied it), I hold that he must have copied it. If Poggio's scribe wrote the ownership note, why did he not do the same in the other two volumes of Livy? This would be the only one of Poggio's twenty or more books in which he did not himself enter his name as owner. Is not that fact in itself a strong argument in favor of my view?

I still hold to what Prof. Dunston quotes against me, that " while I am confident that the Cicero and Livy manuscripts were

---

[3] E. Walser, *Poggius Florentinus* (Leipzig, 1914), p. 420.

[4] Walser (*op. cit.*, p. 422) in fact identifies the manuscript with the one mentioned in the inventory, but the ownership claim is definitely not in Poggio's writing but that of the manuscript itself.

copied by Poggio, we must not forget that the identification of handwriting is not always certain ". But it is sometimes just as difficult to be sure of the opposite, that the handwriting of two manuscripts is not identical. I can only plead that after studying the script of all the manuscripts unquestionably transcribed by Poggio I concluded that the manuscripts under discussion were copied by him.

To take up Dunston's points in order, let me begin with Poggio's copies in *manus velox*, Madrid 8514 and Vat. lat. 11458, together with the small ✕, or cross, in the margins to indicate places where corrections should be made. One might get the impression from Dunston (which he surely did not intend) that these marks are unique. They are in fact very common in manuscripts of this period. Dunston makes much of his claim that in the two manuscripts mentioned the crosses are in the same ink as the text, but in the Livy manuscripts they are in a different ink. For one thing one might urge that the Livy manuscripts are fair copies, the other two are rapidly written first drafts, in which the procedure might have been different. The rough drafts were copied from older manuscripts, the fair copies were presumably made from corrected first drafts [5]. But my main answer is that, after a very careful examination of the Livy manuscripts, I concluded that not all of the crosses are in a different ink: some are, some are not, some are so faint and colorless that one cannot tell, and sometimes the ✕ is erased. In Vat. lat. 1849, f. 36r, two crosses are lighter than the text script, one where no correction was made, one where there was a correction. On f. 54r the ink is the same but there is no correction. On f. 116v I found no ✕, as Dunston claimed. On f. 159r the ✕ is lighter, as Dunston says, but of the same color as the marginal correction. In Vat. lat. 1852, on f. 12r, 66r, 66v, the ✕

---

[5] See my quotations from Poggio's letter in my *Origin and Development of Humanistic Script*, p. 46, and compare with the copies made by Niccoli on paper, evidently to be copied on parchment (*ibid.*, p. 61 ff.). Poggio's exact words are worth quoting (Tonelli, I, p. 264): "Laudo tuam diligentiam de quarta Decade: ea nunc scribitur: non multum autem curo, antea ne, an postquam scripta fuerit, emendetur, quamquam duo habeo volumina satis tolerabilia inter mendosa. Huic quartae Decadi, ut conjicio, multa multis in locis desunt." Note especially the sentence beginning "non multum autem curo."

is in the same ink as the text but the corrections are darker. On other pages the × is in the same ink but no correction was made (f. 70r, 71r, etc.). On f. 74v, 75v, 77r, 81v, etc., the ink may be different. In Vat. lat. 3245, which Dunston accept as Poggian, I found that the ink of the × was now the same as that of the text, now different. This is contrary to Dunston's principle that Poggio made the × as he copied the manuscript. The ink is different on f. 50r, 58r, 60r, 63r, etc. In Laur. 48, 22 and 50, 31, both genuine Poggio, there are few crosses, but some are in the same ink as the text, some are not. This whole matter seems to me to be entirely without significance and should not be used as a test for Poggio's writing. The color of the ink of the crosses proves only that in some cases Poggio marked passages for correction at the time he copied or used the same ink in rereading or that he entered his marks in a different ink while rereading.

As to Vat. lat. 3245, which we both agree was copied by Poggio, another question is involved. We have only the statement of Poggio's son Iacopo at the end of the manuscript that his father copied it in the pontificate of John XXIII. John was pontiff from 1410 to 1415, Iacopo was born in 1442. How could the son have known that his father copied the manuscript some thirty years, more or less, before he was born? Perhaps his father told him while dandling the boy on his knees? No, there must originally have been a note of Poggio's, similar to those he wrote in other manuscripts. He liked to mention the name of the Pope in dating. He says that he wrote Laur. 67, 15 in the pontificate of Gregory XII, and that he copied Laur. 50, 31 while secretary of Martin V. But Dunston argues that the Vatican manuscript is complete, that nothing has been lost. True, as far as the manuscript proper is concerned. There are two unnumbered flyleaves; there might have been a third. Only four of the manuscripts copied by Poggio have his signature at the present time, all signed either at the end or within the volume. Two of the four, however, have tables of contents by Poggio on flyleaves. Could not Vat. lat. 3245 once have had such a flyleaf, this time signed by Poggio? Ricc. 504, probably copied by Poggio, has a table of contents on f. 1v (flyleaf), followed by « Liber Poggii ». Iacop's knowledge absolutely must be accounted for. To clinch matters, this manuscript is said in the inventory (No. 13) to be « manu Poggi ». I believe that such entries in the inventory were based on Poggio's entries in his manuscripts. As I have said, we have four such manuscripts. For Laur. 50, 31 and 67, 15 the inventory has « manu Poggi ». It does not have it for Laur. 48, 22 and Berlin, Ham. 166, but the latter is not in the inventory at all, having been given or sold to Cosimo de' Medici before 1418. Only three other manuscripts in the inventory of 95 items are marked as being « manu Poggii » (Nos. 2, 11, 47), and these are lost. On the other hand, Nos. 1, 3, 19 of the inventory, which I have claimed for Poggio, do not add the words « manu Poggii », nor, of course, does the one Livy which I have identified in the inventory (Vat. lat. 1852, No. 37).

I have examined the manuscripts under discussion with Dunston's comments before me. At the end of Vat. lat. 1843 we read «liber Aurispae (changed from "Poggii") secretarii apostolici». I accept Dunston's statement that the last two words are in a different ink; it is gummy and therefore tends to flake. But I still think the writing is that of Poggio. Dunston suggests that Aurispa added these words after he became papal secretary in 1437; I believe that Poggio wrote them after he was appointed to this position, though perhaps he did not do so immediately. He took the office in 1423 but did not write Niccoli about copying Livy until 1425. In any event, Poggio wrote the two words; Aurispa could not possibly have done so. In Vat. lat. 1849 Poggio omitted « secretarii apostolici », but in Vat. lat. 1852 « secretarii » was written at the same time as « Liber Poggii ». It seems to me that my original suggestion for the date of writing (1425-26) still holds, and that Poggio did not think about adding his stile until later.

That the ownership notes in Vat. lat. 1843 and 1852 were written later and that of Vat. lat. 1849 at the same time as the *explicit* proves nothing, in my opinion, except that Poggio was not a man of habit so mechanical that he would never change his way of doing things.

I cannot agree with Dunston that the hand of the ownership notes in Vat. lat. 1843 and 1852 is not that of the text. In 1843 the L of *liber* is like that of *apostolici* and that of the title of

Book VIII on f. 141r. *Liber* is written in *exactly* the same ink as *explicit*. The E of *liber* can be matched in *secretarii* and elsewhere in the book. The R varies in width at the bottom from about four mm to five mm (*feliciter*). In *liber* it is narrower than in the *liber* of line 1 and in *feliciter*, but its width is about the same as those in *urbe* and *secretarii*. The *ii* of this last word is written in typical Poggian fashion: the second *i* is taller than the first.

As to f. 30r in Vat. lat. 1852, the marginal note « deficit liber tertius » is written in exactly the same light red ink as the title opposite it. If the note is by Poggio (and I agree with Dunston's conviction that it is), then the title too was written by him. So far as I know, no other note is written in red ink; *ergo*, it must have been written when the title was written. If Poggio had written the note later, he would have used black (or brown) ink, as he did in thousands of other places in the three volumes.

We turn now to the script itself. If one looks at the plates and reads my discussion in my book on humanistic script, he will note the wide variation in Poggio's practice in the volumes in which he proclaims himself to be the scribe. This is especially true of that characteristic letter of minuscule script, *g*. If one allows himself to be influenced by these differences (some of which are far more serious than those listed by Dunston), then the only logical conclusion is that not a single manuscript copied by Poggio exists today! But let us examine the differences between the Livy manuscripts and those regarded as genuine Poggio, as listed by Dunston. In Laur. 48, 22 and 50, 31 (" genuine " Poggio), the vertical stroke of the *d* tends to fall below the line, Dunston tells us. I find the same phenomenon occasionally in the Livy manuscripts. In Vat. lat. 1852, f. 2r, the second *d* of *dedecorique* is like that of the *sed* cited by Dunston from Plate 18 of my book. Other examples occur on f. 4r, *deterrere*, and f. 6r, *Macedoniam* and *data*, etc.

Again, we are told that in the *-rum* abbreviation the cross-stroke in Laur. 48, 22 and 50, 31 is diagonal, but more nearly vertical in Vat. lat. 1843. But in the latter I find a definite slant in *tribunorum* on f. 83r, etc. In Vat. lat. 1849,

f. 175r, *ceterum*, the top of the stroke is two mm to the right of the bottom. On the other hand, Laur. 50, 31 has some almost vertical examples: f. 1r, 69r, 77r, etc.

The abbreviation stroke for *m* is "more or less horizontal" in Laur. 48, 22 and 50, 31, according to Dunston, but "seems in Laur. 49, 24 and Vat. lat. 1843 to have much more of an upward sweep". I find this upward sweep in an extreme form in Vat. lat. 2208, f. 144r (Pl. 21 of my book; this should be examined with a magnifying glass). This and other examples mingle with straight forms. In Vat. lat. 3245 too there are upsweeping strokes. Some mild examples are to be seen on f. 61v (Pl. 17 of my book), *istam*, *ipsum*; others on f. 1v, etc. Laur. 48, 22 and 50, 31 also furnish examples, e.g., f. 31r of the former, f. 1r, 77 v of the latter, etc. On the other hand, I find straight strokes in the impugned Livy codices. In Vat. lat. 1843 I note the straight stroke in *commodis* (f. 85 v); in *imminentem* on f. 137 r, the first stroke is straight, the second curls upward. In Vat. lat. 1852, f. 74 r, in *nuntiis* the stroke is perfectly straight. On f. 87 v the first stroke of *exeuntium* is quite straight, the second curls.

We come now to the low *ct* ligature (non-Poggian, according to Dunston) versus the high one (genuine Poggio). Admittedly, the low *ct* occurs in Laur. 49, 24 and Vat. lat. 1843, 1849, and 1852. But the high one also occurs: 1849, f. 14r, *auctores*; 14v, *delectum*; 16v *octo* (the very word in which Dunston found the low *ct* on f. 189v of 1843); 20r, *introductis*, etc., etc. On the other hand, a farly low one is found in Vat. lat. 2208, f. 144r (Pl. 21, last line, of my book).

Apart from these negative arguments I should like to call the reader's attention to the positive ones, the striking similarities between Vat. lat. 1843, 1849, 1852, Laur. 49, 24 and the Poggio volumes that are vouched for, e.g., the very unusual 8-shaped -*ur* abbreviation. This occurs also in Vat. lat. 2208. Then there is the curious word division, the forms of *g* and *ii*, the use of accent marks. On these arguments I rest my case.

Reply of Prof. A. J. Dunston

Professor Ullman very kindly send me some time ago a copy of his reply to my article, thus enabling me to make the following observations.

Page 71 [here, p. 483]. Exactly what does Ullman agree is " the weak spot in his armour "?

Page 72 [here, p. 484]. If my conjectured reason for the difference in the illumination of Mss. Vat. Lat. 1843, 1852 and Laur. 49. 24 on the one hand and Vat. Lat. 1849 on the other is correct, then the fact that 1849 is the only one of Poggio's books in which someone else has entered his name as owner is an argument in *my* favour! Poggio had the first copy re-copied in order to have a uniform set (page 67). By that time he had already added the words « Liber Poggii » to the first copy and they were copied by the scribe into the second copy!! I should perhaps have given more stress to this conjecture. The coincidence is remarkable.

Page 72 [here, p. 485]. I did not for one moment intend to give the impression that I thought the × marks unique. It should, however, be noted that Poggio was remarkably consistent in his method of correcting manuscripts.

Page 74 [here, p. 488]. I have not had any opportunity of visiting Italy since writing my article and am therefore not in a position to agree with or refute Ullman's assertions. I can only say that my original and rechecked notes say, for example, of the marginal note *deficit tertius liber* " this in a red ink different from that of the *incipit.* "

Chapter XXVIII

PONTANO'S MARGINALIA IN BERLIN, HAMILTON 471 [1]

Professor A. Campana, the leading connoisseur of the hand-writing of Italian humanists, deserves the credit for discovering Pontano's hand in the margin of the Berlin Ovid (Hamilton 471). When I first examined the photographs Professor Munari sent me I had strong doubts about being able to identify Pontano's work. But my doubts were quickly dissipated, especially when I came to fol. 29v, with two examples of a broken *e* and one of a leng-thened *r* in the "Beneventan" style so characteristic of Pontano and perhaps unique with him in the fifteenth century (see Pl. 32) [2].

The examples of broken *e* on fol. 29v are in *Rem.* 131; are on fol. 28r (*Rem.* 10; see Pl. 30) where it is used as a ca-pital, and fol. 62r (*Am.* III 6, 41 *eu*). Its use as a capital may be seen in Tacitus, fol. 57v. Long *r* appears, in addition to fol. 29v, on fol. 31r (*Rem.* 247), fol. 46r (*Am.* I 13, 11; Pl. 34), and fol. 64v (*Am.* III 8, 59). Sometimes the vertical stroke of the *r* bends backward: fol. 31r (*Rem.* 247, *eras*), fol. 64v (*Am.*

---

[1] [As *Appendice I* in F. Munari, *Il codice Hamilton 471 di Ovidio*, Roma 1965, Edizioni di Storia e Letteratura (Note e discussioni erudite, 9)].

[2] In what follows I refer to the Leiden Tacitus, Periz. 4° 21, the Wolfen-büttel Tibullus, Aug. 82, 6 fol., and the Berlin Propertius, lat. fol. 500 (disco-vered by me many years ago), and to my article in *Italia medioevale e umanistica*, II (1959), pp. 309 ff. [here, Chap. XXII]. Besides the plates in this article I have used the facsimile of the Tacitus (Leiden, 1907), prefaced by G. Wissowa, that of the Tibullus (Leiden, 1910), prefaced by F. Leo, and a microfilm of the Propertius, kindly put at my disposal by Professor Munari, together with pho-tographs of some pages made by me years ago. References to Pontano plates are to those in my artiche [here, Pl. 13-28], references merely to plates are to those in the present volume [i.e. Munari; here, Pl. 30-38].

III 8, 59); cf. Pontano, Pl. 24 (*custodiebatur*); Tacitus, *passim*, especially fol. 2v margin *Tragoedia*; Tibullus, *passim*.

A tall capital T occurs at the end of the word *fluunt* on fol. 30v (Pl. 31); a short one at the end of *proferebant* on fol. 33r (Pl. 33). For parallels see Pontano, Pl. 19, 22; Tacitus, fol. 39r; Tibullus, fol. 3r, etc.

Of lesser importance are these peculiarities of Pontano's script: long ascenders and descenders, including those of *f* and *s,* a characteristic *g,* an *e* that sometimes has a long connecting stroke, *v* often used for *u.* The prolonged connecting stroke of the *e* on fol. 57r of *epistole* (Pl. 36) is paralleled by Pontano, Pl. 24 and Tacitus fols. 27v, 47v margin, etc.

On fol. 28r (*Rem.* 9-10; Pl. 30), 30v (*Rem.* 189-190; Pl. 31), and 46v (*Am.* I 13, 31-32; Pl. 37) two lines are added transversely exactly as in the Propertius, fols. 5r and 5v.

On fol. 29v (*Rem.* 131; Pl. 32) *Temporibus* is written *Tpribus* with an abbreviation sign similar to the figure 2, with a prolonged horizontal final stroke. The same sign is used in *tpibus,* though with a shorter final stroke, in Tacitus, fol. 13r margin. On fol. 14v of Tacitus it is found in the text with *tpa,* as also on fol. 25v. In the margin of fol. 33v of Tacitus we have *Sacerd* (*otis*) *auc*(*tori*)*tas,*with a similar sign over the second word. In the text of this page we see *enu*(*mer*)*are* with this sign. On fol. 44v it occurs in *deg*(*e*)*n*(*er*)*ant* (cf. 46r). The 2 sign is also employed for *-ur,* an old and well-known usage: Tacitus, fol. 58v *fungeretur,* etc.

Characteristic features of manuscripts written or annotated by Pontano are the braces or other flourishes used by him. They take these forms:

1. Two or three dots followed by a curving horizontal line: Pontano, Pl. 13 margin (Tacitus, fol. 47v), two instances at the bottom, at the end of a paragraph; Pontano, Pl. 18, 19, three examples at the end of titles and poems; Pontano, Pl. 20; Tacitus, fols. 2r, 31r, 47r (four examples), 51r, 52v, 53r, 54r (three times), 54v, 55r, 57v, 58v (twice), 59v; Tibullus, fols. 2v, 6r, 7v, etc., after each poem. So too in the Propertius. In the Ovid manuscript examples occur on 38r, 38v, 40v, 44v, 46v (Pl. 37), 52r (Pl. 35), etc. Three of these in a row are on

fol. 28r of the Hamilton manuscript (Pl. 30) at the end of the
Ars. The same occurs in Tacitus, fol. 47r at the end of the
Germania. At the end of Tibullus (fol. 38r) five are found before
the word *finis* and four after it, to fill the line. Two in a row
occur in Pontano, Pl. 18.

2. Two or three dots (usually three) below which there is
a vertical curving line. This is the same as the preceding except
that it is at a different angle. Examples are on fol. 46v (Pl. 37;
before the added lines), 59r, 60r (*Am.* III 3, 23-24), 61r (*Am.*
III 4, 25), 68r (*Am.* III 14, 7-8). Parallels in Pontano, Pl. 19, 22;
Tacitus, fol. 1v, 9r, etc.; Propertius, fol. 7, etc.

3. A third form is the well-known sign consisting of a
vertical line broken at intervals by three or four semicircles. This
is used in the Ovid along with the No. 1 flourish on fol. 46r
in a marginal addition (Pl. 34). The same style is used in Tacitus (though not with an addition): fols. 9r, 16v, 20v, 29r, 29v,
etc. A similar one is used with an addition in Propertius, fol. 5v.

Both the Tacitus and the Propertius were written in March,
1460. In the latter it is indicated that the copying was done at
Naples, as we would naturally suppose; we may well conclude
that the Tacitus was also copied there. The similarity of the script
of the Tibullus leads one to infer that it too was copied about
the same time. Perhaps Pontano's script in the Ovid is sufficiently like that of the three codices just mentioned to suggest
that his activity in this manuscript is not very much later than
1460, but that idea is perhaps too speculative.

A list of Pontano's books presented to the church of S. Domenico at Naples by Pontano's daughter Eugenia has been preserved [3]. Among the books in this list is "Ovidius de arte amandi
cum multis aliis operibus eiusdem". This I take to be the Berlin
manuscript in spite of the fact that only two works (*Rem., Am.*)
are included besides the *Ars* instead of " multis aliis ".

I now list the items which I attribute to Pontano. Some
are followed by a question mark where I could not be certain,

[3] G. Filangieri, *Documenti per la storia le arti e le industrie delle provincie napoletane*, III (Naples, 1885), p. 50; also in E. Pèrcopo, *Vita di Giovanni
Pontano* (Naples, 1938), pp. 313-4.

especially in short words which contained no characteristic letters. Others too may be doubtful. I have not seen the manuscript itself and could therefore not make use of the color of the ink. But it is clear from the photostats (made from a microfilm) that Pontano usually employed a very black ink. Some notes of his are not in that ink because they were made at a different time. I did not, as a rule, include corrections and additions of one or two letters that may have been made by Pontano. It should be remembered that this is not a collation but merely an attempt to identify Pontano's notes [4].

3r	(*Ars* I 161) vel ventos movisse flabello *i. m.* [5]
6r	(I 407) fritillis *i. m.*
6r	(I 415) redeunt *i. m.* (?)
7v	(I 563) euhoe *i. m.* (?)
19r	(III 108) viri *sscr.*
19v	(III 111) grece protulit *i. m.*, aiaci *sscr.*
22v	(III 367) esse *sscr.*
23v	(III 440) sui *sscr.*
27r	(III 749) Scilicet *sscr.*
28r	REMEDIORUM *i. m. sup.*
28r	(*Rem.* 9-10) *i. m. add.*
29r	(60) virum *i. m.*
29r	(73) viciis *i. m.*
29v	(131) aliter Temporibus medicina valet *i. m. inf., sub quo litteris minutis superior textus verior meo iudicio*
30v	(185) suppositos *ex* compositos *corr.* (sup *sscr.*)

30v	(189-190) *i. m. add.*
30v	(207) *alt.* studium *sup.* tamen *scr.*
31r	(247) aliter quicquid eras fueris *i. m.*
32v	(351) aliter collinet *i. m.*
32v	(375) tragicos *i. m.*
33r	(385) libera *i. m.*
33r	(393) crescit *ex* crevit (sc *sscr.*)
33r	(394) noster *sup.* vester *scr.*
33r	(417) genere neutro potius quam feminino veteres proferebant *sup.* mendum
34v	(513) fallet *ex* falle (et *sscr.*) *corr. et* amor *sscr.*
34v	(517) ut *sscr.*
34v	(537) Vtere et *sscr.*
35v	(582) tuo *sup.* tibi *scr.* (?)
36r	(623) sana *sup.* firma
36r	(647) doluisse *i. m.*

[4] No reference is made here to the Plates in the present volume [i.e. Munari]. For the parts of text reproduced in single Plates, see "Indice delle tavole" [here, "Index of Plates"]. Notes by Pontano are in Pl. 30-38.

[5] On fol. 4 r (*Ars* I 269) a humanistic hand wrote *cunctas* in the margin, but the *ct* is in ligature, which Pontano does not use, and the *s* ends at the bottom of the line, whereas Pontano's nearly always goes well below the line. Similarly I reject other readings.

36r (657) non curandus adest *i. m. inf.*

36v (677) amicae *sscr.* (?)

37r (722) vel rapide *sup.* Tu timide

37r (725) sola *sscr.*

37r (727) vit *sup.* dormimus

38r DE AMORIBUS *i. m. sup.*

39v (*Am.* I 3, 13) Inde cessuri nisi dis *i. m.*

39v (I 3, 21) Carmine nomen habet *sscr.*

39v (I 4, 5) vel sinu dextram *i. m.*

43v (I 8, 67) Si quia *sscr.* (?)

43v (I 8, 70) ignibus *sscr.* (?)

44r (I 9, 12) conteret *sup.* exteret

45r (I 10, 15) sordibus *sscr.*

45v (I 11, 4) blandis *sscr.* (?)

45v (I 11, 14) fert *i. m.*

46r (I 13, 11-14) *i. m. inf. add.*

46v (I 13, 23) cum *post* tunc *sscr.,* aliter lacerti *i. m.* (?)

46v (I 13, 33-34) *i. m. add.*

46v (I 13, 44) forma *sscr.*

46v (I 13, 46) furta *sscr.*

46v (I 13, 48) vel est solito *sscr.*

47r (I 14, 15) pectinis *i. m.*

47r (I 14, 26) vel nexilis *i. m.*

47r (I 14, 30) aquas *i. m.* (?)

48r (II 1, 19) bella *sscr.* (?)

48r (II 1, 30) mihi aiaces *i. m. inf.*

48v (II 1, 33) laudataque semper amicae *i. m.*

48v (II 2, 18-27) *i. m. inf. add.*

48v (II 2, 23) faciet *sscr.*

49r (II 2, 52) viderit *i. m.*

49v (II 3, 17) temptare rogabo *ex* temptasse rogamus *corr.* (re bo *sscr.*)

49v (II 4, 5) esse *ex* nosse *corr.* (e *sscr.*)

49v (II 4, 9) irritet *i. m.* (?)

49v (II 4, 27) agili *sscr.*

50r (II 5, 21) remota *sscr.*

50v (II 5, 34) rubor *ex* pudor *corr.* (rub *sscr*).

50v (II 5, 45) compti *sscr.* (?)

50v (II 5, 54) hec ego *sup.* Et volo, nota *sup.* illa, volo *sup.* nota

50v (II 6, 2) ferte *sscr.*

51r (II 6, 12) ante *sscr.*

54r (II 11, 40) spectet *sup.* ventis

54r (II 11, 41) pleni *sup.* soli

54r (II 12, 3) fortis *sup.* firmat

54r (II 12, 17) causa *sscr.*

54v (II 13, 7) genialia *i. m.* (?)

54v (II 13, 17) meruit *i. m.*

54v (II 14, 19) nasci *sscr.*

55v (II 15, 26) ipse *sscr.*

57r (II 18, 19) Artes ante hos edite *i. m.*

57r (II 18, 21) Heroidum epistole *i. m.*

57r (II 18, 26) vel aonio *sscr.,* amica viro *sscr.*

57r (II 18, 27) Responsa SABINI *i. m.*

57r (II 19, 7) est *post* fortuna *sscr.,* possit *sscr.*

57v (II 19, 12) tardo *sscr.*

57v (II 19, 14) ipsa *sup.* esse

57v (II 19, 20) face *sup.* time

57v (II 19, 31) cupit ab (ab *del.*) *sscr.*

58r (III 1, 26) digna *sup.* facta

58v (III 1, 30) iste *sscr.*

58v (III 1, 64) orbe sonor *i. m.*

59r (III 2, 1) vel venio specta-
tor *sup.* sedeo studiosus

59r (III 2, 4) quem *ex* quam (e
sscr.)

59r (III 2, 7) faves *ex* favet
(es *sscr.*)

59v (III 2, 41) vel nigro *sup.*
levi

59v (III 2, 64) imposuisse *ex*
inseruisse (impos. *sscr.*)

59v (III 2, 66) quadriiuges *ex*
quadriiugo (s *sscr.*)

59v (III 2, 70) ad *sup.* moto

59v (III 2, 74) (to)gis *in corr.*

59v (III 2, 75) et ne *sup.* agne

60r (III 2, 78) agmen discolor
i. m.

60r (III 3, 1) credamne? *sscr.*

60r (III, 3, 5) rubore *ex* robore
(v *sscr.*)

60v (III 4, 7) mentem *sup.* corpus, claudas *ex* cladas (u
sscr.)

60v (III 4, 24) tam multos *i.
m. inf.*

61r (III 4, 26) Preda *sscr.*

61r (III 4, 27) amore *ex* more
(a *sscr.*)

61r (III 4, 28) quid *sscr.*

61r (III 4, 29) tantum est *sup.*
cara

62r (III 6, 25) media *sup.* me-
liae

62r (III 6, 29) Alpheon *ex* Al-
phion (e *sscr.*)

62r (III 6, 32) Pthiadum *ex*
Pthiotum (ad *sscr.*)

62r (III 6, 41) euanthe *ex* eban-
the (eu *sscr.*)

62r (III 6, 41) esopide *ex* eso-

piae (de *sscr.*), eosopide
asapide *i. m.*

62v (III 6, 68) vel tepido *sscr.*

62v (III 6, 74) vel tegi *sscr.*

62v (III 6, 90) terras *ex* ras
(ter *sscr.*)

63r (III 7, 1) Aut... aut *ex* At...
at (v *sscr.*), est *sscr.*

63r (III 7, 2) Aut *ex* At

63r (III 7, 3) male *ex* ma (le
sscr.)

63r (III 7, 9) que *sscr.* (?)

63r (III 7, 10) Lascivum *ex* La-
scium (u *sscr.*), supposuit-
que *ex* posuique (sup *et*
t *sscr.*)

63v (III 7, 43) illi *ex* ille (i
sscr.) (?)

63v (III 7, 44) nunc *sup.* cum
(?)

63v (III 7, 55) blanda est *ex*
blanda (est [*abbr.*] *sscr.*)

64r (III 8, 11) stulta *i. m.*

64r (III 8, 17) aliter quisquam
i. m.

64v (III 8, 27) deducere *ex* de-
ducite (ere *sscr.*)

64v (III 8, 50) regna petis *sscr.*

64v (III 8, 59) Liceor *i. m.*

65r (III 9, 22) obstupuisse *ex*
obstipuisse (u *sscr.*)

65r (III 9, 23) etlinon *ex* eli-
non (et *sscr.*) (?)

65r (III 9, 24) invicta *sup.* in
lyra, lyra *sup.* comam

65v (III 9, 49) hic, manibus
sscr.

65v (III 10, 5) cunque *sup.*
quaeque

66r (III 10, 10) cibus *sup.* erat,
torus *sup.* cibus

66r (III 10, 30) Redire semina *i. m.*

66r (III 10, 37) fuit *sscr.*

66v (III 10, 47) cererem *sup.* venerem

66v (III 11, 12) ut *sup.* et

66v (III 11, 28) velit *i. m.* (*pro* queat *eraso i. m.*)

67r (III 11, 52) Quamquam *sscr.*

67r (III 12, 20) vel debuerat *i. m.*

67v (III 12, 37) auriga *ex* auriosa (ga *sscr.*)

67v (III 12, 41) facunda *ex* iucunda (fac *sscr.*)

67v (III 13, 2) con *sup.* tigimus, culta *sup.* victa

67v (III 13, 11) hic *sup.* Hanc

68r (III 13, 27) sancto *sscr.*

68r (III 14, 13) que *sscr.*

68v (III 14, 37) abit *sup.* hebetet

68v (III 14, 42) criminis *sup.* numeris

PLATES

1. Rome, Vat. lat. 3357, fol. 1r. Petrarch, *De vita solitaria.*

2. Rome, Vat. lat. 3357, fol. 24r. Petrarch, *Itinerarium.*

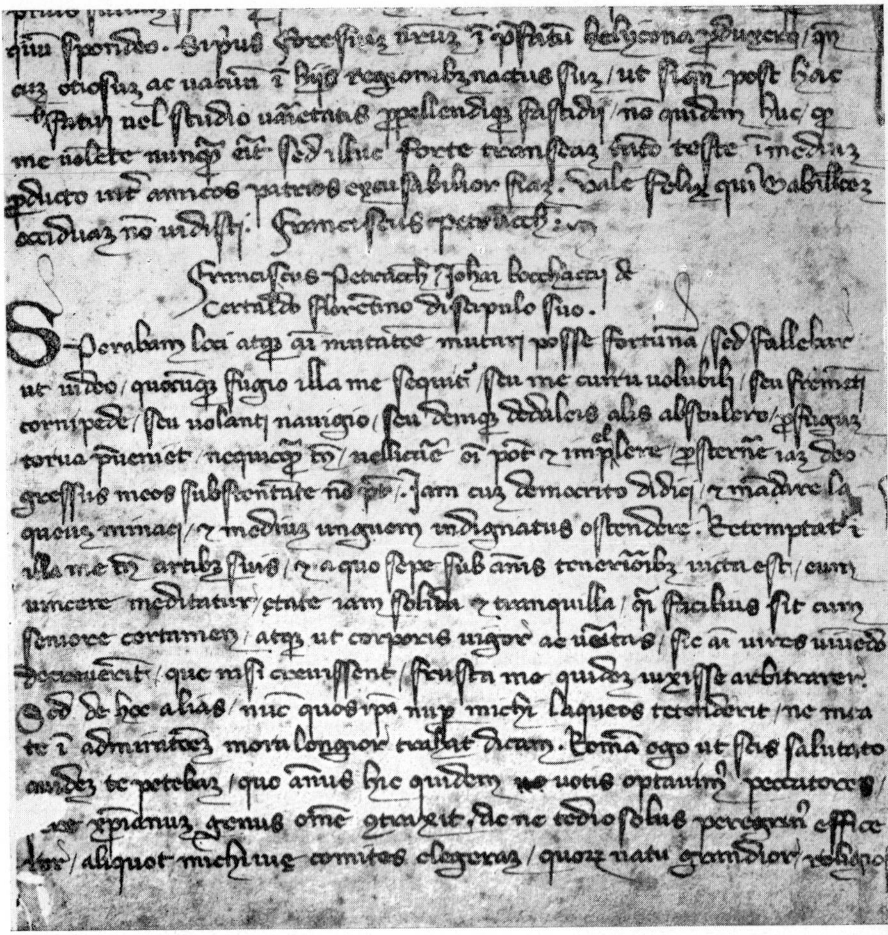

3. Florence, Naz. Conv. Soppr. I, 1, 28, fol. 2r. Petrarch, *Epist.*

accidi$i$, eandē legē optauit. Gessi mõre īgeniose, et amica uito,
legit eã totam, n̄ alicubi substitit, n̄ stens obductioz vox fracto
n̄ lacrime n̄ singultus ĩtuenē, et ĩ fine, Ego igt flesses Nã et pia
res, et reb; ūba acomodata, fletuz suadebant, n̄ ego duri cordis
sim, n̄ q ficta ō credidi et credo. Nam si uera essent, q usq$z$ mulier,
ut romana ut cui lib$z$ gentis, hanc griseldiz equatura sit. Vbi qɨ
tantus amoz ouigat, $\bar{u}$ par fides. $\tilde{u}$ tã ĩsignis patientia, atq$z$ cō
stantia, his uz ego nil respondi, ne rem ac̃ris, amici $\tilde{p}$ collog$z$ se
sta dulcedine, ad acrimoniaz disceptationis adducerez. Erat aut
p$\tilde{n}$a responsio. Esse nō nullos, q qcūqz difficilia eis sint, ĩpossibilia
omib; arbitrentuz, sic mēsura sua omia metientes, ut se omiũ $\tilde{p}$mos
locent. cū tā mīti fuerint sorte et sint, q^h essent facilia, q uulgo
ĩpossibilia uiderentuz. Qu^se est eis exempli $\tilde{g}$a, $q$no Curtiū et Mutios
Nutiū et decios ex extnis aut, Codrū et silenes fr̃es, ut q^{m} defe
minus p̃mo erat, qs ut portia ut ysicrate$z$, ut alcestim, et har$z$
similes, n̄o fabulas fictas putet. Atq$z$ ysorie uere sūt. Et sane q
palio uitaz sp̃nit, q^d n̄o sp̃ie, q^d n̄o pati possit, n̄o ĩtelligo. — Ce
tez et illaz, et aliãz, duas magnas epistolas, ad te nō puenisse nūc
sentio. Ez q^d faciaz pati oz. Indign̄er h n̄o ulciscī. Apparuit et $\tilde{p}$
cisalpinaz galliaz, tediosissimū hoc hoiuz g̃n, custodes passuū, ymo
pestes nuptioz, q tuas aptas ĩtrospiciant, et morosissīme ĩreplet,
q^d dnoz Jussus försan excusat, q ō omiuz $\tilde{p}$scij, trepida ac superba
uita, dese et $\tilde{q}$ se omia dici putant, atq$z$ omia nosse uolūt. Illud
nich excusat, q si odi lenes ipis ĩueniunt, q^d aures asininas
mt̃reat, solebant q dez ĩtrascribendo tp̃s trahē et nuptios detinē.
Nūc crescente licentia, ut digitis suis parcant, abire illos uolent
n̄ lenes. q^d q grauissimū tedij g̃n̄ est, hoc illis maxime faciut, $q$ni
ĩq^{h} ĩtelligunt. Silene de his, $q$uoz ampla et prope gula ē, et lenta
digestio, q male ualitudinj $\tilde{p}$xi sint oportet. Importunitatū taliū

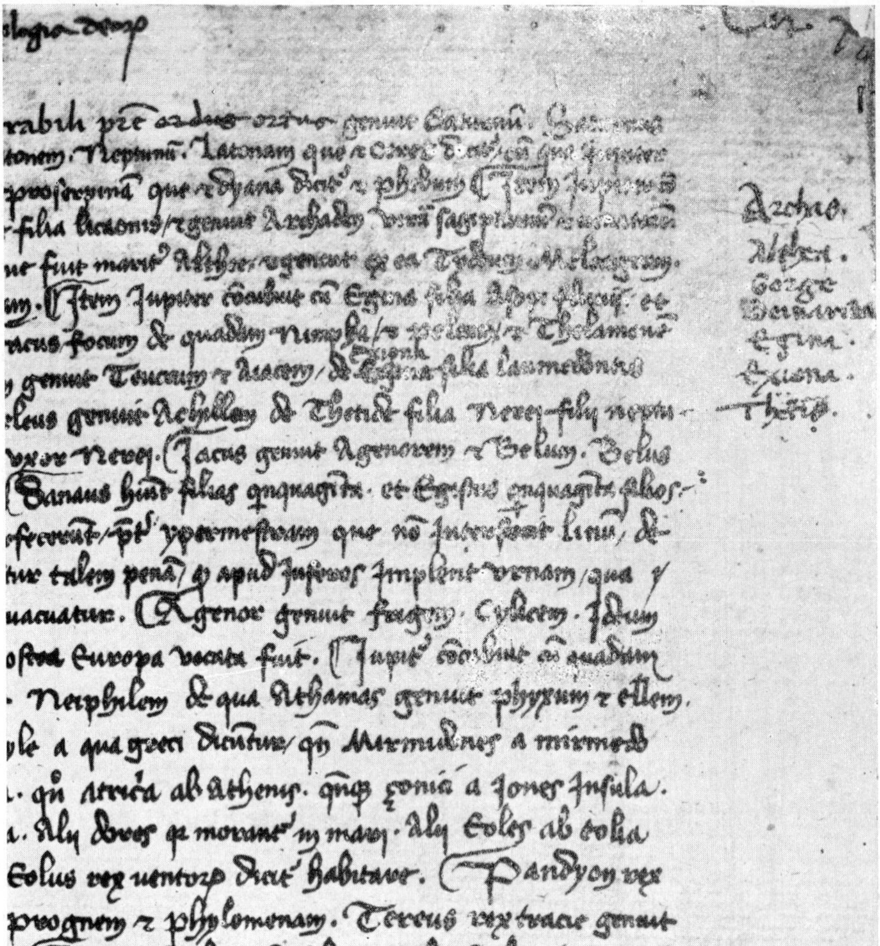

5. Florence, Naz. Conv. Soppr. I, 1, 28, fol. 49r. *Genealogia deorum.*

6. Rome, Vat. lat. 1843, fol. 63r. Livy, copied by Poggio.

7. Florence, Laur. 48, 22, fol. 22r. Cicero, copied by Poggio.

tissime uolens infamem filii uitam parentis
tum uerecundiam esse tum crimen. Vnde
non inconuenienter philosophus in rhetori
cis inquit. Necesse erubescere qdem in talibus
maloʒ que uidentur turpia esse ipsis aut his
de qbus curant. uel secundum aliam translati
onem. Erubescet quis proculdubio secundum
hunc modum scilicet omne quod fuerit ex
malicia fedum uitupabile quando accidit
et aut alicui eoʒ de quibus curat. Et omnes
ferme moralium tractatores admittunt &
uolunt etiam sapientem & uirtuosum ex co
iunctoʒ turpitudine uerecundiam nedum
posse pati. sed perpeti. & ex ipsis quasi pprijs
commoueri. Quod qdem apud philosophum
in ethicis non memeni me legisse. Nam quod
in rhetoricis inqu t in quibus de popularib;
commotoibus agitur ut doceat ex quibus ora
tor auditore it aduersarium poterit com
mouere de uulgo non de sapientibus & uir
tuosis & dictum & intelligendum est. Et ego

8. Florence, Laur. Strozzi 96, fol. 22v. Salutati, *De verecundia*.

nisi eo illum ipsa fortuna uel secunda uel quasi auersa pducit. nihil p̱
te aliud nobisq̱ uota restat. quibus ab illo cui hec cure sint deo si pos
sumus impetremus ut te tibi reddat. ita eni reddet & nobis. Sin at
q̱ mentem illam tuam que respiratione iam diu parturit aliquando in a
uras uere libertatis emergere. Ceni fortasse que uulgo fortuna no
minatur occulto quodam ordine regitur. Nihilq̱ aliud in rebus ca
sim uocamus nisi cuius ratio & causa secreta est. Nihilq̱ mali seu
commodi contingit in parte quod no conuenit aut cogruat etia u
niuerso. Quam sententiam uberrimay doctrinay oraculis. editam re
motiq̱ longissime ab intellectu profanoy se demonstraturam ueris
amatoribus suis. ad qua te inuito philosophia pollicetur. Quiob
re tuo animo cu tibi indigno multa accidunt ne te ipse contempnas.
Nam si diuina prouidentia portenditur usq̱ ad nos quod minime
dubitandum est. mihi crede sic tecu agi oportet ut agitur. Nam
cum tanta quanta sepe admiror indole tua abineunte adolescentia
adhuc infirmo rationis atq̱ labante uestigio. humana uita erroy
omniu plenissimam ingredereris. excepit te circufluentia diuiti
ay que illa etate atq̱ animu. que pulchra & honesta uidebitur.
uite sequente illecebrosis coeperat absorbere gurgitibus. nisi inde
te fortune illi flatus qui putantur auersi eripuissent pene merge
tem. An u si edente te munera ursoy. & nunq̱ ibi antea uisa spec
tacula cuibus nostris theatricus plausus semp prosprimus accepi
set. si stultoy hominu quoy turba est conflatis & consentientibus
uocibus ferreris ad celum. si nemo tibi esse audiret inimicus. si
municipales tabule te non solum ciuiu sed etia uicinoy patronu
ere signaret. collocarentur statue. influerent honores. adderetur

9. Florence, Laur. S. Marco 665, fol. 3r. St. Augustine, *Contra academicos*,

multitudine: uno tempore p̄gressus haud ita longe a cesaris castris con
stitit in campo. Quib; reb; cognitis cesar iube milites q̄ extra munitione
minutarum modeste precesserant. qq; pabulandi legandiq; aut etiam mu
nendi gratia uallem peterant. qq; ad eius rei opus erant omnes intra
munitiones minutarum modesteq; sine tumultu ac timore se recipere
atq; in ope consistere. Equit; autem q̄ in statione fuerant precepit ut
usq; eo locum obtinerent in quo paulo ante constitissent donec ab ho
ste telum missum ad se puenirent: quod si propius accederet q̄ honestissime
se intra munitiones reciperent. Alii qq; equiti edicit uti suo quisq; loco
paratus armatusq; presto esset. Ad hec non ipse p̄se eorum eu de uallo
p̄specularetur: sed mirabili quadam scientia bellandi: in pretorio sedens p
speculatores et nuntios impellat qd fieri uolebat. Animaduertebat en̄
q̄q̄ magnis essent copiis aduersarii freti: tamen sepe a se fugatis pulsisq; p
terretisq; et concessam uitam a ignota peccata: quib; reb; nunq; tanta
supperere ex ipsorum inertia conscientiaq; animi uictorie fiducia ut ca
stra sua adoriri auderent. Preterea ipsius nom̄ auctoritasq; magna ex
parte eorum exercitus minuebat audacia. tu agrege munitiones castro
ru atq; ualli: fossaq; altitudo et extra uallu tali certe mirabilem in mo
dum consita. que sine defensorib; aditum aduersariis prebebant. scor
pionum, catapultaru: eoterioruq; telorum que ad defendendum solent para
ri magnam copiam habebat. Atq; hec propter exercitus sui presentis pau
citatem et tyrocinium procurauerat: non hostium ui et metu commotus.
Sapientem se timidisq; hostium opinioni prebebat. Neq; idcirco copias q̄q̄
erant pauce tyronu̅q; non educebat in aciem quia uictorie sue diffi
deret: sed referre arbitrabatur cuiusmodi uictoria esset futura. Turpe en̄
sibi existimabat tot rebus gestis tantisq; exercitibus deuictis tot tam claris
uictoriis partis ab reliquis copiis aduersarioru ex fuga collectis se cruentam
adeptu existimari uictoriam. Itaq; constituerat gloriam exultationemq;
eorum pati donec sibi ueterani legionum pars aliqua in secundo com

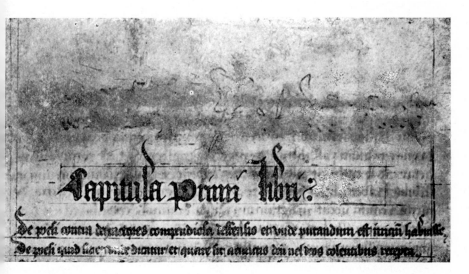

11. London, Brit. Mus. Harl. 1705, fol. 96v. Plato, *Republic* (owned by Duke Humphrey of Gloucester).

12. Rome, Vat. Urb. lat. 694, fol. 179v. Salutati, *De laboribus Herculis* (owned by Duke Humphrey of Gloucester).

Caii Suetonii Tranquilli De viris
liber incipit :-   DE GRAMMAT

GRāmatica romę ne in usu qdem
honore ullo ęrat rudi scilicet ac
tū ciuitate. necdū magnopere liber
uacate. Initiū qq; eī mediocre ęxt
Antiqssimi doctorū qdem et poetę
ęrat liuiu et Enniū dico. q̄ utraq;
forisq; docuisse ac notū ē. nihil a̅r
ī terp̄tabatur aut si q̄d ipsi latine ē
allegabāt. na̅ q̄d no nulli tradūt d
tris syllabisq; ite̅ de metr̄ is ab eo
ture̅ argut. L. cotta no poetę se
nii ēē cui et de augurādi discipl
fęratur. Primus igr̄ quātū opinā
grāmaticę ī urbe̅ intulit crates f
starchi ęqualis q missus ad senatū
iter secudū et tertiū punicū bel
Ennii morte̅ cū regione palatii p
cę foram eius fregisset p omne l
et ualitudinis te̅pus plurimas ꝺep
fecit assidueq; disseruit ac nr̄is e

Duo Enni

C. Suetoni sc̄psit de viris
illustribus cuius exemplū
secutus secutus hieronymus
ipse q̄q; libellū de scp̄toribus
christianis edidit Nup̄ etiā
Bartholomeus facius famil
ariis nr̄ de uiris illustribus
trιs suis libros composuit. q
nec hos Suetonii illustres ui
ros uidere posset mors im
matura effecit. paulo eı̅m
p̄ ei morte̅ in luce̅ rediep
cū multos anos desiderat
a docris ho̅ibus te̅ter Thib;
eı̅m Nicol q̄nt pontficis max
E̅noe Asculan in Galliam et
inde in Germaiam pfecrus
cogredens librorū grā hos
quaquā mendosos et impfos
ad nos retulit. cui sic hnd̄
pꞇatu̅ ut male ipc̄cadū
est Siccon̄io poletono patau
no. q cū de oratoribus ac poetis
epꝺinuenisset ita suppisset
ut ne unquā in luce̅ uenire
posset. quā ego ai̅ patauii
ꝗere̅ tand rep̄ ea ab illo
fuisse co̅bustā ipumq; ar
rogantia ac temeritate im
pulsum ꝺ iunis illustriū s̄n
pꞇorū loquacissime pariter
et inepissime scp̄sisse
Iov Pontanus umber
excripsit

13. Leiden, Periz. 4° 21, fol. 47v. Tacitus, copied by Pontano, 1460.

Hos libellos Jouianus pontanus excripsit
nuper adinuetos et in luce relatos ab Enoc
Asculano quanqua satis mendosos.

M·CCCC·
LX
martio mse

14. Leiden, Periz. 4° 21, fol. 1 v. Tacitus, copied by Pontano, 1460.

CORNELII TACITI·DIALO
GVS·DE·ORATORIBVS·INCIPIT :~

Saepe ex me requiris Iuste Fabi cur cu
priora secula tot eminentiu oratoru inge
niis gloriaq: floruerint nostra potissimu
aetas deserta et laude eloqntiae orbata ui
nomen ipsum oratoris retineat. Neq; enim ita
appellemus nisi antiquos. Horum uero temporu
diserti causidici et aduocati et patroni et qd
uis potius qua oratores uocatur. Cui percetatioi
tuae respondere et ta magnae questionis pondus
excipere ut aut de ingeniis nris male existi
mandum si idem assequi no possumus aut de
iudiciis si nolumus ut hercule audere si mihi
mea sententia proferenda ac no disertissimoru ut
nris temporibus hominu sermo repetendus eet qs
eandem hac qstione pertractantes iuuenis admodum audiui. Ita non ingenio sed memoria et
recordatione opus est. ut quae a prstantissimis
uiris et excogitata subtiliter et dicta grauiter

15. Leiden, Periz. 4° 21, fol. 2r. Tacitus, copied by Pontano, 1460.

16. Rome, Vat. lat. 2837, fol. 1r. Pontano, *De stellis*, autograph, before 1490.

17. Rome, Vat. lat. 2838, fol. 2r. Pontano, *Meteora*, autograph, 1490.

IOVIANI·PONTANI·VMBRI·DE·DIVINIS
LAVDIBVS·LIBER·INCIPIT :·

AD Illustrem Pricipem Joanne Aragonia
q nec auro nec gemis capiatur is q uir
tute colat. sed pietate et Justitia qua
lem eundem esse dici

NON aurum gemmeq; iuuat que cadida uirt
Veraq; diuine gloria mentis alit
Sed pietas rectiq; animo sibi coscius equi
Et nulli imprimis dedita corda probro.
Naq; auro uix sola homini mortalia constat
Virtuti celum sideraq; alta patent.

18. Madrid, Aa 318, fol. 2r. Pontano, *De divinis laudibus*, autograph, 1458.

Sic tibi celestes aderunt. sic alma fauebit
Mater. et humanus sic tibi cedet honos.
Regna parie uirtus. adimit scelus. Inclytus ille e
Quem sua non patrum spledida facta probant

IOVIANI PONTANI VMBRI

DE LAVDIBVS DIVINIS LIB FINIT

AD ILLVSTREM PRINCIPEM AC

DOMINVM JOANNEM

ARAGONIAM

M CCCC LVIII xi die Maij

19. Madrid, Aa 318, fol. 17r. Pontano, *De divinis laudibus*, autograph, 1458.

Nicolaus Maria buçutus insignis eques neapolitanus
hoc uolumen dono dedit Iouiano pontano vmbro
cum ad eum diuertisset euitande pestis gratia,
Anno dn. M. CCCCLVIII. iii die Junij

20. Rome, Vat. Barb. lat. 146, fol. 196r. Pontano autograph, 1458.

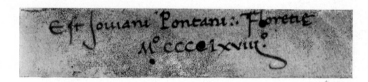

Est Iouiani Pontani. Florentie
M° CCCCLXVIII.

21. Munich, lat. 822, fol. 81r. Pontano autograph, 1468.

Andreas flocus honestis parentibus
florentie in etruria nascitur. Adolescens liberalibus studijs operam dedit.
post in curiam romanam concessit.
ubi diu scriptor apostolicus: & came-
re clericus uixit: dum ab eugenio
pontifice maximo inter familiares
asciscitur, Pontifice Florentie
agente moritur: annos natus cir-
citer septuaginta quo tempore
hec scripsit: que post eius morte
in lucem ab Amicis data sunt:

Io. Pontanus

22. Munich, lat. 822, fol. IIv. Pontano autograph, 1468.

paul. lepid. emilia.l   filioz

Venit in exequias tota caterua meus.

Causa porata est. flentes me/surgite testes
Du precium uite grata pependit humus.

Moribus et caelu patuit. sum digna merodo
Cuius honoratus ossa uehantur aquies.

AVRELII PROPERTII. mors extrema
triumphi

LIB. IIII FINIT.

M. CCCCLX.
Martio mese
Neap.li

23. Berlin, lat. fol. 500, fol. 66v. Propertius, Pontano autograph, 1460.

Scyllaq; et alternas scissa carybdis aquas
ampathie scythicus uerubus mugisse iuuecos)
Pauerat hos phoebo filia Lamparhie.

Circe e socys ulyssis/rex in sues uertit indito poculis uenenu
solus cum eurylochus illos dux abstinuiss poculis fraudem
euasit: req; omem ulyssi rettulit. quo in piculo, a mer
curio adiutus e tradito unguento, et thymoli flore; Cu
pmisiss e socys qui lethophagoz insula ad quia tempestate
delat fuas explorare illi letho gustata loto, ibidem versa
seruit ob abi suauitate at ulysses hoc coonito inuitos eos
ad se retraxit, Cu in siciliam pueriss ipse dormiete eury
locho tum iscenere aduersus moita arces et tiresu solis
armentum a socys violatum est. qd custodiebatur a la
pethie, phetusa et neera solis filiabus. ?

f. 43 v

24. Berlin, lat. fol. 500, fol. 43v. Propertius, Pontano autograph, 1460.

25. Berlin, lat. fol. 500, fol. 20v. Propertius, Pontano autograph, 1460.

26. Berlin, lat. fol. 500, fol. 60v. Propertius, Pontano autograph, 1460.

27. Berlin, lat. fol. 500, fol. 32r. Propertius, Pontano autograph, 1460.

28. Berlin, lat. fol. 500, fol. 59r. Propertius, Pontano autograph, 1460.

A A B B C C D D E E F F
G G E H h I I K K L L M M
N N O O P P Q Q R R S S T
T V V X X Y Y Z Z Z ç

A a b b c c d d e e f f g g h h h
i j k k l l m m n n o o p p q q r r
ff s t t u u x x y y z z & & ꝓ ꝗ

Vilius argentum ē auro innuch
aurea

S olemuſ mala domuſ noſtre ſcire nouiſſi
mi: & coniugum: ac liberorum uitia uicinis
canentibuſ ignorare. Ieronimuſ ait

N ihil eſt tam ſanctum quod non uiolari, ni
hil tam munitum quod non expugnari pe
cunia poſſit: Cicero ait:

O culi amorem incipiunt, conſuetudo pficit:

PANIGALLIVS IACOBVS

29. Panigallius' *Abecedarium* on fol. 31v of MS. *penes* A. N. L. Munby.

S iqua fides arti quam longo fecimus usu
Credite prestabunt carmina nostra fidem .

S entiat eximus uenerem resoluta medullis
faemina & ex aequo res iuuet illa duos ·

N ec blandae uoces iucundaque murmura cessent
Nec taceant mediis improba uerba iocis

T u quoque cui ueneris sensum natura negauit
Dulcia mendaci gaudia finge sono

I nfelix cui torpet hebes locus ille puella est.
Quo pariter debent faemina uirque frui .

T antum cum finges nesis manifesta caueto
Effice permotum luminaque ipsa fidem

Q uid iuuat & uoces & anhelitus arguat horis
Apud & archanus pars habet ista notas

G audia post ueneris que poscat munus amantem
Illa suas nollet pondus habere preces.

N ec lucem in thalamos totis admitte fenestris
Aptius in uestro corpore multa latent ·

L usus habet. finem. cingnis discedere tempus
Duxerunt collo qui iuga nostra suo ·

U t quondam iuuenes ita nunc mea turba puellae
Inscribant spoliis naso magister erat :—· :—· :~

P· OUIDII NASONIS ARTIS AMATORIE EXPLIC LIB· III·
E IUSDE INCIP REMEDIORUM LIBER PRIMUS ·

L egerat huius amor titulum nomenq; libelli
Bella mihi uideo bella parantur ait

P arce tuum uatem sceleris damnare cupido
Tradita qui totiens te duce signa tuli

N on ego tidides a quo tua saucia mater
In liquidum rediit aethera martis equis

S epe tepent alii iuuenes ego semper amaui
Et siquid faciam nunc quoque quaeris amo

N ec te blande puer nec nostras prodimus artes
Nec noua preteritum musa retexit opus

S iquis amat quod amare iuuat feliciter ardet
Gaudeat & uento nauiget ille suo

A t siquis male fert indignae regna puellae
Ne pereat nostrae sentiat artis opem

C ur aliquis laqueo collum nodatus amator
A trabe sublimi tristis pependit honus

30. Berlin, Ham. 471, fol. 28r. Ovid, *Ars* III 791-812; *Rem.* 1-18 (9-10 Pontano autograph).

Ecce petunt rupes praeruptaque saxa capellae:
Iam referent haedis ubera plena suis.
Pastor inaequali modulatur arundine carmen.
Hec desunt comites sedula turba canes.
Parte sonant alia silvae mugitibus altae
Et queritur vitulum mater abesse suum.
Quid cum compositos fugiunt examina fumos
Ut relevent depto vimina curva favi.
Poma dat autumnus formosa est messibus aestas
Ver prebet flores igne levatur hiemps
Temporibus certis desectas alligat herbas
Et tonsam raro pectine verrit humum.
Ipse potes riguis plantam deponere hortis
Ipse potes rivos ducere lenis aquae.
Venerit insitio sacramum ramus adobtet
Stetque peregrinus arbor operta comis.
Cum semel haec animum coepit mulcere voluptas
Debilibus pinnis irritus exit amor.
Vel tu venandi studium cole saepe recessit
Turpiter a phoebi victa sorore venus.
Nunc leporem pronum catulo sectare sagaci.
Nunc tua frondosis retia tende iugis.
Aut pavidos terre varia formidine cervos.
Aut cadat adversa cuspide fossus aper.
Nocte fatigatum somnus non cura puellae
Excipit et pingui membra quiete levat.
Lenius est studium tamen alite capta
Aut lino aut calamis premia parva sequi.
Velque pisces edat avido male devoret ore
Abdere supremis fera pecu rua cibis.
Aut his aut aliis donec dediscis amare
Ipse tibi furtim decipiendus eris.
Tu tantum quamvis firmis retinebere vinclis
I procul et longas carpere perge vias.
Flebis et occurret desertae nomen amicae
Stabit et in media pes tibi saepe via.
Sed quanto minus ire voles magis ire memento
Perfer et invitos currere coge pedes.
Nec pluvias opta nec te peregrina morentur
Sabbata nec damnis alea notatus

Adgrediar melius tunc cum sua uulnera tangi
iam sinet et ueris uocibus aptus erit.
Quis matrem nisi mentis inops in funere nati
flere uetat? non hoc illa monenda loco est.
Cum dederit lacrimas animumque impleuerit aegrum
ille dolor uerbis emoderandus erit.
Temporis ars medicina fere est data tempore prosunt.
Et data non apto tempore uina nocent.
Quin etiam accendas uitia inritesque uetando
Temporibus si non adgrediare suis.
Ergo ubi uisus eris nostrae medicabilis arti
fac monitis fugias otia prima meis.
Haec ut ames faciunt haec quod fecere tuentur
haec sunt iucundi causa cibusque mali.

alr. Tporibus medicina ualet.
super decimi uersu meo indice.

32. Berlin, Ham. 471, fol. 29v. Ovid, *Rem.* 125-138.

At simul ad metas uenit finita uoluptas
Lassaque cum tota corpora mente iacent.
Dum piget et malle nullam tetigisse puellam
Tacturusque tibi non uideare diu
Tunc animo signa quodcumque in corpore menda e
Luminaque in mutis illius usque tene.
Forsitan haec aliquis nam sunt quoque parua nocibit
Sed quae non prosunt singula multa iuuant.

33. Berlin, Ham. 471, fol. 33r. Ovid, *Rem.* 413-420.

Nunc iuuat in tenera dominae iacuisse lacertis
Si quando lateri nunc bene iuncta meo est
Nunc etiam somni pingues et frigidus aer
Et liquidum tenui gutture cantat auis.
Quod properas ingrata uiris ingrata puellis
Roscida purpurea supprime lora manu.
Prima bidente uides oueratos arua colentes.
Prima uocas tardos sub iuga panda boues.

Ante tuos curru meliu sua sidera seruat
Nauita, ne media nescius erret aqua.
Te surgit quamuis lassus ueniente uiator,
Miles et armiferas aptat ad arma manu.

34. Berlin, Ham. 471, fol. 46r. Ovid, *Am.* I 13, 5-16 (11-14 Pontano autograph).

Per uenerem iuro puerique uolatilis arcum
Me non admissi criminis esse reum :—
Ponendis in mille modos perfecta capillis
Comere sed solas digna capillis deas
Et mihi iucundo non rustica cognita furtu
Apta quidem dominae sed magis apta mihi
Quis fuit inter nos sociati corporis index
Sensit concubitus unde corinna tuos :
Non tamen erubui numue ebo lapsus in ullo
furtuiae ueneris conscia signa dedi :

Ad ancillam cuius stupri sit amica

35. Berlin, Ham. 471, fol. 52r. Ovid, *Am.* II 7, 27-28; 8, 1-8.

Implicuit que suos circum mea colla lacertos .
Et que me perdunt oscula mille dedit .
Vincor & ingenium sumptis reuocatur ab armis
Resque domi gestas & mea bella cano .
Sceptra tamen sumpsi cuiusq; tragoediae nostra
Creuit & huic operi quamlibet aptus eram .
Risit amor pallamque meam pictosque coturnos
Sceptraque priuata tam cito sumpta manum .
Hinc quoque me dominae numen deduxit iniquae
Deque coturnato uate triumphat amor .
Quod licet aut artes teneri profitemur amoris
Ei mihi praeceptis urgeor ipse meis .
Aut quod penelopes uerbis reddatur ulixi
Scribimus & lacrimas phylli relicta tuas .
Quid paris & macareus & quod male gratus iaso
hippolytique parens hippolitusque legant .
Quoque tenens strictum dido miserabilis ensem
Dicat et aoniae lesbis amata lyrae .
Quam cito detoto rediit meus orbe sabinus
Scriptaque diuersis rettulit ille locis .
Candida penelope signum cognouit ulixis .
legit ab hyppolito scripta nouerca suo .
Iam pius aeneas miserere scripsit elisae .
Quod que legat phyllis simodo uiuit habet .

Artes amatoriae edite
Heroidum epystole
Responsa SABINI

36. Berlin, Ham. 471, fol. 57r. Ovid, *Am.* II 18, 9-32.

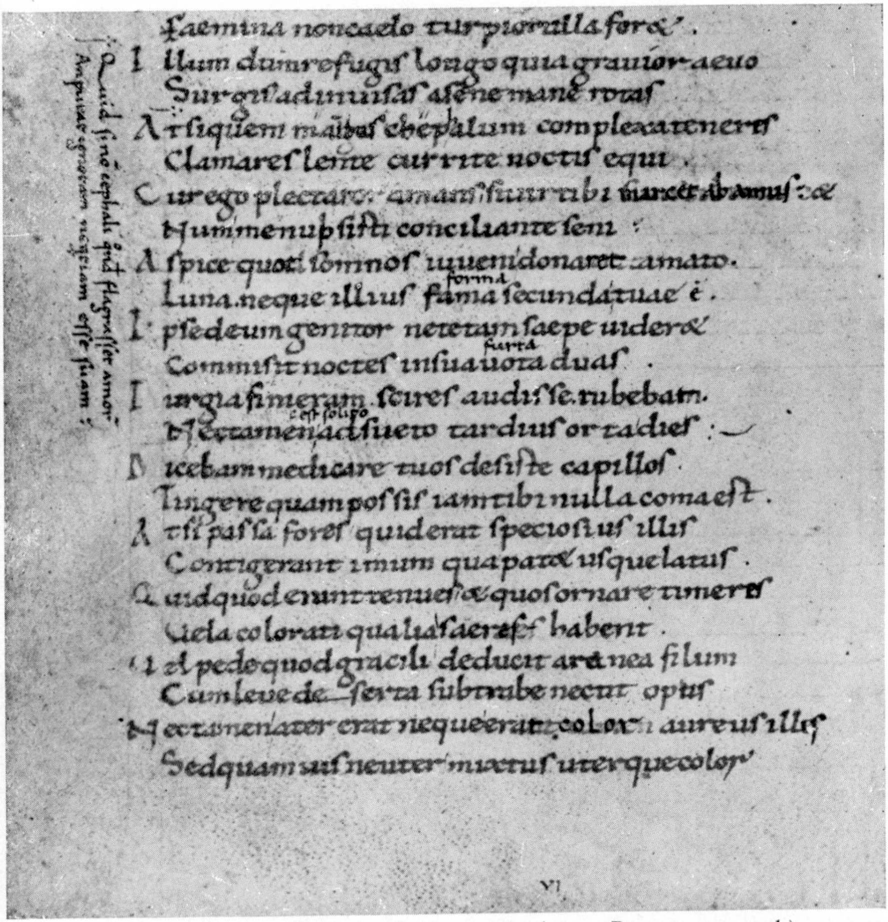

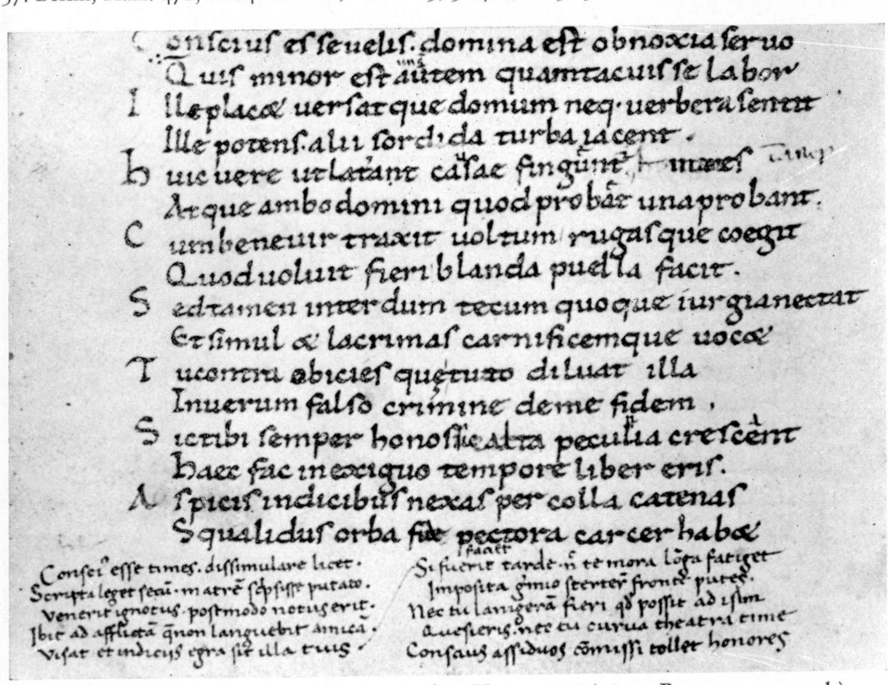

INDICES

by R. Avesani

INDEX OF NAMES

INDEX OF MANUSCRIPTS

(On the pages indicated in italics the MSS. are cited without their references, or only indirectly).

INDEX OF PLATES

TABLE OF CONTENTS

Indices:

STORIA E LETTERATURA

N.B. - Di questa collana sono in vendita, fino al n. 100, due edizioni: una *comune* e una *distinta* di 300 copie numerate. Le copie della edizione distinta *non si vendono separatamente*, essendo riservate a chi acquista tutti i volumi della collana. I nn. 3 e 4 furono stampati solo in edizione distinta. Di ogni volume sono segnati due prezzi: il primo si riferisce alla edizione comune; il secondo alla edizione distinta. Dal n. 101 in avanti, le due edizioni (comune e distinta) sono state unificate.

1. ALFREDO SCHIAFFINI, *Tradizione e poesia nella prosa d'arte italiana, dalla latinità medievale al Boccaccio.* Seconda edizione (ristampa). 1969, pp. 232. L. 4.600.

2. ANDRÉ WILMART, O.S.B., *Le « Jubilus » dit de saint Bernard (Étude avec textes).* Edizione postuma, a cura di JEANNE BIGNAMI-ODIER e AUGUSTE PELZER. 1944, pp. X-292. L. 2.500 e 3.000.

• 3. LIVARIUS OLIGER, O.F.M., *De secta « spiritus libertatis » in Umbria saec. XIV. Disquisitio et documenta.* 1943, pp. XII-116. L. 3.500 (ed. dist.).

• 4. PIO PASCHINI, *Domenico Grimani, Cardinale di S. Marco († 1523).* 1943, pp. VIII-162. L. 3.500 (ed. dist.).

• 5. BRUNO NARDI, *Nel mondo di Dante.* 1944, pp. VIII-384. L. 5.500 (ed. dist.).

6. RAFFAELE CIAMPINI, *Studi e ricerche su Niccolò Tommaseo.* 1944, pp. XXIV-412. L. 4.600 e 5.500.

• 7. MARIO PRAZ, *Ricerche anglo-italiane.* 1944, pp. VIII-372. L. 5.500 (ed. dist.).

8. GIUSEPPE BILLANOVICH, *Restauri boccacceschi.* 1945, pp. VIII-200. L. 1.200 e 3.500.

• 9. ANGELO MONTEVERDI, *Saggi neolatini.* 1945, pp. VIII-388, 2 tavole f.t. L. 5.500 (ed. dist.).

• 10. MARIO TOSI, *Il Torneo di Belvedere in Vaticano e i tornei in Italia nel Cinquecento. Documenti e tavole.* 1945, pp. XXIV-200, 1 ill. e 4 tavv. L. 5.500 (ed. dist.).

* 11. VINCENZO ARANGIO-RUIZ, *Rariora. Studi di diritto romano.* 1946, pp. XII-292. L. 5.500 (ed. dist.).

12. UGO MARIANI, O.E.S.A., *Il Petrarca e gli Agostiniani.* Edizione distinta, 1946, pp. VIII-120, L. 2.500; seconda edizione aggiornata, 1959, pp. 112, L. 3.000.

* 13. ALEXANDRO VALIGNANO, S.J., *Il Cerimoniale per i missionari del Giappone.* Ed. critica, introd. e note di G. FR. SCHÜTTE, S.J. 1946, pp. XVI-360, 28 tavv. f.t. e 2 incisioni. L. 6.000 (ed. dist.).

* 14. MICHELE PELLEGRINO, *Studi su l'antica apologetica.* 1947, pp. XIV-212. L. 3.500 (ed. dist.).

* 15. *Miscellanea bibliografica in memoria di don Tommaso Accurti,* a cura di LAMBERTO DONATI. 1947, pp. XII-222, 5 tavv. f. t. e 23 incisioni. L. 4.200 (ed. dist.).

16. GIUSEPPE BILLANOVICH, *Petrarca letterato. - I. Lo scrittoio del Petrarca.* 1947, pp. XXIV-448. L. 6.000 e 7.000.

17. *Miscellanea Pietro Fumasoni Biondi. Studi missionari raccolti in occasione del giubileo sacerdotale di S. E. il Sig. Cardinale* PIETRO FUMASONI BIONDI, *Prefetto della S. Congregazione « de Propaganda Fide ».* Vol. I, 1947, pp. XVI-192. L. 2.500 e 3.000.

* 18. MARIO SCADUTO, S.J., *Il monachismo basiliano nella Sicilia medievale. Rinascita e decadenza: secoli XI-XIV.* 1947, pp. LX-368 (esaur.; in prepar. la 2ª ediz.). L. 5.000.

19. HUBERT JEDIN, *Das Konzil von Trient. Ein Ueberblick über die Erforschung seiner Geschichte.* 1948, pp. 232. L. 3.000 e 3.500.

* 20. MASSIMO PETROCCHI, *Il quietismo italiano del Seicento.* 1948, pp. 222. L. 3.500 (ed. dist.).

* 21. FEDERICO DA MONTEFELTRO, *Lettere di stato e d'arte (1470-1480).* Edite per la prima volta da PAOLO ALATRI. 1949, pp. XVIII-132, 1 tav. f. t. L. 2.500 (ed. dist.).

* 22. ANNELIESE MAIER, *Studien zur Naturphilosophie der Spätscholastik. I. Band: Die Vorläufer Galileis im 14. Jahrhundert.* 2. erweiterte Auflage (Neudruck mit Nachträgen), 1966, pp. VIII-370.

* 23. TOMMASO BOZZA, *Scrittori politici italiani dal 1550 al 1650.* 1949, pp. 224. L. 4.200 (ed. dist.).

- 24-25. Fausto Nicolini, *Commento storico alla seconda Scienza Nuova,* 2 voll., 1949, pp. 676. L. 9.500 (ed. dist.).

- 26. Sergio Baldi, *Studi sulla poesia popolare d'Inghilterra e di Scozia.* 1949, pp. 184. L. 3.000 (ed. dist.).

- 27. Roberto Weiss, *Il primo secolo dell'umanesimo. Studi e testi.* 1949, pp. 172. L. 3.500 (ed. dist.).

- 28. *Epistolario di san Giuseppe Calasanzio* edito e commentato da Leodegario Picanyol. Vol. I: *Introduzione ed elenco cronologico.* 1950, pp. XLIV-244. L. 4.200 (ed. dist.).

- 29. *Un inedito petrarchesco. La redazione sconosciuta di un capitolo del « Trionfo della fama »,* a cura di Roberto Weiss. 1950, pp. 92. L. 1.800 (ed. dist.).

- 30. *Expositio Quatuor Magistrorum super Regulam Fratrum Minorum (1241-1242). Accedit eiusdem Regulae textus cum fontibus et locis parallelis.* Edidit P. Livarius Oliger, o.f.m. 1950, pp. XVI-208, 4 tavv. f. t. L. 4.000 (ed. dist.).

- 31. Werner P. Friederich, *Dante's fame abroad (1350-1850). The influence of Dante Alighieri on the Poets and Scholars of Spain, France, England, Germany, Switzerland and the United States.* 1950, pp. 592. L. 7.000 (ed. dist.).

- 32. Francesco Petrarca, *Invective contra medicum. Testo latino e volgarizzamento di ser Domenico Silvestri.* Edizione critica a cura di Pier Giorgio Ricci. 1950, pp. 212. L. 3.500 e 4.200.

- 33. Lanfranco Caretti, *Studi sulle Rime del Tasso.* 1973, pp. 282 (ristampa anastatica dell'edizione 1950, con aggiunte e correzioni). L. 6.000.

- 34. Angelo Mercati, *Saggi di storia e letteratura.* Vol. I, 1951, pp. 444, 4 tavv. f. t. L. 4.600 e 5.500.

- 35. *Epistolario di san Giuseppe Calasanzio,* edito e commentato da Leodegario Picanyol. Vol. II: *Lettere dal n. 1 al n. 500 (1588-1625).* 1951, pp. 436. Lire 4.600 e 5.500.

- 36. Joseph Franz Schütte, s. j., *Valignanos Missionsgrundsätze für Japan.* I. Band: *Von der Ernennung zum Visi-*

tator bis zum ersten Abschied von Japan (1573-1582).
I. Teil: *Das Problem (1573-1580).* 1951, pp. XVI-482,
17 tavv. f. t. L. 8.400 e 9.500.

37. ANNELIESE MAIER, *Studien zur Naturphilosophie der
Spätscholastik.* II. Band: *Zwei Grundprobleme der scho-
lastischen Naturphilosophie: das Problem der intensiven
Grösse, die Impetustheorie.* 3. erweiterte Auflage (Neudruck mit Nachträgen), 1968, pp. 412. L. 7.000. (Co-
loro che già possiedono la seconda edizione possono acquistare separatamente gli *Addenda*).

* 38. ERNEST H. WILKINS, *The Making of the Canzoniere and
other Petrarchan Studies.* 1951, pp. XXVIII-432, 2 tabelle
e 3 tavv. f. t. L. 7.000 (ed. dist.).

* 39. EDWARD WILLIAMSON, *Bernardo Tasso.* 1951, pp. XVI-
172, 1 tav. f.t. L. 3.500 (ed. dist.).

* 40. ROBERTO CESSI, *Politica ed economia di Venezia nel
Trecento. Saggi.* 1952, pp. 292. L. 4.600 (ed. dist.).

* 41. ANNELIESE MAIER, *Studien zur Naturphilosophie der
Spätscholastik.* III. Band: *An der Grenze von Scholastik
und Naturwissenschaft: die Struktur der materiellen
Substanz, das Problem der Gravitation, die Mathematik
der Formlatituden,* 2. Auflage. 1952, pp. X-398. L. 6.500
(ed. dist.).

42. ALBERTO VACCARI, S. J., *Scritti di erudizione e filologia.*
Vol. I: *Filologia biblica e patristica.* 1952, pp. XLVIII-408.
L. 6.000 e 6.500.

43. *Epistolario di san Giuseppe Calasanzio,* edito e commentato da LEODEGARIO PICANYOL. Vol. III: *Lettere
dal n. 501 al n. 1.100 (1626-1629).* 1951, pp. 480.
L. 4.600 e 5.500.

44. HYACINTHE DONDAINE, O.P., *Le Corpus dionysien de
l'Université de Paris au XIIIᵉ siècle.* 1953, pp. 164.
L. 3.000 e 3.500.

45. MASSIMO PETROCCHI, *Il problema del lassismo nel secolo XVII.* 1953, pp. 136. L. 2.500 e 3.000.

46. GEORGE B. PARKS, *The English Traveler to Italy.* Vol. I:
The Middle Ages (to 1525). 1954, pp. 672, 19 tavv. f.t.
L. 9.000 e 9.500.

'47. Arnaldo Momigliano, *Contributo alla storia degli studi classici*. 1955, pp. 412. L. 6.500 (ed. dist.).

48-49. *Epistolario di san Giuseppe Calasanzio*, edito e commentato da Leodegario Picanyol. Vol. IV: *Lettere dal n. 1101 al n. 1730 (1629-1631)*. Pp. 450. Lire 4.600 e 5.500. Vol. V: *Lettere dal n. 1731 al n. 2350 (1632-1655)*. 1952, pp. 478. L. 4.600 e 5.500.

50. Franz Kard. Ehrle, *Gesammelte Aufsätze zur englischen Scholastik*, herausgegeben von Franz Pelster, s. J. 1970, pp. xxx-393. L. 9.500.

51. B. L. Ullman, *Studies in the Italian Renaissance*. Second edition with additions and corrections. 1973, pp. 538, 38 ill. f.t. L. 15.000.

• 52. Anneliese Maier, *Studien zur Naturphilosophie der Spätscholastik*. IV. Band: *Metaphysische Hintergründe der spätscholastischen Naturphilosophie*. 1955, pp. vii-414. L. 6.500 (ed. dist.).

53. Augusto Beccaria, *I codici di medicina del periodo presalernitano (secoli IX, X e XI)*. 1956, pp. 508. L. 6.000 e 6.500.

54. Paul Oskar Kristeller, *Studies in Renaissance Thought and Letters*. 1969, pp. xvi-682, 4 tavv. f.t. (offset reprint of the edition published in 1956). L. 11.500.

55. *Le lettere di Benedetto XIV al card. de Tencin*. Dai testi originali, a cura di Emilia Morelli. Vol. I: *1740-1747*. 1955, pp. viii-502. L. 6.000 e 6.500.

56-57. *Epistolario di san Giuseppe Calasanzio*, edito e commentato da Leodegario Picanyol. Vol. VI: *Lettere dal n. 2351 al n. 3000 (1635-1638)*. Pp. 456. L. 4.600 e 5.500. Vol. VII: *Lettere dal n. 3001 al n. 3800 (1639-1641)*. 1954, pp. 480. L. 4.500 e 6.500.

58. *Epigrammata Bobiensia*. Detexit Augustus Campana, edidit Francus Munari. Vol. I: Augusto Campana, « *Heroicum Sulpiciae Carmen. LXX Epigrammata* »: *storia della tradizione* (imminente).

• 59. *Epigrammata Bobiensia*. Detexit Augustus Campana, edidit Francus Munari. Vol. II: *Introduzione ed edizione critica*, a cura di Franco Munari. 1955, pp. 156, 1 tav. f.t. L. 3.000 (ed. dist.).

60. *Epistolario di san Giuseppe Calasanzio,* edito e commentato da LEODEGARIO PICANYOL. Vol. VIII: *Lettere dal n. 3801 al n. 4578 (1641-1648).* 1955, pp. 460. L. 4.600 e 5.500.

61. TOMMASEO-VIEUSSEUX, *Carteggio inedito,* a cura di R CIAMPINI e P. CIUREANU. Vol. I: *1825-1834.* 1956, pp. 424. L. 3.000 e 3.500.

62. ROBERTO CESSI, *Saggi romani.* 1956, pp. 200. L. 2.600 e 3.000.

63. GIORDANO BRUNO, *Due dialoghi sconosciuti e due dialoghi noti: « Idiota triumphans », « De somnii interpretatione », « Mordentius », « De mordentii circino »,* a cura di GIOVANNI AQUILECCHIA. 1957, pp. XXIV-72, 7 tavv. f.t. L. 3.000 e 3.300.

64. VITTORIO GABRIELI, *Sir Kenelm Digby. Un inglese italianato nell'età della controriforma.* 1957, pp. 304. L. 4.200 e 4.600.

65. CHRISTINE MOHRMANN, *Études sur le latin des chrétiens.* Vol. I: *Le latin des chrétiens.* Pp. XXIV-470. Edizione distinta, 1958, L. 7.000; ristampa aggiornata dell'edizione comune, 1961, L. 6.500.

66. VITTORE BRANCA, *Tradizione delle opere del Boccaccio.* Vol. I: *Un primo elenco dei codici e tre studi.* 1958, pp. XL-380. L. 7.000 e 7.500.

67. ALBERTO VACCARI, S.J., *Scritti di erudizione e di filologia.* Vol. II: *Per la storia del testo e dell'esegesi biblica.* 1958, pp. XVI-528, 3 tavv. f.t. L. 6.500 e 7.000.

68. JOSEPH FRANZ SCHÜTTE, S.J., *Valignanos Missionsgrundsätze für Japan.* I. Band: *Von der Ernennung zum Visitator bis zum ersten Abschied von Japan (1573-1582).* II. Teil: *Die Lösung (1580-1582).* 1958, pp. XXXIV-598, 18 tavv. f.t. L. 9.000 e 9.500.

69. ANNELIESE MAIER, *Studien zur Naturphilosophie der Spätscholastik.* V. Band: *Zwischen Philosophie und Mechanik.* 1958, pp. X-394. L. 6.000 e 6.500.

70. MIGUEL BATLLORI, S.J., *Gracián y el barroco.* 1958, pp. 228, 9 tavv. f.t. L. 3.500 e 4.200.

71-73. *Miscellanea in onore di Roberto Cessi.* 1958. Vol. I: pp. LXX-434, 3 tavv. f.t.; vol. II: pp. 528, 3 tavv. f.t.;

vol. III: pp. 416, 3 tavv. f.t. Prezzo dei tre volumi:
L. 21.000 e 25.000.

74. LUIGI PARETI, *Studi minori di storia antica.* Vol. I:
Preistoria e storia antica. 1958, pp. XXIV-408. L. 6.500
e 7.000.

75. ERNEST HATCH WILKINS, *The Invention of the Sonnet
and other Studies in Italian Literature.* 1959, pp. 354.
L. 6.000 e 7.000.

76. RAFFAELE CIAMPINI, *I toscani del '59. Carteggi inediti
di Cosimo Ridolfi, Ubaldino Peruzzi, Leopoldo Galeotti,
Vincenzo Salvagnoli, Giuseppe Massari, Camillo Cavour*
1959, pp. 220. L. 3.000 e L. 3.500.

• 77. ARNALDO MOMIGLIANO, *Secondo contributo alla storia
degli studi classici.* 1960, pp. 508. L. 7.500 (ed. dist.).

78. BRUNO NARDI, *Studi di filosofia medievale.* 1960, pp.
240. L. 3.000 e 3.500.

79. B. L. ULLMAN, *The Origin and Development of Humanistic Script.* 1960, pp. 157, 70 ill. f.t. (offset reprint
1974) L. 4.000.

80-81. WERNER JAEGER, *Scripta minora.* 1960. Vol. I: pp.
XXVIII-418; vol. II: pp. 478, 12 tavv. f.t. Prezzo dei due
volumi: L. 10.500 e 11.000.

82-83. FRIEDRICH LEO, *Ausgewählte kleine Schriften.* Herausgegeben und eingeleitet von EDUARD FRAENKEL. 1960.
Vol. I: pp. LVIII-330; vol. II: pp. 448. Prezzo dei due
volumi: L. 10.500 e 11.000.

84. RENZO DE FELICE, *Note e ricerche sugli « illuminati » e
il misticismo rivoluzionario (1789-1800).* 1960, pp. 248.
L. 5.500 e 6.000.

85. ERIC W. COCHRANE, *Tradition and Enlightenment in the
Tuscan Academies (1690-1800).* 1961, pp. XXIV-272.
L. 4.500 e 5.000.

86. GIOVANNI MUZZIOLI, *Le carte del monastero di S. Andrea
Maggiore di Ravenna.* Vol. I: *896-1000* (imminente).

87. CHRISTINE MOHRMANN, *Études sur le latin des chrétiens.*
Vol. II: *Latin chrétien et médiéval.* 1961, pp. 408.
L. 6.500 e 7.000.

88. AUGUSTO ROSTAGNI, *Virgilio minore. Saggio sullo svolgi-
mento della poesia virgiliana.* Seconda edizione riveduta e
ampliata. 1961, pp. XII-460. L. 6.000 e 6.500.

89. NELLO VIAN, *La giovinezza di Giulio Salvadori. Dalla stagione bizantina al rinnovamento.* Prefazione di B. TECCHI. 1961, pp. XX-352, 19 tavv. f.t. L. 6.000 e 6.500.

90. LUIGI PARETI, *Studi minori di storia antica.* Vol. II: *Storia greca.* 1961, pp. XII-472. L. 7.500 e 8.000.

91. GIAN CARLO ROSCIONI, *Beat Ludwig von Muralt e la ricerca dell'umano.* 1961, pp. XVI-360. L. 2.500 e 3.000.

92. JEAN LECLERCQ, *Recueil d'études sur saint Bernard et ses écrits.* Vol. I. 1962, pp. VIII-380. L. 7.000 e 8.000.

93-94. *Classical Mediaeval and Renaissance Studies in honor of Berthold Louis Ullman.* Edited by CHARLES HENDERSON, Jr. 1964. Vol. I, pp. XXIV-296, 6 tavv. f.t.; vol. II: pp. 556, 14 tavv. f.t. Prezzo dei due volumi: L. 14.000.

95-96. EDUARD FRAENKEL, *Kleine Beiträge zur klassischen Philologie.* 1964. Vol. I: pp. 520; vol. II: pp. 632. Prezzo dei due volumi: L. 18.000 (rilegati in tutta tela con custodia L. 19.800.

97. ANNELIESE MAIER, *Ausgehendes Mittelalter. Gesammelte Aufsätze zur Geistesgeschichte des 14. Jahrhunderts.* I. Bd. 1964, pp. X-518. L. 9.500 e 10.500.

98. GIORDANO BRUNO, *Praelectiones geometricae* e *Ars deformationum,* a cura di GIOVANNI AQUILECCHIA. 1964, pp. 144 con 88 disegni. L. 3.500 e 4.200.

99. GAETANO DE SANCTIS, *Scritti minori.* Vol. I, 1970 (ristampa), pp. 512, L. 9.500.

100. LUIGI PARETI, *Studi minori di storia antica.* Vol. III: *Storia romana.* 1965, pp. 484. L. 9.000 e 9.500.

101. *Le lettere di Benedetto XIV al card. de Tencin.* Dai testi originali, a cura di EMILIA MORELLI. Vol. II: *1748-1752.* 1965, pp. 572. L. 8.000.

102. IVAN DUJČEV, *Medioevo bizantino-slavo.* Vol. I: *Studi di storia politica e culturale.* Introduzione di BRUNO LAVAGNINI. 1965, pp. XXXVI-592 con 10 tavv. f.t L. 9.500.

103. CHRISTINE MOHRMANN, *Études sur le latin des chrétiens.* Vol. III: *Latin chrétien et liturgique.* 1965, pp. 468. L. 6.500.

104. JEAN LECLERCQ, *Recueil d'études sur saint Bernard et ses écrits.* Vol. II. 1966, pp. 416. L. 7.000.

105. ANNELIESE MAIER, *Ausgehendes Mittelalter. Gesammelte Aufsätze zur Geistesgeschichte des 14. Jahrhunderts.* II. Bd. 1967, pp. x-550. L. 10.500.

106-107. *Friendship's Garland. Essays presented to Mario Praz on his seventieth Birthday.* Edited by VITTORIO GABRIELI, 1966. Vol. I: pp. VII-308; vol. II: pp. 471. Prezzo dei due volumi: L. 18.000.

108-109. ARNALDO MOMIGLIANO, *Terzo contributo alla storia degli studi classici e del mondo antico.* 1966. 2 voll., pp. 876. L. 18.000.

110. JEAN BAYET, *Mélanges de littérature latine.* 1967, pp. 376. L. 11.500.

111. LUIGI PARETI, *Studi minori di storia antica.* Vol. IV: *Saggi vari.* 1970, pp. 518. L. 10.500.

112. ANNELIESE MAIER, *Zwei Untersuchungen zur nachscholastischen Philosophie: Die Mechanisierung des Weltbilds im 17. Jahrhundert. - Kants Qualitätskategorien.* 2. Auflage. 1968, pp. 150. L. 3.500.

113. IVAN DUJČEV, *Medioevo bizantino-slavo.* Vol. II: *Saggi di storia letteraria.* 1968, pp. XII-656, con una tav. f. t. L. 9.500.

114. JEAN LECLERCQ, *Recueil d'études sur saint Bernard et ses écrits.* Vol. III. 1969, pp. 448. L. 8.000.

115. ARNALDO MOMIGLIANO, *Quarto contributo alla storia degli studi classici e del mondo antico.* 1969, pp. 756. L. 11.500.

116. CHRISTINE THOUZELLIER, *Hérésie et hérétiques. Vaudois, cathares, patarins, albigeois.* 1969, pp. VIII-275, 2 tavv. f.t. L. 6.000.

117. GAETANO DE SANCTIS. *Scritti minori.* Vol. II: *1892-1905.* 1970, pp. 524. L. 14.000.

118. RAYMOND-JOSEPH LOENERTZ, *Byzantina et Franco-Graeca.* Articles parus de 1935 à 1966, réédités avec la collaboration de PETER SCHREINER. 1970, pp. XXX-634. L. 14.000.

119. IVAN DUJČEV, *Medioevo bizantino slavo.* Vol. III: *Altri saggi di storia politica e letteraria.* 1971, pp. XVI-736, L. 16.500.

120. *La Chine au temps des lumières d'après la correspondance de la mission de Pékin.* Vol. I: JACQUES SILVESTRE DE SACY, *Henri Bertin dans le sillage de la Chine (1720-1792).* 1971, pp. X-175 (imminente).

121. Helene Wieruszowski, *Politics and culture in medieval Spain and Italy.* 1971, pp. xx-681, 6 tavv. f.t. L. 14.000.

122. Gaetano De Sanctis, *Scritti minori.* Vol. III: *1906-1919.* 1972, pp. 636. L. 14.000.

123-124. Gaetano De Sanctis, *Scritti minori.* Vol. IV e V (in corso di stampa).

125-126. Gaetano De Sanctis, *Scritti minori.* Vol. VI: *Recensioni - Cronache e commenti.* 1972. Tomi 2, pp. 1008. L. 18.000.

127-128. Josef Koch, *Kleine Schriften.* 1973. Vol. I: pp. xvi-632; Vol. II: pp. 504. Prezzo dei due volumi: L. 24.000.

129-130. Ludwig Bertalot, *Studien zum italienischen und deutschen Humanismus,* herausgegeben von Paul Oskar Kristeller. Vol. 2 (imminenti).

131-133. Hygini Anglés, *Scripta musicologica,* cura et studio Josephi López-Calo. Voll. 3 (imminenti).

In corso di stampa:

Niccolò Tommaseo, « *Un affetto* ». *Memorie politiche inedite.* A cura di Michele Cataudella.

Arnaldo Momigliano, *Quinto contributo alla storia degli studi classici e del mondo antico.*

Anneliese Maier, *Ausgehendes Mittelalter. Gesammelte Aufsätze zur Geistesgeschichte des 14. Jahrhunderts,* herausgegeben von Agostino Paravicini. III. Bd.

Scevola Mariotti, *Scritti medievali e umanistici.*

Seguirà:

Raymond-Joseph Loenertz, *Byzantina et Franco-Graeca.* Vol. II.

maggio 1973

ABETE
Azienda Beneventana Tipografica Editoriale
Roma - Via Prenestina, 683